RECORD

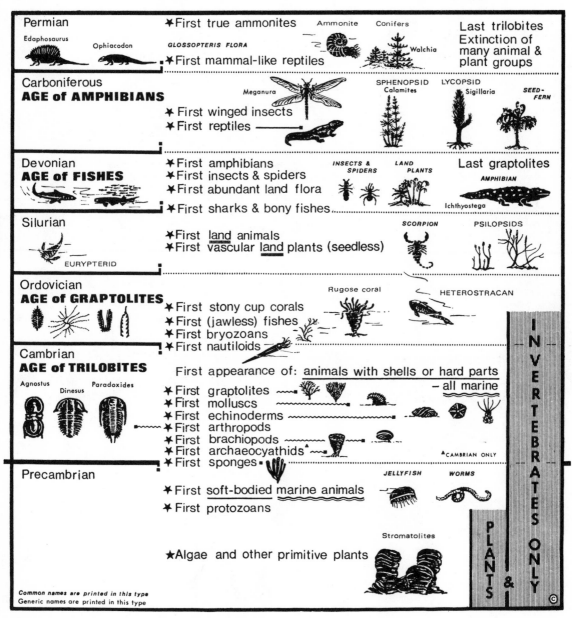

(Courtesy of the Museum of South Australia, Adelaide.)

Plant Biology

KNUT NORSTOG

Northern Illinois University
and
Fairchild Tropical Garden

ROBERT W. LONG

University of South Florida

W. B. SAUNDERS COMPANY

Philadelphia   London   Toronto

W. B. Saunders Company: West Washington Square
Philadelphia, Pa. 19105

1 St. Anne's Road
Eastbourne, East Sussex BN21 3UN, England

833 Oxford Street
Toronto, M8Z 5T9, Canada

Library of Congress Cataloging in Publication Data

Norstog, Knut, 1921–

Plant biology.

Includes index.

1. Botany.   I. Long, Robert W., 1927–   joint author.
II. Title.

QK47.N66 1976   581   75–297

ISBN 0–7216–6864–X

Front cover illustration: Blighia sapida, Priscilla Fawcett.

Copyright © Fairchild Tropical Garden, Miami, Florida.

Plant Biology   ISBN 0-7216-6864-X

Last digit is the print number: 9   8   7   6   5   4   3   2

Preface

Over the past few years there has been a growing awareness that plants as organisms form a vital part of our environment. This tendency to deal with a plant as a whole unit rather than as a series of highly complex physico-chemical reactions has had a salutary effect on the teaching of botany. It is our purpose in this textbook to continue this approach to an understanding of plant life, and to acquaint the beginning botany student with the fundamentals of plant biology by means of an examination of the diversity within the major plant groups. Our emphasis here is solidly on the comparative viewpoint within a conceptual framework of organic evolution. We are interested in the student's becoming aware of the great variety of life style and form that occurs in plants. We also are interested in enhancing his or her appreciation of the importance of plants in everyday life. To a considerable extent, the history of plants is human history, and our understanding of the origins of our civilization can be enriched by an examination of the history of certain plant species.

This book has been designed specifically as a comprehensive introductory text for use in a one-term course in plant biology. We do not presume that the student has had any previous college-level biology preparation. In general, a gradual introduction of terms and concepts prevails throughout the chapters. Plant anatomy and physiology, for example, are included early in the discussion of vascular plants, as well as in their traditional treatment with the flowering plants. One of the main reasons we chose to write this book is our conviction that many present-day textbooks in botany fail to impress upon the student the immense variety to be found among plants, as well as the historical perspective of the science of botany. Although it is impossible to write an entirely balanced account of plant life in a single volume such as this, we have attempted to describe objectively and accept those controversial theories that appear to us to be valid at this time. In some instances we have taken positions that in themselves may be debatable, but we have done this in order to present to the student what appear to us to be the most currently acceptable explanations of certain phenomena.

The text begins with an examination of the roles that plants have played in human history. We then examine the position of botany in modern science and follow this with an examination of the nature of the first cells. Theories regarding the origin of life and the evolution of the most primitive plants are discussed. Next, the "typical plant cell" is described in some detail in order to form a background for later discussions of anatomy, morphology, physiology, and reproduction found among the major plant groups. A brief résumé of photosynthesis and respiration is presented. This is intended to serve both as a review for students who have covered this material perhaps more thoroughly in a "principles" course and as an introduction to the subject for those who have not. In particular, the introduction to photosynthesis and respiration is included here to support the presentation of ecological principles, particularly of energy flow relationships, in the following chapter on plant ecology. The first six chapters are intended to serve as the foundation for the discussion of the major plant groups.

The second group of chapters deals with those simple plants collectively referred to as algae. The several important divisions of algae are described, with special reference to representative life-forms within each division. The slime molds and fungi are covered in a single chapter, with considerable emphasis placed on their societal and economic importance.

The third major group of chapters deals with the bryophytes and the primitive vascular plants that evolved principally in the Paleozoic Era and are ancestral to the modern seed plants, which dominate our landscape today. Finally, a fourth set of chapters is devoted to the biology of flowering plants—their reproduction, structure, and ecology, concluding with a chapter on genetics and a final chapter dealing with growth and development. In this last chapter the theme of plants and human affairs is once again reiterated.

We have standardized the terminology throughout the text and important terms are shown in boldface type. New terms are defined upon their introduction, and most such terms also are defined again in the glossary. Although it is impossible to present modern plant biology without the use of terminology, we have consciously attempted to minimize this aspect of biological science. Trends in evolution and phylogenetic pathways are emphasized, concepts are introduced where appropriate, and specific examples are identified.

We could not have completed this work without the assistance of many friends and colleagues. The original drawings were done by Ms. Priscilla Fawcett of Fairchild Tropical Garden, and by Mr. Jack Schroeder. A number of our professional acquaintances have contributed illustrative material, and are acknowledged in the illustration captions.

Other colleagues have read portions of the manuscript and have offered their suggestions for improvements. We wish to thank especially Drs. Anne Benninghoff, David Benzing, Clinton Dawes, Elon Frampton, William Gray, James Grosklags, Jean Gross, Laszlo Hanzely, Malcolm Jollie, Donald Kaplan, Darrel Lynch, Ole A. Schjeide, John Skok, Paul Sorensen, and Paul Voth. Mrs. Suzanne Todd Cooper and Mrs. Paula Hilsenbeck helped us in many of the bibliographic tasks associated with the production of the glossary and index. In particular, we wish to express our appreciation to Nona Norstog and Gloria Long for their support and encouragement during the planning and writing of this book.

KNUT NORSTOG
ROBERT W. LONG

Contents

CONTENTS

Plant Biology

Primitive agriculture in the New Stone Age in Northern Europe—death and fertility ritual.

Chapter 1

Plants and Human Affairs

THE ORIGIN OF AGRICULTURE • SEX, RELIGION, AND PLANTS • PLANTS AND CIVILIZATION • PLANTS OF DISCOVERY AND EXPLORATION • SPICES • ESSENTIAL OILS AND PERFUMES • FOOD PLANTS • PLANTS AND NARCOTICS • COTTON AND TOBACCO • THE FUTURE OF AGRICULTURE • SUMMARY

We do not know exactly when the human race came into existence. Human-like creatures existed about two million years ago, but *Homo sapiens sapiens* (thinking man) appears to have arrived on the scene in comparatively recent times, perhaps some 50,000 years ago. Whatever their origins were, we believe that our earliest ancestors were food gatherers and spent most of their energies hunting animals, catching fish, and collecting edible plants. About 10,000 years ago our forebears changed from gathering food to producing food. Eventually, through cultivation of plants and domestication of animals, they were able to produce sufficient food to free them of the constant search for their next meal. With a dependable food source, humans could live together, and so villages and towns came into existence. Social organization and civilization followed. Therefore, our history is also the history of our plants, for they have been our partners in survival.

THE ORIGIN OF AGRICULTURE

The discoveries of archeology have increased greatly our knowledge of the origins of agriculture. Recent research has led to a greater understanding of the ecology of prehistoric men and women, and new finds are being recorded each year, throwing light

---

Father have pity on me
Father have pity on me
I am crying for thirst
I am crying for thirst
All is gone—I have nothing to eat
All is gone—I have nothing to eat

ARAPAHOE INDIAN GHOST-DANCE SONG (FROM *Anthropology: The Study of Man,* 3RD ED. BY E. A. HOEBEL. COPYRIGHT 1966 BY MCGRAW-HILL BOOK COMPANY. USED WITH PERMISSION OF MCGRAW-HILL BOOK COMPANY).

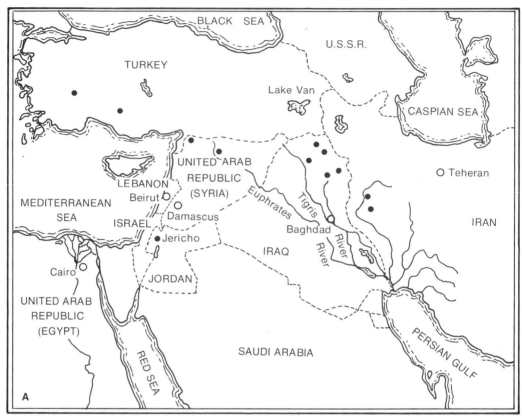

Figure 1–1 Sites of early agriculture in *A*, the Old, and *B*, the New Worlds. Black dots indicate sites at which archeological evidence of early agriculture has been found (Redrawn from Heiser, C. B., Jr.: *Seed to Civilization: The Story of Man's Food,* San Francisco, W. H. Freeman and Co., 1973).

Illustration continued on opposite page.

on the early part of our long struggle for survival. Remains from old camp sites, a few pieces of bone, or charred seeds may not be as spectacular as an ancient Egyptian tomb, but they have great significance when they are correlated with similar finds from other excavations.

Evidence now strongly indicates that agriculture had its origin in the semi-arid mountainous regions near the river valleys of Mesopotamia, in present-day Iraq. Sometime before 8000 B.C., men and women were collecting wild grain plants and keeping domesticated animals such as dogs and sheep. Wheat and barley seeds have been obtained from excavations dated at about 6750 B.C., in Jarmo, Iraq, and deposits later than this date contain remains of many cultivated plants.

The cultivation of plants probably originated in more than one ancient center (Fig. 1–1). In addition to several sites in the Near East known to have supported early agriculture, other centers developed in both the Old and the New Worlds. Archeological evidence suggests that legumes, such as beans and peas, may have been in cultivation in Thailand as early as 7000 B.C. In the New World, agriculture began in Mexico about 5000 B.C., probably near the desert regions of southwestern Tamaulipas. Here the first plants to be cul-

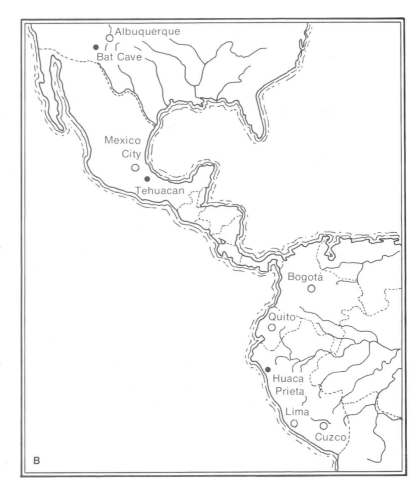

Figure 1–1 *Continued.*

tivated were maize, avocado, squash, and chili peppers. Somewhat later, other plants such as beans, cotton, and various fruits were grown. Recent research has also suggested that agriculture arose very early in Peru in the Andean valleys. It seems probable that agriculture originated independently in at least two regions in the New World—Mexico and Peru—and the earliest site may have been Peru.

We can only speculate as to why primitive people first thought of cultivating plants instead of gathering wild ones. One theory proposes that agriculture was invented by women. Since most of the wild plant gathering (as opposed to hunting) was done by women, it is reasonable to believe that they may have devised the plan of collecting seeds, planting them, and successfully bringing them into cultivation. Some archeologists believe that climatic changes and a growing familiarity with plant and animal resources combined to bring about the invention of agriculture. Others believe that increased population densities forced primitive tribes to attempt to control their environment, and thus led to the invention of agriculture.

One geographer and ethnobotanist, Dr. Carl Sauer, has suggested that the first deliberate planting of food plants was of

Figure 1–2 *A,* Taro corms and tubers (Photo courtesy of Hawaii Visitors Bureau). *B,* Taros on sale in a market in Thailand (USDA Photo).

root crops. He believes this practice began in the humid, southwestern regions of Asia. Plants grown for their roots can be dug up with a simple digging stick; the technology for this kind of agriculture is the simplest type. Perhaps the taro plant, *Colocasia esculenta,* of the aroid family, was one of the first plants cultivated in this fashion. The taro still is grown in the wet, tropical areas of the world, and its fleshy underground parts can be seen in many open-air markets even today (Fig. 1–2).

Although Sauer's theory has much to recommend it, there are some serious objections. The remains of food plants found in early agricultural centers of both the Old and New Worlds are of plants that were propagated by seeds. Seeds generally have higher food value than roots, are less subject to spoilage, and are more readily stored and transported under unfavorable conditions. The development of advanced civilizations was based on grain-forming plants such as rice, wheat, and maize. The cultivation of these grain crops, together with the domestication of animals, formed the basis for the development of civilizations as we presently know them.

Another interesting theory suggests that the origin of agriculture can be traced to the camp dump-heap. The rubbish heaps of primitive camp sites would be rich in organic matter and would be excellent seed beds. As discarded plant parts, especially seeds, were thrown into the dump, they would grow into vigorous plants, because of the abundant supply of organic fertilizers. Perhaps gardens were invented in this way.

SEX, RELIGION, AND PLANTS

We know that primitive religion was tied closely to natural events. Birth, death, and food were of great significance to primitive people. The cycles of growth and death of plants were thought to be related to human life. For example, tree worship was an early form of religion and was carried down to historical times.

Perhaps the most intriguing theory concerning the origin of agriculture suggests that it began with the sowing of seeds as an adjunct to human burial. Primitive people buried food and tools with the dead for use in the next world. This involved burying seeds, and these usually were from annual plants, which were the chief wild-food plants. Since annuals are especially adapted to grow well in soil that is newly cleared, such as at grave sites, the plants would grow vigorously. Primitive folk would conclude that the dead person's ghost was rewarding them for their kind treatment by returning grain from the dead body many times over. Consequently, the people would have noted that plants grew best near the newly-made graves, and may have concluded that new burials would have to be made each year, which could even have led to human sacrifice to secure more plants. In some cases it is known that human bodies were not buried, but were cut up and scattered over fields for their "magical" properties. In this way, according to the theory, primitive societies learned the necessity of turning the soil, and eventually of sowing seeds, for cultivating plants.

Figure 1–3 Indonesian rice harvesters (FAO Photo by Frank Botts). **7**

Finally, we consider one of the most plausible explanations of the discovery of the art of agriculture. Through the ages there has been a close association of religion and planting, and many rituals and ceremonies were associated with the climactic event of prehistoric society, the harvest. Seed offerings were made at harvest time to propitiate the spirit of the wild grain being cut. The seeds were scattered over the fields and buried in the soil in recognition of the earth as the mother god and source of life. The first seed plantings, then, may have been a religious ceremony used to appease the grain gods. The wild seeds would be harvested, but some of the seeds (the "first fruits") would be saved and returned to the gods by way of the soil. As ceremonial plantings became larger, eventually intentional cultivation would have evolved. The fact that improved varieties of grains are of great antiquity may indicate a process of artificial selection. Naturally, only the best of the "first fruits" would have been saved for the gods and returned to the soil. Thus, mankind unconsciously improved cultivated plants.

Human fertility and that of vegetation were believed to be closely related. Mother-goddess fertility cults based on the worship of agricultural symbols were common among primitive societies. Sexual intercourse was believed to be related to the fertility of the grain fields and became a part of the festivals held in the fields at the time of planting to promote the growth of crops. The plow may have been designed originally as a phallic symbol representing man's function to bring fertility to mother earth. From early times, sex was considered to be sacred among people because it was as-

A

B

Figure 1–4 Hoeing and plowing: *A,* as recorded in cave drawings, in Northern Italy, and *B,* on an ancient Egyptian tomb (*A* from *Seed to Civilization: The Story of Man's Food* by Charles B. Heiser, Jr., W. H. Freeman and Company. Copyright © 1972; *B* reproduced with permission of the Egypt Exploration Society, London, England).

sociated with the life-supporting fertility of the village grain fields. Fertility ceremonies persisted through ancient Greek and Roman times, and May Day celebrations presently observed in some of the more advanced countries can be traced to their original purpose, which was to promote the well-being of vegetation.

Although we cannot say definitely how agriculture arose, we can say that its origin changed history. Agriculture may have been discovered accidentally, or it may have come about through trial and error in connection with religious rites and ceremonies. But once established, it spread out rapidly from early agricultural centers and changed our cultural patterns forever. Superstition and magic still surround planting and harvest time in many parts of the world. Even in the United States some farmers still plant their fields during certain phases of the moon. Old beliefs die hard, especially if they have been in religious or traditional use for thousands of years.

PLANTS AND CIVILIZATION

The early history of botany can be traced to the work of philosophers and medical practitioners of the Greek and Roman civilizations. The oldest known botanical work was written by a Greek naturalist-philospher and student of Aristotle named Theophrastus of Lesbos (c. 372–288 B.C.). He devised the first classification of native Greek plants into a catalog or book, writing two fundamental works, *Enquiry into Plants,* and *Causes of Plants* (on plant physiology), and produced detailed drawings and descriptions so that the plants could be identified.

This and later Greek and Roman books on plants became models for later botanical writings, called **herbals.** Herbals were compendia of information about medicinal properties, horticulture, and other uses of plants. Many herbals were produced in the Middle Ages and often were profusely illustrated with woodcuts of great

Figure 1–5 Otto Brunfels, an herbalist of the Middle Ages (From Arber, A. *Herbals, Their Origin and Evolution: A Chapter in the History of Botany,* 2nd ed. (Reprint of 1953 ed.), Hafner, 1970).

originality. Accompanying the illustrations were descriptions of the plants, and these sometimes reflected an aura of magic and folklore traceable to very ancient times. One of the most famous herbals of that period was the beautifully illustrated *Herbarium vivae eicones,* written by Otto Brunfels (c. 1488–1534).

One of the plants mentioned in all the old herbals is the mandrake, a member of the nightshade or tomato family. Mandrake, a native of the Mediterranean region, is a small plant (about 30 centimeters high) having leaflets borne mainly at the base and a root resembling a parsnip (Fig. 1–7). Sometimes the root is branched and, with the use of a little imagination, one may see a resemblance to the human figure complete with arms and legs. In medieval times it was believed that the Creator had indicated the usefulness of certain plants by designing them in the image of the human organs whose diseases they would cure. This belief became formalized in a dogma called the "doctrine of signatures." The walnut, for instance, was supposed to be good for headaches since the walnut shell resembled the human skull and the convoluted nutmeat was like a brain. Since the mandrake plant resembled the whole human body, it was believed to be good for all human ailments. During Roman times, the mandrake root was thought to resemble a human penis, and the Romans used the plant as an aphrodisiac. In Biblical times, mandrake was thought to be a cure for sterility as well as an aphrodisiac.

Figure 1–6 The mandrake, *Mandragora officinarum,* as depicted in an ancient herbal. Dogs were used to pull the plants out of the ground because it was believed that any person who dug up the plant would die (From Arber, A. *Herbals, Their Origin and Evolution: A Chapter in the History of Botany,* 2nd ed. (Reprint of 1953 ed.), Hafner, 1970).

Figure 1–7 The mandrake as it actually is (From *Nightshades: The Paradoxical Plants* by Charles B. Heiser, Jr., W. H. Freeman and Company. Copyright © 1969).

The ancient Greeks boiled the roots of mandrake or soaked them in wine, using the resulting brew to promote drowsiness and sleep. Mandrake also was used to dull pain during surgical operations, and may well have been the first anesthetic. Perhaps it was mandrake that was offered to Christ on the cross, since it was widely used throughout the Middle East in that era.

One might suspect the soporific effect of mandrake may have been due to the wine in which it was steeped, but a chemical analysis done in 1889 showed that it contains a mixture of alkaloids, including a potent one called scopolamine. Scopolamine has the property of deadening pain without inducing complete insensibility. When it is mixed with morphine, a drug obtained from the opium poppy, the resulting product can be used to produce "twilight sleep" during childbirth.

Although mandrake today has been replaced by other more effective sources of scopolamine and by other drugs, this story is only one of many demonstrating the progressive refinements in our use and knowledge of medicinal plants. Typically, primitive people discovered the value of a certain plant without understanding its way of acting; much later, an analysis discloses the principle of its action,

11

and, finally, the active ingredient is synthesized. Sometimes an even better drug is discovered in the laboratory so that the traditional one no longer is used.

PLANTS OF DISCOVERY AND EXPLORATION

When we think of botany and plants, we often conjure up scenes of an innocent past because of the elegance, fragrance, beauty, and fragility of many flowers and plants. Botanists know that this view of the history of plants is far from the truth. Men have gone forth with sword in hand to distant lands, have set out on long and dangerous voyages of discovery, and have conquered empires, all for certain kinds of plants.

Spices

The story of spices is a great romance complete with tales of war, conquest, theft, envy, and hatred. One spice in particular, black

Figure 1–8 *Piper nigrum,* the black pepper (From d'Alechamps, J. *Historia Generalis Plantarum,* 1587).

pepper, holds an important place in history, perhaps the most important of any plant. Although pepper is very common now, in ancient times only the richest could afford it and it was measured out with balances for its equivalent weight in gold. In medieval times it was so highly prized that rich men wrote wills bequeathing pepper to their sons. Beautiful women, fine horses, and expensive jewels could be had for pepper. Many other spices, such as ginger and cloves, also were valuable, for they were used to preserve food, flavor wine, make perfumes, prepare medicines, and even embalm the dead.

Many spices came from India, Ceylon, and the Moluccas. The Venetians monopolized the spice trade and suppressed competition from other European powers. Then, in 1497, the Portuguese explorer Vasco da Gama opened up the spice trade of the Far East by navigating around the Cape of Good Hope. Columbus' discovery of America was inspired by the desire to find a direct route to the spice treasures of the East. The great rivalries between Portugal, Holland, England, and Spain in the sixteenth, seventeenth, and eighteenth centuries were caused by disputes over trading rights in China, India, and the Spice Islands. Although sugar now has replaced spices as the world's chief flavoring material, we should note that it was pepper, cinnamon, and ginger that caused the Spanish, Portuguese, Dutch, and English to make their most daring voyages.

Essential Oils and Perfumes

Spices were used to make food acceptable to the palate, and perfumes were important in making human beings acceptable to one another. The distillation of essential oils from flowers and other plant parts is one of the most ancient crafts of civilization. In ancient Egypt, perfumes were sprinkled on the royal mummies each year. The tomb of Tutankhamen, the boy Pharaoh of 1350 B.C., still contained a fragrance from the alabaster perfume vases after 3300 years.

Perfumes were the rage in the France of Louis XIV and in the England of Elizabeth I. Women of nobility spent fortunes each year just for fragrances. For most of them, the use of perfume substituted for taking regular baths, and doubtless a crowd of aristocrats in those days was quite pungent. The British became so concerned about the use of perfume in the eighteenth century that they passed a law in Parliament making it a criminal offense to employ fragrance to betray a man into matrimony.

Today the fragrance of the living flower is produced synthetically, and the perfume of rose, violet, and jasmine are imitated by artificial essences that produce the great array of scents now available on the market. However, flower petals are still gathered in some countries for the production of natural perfumes, such as lavender and attar of roses.

13

Figure 1–9 An herb garden where essential oils are being distilled for manufacture of spices and perfumes (From Brunschwig, H. *Liber de Arte Distillandi de Simplicibus,* 1500).

Food Plants

Discovery and exploitation also accompanied the search for new food plants. Many have read of Captain Bligh and the mutiny aboard his ship, *Bounty.* In the eighteenth century, British planters of the West Indies used thousands of African slaves to produce sugar cane, and it was necessary to have cheap food for them. The answer to their problem seemed to be the breadfruit of the mulberry family (Fig. 1–10). The fruit is large and is produced abundantly throughout most of the year on a fast-growing tree. It forms an important food for the inhabitants of the South Pacific islands and was considered ideal for use in the great plantations of Jamaica and other islands of the Caribbean.

His Majesty's Ship *Bounty* left England on October 15, 1787, and reached Tahiti on October 24, 1788, after a hard voyage. Saplings of the breadfruit tree were carefully placed on board and the Bounty set off for the long, perilous trip to the West Indies. However, the sailors of the Bounty did not want to leave Tahiti. Furthermore, Captain Bligh was strongly disliked by most of the crew because of his harsh treatment of them. As a consequence, when the ship was three weeks out of Tahiti, mutiny broke out with the acting lieutenant, Fletcher Christian, leading the revolt. The breadfruit plants were dumped unceremoniously overboard by the mutinous crew

A

PF

B

Figure 1–10 *A*, Particularly large breadfruit tree in Guatemala (USDA Photo). *B*, Leaf and fruit of a breadfruit tree.

who had thoroughly detested having to tend to them. A few loyal sailors, the ship's surgeon, the chief botanist and Bligh were placed in an open boat, but miraculously nearly all reached safety after a 41-day trip covering 3618 miles. Much of the drama surrounding these episodes has been recaptured in popular novels and films.

Because of the mutiny, the first large-scale attempt to introduce a new food plant into America was delayed. Sir Joseph Banks, a botanist who had been with Captain Cook on his first voyage and who was then President of the Royal Society of London, persuaded the British Government to send Bligh on a second voyage in 1792, and this time Bligh was successful. Over 2,000 breadfruit trees left Tahiti and 700 of these lived to be planted in Jamaica and in St. Vincent of the Windward Islands. One of these trees, it is said, still survives in downtown Kingston, Jamaica. The irony of the whole episode, involving so much expense, so many lives, and so much effort, was that the slaves found the breadfruit not to their liking and would not eat it. Today, however, breadfruit trees grow wild throughout Jamaica and seem to be a part of the natural vegetation.

An additional touch of irony is supplied by another fruit tree, the akee, seeds of which the slaves themselves brought with them from

Figure 1–11 The sugar beet, *Beta vulgaris* (USDA Photo).

Africa. This tree, which flourishes in the West Indies, is named *Blighia sapida* after Captain Bligh, and its fruit is still enjoyed in the form of the Jamaican national dish, saltfish (cod) and akee.

Other important food plants also have played a role in history. The soldiers of Alexander the Great first reported that the barbarians of the Indus obtained honey from reeds, that is, from sugar cane. The growing of sugar cane spread to Persia and thence to Egypt and Spain, and, by the sixteenth century, to the New World. Sugar soon became a very important commodity in Europe and nations plotted, fought, and struggled for trade supremacy in sugar. Sugar also figured prominently in the Napoleonic wars of the early nineteenth century. The British navy blockaded the continent, closing down the sugar refineries, which had been importing raw sugar and selling it to France, Germany, and other countries. Everywhere there was a sugar shortage and finally, in 1811, Napoleon subsidized the establishment of a sugar-beet industry. Sugar-beet factories by the hundreds sprang up in France, and began producing sugar. The British ridiculed the idea of making sugar from beets and published satirical cartoons, such as one showing a nurse thrusting the end of a root in the mouth of Napoleon's son, saying, "*Suce, mon chéri, suce; ton pére dit que c'est du sucre.*"*

Although Napoleon lost his empire, the sugar beet survived, and botanists were able to breed beets that contain up to 28 per cent sugar. Today, it is one of the best examples of an important crop that has been brought about through the joint efforts of politics and science.

PLANTS AND NARCOTICS

The coagulated latex of the fruit of the opium poppy is called *opium* (Fig. 1–12). Opium has been used since Greek and Roman times, when physicians administered it as a sleeping potion. Its cultivation then spread throughout Asia and, because of its narcotic effects, its use became widespread among rich and poor alike. Along with spices and perfumes, opium was an important cargo in early trading ships.

In the eighteenth century, the English expanded their trade with China, primarily to secure tea for their European markets. Opium was exported from India, and by 1838 over 20,000 chests of the drug were shipped annually. The English did their best to promote opium consumption in China, and soon Chinese money and tea were flowing to world markets and the Chinese people were losing their health and aptitude for work. Although the Emperor of China forbade the importation of opium, the English smuggled it past corrupt Chinese customs officials, many of whom were themselves addicts. A Chinese general, appointed by the Emperor, successfully stopped the illegal traffic in Canton, only to have England declare war on China for destroying opium. After a pathetic war the Chinese surrendered and were forced to accept the opium trade, which then expanded

---

*Translation: "Suck, my dear, suck; your father says it's sugar."

Figure 1–12 Capsules of the opium poppy, *Papaver somniferum*. The capsules have been gashed and are oozing latex, the source of opium (Photo courtesy of W. H. Hodge).

over much of China. Appeals to Queen Victoria went unheeded; profitable business was good business, regardless of what the Chinese wanted. Finally, the Chinese gave up completely and began planting the poppy for themselves. Much later England recognized its immoral position, and, in 1906, the House of Commons put a stop to the narcotics traffic and the Chinese began to recover.

Not all drug plants are narcotics. Beneficial drugs derived from plants include digitalis, a heart stimulant obtained from the foxglove; belladonna, which acts as a stimulant to the sympathetic nervous system, from *Atropa belladonna* of the nightshade family; reserpine, first isolated from the shrub *Rauwolfia* of the dogbane family and used as a tranquilizer and depressant in treating high blood pressure and insanity; and mescaline, from the small peyote cactus, *Lophophora* (Fig. 1–13), a hallucinogen now used in the treatment of certain kinds of mental illness. The Aztec drug *ololiuqui* is obtained from seeds of the Mexican morning glory, and is a potent hallucinogen whose active agents are similar to LSD. LSD itself is derived from ergot, a fungus long known to be toxic. As little as 10^{-8} gram of LSD will produce clinical symptoms, and it is said to be about 10,000 times more powerful than mescaline. The steroid hormones of fertility and birth control pills, as well as cortisone, are obtained by chemically altering substances present in the Mexican yam, *Dioscorea*. Of the more than 300,000,000 prescriptions written by physicians in the United States in 1963, a prescription auditing firm estimated that over 47 per cent contained a natural drug as a major ingredient.

Figure 1-13 The peyote cactus, *Lophophora williamsii* (From *Plants and Civilization,* Second edition, by Herbert G. Baker. © 1970 by Wadsworth Publishing Company, Inc., Belmont, California 94002. Reprinted by permission of the publisher).

COTTON AND TOBACCO

Cotton probably was grown in India as far back as 3000 B.C. The ancient Greeks reported it growing in India as "tree wool" and were greatly attracted by the soft and beautiful muslins of the Far East. By the sixteenth century, chintzes and calicos were being imported into Europe in tremendous amounts, but the demand for these fabrics still could not be met. Because of opposition by English wool manufacturers cotton cloth had to be smuggled into England, but eventually the government relented and cotton cloth began to be woven in England.

The first cotton was exported from the American colonies to England in 1747, and later Eli Whitney's cotton gin gave great impetus to the cotton industry. Soon cotton became the most important plant in the southern United States, and there was a great labor shortage in the cotton fields. Cheap labor was required, and slaves from Africa were imported in great numbers. Cargo ships, many of them British, made a profitable, three-cornered voyage: slaves were brought from Africa to North America; the ships then were reloaded with cotton, tobacco, rum, and molasses for the trip to England; and, for the third voyage of the triangle, the ships were reloaded in England with manufactured goods to exchange for slaves in Africa. By the beginning of the nineteenth century, over 10,000 slaves were

19

being brought to America each year. By 1830, differences arose between the southern and the northern states over slavery, culminating in the Civil War and the freeing of the slaves in 1865.

In the Old World, the cotton plant was one of the chief causes of the final break between England and India. The importation of cheap cotton cloth into India enabled England to profit, but the Indian peasant grew poorer and poorer. England took the raw cotton from India, manufactured the cloth, and then sold it back to India, meanwhile preventing the manufacture and marketing of native Indian cloth. Gandhi and his spinning wheel became the symbol of resistance to the British, and finally the boycott of British cloth made the occupation of India unprofitable.

Tobacco, another plant of considerable importance, was being smoked by the Carib Indians when Columbus landed in 1492. It was introduced into Europe in 1519 and popularized by such buccaneers as Sir Walter Raleigh. The cultivated tobacco plant probably arose through hybridization and chromosome doubling of two wild species (see Chapter 19). The wild species do not contain much nicotine in their mature leaves, but the best smoking varieties of cultivated tobacco have about one per cent nicotine. Apparently in the passage of time the tendency was to select plants that contained some nicotine in their older leaves as well as in the young leaves. Now the mature leaves are the ones that are cured in the production of tobacco. Today the United States is the largest producer of tobacco in the world, and production and use seem to be increasing each year.

It is difficult to think about tobacco without reflecting on the problems in human health that its widespread use has created. Despite numerous warnings of the dangers of prolonged smoking in terms of cancer, emphysema, and cardiovascular disease, there appears to be no abatement in the number of people who use tobacco. Were it solely a matter of the freedom of the individual to choose whether or not to harm one's self, society could restrict its role in the matter to making sure the dangers are clearly understood. However, treatment of the diseases associated with tobacco places an unwarranted strain on medical and social facilities. For this reason it would seem that further legislative action is needed, perhaps in the form of a special tax on the tobacco industry to underwrite the cost of research into the prevention and cure of tobacco-associated disease.

Marijuana, or hashish, which, like tobacco, may be smoked or eaten, is a product of the Indian hemp plant and contains a powerful alkaloid, tetrahydrocannabinol (THC), which essentially acts as a depressant. While its use in Asia goes back into antiquity, its present distribution and use is a matter of widespread medical, social and political concern. Objections to its use are not so much based on its direct effect on the user (it appears to be a relatively mild and non-addictive drug) as on the fear that it predisposes the individual toward addiction to more dangerous drugs. There may be some truth to this, in that the illegality of marijuana puts the purchaser into contact with the illicit drug trade, where the hard drugs are also avail-

Figure 1–14 *Cannabis sativa,* the marijuana or hemp plant (Courtesy Carolina Biological Supply Company).

able. Whether or not prolonged use of marijuana may produce harmful side effects, as does tobacco, remains to be determined.

THE FUTURE OF AGRICULTURE

All our food ultimately comes from plants, for plants are the only organisms capable of synthesizing foods from such basic raw materials as water and carbon dioxide, using sunlight for energy. In addition, we rely on plants for building material, books, and other paper products, fibers for natural and synthetic textiles, fuel, drugs, cosmetics, among many other uses.

Many great changes have been made in agricultural processes in the twentieth century. Cumulatively, these have had a spectacular effect on human life and are now being referred to as the **green revolution**. Usually, this term is employed with reference to the ever-increasing manipulation of plants toward rather short-term ends, and thus may encompass hybrid corn, "miracle rice," mechanical harvesting of crop plants genetically "tailored" for this purpose, use of herbicides for weed control and insecticides for insect control, regulation of flowering time by hormones and artificial light, use of high-potency chemical fertilizers, and, with only a small stretch of the imagination, abandonment of the family farm.

Inevitably, such great changes in our way of growing plants have become controversial. Immense areas of natural vegetation

21

have been destroyed to provide land for growing crops. In Illinois, the destruction of the original prairie vegetation is so complete that an artificial prairie has been created near Chicago so that people may see how the land once looked.

In places where formerly there was natural vegetation, with perhaps a hundred or more species of plants, there may now be only corn, wheat, or soybean fields. This practice of growing only one kind of plant on a large tract of land has been termed **monoculture**, and, although it has advantages, it also has serious drawbacks. Recently we have seen one of the perils of monoculture. In the summer of 1970, which was unusually humid, a fungus disease produced a corn blight that devastated the vast, hybrid corn (maize) fields of the American Midwest. Monocultures are very susceptible to disease outbreaks because there are no buffer regions of non-susceptible plants between the susceptible crops. However, monocultures and epidemics of plant diseases are not a new phenomenon. About 130 years ago, the whole of Ireland was essentially a potato monoculture. A fungus infection wiped out the crop for two years in succession, and millions of Irish starved and died or were forced to emigrate. Imagine what an epidemic of similar proportions would do to the economies of any of our present industrialized societies!

Figure 1-15 This artificial prairie at the Morton Arboretum near Chicago, Illinois, which has been completed recently. The land had been farmland, but has been replanted with native prairie species (Photo courtesy of Morton Arboretum).

Figure 1–16 The potato famine of Ireland in 1846. This drawing depicts the fate of starving women and children (From O'Brien, M., and O'Brien, C. C. *The Story of Ireland.* New York: The Viking Press, 1972).

Despite the dangers, we are committed to monoculture patterns of agriculture. Populations in nearly all countries are too great to be sustained by natural vegetation, or even by crops grown under primitive methods (sometimes called "natural" or "organic" farming). This important topic will be taken up in greater detail in Chapters 5 and 6.

Although there may be local overproduction of food in some parts of the world, for most there is present or potential famine. Unless new sources of food are found, and soon, the spread of hunger and disease will continue. There will, of course, have to be an acceleration of efforts to control human populations. But even if we had an immediate solution to the problem of human overpopulation, several generations would pass before the present stress on our resources would be alleviated.

Some suggest we turn to the sea for our food. Long ago we passed the point where we could rely on wild land animals for food. Why, then, would the wild animals of the sea constitute an inexhaustible supply of animal protein? They often are in as delicate a state of ecological balance as the populations of terrestrial wildlife, and are similarly vulnerable to exploitation and destruction of habitats. Instead, a re-evaluation of our use of arable land is urgent.

Probably it will be necessary to rely more and more on plants as a direct food source, for some are high in protein and might thus

23

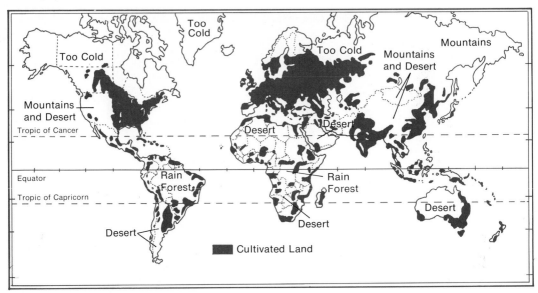

Figure 1-17 Approximate distribution of cultivated land in the world today (Redrawn from Heiser, C. B., Jr.: *Seed to Civilization: The Story of Man's Food,* San Francisco, W. H. Freeman and Co., 1973).

serve as a primary source of protein for humans (see Figure 1–18). For example, soybeans are a good source of protein, and can be processed to produce palatable foods. Food yeasts are another promising source of cheap, high-protein foods. Brewer's yeast has had some use already. It is not very tasty, however, nor is it espe-

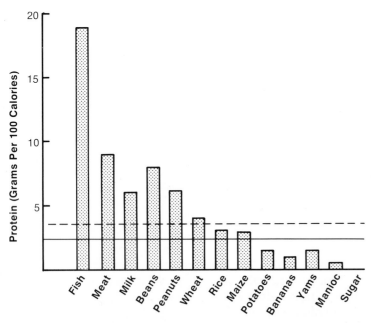

Figure 1-18 Protein-calorie ratios of various foods. The approximate daily requirements for children (dashed line) and adults (solid line) are indicated (Redrawn from Heiser, C. B., Jr.: *Seed to Civilization: The Story of Man's Food,* San Francisco, W. H. Freeman and Co., 1973).

cially high in protein. Attention has become focused on another yeast, *Candida utilis,* which can be produced rapidly, has a pleasant flavor, and is a rich source of protein and vitamins. Its future appears greatest where sugary waste materials are available for growing the yeast and where supplemental protein is needed.

Algae also have been described as the "food of the future." Most experimental work has involved the unicellular green alga, *Chlorella,* for which culture conditions can be changed to yield varying amounts of protein, oils, and carbohydrates. Yields of *Chlorella* are far higher per acre of culture than are obtainable with any terrestrial crop (see Chapter 7).

Large scale experiments involving the production of food from algae have been conducted in Texas and California. Algae are grown in culture solutions containing the necessary inorganic chemicals in proper balance. The suspensions are constantly stirred, and carbon dioxide is bubbled through the culture while it is exposed to bright light. Algae are harvested every few days and concentrated by centrifugation. The chlorophyll is extracted by methyl alcohol, leaving a residue containing up to forty per cent protein, and yields may be as high as fifteen tons of protein per acre. The problem of making the protein produced acceptable for dietary use, however, still remains. Thus, the experience of the English planters who introduced the breadfruit tree to Jamaica only to discover after all the effort that the fruit was unacceptable as food, is repeated in modern-day efforts to make algae acceptable as food. The potential is there, however, for a highly productive source of plant protein, and perhaps techniques to make it more palatable will be developed.

SUMMARY

How could we live without plants? From the time of our most primitive ancestors, plants have been a source of food, shelter, medicines, and enjoyment, and are no less so today. Plants are used to express our deepest sympathy in times of sickness and sorrow. We also symbolize our love of one another with the gifts of plants. Yet, in considering plant life it is important to avoid making undue, human-centered value judgments on the utility or non-utility of plants of all kinds. The mosses that are such an interesting and vital component of the Arctic tundra are fully as important objects of our interest and appreciation as are the wheat fields of Kansas. Whenever we attempt to manipulate one kind of natural resource, we risk another. Thus, an Arctic oil pipeline may upset a delicate ecological balance in Alaska, just as the virgin prairies of Kansas were destroyed to make room for fields of wheat.

Sometimes we are led into a kind of rebellion against the exploitation of nature and feel that we should return to the simple primitive life in which only naturally grown plants are gathered for food and other uses. But this may be equally harmful. Human populations are much too great to be sustained by wild plants and animals. Therefore, if synthetic means are found whereby we can obtain such essential commodities as food, fiber, drugs, and construction materials necessary for the maintenance of life and at the same time relieve the stress on wild populations, we will have made some progress toward saving the natural quality in our environment, which is so much desired today. Application of scientific principles to agriculture in a thoughtful way will enable us to sustain and perhaps expand our food production without further despoliation of natural areas. Unfortunately at present we are destroying much of our arable land through urbanization, mining, fire, and sheer irresponsibility. Whether this trend will be reversed through greater ecological awareness remains to be seen. We have reached the position where we have the power to ruin our world. Whether we can, through our intellectual resources, wisely use and control this planet (and possibly others as well) also remains to be seen. Botany can make it possible for us to have our plants, and the appreciation of those plants can be our key to continued existence.

DISCUSSION QUESTIONS

1. How did primitive people obtain food before the invention of agriculture?
2. From archeological and ethnobotanical evidence, where did agriculture begin? Was there more than one center of early plant cultivation? Explain.
3. Discuss the probable relationship between certain religious practices of early mankind and the cultivation of grain crops.
4. Briefly describe the theory that explains the origin of agriculture as the result of primitive burial practices.
5. Who was Theophrastus? What is the significance of herbals in the history of botany?
6. The mandrake plant was thought to have magical powers by the ancients. Was there any scientific basis for its use as a medicine? If so, explain. What was the doctrine of signatures?
7. Why were spices so important in medieval trade? List three of the important spices of commerce during the fifteenth to eighteenth centuries.
8. Briefly outline the history of the introduction of the breadfruit tree into the New World.
9. Both the potato and sugar cane were responsible for social and political problems in the nineteenth century. Explain.
10. The opium trade was once an important aspect of British trade. Explain.
11. Two plants, cotton and tobacco, were important in the development of colonial America. Describe the famous "three-cornered" voyage of trading ships during this period.
12. Discuss some examples of so-called "foods of the future." Do any of these appear to be promising new sources of food?

SUPPLEMENTAL READING

Anderson, E. *Plants, Men and Life.* Boston: Little, Brown, 1952. (Available as a paperback from the University of California Press, Berkeley, 1967).

Arber, A. *Herbals, Their Origin and Evolution.* New York: Cambridge University Press, 1953.

Baker, H. H. *Plants and Civilization*, 2nd ed. Belmont, California: Wadsworth Publishing Co., Inc., 1970.

Bates, M. *Man in Nature*, 2nd ed. Englewood Cliffs, N.J.: Prentice-Hall, Inc., 1964.

Heiser, C. B., Jr. *Nightshades, the Paradoxical Plants.* San Francisco: W. H. Freeman and Co., 1969.

Heiser, C. B. Jr. *Seed to Civilization, the Story of Man's Food.* San Francisco: W. H. Freeman and Co., 1973.

Hoebel, E. A.: *Anthropology: The Study of Man,* 3rd ed. New York, McGraw-Hill, 1966.

Janick, J., R. W. Schery, F. W. Woods, and V. W. Ruttan (eds.). *Plant Agriculture: Readings from Scientific American.* San Francisco: W. H. Freeman and Co., 1970.

Sauer, C. O. *Agricultural Origins and Dispersals.* Cambridge: M.I.T. Press, 1969.

Schery, R. W. *Plants for Man,* 2nd ed. Englewood Cliffs, N.J.: Prentice-Hall, Inc., 1972.

A tropical rain forest as viewed in Darwin's day (From Moorhead, A. *Darwin and the Beagle*. Harmondsworth, England: Penguin Books, Ltd., 1971).

Chapter 2

Plants and Science

THE NATURE OF PLANTS • **THE NATURE OF SCIENCE** • **THE CLASSIFICA-
TION OF PLANTS** • **SCIENTIFIC NAMES** • **LINNAEUS** • **DARWIN AND
EVOLUTION** • **NEO-DARWINISM** • **PRESENT SYSTEMS OF CLASSIFICATION**
• **BOTANICAL SCIENCE IN THE MODERN WORLD** • **SUMMARY**

THE NATURE OF PLANTS

When we speak of plants in ordinary conversation, it is generally
understood that we mean the leafy, green plants of fields, gardens,
and woods. These plants are highly advanced organisms of complex
structure and are the products of millions of years of evolutionary
changes. In botany, we are interested not only in the complex plants
but in their simpler fossil ancestors. We also include in our studies
contemporary one-celled and few-celled plants that apparently have
undergone little evolutionary change.

Since so many organisms are called plants, it is useful to have
fairly comprehensive definitions that allow for the great variations as
well as common attributes. Plants range from such one-celled types
as algae and bacteria, through the associations of algal cells
(termed *colonies*) to many-celled higher plants with their diversity of
cell types. What things do these plants have in common? Perhaps
our first thought is that most plants are green. More specifically,
they contain chlorophyll and are photosynthetic. Plants, unlike
animals, are able to make their own food, using solar energy. The
exceptional plants that are unable to photosynthesize—mostly bacteria and fungi—have other characteristics that seem plant-like. The
presence of walls around each cell is one such characteristic. Another is the way in which substances enter and leave the cell. Plants
have neither digestive tracts nor excretory organs. All substances
moving into or out of plant cells do so in water solution, passing
through the porous cell walls and the selectively permeable outer
membranes. Generally speaking, this requirement for soluble food
confers on plants a sedentary life. Plants do not pursue food, although a few have perfected means of trapping and digesting prey.
Certain fungi snare minute nematode worms in the soil and some in-

---

"Delight is a weak term to express the feelings of a naturalist who for the first time
finds himself in a Brazilian forest."

CHARLES DARWIN, *Voyage of the Beagle*

sectivorous plants trap, entangle, or drown ants, flies, and other small insects.

Still another characteristic of many plants is their pattern of growth. Unlike most animals, plants continue to grow as long as they live. This is called *indeterminate growth,* and is in contrast to the determinate growth of many animals that results in the production of mature, non-growing adults.

We see, therefore, that while it is possible to make general statements about the nature of plants, it is impossible to make absolute, scientifically correct definitions. There are always exceptions to be seen, and the reasons for these uncertainties are to be found in the nature of science itself.

THE NATURE OF SCIENCE

The student of any biological science should be aware of the conceptual nature of science. Our groupings of plants are made according to our concept of their evolutionary relationships. Conceptual constructions of this kind are based on a combination of interpretations regarding the natural orders and states of living things and are termed *models.* Although these models are usually accurate within the limitations of the observations upon which they are based, they are still oversimplified generalizations and are subject to future modifications and sometimes even drastic revision or abandonment.

The nature of scientific concepts can be explained in terms of the well-known Indian fable of the three blind Brahmins and the elephant. One Brahmin felt the elephant's trunk and conjectured that an elephant was like a rope; another felt a leg and conceived the animal as tree-like; the third, upon leaning against the elephant's broad side, imagined him to be like a wall. A synthesis of these three concepts might produce a model bearing some resemblance to the

Figure 2–1. Cartoon depicting the evolution of a scientific model. The manner in which hypotheses sometimes diverge from observations and reality is satirized (Redrawn from *Deciduous Forest Newsletter,* 1972).

real animal but additional data would be required to achieve a model that would be recognized by an individual with sight.

The reader with an interest in fossils will recognize that the simple example above has something in common with the elegant reconstructions of extinct plants such as *Lepidodendron* and *Calamites* (see Chapter 13). Such models are constructed by the imaginative interpretation of carefully prepared specimens obtained from scattered bits of fossilized plants. Since these models were based at least in part on direct observation, we believe that they are reasonably close to reality. On the other hand, the task of constructing useful models becomes increasingly more complicated as the data tend to consist of indirect observations. A good example of this is Dr. James Watson's description in his book, *The Double Helix,* of his weekend of making paper cutouts of the nucleotides of DNA (deoxyribonucleic acid) and then attempting to fit them together in a meaningful way. His imaginative concept of a double helix consisting of matched base-pairs was constructed in part on ratios of such pairs established by chemistry and in part on his understanding of genetics, which led him to think in terms of paired structures. Subsequent verification of the double helix model by x-ray diffraction patterns of actual DNA was in itself a marvel of interpretation from indirect observations.

It is important also to realize that the scientific information presented in a textbook such as this is based upon the authors' selection of concepts that they believe lead to an integrated presentation of subject matter. Since a science is built up from the contributions of many research writers, considerable selectivity must be employed, and erroneous or misleading interpretations are always possible.

THE CLASSIFICATION OF PLANTS

The classification of plants has been an intellectual pursuit of humans since they first began to reason. Early men and women doubtless recognized plants according to their usefulness or their danger; for example, it was probably discovered rather quickly that some plants were efficacious in relieving symptoms of physical distress. The naming of plants was a matter of survival for ancient peoples, because they were directly dependent upon them for food, for shelter, and often for medicines and pleasures. It was often necessary to communicate with others in order to find and collect these materials, and thus over the centuries a folklore of common or aboriginal names came into being, many of which have come down to us today. All primitive peoples have their own set of useful local plants; and all have their own names and particular descriptions for them. All have names for the magical plants, for plants important in religious ceremonies, and for harmful plants.

With the origin of agriculture around 8000 B.C. and the rise of civilization, the importance of plant names grew to the point where rudimentary classifications were produced to aid in identification of native plants. Useful plants were cultivated widely in the Old World empires of Egypt, Mesopotamia, and Israel, and the Maya of the New World. Drug, spice, and medicinal plants, as well as food plants, spread widely around the Mediterranean Basin. The first rational classification of plants was produced in ancient Greece. Theophrastus' *Enquiry into Plants,* mentioned earlier, classified plants into four large groups: herbs, undershrubs, shrubs, and trees, and descriptions of about 500 different plants were included together with their real or imagined medicinal values. As Greek learning spread, so did systematic knowledge of plants. The Romans inherited the Greek philosophical tradition and also imitated their system of naming plants. Dioscorides (born c. 64 A.D.), a physician and surgeon in the armies of Emperor Nero, wrote a a book he called *De Materia Medica* in which were illustrated 500 plants of supposed medicinal usefulness. This book was called an **herbal,** and became the cornerstone of medical botany for 15 centuries. It was faithfully copied by generations of scholars, and it exerted tremendous influence on the development of plant lore. The copies and elaborations of Dioscorides' book also were called herbals, and constituted the body of knowledge about plants into the Renaissance.

SCIENTIFIC NAMES

Herbals were usually illustrated with woodcuts, and the plants were described by a long Latin sentence or phrase. For this reason naming was a ponderous operation that could be performed only by scholars and physicians. In the seventeenth century, a Frenchman named Tournefort (1656–1708) brought some order out of this chaos by assigning group names to cover assemblages of plants that scholars had agreed were similar; such a group name is called the **genus**. Thus, the oaks belong to the genus *Quercus,* which is the old, classical name for this important group of trees. This and several other plant-naming systems in a sense set the stage for the great systematic work of the eighteenth and nineteenth centuries.

Carolus Linnaeus

The present system of scientific names was finally perfected by the Swedish botanist, Karl Linné (Carolus Linnaeus) (1707–1778), who gave each plant two names (binomial) in place of the many names (polynomial) in popular use before his time. This proved to be quite a breakthrough; to this day we have found no better way of naming plants and animals.

Every plant (and every animal) has only one correct scientific name, composed of the generic and specific names. The scientific name that Linnaeus gave to the live-oak tree was *Quercus virginiana, Quercus* because it produced acorns as do European oaks,

Figure 2–2 Page from an herbal illustrating *Zea mays,* also known as Indian corn and maize (From Arber, A. *The Gramineae:* Cambridge, The University Press, 1934).

and *virginiana* because the first specimen was collected by one of his students in the Virginia colony. There are many species of oak, but there is only one correct scientific name for the live-oak, and that is its name over the world.

People sometimes ask, "Why does a plant or animal have to have a Latin name?" The answer is so that a single, universally accepted name can be used, instead of many local or common names. Latin is used because its use offends the sensibilities of no nation, and because it traditionally was the language of scholarship.

During the eighteenth century, several extensive systematic works were published by such distinguished botanists as Linnaeus, Lamarck, DeJussieu and DeCandolle. In these systematic treatments there was acknowledgment of the relationship of plants, both as individuals and as members of larger groups. However, they were, first and foremost, information retrieval systems. Once having identified and named a plant (or animal), how best to insure that it, and its name, does not become lost again? It seems obvious to us now that a system in which related species are grouped in genera, genera in families, and families in even higher categories would be most adaptable to a retrieval system. Such a system, however, often implies evolutionary relationship, a concept as yet unformalized in Linnaeus' time.

Figure 2-3 The frontispiece of *Hortus Cliffortianus,* the first major publication of Linnaeus. Cherubs are shown surrounding a goddess figure and bearing Linnaeus' contributions to science. One cherub is pictured holding a Centigrade thermometer, which was actually invented by Linnaeus even though it is credited to Celsius.

Linnaeus, who was the greatest botanist of the eighteenth century, firmly ensconced the binomial system of nomenclature, but designed a system of classification that had a numerical basis and was almost completely artificial and unnatural. He established a number of classes based on stamen numbers and arrangements—Monandria for flowers having only one stamen, Diandria for those with two stamens, Triandria for those having three stamens, and so on. Additional classes were erected to include plants with other floral peculiarities. Widely unrelated genera were lumped together on this basis. Class Monoecia (unisexual flowers), for instance, included the cat-tail, which is a monocotyledon; the oak, a dicotyledon; and the arbor-vitae, a cone-bearing gymnosperm.

Nevertheless a great many of Linnaeus' binomials are valid to this day. It is customary to abbreviate the author's name after a scientific name, so the name for the live-oak correctly is *Quercus virginiana* L. A brief scanning of the pages of Gray's *Manual of Botany* shows that, of 109 plants picked at random by the author, the

Linnaean species name is still used for 33, while in others the Linnaean name has been preserved in a new combination. A name such as *Asimina triloba* (L.) Dunal., for the paw-paw, represents a revision of a Linnaean name by another botanist. It is a remarkable testimony, not only to Linnaeus but to many other plant taxonomists, that the species designations have retained a high degree of accuracy to this day.

DARWIN AND EVOLUTION

In the year 1831, a 22-year-old theological student and amateur naturalist embarked on a voyage of scientific exploration that was to have far-reaching consequences for scientists and philosophers the world over. This young man, Charles Darwin, had been recommended to Captain Robert FitzRoy, commander of H.M.S. *Beagle,* for the position of naturalist on an around-the-world voyage. FitzRoy, who was but 23 years of age, disliked Darwin at first sight. For one thing, he thought Darwin's nose was too short to denote strong character (FitzRoy, himself, had a large nose). However, within an hour or so he became completely charmed by Darwin's cheerful nature and sincere manner. And so Darwin was appointed naturalist on the Beagle, and shortly thereafter the epic voyage began. It was to last four and one half years.

Early in the voyage, Darwin became immensely impressed with the abundance and variety of life in the tropics. Later, he discovered rich deposits of fossils of large, extinct mammals in Argentina, and, subsequently, he was to observe and speculate upon the island-

Figure 2–4 Darwin as a young man (From Moorhead, A. *Darwin and the Beagle.* Harmondsworth, England: Penguin Books, Ltd., 1971).

building activities of corals and the uplifting and subsidence of land masses. These and other experiences led him to think about the changing patterns of past and present life, on the extravagance of reproduction in nature, and on the great span of time involved in island-formation and the rising and sinking of great land areas. After his return to England, a life of quiet contemplation led, in 1859, to the publication of *The Origin of Species,* in which Darwin firmly set forth the concept of evolution of life-forms as a consequence of natural selection. His presentation was so well-documented with numerous examples from nature and from plant and animal breeding that his concepts received wide acceptance in the scientific community of his day.

Darwin's theory of evolution was based on the following premises:

(a) organisms produce many offspring, but very few of these live to reproduce;

(b) no two organisms are exactly alike, all differing from each other to varying degrees;

(c) the competition among the members of a generation of progeny is fierce;

(d) those individuals best adapted (having the optimum combination of physical and physiological attributes) to survive live to reproduce, while the others perish; and

(e) this selection by nature of individuals best adapted for survival exerts a slow but appreciable change in the structural and functional nature of the organisms.

Although such adaptive modifications may appear relatively minor over short periods of time, great evolutionary changes may result in the long run from the cumulative effects of many such changes.

Darwin, however, knew of no processes that would explain the transmission of structural and functional variations from generation to generation, and he was unaware that an obscure Austrian monk named Gregor Mendel had worked out an explanation for the inheritance of such variations. Mendel's principles of heredity had not been accepted up to this time; it was not until the early 1900's that they were rediscovered and applied to the theory of evolution. Subsequently, **mutations** were discovered, first as spontaneous changes in hereditary characteristics and, later, as the products of treatment of cells and organisms with x-rays, other forms of radiation, and various chemicals. The combination of modern genetic theory and Darwin's concept of natural selection has been termed **Neo-Darwinism.**

NEO-DARWINISM

In his theory, Darwin stressed greatly the survival of the *individual* organism. For example, the strongest male capable of attracting and defending a harem passed on his strengths to his offspring while weaker males perished without producing progeny, so that only the "fittest" organisms survived. Now it is recognized that selection and evolution operate most effectively at the level of a population of organisms, and that fitness to survive is a *group* characteristic. Many individual traits, some highly advantageous in a given environment, as well as others of slight or no survival value, occur among the individuals in a population. These traits form the basis of the variation upon which natural selection operates. Evolution, in the modern view, seems to be a change in the characteristics of a population over a period of time during which individual organisms share to varying degrees a common stock of hereditary traits having adaptive values in particular environments.

Darwin had no understanding of the hereditary units we call **genes,** hence he was ignorant of the cause of the variations occurring between individual plants and animals. He tended to assume a direct transfer of the inherited traits themselves rather than the inheritance of hereditary units which in turn could control and determine such traits, a process we call **gene expression**. Spontaneous changes in the genes are known to occur from time to time. Such changes, or mutations, usually are deleterious when expressed, but sometimes have positive effects. Most often this is the case when the environment is changing and a population faces new challenges. For instance, genes for dwarfness might be advantageous should there be a climatic shift from warm and wet to cool and dry conditions. Thus, formerly deleterious genes might have adaptive value in the new situation. In such instances some of the mutant genes present in the population may be expressed in combinations of traits favoring the survival of a segment of the population. This segment may flourish and expand so that the overall nature of the population eventually undergoes evolutionary change.

Modern evolutionary theory represents a refinement of Darwinian evolution, so that now the variation upon which natural selection operates is seen as a product of gene mutation, and attention is focused on the evolution occurring in populations rather than in individuals.

Not all biologists support the concepts of Neo-Darwinism. For example, certain features of plants and animals are perpetuated even though they appear to have no adaptive significance, and sometimes hereditary changes in individuals making up a population appear to have occurred in a random fashion rather than to have been directed by natural selection. Others feel that Neo-Darwinism offers a satisfactory explanation for minor evolutionary changes but not for the great differences that exist among major groups of organisms. Despite such reservations, evolution through natural selection seems to offer the most satisfactory scientific explanation for a number of trends observable in organisms of the past and present. Among these are:

(a) the existence of fossil plants and animals of great antiquity that either are quite unlike present day organisms or else appear to be primitive counterparts of living forms;

(b) the appearance in the fossil record of apparent lineages of organisms in which progressive structural modifications may be discerned (the evolution of the horse is a well-known example, and similar examples may be seen among plant groups such as ferns, club mosses, and conifers);

(c) the occurrence of similar structural characteristics in unrelated and widely separated groups of organisms living in similar environments (convergent evolution); and,

(d) the great structural diversity sometimes seen in closely related forms (apparently of common ancestry) in isolated regions (adaptive radiation).

As we look at the fossil record of plants and animals we often see bizarre forms of life (such as the dinosaurs) that are difficult to imagine as ancestral to modern organisms. Evolutionary processes often have produced such highly specialized plants and animals, which are termed evolutionary "dead-ends" because they appear to be incapable of development into new forms of life. This is not to say that such dead-end groups are unsuccessful; they have

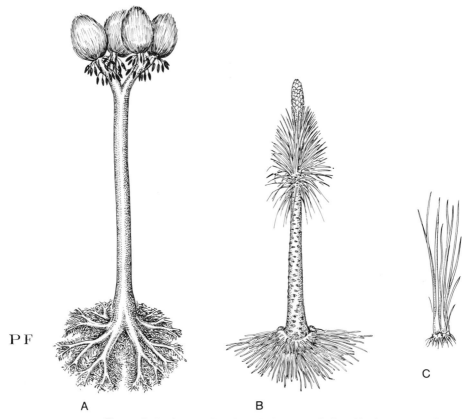

P F

A   B   C

Figure 2–5 A postulated evolutionary relationship between a *Devonian tree form, Sigillaria* (ca. 300 million years ago), A Mesozoic plant, *Pleuromeia,* (ca. 200 million years ago), and *Isoetes,* a living plant. In this case the trend has been modification through reduction and loss of parts. However, all three share such common features as leaf form, attachment pattern of roots, lobed stem bases, and have similar reproductive organs.

Figure 2–6 Convergent evolution is exhibited by an African euphorb (*right*), an American cactus (*left*), and an African *Stapelia* (*foreground*). Though these three species are classified in different families, all show a number of similar characteristics that are considered to be adaptations to desert conditions.

flourished in the past and some continue to survive to the present. A few, such as the horse-shoe crab and the mosses, are "living fossils," and appear to be little changed from their ancestors of millions of years ago.

Since we cannot visualize the continuing evolution of new plant and animal forms from highly specialized ancestors, we see the evolutionary process as, initially, the development of relatively unspecialized organisms, followed later by the development of more highly specialized groups. When visualized diagrammatically, an evolutionary family tree becomes a shrubby, multi-branched structure with unspecialized ancestral types at the forkings and many terminating side branches. Often we know more about these dead branches than we do about the forks in the tree, and our search for fossils of unspecialized ancestors that might have given rise to major groups of plants and animals is never-ending.

Among the explanations offered to account for the great diversity we see among living organisms, as well as their relationships with those of the past, are:

(a) duplication of structure, including multiplication of cells, tissues, and organs (according to this explanation, unicellular organ-

Figure 2–7 Adaptive radiation exhibited on the Canary Islands by members of the genus *Aeonium* (From Carlquist, S. *Island Life, A Natural History of the Islands of the World.* Garden City, N.Y., The Natural History Press, 1965).

isms are thought to have given rise to multicellular organisms, unbranched plants to many-branched forms, and plants with simple systems of conductive tissue to those with multiple conduction systems);

(b) increases in structural complexity, as for example the modification of some cells of a simple multicellular organism composed of like cells, or in the specialization of some branches in a simple branched form in such a way that leaf shapes are produced;

(c) reduction and loss of parts (decrease in complexity), as in the elimination of petals in flowers of certain plant groups or elimination of leaves in some desert plants; and

(d) modifications in vegetative and reproductive patterns, such as the timing of flowering to coincide with favorable climatic pat-

40

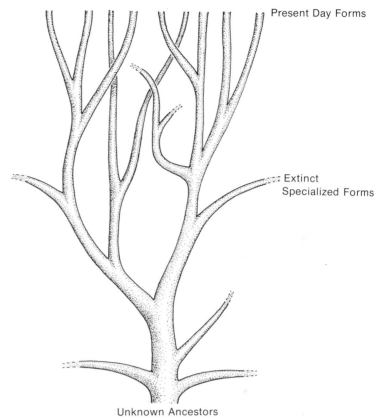

Present Day Forms

Extinct
Specialized Forms

Unknown Ancestors

Figure 2–8 Model of an evolutionary family tree. The forks in the tree represent unspecialized forms, from which have evolved both highly specialized forms and further advanced (but still relatively unspecialized) types.

terns or the germination of seeds of desert plants only after heavy rainfall.

Examples of these and other evolutionary trends will be seen in coming chapters.

PRESENT SYSTEMS OF CLASSIFICATION

Our present system of plant classification is derived from the work of Engler and Prantl, whose 20-volume *Die Natürlichen Pflanzenfamilien* has undergone some revision since its appearance in 1899, but is so monumental as to defy abandonment. *Die Natürlichen Pflanzenfamilien* is a phylogenetic (evolutionary) classification, as all post-Darwinian systems tend to be. It attempts to arrange the plant groups according to certain principles of primitive vs. advanced characteristics. As one can imagine, there have been many arguments about such characteristics and how they should be applied. Consequently, several modern classifications, principally at the levels of Order, Class and Division (Phylum), have been superimposed on the Engler and Prantl system. The system of plant clas-

41

sification adopted for this book is based on a recent one devised by Dr. Arthur Cronquist of the New York Botanical Garden, and is printed on the inside back cover.

Since we have already talked about the live-oak, let us see how it might appear in a classification system:

KINGDOM: Plantae
  Division: Magnoliophyta (flowering plants)
  CLASS: Magnoliopsida (dicotyledons)
  Order: Fagales (beech order)
    FAMILY: Fagaceae (beech family)
    Genus: Quercus (oaks)
    Species: *virginiana* (live-oak)

Every species is classified in this fashion and the arrangement is such as to reflect supposed evolutionary relationships of plants. The category to which a name belongs is shown by the suffix of the Latin (or Greek) word. Thus, division names end in -phyta, class names in -opsida (or -ae), order names in -ales, and family names in -aceae. Unfortunately many students believe that botany consists only of long lists of unpronounceable Latin and Greek words. This is, of course, far from the truth, for naming and classification are only one area of activity in the broad field of plant science. However, the

Figure 2–9 The live-oak, *Quercus virginiana.* Note the Spanish moss, a flowering plant of the pineapple family, hanging from the boughs; such a plant is said to be an **epiphyte** (see Chapter 6).

name of the plant is the key to all the information we have about it, and accurate names are essential to progress in the science. Classification enables us to understand natural relationships and evolution, and makes it possible to predict properties of newly discovered species through comparison with known species of plants.

BOTANICAL SCIENCE IN THE MODERN WORLD

Botany is both one of the oldest sciences of Western civilization and a modern science. In its early history, botany naturally emphasized observation, description, and interpretation. These activities are still important, but they are not the only methodologies in use. Controlled experiments, in which test samples are compared to control samples, are widely used, particularly in plant biochemistry, plant physiology, plant genetics, and developmental studies. In many botanical studies, sophisticated instruments are employed at

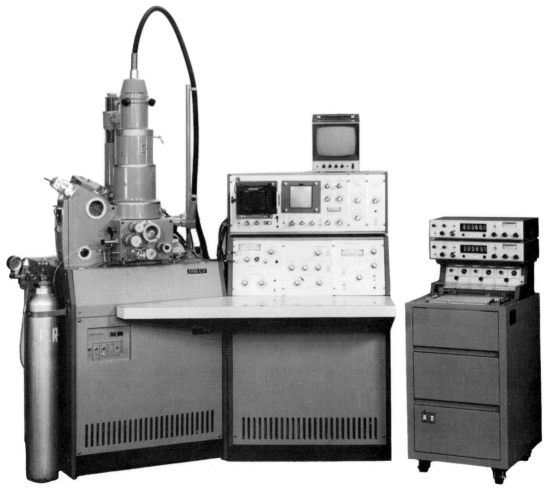

Figure 2–10 A scanning electron microscope (Photo courtesy of JEOL U.S.A., Incorporated, Medford, Massachusetts).

universities, institutes, and research laboratories where phytotrons, ultracentrifuges, electron microscopes, and other facilities make experimentation possible.

In this book, we will devote considerable space to discussions of major plant groups and their relationships. This aspect of plant biology, called **systematic botany,** includes the study of classification and relationship, especially from the evolutionary standpoint. Many fields of biology contribute to our understanding of this part of plant biology, including **genetics** (study of heredity), **ecology** (study of organisms and their relationships to one another and to the environment), **cytology** (study of cells), **anatomy** (study of structure of tissues and organs), and **morphology** (study of form and development). In addition, there are branches devoted to the study of particular groups of plants, such as **phycology** (study of algae), **mycology** (study of fungi), **bryology** (study of mosses and liverworts), **lichenology** (study of lichens), and **pteridology** (study of ferns). Chromosome number, chromosome behavior, genetic testing through hybridization experiments, as well as detailed anatomical and morphological comparisons, have made important contributions towards improving our interpretations of plant diversity.

In recent years, new tools have been added to the laboratory of the systematic botanist, chiefly from the laboratory of the biochemist. For example, flowering plants produce thousands of chemical compounds, a number of which are of uncertain function in the plant. Many of the latter are metabolic by-products and are sometimes referred to as **secondary compounds.** They apparently are not essential to the life of individual cells, but seem to be part of the total adaptation of the plant to a particular environment. Examples of secondary compounds are the red and blue flower pigments, **anthocyanins,** and hundreds of related compounds called **flavonoids,** each of which is a slight modification of a basic molecular structure.

One of the most interesting examples of a group of pigments that have evolutionary and systematic significance is the **beta-cyanins.** There are about ten families of plants that produce betacyanins, and all are classified in the same order. Families of plants that produce betacyanins apparently cannot produce anthocyanins, and vice versa.

The identification of groups whose relationships are uncertain can be aided by determination of the kind of chemical markers present. Certain chemical compounds found in *Casuarina,* the Australian pine, suggest that it is more closely related to certain non-flowering plants, though presently it is classified as a flowering plant. Its relationship has been in dispute for many years; some botanists consider it to be a primitive flowering plant, while others believe it to be a highly specialized plant related to the common sycamore tree. Its chemical markers relate it to the non-flowering seed plants known as conifers, particularly those of the genus *Podocarpus.*

One technique of making comparisons between pigment markers in flowering plants is use of **two-dimensional paper chro-**

matography. The flower pigments are extracted in a solvent, and then this extract is concentrated. The individual pigments are then separated by means of their different absorptive properties with respect to paper, as follows:

The pigment concentrate is placed in one corner of the paper. An adjacent edge of the paper then is dipped in a solvent that rises by capillary action, carrying the pigments to various heights. The paper then is dried and turned 90°; the second edge that was adjacent to the original spot is dipped in another solvent, carrying the pigments at right angles to the first direction. The resulting two-dimensional pattern of individual pigments formed on the paper, when viewed under ultra-violet light and in the presence of ammonia fumes, has been found often to be specific for species. The spots of pigment then can be analyzed further for identification of specific compounds. In this way the chemical markers can be discovered for particular species or groups of species.

Enzymes and other proteinaceous components also can be used to identify plant groups and to study their relationships. Individual proteins in plant extracts can be separated and a number of constituents in the extracts can be compared individually with those of other species. This technique is essentially an immunological analysis and involves many of the same methods used in blood typing and serum analysis.

Antisera are produced in rabbits from crude saps taken from a plant. Extracts from another plant, whose relationship to the first plant is in question, are added to the antisera. Well-marked precipitation lines develop against the extracts in accordance with the similarity of protein composition of the unknown to that of the known plant. The degree of precipitation will be proportional to the relationship of the plants. Generally, serological investigations of this kind have produced schemes of relationship between species that are similar to those already postulated on the basis of morphological evidence. The importance of serological approaches to the study of relationship lies in the fact that they represent another method of measuring differences between species and groups of species that can be used, along with other data, to make final appraisal of the probable course of evolution in the group under investigation.

Botany is an important division of biology, the science of living things, and is related to many similar specialties and branches in **zoology,** the science of animals, and **microbiology,** the science of bacteria and other microbes. Many activities in the biological sciences cut across the botanical and zoological sciences, such as **molecular biology, biochemistry** and **physiology** which deal with the physico-chemical composition and reactions of living matter.

In the chapters that follow, the principal concepts of botany, particularly those dealing with the great groups of plant species, will be discussed. The general structures of plants, their reproduction, and evolutionary pathways of descent will be examined. And finally, plants and plant life in relation to today's society, the ecological importance of vegetation, and the usefulness of plants in solving some of today's pressing problems will be considered.

Text continued on page 50.

45

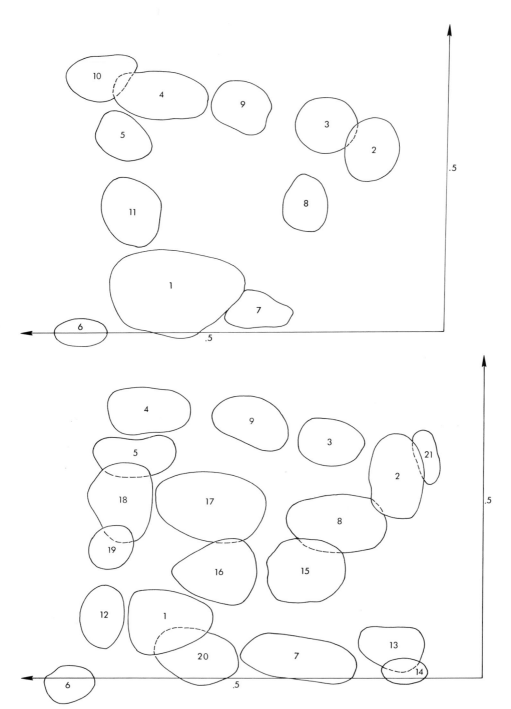

Figure 2–11 Four two-dimensional paper chromatograms of corolla pigments from four taxa of the genus *Ruellia* (family: Acanthaceae). Each spot on the chromatogram represents a phenolic compound, and identical compounds occurring in different taxa bear the same number.

In Table 2–1 on the opposite page is a summary of the occurrence of phenolic compounds in the four taxa. Note that there are nine compounds that are common to all taxa. The two varieties of *Ruellia nudiflora* differ by only three compounds, but *R. tuberosa* and *R. caroliniensis* differ by 12 compounds. The latter two species are also very distinct morphologically. The chromatographic evidence would further suggest that *R. nudiflora* is more closely related to *R. tuberosa* than is *R. caroliniensis*, since these taxa differ by only six compounds.

These conclusions regarding the relationships of these taxa are also corroborated by the genetic evidence produced by means of artificial hybridization tests.

Illustration continued on opposite page.

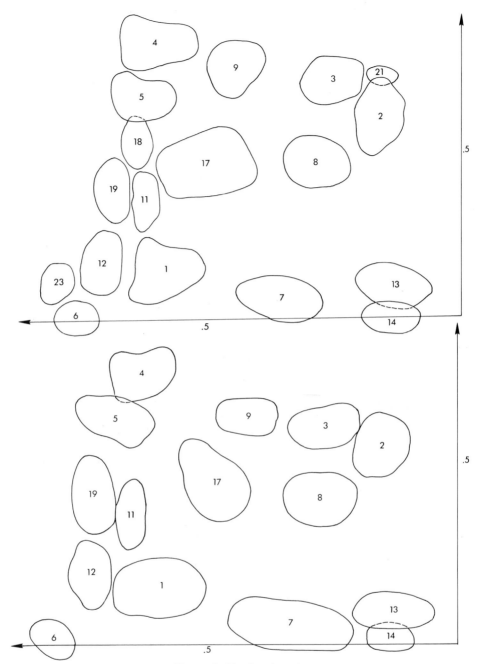

Figure 2–11 *Continued.*

Table 2–1. DISTRIBUTION OF FLAVONOID AND OTHER PHENOLIC COMPOUNDS IN *RUELLIA* SPECIES

Nos.	1	2	3	4	5	6	7	8	9	10	11	12	13	14	15	16	17	18	19	20	21	22	23	24	25	26
TAXON																										
Ruellia tuberosa	x	x	x	x	x	x	x	x	x	x	x	x														
Ruellia nudiflora var. *nudiflora*	x	x	x	x	x	x	x	x	x	x		x	x	x	x		x		x							
Ruellia nudiflora var. *occidentalis*	x	x	x	x	x	x	x	x	x	x		x	x	x	x		x	x	x		x[1]		x			
Ruellia caroliniensis var. *caroliniensis*	x	x	x	x	x	x	x	x	x	x		x	x	x	x	x	x	x	x	x	x					

[1]Weak.

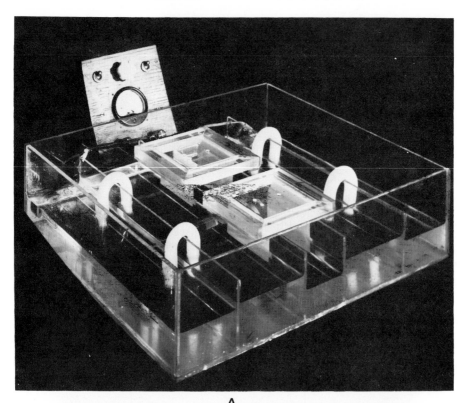

A

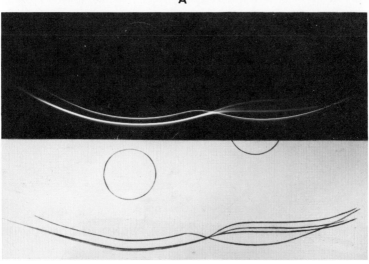

B

Figure 2–12 *A,* Immuno-electrophoresis apparatus. *B,* Precipitation lines formed by interactions between plant proteins and antibodies of rabbit serum. *C* (opposite page), Reactions between extracts of several species of wild potato (*Solanum*) are shown. It is apparent that some species have more precipitation lines in common than do others. The latter presumably are less closely related to members of the first group. (From Gell, P. G. H., J. G. Hawkes, and T. C. Wright: *Proc. Royal Soc. B.,* 151:364, 1959.)
Illustration continued on opposite page.

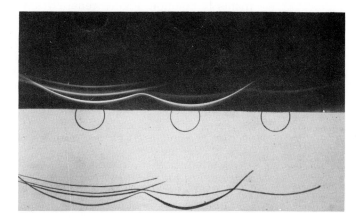

4 lines	2 lines	1 line
Series IV	Series V	Series III
BUL	*CPH*	*MOR*
Series XII	*SMB*	
VER	*EHR*	
SEM	Series VI	
DEM	*JAM*	
GRR	*PIN*	
SPT		
Series XIII		
PLT		
STO		
Series XIV		
POL		
Series XVII		
TUB		

BUL = *S. bulbocastanum*
VER = *S. verrucosum*
SEM = *S. semidemissum*
DEM = *S. demissum*
GRR = *S. guerreroense*
SPT = *S. spectabile*
PLT = *S. polytrichon*
STO = *S. stoloniferum*

POL = *S. polyadenium*
TUB = *S. tuberosum*
CPH = *S. cardiophyllum*
SMB = *S. sambucinum*
EHR = *S. ehrenbergii*
JAM = *S. jamesii*
PIN = *S. pinnatisectum*
MOR = *S. morelliforme*

C

Figure 2–12 *Continued.*

SUMMARY   While it is rather difficult to find a simple definition that will fit all plant-like organisms, several concepts that are generally useful may be applied. Plants for the most part are photosynthetic organisms. Those that are not (fungi, bacteria and a few flowering plants) have other plant-like characteristics. The cells of plants are almost always enclosed within rigid walls. While animals generally ingest particulate matter, plants usually take up nutrients in solution. Plants generally are stationary, although a few simple types are motile. Finally, many plants have an indeterminate growth pattern; that is, they continue to grow as long as they live.

Plant science (botany) is largely a conceptual science. We see this in our concept of plant evolution, which depicts a progression of more and more diverse life forms. Knowledge of evolution and plant relationships requires a means of keeping track of all of the diverse kinds of plants. Present plant classifications attempt to arrange plants in such a way that evolutionary relationships are evident. Of great importance is agreement on the name to be applied to any particular kind of plant; each plant is given a binomial (genus and species, usually in Latin), which is accepted by scientists all over the world.

Modern botany encompasses much more than the naming and classification of plants. It includes the study of cells (cytology) often with the most sophisticated instruments (such as electron microscopes and ultracentrifuges); the chemical and physical nature of plants (biochemistry and physiology); as well as plant form and structure (morphology and anatomy); plant genetics, and many others.

DISCUSSION QUESTIONS

1. What characteristics are shared by all plants? By most plants? By only some plants?
2. What is meant by a scientific model? Give an example.
3. About how long has agriculture been in existence?
4. What is meant by an artificial system of classification? Give an example.
5. What kinds of plant designations antedated binomials?
6. List four premises upon which Darwin based his theory of evolution.
7. What is meant by Neo-Darwinism? How does it differ from Darwinism?
8. What plants might be used to illustrate convergent evolution?
9. What observations and circumstances might be used to argue against Darwinian evolution?
10. Define cytology, morphology, ecology, phycology, mycology, bryology, and pteridology.
11. Discuss how biochemical approaches to systematic problems of classification may aid the botanist in solving difficult problems of relationship.
12. Briefly explain how systematists use two-dimensional paper chromatography to study plant species relationships.

SUPPLEMENTAL READING

Alston, R. E., and B. L. Turner. *Biochemical Systematics.* Englewood Cliffs, N.J.: Prentice-Hall, Inc., 1963.

Benson, L. *Plant Classification.* Boston: D.C. Heath and Co., 1957.

Briggs, D., and S. M. Walters. *Plant Variation and Evolution.* New York: McGraw-Hill Book Co., 1969.

Corner, E. J. H. *The Life of Plants.* New York: The World Publishing Co., 1964.

Gray, A. *Manual of Botany,* 8th ed. New York: Van Nostrand Reinhold, 1950.

Lawrence, G. H. *Taxonomy of Vascular Plants.* New York: The Macmillan Co., 1951.

Moorhead, A. *Darwin and the Beagle.* Harmondsworth, England: Penguin Books., 1971.

Watson, J. *The Double Helix.* New York: New American Library, 1969.

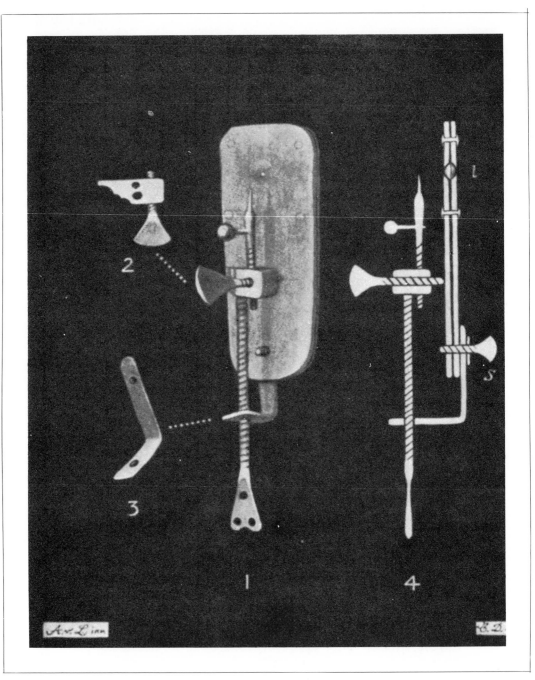

Drawing showing details of Van Leeuwenhoek's microscope.

The First Cells

Visitors to the north shore of Lake Superior cannot help but be impressed by the extensive masses of exposed rock visible on hillsides, slopes, and in gorges cut by fast-flowing streams. These expanses of rock are part of the great Canadian Shield or Precambrian Shield and are, in fact, the bedrock backbone of North America. They were laid bare by the bulldozing advances of a series of ice sheets that moved as far south as where St. Louis now stands and deposited the scraped-off soil and sediment over the land surfaces in their path.

The Canadian Shield contains the oldest known sedimentary rocks on the continent; in these rocks are found the fossilized remains of plant cells, including authentic colonies of blue-green algae thought to be nearly two billion years old.

Even older Precambrian fossils, believed to be those of bacteria, are found in the three-billion-year-old rocks of the fig tree formation of South Africa. Thus we see that unicellular organisms have existed for more than half of the 4.5 billion years of the earth's history.

THE ORIGIN OF LIFE ON EARTH

For the first billion and a half years of its existence, our world was a lifeless planet, surrounded by steaming clouds of water vapor, ammonia, carbon dioxide, nitrogen, hydrogen, and methane. The recent exploration by the space vehicle Pioneer 11 of the planet Jupiter, the largest planet in our solar system, uncovered evidence indicating a similar atmosphere. This oxygen-free atmosphere has been termed a **reducing atmosphere,** since substances exposed to

---

"There was, further, a fourth sort, which were so small, that I was not able to give them any figure at all. These were a thousand times smaller than the eye of a big louse."

A. Van Leeuwenhoek

Figure 3–1 The Canadian Shield near Thelon River, Northwest Territories. The deep parallel grooves gouged out by the glaciers indicate the direction of their advance (Courtesy of Royal Canadian Air Force).

it would tend to undergo chemical reduction, unlike earth's present atmosphere, in which substances tend to become oxidized (witness, for example, the rusting of iron). This concept of a primordial atmosphere is basic to theories that **chemical evolution** was a necessary prelude to the evolution of living things.

Although our present atmosphere, because of the shielding effect of its oxygen, screens out much of the ultraviolet radiation (UV) from the sun, those of us who have developed severe sunburns can easily accept the fact that such radiation is damaging to living cells. The ultraviolet radiation that reached the earth was much more intense in the period prior to the presence of life on earth (Azoic Era), since oxygen was supposedly absent.

Although our present atmosphere, because of the shielding effect of its oxygen, screens out much of the ultraviolet radiation (UV) from the sun, those of us who have developed severe sunburns can easily accept the fact that such radiation is damaging to living cells. The absorption of energy from ultraviolet radiation by simple

54

Figure 3–2 Fossilized blue-green algae from Precambrian rocks of the Canadian Shield. The concentric rings are composed of calcium carbonate deposited by the algae when living (Courtesy of Geological Survey of Canada).

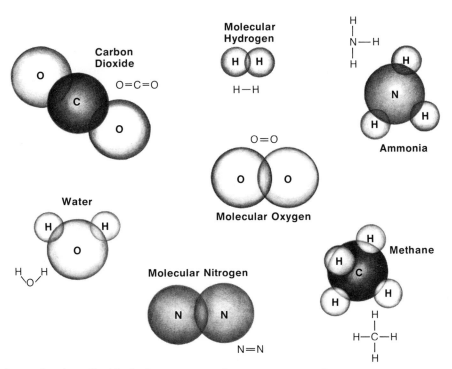

Figure 3–3 Structures of carbon dioxide, hydrogen, ammonia, water, oxygen, nitrogen, and methane molecules.

55

molecules such as water, ammonia, methane, and hydrogen causes them to become more capable of combining with one another to form new chemical compounds. It is believed that the intense radiation present during the early history of our earth brought about the interaction of the simple chemicals in the primitive atmosphere in such a way that more complicated molecules were formed. The accumulation of these chemicals in the ancient environment led, in turn, to even more complex chemicals and, eventually, to living cells. It is interesting to note that such chemicals would not last very long in today's environment. They would be consumed rapidly by bacteria and other organisms or broken down by oxidation. Since bacteria and other organisms had not yet evolved and, in addition, the atmosphere contained little oxygen, it is entirely possible that these chemicals accumulated during the early history of the earth.

There is some experimental evidence to favor this concept of the evolution of life such as the now familiar experiments of Drs. Stanley Miller and Harold Urey, in which a synthetic "primordial atmosphere" contained in a retort and exposed to radiation produced a number of organic molecules (organic molecules are composed primarily of carbon, hydrogen, and oxygen, and are characteristic of living matter). Other experiments have demonstrated that some kinds of organic molecules may assemble *in vitro* (in a test tube or a flask) spontaneously to form structures resembling cell membranes and that others may be able to replicate themselves and also to direct the synthesis of other molecules.

One of the interesting puzzles presented by the theory outlined above is that ultraviolet radiation, which seems essential for chemical evolution, is fatal to living cells; the ultraviolet radiation that caused the formation of complex molecules would have been damaging to the life formed as a result. This paradox is circumvented to a degree by supposing that the first cells lived in the biochemical debris at the bottom of bodies of water where the water might filter out harmful radiation.

There are also, as we know, other theories regarding the origin of life on earth. Those that require supernatural intervention are not within the scope of this presentation. However, there is a possibility that earth's life may have originated elsewhere in the universe. We have seen that space agencies have gone to great lengths to disinfect space vehicles in order to prevent either the contamination of the moon and the planets or the introduction of foreign life-forms to our planet. Life may represent a state of matter continually in existence in various levels of complexity, carried by meteorites from planet to planet in much the same manner as we maintain bacterial cultures by first growing, then freeze-drying, and finally, by inoculating them into fresh culture chambers.

THE GEOLOGICAL TIME TABLE

It is interesting that Charles Darwin modified his views on the rate of evolutionary changes to some extent because he was led to

Table 3–1. THE GEOLOGICAL TIME SCALE

Relative Duration of Eras	Era	Period	Epoch		Million years ago
	CENOZOIC	QUATERNARY 1-2 million years	RECENT — about 10,000 years	Humans	
			PLEISTOCENE - 1-2 million years		1-2
		TERTIARY about 63 million years	PLIOCENE about 5 m.y.	Hominids	c. 7
			MIOCENE about 19 m.y.	Primates	c. 26
			OLIGOCENE about 12 m.y.	Insectivores	c. 38
			EOCENE about 16 m.y.	Hoofed Mammals	c. 54
			PALAEOCENE about 11 m.y.	Grasslands	c. 65
	MESOZOIC	CRETACEOUS about 70 m.y.	First Grasses / Last Seed Ferns / Early Mammals		c. 135
		JURASSIC about 55 m.y.	First Birds / First Flowering Plants		c. 190
		TRIASSIC about 35 m.y.	Dinosaurs, Conifers, and Cycads		c. 225
	PALEOZOIC	PERMIAN about 55 m.y.	Last Trilobites		c. 280
		CARBONIFEROUS about 65 m.y.	Seed Ferns / First Reptile		c. 345
		DEVONIAN about 50 m.y.	First Amphibians / Club Mosses / First Insects		c. 395
		SILURIAN about 45 m.y.	First Land Plants / First Land Animals		c. 440
		ORDOVICIAN about 60 m.y.	Corals / Algae		c. 500
		CAMBRIAN about 70 m.y.	Trilobites / Sponges / Algae		c. 570
		PRECAMBRIAN	Algae and Other Primitive Plants / First Protozoans		

Relative Duration of Eras scale markings: 1,000 m.y., 2,000 m.y., 3,000 m.y., 4,000 m.y.

Oldest-known earth rocks — about 3,600 m.y.

Formation of the earth — more than 4,500 million years ago

1971

believe that the age of the earth was considerably less than he thought would have been required for great changes to occur. The estimates of the earth's age necessitating these revisions came to him from the physicists of his day who knew of no mechanisms capable of producing solar energy for extremely long periods of time. Long after Darwin's death, the discovery of atomic fusion (the hydrogen bomb) and the understanding that this is the sun's source of energy have greatly extended the estimates of the age of the solar system, as have isotopic datings of ancient rocks and sediments.

Isotopic dating is based on the principle of slow decay of certain radioactive types of atoms (**isotopes**), with the ultimate formation of other, non-radioactive forms (also called isotopes) of the same kind of atoms or of atoms of other elements. For example, uranium^{238} (a uranium atom with an atomic weight of 238) slowly decays to form lead. The time interval since the original formation of the uranium^{238} can be estimated by measuring the ratio of the isotope to its decay product (or products), and in this way the approximate age of the deposit containing the isotope can be determined. About 4.5 billion years are required for half the initial deposit of uranium^{238} to decay to lead (this is termed the **half-life** of the isotope). The half-life of another isotope, carbon^{14}, is about 5700 years. Carbon^{14} dating is useful in covering dates from 1000 to about 60,000 years before the present (BP). A certain constant amount of carbon^{14} is present in the atmosphere at all times in proportion to ordinary carbon (carbon^{12}). Both forms are present in carbon dioxide and are taken up by plants in photosynthesis. They are incorporated into plant structures and products in the ratio occurring in the atmosphere. Animals eating the plants then also incorporate carbon^{14} and carbon^{12} in the same ratio.

When plants and animals die they no longer take up additional carbon from the atmosphere. As time passes, the carbon^{14} slowly decays to form carbon^{12} and the age of the fossilized remains can be estimated by the ratio of the two carbon isotopes. Because carbon^{14} is radioactive and carbon^{12} is not, the relative amounts of each can be determined simply by using a Geiger counter or other similar device. A present concept of geological and biological history of the earth is printed on the inside front cover of this book and should be referred to when reading accounts of plant and animal life of the past presented in this and in subsequent chapters.

THE FIRST CELLS

It is believed by many scientists that the first cells on earth were formed in an aqueous environment. This environment, containing many nutrients and sometimes called the "primordial soup," developed by the processes of chemical evolution previously described. Although the oldest known fossil cells are those of bacteria, we do not believe they were the earliest cells to evolve. As simple as they may seem to us, they are still too complex to represent the first steps toward cellular life.

What may those first cells have been like? We suspect that they resembled in complexity a group of present-day organisms, the **mycoplasmas,** which are the simplest living cells known. The mycoplasmas are classified with the bacteria, though they are smaller and less complex than other bacteria. A typical mycoplasma cell is about 0.15 micrometer (μm) in diameter, somewhat irregular in shape, and enclosed in a delicate membrane composed of proteins and lipids, the **plasma membrane.** This membrane type is characteristic of all living cells. However, the cells of typical bacteria, blue-green algae, and nearly all other plants are further enclosed within a durable wall of non-living material, the **cell wall.**

Mycoplasmas have been estimated to contain about 1200 types of large, biologically important molecules, among them enzymes and nucleic acids. Although the number of these molecules is considerably less than one would expect to find even in a typical bacterial cell, they are sufficient to do the work of the cell.

Enzymes are structurally complex proteins that increase the probability that specific chemical processes or reactions will occur. For this reason they have been termed organic catalysts. They are very specific in their actions; each enzyme normally catalyzes only a single operation in a biochemical process. Since major chemical processes occurring in cells, such as the oxidation of foods (by fermentation and respiration), the making of foods (chiefly by photosynthesis), and the manufacture of amino acids and other kinds of

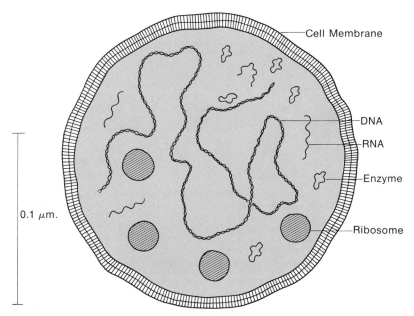

0.1 μm.

Cell Membrane

DNA

RNA

Enzyme

Ribosome

Figure 3–4 Diagrammatic representation of a *Mycoplasm* cell (Redrawn from The Smallest Living Cells, by H. J. Morowitz and M. E. Tourtellotte. Copyright © 1962 by Scientific American, Inc. All rights reserved).

59

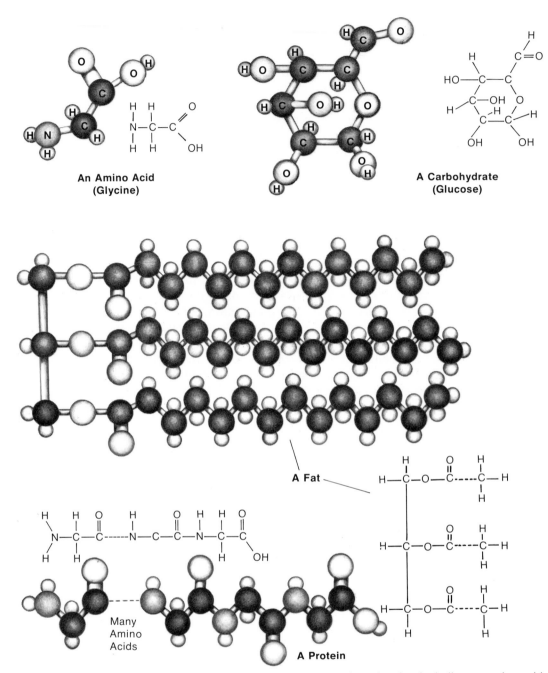

Figure 3-5 Structures of some simple organic molecules, including an amino acid, a carbohydrate, a lipid (fat), and a portion of a protein showing its composition of amino acids.

molecules involve many operations, a considerable number of different enzymes are employed.

The nucleic acids include DNA (deoxyribonucleic acid) and several kinds of RNA (ribonucleic acid). All are composed of subunits, termed **nucleotides,** that are made up, in turn, of molecules of sugar, phosphoric acid, and one or another of several base molecules (adenine, guanine, thymine, cytosine, or uracil). DNA is composed of chains of nucleotides containing the five-carbon sugar deoxyribose, a phosphate, and either adenine, guanine, thymine, or cytosine. The nucleotides are held together by sugar-phosphate linkages, and are arranged sequentially in long strands. A number of nucleotides constitute a **gene** (conventionally a gene is said to be that portion of DNA that contains instructions for making one specific kind of protein molecule). Cellular DNA is composed of two such strands intertwined to form a double helix (Fig. 3–6). RNA is similarly composed of nucleotides but these differ from those of DNA in that they contain ribose rather than deoxyribose and uracil rather than thymine. Moreover, cellular RNA exists in the form of a single strand rather than a double helix.

Nucleotides also help to make up other important molecules, such as the energy transfer molecules ATP (adenosine triphosphate), NAD (nicotinamide adenine dinucleotide), FAD (flavin adenine dinucleotide) and several others. These are associated with the transport of chemical energy in photosynthesis, respiration, and other processes.

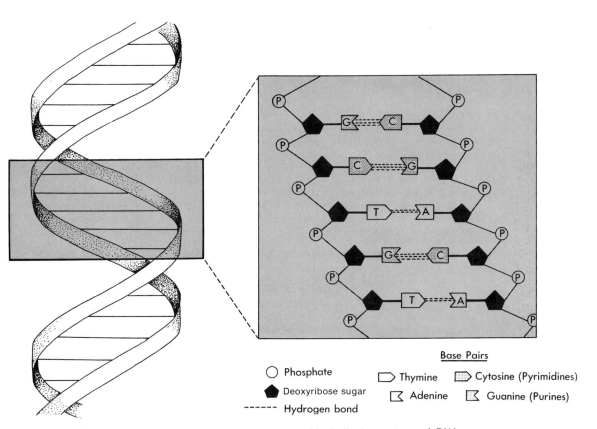

Figure 3–6 Diagrammatic representation of the double helical structure of DNA. Note that the four bases are directed inwardly, and that adenine is coupled with thymine while guanine is coupled with cytosine (Redrawn from Gerking, S. D. *Biological Systems,* 2nd ed. Philadelphia, W. B. Saunders Co., 1974).

Although mycoplasmas are relatively uncomplicated organisms, it is a mistake to conceive of them as simply "bags of enzymes," as some early biochemists were prone to believe. Instead, they are well-organized and smoothly running biological machines. Even so, they are unable to make foods or even to utilize many of the kinds of foods that bacteria thrive on. Rather, they parasitize other organisms and can be grown in culture only by the use of complex and sophisticated nutrient solutions. Might not such solutions be compared to the "primordial soup" in which lived the first cells on earth? If so, we think the time came when increasing populations of such cells began to deplete the nutrients that sustained them. The law of Malthus, that populations of organisms tend always to increase beyond the capacity of the environment to support them, often mentioned in connection with today's overpopulation, must be universal in its application, and apparently applied even to the earliest of organisms.

How did these organisms adjust to their dwindling food supply? Changes doubtless occurred in the genetic code; that is, in the sequence of the nucleotides of their DNA. In living cells the DNA code is copied by RNA through a process termed **transcription.** This RNA serves as a message from the DNA which is transferred to other RNA-containing structures called **ribosomes** where, in conjunction with amino acids attached to another form of RNA, called **transfer RNA,** the message is *translated* into a specific sequence of connected amino acids (a protein). Additional details of this important process are presented in Chapter 19 and in Figure 19–13. The changes, which we call **mutations,** occurring in the genetic code in those primitive organisms might, therefore, have resulted in the production of new and different enzymes and other proteins. The result may have been that light-absorbing pigments were produced by the new enzyme systems and, in some cases at least, those pigments were capable of transferring the absorbed solar energy to other molecules which then in turn might serve as food. This process, called photosynthesis, will be considered in greater detail in subsequent chapters.

The evolution of photosynthetic organisms did not occur in one great evolutionary jump; the study of photosynthetic systems in photosynthetic bacteria, in blue-green algae, and in higher plants suggests that it was an additive process. The photosynthetic systems of organisms became progressively more complicated involving more and more pigments (the most important and widespread of which is chlorophyll), as well as enzymes, raw materials, products, and by-products.

Eventually one of these organisms attained the ability to use the hydrogen ions and electrons of water and add them to carbon dioxide to make carbohydrates, leaving oxygen free to be released into the atmosphere. This step was a culmination in the evolution of photosynthesis, for such cells could live in complete independence from organic foods from other sources, and would require from the environment only the energy of the sun and a few simple minerals, such as water and carbon dioxide.

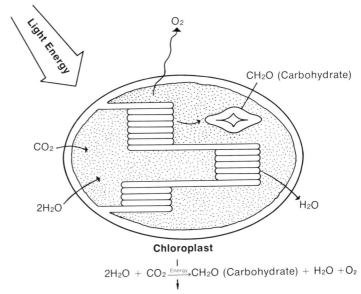

Figure 3-7 Diagrammatic simplification of the process of photosynthesis occurring in the chloroplast. The role of water, carbon dioxide, and solar energy in the production of food is illustrated.

THE EVOLUTION OF THE ATMOSPHERE

As we have seen, the first apparently *bona fide* fossilized cells of once-living organisms are associated with certain ancient shale rocks of the Proterozoic Era (Precambrian Era). These fossils, called **stromatolites** (see Figure 3-2), appear to have been spherical colonies of organisms similar to the present-day blue-green algae; they are composed of concretions of limestone surrounding cellular remnants. The oldest stromatolites exhibiting cellular structure are those of the Gunflint Chert in Canada and are dated at about 1.7 billion years BP. Older stromatolites containing no cellular detail are present in African sediments dated at approximately 2.7 billion years BP.

In photosynthesis occurring in blue-green algae (as in other green plants) oxygen is given off into the environment. After the advent of photosynthetic life, the earth's atmosphere slowly changed from one that contained little, if any, oxygen to one in which oxygen began to accumulate, eventually reaching its present 21 per cent level. The change made it possible for **aerobic** (oxygen respiring) organisms to evolve. Beginning at about 600 million years ago, a great increase both in kind and number of aerobic animals and photosynthetic plants seems to have occurred. The plants and animals that arose during this period of time, the Cambrian, included animals such as starfishes, trilobites, brachiopods, and plants such as green and blue-green algae. They were water-dwelling and usually armored with siliceous or lime exoskeletons, shells, or walls. Proponents of atmospheric evolution believe that these coverings functioned as defensive systems against the somewhat higher ultraviolet radiation levels of the atmosphere of that Period.

63

FOSSIL PLANTS AND ANIMALS

Subsequently, increased oxygen levels in the atmosphere due to photosynthesis provided a barrier to much of the harmful ultraviolet radiation. This was an important factor in the evolution of land plants and animals. Nearly all of the major phyla and divisions of plants and animals appeared during the Paleozoic Era (570 to 225 million years ago). We see in the fossil record the occurrence, during the Silurian and early Devonian Periods, of the primitive land plants and air-breathing animals. These were followed by more complex types of plants, including ferns and primitive seed plants, that flourished in the Carboniferous Period of the Paleozoic Era and produced many of the earth's great coal deposits. The next great Era was the Mesozoic Era, the age of conifers and large reptiles. Mammals and flowering plants originated in the Mesozoic Era, or even earlier, but are not so representative of that Era as they are of the Cenozoic Era, which extends to the present. Against this great panorama it is somewhat humbling to look for our own immediate ancestors. Thinking man (*Homo sapiens sapiens*) has been a part of the landscape for an incredibly short period of time. Yet it is truly remarkable that, in this eye-wink of geological history, he has managed to change the face of the earth to such an astonishing degree and perhaps even sow the seeds of his own destruction.

THE PROKARYOTIC CELL

The blue-green algae, bacteria, and mycoplasmas are all organisms whose study requires the use of microscopes. Hence, they are termed microorganisms, a very broad category of unicellular and multicellular creatures. Customarily, the microorganisms are divided into two groups, the **prokaryotes** and the **eukaryotes.** The eukaryotes have their DNA packaged in chromosomes, and these in turn are enclosed within a membrane system referred to as the nuclear envelope. The DNA of prokaryotes, on the other hand, is said to be naked, that is, it is not organized into chromosomes and is not enclosed by a nuclear envelope. There are other differences as well; eukaryotic cells contain **organelles** (little organs) such as mitochondria, plastids, and Golgi bodies, while prokaryotes do not have these. However, both kinds of cells contain ribosomes, and utilize similar metabolic systems and methods of translating their genetic codes in the synthesis of proteins.

There are only two groups of prokaryotes known, the Cyanophyceae, or blue-green algae, and the Schizomycetes, which include bacteria, mycoplasmas, rickettsias, and other forms. Rickettsias, like the mycoplasmas, are small, parasitic cells, one type of which is responsible for Rocky Mountain spotted fever. Although these organisms traditionally have been classified as members of the plant kingdom, there is a growing trend toward grouping them separately in the kingdom **Monera,** composed solely of prokaryotes. Viruses, although disease-causing, are not considered to be prokaryotes be-

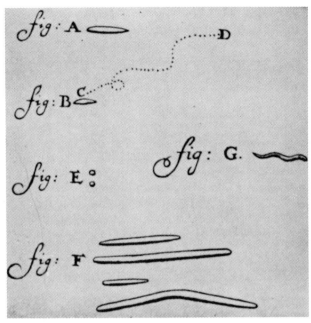

Figure 3–8 Van Leeuwenhoek's sketches of microorganisms. *A*, Motile bacterium. *B, Spirillum. C*, Cocci. (From Frobisher, M., *et al. Fundamentals of Microbiology*, 9th ed. Philadelphia, W. B. Saunders Co., 1974).

cause they are non-cellular. Their nature is discussed later in this chapter.

In the year 1676, a remarkable letter was read before the Royal Society of London. Its author described some hitherto unknown and extremely small organisms that he had observed with a simple microscope of his own design and making. He wrote that he had seen animals "a thousand times smaller than the smallest grain of sand," having numerous "thin little legs." Clearly, these were ciliated protozoa. Others, "so exceedingly small that they almost escaped my sight," were bacteria.

As a consequence of such research, Anton van Leeuwenhoek, a Dutch merchant, has become known as the father of both protozoology and bacteriology, and the discoverer of some of the most primitive and yet most important groups of organisms known to mankind, the bacteria.

We all know bacteria are extremely small and can be seen clearly only with the most powerful of microscopes. How, then, was van Leeuwenhoek able to see them so distinctly? First of all, he must have been a most persevering man. Secondly, he was a remarkably good technician. His microscopes were quite uncomplicated, but were capable of high performance, even by today's standards. Nine authentic van Leeuwenhoek microscopes have survived to this day. One of them, now in the Utrecht Museum, has a magnification of about 275× and a resolution of approximately 1 micrometer (1 μm), which is very close to that attainable with the best microscopes today.

At this time it may be helpful to review the expressions of

dimensions currently used in microscopic studies. That most frequently encountered is the micrometer (μm). A typical plant cell may be about 50 μm in diameter, a bacterium 2 μm in diameter. A micrometer is 1/1,000,000 or 10^{-6} meter. Electron microscopy often employs the nanometer (nm), 1/1000 μm or 1/1,000,000,000 (10^{-9}) meter, and frequently the Ångstrom unit (Å), 1/10 nm.

BACTERIA
The Bacterial Cell

Although bacteria vary somewhat in size (1 to 2 μm in diameter) and form, a typical cell can be conceptualized (Fig. 3–9). Such a cell consists of a living component, the protoplast, that includes the outer, bounding membrane, the plasma membrane, and the cytoplasm, within. The cytoplasm contains small particles (20 nm), the ribosomes, specialized membranous structures such as the **mesosomes,** and the photosynthetic pigment bodies present in some bacteria. The mesosomes are membrane whorls that appear to have some function in the division of the cell. The cytoplasm also contains a comparatively long loop or circle of DNA, folded and coiled in the center of the cell. The DNA of a bacterial cell is the equivalent of the chromosomes of a higher plant or animal cell, and similarly, bears the cell's genetic information in the form of genes; hence, it is often termed the **genophore** (gene bearer). The common sewage and intestinal bacterium, *Escherichia coli,* often used for genetic research, has a long, circular genophore. When *E. coli* cells are broken up in such a way that the genophore opens out, the loop of DNA may be as much as 1 millimeter long, or about 500 times longer than the cell from which it came.

The protoplast of a bacterium is surrounded by a rigid wall made up of several layers of a **mucoprotein** material composed of sugars and proteins combined with each other to form larger, structural molecules. The cell wall is inert and non-living, as is always

Table 3–2. **A TABLE OF METRIC EQUIVALENTS**

1 kilometer	= 3250 feet (0.6 mile) = 1,000 meters
1 meter	= 39 inches = 0.001 (10^{-3}) kilometer
1 centimeter	= 0.39 inch = 0.01 (10^{-2}) meter
1 millimeter	= 0.039 inch = 0.001 (10^{-3}) meter
1 micrometer	= 0.000039 inch = 0.000001 (10^{-6}) meter or 1 micron
1 nanometer	= 0.000000001 (10^{-9}) meter or 1 millimicron
1 Ångstrom	= 0.1 nanometer
1 metric ton	= 2205 lbs. (1.1) tons = 1,000 kilograms
1 kilogram	= 2.2 lbs.
1 gram	= 0.035 oz.
1 milligram	= 0.001 (10^{-3}) grams
1 microgram	= 0.000001 (10^{-6}) gram or 1 gamma (γ)
1 nanogram	= 0.000000001 (10^{-9}) gram
1 picogram	= 0.000000000001 (10^{-12}) gram
1 liter	= 1.057 quarts
1 milliliter	= 1 cubic centimeter = 0.001 (10^{-3}) liter
1 hectare	= 2.471 acres = 10,000 square meters

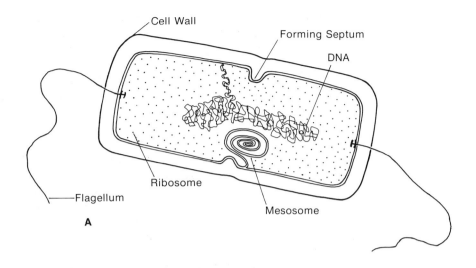

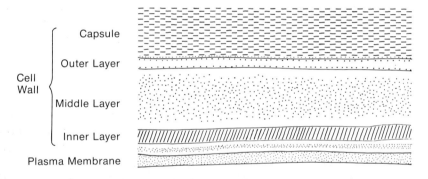

Figure 3–9 A bacterial cell. *A*, Cell in longitudinal section. *B*, Expanded view of the outer layers. Note that the cell wall is composed of several layers, and may or may not include a capsule (Redrawn from The Blue-green Algae, by P. Echlin. Copyright © 1966 by Scientific American, Inc. All rights reserved).

true for any plant cell. Its principal function is protection, not so much against abrasion as against pressure. Cells tend to take up water from their environment by osmosis, which often produces a pressure buildup within the cell. In bacteria and many other plant cells, this pressure is contained by the cell wall in somewhat the same way as the leather cover of a basketball resists the air pressure within the rubber bladder. The importance of the cell wall can be understood from the activity of the antibiotic, penicillin. Penicillin interferes with the ability of a bacterial cell to make a new wall when it reproduces; consequently, wall-less bacteria sometimes are produced and these must be maintained on media having high solute concentrations in order to prevent excessive osmotic uptake of water by the protoplast. When placed in water, they swell up and burst. This action of penicillin is responsible for its effectiveness against certain bacteria.

The cell wall is permeable to solutions but not to particles; hence, all food taken up by bacteria must be dissolved in water.

67

Bacteria produce and secrete many kinds of enzymes that are able to break down and solubilize food materials so that they may then be taken up. Such enzymes are called **exoenzymes** because they act outside the cell.

Some types of bacteria possess **flagella** and are motile. The bacterial flagellum is composed of a single fiber of protein, and propels the cell by its whip-like movements. The flagella are so slender that they ordinarily are not seen with the microscope and special flagella stains must be used.

Still another characteristic of some bacterial cells is the formation of thick-walled **endospores** within the parent cell. Endospores are highly resistant to heat, cold, and drying. They are released upon the death of the parent cell and survive most conditions that kill ordinary bacteria. Non-sporulating bacteria are quite sensitive to heat, ultraviolet light, drying, and chemicals of various kinds (including many antiseptics), but endospores are more resistant to these treatments. The bacteria that produce the deadly **toxins** (poisons) of tetanus and botulism (a type of food poisoning) are spore formers. Not only are the toxins dangerous in almost infinitesimal amounts (one billionth of a gram of botulism toxin may kill a man), but the spores make it difficult to eradicate the organisms in food and soil. Some of these bacteria (of the genus *Clostridium*) have been used in germ warfare research because of these characteristics.

Bacterial Morphology

The study of the forms of different bacteria is called bacterial morphology. Bacterial cells are simple in form, and there are only a few main structural types (Fig. 3–10). Spherical bacteria are called **cocci,** rod-like bacteria are called **bacilli,** and spiral-shaped species are known as **spirilli.** Chains of cocci are characteristic of the species of *Streptococcus* that produce "strep" throat and scarlet fever. *Staphylococcus* species form irregular clumps and grapelike clusters of cocci; pathogenic species of this genus produce boils and abscesses in humans. Colonies composed of pairs of cocci are exemplified by *Diplococcus pneumoniae,* the pneumonia pathogen, and *Neisseria gonorrhoeae,* the cause of the venereal disease, gonorrhea. Other cocci, such as *Gaffkya,* form four-celled squares; while others, such as *Sarcina,* form cubical packets of eight cells. Still other bacteria are in the form of flexible spirals or **spirochaetes,** one of which, *Treponema pallidum,* causes syphilis, and the **actinomycetes,** which form long tubular filaments known as **hyphae.**

Bacterial Growth and Nutrition

Bacteria grow and reproduce in a variety of environments and on many different **substrates** (nutrient sources). They are abundant in soil, in water (especially if the water is contaminated by sewage), and on foods of all kinds. In fact, they may be found in any situation where there is material on which to feed, including petroleum in oil wells, bottom ooze in the ocean depths, sulfur springs, and

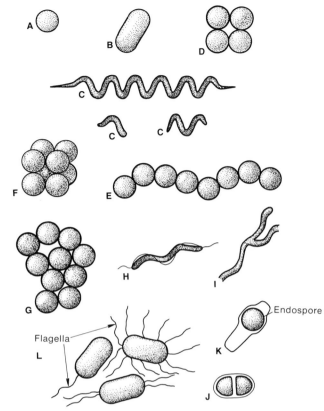

Figure 3-10 Some morphological types found among the bacteria. *A,* Coccus. *B, Bacillus. C,* Spirilli. *D, Sarcina. E, Streptococcus. F, Gaffkya. G, Staphylococcus. H,* Spirochaete. *I,* Actinomycete. *J, Diplococcus. K, Bacillus* with endospores. *L, Bacillus* with flagella.

many places that seem inhospitable to any form of life. Generally, however, their growth is favored by moist and warm conditions.

Bacteria are also characterized as being **heterotrophic** or **autotrophic.** Heterotrophic organisms obtain energy by breaking down energy-rich organic compounds, such as carbohydrates, fats, and proteins, while autotrophs use energy obtained from oxidation of inorganic substances such as nitrogen, sulfur, or iron, or energy from sunlight, for building energy-rich organic compounds. If their energy is obtained from oxidation of inorganic materials, the bacteria are said to be **chemosynthetic,** while those that use radiant energy are **photosynthetic**. The chemosynthetic bacteria are particularly important in the environment because of their participation in the natural cycles discussed in Chapter 6.

Bacteria also may be grouped as **aerobes** or **anaerobes,** depending on their requirements for atmospheric oxygen. Anaerobic bacteria do not require atmospheric oxygen for their metabolism, but instead obtain energy from their food by processes called **anaerobic respiration** and **fermentation**. Anaerobic respiration employs inorganic molecules, such as nitrate, as a substitute for oxygen; fermentation uses organic molecules as oxidants. Both are described in greater detail in the next chapter. The fermentative processes are all fundamentally alike, differing mainly in byproducts

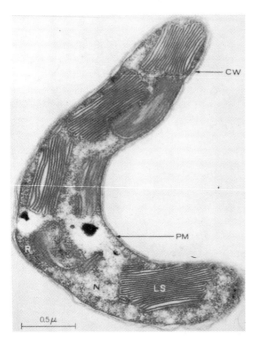

Figure 3-11 Electron micrograph of a photosynthetic bacterium (longitudinal section). The photosynthetic pigments are located within involutions of the cell membrane. CW—cell wall, PM—plasma membrane, R—ribosomes, N—DNA, LS—stacks of photosynthetic lamellae (From Hickman and Frankel, J. Cell Biol. 25:261, 1965).

produced by the bacteria; some are of commercial importance, being used in the production of various organic acids, alcohols, and solvents such as acetone. Aerobic bacteria require atmospheric oxygen in order to obtain energy from their food. Still other forms, known as **facultative** organisms, may function either with or without oxygen.

Heterotrophic bacteria may be **saprobes, parasites,** or **symbionts** and either aerobic, anaerobic, or facultatively anaerobic. Saprobes live on dead plants and animals or on their products. Parasites and symbionts live in or on living host organisms. However, parasites are either neutral or damaging to their hosts, whereas symbionts contribute to the well-being of their hosts and are themselves benefited. There are many examples of symbiosis involving bacteria. Well-known bacterial symbionts are those living in the digestive tracts of animals, including those of the intestinal flora of humans. The intestinal bacteria normally are not harmful and it has been shown that they confer upon their host resistance to pathogenic bacteria. Ruminant animals, including sheep, goats and cows, use bacteria in their stomach chambers to digest the cellulose in the hay that they eat. Cellulose is a glucose **polymer** (a long molecule made up of units of the sugar glucose); these bacteria possess enzymes capable of breaking cellulosic chains into the constituent glucose molecules. Ruminants are able to digest paper with the aid of their bacteria. In one experiment, a ram whose diet was supplemented with 150 grams of filter paper daily was found to have digested up to 90 per cent of this nearly pure form of cellulose. Plants also profit from bacterial symbionts. The nitrogen-fixing bac-

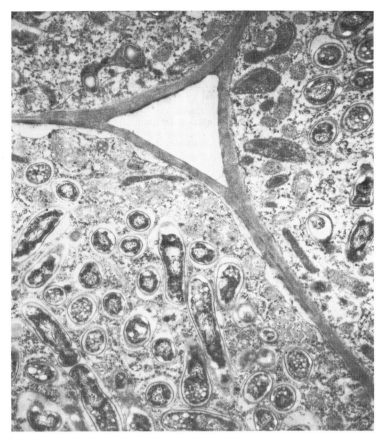

Figure 3–12 *Rhizobium japonicum,* a symbiotic species of bacteria, as seen in the root nodule cells of the soybean, × 20,100 (From Goodchild, D. J., and Bergerson, F. J. Electron Microscopy of the Infection and Subsequent Development of Soybean Nodule Cells. *Journal of Bacteriology 92:*204, 1966).

teria that live with the root cells of legumes (Fig. 3–12) are probably the best example of this. They convert atmospheric nitrogen gas into ammonia and amino acids required by the host plants for their metabolism. In return they appear to receive certain nutrients as well as shelter from their host.

Bacteria and Disease

Bacterially-caused disease is a severe form of parasitism in which pathogenic bacteria produce chemical substances that are harmful to their hosts. These substances, called **toxins,** may be components of the bacterium (such as portions of the wall), or they may consist of exoenzymes that destroy cells or cellular components and products (such as intercellular cementing substance, sera, and blood clots) that would otherwise limit the spread of disease. Some bacteria, such as those causing pneumonia, overwhelm their hosts by first overcoming their natural lines of defense and then producing large populations. Others, such as the tetanus bacterium *(Clostridium tetani),* may remain at the point of infection as a small population while producing powerful and even lethal toxins. Others do not grow within the host at all but instead affect their victims solely by their toxins, already present in food previously contaminated; *Clostridium botulinum* is an almost classic example of a species of bacteria that acts in this manner.

In addition to those diseases previously named, bacterially-caused diseases of humans include tuberculosis, anthrax, cholera, bubonic plague, leprosy, diphtheria, typhoid, gangrene, bacterial dysentery, meningitis, and tularemia. Plant diseases caused by bacteria include soft rot of potatoes, black rot of cabbage, crown gall of grapes, and fire blight of apples and pears.

Bacterial Reproduction

Under ideal conditions, bacterial cells may divide every twenty minutes, forming huge populations in a short time. Theoretically, the progeny of a single bacterium, dividing maximally, would equal the earth's mass in a single day. Fortunately, bacterial colonies soon outstrip their food supplies and begin to die. The growth curve exhibited by bacterial populations is characteristic of all life when reproduction is unimpeded. There is an introductory period of slow growth followed by a very rapid population expansion, the logarithmic growth phase. Then there is a plateau period as environmental factors become limiting, and a period of rapid decline brought on by starvation, environmental pollution, and space factors. Finally, there comes a time when a much-depleted population struggles for survival in an impoverished environment (Fig. 3–13). It is not at all difficult to see parallels between life and death in bacterial and human populations.

Most bacteria reproduce by a non-sexual process known as **fission.** Fission requires the replication of the cell's DNA and the division of the protoplast by the formation of a new cell wall. The new wall generally forms as a **septum,** or divider, growing inwardly from the edges of the cell until the cell is completely divided. The new cells may separate completely or may adhere together to form the distinctive chains, clumps, and packets previously described.

Some bacteria engage in a fragmentary exchange of genetic material termed **para-sexuality,** or **conjugation,** in which a portion of the genophore of one bacterium is transferred to another over a cytoplasmic bridge. This process is as near to sexuality as has yet been observed among prokaryotes. True sexuality as it occurs among higher organisms involves complete exchange of genetic material through the fusion of special sex cells, or **gametes.**

Under some conditions, bacteria are capable of taking up pure DNA from their surroundings and incorporating it into their genophores. When bacteria are grown on the surface of a culture medium, they often produce colonies of closely packed cells. Those of *Diplococcus pneumoniae,* the pathogen that causes pneumonia, are usually smooth and glistening because of a slime-sheath or capsule that surrounds each cell. Cells of a mutant form lack capsules and produce rough-looking colonies. The smooth form (S-form) is path-

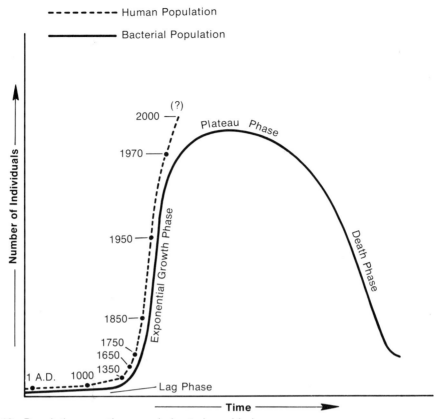

Figure 3–13 Population growth curves in bacteria and in humans.

ogenic, but the rough form (R-form) is not, and it would appear that the capsule is related to pathogenicity. A classic experiment of the 1940's by Dr. O. T. Avery and co-workers at the Rockefeller Institute in New York City demonstrated that DNA from broken-up, non-living S-form cells was taken up by living R-form cells, transforming them into S-form cells. This process (transformation) constituted the first clear proof that DNA is the genetic-determining substance of cells.

Culture and Identification of Bacteria

In the eighteenth and nineteenth centuries, a heated controversy raged over the origin of bacteria. Nutrient broths, though boiled for hours, soon teemed with bacteria after cooling. This led some scientists to the conclusion that bacteria were formed spontaneously by a reaction between air and the organic constitutents of the brew in which they grew. That concept, sometimes called **abiogenesis,** was finally disproved by Louis Pasteur in 1864. He employed flasks with S-shaped necks and showed that nutrient broths would not develop bacteria after boiling and cooling even though they had free access to the air. Some of Pasteur's flasks have remained free of bacterial contamination for a century. The down-swept portion of the neck traps bacteria and prevents them from entering and contaminating the broth.

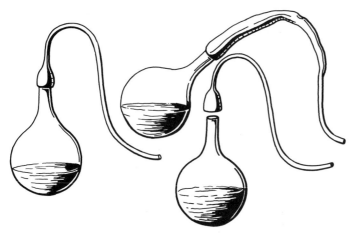

Figure 3–14 Original Pasteur flasks (Redrawn from Stanier, R. Y., et al. *The Microbial World,* Second Edition. Englewood Cliffs, N. J., Prentice-Hall Inc., 1963).

Today, bacteria are cultured using many of the techniques developed by Pasteur and other bacteriologists of his day. Nutrient broths containing beef extract or other suitable food are sterilized in a type of pressure cooker called an autoclave, which develops enough moist heat to destroy any microorganisms and spores that may be present. Then the broth is cooled and inoculated with the desired bacteria.

The objectives in culturing bacteria are many and varied, but the initial desire usually is to obtain pure cultures of a single bacterial type so as to know what organisms are involved. Once this has been achieved, one may progress toward identification of species, determination of pathogenicity, susceptibility to antibiotics, or toward industrial production if it turns out that the species is one that manufactures a useful byproduct.

Isolation of a single bacterial type from a mixture of bacteria is challenging; it can be accomplished by spreading a very small drop of the bacterial culture over the surface of a fresh medium solidified with a jelly-like substance known as agar-agar. This spreading process, if carefully done, will isolate some individual bacterial cells and the colonies developing from them will contain only one kind of bacteria. Pure colonies of this kind may be used to start new cultures for further study.

Identification and classification of bacteria often are complicated. Since there are only a few morphological types (such as spheres, spirals, and rods with or without endospores and flagella), visual identification usually is employed only in preliminary screening for the purpose of narrowing the range of possibilities. The staining reactions of bacteria also are useful at this point. There is a staining protocol named **Gram's stain** after its inventor, Hans Gram (1853–1938). Bacteria that stain permanently with crystal violet are termed Gram positive, those from which this stain can be removed are said to be Gram negative. It is noteworthy that most pathogenic bacteria are Gram positive.

In the final analysis, complete identification of bacteria usually requires study of their biochemical reactions. This is accomplished by culturing them on various kinds of nutrient media. For example, certain bacteria are able to utilize the sugar maltose, others cannot use maltose but will utilize lactose. Some digest gelatin, others break down starch, and so forth. Still others form acids or produce some characteristic byproduct. The modern bacteriologist uses an almost bewildering array of special media and sophisticated techniques.

One of the interesting stories about bacteria has as its central figure the biochemist-bacteriologist, Chaim Weizmann. During World War I, the English were cut off from their supply of acetone, which they used in the manufacture of cordite, an explosive. Dr. Weizmann, then a lecturer at the University of Manchester, had developed a method of obtaining acetone from cultures of a species of the genus *Clostridium.* He took his process to the First Lord of the Admiralty, Winston Churchill, who set him to work making tons of acetone. As a result of his cooperation, Weizmann became friendly with Churchill and with his successor, Lord Balfour, and soon came to have considerable political influence. Weizmann was an active Zionist and persuaded Balfour to establish a homeland for homeless Jews. This resulted in the famous Balfour Declaration of 1917 and eventually in the establishment of the new state of Israel with Chaim Weizmann as its first president.

THE BLUE-GREEN ALGAE

The blue-green algae are common prokaryotes found in lakes, streams, and moist soil. Blue-green algae are capable of living under very rigorous environmental conditions. Some grow in snow and ice, others thrive in waters of hot springs (which often approach the boiling point) and even in desert soils.

Cells of Blue-Green Algae

Blue-green algae resemble bacteria in that they have only a few basic cell forms. Short cylinders and spheres are common, but rods and spirals also occur (Fig. 3–15). A cell wall composed of several layers is always present and, as in the bacteria, it is composed primarily of mucoprotein, although cellulose also has been reported to be present in the walls of some species.

The protoplasts are not highly organized. A genophore composed of DNA lies in the center of the cell, and the surrounding cytoplasm contains ribosomes, as well as small particles and crystals of unknown function. Sometimes gas vacuoles are present and make the cells more or less buoyant. An internal membrane system also is seen in electron microscopic pictures. These membranes, called **lamellae** or **thylakoids,** are parallel to each other and are formed by infolding of the plasma membrane. Photosynthetic pigments are located in the lamellae, among them green **chlorophyll a,** orange and yellow **carotenoids,** blue **phycocyanin** and red **phycoerythrin.** The presence of these pigments in varying proportions results in cells of different colors, ranging from grass-green

75

through blue-green, olive and red to deep violet. The Red Sea is red with blue-green algae whose cells reflect wavelengths of red light.

Reproduction in Blue-Green Algae

As in the bacteria, true sexual reproduction is unknown in blue-green algae. However, some recent studies show that genetic recombination occurs in blue-green algae but the manner of gene transfer is unknown. Asexual reproduction occurs by cell division and includes genophore replication, although this part of the process is not well understood. After DNA replication, the protoplast becomes divided by septation similar to that occurring in bacteria, in which new walls are formed by inward growth.

The cells of blue-green algae are almost always associated in colonies—usually in chains, but also in sheets, cubes and spherical masses (Fig. 3–16). A chain of cells is called a **trichome.** Trichomes

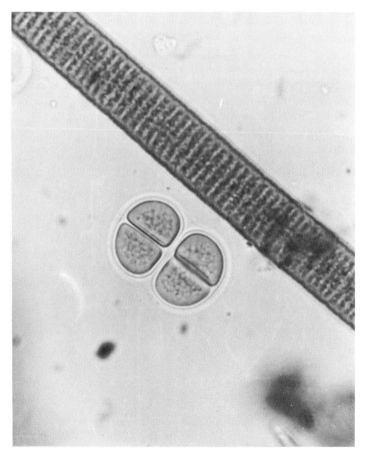

Figure 3–15 Living blue-green algae. Filamentous *Oscillatoria* has disk-like cells and a thin sheath; *Chroococcus* has semi-spherical cells dividing at right angles to plane of former division and several sheath layers are seen.

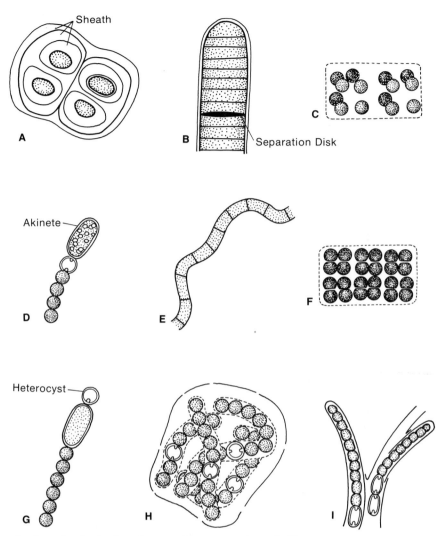

Figure 3–16 Types of cells and colonies found among blue-green algae. *A, Chroococcus. B, Oscillatoria. C, Anacystis. D, Anabaena. E, Spirulina. F, Agmenellum. G, Cylindrospermum. H, Nostoc. I, Tolypothrix.*

are surrounded by the jelly-like sheath material of the cell walls. Sometimes the sheath material is especially thick, so that many filaments adhere together to form large, baseball-sized masses as in *Nostoc* or the fossilized blue-green algae found in rocks of the Precambrian Era.

In some members of the group, specialized cells called **heterocysts** occur. They are involved in a cellular process termed **nitrogen fixation** in which gaseous nitrogen is converted to other forms useful to plants. Heterocysts are also related to the separation of longer trichomes into shorter chains. Heterocysts also may function as reproductive cells, eventually dividing to form daughter cells. In some other groups, as in *Oscillatoria,* living cells may become separated by degenerated cells and eventually become detached as trichome segments, known as **hormogonia.** Simple fragmentation of trichomes also serves to establish new colonies.

Large resistant cells, containing reserve food, are formed by some blue-green algae such as *Anabaena* and *Cylindrospermum.* These cells, the **akinetes,** have thick walls and carry the organisms through adverse conditions, dividing later to produce new colonies. A few species of blue-green algae also produce endospores.

Motility of Blue-Green Algae

Blue-green algae, though they lack flagella, sometimes display a gliding motion or undulation. This seems to be caused by a sub-microscopic rippling of the outer, jelly-like layer of the cell wall, termed the **sheath.** The rippling is thought to be produced by movement of fibers in one of the inner layers of the wall.

Blue-Green Algae and the Environment

Blue-green algae are important pollution indicators. Recent studies in Lake Erie have shown increasing concentrations of *Oscillatoria, Anacystis,* and *Anabaena,* which are considered to be indicator species of pollution. A population explosion, or **bloom,** of these algae covering 800 square miles was observed in this lake in September, 1964. During a bloom, algal photosynthesis brings about temporary increases in the oxygen content of a body of water, but the huge population then dies and decay-causing bacteria increase drastically. These bacteria use up so much oxygen in consuming the dead algae that the end result may be severe oxygen depletion and the death of fish and other oxygen-requiring forms of aquatic life. The algae also contribute noxious tastes and odors and even toxic substances to the water.

Blue-green algae also are able, as we have noted, to fix nitrogen as do some bacteria. Rice paddies develop large populations of blue-green algae, and these contribute significantly to the maintenance of soil nitrogen. Blue-green algae are found also within nodules on the roots of a group of tropical plants called the cycads, and they probably function symbiotically in somewhat the same fashion as do the nitrogen-fixing bacteria of legumes.

VIRUSES

Viruses are associated with cells of all kinds, prokaryotes as well as eukaryotes. While some viruses destroy cells, others do not, and it is currently believed by some scientists that viruses are basically cellular products that evolved very long ago, perhaps as early as the oldest prokaryotes. It is thought that their major role may be to effect genetic recombination between cells, and that cells evolved modes of gene transfer via virus particles, a process alluded to earlier as transduction.

However, certain viruses take over the genetic machinery of cells completely, using it to turn out great numbers of new viruses and disrupting and destroying the cells. Viruses, generally speaking, are composed of an outer shell of protein, enclosing a single or double strand either of DNA or RNA. The DNA or RNA contains the genetic instructions for making a new virus particle, but the virus itself has no ribosomes, and no other means of making proteins or of replicating DNA and RNA. The **bacteriophage** for example, after attaching to a bacterium, injects its DNA into the host cell. The DNA is somehow inserted in the DNA of the host and there it does three things: (a) it stops the multiplication of host cell DNA; (b) it represses the transcription of bacterial genes; and (c) it begins the transcription of its own DNA. As a result, enzymes are made for replicating virus DNA and structural proteins are made for all of the components of the protein shell. These components apparently are self-assembling and eventually the bacterium becomes filled with new virus particles. It dies and releases numerous virus particles upon disintegration.

In a general way all viruses, both benign and virulent, are reproduced as outlined above. However, the benign viruses remain latent for long periods of time prior to replication, while the virulent

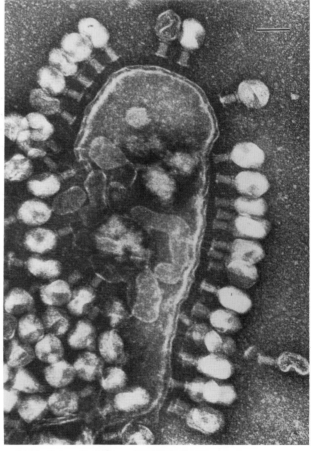

Figure 3–17 Bacteriophages attached to a bacterial cell wall, × 130,000. Bacteriophage viruses attach themselves to certain receptor sites on the surface of a bacterium. These sites are composed of molecules that have an affinity for molecules in the tail-piece of the virus, so that binding of virus to host occurs upon contact between the two (From Simon, L. D., and Anderson, T. F. The Infection of Escherichia coli by T2 and T4 Bacteriophages as Seen in the Electron Microscope. *Virology 32*:279, 1967.)

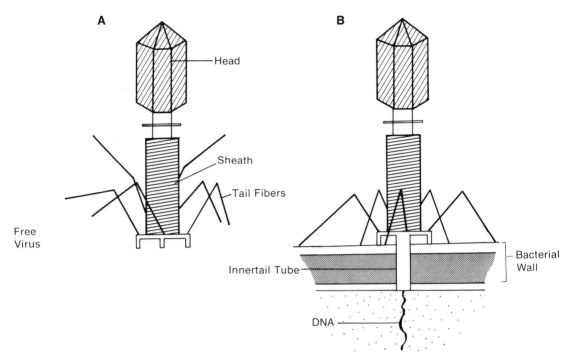

Figure 3–18 T-even virus. *A,* Free virus prior to the discharge of DNA. *B,* Virus on host cell at time of discharge of DNA (After Simon, L. D., and Anderson, T. F. *Virology* 32:279, 1967).

ones are replicated rapidly. Human virus-caused diseases include smallpox, mumps, measles, chickenpox, poliomyelitis, rabies, influenza, warts, mouth cankers, cold sores, the common cold, and probably cancer. Plants also succumb to viruses. In addition to the phages that attack bacteria, the tobacco mosaic virus infects tobacco and tomato plants and other members of the Solanaceae. Bean plants suffer from the bushy stunt virus and there are a number of other examples.

SUMMARY

We have seen that simple cells of the type we call prokaryotes have existed on earth for nearly 3 billion years, and that modern bacteria and blue-green algae have descended virtually unchanged from those early, ancestral cells. It is thought that the first cells evolved in a mixture of organic compounds that had developed by chemical evolution. These cells no doubt began to exhaust their food supplies as their populations increased. Mutations in the genetic information of such cells may have resulted in the evolution of photosynthetic cells, perhaps like photosynthetic bacteria and the blue-green algae. The latter produce oxygen as a byproduct of photosynthesis, and there is a nice correlation between the geochemical theory that oxygen first began to appear in the atmosphere about 2 billion years ago and a similar dating for the age of blue-green algae.

Present-day bacteria and blue-green algae are very important in maintaining nutrient and energy equilibria in nature. Bacteria recycle the wastes of living and the components of dead organisms by actively participating in decay processes. Blue-green algae produce food and oxygen by photosynthesis and these are used both by plants and animals in their metabolic processes. Both bacteria and blue-green algae enrich the soil by nitrogen fixation. Bacteria, especially, are important to man in a variety of ways, which are often overlooked because of the disease-causing aspects of some bacteria.

A simplified classification of bacteria and blue-green algae covered in this chapter follows:

Division Schizophyta. So-called "Fission Plants," prokaryotes living as single cells or colonies and reproducing by fission, a simple cell division process. Most have cell walls composed of mucoproteins.

CLASS SCHIZOMYCETES. Autotrophic and heterotrophic bacteria (about 1,500 species). Examples: *Bacillus, Spirillum, Streptococcus, Diplococcus, Neisseria, Treponema, Mycoplasma, Rickettsia.*

CLASS CYANOPHYCEAE. The blue-green algae, non-sexual, photosynthetic cells and colonies of cells, always non-flagellate (about 1,500 species). Examples: *Oscillatoria, Coccochlorus, Anabaena, Agmenellum, Anacystis, Spirulina, Nostoc.*

DISCUSSION QUESTIONS

1. How is the discovery of prokaryotes linked with the invention of microscopy?
2. If abiogenesis were a valid theory, what might some of the consequences be? For medicine? For food? For sanitation?
3. In what way, if any, do theories of abiogenesis differ from modern theories of the origin of life?
4. How would you define a prokaryote in morphological, cytological and biochemical terms?
5. What is a mycoplasma and what are its theoretical implications for prokaryote evolution?
6. What distinguishes viruses from prokaryotes?
7. What is the significance of bacterial transformation?
8. What is an exoenzyme and how is it related to disease?
9. What is the relationship between blue-green algae and rice paddies?
10. How do saprobes, parasites and symbionts differ?
11. Do you know of any specific instances in which human societies have followed a population growth curve like that characteristic of bacteria? If so, discuss the case briefly.
12. What is the relationship between blue-green algae and the present atmosphere?
13. Since blue-green algae are oxygen producers, why should they be associated with pollution, eutrophication and death of fish and other aerobic animals?

SUPPLEMENTAL READING

Adler, I. *How Life Began.* New York: The John Day Co., Inc., 1957.

Block, T. D. *Milestones in Microbiology.* Englewood Cliffs, N.J.: Prentice-Hall, Inc., 1951.

Bradbury, S. *The Evolution of the Microscope.* Oxford, England: Pergamon Press, 1967.

Dobell, C. D. *Antony van Leeuwenhoek and His "Little Animals."* New York: Russell and Russell, Inc., 1958.

Echlin, P. The Blue-green Algae. *Sci. Amer. 214(6)*:74, 1966.

Olson, J. M. The Evolution of Photosynthesis. *Science 168*:438, 1970.

Oparin, A. I. *Life, Its Nature, Origin and Development.* New York: Academic Press, 1962.

Stanier, R. Y., M. Doudoroff, and E. A. Adelberg. *The Microbial World,* 3rd ed. Englewood Cliffs, N.J.: Prentice-Hall, Inc., 1970.

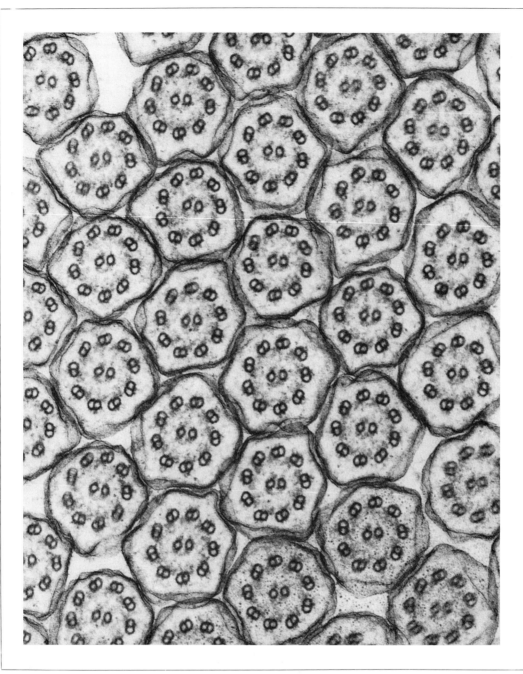

Electron micrograph of the flagella of *Zamia integrifolia*, × 200,000.

Chapter 4

The Plant Cell

THE CELL THEORY • THE EUKARYOTIC CELL • MITOSIS • MEIOSIS •
LIFE CYCLES AND ALTERNATION OF GENERATIONS • PLANT CELLS •
CELL WALL—MERISTEMS • PROTOPLASTS • ORGANELLES • EVOLUTION
OF EUKARYOTES • SUMMARY

For more than two thousand years philosophers and scientists
were forced to describe plants and animals in terms of features observable with the unaided human eye. We have noted that about 300
years ago the Dutch cloth merchant van Leeuwenhoek invented a
microscope capable of revealing the unseen world of microorganisms. Still, van Leeuwenhoek's instruments looked at the outside
of organisms, not at their inside where information on the fundamental organization of life resides. However, a few years earlier, in
1665, a clever Englishman named Robert Hooke described an exer-
cise in which he sliced a piece of cork very thinly and examined it
with a microscope of his own design. He discerned innumerable
minute empty spaces, which he termed cells. If we call van Leeuwenhoek the father of microbiology, then it is equally proper to call
Hooke the father of cell theory.*

There followed a slow advance in the understanding of cells.
Microscopes were improved, and even more importantly, methods
of dissecting organisms and staining them for microscopy were developed. For example, the decade from 1770 to 1780 saw the invention of a cutting instrument (the **microtome**) and the discovery of
stains to make cell structures more visible under the microscope. At
that time plants and animals were variously described as composed
of fibers, bubbles, or vesicles, empty chambers and slime, but by the
early nineteenth century it was recognized that the structural unit of
life was a microscopic body enclosed within a bounding membrane

---

*Hooke's genius is evident also in some other accomplishments that have had
widespread effects on modern science; for in addition to inventing microscopes and
studying the microscopic nature of many organisms, Hooke invented the vacuum
pump used by Robert Boyle in his research on gases and is also credited with the invention of the balance spring, which substituted for the pendulum of clocks and
made pocket watches possible.

"But then I observ'd a third sort of little Animals, that were twice as long as broad,
and to my eye yet eight times smaller than the first. Yet for all this, I thought I discerned little feet, whereby they moved very briskly, both in a round and streight line."

A. VAN LEEUWENHOEK

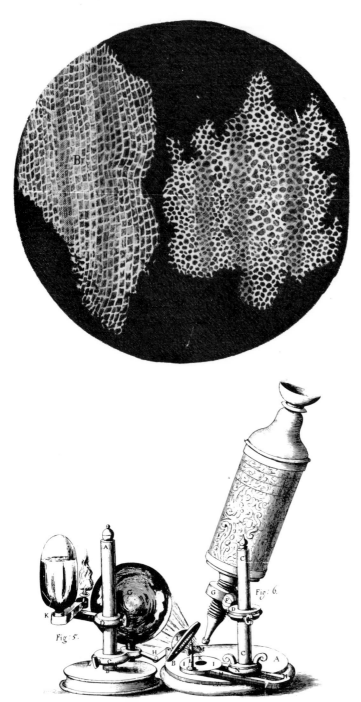

Figure 4–1 Robert Hooke's microscope, and his drawing of the cells in a section of cork (From *Micrographia*, 1665).

and composed of a substance named **protoplasm** (Purkinje, 1839). That cells of higher plants and animals contained a small internal body, the nucleus, also was determined by several nineteenth century microscopists, including Robert Brown, an English botanist who, in addition, described protoplasmic streaming in cells.

We are prone to credit individuals with great scientific advances and to fail to recognize the many individual discoveries that make such advances possible. For example, two Germans, Matthias Schleiden and Theodor Schwann, often are credited with the development, during 1838 and 1839, of the **cell theory,** which states that cells are the structural and physiological units of all life. Yet, a number of earlier scholars and scientists had clearly recognized the cellular nature of organisms. For example, the French evolutionist Jean Lamarck wrote, in 1809, "... cellular tissue is the general matrix of all organization; without this tissue no living body would be able to exist, nor could it have been formed."

THE CELL THEORY

In Chapter 2 we noted that scientific concepts are models that make general statements about natural phenomena. Such models are useful only if they have a high order of predictability; that is, they should enable one to predict the occurrence and interpret the characteristics of new phenomena. No simple statement about cells can fit all of the variations we now know to occur among living organisms, but the cell theory summarizes our basic knowledge of the composition of organisms, and has been found to have high predictive value. Essentially, the cell theory states that:

(a) all living things are composed of cells;
(b) all cells resemble one another in structure and functions;
(c) all cells originate by cell division from pre-existing cells; and
(d) the structure and functions of an organism are produced by the collective organization and actions of its individual cells.

Regardless of who is to be credited with its formulation, the cell theory is considered one of the great scientific generalizations of all time, and it has been compared in importance to the theory of evolution. Indeed, for most people the "spin-off" from the cell theory has had a far greater impact on their intimate lives than has the theory of evolution. Modern medical practice, for example, is based on an understanding of the way in which cells work, both those of our own bodies and of disease-causing organisms. We know that cancer, one of the great scourges of human life, is a disease of cells, and there is growing suspicion that it may be a consequence of viral infections in which a part of the cell's reproductive machinery has been sabotaged. We have even learned methods of removing cells from plants and animals and growing them on nutrient media as we do bacterial cultures. A particular culture of cancer cells named HeLa (after their donor, Helen Lane) is maintained in research laboratories all over the world and has contributed immeasurably to the understanding of cell biochemistry and of cancer. Plant cells also have been very instructive; it is now known that individual plant cells may be isolated in culture and nurtured in such a way that they continue to divide and eventually grow into entire new plants (see Chapter 20).

85

It is impossible to catalog in a book such as this all of the important discoveries made in the cell sciences since the pioneering days of microscopy, so a few additional highlights will have to suffice. Cell division was discovered by several microscopists between 1826 and 1832, and mitosis was described in some detail by a German botanist, Hugo von Mohl, from his observations of plant root tips and buds between 1835 and 1839. However, the nature and action of chromosomes and their role in cell division and reproduction escaped him and it remained for several other scientists, including Strasburger, Flemming and van Beneden, to uncover in the decades between 1870 and 1900 the basic knowledge of cell division and chromosome structure and behavior.

The last two decades of the nineteenth century were the most productive years in the history of the study of cells by light microscopy, and the following 50 years were almost anticlimactic. Steady progress was made in instrumentation and additional observations were recorded as to the composition and action of cell components, but a student in a beginning biology class in 1950 would really not have been told much more about the structure of cells than would his father or even his grandfather before him. Then, in the early 1950's, the newly-perfected electron microscope was turned to the examination of cells, and a whole new world of cellular ultrastructure was revealed. Much of what we now know about the subcellular organization of life has been discovered only in the last two decades, and the biological sciences currently are busily digesting an enormous amount of new information dealing with cellular structure and function. It is indeed an exciting and challenging time in which to be a student, a teacher, or a researcher in the biological sciences.

THE EUKARYOTIC CELL

We recognize two major groups of organisms: those with cells having nuclei and those with cells lacking nuclei. The great majority of types have nucleated cells and are termed **eukaryotes.** The remainder are the bacteria and blue-green algae; these lack nuclei and are termed **prokaryotes.**

As we have noted in Chapter 3, the cells of prokaryotes, though lacking nuclei, have central regions in which DNA is located. Eukaryotic cells, on the other hand, have the bulk of their DNA contained within **chromosomes,** and these in turn are enclosed by a double membrane system called the **nuclear envelope.** The entire nucleus is composed of the chromosomes, one or more spherical, RNA-containing bodies called **nucleoli,** the nuclear cytoplasm or **nucleoplasm,** and the surrounding nuclear envelope.

MITOSIS

The number of chromosomes in any given cell corresponds to a definite number characteristic for each species of plant or animal.

The lowest chromosome number known is four (in some flatworms and *Haplopappus,* a desert plant). There are eight in the fruit fly, 14 in garden peas, 46 in humans, 254 in the hermit crab, and 1260 in the adder's tongue fern, to name a few examples. This characteristic number is maintained in each species through countless generations of cells, both in unicellular and multicellular eukaryotes, by mitotic cell division. The essence of **mitosis** is that it is a process in which each chromosome is duplicated prior to the formation of two new daughter cells, and that each duplicate chromosome is directed to a different daughter cell. This insures that all cells will have the same chromosome number, and that each new cell will have the identical complement of individual chromosomes as the parent cell.

Each chromosome carries in its DNA a portion of the genetic information of the cell. This information is in the form of **genes** (spe-

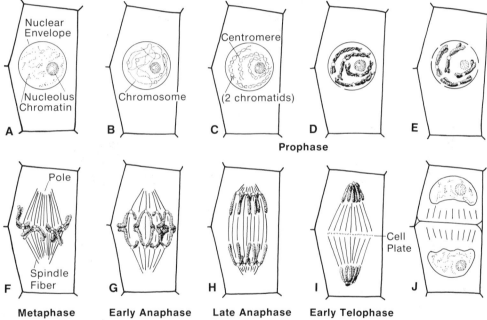

Figure 4–2 Mitosis in a eukaryotic plant cell. *A,* **Interphase.** Pictured is a metabolic, non-dividing cell. The chromosomes are extended as extremely fine threads and granular regions of *chromatin.* A nucleolus is present, and the nuclear envelope is intact.

B to *E,* **Prophase,** the early stage of cell division. The chromosomes become progressively shorter and more distinct as a result of coiling. Each chromosome is visibly double; its two strands, known as **chromatids,** are conjoined at the **centromere.** The nucleolus disappears in late prophase.

F, **Metaphase.** The chromosomes are arranged in the center of a fibrous body called the **spindle.** Both the nucleolus and the nuclear envelope have disappeared completely. The centromere has been duplicated.

G and *H,* **Anaphase.** The chromosomes become separated into two equal sets as a result of attachment of a **spindle fiber** to the centromere of each chromatid pair, followed by the drawing apart of the individual chromatids toward opposite poles of the spindle.

I and *J,* **Telophase.** During this stage, the chromatids complete their movement to opposite poles. A new cell wall, or **cell plate,** forms in the center of the spindle. Subsequently the spindle disappears and nuclear envelopes are reconstituted around each set of chromatids. The new cell wall is completed in each daughter cell, and each chromatid becomes a complete chromosome through synthesis of additional DNA (Redrawn from Weier, T. E., Stocking, C. R. and Barbour, M. G. *Botany, An Introduction to Plant Biology,* Fifth Edition. John Wiley & Sons Inc., New York, 1974).

87

cific groupings of nucleotides), which are now known to have a rather constant linear arrangement along each chromosome. Duplication of the chromosomes and their separation and systematic distribution to daughter cells by mitosis insures that each new cell will have acquired the same genetic information as its sister cells. This is of great importance if the cell is to carry on all of its functions. Cells sometimes fail to receive their full complement of chromosomes as a result of malfunctions in mitosis, and it is observed that such cells usually do not survive.

If we were to use a light microscope to examine the chromosomes of a eukaryotic cell, we would find subtle structural differences, principally in length and in the location of centromeres, that would enable us to distinguish individual chromosomes. Furthermore, with rare exceptions it can be shown that certain cells of plants have twice as many chromosomes as others. These cells are said to be 2N in chromosome number, while the others are said to be 1N in chromosome number. Moreover, the chromosomes of these 2N cells are present in pairs, whereas those of 1N cells are not. For example,

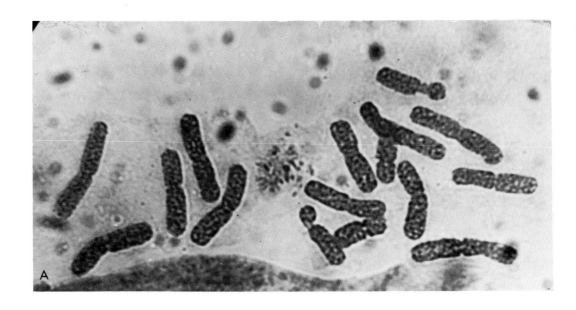

Figure 4-3 The chromosomes of the Florida cycad, *Zamia integrifolia. A,* Preparation of the dividing cells in a young leaf. Careful inspection of this preparation reveals that the 16 chromosomes consist of eight distinguishable pairs, as shown in *B.*

if the 1*N* number of chromosomes in some cells of a certain plant is eight, then the 2*N* number of chromosomes in other cells of this plant will be found to have two matching sets of eight chromosomes, for a total of 16 (see Figure 4–3). The basic or reduced number of chromosomes is termed the **monoploid** number, while the 2*N* condition is called the **diploid** number.

MEIOSIS

Changes in chromosome number are associated fundamentally with sexual reproduction in eukaryotes. Chromosomes from two sex cells (with the 1*N* number of chromosomes) combine to form a 2*N* line of cells. Then, in a process known as **meiosis,** these chromosome sets are again separated prior to the formation of sex cells. Every 2*N* cell of plant or animal origin can be traced, at least theoretically, to a single cell, the **zygote,** formed by the union of two sex cells or gametes, each having the 1*N* number of chromosomes. The gametes, in turn, were either themselves produced directly by meiosis occurring in a 2*N* cell or indirectly by a series of mitotic divisions of 1*N* cells following meiosis in a 2*N* cell. The former method is characteristic of animals, while the latter is more typical of plants.

Meiosis always involves the division of the nucleus and usually the cytoplasm of a 2*N* cell. Typically, meiosis consists of two sequential nuclear divisions. The first of these, the **reductional**

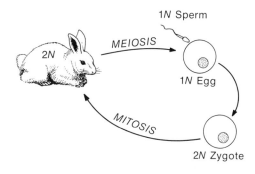

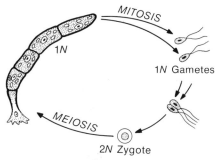

Figure 4–4 Diagrammatic summary of the roles of mitosis and meiosis in the life cycles of plants and animals.

division, involves the segregation of each member of a chromosome pair into a different daughter nucleus. At its terminus, in a plant having a 2N set of chromosomes numbering 16, for example, each daughter nucleus will have one set of eight chromosomes. The second meiotic division, sometimes termed an **equational division,** resembles mitosis in that the chromatids of each chromosome are segregated in daughter nuclei so that a total of four nuclei are formed, each having an equal number of eight chromosomes. Usually the division of nuclei is accompanied by cytoplasmic division so that four daughter cells are produced. However, exceptions are known in both plants and animals.

Commonly in animals, the four daughter cells formed in meiosis are transformed directly into gametes and fertilization ensues, so that a 2N zygote is produced at once. But in plants, the cells formed by meiosis ordinarily have a different destiny. They give rise by repeated mitotic divisions to a generation of 1N cells (known as the **gametophyte generation,** because such cells eventually will produce gametes). The nature and duration of the gametophyte stages, as well as that of 2N stages, differ among plant groups.

The significance of meiosis and fertilization is not so much that 1N and 2N chromosome numbers occur in cells as it is that chromosomal and genetic segregation takes place as a result of meiosis. Then, as a result of fertilization (which brings chromosomes from

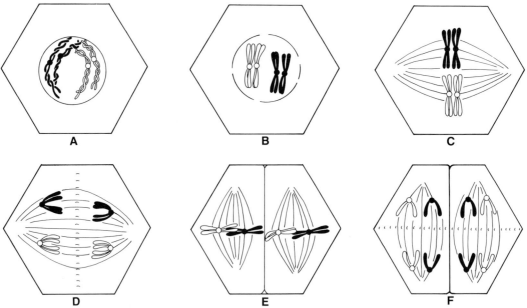

Figure 4–5 Summary of the major steps constituting **Meiosis I,** A and B, mid and late prophase. The chromosome pairs become closely associated (**synapsis**) and each chromosome separates into two chromatids in a 2N cell undergoing meiosis.

Metaphase, C, and anaphase, D, of the first, or reductional, division of meiosis. Each member of a chromosome pair becomes separated from its partner and is segregated to opposite daughter nuclei.

Meiosis II, Metaphase, E, and telophase, F, of the second, or equational, division of meiosis. The sister chromatids become separated from one another and are segregated into opposite nuclei; thus, this division somewhat resembles mitosis.

different parents together), genetic recombination results. From time to time, both major and minor variations (mutations) occur in the genes of any organism. In any given set of environmental conditions, these changes may prove to be either deleterious or fortuitous, the latter more often during periods when the environment is changing. If such genetic changes prove to have survival value for the cell or organism, their distribution to other cells and organisms via the process outlined above may be of benefit to both population and species.

PLANT LIFE CYCLES AND ALTERNATION OF GENERATIONS

Plants vary greatly in structural complexity, from simple unicellular types found among the algae to highly organized assemblages of diversified cell types of the larger land plants. Despite these differences, meiosis and fertilization occur in all these plants as correlated events in their respective life cycles. Were fertilization to occur generation after generation without meiosis, the chromosomes would soon increase to an unsupportable number. That chromosomal multiplication may occur in nature is shown by the frequent occurrence of plants having higher chromosome numbers than are usual for the species. These are called **polyploids,** and plants with four sets of chromosomes (**tetraploids**), eight sets of chromosomes (**octoploids),** and other ploidy levels are known in naturally occurring plant populations.

The alternation of $1N$ and $2N$ stages in a life cycle, the manner in which these stages are attained, their duration, and their relative complexity are of great importance in characterizing species and groups of plants according to their evolutionary and ecological relationships. In many algae and fungi the only $2N$ stage is the zygote. When the zygote divides it does so by meiosis, producing vegetative cells that are $1N$ in chromosome number. These, in turn, repeatedly divide by mitosis, which maintains the $1N$ number. But eventually, often as a result of seasonal environmental changes, some or all of the vegetative cells either become transformed into gametes or else produce specialized gametes by processes characteristic of the species. When the gametes combine in fertilization, a zygote again is formed and the life cycle has been completed. In subsequent discussions this kind of life cycle will be termed **life cycle I.** A second life cycle type **(life cycle II)** is similar, but differs from life cycle I in that meiosis occurs directly before production of gametes (gametic meiosis). It is typical of most animals, and is found in a few algae.

In other algae and fungi and in all higher plants including mosses, ferns, conifers, and flowering plants, however, a complicated life cycle known as **alternation of generations** occurs. The details of this process vary from plant group to plant group, but the essentials are very similar in all groups. The $2N$ zygote in such plants divides by mitosis rather than meiosis and forms a $2N$ plant called a **sporophyte.** Some cells of the sporophyte undergo meiosis and form **meiospores**

91

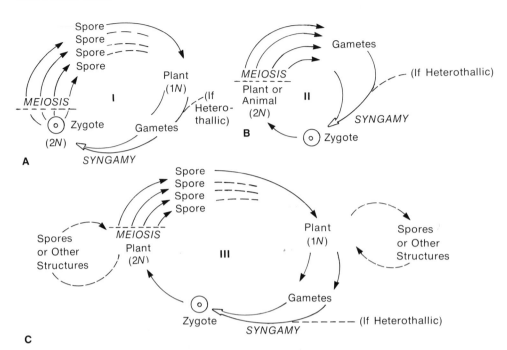

Figure 4–6. Sexual life cycles among algae, fungi, and higher plants. *A,* Life cycle without alternation of generations, as seen in many algae and certain fungi, in which meiosis occurs in the zygote (life cycle I). *B,* Life cycle without alternation of generations in which meiosis results directly in the production of gametes; this is seen in some algae and in most animals, and is referred to as life cycle II. *C,* Life cycle with alternation of generations; this is seen in some algae and fungi and in all higher green plants, and is referred to as life cycle III. Note that asexual reproduction also may occur in conjunction with various phases of such life cycles.

that are 1*N* in chromosome number. The meiospores then divide by mitosis, forming a second plant generation termed the **gametophyte.** The gametophyte is 1*N* in chromosome number and upon maturity produces gametes that also are 1*N.* After fertilization, a 2*N* zygote is formed and the cycle is complete. This life cycle will be referred to as **life cycle III.**

THE EUKARYOTIC PLANT CELL

Plant cells come in all shapes and sizes. Many one-celled algae have flagella and are motile, as are also the male gametes of many multicellular plants. Some plant cells are boxlike and uninucleate, others are tubular and multinucleate. Within all such cells are found a number of membrane-bounded structures, the **organelles,** which also vary in form, number, and distribution from cell type to cell type. For this reason, in speaking or writing about plant cells in general, it is necessary either to select an unspecialized kind of cell as a representative cell or else to invent a "typical plant cell" that incorporates most of the structures found in the majority of cells. In ei-

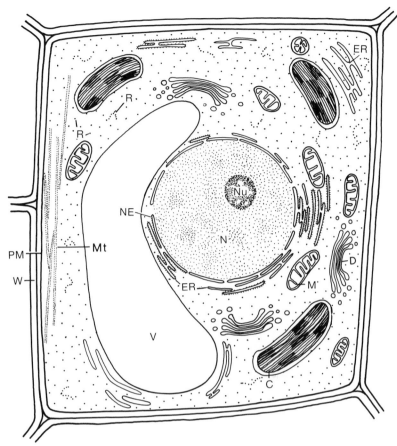

Figure 4-7 Cell wall and protoplast of a "typical" plant cell, with some of the more commonly recognized structures: W, cell wall; PM, plasma membrane; ER, endoplasmic reticulum; C, chloroplast; D, dictyosome; M, mitochondrion; R, ribosomes; Mt, microtubules; NE, nuclear envelope; Nu, nucleolus; N, nucleus; V, vacuole (Redrawn from Wilson, C. L., W. E. Loomis, and T. A. Steeves. *Botany,* 5th ed. New York, Holt, Rinehart and Winston, 1971).

ther case, it is important to know that such a "typical cell" represents only our concept of the average cell; the average cell, like the average person, exists only in the mind.

The Cell Wall—Meristems

The walls of green plant cells are composed of cellulose fibers that are randomly oriented in the first-formed part of the wall, the **primary wall,** and spirally or longitudinally oriented in the **secondary wall.** In most cells, the starting point in wall formation is never a completely naked protoplast. The only naked cells are the gametes, which obviously would have great difficulty in uniting if they were enclosed by walls. The zygote develops a primary wall and in all subsequent cell divisions the new cells inherit portions of this original wall, developing new walls in the plane of cell division and adding more material to older walls.

The first partitioning layer to form in a dividing cell is the **cell plate.** The cell plate is shared by each daughter cell, and these daughter cells deposit cellulose fibers on their respective sides, thus forming primary walls. The cell plate material persists as the **middle lamella.** The middle lamella is composed of **pectin,** a polysaccharide-like substance that acts as a cementing agent between adjacent cells.

In many species of algae every cell is at least potentially a dividing cell, but in more complex, multicellular plants such as ferns and flowering plants, growth and development are generally restricted to certain regions known as **meristems** and their adjacent tissues. These usually are located at the tips of stems and roots, but also may be present in other regions. Most woody plants, for example, have a cylindrical meristem (the **cambium**) located within their stems and roots. Division of cambial cells produces lateral growth and adds to the girth of plants. Terminal or **apical meristems** produce longitudinal growth of stems and roots.

Newly formed cells are relatively small, but soon undergo considerable expansion. This expansion is due in part to added cytoplasm, but is mostly the result of enlargement of the cell **vacuole,** a membrane-lined reservoir filled with a sap composed of water, sugar, and other solutes. The mature cell typically is considerably larger than the meristematic cell. During the period of expansion, the protoplast is enclosed only by a primary wall that is rather elastic, in part because of the random orientation of its cellulose fibers and in part because of the action of certain plant hormones that promote the extensibility of the wall. As a cell attains its mature dimensions, the protoplast lays down a more rigid secondary wall on the inner side of the primary wall. The fibers of the secondary wall are parallel and several layers may be present, (each oriented in a different direction.) The wall is penetrated at many points by cytoplasmic strands known as **plasmodesmata,** which maintain cytoplasmic continuity between neighboring cells.

Some kinds of cells undergo self-digestion (**autolysis**) of their protoplasts so that nothing remains of the formerly living cells but their walls; the water-conducting **xylem** cells of higher plants are included here. Xylem cells have thin areas in their walls, called pits, that permit rapid movement of water and solutes from cell to cell. The pit should not be considered a hole in a cell wall, but instead as a thin, permeable membrane composed of primary wall material.

Finally, in some tissues the cells may have additional substances deposited in the interstices of cellulose fibers that further modify the composition and characteristics of their walls. The cells of cork tissue, for example, contain deposits of a waxy material called **suberin,** which is responsible for the water- and wine-proof nature of cork. Xylem cell walls characteristically contain **lignin,** a substance that adds rigidity to cells.

It should be emphasized that not all plants have walls of the kind just described. Fungi have cell walls composed of materials other than cellulose and have a plan of cellular organization that is entirely different from that found in most green plants. The body of a

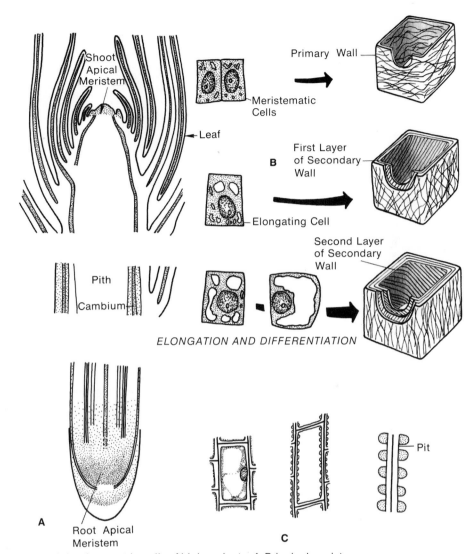

Figure 4-8 Growth and development in cells of higher plants. *A,* Principal meristems. *B,* Cell wall development in an expanding cell. *C,* Formation of a xylem cell. (Redrawn from Wilson, C. L., Loomis, W. E., and Steeves, T. A. *Botany,* 5th ed., and from Weier, T. E., Stocking, C. R., and Barbour, M. G. *Botany, An Introduction to Plant Biology,* Fifth Edition. New York, John Wiley and Sons, Inc., 1974.)

fungus is composed of intertwining tubes, called **hyphae,** rather than multilayered ranks of angular cells. Other kinds of cellular organization also are found within some groups of algae. These will be discussed in greater detail in the appropriate chapters.

The Protoplast

The living part of the plant cell is called the protoplast. Its outer boundary is a delicate **plasma membrane** composed of two layers of lipid molecules in which protein molecules are interspersed (Fig. 4–10). The plasma membrane is a dynamic structure that functions not only to protect and enclose the cytoplasm but also to maintain a

95

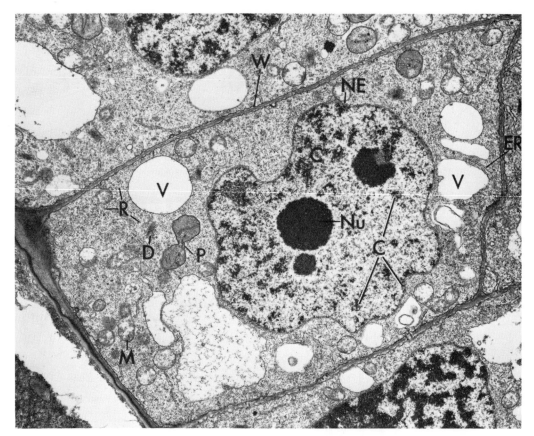

Figure 4–9 Electron micrograph of a relatively unspecialized cell of barley, × 11,500. W, cell wall; M, mitochondrion; ER, endoplasmic reticulum; NE, nuclear envelope; Nu, nucleolus; C, chromosomal material (chromatin); D, dictyosome; P, proplastid; R, ribosomes; V, vacuole.

traffic of substances passing in and out of the cell. The materials of the cell wall, for example, are secreted through the plasma membrane during wall-building, and water and solutes necessary for maintaining the life of the cell must enter through the plasma membrane. The plasma membrane is said to be **selectively permeable,** for it has the property of permitting the passage of some kinds of molecules while excluding other kinds. On the other hand, the cell wall is perfectly permeable to water and solutes but not at all so to particles (for example, soil particles). Hence, plant cells take up solutions only from the environment; even gases such as oxygen and carbon dioxide are dissolved in water when taken up or excreted by cells.

The protoplast is composed largely of water. In addition to the "free" water present in its vacuoles, "structural" water constitutes 75 to 95 per cent of the cytoplasm and nucleoplasm. This water is an integral part of the protoplast, not simply a dissolving medium. The living protoplasm is a somewhat viscous or glue-like substance composed of many kinds of molecules held together by various kinds of chemical bonds.

It is customary to divide the protoplast into cytoplasm and nucleoplasm. The ground substance of the cell makes up the bulk of

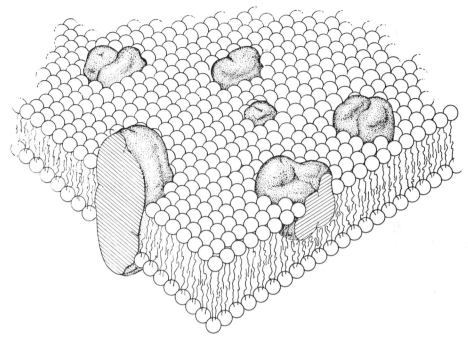

Figure 4–10 Model of a hypothetical cell membrane. The plasma membrane and other membranes of cells are hypothesized as consisting of outer and inner lipid layers, with protein molecules interspersed (From Singer, S. J., and Nicolson, G. L. The Fluid Mosaic Model of the Structure of Cell Membranes. *Science, 175*:720–731, 18 February 1972. Copyright 1972 by the American Association for the Advancement of Science).

both regions and, during metaphase, when the nuclear envelope is absent, the boundary between nucleoplasm and cytoplasm is indistinguishable. In both regions, the ground substance has a faintly fibrous appearance when viewed by electron microscopy.

Organelles

Embedded or suspended in the cytoplasm of a typical plant cell are specialized, membranous bodies called **organelles.** Perhaps the most obvious of these are the **nucleus,** the **plastids,** the **mitochondria,** the **endoplasmic reticulum,** the **dictyosomes,** and the **vacuoles.** The nucleus and its components have already been described; we now proceed to brief descriptions of the other organelles.

Plastids. Plastids are organelles associated with photosynthesis, the formation and deposition of starch, oils, and carotenoid pigments. Not all of these functions are carried on by any one particular plastid type, but rather by several kinds of plastids. Meristematic cells very often have **proplastids.** These are small bodies, usually less than 1 micrometer in diameter, of comparatively simple structure. Proplastids give rise to other plastid types as the cell matures. **Chloroplasts** carry on photosynthesis and also produce starch and sometimes oil. **Leucoplasts** are non-photosynthetic; they store starch and oil. The **chromoplasts** are the red and yellow, carotenoid-con-

97

taining plastids found in fruits and vegetables such as tomatoes, oranges, and carrots. All of these plastid types are interconvertible; for example, the plastids in a tomato fruit may first be proplastids, then become chloroplasts and finally chromoplasts as the fruit grows and ripens.

Chloroplasts. Much attention has been given to chloroplasts because in eukaryotic plant cells all photosynthesis occurs in them. If we examine the chloroplast of a typical plant cell with a light microscope, we find it to be a football-shaped organelle about 5 to 10 micrometers long and perhaps 3 to 4 micrometers in diameter. We may by chance see one dividing, since chloroplasts reproduce independently of cell division. Within the chloroplast small green disks (the **grana**), suspended in a colorless matrix (the **stroma**), are faintly discernible.

The electron microscope gives us a much more detailed view of chloroplast structure (Fig. 4–12). The outer covering of the chloroplast is composed of two membranes, one within the other. Within the chloroplasts are parallel arrays of membranes, known as

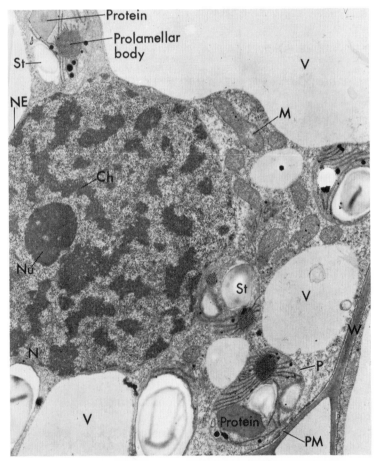

Figure 4–11 Electron micrograph of a young leaf of *Encephalartos,* a cycad, ×15,000. The plastids are undergoing transformation from proplastids to chloroplasts; Ch, chromatin; P, plastid; M, mitochondrion; N, nucleus; Nu, nucleolus; NE, nuclear envelope; St, starch; W, cell wall; V, vacuole. The mesh-like structure known as the prolamellar body is a transitional phase in the formation of chloroplast lamellae.

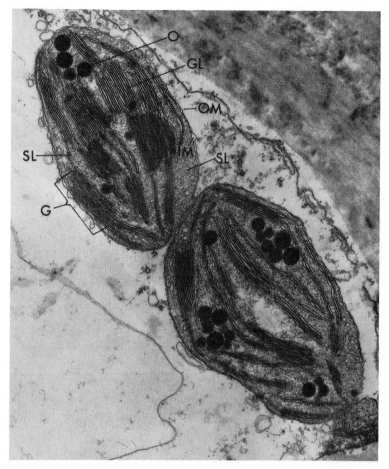

Figure 4–12 Electron micrograph of chloroplasts of *Ceratophyllum,* an aquatic flowering plant, × 28,000. OM, outer chloroplast membrane; S, stroma; O, oil; G, granum; GL, grana lamellae; SL, stroma lamellae (From Rebechini, H. M., and Hanzely, L. *Z. für Pflanzenphysiologie 73*:377, 1974).

lamellae or **thylakoids.** In some places these are closely associated in stacks, resembling stacks of pancakes, and are more deeply stained.* The stacks are the grana and the deeply stained portions are occupied by the photosynthetic pigments. Starch grains, deeply-staining globules of oil, and ribosomes also are present, and it is sometimes possible to discern some fibers of chloroplast DNA.

Since chloroplasts are reproduced independently of cell division, we wonder whether they actually make some or all of their own components or whether they depend on the mother cell in which they live for the membranes, pigments, enzymes, and other elements of which they are made. Studies now show that the chloroplast is surprisingly independent of the mother cell and is able to make a number of its own components. In doing this it uses its own DNA, RNA, and ribosomes. However, it is not completely autonomous, for some of its constituent molecules are supplied by the cell.

---

*In electron microscopy, heavy metals such as lead and uranium are used for staining and present a dark appearance.

99

Mitochondria. Mitochondria resemble chloroplasts in some structural features but are smaller (usually 1 to 2 micrometers in diameter). Both organelles have outer double membranes and both have internal membrane systems. The inwardly projecting membranes of mitochondria are termed **cristae,** and seem to consist of flattened bags or, more commonly in plants, of tubules.

Mitochondria are the sites of **aerobic respiration** in eukaryotes, an oxidative process in which cells make the energy stored in food available for cell functions. In addition, mitochondria have their own DNA, RNA, and ribosomes, and, like the chloroplasts, appear to be self-reproducing and semi-autonomous bodies.

Endoplasmic Reticulum. The endoplasmic reticulum is an internal membrane system present in the cytoplasm of cells. Its usual appearance is that of a pair of parallel membranes that seem rather randomly oriented in the cytoplasm. In its three-dimensional aspect the endoplasmic reticulum is composed of flattened tubes or bags, known as **cisternae.** One kind of endoplasmic reticulum, the **rough**

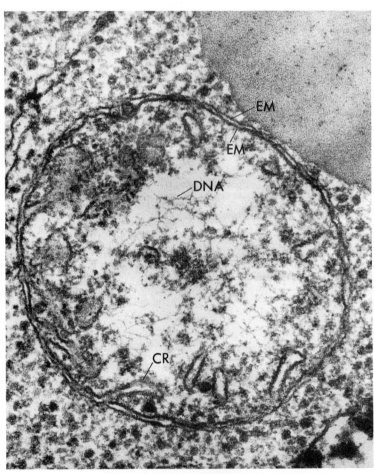

Figure 4–13 A mitochondrium from the root tip of garlic (*Allium sativum*), × 220,000. Note the two external membranes (EM) constituting the mitochondrial envelope and internal cristae. DNA fibrils also are present (From Hanzely, L., and Schjeide, O. A. *Cytobiologie* 4:207–215, 1971).

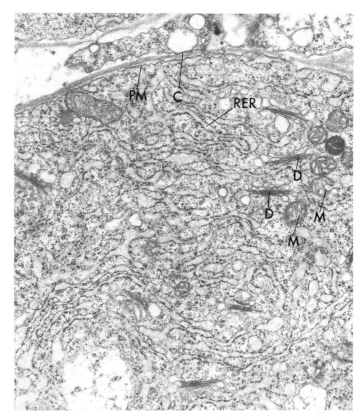

Figure 4–14 Rough endoplasmic reticulum (RER) in an endosperm cell of barley. The endosperm is the principal storage tissue of the seed and is very active in the synthesis of large molecules. Also note dictyosomes (D), mitochondria (M), cell wall (C), plasma membrane (PM), and numerous ribosomes, some free, others on the endoplasmic reticulum.

endoplasmic reticulum, has ribosomes attached to the outer surface of its membranes and is thought to be associated with protein synthesis and secretion. The **smooth endoplasmic reticulum** lacks ribosomes and may be concerned with the synthesis and perhaps the transport and secretion of carbohydrate substances. It appears to be associated with plasmodesmata and has been reported to be continuous with the plasma membrane in some kinds of cells.

Dictyosomes. The dictyosomes, also called **Golgi bodies,** are composed of several (often five to seven) flattened cisternae. They are often seen in profile view in electron micrographs where their cisternal nature is apparent, but in surface views they appear somewhat disk-like and also have been likened to a stack of pancakes. Associated with the margins of dictyosomes are small sac-like **vesicles,** and it is thought that these vesicles contain cell wall substances and participate in the formation of the cell plate. One class of dictyosome vesicles contains digestive enzymes and is termed **lysosomes.** Lysosomes are active in digestion and secretion and have been observed in root-cap cells, but are more common in animal cells than in plant cells.

Vacuoles. Most plant cells have vacuoles, and these, though not in themselves living components, are important in maintaining

101

vital functions of cells, such as osmotic relationships and cell enlargement. Meristematic cells have several small vacuoles, but these coalesce as the cell grows so that the mature cell usually has just one large vacuole. In addition to water, sugar, and various solutes, many vacuoles contain **anthocyanins.** The yellows, pinks and blues of flower petals are often due to anthocyanin and anthocyanin-like pigments within vacuoles. Red cabbage and red beets also owe their color to such pigments in vacuoles.

Microtubules. One of the most recently discovered cytoplasmic components is the **microtubule.** Improvements in the chemicals used to preserve cells for electron microscopy have led to a realization that microtubules are of widespread occurrence in eukaryotic cells. The fibers that form the spindle of a dividing cell make up one class of microtubules, as do the elements of cilia and flagella. A band of microtubules, the **preprophase band,** present only during mitosis, encircles the meristematic plant cell just within the plasma membrane and seems to establish the plane of cell division. Other microtubules form **cytoskeletons** in such motile cells as free-swimming algae and the motile male gametes of some land plants. Microtubules are about 25 nanometers in diameter, of varying length, and

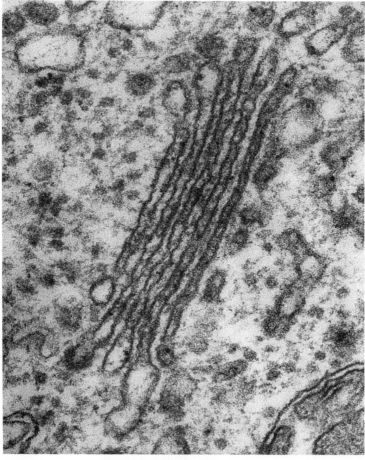

Figure 4–15 The dictyosome of a root cell of garlic, × 270,000 (Photo courtesy of Dr. Laszlo Hanzely).

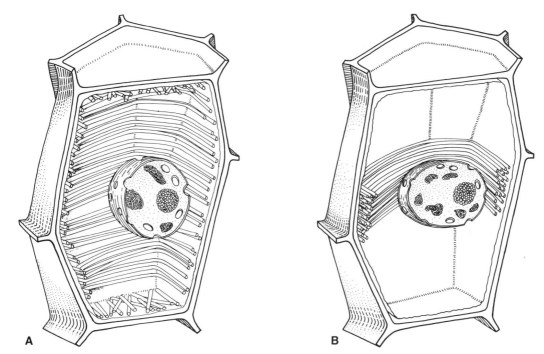

A   B

Figure 4–16 Microtubules. *A,* Mictotubules have a random orientation in an inter-phase cell. *B,* In a cell in mitotic prophase, the microtubules form a preprophase band equatorially in the plane of cell division (Redrawn from Ledbetter, M. C., and Porter, K. *Introduction to the Fine Structure of Plant Cells.* New York, Springer-Verlag, 1970).

are composed of a dense protein wall and a transparent core. Strictly speaking, microtubules are not organelles since they are not membranous structures.

Flagella. Most cells of multicellular plants are immobile. In fact, one of the characteristics associated with plants is that they are stationary even though capable of certain in-place movements, such as bending in response to light, folding of leaves and flowers, and, in one case, snapping shut on insects. But we should not overlook the point that a number of unicellular algae are very mobile indeed, swimming about energetically, and that a few terrestrial plants, such as slime molds, creep from place to place by cytoplasmic flowing. Moreover, in every major plant group but three (the blue-green algae, red algae, and flowering plants), there are at least some species that have flagellated, free-swimming male gametes (Fig. 4–17).

The locomotory organelle of free-swimming plant cells is the **flagellum,** an elongated, cylindrical structure enclosed by an extension of the plasma membrane and containing an internal system of longitudinal fibers. In all flagellated plants except bacteria, there is a basic flagellar pattern of nine peripheral sets of fibers and two central ones. This pattern also is found in nearly all flagellated animal cells.

Microbodies. Small bodies, about 0.5 micrometer in diameter, termed **microbodies,** have been found in some plant and animal cells. They appear to have certain oxidative functions and also are termed

103

peroxisomes and **glyoxisomes.** Their functional significance in the cell at present is poorly understood.

Ribosomes. The structures enumerated above are not the only ones present in the cytoplasm of a cell. Low magnification electron micrographs often show the cytoplasm as having a granular appearance. At higher magnifications, these granules in eukaryotic cells are seen to be sub-spherical bodies about 25 nanometers in diameter. They are the **ribosomes** and are the sites of protein synthesis in the cell. Ribosomes often occur in chains and then are referred to as **polyribosomes** or **polysomes.** They also occur within chloroplasts, mitochondria, and the nucleus. Those destined for the cytoplasm are made and stored temporarily in the nucleolus. When ribosomes are bound to the outer surface of the cisternae of the endoplasmic reticulum, they form the rough endoplasmic reticulum.

Other Cytoplasmic Bodies. Inorganic crystals of various shapes accumulate in many kinds of plant cells, as do deposits of tannins and other substances. Most of these are thought to be waste products that have been precipitated in an inactive form. It should be remembered that plant cells do not excrete solid wastes, since the cell wall is impermeable to particles.

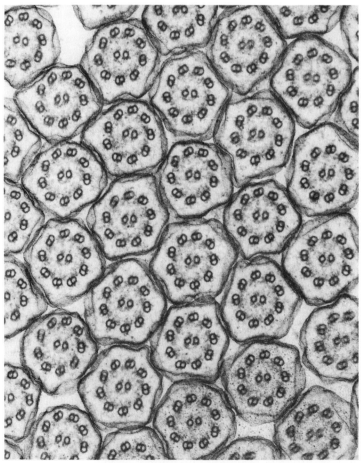

Figure 4–17 Electron micrograph showing transverse sections of the flagella of the sperm cell of *Zamia integrifolia,* a cycad, × 200,000. Note that each flagellum contains nine outer pairs of fibers (doublets), and two inner, single fibers.

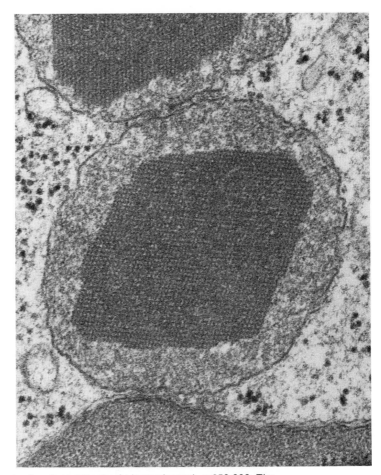

Figure 4–18 Electron micrograph of a plant microbody (peroxisome), × 250,000. The angular, crystalloid body is composed of molecules of the enzyme peroxidase (Photo courtesy of Dr. Eugene Vigil).

Very recently, small proteinaceous fibers about 10 nanometers in diameter, have been observed in some plant cells; these fibers are called **microfilaments** and apparently are required for a form of cytoplasmic movement termed **streaming** or **cyclosis.**

Evolution of the Eukaryotic Cell

We do not know how or when the first eukaryotic cells evolved. Fossils of apparently nucleated cells are seen in late Precambrian deposits about one billion years old, but these tell us little of their origin. Various suggestions have been offered to explain the origin of such organisms and their organelles. Blue-green algae or similar cells may have formed nuclei by folding in their cell membranes around their DNA fibers, or evolved chloroplasts by similarly enfolding their photosynthetic membranes, and mitochondria might have evolved in a like manner. Unfortunately there are no intermediate stages, either fossil or living, to illustrate such an origin for eukaryotes, nor does there seem to be good supporting evidence of a circumstantial nature for this hypothesis. On the other hand, the hypothesis that eukaryotic organisms arose as a result of symbiosis

105

in which several primitive cell types, living together very intimately, produced the eukaryotic cell type seems to be gaining favor. This theory, the **symbiotic theory of evolution,** is particularly associated with Dr. Lynn Margulis of Boston University.

It is suggested in the symbiotic theory of evolution that, during Precambrian times, three general kinds of organisms may have existed: bacteria living in and metabolizing organic debris such as dead cells and cellular byproducts; photosynthetic prokaryotes (such as photosynthetic bacteria and blue-green algae); and a hypothetical amoeba-like predator that may or may not have had a nucleus, but certainly lacked mitochondria and chloroplasts and had no cell wall. This organism, unlike bacteria and blue-green algae, had the ability to ingest food particles in much the same way as present-day amoebas. Perhaps, like some kinds of amoebas, this organism also had a flagellum. If so, it would have been of the 9 + 2 pattern, we think, for most biologists believe that the occurrence of a single flagellar pattern among all eukaryotes is evidence of their common origin.

Not having their own photosynthetic or aerobic respiratory systems, some eukaryotic predators may have "borrowed" those of blue-green algae or, perhaps, bacteria. They may have engulfed such prokaryotic cells and, through modifications of their internal membrane systems, preserved a few such cells in a permanent, symbiotic association. Further adjustments, such as the shedding of cell walls and elimination of nonessential parts of their genetic information with increased dependence on the genes of the host cell for certain enzymes, might have resulted in the conversion of these symbionts into the structures we recognize as chloroplasts and mitochondria. Some steps in this novel and interesting theory are shown in Figure 4–19.

The concept outlined above is, of course, highly speculative, and one is justified in asking whether there is evidence that such evolution might actually have taken place. A number of clues have been used in formulating the hypothesis. Symbiotic associations in which prokaryotes reside in the cytoplasm of eukaryotes are known (Fig. 4–20). Blue-green algae of several species apparently function as substitutes for chloroplasts in some protozoa, and even in other algae, and in the association depicted in Figure 4–20 the blue-green algae further resemble chloroplasts in that they lack cell walls. Also, the chloroplasts of some cells, notably those of red algae, resemble blue-green algae both in the nature of their membranes and in their pigments.

Other similarities exist between mitochondria, chloroplasts, and prokaryotic cells. The DNA in bacteria and mitochondria is in the form of loops and circles, and recent studies suggest that this is true also of chloroplast DNA. The form of DNA in blue-green algae is not known except that it appears to resemble that of bacteria. A procedure called **hybridization,** in which RNA and DNA from different sources are mingled, shows that RNA and DNA tend to stick together where their respective nucleotides match (i.e., where they have identical genetic information). The degree to which this occurs is supposed to indicate the closeness of the evolutionary relation-

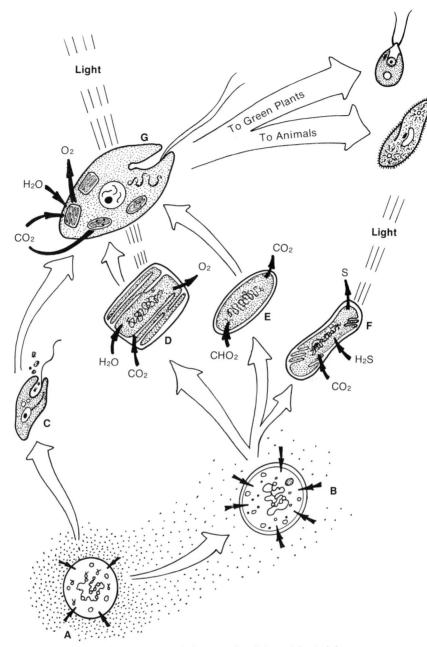

Figure 4–19 Hypothetical evolution of eukaryotes. *A*, Ancestral cell in nutrient-rich sea. *B*, Primitive cell capable of photosynthesis (which aids in nutrient uptake). *C*, Primitive, anaerobic, eukaryotic predator. *D*, Blue-green algal cell. *E*, Aerobic bacterium. *F*, Photosynthetic bacterium. *G*, Ancestral eukaryote having blue-green algal cell and bacteria in symbiotic relationship.

ship between the two organisms from which the DNA and RNA were obtained. It has been shown that RNA from blue-green algae shows a higher degree of matching when tested against chloroplast DNA than does the cytoplasmic RNA of the chloroplast's own cell. Somewhat similar hybridization experiments show a much higher affinity between DNA in humans and monkeys than between that in humans

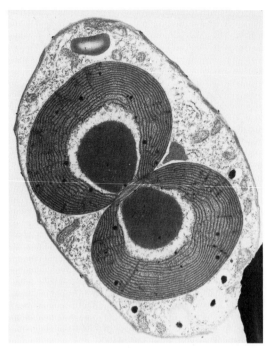

Figure 4–20 *Cyanophora paradoxa,* a flagellated eukaryote, containing *Cyanocyta korschekoffiana,* a blue-green alga, × 18,000. The algal cells replicate within the host cells and are carried over into the daughter cells when the host cells divide (From Pickett-Heaps, J. Cell Division in *Cyanophora paradoxa. New Phytol. 71*:561–567, 1972).

and chickens. This is what we would expect, and tends to indicate the validity of this method.

If mitochondria and chloroplasts are descended from intracellular symbionts, they ought to be at least partially independent with respect to their reproduction. This, as we know, is the case. Furthermore, many studies done with the photosynthetic one-celled organism *Euglena* have shown that, when chloroplasts are totally eliminated as a result of heat or chemical treatment, such "bleached" *Euglena* cells never recover their chloroplasts and must live as heterotrophs. Moreover, recent experiments with wall-less tobacco cells of an albino (non-green) mutant strain have shown that such cells can take up isolated chloroplasts and adopt them, thus becoming green cells. With respect to their ribosomes, mitochondria and chloroplasts both resemble prokaryotes in having a smaller type, unlike the larger variety found in the cytoplasm of eukaryotes. Additionally, the same antibiotics that inhibit protein synthesis by bacterial ribosomes also affect those of mitochondria and chloroplasts, but not the ribosomes of eukaryotic cytoplasm.

Not all of the arguments support this view, however. There are reports indicating derivation of mitochondria from chloroplasts, and derivation of both from the nuclear membrane. These, if substantiated, are at variance with the view that such organelles are autonomously reproducing bodies. The complex development of chloroplasts from proplastids seems to have no parallel in blue-green algae. Moreover, since the symbiotic theory of evolution is based almost entirely on circumstantial evidence, it must be weighed against the lack of either fossil or living forms of life that would typify some of the important evolutionary stages.

SUMMARY

Eukaryotes, in contrast to prokaryotes, are characterized by the complexity of their cell structure and by sexual as well as asexual reproduction. The term eukaryote denotes a cell with a nucleus, whereas the term prokaryote denotes a cell lacking a nucleus although it contains DNA in a central region of the cell. Additional distinctions may be noted in connection with the nuclei of eukaryotes. These contain chromosomes and are replicated in two distinct processes: by mitosis, an asexual process in which cells and their chromosomes are duplicated in such a way that the chromosome number remains constant, and by meiosis, normally a part of the sexual cycle in which the chromosome number is reduced by one half.

In addition to the nucleus, other structures not present in prokaryotes occur in eukaryotes. Among these are the mitochondria (in which aerobic respiration takes place), and the chloroplasts (in which photosynthesis occurs).

How did eukaryotes evolve? One possibility is that they developed as a result of modifications occurring in the membrane systems of prokaryote ancestors. Another hypothesis, termed the symbiotic theory, suggests that the eukaryotic cell as we know it is a product of symbiosis, that perhaps primitive eukaryotes engulfed blue-green algae and bacteria and preserved them in a permanent symbiotic relationship. Eventually some of these prokaryotes became greatly modified and incorporated into the cytoplasm of their host cells as plastids and mitochondria.

DISCUSSION QUESTIONS

1. What is the relationship between chromosome number and mitosis? Meiosis?
2. In what phase of mitosis are chromosomes numerically replicated?
3. What is the relationship between the chromosomes of a 1N cell and those of a 2N cell?
4. Specifically, what process occurs in the first division of meiosis? In the second division of meiosis?
5. What is meant by polyploidy? How might polyploid cells be formed?
6. What is the relationship between the primary wall and secondary wall of a plant cell in terms of cell growth and development?
7. Are all cells in a complex, multicellular plant living? Explain.
8. How do substances get into and out of plant cells? What is the role of the cell wall, if any, in such movements?
9. Name five cell organelles and give a function for each.
10. Eukaryotes may have acquired plastids through symbiosis with blue-green algae. What evidence favors this theory?

SUPPLEMENTAL READING

Goodenough, U. W., and R. P. Levine. The Genetic Identity of Mitochondria and Chloroplasts. *Sci. Amer. 223(5)*:22–31, 1970.

Loewy, A. G., and P. Siekevitz. *Cell Structure and Function,* 2nd ed. New York: Holt, Rinehart and Winston, Inc., 1969.

Margulis, L. *Origin of Eukaryotic Cells.* New Haven: Yale Univ. Press, 1970.

Margulis, L. Symbiosis and Evolution. *Sci. Amer. 225(2)*:48–57, 1971.

Raff, R. A., and H. R. Hahler. The Non-symbiotic Origin of Mitochondria. *Science 177*:375–381, 1972.

Wolfe, S. L. *Biology of the Cell.* Belmont, California: Wadsworth Publishing Co., Inc., 1972.

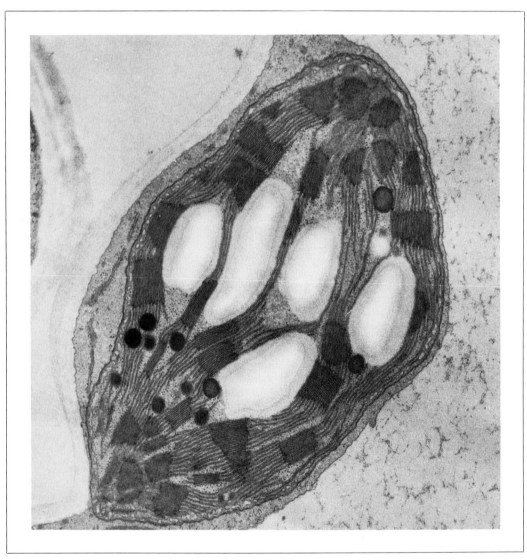

Chloroplast of *Muhlenbergia racemosa,* × 15,000 (Photo courtesy of Dr. Watson Laetsch, University of California at Berkeley).

Chapter 5

Photosynthesis and Respiration

PHOTOSYNTHESIS • LIGHT QUALITY AND QUANTITY IN PHOTOSYNTHESIS
• FACTORS LIMITING PHOTOSYNTHESIS • PHOTOSYNTHESIS AND HUMAN
POPULATIONS • RESPIRATION • SUMMARY

Plant power supports the world! As we view our dwindling energy resources, we increasingly turn our thoughts to natural, non-polluting energy. The wind, the sun, and the tides often are mentioned as possible allies in our attempts to meet our future energy needs. Because we cannot afford to ignore any potential source of new energy, we have an obligation to develop all such inexhaustible, non-polluting supplies of energy. Of these, the sun seems to hold the greatest promise, and methods of direct conversion of sunshine into useful thermal and electrical energy are even now in use. Houses are heated with solar energy, and space satellites are operated with electricity obtained from light-absorption by special photoelectric panels. Important as these may be in the future, the most important energy source in the world today is photosynthesis by green plants.

It has been estimated that each year about 90 billion metric tons of high energy fuel in the form of sugar are produced by green plants. This is about 100 times the total amount of energy produced in the world by human activities, including coal mining, oil wells, nuclear energy, thermal energy, and wind and water power. Moreover, if we consider that coal and petroleum both were produced by photosynthesis in the green plants of long ago, we see that photosynthesis eclipses all other energy sources by a vast margin. Clearly it is not a question of production of energy that confronts the world, but a problem of proper utilization of energy produced by photosynthesis. It is a problem that will require much greater attention in the future by governments, industries, and scientists before it is resolved.

"All plants possess a power of correcting, in a few hours, foul air unfit for respiration; but only in clear daylight, or in the sunshine."

JAN INGEN-HOUSZ, 1779

PHOTOSYNTHESIS

It is possible to view photosynthesis by considering it in terms of a black box. In this approach, we conceive of substances going into the box, together with the energy to operate its machinery, and new products coming out of the box; then, we attempt to imagine what is going on inside the box. If we consider the chloroplast as the black box of photosynthesis, then we see molecules of water and carbon dioxide going in, light energy furnishing power to the box, and carbohydrate coming out as the product. The black box also produces by-products in the form of oxygen and water. The question: How does it operate?

One approach to solving the mystery is to try to separate it into smaller boxes, and then observe intermediate steps in the processing of raw materials, use of energy, and product and waste product output. In historical terms, the development of our understanding of photosynthesis can readily be likened to the black-box approach. Initially, the box was the whole plant, then the chloroplast, and now the components of the chloroplast down to the molecular level.

The efforts of many distinguished scientists during the past 200 years have been concentrated on understanding photosynthesis. Joseph Priestley (1733–1804), who also discovered oxygen, showed that green plants could replenish an atmosphere from which oxygen had been removed by a living animal or a candle flame. He was the first scientist to recognize this fundamental relationship between plants and animals. In the eighteenth and nineteenth centuries other scientists discovered the necessity for light and water in photosynthesis, explained the role of carbon dioxide and oxygen, identified the end product as carbohydrate, and localized the action in the chloroplast. So then the black box of photosynthesis looked like this:

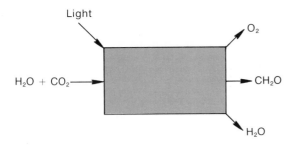

Then, early in the twentieth century, it was found that photosynthesis consisted of two phases, the **light reaction** and the **dark reaction.** The black box had become two boxes:

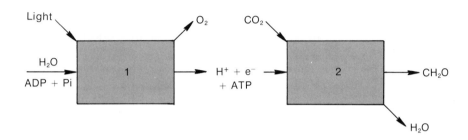

In Box 1 (the light reaction), the energy input is light, the raw material is water, and the by-product is oxygen. In Box 2 (the dark reaction), the raw material is carbon dioxide, the primary energy supply is electrical energy (electrons) produced by the light reaction (Box 1); also utilized are hydrogen ions and molecules of adenosine triphosphate (ATP). The latter is an energy-rich molecule of widespread occurrence in biochemical reactions; it furnishes chemical energy for cellular reactions in which molecules are assembled and disassembled. In the light reaction some of the energy derived from light is used to generate ATP from ADP and phosphate, some is used in splitting apart water molecules, and much of it is passed on to the dark reaction in the form of electrons.

Why is water both a raw material and a by-product in photosynthesis? The answer lies in the somewhat devious method the plant employs in converting energy and in transforming one kind of molecule into another. At one time it was thought that water molecules were added directly to the carbon molecules of carbon dioxide to make carbohydrate (CH_2O) and the oxygen of CO_2 was given off as a by-product. Now it is known that only the hydrogen of the water molecule is attached to the carbon dioxide, so the oxygen given off comes from water initially put into the reaction. About twice as much water is used in photosynthesis as is given off. The waste water is produced as a result of the combining of some hydrogen (derived from the splitting of water) with one of the oxygens of the CO_2 molecule.

The essential nature of the photosynthetic process is set forth in the brief explanation above, and may be sufficient to understand the basic aspects of energy flow in the environment. However, in order

113

more fully to understand the mechanism of photosynthesis, it is necessary from this point on to subdivide further the light and dark reactions.

The Light Reaction

In the light reaction, light energy is absorbed by chlorophyll and is converted into chemical energy that is then stored in several kinds of high-energy molecules. During this process water molecules are separated into their constituent hydrogens and oxygens; the hydrogens are used to **fix** carbon dioxide, that is, to produce carbohydrates by adding hydrogen to carbon and oxygen; surplus oxygen is then released into the atmosphere or is used in the plant cell's own respiration. The entire process of photosynthesis may be summed up as:

$$2H_2O + \text{Light Energy} + CO_2 \xrightarrow{chlorophyll} CH_2O \text{ (Carbohydrate)} + H_2O + O_2.$$

This equation conceals the numerous steps actually involved in photosynthesis and does little to explain the complexities and relationships of the light and dark reactions. It may be helpful, therefore, to subdivide the equation as follows:

$$2H_2O + \text{Light Energy} \xrightarrow{chlorophyll} 4H^+ + 4e^- + O_2$$

in which the light energy absorbed by chlorophyll is used to break down water and produce hydrogen ions, electrons, and oxygen. Later we will see that an energy-rich molecule, ATP, also is produced in the light reaction and interacts in the dark reaction. The second half of the equation may be written:

$$CO_2 + 4H^+ + 4e^- \xrightarrow{chloroplast} CH_2O + H_2O$$

in which we note that hydrogen ions and electrons are employed to fix (i.e., to reduce chemically) CO_2 and to form carbohydrate. This half-equation also shows that the water appearing on the right side of the equation results from the removal of oxygen from CO_2 and that all of the oxygen formed in the process of photosynthesis results from the dissociation of water molecules in the light reaction.

At this point we pause briefly in the discussion of photosynthesis to consider the nature of energy relationships in cells and among cell constituents. As we have seen above, hydrogen ions and electrons are transferred from molecule to molecule. Those giving up electrons (or hydrogen atoms that contain electrons) are said to be **oxidized** (even though oxygen itself is not always present), while molecules receiving electrons (or hydrogen atoms) are said to be

reduced. The rule in such energy or electron transfers is that molecules rich in energy (electrons) may transfer energy (electrons) to those that are not as rich. The drop in energy of the contributing molecules may be accompanied by processes in which some of the energy is conserved in the form of high-energy molecules such as ATP. For the reverse process to occur, in which electrons flow from relatively low-energy molecules to higher-energy molecules, the input of additional energy from other sources is required. Essentially, this is the difference between photosynthesis and respiration. Photosynthesis puts energy from sunlight into relatively energy-poor molecules (H_2O and CO_2) to make high-energy molecules (CH_2O), while respiration (also called **biological oxidation**) consists of the degradation of high-energy molecules formed by photosynthesis (CH_2O) and release of energy, which is then used in various cellular activities, and work is performed.

A number of different kinds of molecules are involved in such energy transfers. Among these are **enzymes**, which greatly accelerate chemical reactions, and **coenzymes**, which cooperate with enzymes to remove electrons from substrate molecules. The coenzymes then pass the electrons on to other molecules called **electron carriers.** These, in turn, transfer electrons to certain ultimate electron acceptors, as for example O_2 in aerobic respiration. The coenzymes include **NADP** (nicotinamide adenine dinucleotide phosphate), **NAD** (nicotinamide adenine dinucleotide), **FAD** (flavin adenine dinucleotide), and others. Their action is illustrated as follows:

$$NADP + 2H^+ + 2e^- \longrightarrow NADPH_2^*$$

In some cases a pair of hydrogen ions accompanies each pair of electrons in their passage from molecule to molecule; in other cases, only electrons are transferred but the hydrogen ions are usually available for eventual recombination. Electron carriers include the **cytochromes,** a group of iron-containing compounds, as well as others active in photosynthesis and respiration.

Energy is released as electrons pass from one electron carrier to the next, and at some electron transfers enough energy is released to be conserved in energy-rich molecules of ATP. ATP does not receive electrons, but stores energy in the form of high-energy phosphate bonds, written $\sim$P. Thus

ADP (Adenosine Diphosphate) + P_i (Phosphoric Acid) +

$$Energy \longrightarrow ADP \sim P \ (ATP)$$

Participation of some of the kinds of molecules named above in the

---

*Often written as $NADP^+ + 2H^+ + 2e^- \longrightarrow NADPH + H^+$

cell's energy flow processes may be illustrated in a highly diagrammatic way as follows:

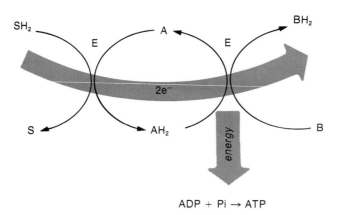

$$ADP + Pi \rightarrow ATP$$

where SH_2 is a substrate or food molecule, and A is a coenzyme, such as NADP, associated with enzymes (E) in the transfer of hydrogens and electrons from SH_2 to B, which is an electron acceptor. During the course of this reaction, in a process known as **phosphorylation,** some of the energy released is diverted into the formation of ATP.

A rather fascinating experiment demonstrates the importance of ATP in cellular reactions. The light-emitting compound **luciferin,** occurring in luminescent fungi and algae and in fireflies, can be extracted but will not emit light energy spontaneously. An enzyme **luciferase** catalyzes light production, but the actual production of light also requires energy from ATP. If luciferin and luciferase are mixed in a test tube, nothing happens, but once ATP is added, the contents of the tube will begin to glow immediately and will continue to emit light until the ATP is exhausted (i.e., until it has given up all its high-energy $\sim$ P bonds and has reverted to ADP and P_i).

Returning again to the action of light in photosynthesis, let us center our attention briefly on the actual absorption of light by chlorophyll. It is not known exactly how light energy is trapped by chlorophyll, but when a unit of light energy, called a **photon,** is absorbed by a chlorophyll molecule its energy appears to be transferred somehow to an electron of that molecule. This electron is raised from its normal energy level, or **orbital,** to a higher energy level (new orbital), and is said to be "excited." This higher state is unstable and the excited electron will tend to fall back to its normal orbital. In so doing, it gives up its absorbed energy by re-emitting visible red light (**fluorescence**). This would indicate that chlorophyll by itself is incapable of converting light energy into chemical energy. But once light energy has raised a chlorophyll electron to a higher energy state in an intact chloroplast, other components of the photosynthetic system come into action, and this energy is made available for further progression of the photosynthetic process.

In actuality, photosynthetic cells rely on pigment complexes composed of chlorophyll *a* (alone or in combination with either chlorophyll *b*, chlorophyll *c*, or chlorophyll *e*, depending on plant group) as well as on accessory pigments such as carotenoids. No matter which of these initially traps a photon, the energy of the photon passes from pigment molecule to pigment molecule until it ends up in a reaction center, possibly composed of a particular kind of chlorophyll *a* molecule. The reaction center then transfers its excited electron to a specific electron acceptor, initiating a series of electron transfers that supplies sufficient energy to operate the synthetic phases of the light and dark reactions.

The fixation of CO_2 in the dark reaction requires two kinds of high-energy molecules originating in the light reaction, i.e., $NADPH_2$ and ATP. These are generated in a series of interactions between two complexes of pigments and carrier molecules, called **photosystem I** and **photosystem II.** Photons striking the pigments of PS-I generate excited electrons that are passed through several electron carriers, ending up in $NADPH_2$. Light absorbed by PS-II, in some way not well understood, "splits" water molecules, thus removing electrons and hydrogen ions and leaving a residue of O_2 molecules. These electrons from water are raised to the excited state by a chlorophyll of PS-II and then are transferred through a chain of

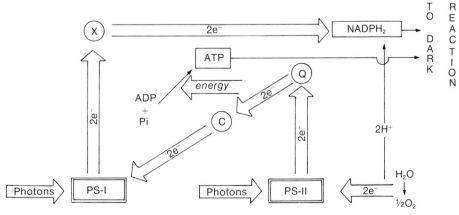

Figure 5–1 Diagrammatic summary of events occurring in the light reaction. $NADPH_2$, X, Q, and C represent some (but not all) of the electron carriers employed in the light reaction. X is an uncharacterized molecule associated with the reduction of ferredoxin, one of the electron carriers; Q is an unknown acceptor molecule referred to as a fluorescence quencher, and C represents several cytochromes associated with the light reaction.

117

electron carriers associated with PS-I, eventually replacing those supplied by PS-I to NADPH$_2$. Electrons, during their passage from PS-II to PS-I, release sufficient energy to generate some ATP. The energy flow in the light reaction is shown in Figure 5–1.

The Dark Reaction

Coupled with the light reaction of photosynthesis is the dark reaction, so-called because it does not directly require light even though it occurs during daylight hours. While it now appears that there may be several different dark reactions in plants, the most widely occurring of these is the **Calvin cycle,** discovered by Dr. Melvin Calvin and his associates at the University of California, for which Dr. Calvin received the Nobel Prize in 1961. A second cycle, the **C-4 pathway,** has been described recently in a small number of tropical and temperate zone plants, including sugar cane. It can utilize higher light intensities to fix CO$_2$ than can the Calvin cycle alone; however, plants having the C-4 pathway also have the Calvin cycle in operation in their chloroplasts.

When light shines on chloroplasts of green plants the immediate products are ATP and NADPH$_2$. Within a few milliseconds these two high-energy molecules are employed in reactions occurring in the chloroplast's stroma that result in the reduction of molecules of CO$_2$ and the formation of carbohydrates. The reduction of one molecule of CO$_2$ is stated simply in the following equation:

$$CO_2 + 2NADPH_2 + 3ATP \longrightarrow CH_2O + 2NADP + 3ADP + 3P_i + H_2O$$

Calvin and his colleagues, using carbon-14 (the radioactive isotope of ordinary carbon whose progress through chemical reactions can be traced with a Geiger counter), showed that when a molecule of CO$_2$ enters an illuminated chloroplast, it is immediately attached to one end of a larger molecule, the 5-carbon sugar **ribulose diphosphate.** The resulting 6-carbon molecule then cleaves into two 3-carbon molecules and the recently-added CO$_2$ is reduced to the aldehyde state characteristic of sugars. This process is accomplished by the transfer of energy-rich bonds from ATP and of electrons and hydrogen ions from NADPH$_2$. Thus, two 3-carbon sugars are formed but at the cost of one 5-carbon sugar. In the balance of the Calvin cycle ribulose diphosphate is produced and 6-carbon sugars, such as glucose and fructose, are formed (Fig. 5–2).

Light Quality and Quantity in Photosynthesis

Photosynthesis requires energy in the visible range of the spectrum of light. Sunlight as we perceive it appears white, but it is actually composed of a spectrum of colors, or wavelengths, as in the fa-

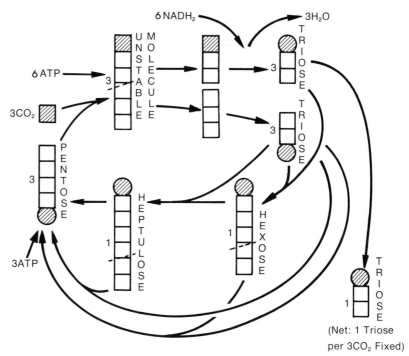

Figure 5–2 Highly diagrammatic summary of the Calvin-Benson cycle. In operation, three molecules of CO_2 with the input of energy from ATP combine with three molecules of five-carbon sugar (pentose) to form three unstable intermediate molecules. Each breaks down into two three-carbon fragments of an organic acid (phosphoglyceric acid). The acid molecules are reduced by $NADPH_2$ from the light reaction, and are converted into trioses. Five of the six trioses combine with each other or with fragments of intermediate sugar molecules (such as six-carbon hexose and seven-carbon heptulose) to form three pentoses, which in turn replace those used in the initial fixation of CO_2. There is a net gain of one triose from these reactions; in two such cycles, one hexose would be produced. In this diagram, the number of segments composing the molecule correspond to the number of carbons per molecule, and the circular segments represent the portion of the molecule most characteristic of a sugar (aldehyde or ketone group).

miliar rainbow. The visible light spectrum ranges from shorter wavelengths of blue light through progressively longer wavelengths of green, yellow, orange, and red light. A chloroplast absorbs a portion of the light of the spectrum and reflects the remainder, and it is principally red and blue light that is absorbed and green light that is reflected. It is this selective absorption that accounts for the green color of chlorophyll. That this absorbed light specifically is active in photosynthesis can be shown by measuring photosynthetic output against absorbed wavelengths of light. An elegant experiment was done as long ago as 1882 by the Dutch botanist T. W. Engelmann, in which a filament of green algal cells was illuminated by a spectrum of light transmitted through a microscope slide. The slide also contained numerous motile aerobic bacteria in addition to the algae, and these clustered about the algal cells in those regions where

119

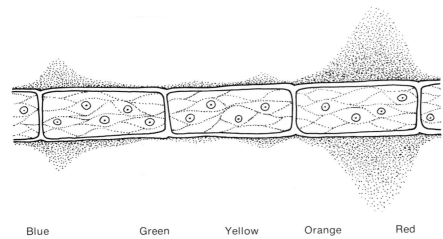

| Blue | | Green | Yellow | Orange | Red |

Figure 5–3 Engelmann's photosynthesis experiment. A green alga was placed on a microscope slide together with motile, aerobic bacteria. The algal filament then was illuminated with a spectrum of the wavelengths of visible light. The bacteria tended to cluster in those regions where oxygen was produced (Redrawn from Greulach, V. A., and Adams, J. E. *Plants: An Introduction to Modern Botany,* 2nd Ed., 1967. New York, John Wiley and Sons).

oxygen was being produced by photosynthesis. Engelmann observed the highest concentration of bacteria where the algal cells were illuminated by red and blue light. This relationship may be called an **action spectrum,** because it measures a photosynthetic response to

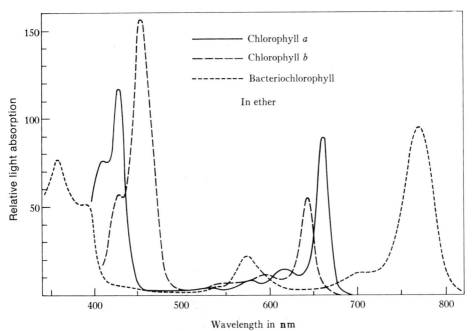

Figure 5–4 Absorption spectrum of chlorophylls *a* and *b* and bacteriochlorophyll (From Clayton, R. K. *Molecular Physics in Photosynthesis.* Blaisdell Publishing Company, 1965).

a spectrum of light. It may be compared with the wavelengths of light actually absorbed by chlorophyll, the **absorption spectrum** (Fig. 5–4). When this is done it is seen that it is the red and blue wavelengths that are absorbed by chloroplasts, just as it is these same wavelengths that are most active in photosynthesis.

Only about one to five per cent of the light energy that reaches the surface of the earth is actually absorbed by chloroplasts; much is reflected or is absorbed by objects other than plants, and even the light that reaches the chloroplast is absorbed selectively, as we have seen. Estimates vary as to the actual efficiency of the energy conversion occurring in chloroplasts, but it is thought to be between 12 and 24 per cent, with recent evaluations favoring the higher figure. Nevertheless, an enormous amount of organic material is produced by photosynthesis in green plants. It is estimated that the world total is somewhere between 10^{10} and 10^{11} tons of sugar each year, more than enough to cover the surface of a state the size of Ohio to a depth of three to four meters.

Factors Limiting Photosynthesis

Light intensity normally is not a limiting factor in photosynthesis. In most cases chloroplasts become light-saturated at levels lower than normally available. Day length, however, may be a limiting factor, particularly when plants are grown in greenhouses during the winter.

Since CO_2 and H_2O are both consumed in photosynthesis, suboptimal amounts of either may limit photosynthesis. Water may be a critical factor in dry climates or during droughts. Although CO_2 is not normally considered an important limiting factor, plants actually are able to use several times as much CO_2 as occurs in the atmosphere (0.03 per cent). It has been shown that photosynthesis increases under experimental conditions until the concentration of CO_2 is about five times that in the atmosphere.

Photosynthesis and Human Populations

Nations of the world are characterized as developed or underdeveloped on the basis of their industrialization and the nature of their agricultural economy. Only about one third of the world's people live in developed countries, almost exclusively in temperate latitudes. These people enjoy per capita wealth three to ten times that of the other two thirds, who live principally in the tropics and subtropics. One of the marked differences between the two groups is the productivity of their agriculture. Crop yields are three to five times higher per unit of area in the developed countries. In Cuba, the sugar cane yield per hectare is less than one third that of Hawaii; wheat yields in India are about one fifth those of the Netherlands; less than one third as many soybeans are produced in Indonesia as in Canada; and the rice yield in Japan is three times that

121

of Brazil. One might attribute these differences to climate or to soil fertility. However, primary productivity (photosynthetic yield) under natural conditions tends to decrease northward and southward from the equator, because of climatic factors; therefore, we must look for another explanation.

The higher agricultural productivity in developed countries is due not to any intrinsic superiority of soil and climate, but to the **energy subsidy** of their agriculture. This energy subsidy is in the form of fuel burned to run tractors and other equipment, and also includes energy used to make fertilizers, pesticides, and even the energy used in supporting education and research in agriculture. A large proportion of the energy required, directly or indirectly, to sustain these operations also comes from photosynthesis in the form of fossil fuels such as coal, oil, and natural gas. Advanced agricultures have much higher energy subsidies than do primitive ones. The Netherlands, where the land has been reclaimed from the sea, is a good example of a country with a high energy subsidy of its agriculture. Without oil, imported principally from the Middle East, countries such as the Netherlands would rapidly become impoverished.

But it is not only the amount of food produced per hectare that is important; sugar cane, for example, is the most productive plant of any of the world's crops, yet sugar, by itself, is not a suitable food to sustain human life. An adequate protein supplement is needed for a healthy people, and this is lacking in underdeveloped countries. Agricultural productivity must be sufficiently great to support the production of high-protein foods. In most cases these are obtained from livestock, poultry, or fish. Plant proteins also may be used, but these require processing and supplementation since ordinarily they are deficient in one or another of the essential amino acids.

One of the most depressing aspects of the agricultural economies of underdeveloped nations is that low crop yields often coincide with high rates of population increase, which are, on the average, more than 200 per cent higher than those of developed countries. There seems to be little hope that improvements in agricultural practice in these poorer lands will do much good as long as their populations continue to grow.

The Energy Crisis

One of the major reasons that agriculture is so productive in the United States is that it is highly mechanized. If the energy required to operate our farms were to fail, it is probable that we would not have a sufficient amount of food. Our population has about doubled since the days when our farms were operated by manpower and horsepower. To return to such conditions would require the return of millions of Americans to farming from industry. Because our nation is outstripping its fuel resources and becoming increasingly dependent on foreign fuel sources, we may find ourselves losing control of our agricultural output. It is in the national interest, as well as the world's interest, that we attempt to develop alternate sources of energy and that we conserve our present fuel supplies. Photosynthesis is the greatest source of energy we know. Research into the energy conversion processes of green plants may show us how to use solar energy directly to run our machines and to heat, cool, and light our homes.

RESPIRATION

In our preoccupation with photosynthesis, we may lose sight of the fact that respiration also occurs in all plant cells—those that photosynthesize as well as those that do not. Fungi and most bacteria are completely non-photosynthetic; that is, they are completely heterotrophic. All higher forms of green plants are partial heterotrophs, for they have non-photosynthetic tissues in their leaves, stems, roots, and reproductive organs, and these are completely dependent on the photosynthetic cells of their leaves and stems. Additionally, a number of higher plants obtain some food from the environment as a consequence of symbiotic relationships with soil fungi or, in a few cases, because they are able to trap and digest insects. A few flowering plants are complete heterotrophs and thus entirely dependent on other plants for their nutrition; among these are dodder, a bright orange-colored parasitic vine; *Rafflesia,* a tropical parasite with enormous flowers; and the Indian pipe, *Monotropa.*

Although all photosynthetic plants use the products of their photosynthesis in their own respiration, they produce more food than is immediately required. A large amount of this surplus is used in the production of wood. Much also is stored in reproductive structures, such as fruits, seeds, and spores. Most of this stored food is eaten or otherwise taken up by consumer organisms and only a fraction survives long enough to support the growth of new plant life.

Respiration originally meant the exchange of gases between an organism and its environment. As understanding of physiological processes grew, respiration came to have another meaning as well. Now we consider respiration to include a number of chemical reactions in which food is oxidized and its energy is released to do work within cells.

The overall equation for respiration seems at first sight to be the exact reverse of photosynthesis:

$$CH_2O + O_2 \longrightarrow Energy + CO_2 + H_2O.$$

However, we realize that the pathways in the two processes are quite different. Even so, respiration and photosynthesis are complementary in terms of products and by-products, and this helps us understand their importance in the maintenance of the ecosystem.

Just as photosynthesis is separable into phases, so too is respiration. The first phase is *glycolysis* (sugar-splitting), and occurs in

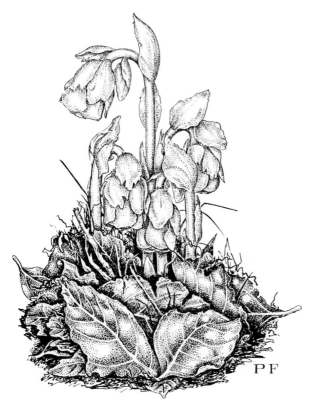

Figure 5–5   The Indian pipe, *Monotropa,* a non-photosynthetic, heterotrophic flowering plant. This plant derives its nourishment from the roots of host trees or from decomposing vegetable matter.

the cytoplasm, both in prokaryotes and eukaryotes. Glycolysis may be summarized as follows:

$$\text{Glucose} + 2\text{NAD} \longrightarrow 2\text{Pyruvic acid} + 2\text{NADH}_2 + 2\text{H}_2\text{O}$$

$$\downarrow energy$$

$$2\text{ADP} + 2\text{P}_i \longrightarrow 2\text{ATP}$$

The second phase occurs in the cytoplasm of prokaryotes but only in mitochondria of eukaryotes, and is termed the **citric acid cycle (Krebs cycle).**

In the citric acid cycle, pyruvic acid from glycolysis is partially oxidized to form an unstable 2-carbon intermediate molecule (acetyl-CoA), which immediately combines with a 4-carbon molecule (oxaloacetic acid) to form citric acid, a 6-carbon molecule for which the cycle is named. In ensuing reactions electrons, hydrogen ions, and CO_2 are successively removed from a series of intermediate molecules, resulting in the generation of ATP and several carrier molecules ($NADH_2$ and $FADH_2$). The final intermediate is oxaloacetic acid, which then may combine with another 2-carbon acetyl-CoA molecule to begin the whole process over again.

The molecules of $NADH_2$ and $FADH_2$ generated in respiration transfer their hydrogens and electron to an acceptor molecule of a series of carrier molecules (cytochromes) constituting the **electron transport system.** This system functions in the manner shown on page 116, and the electrons pass from cytochrome to cytochrome with the energy released in these transfers used to form three ATP for every $NADH_2$ and two ATP for each $FADH_2$. The last cytochrome in the series passes electrons and hydrogen ions to a final electron acceptor molecule (which is usually oxygen, and results in the formation of water). A total of 38 ATP molecules are formed from the oxidation of one glucose in glycolysis, the citric acid cycle, and the electron transport system.

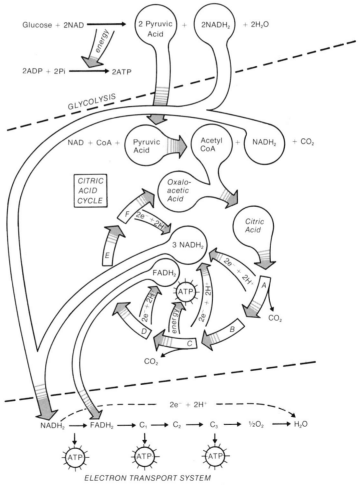

Figure 5–6 A graphic summary of the events in respiration. A to F are intermediate molecules of organic acid from which electrons and hydrogen ions are successively removed or in which molecular rearrangements have occurred without oxidation.

Fermentation

We have noted that some cells (especially bacteria, but also some eukaryotes, such as yeasts) may live without oxygen. The processes whereby they obtain energy from food are **anaerobic respiration** and **fermentation.** In fermentation, the citric acid cycle is not involved; rather, glycolysis is the source of ATP and pyruvic acid acts as the terminal electron acceptor for $NADH_2$. The process may be summarized as follows:

1. Glucose + 2NAD $\longrightarrow$ 2Pyruvic Acid + $2NADH_2$ + $2H_2O$

energy

2ADP $\longrightarrow$ 2ATP
+
$2P_i$

2. 2Pyruvic Acid + $2NADH_2$ $\longrightarrow$ 2 Ethyl Alcohol + $2CO_2$ + 2NAD

Both CO_2 and ethyl alcohol are by-products of fermentation. Since the higher-yielding electron transport system is not in operation, the net yield of ATP is very low, only two ATP per glucose molecule. Substrates other than glucose may be the starting point of fermentation in various ·species of bacteria, and waste products other than ethyl alcohol may be produced. These waste products, which include other alcohols, organic solvents, and several organic acids, are often of importance in industrial processes, as we have seen in the case of acetone in the manufacture of explosives.

Anaerobic Respiration

Though confined to bacterial cells, anaerobic respiration is of interest in the present context because it uses inorganic molecules other than oxygen as terminal electron acceptors from the cytochromes of the electron transport system. Thus, in some cases, nitrate (NO_3^-) may be the terminal electron acceptor and N_2 and H_2O the products of this terminal oxidation. Unlike fermentation, the energy yield from anaerobic respiration may be as great as that derived from aerobic respiration.

SUMMARY

Photosynthesis is the most important natural process of chemical synthesis in the world. It is the prime source of energy in all natural cycles. In addition, most of our industrial plants, our homes, and our automobiles are run with the energy produced by photosynthesis long ago and locked up in fossil fuels. One can predict with reasonable assurance that at some future date scientists will learn to duplicate the energy conversion processes of the light reaction. When this happens, the new process may well overshadow all the other sources of energy available to us.

Respiration is intimately associated with photosynthesis, for the energy involved in respiratory processes in plant and animal cells comes either directly or indirectly from photosynthesis. Ultimately, of course, all such energy comes from the sun, but photosynthesis is the only process we know of that is capable of transforming light energy into food energy.

Another important relationship between photosynthesis and respiration is indicated by the requirement for oxygen in aerobic respiration, together with the production of oxygen in the light reaction of photosynthesis. A further correlation between these two life processes is noted by the requirement for carbon dioxide as a raw material in photosynthesis, and the production of carbon dioxide in respiration. Thus, photosynthesis and respiration are prime examples of ecological interdependence and coexistence.

Cellular respiration is summarized as:

$$CH_2O + O_2 \longrightarrow Energy + CO_2 + H_2O,$$

and photosynthesis as:

$$CO_2 + 2H_2O + Light\ Energy \xrightarrow{\text{\textit{chlorophyll}}} CH_2O + H_2O + O_2.$$

But these processes are much more complex than these simple equations seem to indicate. Furthermore, one is not the reverse of the other, for greatly different metabolic pathways occur in them. However, photosynthesis and respiration are complementary in terms of products, by-products, and energy flow.

DISCUSSION QUESTIONS

1. What are the raw materials of photosynthesis? The products? The by-products?
2. The two important products of the light reaction are $NADPH_2$ and ATP. How are they formed? Where are they used? What is an important by-product of the light reaction?
3. What wavelengths of light are active in the light reaction? Essentially what is cycled in the Calvin cycle? What happens to CO_2 in the Calvin cycle?
4. What is meant by the energy subsidy of agriculture? What are its implications in terms of future energy needs?
5. Define glycolysis; fermentation; anaerobic respiration.
6. What is meant by the statement, "all higher plants are partial heterotrophs"?
7. Are any flowering plants completely non-photosynthetic? Explain.
8. What is meant by the term *cycle* in relation to the citric acid cycle?
9. List the essential aspects of the relationships between plants, animals, and the environment.
10. What new sources of energy for support of human societies do you envision in the years ahead?

SUPPLEMENTAL READING

Bassham, J. A. The Path of Carbon in Photosynthesis. *Sci. Amer. 206(6)*:88–100, 1962.

Fogg, G. E., *Photosynthesis.* 2nd ed. New York: American Elsevier Publ. Co., Inc., 1972.

Levine, R. P. The Mechanism of Photosynthesis. *Sci. Amer. 221(6)*:58–70, 1969.

Rabinowitch, I. E., and Govindjee. The role of chlorophyll in photosynthesis. *Sci. Amer. 213(1)*:74–83, 1965.

Salisbury, F. B., and C. Ross. *Plant Physiology.* Belmont, California: Wadsworth Publ. Co., Inc., 1969.

Overflight view of the Greenland Ice Cap.

Chapter 6

Plants and Ecology

THE ECOSYSTEM • ENERGY FLOW IN THE ECOSYSTEM • ESSENTIAL MIN-
ERALS AND NATURAL CYCLES • BIOTIC FACTORS • PLANT COMMUNITIES
• LIFE STRATEGIES • ECOLOGICAL SUCCESSION • WORLD CLIMATES
AND MAJOR ECOSYSTEMS • THE TUNDRA • THE BOREAL FOREST • THE
TEMPERATE DECIDUOUS FOREST • GRASSLANDS • TROPICAL SAVANNA
• DESERTS • TROPICAL RAIN FORESTS • OCEANIC ECOSYSTEMS •
POLLUTION, EROSION, AND DEPLETION • SUMMARY

Many airlines still fly the "great circle route" pioneered by
Charles and Anne Morrow Lindbergh in the early 1930's. Before the
jet age, transatlantic flights left New York City, flew northeast over
New England, then over Nova Scotia and Newfoundland, and on to
Goose Bay, Labrador, for refueling. From Labrador the journey continued over the Greenland Ice Cap to Iceland for another refueling
stop, and, finally, to Ireland. The propeller-driven aircraft of that era
flew at relatively low altitudes and speeds and offered the traveler a
marvelous view of the changing landscape. First, beneath one's
window were the **temperate deciduous woodlands** of New England,
grading into pine forests transitional to the vast expanses of spruce
of the Canadian **boreal forest** or **taiga.** Over Newfoundland and
Labrador the **muskeg** (a boggy type of vegetation interspersed with
alders, willows, and spruce) gave way to the stony, moss- and
lichen-covered **tundra.** Finally, over Greenland, the massive ice cap
with its great, gray-white glaciers came into view. Glimpses of these
scenes can still be obtained from jet airliners, but not so clearly
because of the great altitudes and high speeds at which they fly. Regardless of how they are viewed, sights such as these permit per-
ception of the zonation of major vegetation types, especially in relation to climate.

Distribution of vegetation types generally is dependent upon
latitude in all parts of the world, being especially affected by the
increasingly colder climates occurring toward the poles. Similar

See matter next, with various life endued,
Press to one center still, the gen'ral good:
See dying vegetables life sustain,
See life dissolving vegetate again.
All forms that perish other forms supply
(By turns we catch the vital breath, and die),
Like bubbles on the sea of Matter borne,
They rise, they break, and to that sea return.

ALEXANDER POPE: *An Essay on Man*

vegetation zones may be seen in mountains. Such zones are altitudinal rather than latitudinal, and result from the colder climates encountered at progressively higher altitudes. Nevertheless, a latitudinal influence also is present; for example, a tundra-like vegetation is present at high elevations on many mountains, but this zone occurs only at the highest altitudes in the tropics (above 4000 meters), whereas in temperate regions it is found at considerably lower elevations (above 1500 meters). Such distributions of plants and animals in relation to features of the earth's surface and to climates is an aspect of ecology often referred to as **biogeography.**

Another approach to the distribution of plants and animals is the historical approach. We know, for instance, that the ice caps have expanded greatly during certain periods in the past and have contracted drastically during others. As a consequence the latitudinal zones also have shifted, with the result that regions now having vegetation types characteristic of temperate climates were at one time tundra and at other times may have had subtropical flora and fauna.

A third approach to plant ecology is study of the evolution of the plants themselves rather than of changes in their geographical distribution. Half a billion years ago the land surfaces may have been as barren as those left in the path of a retreating glacier (see Figure 3–1). Evolving plants and animals invaded this seemingly hostile environment and changed it, their continued evolution producing a series of vegetation types, including the flora of the coal age, the conifers of the Mesozoic Era when the great dinosaurs flourished, and many others. The study of fossil plants themselves is termed **paleobotany;** that of the ecological relationships of fossil plants and animals is **paleoecology.**

THE ECOSYSTEM

The associations of various plants composing the major vegetation zones described above, as well as many others, together with their various interrelationships with each other, with other organisms, and with a variety of additional environmental factors, constitute dynamic ecological units termed **ecosystems.** Ecosystems may be as small as a laboratory culture or as large as the Arctic tundra. The concept is a broad one, and encompasses both natural communities of organisms and artificial *model systems,* such as balanced aquaria. All ecosystems have the following in common:

(a) energy flow, including an initial input of energy, and **food web** relationships between **producer** and **consumer** organisms;

(b) an inorganic component consisting of essential chemical elements;

(c) biotic factors, including communities of interdependent livings organisms and the organic substances produced by them;

(d) characteristic physical factors, such as temperature, humidity, and light; and

(e) a developmental history (ecological succession).

Energy Flow in the Ecosystem

The unit employed in describing energy relationships in ecosystems is the **calorie** (the amount of heat required to raise the temperature of 1 gram of water 1°C at 15°C). Energy transactions take place between two very broad categories of organisms: **producer organisms,** most of which are photosynthetic plants; and **consumers,** which include those that feed on plants (the herbivores), on other consumers (the **predators**), and other specialized categories, such as **parasites, saprobes,** and non-photosynthetic **symbionts.** The initial input of energy into the ecosystem is sunlight. This light energy is converted by photosynthesis into chemical energy in the form of energy-rich molecules of organic compounds. Such chemical energy, in the form of foods of various kinds, passes from consumer organism to consumer organism until eventually all of the energy in the food has been used in cellular respiration (biological oxidation of food in cells). Since respiratory processes at their best are somewhat inefficient, considerable energy is wasted. This waste energy is in the form of heat, which sooner or later is radiated out into space and lost.

Various terms have been used to describe the energy relationships between producers and consumers. The term **food chain** suggests a succession of organisms beginning with plants and extending through various levels of consumer organisms. These relationships are not usually linear in form but are interwoven; therefore, the term **food web** seems preferable. Another descriptive term, **pyramid of numbers,** indicates that in many ecosystems the producers are more numerous than the herbivores and that generally the predators tend to diminish in number with each higher link in the food chain. The links or steps in producer and consumer relationships are called **trophic levels** (feeding levels).

There is another way of stating the pyramidal relationship of organisms. If one totals the weights of all of the individuals in a trophic level of a food chain or web, the **biomass** is obtained. The pyramid of numbers then may be converted into a pyramid of biomasses, which is more revealing because numbers of individuals are not always a true measure of food relationships. Herbivores may range in size from insects to elephants, and similar ranges in size and numbers may occur at other trophic levels, although the overall trend often is toward larger individuals and fewer numbers. For this reason, a clearer image of a food pyramid is presented when it is shown that biomass diminishes at each trophic level.

At each trophic level in a food pyramid some energy is lost. This is due in part to the inefficiency of cellular respiration, but mostly to the use of energy in the metabolism of organisms. Only a portion of

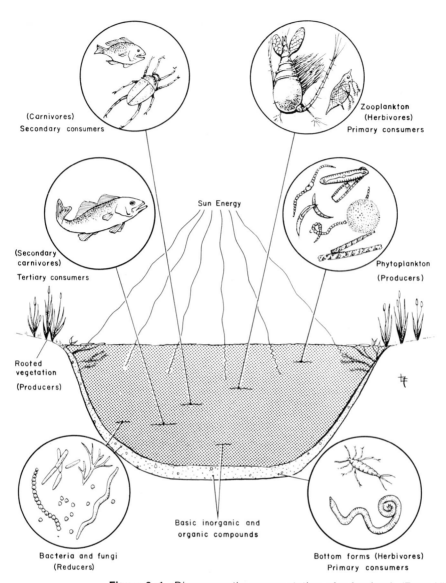

(Carnivores)
Secondary consumers

Zooplankton
(Herbivores)
Primary consumers

Sun Energy

(Secondary carnivores)
Tertiary consumers

Phytoplankton
(Producers)

Rooted vegetation
(Producers)

Basic inorganic and organic compounds

Bacteria and fungi
(Reducers)

Bottom forms (Herbivores)
Primary consumers

Figure 6–1 Diagrammatic representation of a food web (From Villee, C. A. *Biology*, Sixth Edition. Philadelphia, W. B. Saunders Co., 1972).

the food taken in by consumer organisms is conserved as food that may be consumed by organisms of the next trophic level; therefore, the useful energy that passes from one level to the next in the food pyramid steadily declines. In a Georgia farm pond managed for fish production, available light energy was calculated at 730,000 kilocalories (Kcal) per square meter of pond surface per year (1 kilocalorie = 1000 calories). Only about 7400 Kcal of this light energy actually was used by algae in photosynthesis. Worms and crustaceans consumed algae with a food value calculated at 1900 Kcal. Insect larvae consumed crustaceans equivalent in food value to 200 Kcal, and in turn sunfish ate worms, crustaceans, and insect larvae equivalent to 350 Kcal. Bass ate sunfish equivalent to 30 Kcal of food energy, and

132

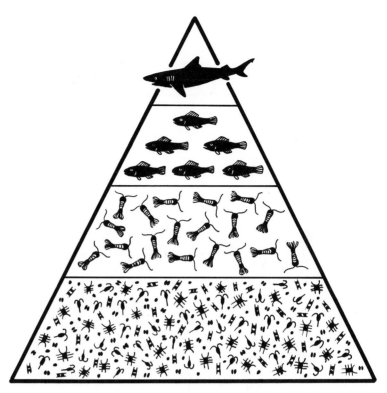

Figure 6-2 A pyramid of numbers in the sea (Redrawn from Buchsbaum, R. W. and Buchsbaum, M. *Basic Ecology*, Pittsburgh, Boxwood Press, 1957).

humans obtained 20 Kcal from eating the bass. Thus total human intake of calories per square meter of pond surface was less than 0.0004 per cent of the light energy potentially available for conversion into food, and only about 0.04 per cent of that taken up by algae. Similar but more complex energy relationships determine the number, kinds, and distributions of organisms in natural ecosystems.

Human impact on the environment has served to make the food web more direct by eliminating some of the trophic levels. For example, a natural meadow abounding in insects, birds, and mammals is converted into a corn field from which consumers are excluded by insecticides, traps, scarecrows, fences, and other means. Nearly all of the food produced by the field then may be fed to hogs, and the hogs in turn are almost totally consumed by humans. The result is increased efficiency from the human standpoint, but at the expense of the natural balance in the environment. Moreover, such manipulation of the environment almost always is accompanied by increased depletion of soil nutrients, soil erosion, and by soil and water pollution.

Essential Minerals and Natural Cycles

Of the total of 104 elements known to science, fewer than 20 seem to be absolutely essential for maintaining life processes. These

133

Figure 6–3 Human impact on the ecosystem (Redrawn with modifications from Dansereau, P. M. *Biogeography: An Ecological Perspective.* New York, Ronald Press Co., 1957).

essential elements are subdivided into two groups: the **major essential elements,** generally considered to be required by plants and animals; and the **trace elements,** required in lower concentrations. Both groups are listed in the following table:

Major Essential Elements	*Trace Elements*
Carbon	Zinc
Hydrogen	Cobalt
Oxygen	Manganese
Nitrogen	Molybdenum
Sulfur	Boron
Potassium	Copper
Magnesium	Sodium
Phosphorus	Chlorine
Calcium	Iron
	Iodine

Additionally, vanadium, fluorine, selenium, and silicon are required by some organisms.

All organic compounds contain carbon, hydrogen, and usually oxygen. Lipids (fats and oils) and carbohydrates are composed of carbon, hydrogen, and oxygen only. Proteins contain these three elements plus nitrogen (in their amino groups, NH_2^-) and nearly always some sulfur. Calcium is a component of pectin, the cementing material of the middle lamella between the walls of adjacent plant cells, and cells of plants deprived of calcium tend to become disorganized. Phosphorus is a component of the nucleic acids ADP and ATP, coenzymes, and phospholipids occurring in the cell membranes. Magnesium is a component of chlorophyll. Iron is found in the cytochromes and in hemoglobin. (It may come as a surprise that soybeans have hemoglobin in their root nodules, where it appears to act as an oxygen-transporting molecule, just as in animals.) Sodium, potassium, and chlorine are important in osmoregulation, the process controlling the entry and departure of water and solutes into and out of cells. Silicon is a component of cell walls of diatoms and some other plants. Iodine does not seem to be necessary for plants but is required for the production of thyroid hormones in vertebrate animals.

The trace elements are required for the functioning of enzymes, and on this account are termed cofactors. Some trace elements also are required in the synthesis of vitamins, as, for example, cobalt in vitamin B_{12} (cobalamine).

There is a limited amount of each of the essential elements in the environment. Were plants and animals to use them without returning them to the environment in a reusable condition, all life would have ended long ago. In the first place, not all of the earth's minerals are available to cells; many are buried far beneath the surface or are present in the form of relatively insoluble substances. For example, a great deal of calcium and carbon is "locked up" in the form of limestone (calcium carbonate, $CaCO_3$) and becomes available only as the stone slowly dissolves. The elements in coal, iron ores, sulfur deposits, phosphate rocks, and many other compounds are similarly inaccessible. Those elements that are soluble or in solution and thus available for use by cells are used over and over again. It is possible theoretically to follow the fates of all of the essential elements through a succession of cycles of birth, life, death, and decay of cells and organisms; the few mentioned on this and the following pages will serve to illustrate the principle of natural cycles.

The Water Cycle

Water makes up the bulk (60 to 95 per cent) of living cells and, together with CO_2, is a raw material of photosynthesis. When carbohydrates and other organic compounds are oxidized in cellular respiration, water is released. Water is the solvent in which cell nutrients are dissolved and is the medium in which all molecular traffic

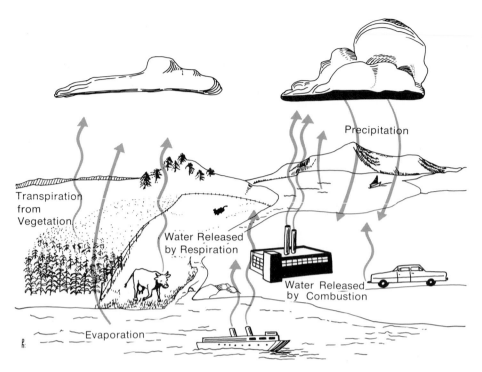

Figure 6–4 The water cycle (Redrawn with modifications from *Botany*, Fifth Edition by C. E. Wilson, W. E. Loomis, and T. A. Steeves. Copyright © 1971 by Holt, Rinehart and Winston, Inc. Used by permission of Holt, Rinehart and Winston, Inc.).

moves into, within, and out of cells. Water is cycled in the environment as well as in cells (Fig. 6–4). Atmospheric water falling to the earth as rain, snow, mist, fog, and dew is absorbed by the soil or collected by lakes, streams, and oceans. Much of the soil water is absorbed by plants. Some of this absorbed water is used in photosynthesis, but very much of it leaves plants by evaporation through pores (**stomata**) in the leaves and the stems, a process termed **transpiration.** Water also is taken up by animals and is excreted in the form of waste products. Sunlight striking the earth's surface evaporates great quantities of water, returning it to the atmosphere. The circulation of water between the earth's surface and the atmosphere is called the **hydrologic cycle** (Fig. 6–4).

The Carbon Cycle

The carbon cycle consists of the two major life processes, photosynthesis and respiration. Carbon dioxide, either in the atmosphere or dissolved in water, is taken up by green plants and converted by photosynthesis into organic compounds. These compounds may be utilized solely by plants in the course of their growth and reproduction, or they may also be used by other organisms that later consume the plant. Eventually death and decay of plants and their consumers, a process in which fungi and bacteria participate, liberates CO_2 that has not already been returned to the atmosphere by cellular respiration. However, some plant material may be preserved in the fossil forms of carbon (peat, coal, petroleum,

136

Figure 6–5 The carbon cycle, as depicted diagrammatically (From Villee, C. A. *Biology,* Sixth Edition. Philadelphia, W. B. Saunders Co., 1972).

or natural gas), which is not cycled into the atmosphere as CO_2 until these materials eventually are burned.

Both oxygen and water are directly involved in the carbon cycle. Water is the source of hydrogen for the fixation of carbon dioxide in photosynthesis, and oxygen is a byproduct. Consumer organisms nearly all use oxygen in cellular respiration, liberating the energy

137

stored in food by photosynthesis and giving off water and CO_2 as by-products.

The Nitrogen Cycle

The nitrogen cycle involves organisms at all trophic levels. Green plants use both nitrate (NO_3^-) and ammonia (NH_3) forms of nitrogen obtained from the soil in making their proteins, but are unable to use gaseous nitrogen (N_2), which makes up 80 per cent of the atmosphere. However, some bacteria and blue-green algae, living freely in the soil or living within root nodules of higher plants, are

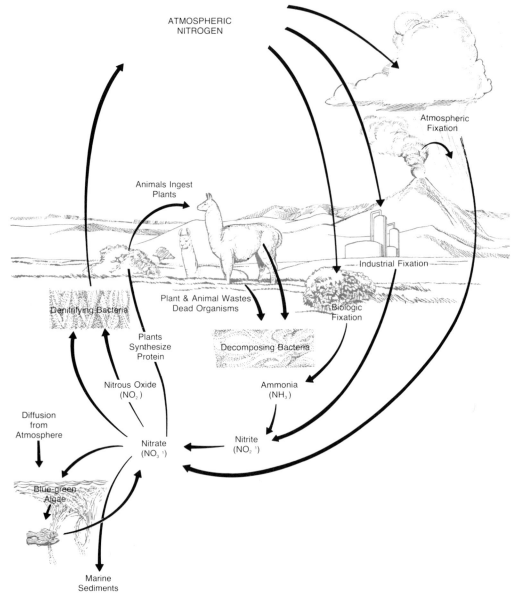

Figure 6–6 The nitrogen cycle (From Villee, C. A. *Biology,* Sixth Edition. Philadelphia, W. B. Saunders Company, 1972).

able to take up gaseous nitrogen and produce ammonia, which in turn is used by other plants. Some atmospheric nitrogen also is converted into nitrates by lightning and in industrial processes. Nitrogen in the form of urea from animal excreta or ammonia produced by the bacterial decay of organisms are other sources of the nitrogen used by green plants.

Animals are able to synthesize proteins, but must rely on plants, either directly or through food webs, for several essential amino acids from which proteins are made. This dependence results from the fact that the animals are unable to synthesize amino groups (NH_2^-) directly; only plants can do this.

If the nitrogen cycle is to be complete, nitrogen must be returned to the atmosphere. A chain of processes, involving several groups of bacteria and green plants, accomplishes this. Certain decay bacteria break down proteins and amino acids and liberate nitrogen in the form of ammonia. Some bacteria convert ammonia into nitrate, in which form it may be taken up by plants. Other bacteria, termed **denitrifying bacteria,** convert nitrates into N_2 that escapes into the atmosphere.

Biotic Factors

Biotic factors in a plant community consist of those interactions between organisms and their products and by-products that influence the development of that plant community. When we include the various animal and microbial components of an ecosystem in our view of a plant community, we see complicated plant–plant, plant–microbe, and plant–animal interactions. Many of these are so closely linked that they must be considered evolutionary life-strategies.

Plant–plant interactions are not uncommon in plant communities. Lichens are composite plants consisting of fungal cells and blue-green or green algae. This relationship is thought to be one of **symbiosis** or **mutualism,** in which both partners contribute toward maintaining the association. Many forest trees have an association with fungal cells (called a **mycorrhiza**) surrounding or invading some of their smaller roots. The mycorrhizae have been shown to take up soil nutrients and pass them on to the trees. **Epiphytes** are plants that are supported mechanically (but not nutritionally) by other plants (usually trees). They are not parasitic and do not appear to damage the plants upon which they grow. Many **bromeliads** (epiphytic members of the pineapple family), including the Spanish moss of the American South, are highly specialized for an aerial existence. They have modified roots and leaves, enabling them to trap and hold moisture and absorb minerals coming to them in dust, and in runoff from the stems and leaves of supporting trees.

An interesting plant–plant, plant–animal relationship in some tropical epiphytes has recently been described by Dr. Daniel Janzen of the University of Michigan. In an area in Malaysia noted for its poor, sandy soil and scrubby vegetation, epiphytes grow that have

Figure 6–7 A bromeliad. The leaves form a central cup, or "tank," capable of holding water.

exceptional nutritional strategies. The epiphytes have enlarged stems that are inhabited by ant colonies. The ants actively harvest animal parts from dead and dying insects, depositing them in special cavities inside the swollen stems and in the process furnishing fertilizers that support the growth of the epiphytes. The ants actually grow the epiphytes by harvesting the seeds and planting them in soil along the stems of small trees.

Other plants, such as the mistletoes, are semi-parasites; that is, they are photosynthetic but also have absorbing organs, termed **haustoria,** that penetrate the tissues of the host plant and take up water and nutrients. Still others, such as the dodder, are non-photosynthetic and are **obligate parasites.** A curious plant–plant relationship exists between dodder, a parasitic, non-green flowering plant, and its host, which may be any of several flowering plants. If dodder is growing on a plant requiring a short-day photoperiod to flower, then the dodder also is a short-day flowering plant. Conversely, if dodder parasitizes a long-day flowering plant, it too becomes a long-day plant. This phenomenon may be explained by the hypothesis that a substance that induces flowering is produced in the host plant as a result of the particular photoperiod and is

Figure 6–8 Myrmecophytes (ant colony plants) growing epiphytically on Malaysian trees. *A,* A cluster of ant colony epiphytes (myrmecophytes) on the trunk of a tree. *B,* The swollen tuber of a myrmecophyte is shown here, and entrances to the ant burrows within are visible. An orchid is present on the tuber of the myrmecophyte (an epiphyte on an epiphyte). *C* and *D,* A smaller epiphyte before and after sectioning, showing the inner cavities occupied by the ant colony. (From Janzen, D. H. Epiphytic Myrmecophytes in Sarawak: Mutualism through Feeding of Plants by Ants. *Biotropica* 6:237, 1974).

141

Figure 6–9 Dodder, a parasitic, non-photosynthetic flowering plant (From *Botany*, Fifth Edition by C. E. Wilson, W. E. Loomis, and T. A. Steeves. Copyright © 1971 by Holt, Rinehart and Winston, Inc. Reproduced by permission of Holt, Rinehart and Winston, Inc.).

transferred to the parasite through its haustoria. Dodder parasitizes annual plants or perennials having annual above-ground parts. Since many of these wither and die shortly after flowering, it is important that the flowering period of the parasite be synchronized with its host; otherwise, it will not have produced seeds before the death of the host brings about the death of the parasite.

Plant–microbe interactions are seen in the relationship between bacteria living in root nodules of some flowering plants. In these cases the bacteria fix gaseous nitrogen (i.e., they reduce N_2 to ammonia, NH_3). The fixed nitrogen is then taken up by the host plant and used in the formation of amino acids and proteins. The bacteria, in turn, are thought to obtain food and other nutrients from the host plants, which in these relationships are members of the pea family (legumes) and include peas, soybeans, alfalfa, clovers, vetches, locust trees, acacias, and many others. One of the reasons that the soybean is such an important crop is that it does not require the use of nitrogen fertilizers. The manufacture of nitrogen fertilizers requires great quantities of energy, a factor in agriculture of ever-increasing importance as our energy resources continue to dwindle. One of the hopes of experimental botanists is that their research will yield means of inducing nitrogen-fixing bacteria to form nodules on non-leguminous crop plants. More will be said about these studies in Chapter 20.

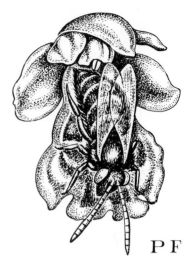

P F

Figure 6–10 Pseudocopulation, as seen in the orchid *Ophrys lutea.* The color patterns of this flower mimic those of the female insect.

Some examples of plant–animal relationships are the insect pollinator–flower interdependencies, which are often highly specialized. There is an orchid flower that mimics the form and color of a female wasp. When a male wasp attempts to copulate with it, pollen is transferred, ensuring cross-pollination.

Peat bogs are usually deficient in nitrogen, but certain bog plants have evolved insect-trapping strategies that supply them with nitrogen. Pitcher plants, sundews, and Venus' flytrap are examples, each having a different mechanism but a similar strategy. Contrary to science fiction, cartoons, and horror movies, there are no plants capable of capturing large animals, at least not on this planet.

Easily the most important biotic factors in plant communities are human-related. The disruption of the ecosystem by human activities alters the landscape, increases the incidence of forest fires, adds noxious gases to the atmosphere, and raises the temperature of bodies of water through thermal pollution. Agricultural practices deplete the soil of mineral nutrients, and the runoff from fields often contains fertilizers, such as phosphates and nitrates, as well as insecticides and herbicides, that pollute streams and lakes. The sewage and other effluents from cities increase the organic and mineral content of lakes and rivers and bring about aging or **eutrophication** processes in such bodies of water. All of these activities create severe stresses on the environmental complex that supports plant life.

Plant Communities

Terrestrial ecosystems often take their names from their plant communities; for example, the term **tropical rain forest** is employed to describe a distinctive kind of ecosystem. This use of the vegetational component to characterize the complex association of physi-

143

Figure 6–11 Insect-capturing plants. *A, Sarracenia purpurea,* the pitcher plant. The brightly colored pitcher is a highly modified leaf. Insects that enter the pitcher are unable to crawl out because of the presence of downward projecting hairs on the inner surface of the leaf. These insects eventually fall into the watery liquid in the base of the leaf where they drown and decay. *B, Dionaea muscipula,* the well-known Venus' flytrap, which bears a highly modified leaf equipped with a trigger mechanism. When an insect touches any two or all three of the hairs of the trigger mechanism, the resulting reaction causes the two sides of the trap to close suddenly, engulfing the insect. Digestive enzymes are then secreted by gland cells in the leaf epidermis (Photos courtesy of W. H. Hodge).

cal factors, energy flow relationships, producer and consumer organisms, and climatic factors is an expedient device, employed because vegetation is the most obvious feature of ecosystems. It should be kept in mind, however, that the vegetation is but one component of the ecosystem, although it is an indispensable one.

Plant communities comprise more or less constantly associated plant species that occur within rather specific climatic and geographic regions. Plant communities have some characteristics in common with human society. People become arranged in socioeconomic classes that define their relationships to individuals of other classes. All the individuals of a class perform similar functions in the society as a whole, and the structure of the human community is determined by the kinds of classes that make it up and their relative importance in maintaining the society. Similarly, the individuals of plant communities form classes based on their positions in the community. The species of plants making up each such class are described as having a certain **life-form,** such as tree-form, shrub-form, herb-form.

One of the main features of a plant community is its **stratification,** each stratum being composed of plants of similar life-form (trees, shrubs, herbs), as well as other forms (such as the plants supported by other plants—vines, epiphytes, and parasites). The members of each stratum all make similar demands on the same environmental resources, so that competition for such resources is most direct between plants within each stratum. The term *habitat* sometimes is applied to a plant community but more often to a stratum within the community.

Let us consider, as an example of a plant community, one of several making up the **temperate, deciduous forest** of eastern North America. Typically, the trees in one of these communities form two layers—one of tall trees, and one of shorter trees. Below are several layers of shrubs and herbs. A layer of mosses often occurs at the ground level. The soil also is stratified and contains such plants as fungi, bacteria, and algae growing at the surface or occupying the spaces between soil particles.

Another example is a **tropical rain forest** on a Caribbean island, where we observe that the strata are more numerous and their spacing and stratification is less apparent than in the temperate forest. To many people, a tropical forest appears chaotic and structureless. Every available space appears to be filled with plant leaves, aerial roots, and stems of all kinds. However, undisturbed rain forests are not impenetrable **jungles;** the term jungle is properly applied to dense and impenetrable thickets containing a preponderance of quick-growing "weedy" plants that follow upon the disturbance or destruction of the rain forest.

Upon close inspection of a rain forest, generally there are five strata: three strata of trees, a layer of shrubs and large herbs, and a ground layer of shrubs and undershrubs; vines and epiphytes occupy positions in all of these layers. This same arrangement is found again and again in rain forest communities in America, Africa, Australia, and Asia. The proportion of life-forms in plant communities

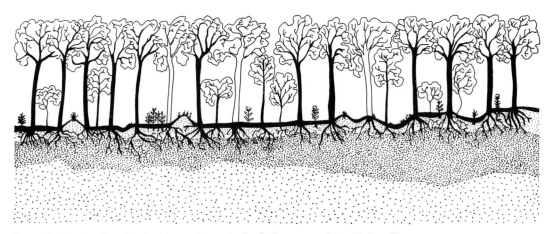

Figure 6–12 Profile of a deciduous forest in the St. Lawrence River Valley. The upper, dark, horizontal layer represents humus. Note that there are relatively few life-forms and species represented, in contrast to the tropical rain forest.

Figure 6–13 Diagram illustrating the structure of a tropical rain forest. Note the strata; epiphytes and lianas are not shown (From Richards, P. W. *The Tropical Rain Forest.* New York, Cambridge University Press, 1952).

occupying similar climatic regions is much the same on all major land masses, probably because a particular arrangement of life-forms is best adapted to exploit a given type of environment no matter where it occurs.

Whether we look at communities in the eastern temperate forest of the United States or at those of a tropical rain forest, an important characteristic of these communities is the presence of certain **dominant species.** The ecologist characterizes the community by these species, and can often detect what is happening to a plant community by studying the relative reproductive vigor of the dominant species. Any deviation can signal a change in the overall character of the community.

Life Strategies

The strata in a particular plant community, as we have noted, consist of characteristic species that have similar physiological requirements and that, consequently, are in direct competition with one another for the same requirements from the environment, whether light, space, or soil nutrients. There also may be degrees of competition between plants in different strata of the same community, but such competition is not so acute as that between plants of the same stratum.

Plants have evolved various strategies that minimize the negative effects of severe competition. The term *strategy* is used to describe adaptations that have survival value, and is not meant to imply that a plant follows a particular plan in its ecological relationships. Rather, it refers to physiological and structural specializations that tend to take plants out of direct competition with one another for nutrients and for other environmental advantages.

One of the most important strategies is variation in the timing of such events as seed germination, seedling growth, flowering, fruiting, release of seeds, and dormancy. In a temperate, deciduous forest, herbs such as orchids, jack-in-the-pulpit, mandrake, dogtooth violet, and spring beauty may grow up, photosynthesize, flower, and set seed before the trees develop a full set of leaves. Such annual periodicities may be established by seasonal patterns of rainfall and temperature extremes or by day and night lengths and by light intensities, to which some plants react in one way and others in another way. Natural, undisturbed plant communities are highly integrated organizations of different life-forms exhibiting a wide variety of periodicities.

The principal physical factors that influence plant life strategies are: soil, water, temperature, light, atmosphere and fire. The close relationship of plants to soil types has been recognized by ecologists for a long time. Communities can be characterized by the soil preference of their dominant species. Acid-loving plants (called **oxylophytes**), salt-loving plants (called **halophytes**), and rock-loving plants (called **lithophytes**) are examples of plants that have evolved specialized strategies based on abilities to flourish in such conditions.

Responses to Water.   Plants display a wide array of strategies in response to the availability of water. **Hydrophytes** (aquatic plants), such as the water hyacinth and water lily, have large, intercellular air spaces in their leaves that store gases used in photosynthesis and respiration.

In all of the dry regions of the world there are plants that have evolved strategies enabling them to cope with water shortages. These plants are termed **xerophytes** and include cacti and euphorbs (the latter are members of the family Euphorbiaceae) and similar plants having thick, succulent stems that enable them to store water; other types, such as the bristlecone pine and mesquite, have very deep underground water sources. Some xerophytes have evolved mechanisms that permit the curling or folding of leaves during times of water stress, thus reducing the amount of exposed leaf surface subject to water loss. Others have reduced or eliminated their leaf surfaces altogether. These latter types have photosynthetic stems, and include most cacti and many euphorbs. Still others have developed extremely short reproductive cycles and are able to go from seed germination through flowering and seed production in about two weeks following an infrequent rainfall.

Not all structures that seem to be xerophytic adaptations are necessarily so, however. Leaf hairs that are sometimes said to insulate plants from the drying effects of desert sunlight are also seen in some rain forest plants where water conservation is not such an important factor in survival. Thorns are said to protect xerophytes from the effects of grazing animals, and doubtless do so. However, thorns also are found in rain forest plants, which are not usually subjected to such grazing. A measure of caution must be

Figure 6–14 A and B *Illustration continued on opposite page*

Figure 6–14 *Continued* Some highly specialized plant forms. *A,* Stone plants, or litho-phytes. *B, Salicornia,* the glasswort, a halophyte. *C,* A cactus and *D,* A euphorb. Both are xerophytes (*A* courtesy of W. H. Hodge).

used in ascribing a function to every structural feature seen in plants.

Responses to Temperature. The temperature is of particular im-portance to the life-supporting activities of plants. The rates of water absorption, conduction, photosynthesis, and of other processes are affected by temperatures. The temperature range for common bio-logical processes is in the 0–40°C range, yet we find plants living under temperature extremes from the arctic (–50°C) to the equato-rial desert (+60°C). Unlike animals, most plants are immobile and must adapt to these temperature variations (usually by dormancy) since they cannot escape them. For each plant species there are **cardinal temperatures,** which include minimum and maximum tem-peratures, beyond which life functions do not occur, and **optimum temperatures,** at which functions go on at maximum velocity. For in-stance, the optimum temperature for the growth of lupine is about 28°C, for corn about 33°C, and for cucumber, about 38°C.

Many plants respond to rhythmic fluctuations in temperature; this is called **thermoperiodism.** Tomato plants, for example, have an optimum night temperature for growth of about 18°C, but during the day the optimum temperature is about 26.5° C. They grow faster if day and night temperatures differ in this way than if a constant tem-perature is maintained. Thermoperiodism also accounts for germi-nation in some plants. This effect is seen in celery and in blue grass, in which germination will occur only after a period of alternating high and low temperatures.

Responses to Light. Light is of tremendous importance in controlling plant growth not only because of its role in photosynthesis but also because it is a factor in a number of physiological and growth responses. The effect on flowering of relative length of daylight and darkness (known as **photoperiodism**) has long been noted, and in this regard plants fall into three categories: **short-day plants,** which require more than a critical number of hours of darkness for flowering; **long-day plants,** which require less than a critical number of hours of darkness for flowering to occur; and **day-neutral plants,** which do not require a specific photoperiod for flowering. For many species of plants, the critical dark period is between 10 and 12 hours.

Seed germination also may be affected by light. The seeds of some types of lettuce, for instance, require a brief exposure to light if germination is to occur. If seeds are buried in the soil, only those will germinate that are exposed to light either through cultivation or by such natural forces as wind and water erosion. The remainder may remain viable for a number of years before producing new plants. Thus, plants survive even though adverse conditions may have prevented additional seed production or germination for a number of years.

Another reaction to light is the growth movement called **phototropism,** in which the stems of plants grow toward the source of light. This has particular significance in situations in which plants are in competition for light energy. The physiological mechanisms controlling photoperiodism, phototropism, and seed germination are discussed in Chapter 20.

Responses to Wind. Wind action also affects plants and is an ecological factor of considerable importance. The borderline between woodland and alpine tundra at high mountain elevations is called the **timberline.** Trees at the timberline are often exposed to high winds and as a result become deformed. Such deformed vegetation is termed **krummholz,** and is very characteristic of alpine woodlands.

Wind damage and salt spray effects can be seen on plants along sea coasts, and severe winds of hurricane force can do extensive damage to coastal vegetation. Wind also is an important factor in soil erosion and soil movement. Extensive ecological studies have been made of plant communities on sand dunes where a constant cycle of wind erosion, dune movement, and dune stabilization by vegetation occurs.

On the positive side, wind is an agent in spore and seed dispersal and in pollination of seed plants. The spores of nearly all nonseedbearing land plants (such as mosses, ferns, fungi, and the like) are dispersed by wind. The pollen of all coniferous seed plants (for example, pines, spruces, and cycads) are windborne, as are those of many flowering plants including the grasses and many trees in temperate regions (among these oaks, willows, and hickories). Examples of seeds and fruits of plants that show adaptations for wind dispersal include the parachute-like types of dandelions and milkweeds and the winged types found in conifers, ashes, and maples. These

Figure 6–15 Krummholz at the timberline of a mountain. Note that the branches of the trees are twisted in the direction of the prevailing wind (USDA Photo).

are good examples of evolutionary plant strategies associated with physical factors in the environment.

Responses to Fire. Fire is a significant ecological factor wherever there is sufficient vegetation to burn. Fire breaks down dead vegetation and releases nutrient minerals to the soil. In some cases it may stimulate plant growth, as in the case of the quaking aspen, where it promotes the growth of suckers and stimulates stem elongation. The cones of some pines do not open until they have been exposed to unusually high temperatures or fire. As a result, seedling pines grow in the wake of forest fires when competition from other plant life is minimal. Fires in grasslands eliminate competition from woody plants and tend to maintain the prairie ecosystems. The underground stems (**rhizomes**) of grasses are undamaged by the fires that destroy woody plants, and the burned vegetation yields minerals that are available for new growth. Not all woody plants are destroyed in such fires, however. A few like the bur oak *(Quercus macrocarpa)* have thick, heat-resistant bark, and survive grass fires. Ecologists have used the distribution of bur oaks as an indicator of the extent of grasslands and of prairie fires before the settlement of America by Europeans. In California a brushland community, the

151

chaparral, is maintained by periodic fires, and nearly pure stands of redwoods *(Sequoia)* and big trees *(Sequoiadendron)* are thought to owe their existence to their very thick, fire-resistant bark.

Ecological Succession

The establishment of a stable plant community, or **climax community,** occurs as a result of a series of developmental stages in the ecological process of succession. Successions are of two basic kinds; if the starting point is bare rock, gravel, sand, or open water, **primary succession** will take place, while if a soil already has been established by a prior vegetation, succession on such a site is termed **secondary.** This latter type is found in situations where the plant community has been disturbed, as after a severe fire, killing drought, or as a consequence of man's activities in such settings as abandoned fields, railway embankments, or clear-cut forests. In a neglected garden, we note that a crop of weeds soon becomes established, forming a ground cover that is essential if later stages of succession are to develop. Actually, some of our common garden plants have evolved through human selection and cultivation of certain wild, weedy plants. Radishes and lettuce are good examples of these; both species have many weedy, wild relatives in the mustard and composite families, respectively. Weeds are ecological pioneers and are characterized by annual or biennial rather than perennial life cycles, rapid growth, and great tolerance of fluctuations in soil moisture and temperature. They usually are prolific seed producers and possess very efficient seed dispersal mechanisms.

After a weedy vegetation has been established, perennial grasses and herbs take over. They are less tolerant of fluctuations in soil moisture and temperature than are the weeds, and become established only after pioneer plants have developed a ground cover. Once established, their perennial nature results in their choking out and eventually eliminating most (but usually not all) of the shorter-lived weedy plants. Depending on the prevailing climate, succession may stop here with a grasslands ecosystem if that is the natural ecosystem of the region. Otherwise, succession will continue with pioneer species of woody plants appearing and being replaced, in turn, by the dominant species of the distinctive forest community of the region.

Primary succession on rock surfaces **(xerarch succession)** is very slow and involves reducing the solid rock to fragments by various erosive forces, such as freezing and thawing, wind and water action, and the dissolving of its minerals by water. Often the first plants to become established are the lichens and mosses. Eventually sufficient soil is accumulated for higher plants to grow, and their roots further break down the parent rock material and provide additional soil matter. As plants die, they add organic material, or **humus,** to the soil. This humus contributes to the development of the soil **microflora** (composed of fungi and bacteria living on the dead plant material). The structure of fertile soil is due in large measure to the humus that decay-producing organisms have provided. Their action produces **aggregation,** in which various-sized mineral particles, ranging from clay to sand, are bound in clumps or aggregates. Without such aggregation, an otherwise fertile soil would become compacted and so dense that root growth would be hindered.

Primary successions on rock have been observed on lava flows in Hawaii, the island of Krakatoa in the South Pacific, and in Iceland,

| Sand, present initially. | Sand, added by waves and wind. | Humus, added by plants and animals. |

HPM

Figure 6–16 Dune succession. Diagram illustrating stages in succession. Note the beach grasses on the fore dunes, shrubs on older dunes, and ancient dunes with an established forest in the background (Redrawn with modifications from Buchsbaum, R., and Buchsbaum, M. *Basic Ecology.* Pittsburgh, Boxwood Press, 1957).

and it has been found that eventually plant communities typical of the region become established. A more rapid primary succession occurs on sand dunes, where fragmentation of rock has already occurred as a result of wind and wave action. Beach grasses dominate in early stages, and are followed by shrubs and trees.

When primary succession begins in a freshwater pond or lake the productivity at first may be rather low, with relatively few producer and consumer organisms present. However, with the accumulation of nutrients from decay products and, perhaps, pollution, the pond or lake becomes increasingly productive, with abundant vegetation and high oxygen concentrations resulting from photosynthesis. Numerous consumers, often including numbers of large fish, can be found. Later stages of succession may be characterized by low oxygen levels, excess nutrients, large populations of oxygen-depleting decay bacteria, accumulated sediments, and reduced fish populations. This advanced stage in pond or lake succession is

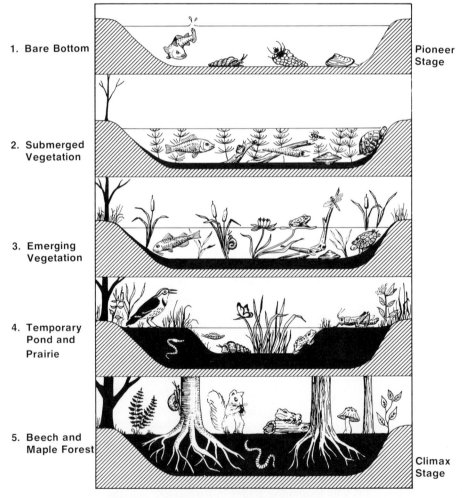

1. Bare Bottom

Pioneer Stage

2. Submerged Vegetation

3. Emerging Vegetation

4. Temporary Pond and Prairie

5. Beech and Maple Forest

Climax Stage

Figure 6-17 Primary succession in a pond. Stages in the transition from a water habitat to a land habitat are diagrammatically illustrated (Redrawn with modifications from Buchsbaum, R., and Buchsbaum, M. *Basic Ecology.* Pittsburgh, Boxwood Press, 1957).

Figure 6–18 The red mangrove, *Rhizophora mangle,* in Florida.

termed **eutrophication.** Eventually, the pond becomes sufficiently shallow to support emergent rushes, sedges, cat-tails and other marsh plants. Finally the accumulated dead plant material forms a thick layer of partially decomposed vegetation called **peat** and land plants can become established.

In colder northern lakes and ponds, a series of successional stages may be observed in which acid bogs are formed from the accumulated remains of the peat moss, *Sphagnum.* This process is described in Chapter 12.

Still another kind of aquatic succession may be seen in some marine environments. Coastal mud flats and river deltas may be inhabited by a distinctive plant life-form, the **mangrove.** Mangrove plants are adapted to grow in shallow water and often are equipped with stilt roots and sometimes with upright, emergent organs called **pneumatophores,** which have air passages and contribute to the aeration of underwater parts. Some species, such as the red mangrove *(Rhizophora mangle),* germinate by a process termed **vivipary,** in which the seeds germinate while the fruit is still on the tree and each produces an arrow-like elongated seedling. When the seedlings are released, they stick in the mud or float off to germinate elsewhere.

The mangrove ecosystem is a very productive one, harboring

155

Figure 6–19 Fruit and seedling of *Rhizophora mangle.*

many kinds of marine organisms including important food fish. Mangroves create sheltered backwaters where silt and plant debris accumulate and land-building occurs, producing a type of ecological succession superficially similar to that occurring in freshwater ponds. Many of the low islands in Florida Bay originated as mangrove communities growing in shallow water.

WORLD CLIMATES AND MAJOR ECOSYSTEMS

Approximately 15 major terrestrial ecosystems or biomes are distributed around the world. Each has a distinctive vegetational aspect related to a prevailing climate. They are essentially latitudinally oriented, but tend to be skewed poleward along coastal areas by warm ocean currents such as the Gulf Stream or toward the equator by cold counter-currents such as the Labrador Current. Because of such warm ocean currents, England, with a latitude approximately equal to that of Labrador, has an average January temperature equivalent to that of the Carolinas and Northern Georgia. Other factors, such as prevailing winds, mountain ranges, and large inland

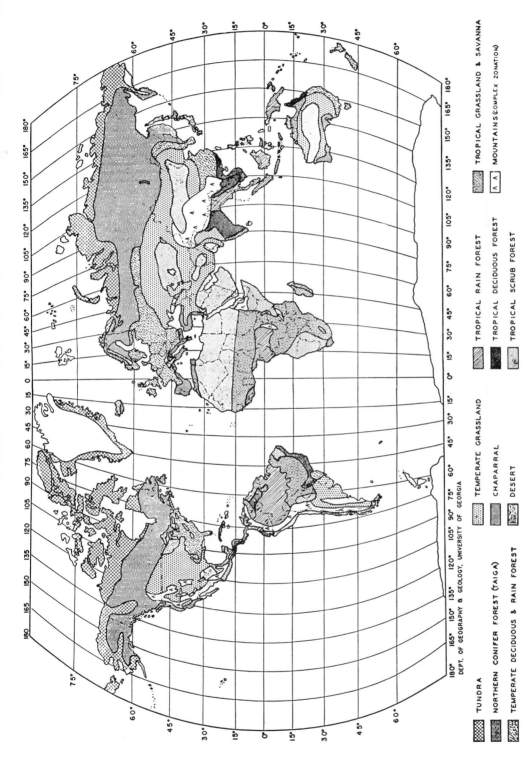

Figure 6–20 Biomes of the world (From Odum, EP. *Fundamentals of Ecology*, Third Edition. Philadelphia, W. B. Saunders Co., 1972).

TUNDRA

NORTHERN CONIFER FOREST (TAIGA)

TEMPERATE DECIDUOUS & RAIN FOREST

TEMPERATE GRASSLAND

CHAPARRAL

DESERT

TROPICAL RAIN FOREST

TROPICAL DECIDUOUS FOREST

TROPICAL SCRUB FOREST

TROPICAL GRASSLAND & SAVANNA

MOUNTAINS (COMPLEX ZONATION)

DEPT. OF GEOGRAPHY & GEOLOGY, UNIVERSITY OF GEORGIA

AVERAGE JANUARY TEMPERATURE (°F)

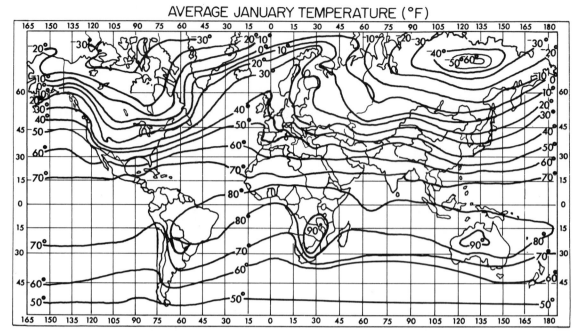

Figure 6–21 January isotherms around the earth (Redrawn from *Climate and Man,* Yearbook of Agriculture, Washington, D.C., U.S. Dept. Agric., 1941).

lakes, also introduce climatic variations and influence the patterns of regional vegetation.

Some of the more widespread biomes are **tundra, boreal forest** or **taiga, temperate deciduous forest, grassland, desert, tropical rain forest,** and **tropical savanna.**

The Tundra

The Arctic tundra occurs on land masses surrounding the Arctic Ocean. No corresponding vegetation occurs in Antarctica because the southern oceans occupy the same relative position as the tundra does in the Northern Hemisphere. However, on the Antarctic Peninsula there is a sparse coastal vegetation composed of mosses, lichens, and two species of flowering plants. We have noted earlier in this chapter that a tundra-like vegetation, the **alpine tundra,** occurs on mountains at high altitudes where the prevailing climate resembles that of the Arctic tundra.

Both kinds of tundra are characterized by low vegetation, consisting mostly of a few species of sedges and grasses together with mosses and lichens and occasionally interspersed with woody heath plants and trees such as dwarf willows and birches. In wetter areas *Sphagnum* moss occurs, as does cotton grass and even a few small orchids.

The winter is long in the Arctic tundra and there is an extended period of twilight and darkness when the sun is below the horizon the entire day. The result is that the growing season is very short, and the subsoil is perennially frozen **(permafrost).** Low tempera-

158

Figure 6–22 Tundra vegetation in Iceland. *Above,* Overview. *Lower,* Close-up view of some tundra plants.

tures and reduced light are critical factors that control this ecosystem, and the productivity is quite low (about 200 Kcal of food energy per square meter of land surface per year). Animal life may be abundant, especially in summer. Nesting migrant birds, caribou, musk oxen, wolves, arctic foxes, snowy owls, ptarmigan, hares, and lemmings constitute elements in the food web.

The Boreal Forest (Taiga)

A broad band of coniferous forest extends across the continents of the Northern Hemisphere immediately south of the tundra. This region has a rigorous climate; permafrost occurs in many areas, but unlike the tundra the soil may be frost-free during the summer.

159

Figure 6–23   The northern coniferous forest, or boreal forest.

Winter darkness and severe cold are the controlling factors, however, and productivity is fairly low (about 400 to 2000 Kcal/m²/yr.). This taiga, or boreal forest, forms the major forest ecosystem of Canada and Siberia and, interspersed with tundra vegetation, extends into Alaska. Southward, it integrates with the coniferous forests of New England and the Great Lakes region, the Rocky Mountains, the Cascade Mountains, and the Pacific coastal range. The dominant trees in the North American boreal forest are white spruce and balsam fir, while birch and jack pine are secondary species. In bog areas, tamarack and black spruce are dominant. Moose, wolves, otter, ravens, wolverines, lynx, white-tailed deer, ruffed grouse, horned owls, and species of varying hare, are included among the animal life in the ecosystem.

The Temperate Deciduous Forest

Extensive deciduous forests are found in Central and Eastern North America, Western Europe, Eastern Asia, and the southern tip of South America. Most of the vegetation loses its leaves and remains dormant through the winter, hence the term deciduous forest. These are areas with moderate temperatures, well-defined seasons, and moderate to heavy annual precipitation (80 to 160 cm. per year). The net productivity of the ecosystem is fairly high (up to about 3000 Kcal/m²/yr.). At its center, the North American temperate forest is characterized by an association of trees called the **mixed mesophytic** (humid but not wet) **forest** in which there occur such species as beech, maple, buckeye, *Magnolia*, tulip poplar, basswood, hickory, elm, ash, oak, and hemlock. To the north, beech and maple tend to predominate. Maple–basswood dominated communities occur toward the northwest (Minnesota), and an oak-chestnut forest prevailed in the eastern Appalachians until the first two decades of this century, when a blight destroyed the chestnut *(Castana)* populations, thus permitting oaks, maples, and hickories to take their place.

South and west of the center, and elsewhere in drier habitats, an association of oaks and hickories is characteristic. Wetlands vegetation may range from nearly pure stands of white cedar or cypress to typical swamp hardwoods, such as red maple, elms, and ashes.

Where the deciduous forest borders the boreal forest, a transitional zone of hardwoods and conifers occurs. Vast tracts of land in this region were once covered with magnificent stands of white and red pines, but these were completely decimated as a result of extensive and wasteful lumbering in the latter nineteenth and early twen-

Figure 6–24   A beech-maple forest in New England (USDA Photo).

tieth centuries. An extension of this zone (mixed hardwood and conifers) reaches down into the Appalachian Plateau. Extensive pinelands also are found in the southeastern United States in areas that are subjected to repeated burnings. Factors controlling the temperate forest ecosystem are moderately low winter temperatures with generally humid conditions, although periodic droughts occur toward the west.

A wide variety of animal life occurs in the deciduous forests of the Northern Hemisphere, although their numbers have diminished because of the nearly total removal of the forest and its replacement by cropland. Common fauna are the white-tailed deer, red, gray, and fox squirrels, black bear, red and gray fox, wild turkey, cottontail rabbits, and many others. The passenger pigeon, once multitudinous and now extinct, depended on the fruits produced by forest trees, and its demise doubtless was hastened by the destruction of the forest as well as by hunters who killed them by the thousands for the eastern market.

Grasslands

The great grassland regions of the world are the prairie of North America, the steppes of Eurasia, the pampas of South America, and the veld of South Africa. Grasslands occur in regions of low to moderate precipitation (25 to 75 cm. of rainfall per year), generally with cool to cold winters and hot, dry summers, climates that often are termed continental.

Several communities make up the **North American Prairie** ecosystems, and they are typified by the forms of grass predominating in each. Ranging from east to west are the **tall grass prairie, mixed grass prairie,** and the **short grass prairie.** These regions correspond approximately to the corn belt of Illinois, Iowa, and Missouri (tall grass), the wheat belt of Canada, the Dakotas, Kansas, Nebraska, and Oklahoma (mixed grass), and the cattle belt of Montana, Wyoming, Colorado, New Mexico, and western Texas (short grass).

Grassland productivity is lower than that of the deciduous forest, and averages about 2500 Kcal/m^2/yr. However, the generally flat to rolling contours of this region permit very intensive cultivation, so that total agricultural productivity is very high.

Wildlife formerly occurring extensively in the grasslands of North America included the grizzly bear, bighorn sheep, bison, elk, and prairie dog. The coyote, pronghorn, mule deer, white-tailed deer, sharp-tailed grouse, pinnated grouse, rabbits, and many others still occur in considerable numbers.

Tropical Savanna

True tropical savannas, grasslands with scattered trees and shrubs, are found in central Africa, South America, and Australia. Rainfall in these regions is moderately high (75 to 150 cm. per year), but very seasonal, and the ecosystem is controlled in part by a long dry period each year during which fires sweep over the vegetation.

Figure 6–25 Tropical savanna vegetation (Photo by Diana Harrison).

The productivity is about 3000 Kcal/m^2/yr. The periodic fires that force the migration of large animal populations are often shown in films depicting the African savanna. The savanna in Kenya and Rhodesia is famous for its large and diverse populations of animal life, which include lions, elephants, rhinoceros, giraffes, gazelles, and antelope.

It is believed that this region is the cradle of human life. The anthropological investigations made in the Olduvai gorge and near Lake Rudolf in Tanzania by the late Dr. Louis Leakey and being continued by his wife, Mary, and son Richard, have uncovered the oldest skeletal remains that can be attributed to the human line of evolution.

Deserts

Deserts occur on the leeward side of mountain ranges, coastal areas bordered by cold oceanic currents, or in areas where the prevailing winds have already lost their moisture. The controlling factor in the environment is the characteristically low annual rainfall (normally less than 25 cm. per year), but temperatures may vary greatly for there are both cold deserts (such as the Gobi in Asia) and hot ones (such as the Mojave in the United States and the Kalahari and Sahara in Africa). Although productivity is low (as low as 200 Kcal/m^2/yr.), deserts are far from lifeless. The vegetation typically consists of deciduous thornscrub, and includes plants that have extensive water-storing tissues (e.g., cacti, euphorbs) and quickly growing annuals with short reproductive cycles. Among the animals present in the desert of the southwestern United States are peccary,

163

Figure 6-26 Desert vegetation in the Southwestern United States. (From Odum, E. P. *Fundamentals of Ecology,* Third Edition, Philadelphia, W. B. Saunders Company, 1971).

quail, coyotes, foxes, civet cats, ring-tailed cats, kangaroo rats, hawks, and owls.

Tropical Rain Forest

There is no true tropical rain forest within the continental United States, but portions of Hawaii, Puerto Rico, the Virgin Islands, as well as some other Caribbean islands, Mexico, and Central America have more or less isolated areas of this distinctive forest type. A temperate rain forest is found in the Olympic mountain range in Washington and has some attributes of the tropical rain forest, such as high rainfall and humidity and an abundance of epiphytic vegetation, but it lacks the diversity of species occurring in tropical rain forests.

The great rain forest regions of the world are those of Brazil, the Congo Valley, Malaysia, the East Indies, and New Guinea. All of these areas are equatorial or sub-equatorial and are controlled climatically by high temperatures and high rainfall with little seasonal variation in either. Productivity is very high in this ecosystem, as much as 20,000 Kcal/m^2/yr.

Tropical rain forests are unique in the great number of species they contain, although the number of life-forms encompassed may not be correspondingly great. Approximately 2500 species of the large tree life-form are known from the Malaysian rain forest, whereas the temperate deciduous forest has perhaps two dozen predominating species of this life-form.

A mature, undisturbed rain forest is characterized by a very dense canopy usually made up of three strata: an upper layer of scattered, tall, emergent trees, a dense intermediate layer of large trees, and a lower level of smaller trees. The forest floor consequently lies in deep shade and is rather open except for a scattering of seedling plants, saprobic flowering plants, ferns, club mosses, and fungi.

A conspicuous feature of a majority of the trees, both large and small, is their smooth, thin, lichen-covered bark and their flaring buttresses or, in the case of some smaller trees, stilt-like prop roots. Many trees are **cauliflorous;** that is, they bear flowers and fruit up and down their trunks and branches, rather than on the smallest

Figure 6–27 Phenomena commonly encountered in tropical rain forests. *A,* Tree buttresses on a kapok tree. *B,* Bromeliads. *C,* A strangler fig growing on a dead palm tree trunk. *D,* The candle tree, an example of cauliflory (*A* courtesy of W. H. Hodge).

twigs as woody plants usually do in temperate regions. Nearly all the plants are evergreen and their leaves tend to be large and leathery and equipped with "drip-tips" that resemble the spout of a pitcher. The rubber plant, a common house plant, has leaves with drip tips, and in nature, is a large rain forest tree.

Air plants, epiphytic bromeliads, and orchids with aerial roots are abundant. Lianas (vines) with rope-like, often twisted stems hang from the tops of trees and give the forest an appearance of a ship's rigging. Strangler figs encircle some of the trees, sometimes completely encasing and killing them. Birds and insects abound and the rain forest is a particularly favorable habitat for reptiles and amphibians. Monkeys and sloths inhabit the canopy which, somewhat romantically, has been likened to a hanging garden.

At higher elevations, cloud forests of perpetual mists are found; these sometimes consist of elfin woodlands in which mosses, lichens, club mosses, and ferns give the effect of a miniaturized version of the larger forest closer to sea level.

Oceanic Ecosystems

Although the oceans of the world constitute more than two-thirds of its surface, the open oceans are not particularly productive per unit area. The communities of the open sea are called **pelagic communities** and are composed of **phytoplankton,** principally of unicellular algae of various kinds, especially diatoms and dinoflagellates, and **zooplankton,** consisting of protozoans, small crustaceans (copepods), coelenterates, worms, and larvae. The phytoplankton organisms are the producers, and zooplankton organisms the primary consumers (which are, in turn, the food of larger animals, such as fish and whales). The nutrients present in the open sea are relatively scarce, because particulate matter constantly settles into the depths, thus leaving circulation. Since the relative scarcity of nutrients limits the populations of phytoplankton that can be supported, productivity by photosynthesis is considerably less than most terrestrial ecosystems (on the order of 1000 Kcal/m²/yr.). However, the total productivity of the oceans is very great because of their great expanse.

The richest oceanic regions are those of the continental shelves, where the constant upwelling of deeper waters brings up nutrients from the depths, and where nutrients are washed out into the sea from the mouths of rivers and streams. Red, brown, and green algae and, in shallow water, higher plants such as turtle grass are the producers (productivities in upwelling zones range from 2000 to 6000 Kcal/m²/yr.). Coral reefs are shallow water ecosystems, and plants have an important role both in their building and in their maintenance. Certain red algae, termed **coralline algae,** secrete calcium carbonate and are important reef builders. Unicellular algae live among the cells of the coral polyps, and studies have shown that corals must obtain part of their food from photosynthesis by such algae since there is insufficient zooplankton to support their existing populations. In this association the algae are not consumed by the polyps but exist in a symbiotic relationship.

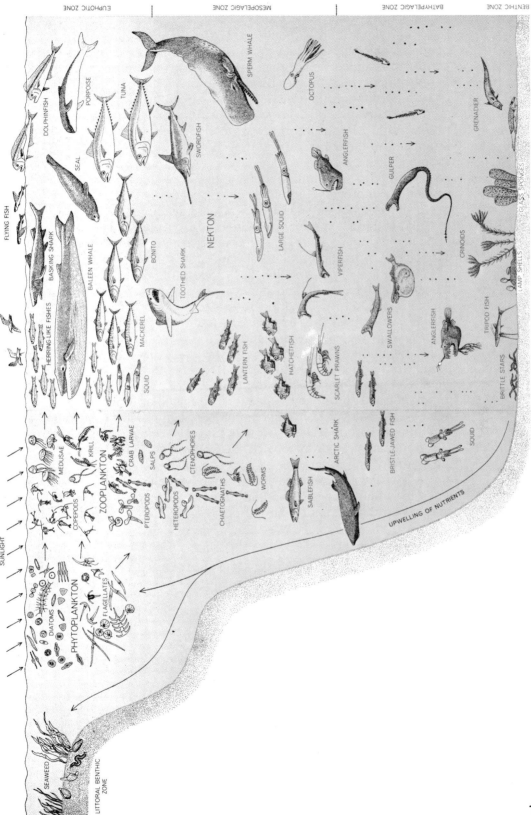

Figure 6–28 An ocean food web (From The Nature of Oceanic Life, by John D. Isaacs. Copyright © 1969 by Scientific American, Inc. All rights reserved).

Pollution, Erosion, and Depletion

A certain amount of pollution, erosion, and depletion has always occurred naturally in ecosystems. Fires, started by lightning, swept across grasslands and forests in prehistoric times, and aboriginal peoples in all regions have used fire to drive wild animals into traps or to keep dangerous predators at bay. Both living and dead plants are known to give off hydrocarbon vapors that cause atmospheric hazes. Spring floods have always occurred, and the soils in many regions have been eroded and moved about by them and by the less spectacular erosion caused by rains. Winds have also played their part in eroding and shifting the soil. However, in natural ecosystems vegetation kept these forces in check so that destruction, when it occurred, was not extensive. Now we are seeing the acceleration of destructive forces in the environment and are concerned that irreparable damage may be done to our environment beyond the recovery capacity of vegetation and other natural forces.

Dramatic examples of the destruction of natural ecosystems by the effects of air pollution can be seen in the vicinity of copper smelters in Sudbury, Ontario; Butte, Montana; and Copperhill, Tennessee. In each of these places, all plant life has been completely destroyed in an area of considerable size by poisonous sulfurous gases emanating from the smokestacks of the smelters. Similar though not complete destruction of vegetation may be seen in the vicinity of paper manufacturing plants where pulpwood is converted into paper by sulfuric acid digestion. Spectacular though such damage is, it probably is minor in comparison with the less visible but almost universal pollution of air, soil, and water going on around us.

Increased concentrations of carbon dioxide given off into the atmosphere by the burning of all kinds of fuel may actually be producing long-term climatic changes by the so-called "greenhouse effect," in which heat is prevented from escaping from the earth into space. Particulate matter, on the other hand, may have an opposite

Figure 6–29 Effects of air pollution at Copperhill, Tennessee. Fumes from copper smelters have exterminated all plant life (U.S. Forestry Service Photo).

Figure 6–30 *A*, Close-up view of the water hyacinth. *B*, Water hyacinths growing in a Florida waterway.

effect by shading the earth from the rays of the sun. In any event, the changes produced in the biosphere (i.e., the earth and its atmosphere) by pollution are on the increase everywhere and are matters of deep concern for all of us.

Eutrophication, the acceleration of lake succession, is caused by the enrichment of water by effluents containing phosphates, nitrates, and organic substances, and is a serious problem, not only in inland waters, but also in oceans. Such enrichment produces algal blooms, which add to the accumulating organic debris. When saprobic bacteria oxidize this material, they may so deplete the water of dissolved oxygen that it is impossible for many kinds of animal life to survive.

Biotic pollution through the introduction of **exotic** (foreign) plants and animals has always been a serious problem. The water hyacinth, introduced to Florida in the early 1870's, today clogs and chokes lakes and waterways, thus greatly accelerating succession.

Soil depletion, the loss of nutrients caused both by the leaching of soluble minerals and their uptake by crop plants, is a leading cause of soil impoverishment. When plants are harvested and sent to market, part of the wealth of the soil goes with them.

Erosion due to road building, housing developments, strip mining, and most importantly agriculture, is directly related to expanding populations. Even with the most careful of management practices, soils and vegetation will tend to diminish, and it is imperative that people everywhere learn to know the relationships between the various factors in our environment that control not only our well-being but that of our ecosystem.

SUMMARY

The major biogeographic provinces are called biomes. They are not merely aggregations of plants and animals, but are highly integrated ecosystems in which each organism functions as a unit in energy relationships with other organisms. The primary energy of ecosystems comes from the sun, and this light energy is converted into chemical energy by photosynthesis. Chemical energy then flows through the food web from one trophic level to the next, losing some energy at each level until all of the energy becomes converted into heat and is released into space. In addition to the sun's energy, cycling of elements is essential in the functioning of ecosystems. The carbon cycle, involving photosynthesis and the functioning of respiration, the nitrogen cycle, and other natural cycles furnish the essential elements for normal plant growth and reproduction.

The principal plant association in the ecosystem is the community. The community often is composed of strata, each one made up of species all having the same or similar life-forms. Plants have evolved various strategies to minimize the negative effects of competition, although competition between individuals of the same stratum may be very severe. Differences in flowering, fruit maturation, seed dispersal, seed germination, and periods of rapid growth tend to reduce competition between different species of the same stratum. The principal factors that lead to intra- and interspecific competition are soil factors, water requirements, temperature, light, certain atmospheric factors, fire, and relationships with other organisms.

Climax plant communities are in dynamic equilibrium with their environment and have evolved through a long series of developmental stages called, collectively, plant succession. The world ecosystems are oriented primarily in relation to prevailing climatic conditions. Across the earth are climatically determined plant communities, such as tundra, taiga, deciduous forest, grassland, desert, tropical rain forest, and savanna. Present evidence suggests that human life evolved in the African savanna ecosystem.

The destruction of natural ecosystems by man's activities can be observed all around us today. Air and water pollution, together with depletion of our natural resources, threaten the continued health of modern society. Whether we will be able to bring these ecologically detrimental processes under control remains to be seen.

DISCUSSION QUESTIONS

1. In what form does energy first reach the ecosystem? In what form does it finally leave the ecosystem?
2. Distinguish between the concepts of "pyramid of numbers" and "food web." Explain your answer by means of specific examples.
3. In what form does carbon enter the ecosystem? Name some other minerals or chemicals that are necessary for the proper functioning of an ecosystem.
4. How does nitrogen enter the ecosystem? Discuss the role of microorganisms in the nitrogen cycle of ecosystems.
5. List the major essential elements necessary for normal plant growth. List the "trace" elements required by plants in much smaller concentrations.
6. How would you explain the difference in the number of strata in a tropical rain forest as compared with those of a temperate forest?
7. How have plants been able to adapt to the problem of severe interspecific competition for water, nutrients, and energy?
8. Define the terms halophytes, hydrophytes, xerophytes, and oxylophytes.
9. Distinguish clearly between primary and secondary succession. Explain the concept of climax and relate it to succession.
10. What are mangroves, and what is their role in ecological succession?
11. Explain the differences between zooplankton and phytoplankton. In what kinds of ecosystems do these organisms occur?
12. List the seven major terrestrial biomes found worldwide. In which of these did the human species originally evolve, as suggested by the evidence? How do these systems differ in productivity, and what might be the explanation for such differences?
13. What activities are principally responsible for the destruction of natural ecosystems? Discuss what measures are necessary to reverse the present trend towards ever-increasing pollution and depletion of natural resources.

SUPPLEMENTAL READING

Billings, W. D. *Plants and the Ecosystem.* Belmont, California: Wadsworth Publishing Co., Inc., 1964.

Dansereau, P. *Biogeography: An Ecological Perspective.* New York: Ronald Press Co., 1957.

Eyre, S. R. *Vegetation and Soils, a World Picture.* Chicago: Aldine Publishing Co., 1963.

Eyre, S. R. (ed.) *World Vegetation Types.* New York: Columbia University Press, 1971.

Hanson, H. C., and E. D. Churchill. *The Plant Community.* New York: Reinhold Publishing Corp., 1961.

Oosting, Henry, Jr. *The Study of Plant Communities.* San Francisco: W. H. Freeman and Co., 1956.

Richards, P. W. *The Tropical Rain Forest.* Boston: Cambridge University Press, 1952.

Wagner, R. H. *Environment and Man.* New York: W. W. Norton and Co., 1971.

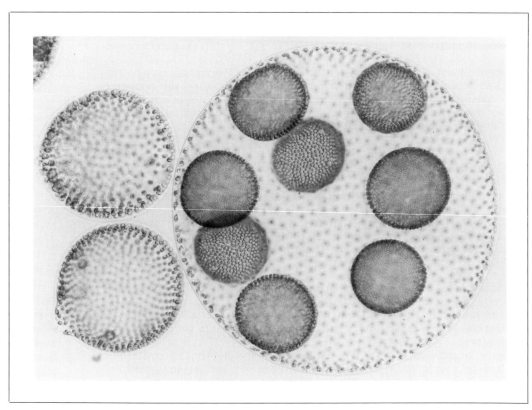

Volvox aureus (Courtesy Carolina Biological Supply Company).

Chapter 7

The Green Algae

THE ALGAE • THE BIOLOGY OF THE GREEN ALGAE • SEXUAL EVOLUTION OF GREEN ALGAE • THE MAJOR GROUPS OF GREEN ALGAE • MOTILE COLONY ALGAE • NON-MOTILE AND FILAMENTOUS ALGAE • SIPHONOUS ALGAE • OTHER GREEN ALGAE • ECOLOGY OF GREEN ALGAE • ALGAE AS FOOD • EVOLUTIONARY IMPORTANCE OF GREEN ALGAE • SUMMARY

THE ALGAE

The term *algae* describes simple, mostly aquatic, photosynthetic plants with structures ranging from single cells, colonies, filaments, and plates to forms superficially similar to some of the higher land plants. There are more than 18,000 species of eukaryotic algae found in a great variety of habitats throughout the world, and, as we have learned in Chapter 6, they are extremely important producer organisms in most of these habitats.

Although it is convenient to group a variety of organisms under the general classification of algae, this treatment is very artificial. We find it much more satisfactory to divide the known algae among several divisions, basing these divisions on the nature of their pigments, food reserves, the chemical make-up of the cell walls, and the detailed structure of their reproductive bodies. There is actually more diversity among the algae than there is among any of the more conspicuous land plants.

Despite the differences among the divisions of algae, all share a number of common features. All possess chlorophyll and are photosynthetic. All require oxygen for respiration, and all produce oxygen in photosynthesis. All differ from the higher land plants in not having roots, stems, and leaves, and with the exception of the giant seaweeds known as **kelps,** none of the algae develop conduction systems within the plant body.

At the present, the eukaryotic algae are classified into six major divisions, which are believed to have evolved along parallel lines. The largest group is the green algae **(Division Chlorophyta),** with about 7000 species. The green algae are generally believed to have given rise to the higher green plants.

"Such are the citizens of the algal kingdom; their number is legion; their abodes are many; their patterns are varied; they are largely our friends. We may name all of them, in spite of their dissimilarities, *Algae.*"

L. H. TIFFANY: *Algae, The Grass of Many Waters,* 2nd Ed. CHARLES C THOMAS, 1968.

Biology of the Green Algae

The basic structure of the green algal cell is like that of higher green plants (see Chapter 4). The living protoplast contains nuclei, nucleoli, vacuoles, ribosomes, mitochondria, chloroplasts, and endoplasmic reticulum. The chloroplasts contain two predominantly green pigments: chlorophyll *a,* found in all photosynthetic eukaryotes; and chlorophyll *b,* also occurring in higher plants. In addition, yellow pigments (xanthophylls) and orange pigments (carotenes) are present; they are referred to as accessory pigments, and collectively are called carotenoids. The chloroplasts contain lamellae, which may consist of two to six membrane layers, but grana are not present.

Cells also may contain structures called **pyrenoids,** which function in starch storage and are found within chloroplasts. **Eyespots** are found in motile cells and are made up of three to eight rows of

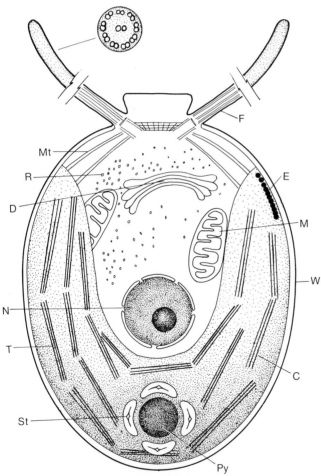

Figure 7–1 Diagrammatic representation of a motile, unicellular green alga. C, Chloroplast; W, cell wall; N, nucleus; M, mitochondrion; F, flagellum; E, eyespot; D, dictyosome; Py, pyrenoid; St, starch; Mt, microtubule; R, ribosomes; T, thylakoids.

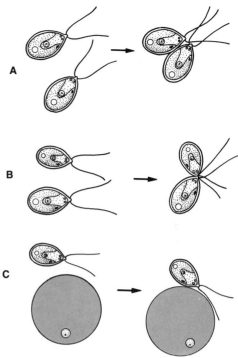

Figure 7–2 The three modes of sexual reproduction found among the green algae. *A*, Isogamy. *B*, Anisogamy. *C*, Oogamy.

compacted granules of carotenoid pigment. It is believed that they serve to orient the cell in relation to light. The motility of green algae is achieved by flagella, which exhibit the typical eukaryotic pattern of nine outer fibers and two central ones. The flagella of green algae are of the **whiplash type,** with a smooth outer surface; they commonly number two to four (although occasionally there are more), and are of equal length.

The green algae exhibit a greater variety of forms and reproductive processes than does any other division of plant life. In a number of multicellular types, asexual reproduction occurs by fragmentation of colonies. Asexual spores may also be seen in many green algae. Such spores may be termed **mitospores,** because they are produced by mitosis; if motile, they are called **zoospores.** Sexual reproduction occurs in almost all green algae. One of the exceptions in which no sexuality has yet been discovered is *Chlorella,* employed in photosynthetic experiments and in pilot studies for food production. There are three variations in sexual reproduction among algae: union of identical and usually motile gametes, or **isogamy**; union of motile gametes, one of which is larger than the other, called **anisogamy;** and union of a motile male gamete or sperm with a nonmotile egg known as **oogamy.** Isogamous sexual systems usually are found in less advanced forms, while anisogamy and oogamy are characteristic of more highly evolved plants. In all cases the gametes of algae are formed in special cells called **gametangia.** After their release the gametes, if motile, swim about for a short time, then combine in pairs to form zygotes.

Sexual Evolution of Green Algae

We have noted that in the most primitive cells, the prokaryotes, sexual reproduction by gametes does not occur. It is believed to be true for eukaryotes that asexual reproduction is the more primitive condition and that sexual reproduction has in some way evolved from asexual reproduction. The isogametes of some green algae are very similar to zoospores, although they are smaller and physiologically weaker. Sexual reproduction may be correlated with a cooperative adaptation on the part of such weakened zoospores that has resulted in cell fusion, the basis of sex. Meiosis results in the restoration of the 1N chromosome condition. The evidence provided by green algae suggests that sexual reproduction arose from asexual reproduction as a response to environmental conditions. However, the evolutionary significance of sexual reproduction is considerably greater than simply as a method for surviving "bad times." The great variability we observe in many living things is largely due to this kind of reproduction. Sexual reproduction has been important in the origin of new species and in providing a reserve of genetic information sufficient to enable the species to adapt to changing conditions.

Major Groups of Green Algae

In the green algae, three major groups may be distinguished on the basis of cellular organization. One group consists of single motile cells or colonies in which all of the vegetative cells are motile. A second group includes forms in which the basic organization is a colony composed of non-motile cells. A third group contains algae having a tubular, multinucleate organization. Although most green algae can be placed in one or another of these three categories, other modes of organization are known, including the beautiful water net, *Hydrodictyon* (all of whose cells are formed at one time), as well as other equally interesting types to be described.

The Motile Colony Algae

The members of this group are motile, unicellular or colonial forms that exhibit a pattern of variation based on a common cell type. The simplest and presumably most primitive example is the motile, freshwater *Chlamydomonas.* This unicellular alga may occur in vast numbers in quiet, standing pools or ditches, causing discoloration of the water and forming a so-called algal bloom. The cell is composed of a rigid cellulosic wall, two contractile vacuoles, a single nucleus, one cup-shaped chloroplast containing a pyrenoid and an eyespot, and two whiplash flagella attached at the anterior end of the cell. Non-motile forms of *Chlamydomonas* also occur, and cells may be found embedded in jelly-like masses during adverse growing conditions.

Rapid multiplication of cells occurring in algal blooms is brought about by asexual reproduction when nutrients are abundant

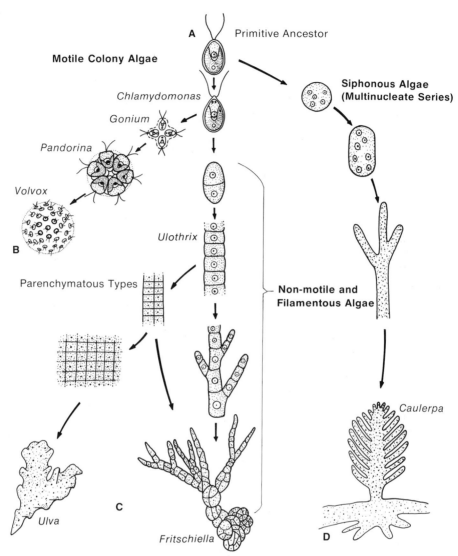

Figure 7-3 The major groups of green algae (highly diagrammatic). *A*, Ancestral motile cell. *B*, Motile colony algae. *C*, Nonmotile and filamentous algae. *D*, Siphonous algae (Redrawn from Scagel, R. F., et al. An Evolutionary Survey of the Plant Kingdom. Belmont, Calif., Wadsworth Publishing Co., Inc., 1966).

and other conditions, such as light and temperature, are optimal. This is the usual reproduction of *Chlamydomonas* and other unicellular types; the cell divides mitotically up to four times and produces as many as sixteen miniaturized replicas of itself. Repeated asexual cycles of this kind soon can produce tremendous population increases; a single cell may divide as many as eight times in one day.

If environmental conditions are less than ideal *Chlamydomonas* may reproduce sexually, for sexual reproduction is not only a means of exchanging genetic material but in many algae it is a prelude to the formation of **zygospores** (resistant cells). A protoplast divides four, five, or six times, thereby producing 16, 32, or 64 very small replicas of itself. The mother cell wall breaks open and these cells,

177

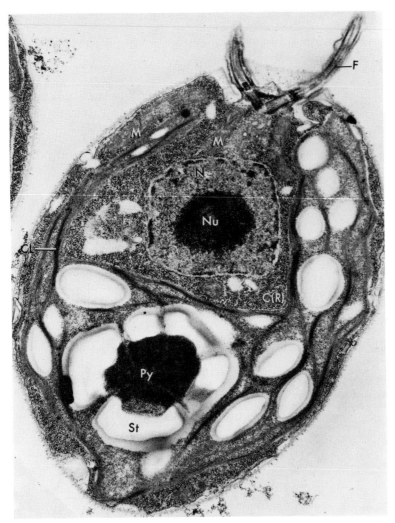

Figure 7–4 Electron micrograph showing a longitudinal view of a cell of *Chlamydomonas*. CL, Chloroplast lamellae; Py, Pyrenoid; F, Flagellum; N, Nucleus; Nu, Nucleolus; St, Starch; M, Mitochondrion; C(R), Cytoplasm packed with ribosomes (From Ringo, D. L. Flagellar motion and fine structure of the flagellar apparatus in *Chlamydomonas*. *J. Cell Biol. 33*:543, 1967).

the **isogametes,** swim out. Unlike zoospores, the isogametes begin to fuse in pairs in a process termed **syngamy.** The resulting fusion cell, the **zygote,** then forms a thick wall around itself and becomes a dormant zygote or zygospore. Since gametes are 1*N* cells, the zygote resulting from their fusion is a 2*N* cell. This condition persists in the zygospore until it becomes active at the end of its dormant period, usually after the return of favorable environmental conditions. Then the zygospore nucleus divides by meiosis, forming four 1*N* zoospores. This kind of zoospore also may be called a **meiospore** (life cycle I; see Figure 4–6), since it is formed directly by meiosis. The zoospores become motile when the zygospore wall breaks open, and they swim out and become independent vegetative cells, reproducing asexually until such a time as conditions lead to the generation of a new sexual cycle.

In some species of *Chlamydomonas,* isogametes produced by one cell can fuse with one another; this form of sexual reproduction is called **homothallism.** In other species, isogametes must fuse with other isogametes formed by mother cells of a different mating type. This requires the union of isogametes of two kinds, which are designated by plus and minus signs to indicate that they are of opposite mating types. Sexual reproduction of this type is called **heterothallism.** Both homothallism and heterothallism occur widely in algae and fungi.

In *Chlamydomonas,* sexual reproduction appears to be related to environmental stresses. The alga continues to reproduce asexually as long as nutrients and other environmental requirements are in adequate supply. Sexual reproduction can be induced experimentally in certain species of *Chlamydomonas* by reduction of nitrogen in the culture medium; in other species sexual reproduction can be inhibited by the addition of nitrogen. Although the role of ni-

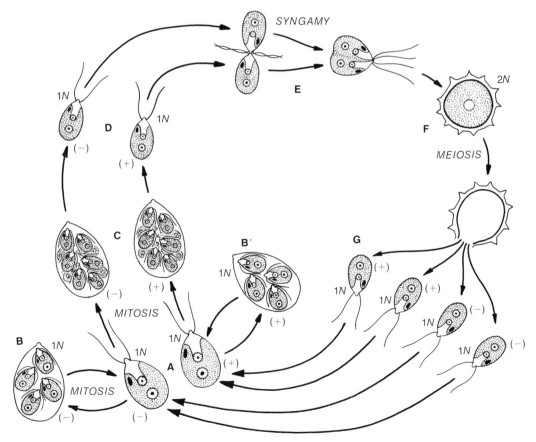

Figure 7–5 Highly diagrammatic representation of the life cycle of *Chlamydomonas.* *A,* Vegetative cells of the plus and minus mating types. *B* and *B',* Vegetative or asexual reproduction by mitosis. *C,* The production of gametes by mitosis. *D,* Plus and minus gametes. *E,* Fusion of gametes by syngamy. *F,* Resulting zygospore. *G,* Meiospores resulting from meiosis (Redrawn from Scagel, R. F., *et al. An Evolutionary Survey of the Plant Kingdom.* Belmont, Calif., Wadsworth Publishing Co., Inc., 1966).

trogen in reproduction is not fully understood, it is clear that reproduction is closely related to prevailing ecological factors.

An advance in the motile series may be observed in the motile colony known as *Pandorina.* From four to 32 cells form a colony in which the cells are arranged in a jelly-like matrix to form a hollow sphere. Individually, each cell resembles *Chlamydomonas,* and the zoospores and gametes also resemble those of *Chlamydomonas.* The colony can reproduce either asexually or sexually. Any cell may divide internally and produce from four to 32 zoospores. When these are released suddenly from the mother cell ("Pandora's box"), they escape as a unit and immediately form a miniature new colony. Also, the cells may divide repeatedly to form gametes. In some species of *Pandorina* the gametes are all motile, but are dissimilar in size **(anisogamy).** When the gametes are released, the smaller, more active ones fuse only with the larger, less active ones. The resulting zygote forms a zygospore that later undergoes meiosis and produces zoospores. Finally, each zoospore divides mitotically to form a new *Pandorina* colony.

The highest form in the motile colony series is *Volvox,* a hollow, spherical colony composed of 500 to 50,000 cells. The individual cells still bear a striking resemblance to those of *Chlamydomonas* despite the greater complexity of colonial organization, and for this reason it is possible to postulate the origin of *Volvox* from unicellular, motile forms.

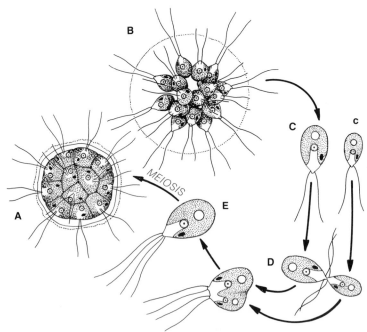

Figure 7–6 The life cycle of *Pandorina. A,* Vegetative colony. *B,* A group of female gametes. *c* and *C,* Male and female gametes, respectively. Note that the female gametes are larger than the male gametes; this is termed isogamy. *D,* Syngamy. *E,* Zygote (Redrawn with modification from Smith, G. M. *Cryptogamic Botany,* Volume 1. Second Edition, New York, McGraw-Hill Book Co., Inc., 1955).

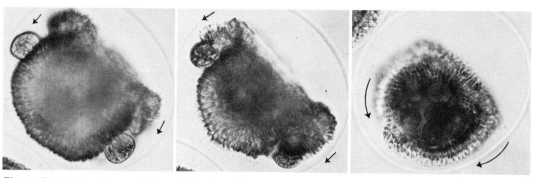

Figure 7–7 Time-lapse studies of the inversions of an autocolony of *Volvox*. The direction of the inversion is indicated by arrows (Photos courtesy of R. Starr, Indiana University).

Volvox occurs in large numbers in freshwater ponds and lakes, and often the colonies may be large enough to be seen with the unaided eye. These colonies swim about rather ponderously, with a rolling motion, which indicates a high degree of cooperation among the body cells, all of which have two outwardly-projecting, whiplash flagella. As in other colonies in this series, *Volvox* may reproduce asexually or sexually. A cell in the colony may enlarge, then divide mitotically to form a mass of cells; these cells form a hollow sphere with their flagella directed inwardly. The sphere, which is complete except for a small opening, then proceeds to turn itself inside out and floats freely within the parent colony. This spectacular feat, which has been recorded by time-lapse photomicroscopy, results in the establishment of a **daughter colony** closely resembling the parent colony in all respects except size. Several of these daughter colonies, or **autocolonies,** may occur within one mature *Volvox*, becoming free-living only when the mother colony breaks apart.

Sexually, *Volvox* has achieved the highest level of evolutionary development in the motile series, producing eggs and sperms that are characteristic of oogamous reproduction. The resulting zygotes form zygospores and these eventually divide, first by meiosis and then mitotically, to establish new colonies.

Many variations occur among the motile colony algae represented here by *Chlamydomonas, Pandorina,* and *Volvox,* but basically this evolutionary pathway has been toward large, motile colonial forms that reproduce oogamously. Although this group appears to be a highly successful one as measured by the ability to colonize many aquatic habitats and to reproduce in great numbers, it is not believed to have given rise to more complex motile plant forms.

Non-Motile and Filamentous Algae

This group includes non-motile unicells and filamentous forms as well as more complex multicellular types that are among the most highly evolved examples of green algae. An example of the simplest and probably the most primitive members of the series is *Chlorococcum,* an inhabitant of soils and fresh water that reproduces asex-

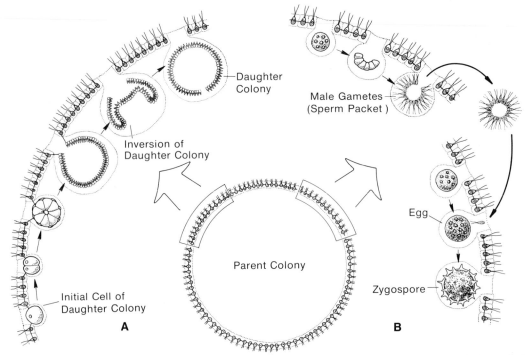

Figure 7–8 Diagrammatic representation of the life history of *Volvox. A,* Stages in the development of a daughter colony. *B,* Sexual reproduction.

ually by forming zoospores, which swim about for a time but then lose their flagella and become non-motile. Sexual reproduction in *Chlorococcum* resembles that of *Chlamydomonas.* A more advanced non-motile alga is *Tetraspora,* in which vegetative cells similar to those of *Chlorococcum* adhere together in irregular masses. *Tetraspora* also produces zoospores and gametes that resemble cells of *Chlamydomonas.* For this reason we assume that algae such as *Chlorococcum* and *Tetraspora* have evolved from ancestors resembling *Chlamydomonas.*

From ancestral algae resembling *Tetraspora* have descended the filamentous forms (both simple and branched) and the parenchymatous forms, which have flattened, leaf-like plant bodies. Simple filamentous forms may be illustrated by the freshwater alga *Ulothrix.* In addition to photosynthetic vegetative cells the mature alga also has basal holdfast cells that may be non-photosynthetic and serve to anchor the filament to the substrate. Asexually, *Ulothrix* forms zoospores that resemble *Chlamydomonas* but have four flagella. The zoospores swim about for a time and then settle down on a suitable substrate to form a **holdfast cell.** The holdfast cell anchors the plant and initiates growth of the new filament. This species is heterothallic; at maturity, certain cells produce biflagellate isogametes that are released into the surrounding water where they fuse with isogametes from other *Ulothrix* filaments. The zygote formed by the union of isogametes is motile for a time and resembles a four-flagellate zoospore. It soon loses the flagella, forms a thick wall, and becomes a zygospore. Eventually this zygospore undergoes meiosis and forms four motile zoospores, each of which can establish a new filament.

Other filamentous green algae include *Stigeoclonium,* a common branching alga found growing on rocks in streams. Though somewhat more complex in organization than *Ulothrix,* its reproductive processes are similar. Another green alga, *Fritschiella,* is interesting to many botanists because the organization of its plant body is in part **parenchymatous;** that is, its cells may divide into three planes, forming regions of several cell layers as in higher plants. *Fritschiella* is thought also to have a life cycle similar to that of the marine green alga *Ulva* (see below), and this too is believed to indicate evolutionary advancement.

The parenchymatous algae may be illustrated by the sea lettuce, *Ulva.* Plants of *Ulva* may be washed up on seashores in large

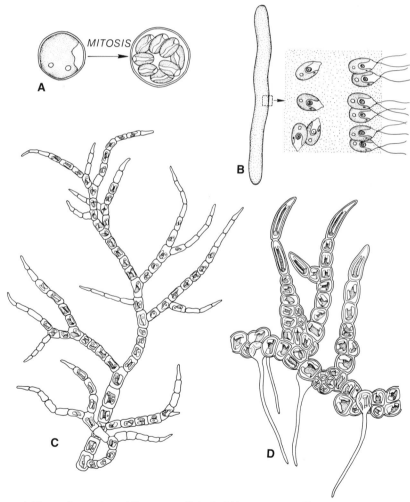

Figure 7–9 Non-motile and filamentous algae (diagrammatic). *A, Chlorococcum. B, Tetraspora. C, Stigeoclonium. D, Fritschiella* (Redrawn in part from Scagel, R. F., *et al. An Evolutionary Survey of the Plant Kingdom.* Belmont, Calif., Wadsworth Publishing Co., Inc., 1966).

183

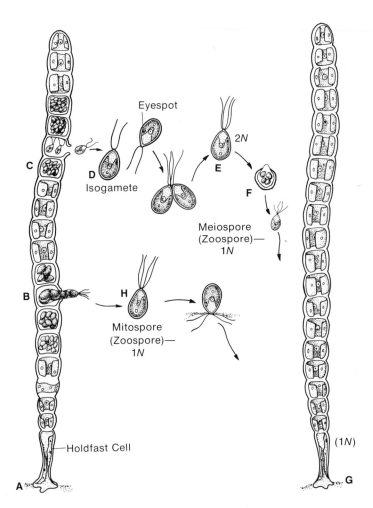

Eyespot

C

D
Isogamete

2N

E

F

Meiospore
(Zoospore)—
1N

B

H

Mitospore
(Zoospore)—
1N

—Holdfast Cell

(1N)

A

G

Figure 7–10 The life history of *Ulothrix,* shown diagrammatically. *A,* Plant in which can be seen zoosporangia (*B*), gametangia (*C*), formation of isogametes (*D*), a zygote (*E*), and meiospores (*F*). Both mitospores and meiospores give rise to new vegetative filaments (*G*). The motile cells are drawn larger than scale.

numbers or may be found attached to rocks or other submerged objects in shallow water. *Ulva* is a flat, membranous plant composed of two layers of cells. Reproductively, *Ulva* is isogamous, producing large numbers of isogametes, which upon release fuse with those from other plants to form zygotes. The zygotes germinate to form 2N *Ulva* plants, identical in appearance to plants producing isogametes, but differing in chromosome number. When the 2N *Ulva* plant matures, it produces 1N zoospores through meiosis. Such zoospores may also be termed meiospores. After their release, they settle upon a substrate and grow into 1N *Ulva* plants. Later, these plants produce isogametes. So in *Ulva* an alternation of generations occurs. Because it involves plants that look alike, it is termed **an isomorphic alternation of generations,** and neither the 2N generation nor the

1N generation is predominant in the life cycle (life cycle III; see Figure 4–6).

All of the higher green plants to be studied in later chapters have similar alternations of generations, although these are not isomorphic since the meiospore- and gamete-producing phases are dissimilar. The terms **sporophyte** (for the meiospore-forming generation) and **gametophyte** (for the gamete-forming generation) usually are used in describing alternations of generations.

The filamentous algae are considered the most advanced line of

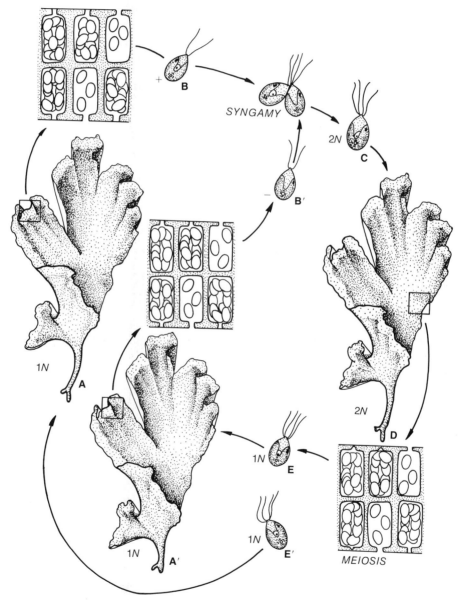

Figure 7–11 Life history of *Ulva* (shown diagrammatically). *A* and *A'*, Plus and minus gametophytes, respectively. *B* and *B'*, Plus and minus gametes. *C*, Zygote. *D*, Sporophyte plant. *E* and *E'*, Meiospores of the two mating types. (Redrawn from Scagel, R. F., *et al. An Evolutionary Survey of the Plant Kingdom.* Belmont, Calif., Wadsworth Publishing Co., Inc., 1966).

specialization among the green algae as regards the evolution of plants. The branched, filamentous algae, such as *Fritschiella,* are thought to resemble intermediate stages in the evolution of higher green land plants, which also are characterized by parenchymatous organization as well as by alternation of generations.

The Siphonous Algae

A third important group of algae is characterized by its multinucleate condition. Each cell contains several nuclei rather than the single nucleus characteristic of other green algae. A plant with this kind of cellular organization is called a **coenocyte,** and examples of coenocytic plants are found among both algae and fungi. However, we know of no higher green plants having this condition; therefore we must exclude the siphonous algae from our concepts of the ancestry of higher green plant forms.

Multinucleate forms may have evolved through loss of capacity for cell wall formation following mitosis, and it is possible that simple coenocytes may have arisen among the green algae from *Chlamydomonas*-like ancestors in this way.

Some of the siphonous marine algae, such as *Valonia,* are easily seen with the unaided eye, even though they are unicells. One of the

Figure 7-12 *Acetabularia crenulata,* the mermaid's wineglass.

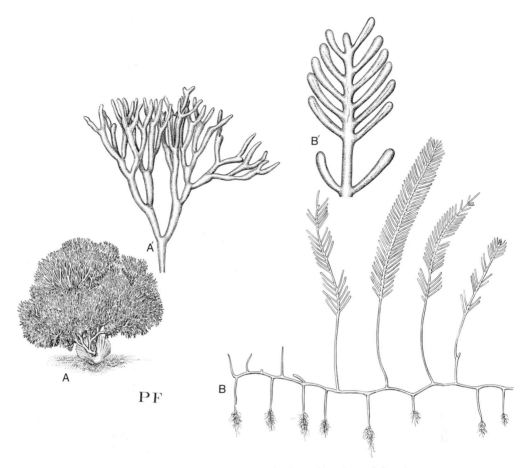

Figure 7–13 Some siphonous, green, marine algae. *A, Codium. A'*, enlarged drawing of a *Codium* branch. *B, Caulerpa*, with its rhizomatous habit. *B'*, enlarged drawing of a portion of a branch of *Caulerpa*. Both algae have been compared to a single giant cell with many nuclei and continuous cytoplasm.

most beautiful and interesting forms is *Acetabularia,* the mermaid's wine glass, found in shallow tropical seas. It can be found growing in great abundance along stretches of the overseas highway to Key West, Florida, bordering on Florida Bay. *Acetabularia* has been used in some important research on nuclear and cytoplasmic relationships. During most of its life cycle the plant has but one large nucleus near its base. Grafting the stalk of one species to the basal, nucleated part of a second species results in the formation of new, intermediate types. This indicates that both the nucleus and the cytoplasm control the form a plant takes in its development.

Reproduction is highly varied in the siphonous green algae. Asexual reproduction may occur by means of zoospores, and sexual processes include either isogamy, anisogamy, or oogamy. In *Acetabularia* meiosis immediately precedes gamete formation (life cycle II; see Figure 4–6).

Other coenocytic green algae include *Codium,* a marine form with forked branches. *Codium* often attaches itself to shellfish and can be very destructive to oysters, mussels, and scallops. Other

187

common siphonous types are *Bryopsis,* with its fern-like vertical branches arising from a horizontal, stem-like part, and *Caulerpa,* with leaf-like blades, stemlike horizontal parts, and root-like holdfasts. Some of these individual plants may be quite extensive (perhaps a meter or more in length). Even these, however, are morphologically a single cell with continuous cytoplasm. They commonly inhabit shallow marine waters, and some members secrete particles, scales and encrustations of calcium carbonate and upon death contribute to the formation of limestone deposits and calcareous sands.

Some Additional Interesting Algae

One of the more interesting and specialized groups in the Chlorophyta is the order **Zygnematales**. Sexual reproduction occurs in this group as a consequence of the fusion of amoeboid gametes in a process called **conjugation**. There are no flagellated cells such as are present in the three series just discussed. Conjugation results in the formation of a 2*N* zygote, which forms a thick wall and becomes a resting cell. Meiosis occurs at the time this cell germinates and the 1*N,* vegetative stage is initiated. *Spirogyra,* a well-known member of the Zygnematales, is characterized by its spiral chloroplasts (see Figure 7–14). Other interesting members of this order are the **desmids,** which are unusual because the vegetative plant is composed of two halves, called **semicells,** identical to each other and having one nucleus. When a desmid divides, each of the daughter cells retains one of the old **semicells** and proceeds to grow a new half-cell. Desmids are important elements of the **phytoplankton,** the floating microscopic plant life found in both fresh and marine water.

The green alga *Hydrodictyon,* also known as the **water net** grows on the bottom of clear pools of fresh water and in quiet streams. Its overall form is that of a bag-like net with meshes formed by tubular cells. Mature colonies may be nearly a meter long. The reproduction of a water net is a marvelous process. Within a single net cell, many tiny zoospores arrange themselves in the form of a tiny net within the mother cell wall. When the mother cell breaks open, the miniature net escapes and begins to grow. Even though it expands greatly in size by the time it becomes mature, no further cells are formed. A colony formed in this way is called a **coenobium**.

In still another algal group is the freshwater, filamentous alga *Oedogonium.* Multiflagellated sperm and zoospores characterize this alga, and sexual reproduction is oogamous. The **oogonia,** as gametangia that produce eggs are called, are the most conspicuous feature of filaments, and in some species, very small, "dwarf male" filaments grow epiphytically on the female filaments. In most other respects the life cycle of *Oedogonium* resembles that of *Ulothrix.*

Another interesting group of green algae is the **stoneworts.** The fossil record for this group goes all the way back to the Silurian Period. A living representative, *Chara,* is a submerged, bottom dweller in clear, freshwater ponds. *Chara* is a comparatively large

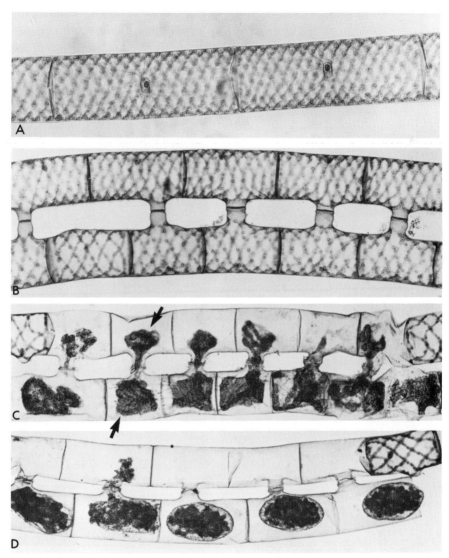

Figure 7–14 Stages of reproduction in *Spirogyra. A,* Vegetative cells; note the spiral chloroplast and numerous pyrenoids present in each cell. *B,* Conjugating filaments; note the conjugation tubes. *C,* Gametes (arrows) passing through conjugation tubes. *D,* Exconjugant cells containing zygotes (Courtesy Carolina Biological Supply Company).

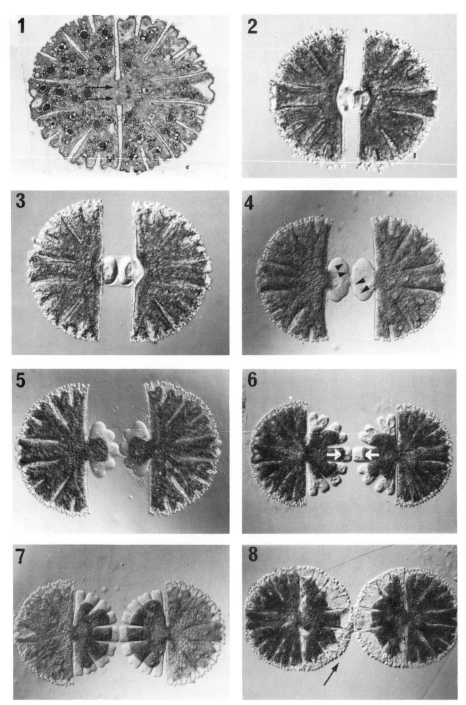

Figure 7–15 Division and development of new semi-cells in *Micrasterias*, a desmid, as shown by these sequentially-numbered time-lapse photographs (From Tippit, D. H., and Pickett-Heaps, J. D. Experimental Investigations into Morphogenesis in *Micrasterias Protoplasma 81*:271–296, 1974).

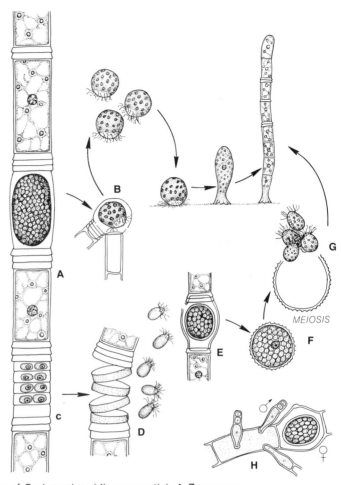

Figure 7–16 Reproductive structures of *Oedogonium* (diagrammatic). *A*, Zoosporangium. *B*, Escape of zoospore and subsequent germination. *C*, Antheridia. *D*, Escape of sperm from antheridia. *E*, Oögonium and egg. *F*, Zygote. *G*, Meiospores. *H*, Form having dwarf male plants.

green alga with whorls of branches, both horizontal and vertical stems, and anchoring structures known as **rhizoids.** The growth of a plant of *Chara* is apical, like that of higher plants. An apical cell gives rise by mitotic divisions to cells further down the branch that develop into several kinds of structural and reproductive types (Fig. 7–17). Most stoneworts have calcified walls and complex gametangia. The relationship of the stoneworts to other green algae is remote, and some algologists prefer to place them in a separate division. Based on their general cell structure and biochemical characteristics, they probably share a common evolutionary history with other green algae. Their distinctive form suggests that they have been separated from the rest of the Chlorophyta for a very long time.

191

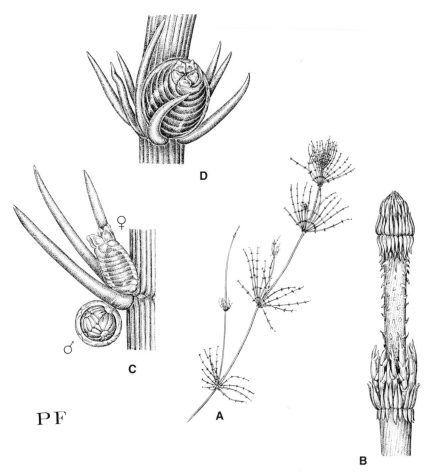

PF

Figure 7–17 *Chara,* a stonewort. *A,* Portion of a plant showing nodes, internodes, and habit of branching. *B,* A stem tip in which growth occurs by divisions of an apical cell and its progeny. *C,* Developing gametangia. *D,* Female gametangium following fertilization. Five helically disposed tubular cells enclose the oogonium.

Ecology of the Green Algae

It has been estimated that as much as 50 per cent of all photosynthetic activity occurring on earth is carried on by phytoplankton. They serve as the basic food-producing organisms in marine and freshwater food chains. Among these planktonic algae are many species of green algae, although members of other algal divisions also are represented and in some situations may even predominate. Also important in aquatic environments are the **benthic** algae (those that grow on the bottom of a body of water). About 95 per cent of benthic species in marine waters are either red or brown algae; the remainder include such green algae as *Ulva, Acetabularia, Caulerpa,* among others.

Green algae also are found in terrestrial and even aerial environments. *Chlorococcum* is an alga widespread in soils, and *Desmococcus (Pleurococcus)* grows as an epiphyte on the bark of trees and is sometimes mistaken for a moss. Many other species of green algae also grow in soil, on moist rocks, on the bark and leaves of trees, and some even exist while carried aloft by currents of air.

No other group of algae has such a wide range of ecological habitats as do the green algae. If light and some moisture are present, then members of the Chlorophyta usually can be found growing somewhere in the vicinity. Species of *Chlamydomonas* can grow in the snow and ice of polar regions and in the alpine zones of high mountains. Most "snow algae" are green algae, although their green pigmentation is masked by a red pigment. Algae of salt lakes are mostly members of the Chlorophyta and, interestingly, appear to be more closely related to freshwater species than to marine types. Probably this reflects the ecological history of such bodies of water, which originally were freshwater and had typical freshwater algae.

Green algae also occur in some rather unusual places. *Basicladia* grows on the backs of freshwater turtles, while *Desmococcus*-like algae can be found in the hair of the three-toed sloth, giving the animal a greenish hue. A number of green algae live as endophytes within other organisms. Species of *Chlorella* live within the bodies of the coelenterate animal *Hydra,* and *Chlorococcum* can be an algal symbiont in lichen, which is an association of algae and fungi (see Chapter 11). A few Chlorophyta are colorless and therefore cannot carry on photosynthesis. They are saprobic or parasitic forms, apparently degenerate species of green autotrophic algae. Some are parasites of animals and plants. *Cephaleuras* is a parasite that attacks cultivated tropical plants, such as tea and pepper.

Algae as Food

Chlorella, a simple one-celled freshwater alga, has been used in pilot studies of food production from algae. It is cultivated in large, aerated vats containing nutrient solutions. On an experimental level, the quantity of food produced per unit area is quite high. Laboratory experiments have resulted in dry weight yields equivalent to 40 tons per acre of surface per year; this compares very favorably with the approximately two to five tons of total dry organic matter per acre of surface produced each year by crop plants. The protein content of *Chlorella* also is high (about 50 per cent), as is the content of carbohydrates (20 per cent), of fats and oils (20 per cent), and of minerals (10 per cent). In addition, various important vitamins are produced. Presently, however, the cost per pound of dry organic matter produced is so high that such an operation would be economically unsound. Before algal farming can become practical, two major problems have to be solved: first, we must learn how to

193

design and operate culture ponds large enough to be efficient and economically profitable; and second, we must learn how to process the algae so as to make them palatable to people who presently are unaccustomed to their taste.

Evolutionary Importance of Green Algae

The fossil history of Chlorophyta goes back to the early part of the geological history of the earth. Green algae existed at least as far back as the Paleozoic Era, and probably earlier. Other divisions of eukaryotic algae are believed to have evolved from green alga—like ancestors along more or less parallel lines of development. Although the evidence is not conclusive, the green algae may have evolved from photosynthetic bacteria, perhaps at the same time as the blue-green algae and the heterotrophic bacteria were evolving. Another possibility is the symbiotic association of primitive eukaryotic cells with blue-green algae or photosynthetic bacteria to form cells with chloroplasts (see Chapter 4). The similarity of certain structural features in the blue-green algae and the red algae (Division Rhodophyta) has led some algologists to postulate the origin of eukaryotic cells along more than one line of specialization, and the blue-green algae may have been progenitors of the red algae.

Many botanists have concluded that the filamentous line of green algae were the group giving rise to the higher land plants. The similarity of pigments, cell wall structure and composition, parenchymatous growth, and the nature of food reserves support this theory. *Fritschiella* has been suggested as an alga exemplifying the ancestral form from which simple land plants may have evolved.

Because higher green plants all exhibit an alternation of spore-producing and gamete-producing generations (life cycle III), the postulated green algal ancestor may have had a life cycle resembling that of *Ulva* or *Fritschiella.* Recently, however, Dr. J. Pickett-Heaps of the University of Colorado has proposed that higher green plants probably are not as closely related to these and other filamentous and parenchymatous algae as formerly believed, but that the latter may be an early offshoot from the evolutionary line that gave rise to higher plants. The evidence for this theory is the mode of cell wall formation found in all higher green plants during mitosis, but in only a few genera of green algae, such as *Chara, Spirogyra,* and two others not mentioned previously in this chapter, *Klebsormidium* and *Coleochaete.* These plants all form cell plates or **phragmoplasts** during mitosis. However, other species of algae, including *Fritschiella,* do not have phragmoplasts, but instead have unique structures termed **phycoplasts.** *Chlamydomonas* and other motile colony algae also have phycoplasts. As a consequence of these and other studies, Dr. Pickett-Heaps and his colleagues have proposed an evolutionary scheme in which *Chlamydomonas* and other algae with phycoplasts, as well as algae and higher plants having phragmoplasts (i.e., all higher green plants) are descended from simpler unicellular and multicellular forms as yet unknown.

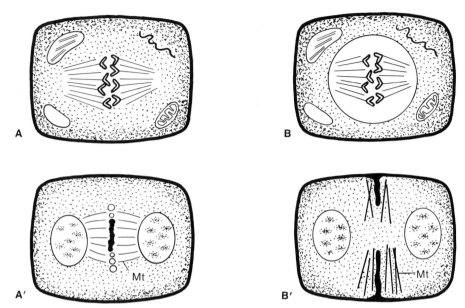

Figure 7–18 Cell wall formation among green algae and higher green plants, shown diagrammatically. *A* and *A'*, The phragmoplast type. The nuclear envelope breaks down prior to formation of the mitotic spindle, and the phragmoplast forms as a disk of vesicles among the pole-to-pole spindle microtubules. *B* and *B'*, The phycoplast type. The mitotic spindle forms within the nuclear envelope and after nuclear division the phycoplast, which consists of microtubules (Mt) bordering the ingrowing new cell wall, can be seen.

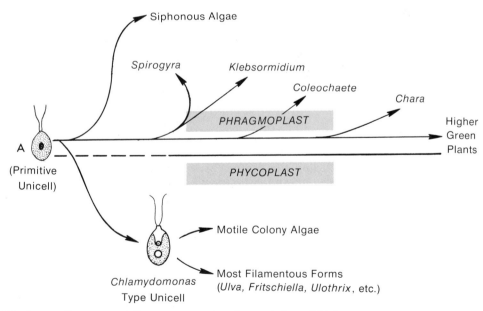

Figure 7–19 A recently-proposed theory concerning the evolution of higher green plants from privitive algal forms. *A* represents an ancestral unicellular form similar to *Chlamydomonas* in many respects but lacking both a phragmoplast and a phycoplast and perhaps undergoing cell division by furrowing. The position of the siphonous green algae is speculative, but present evidence suggests that they are not closely related to the phycoplast forms such as *Ulva, Fritschiella,* and *Ulothrix* (Modified from Pickett-Heaps, J. D., and Marchant, H. J. The Phylogeny of the Green Algae: A New Proposal. *Cytobios 6*:255–264, 1972).

195

SUMMARY   There are about 18,000 species of eukaryotic algae of various types, and these include about 7000 species of green algae, members of the division Chlorophyta.

We have chosen the unicellular green alga *Chlamydomonas* to represent the cellular organization of the green algae, although many variations in cell structure are recognized among the members of the group. The protoplast of *Chlamydomonas* is enclosed in a cellulose wall and features all of the organelles of the typical plant cell. These include chloroplasts, mitochondria, vacuoles, dictyosomes, endoplasmic reticulum, and flagella. In addition, the chloroplasts possess pyrenoids and eyespots.

Although many green algae are composed of cells other than the kind described above, one group, the motile colony series, consists solely of aggregates of *Chlamydomonas*-like cells. Other evolutionary developments in the green algae are the algal forms having a filamentous association of non-motile cells, and the siphonous group, in which the organization is that of a multinucleated, tubular or branching cell. Even in these groups we find motile reproductive cells closely resembling *Chlamydomonas* in their basic structure.

Green algae are important members of environments on land and sea. They add to the formation of limestone reefs and sands in oceans and are at the base of food chains in all aquatic habitats. The green algae are classified as follows:

Division Chlorophyta: These are the green algae. There are about 350 genera comprising 7000 species. They are eukaryotic, autotrophic plants, having chlorophylls *a* and *b*, carotenes, and xanthophylls. Starch is the storage product. Walls are composed of cellulose and pectic materials. Flagella are of the whiplash type. Modes of reproduction are varied.

CLASS CHLOROPHYCEAE: These are the typical green algae, and included are the motile colony algae, represented by the genera *Chlamydomonas, Pandorina,* and *Volvox;* the non-motile, filamentous, and parenchymatous algae; among these the genera *Chlorococcum, Chlorella, Coleochaete, Klebsormidium, Stigeoclonium, Fritschiella, Tetraspora, Ulothrix,* and *Ulva;* the siphonous algae, including the *Valonia, Acetabularia, Codium, Bryopsis,* and *Caulerpa.* Some additional types are the coenobic algae, represented by the genus *Hydrodictyon;* the Zygnematales, represented by the genera *Spirogyra, Cosmarium, Closterium,* and *Micrasterias;* and Oedogoniales, including the genus *Oedogonium.*

CLASS CHAROPHYCEAE: These are complex green algae with apical growth, relatively complex sex organs, and a number of specialized cell types. The genus *Chara* represents this class.

DISCUSSION QUESTIONS

1. From the strictly practical standpoint, do you think that algae ever will become important sources of food for humans? Give reasons for your answer.
2. On the basis of your knowledge of events in the life history of *Chlamydomonas,* is the vegetative stage 1*N* or 2*N*?
3. What are the characteristic pigments of the Chlorophyta?
4. Sexual reproduction occurs in three basic patterns in algae. Describe them and comment on their similarities and differences.
5. In comparing the cell of *Chlamydomonas* and the typical, higher plant

cell discussed in Chapter 4, what features are present in *Chlamydomonas* and not in the typical cell?

6. The motile colony series has been described by some botanists as an evolutionary "dead end." Why?
7. How are the autocolonies of *Volvox* formed?
8. The non-motile, filamentous series is believed to be the most important in the evolution of the Chlorophyta. Why?
9. What is unique about the structures of *Codium* and *Bryopsis*?
10. Explain in what important way the reproductive cycle of *Ulva* differs from that of *Ulothrix*. What possible significance does this have with respect to higher land plants?
11. What relationships are there between oceanic reefs, sands, and some of the siphonous algae?
12. What is the significance of algae in the aquatic ecosystems of the world?

SUPPLEMENTAL READING

Dawson, E. Y. *Marine Botany: An Introduction.* New York: Holt, Rinehart and Winston, Inc., 1966.

Pickett-Heaps, J. D., and H. J. Marchant. The Phylogeny of the Green Algae: A New Proposal. *Cytobios* 6:255–264, 1972.

Prescott, G. W. *How to Know the Freshwater Algae.* Dubuque, Ia.: Wm. C. Brown and Co., 1954.

Round, F. E. *The Biology of Algae.* London: Edward Arnold, Ltd., 1965.

Smith, G. M. *Freshwater Algae of the United States,* 2nd ed. New York: McGraw-Hill Book Co., 1950.

Tiffany, L. H. *Algae, the Grass of Many Waters,* 2nd ed. Springfield, Ill.: Charles C Thomas, 1958.

Trainor, F. R. Control of Sexuality in *Chlamydomonas. Amer. J. Bot. 45*:621–626, 1958.

Ship stranded on the Sargasso Sea (Photo courtesy of The Bettmann Archive).

Chapter 8

The Brown Algae

IMPORTANCE AND USES OF BROWN ALGAE • THE SARGASSO SEA • BIOLOGY OF THE BROWN ALGAE • THE ISOGENERATAE • THE HETEROGENERATAE • THE CYCLOSPORAE • ECOLOGY OF THE BROWN ALGAE • EVOLUTIONARY RELATIONSHIPS • SUMMARY

Importance and Uses of Brown Algae

Everyone who lives near the coastlines of the United States has had an opportunity to see examples of brown algae. They are often washed ashore, particularly after storms at sea, and at times are seen floating in large numbers in bays, inlets, and harbors. Among them are the largest of all the algae, the giant kelps, which reach lengths in excess of 50 meters. Along the West Coast, kelps are harvested by specially built ships fitted out with large mowers which cut them off about a meter below the water's surface. They regrow rapidly (at a rate greater than one-half meter per day) so they may be harvested repeatedly without harm. The economic importance of the brown algae has increased markedly in the past two decades. In Japan and China a food called **kombu** has been used for centuries. Kombu is made from dried and pressed brown algae and is a popular food in many parts of the Far East. It is cut into thin slices and served as a vegetable, or it may be cooked with meats or shredded and used in soups and sauces. It can even be coated with sugar and served as a dessert. **Haidai,** or "sea belt," is a kelp that has been widely used by the Chinese as medicine and food for 1500 years. It is usually cooked with pork and soybean sauce, and is popular during the season of the year when green vegetables are not plentiful. Mass cultivation of the kelp is now in progress in China, and kelp culture is considered one of the chief accomplishments of aquaculture programs run by the government.

Day after day, day after day,
We stuck, nor breath nor motion;
As idle as a painted ship
Upon a painted ocean.

SAMUEL TAYLOR COLERIDGE: *The Rime of the Ancient Mariner*

The Sargasso Sea

The Atlantic Ocean between the West Indies and the Azores contains a large tract of calm, warm waters covered by floating masses of seaweed. This is known as the Sargasso Sea, an area about 1000 miles by 2000 miles with a long axis more or less east to west. A great deal of legend has grown up from tales told by sailors who have passed through this region. The remains of keels of ships weighted with barnacles and shells, great numbers of wrecks, dead men at their posts on deserted warships, skeletons of slaves still locked in their chains, all have been reported by terrorized seamen. This legend is still believed by some, but actually the Sargasso Sea is a sunny, quiet place, with floating patches of the brown alga *Sargassum* and a considerable amount of open water. Columbus sailed through it on his first voyage to the New World, and although his men became worried lest they become stranded, they passed through it easily.

The Sargasso Sea is unique. It is not known how the *Sargassum* became so concentrated, although apparently the process has been going on for a long time. Through evolution the plants have adapted to the open water, so that they are naturally floating, not attached to rocks. They reproduce vigorously by vegetative budding and are remarkably well-fitted for their floating existence. The leafy stems

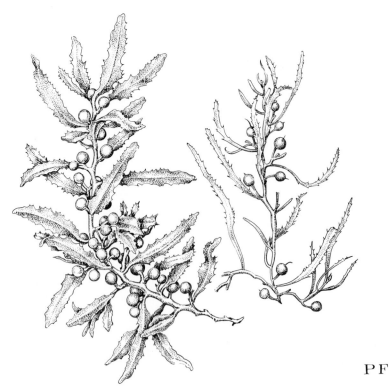

P F

Figure 8–1 The brown alga *Sargassum.* The small, berry-like spheres are gas bladders.

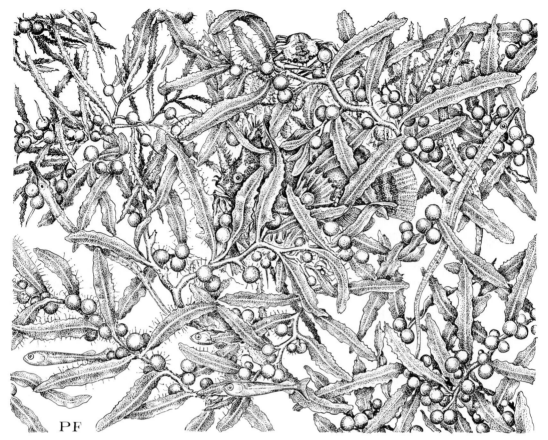

Figure 8–2. *Sargassum* association; an artist's conception of life as it exists in a *Sargassum* bed, such as in the Sargasso Sea.

bear grapelike bladders that give them buoyancy. Other marine life-forms in the Sargasso Sea are also specially adapted to this region. Some animals have taken on the appearance of the alga; there are crabs, fish, and sea slugs that blend in with their surroundings. Eels migrate from the eastern rivers of the United States, the Mediterranean area, and from Europe to mate and die under the *Sargassum* beds. From the Sargasso Sea the tiny eel larva must make the long journey back to its native rivers and streams thousands of miles away.

Biology of the Brown Algae

The brown algae belong to the division Phaeophyta, which contains approximately 1500 species. They occur in the oceans and seas, especially in cold, northern latitudes, with very few forms adapted to fresh water. Brown algae resemble green algae in their cell wall construction, with the inner layer cellulosic and the outer one pectic. They differ from green algae in the composition of the cell wall, cellular contents, and in the structure of the motile cells. Complex colloidal substances called **phycocolloids** are found in the cell walls. Two important phycocolloids, **algin** and **fucoidin,** are substances that make the brown algae of importance to man. Algin in particular is used in many ways; the salts of alginic acid (alginates) are used in the manufacture of beer, toothpaste, ice cream and other dairy products, paint, shaving cream, medicine, soaps, and in a host of other applications including photography. The algin of the cell wall takes up and holds water very effectively, actually absorbing up to 20 times its own weight in water, and this aids the alga in resisting drying out while exposed to the air during low tides. It enables brown algae to grow in intertidal areas where other marine plants or terrestrial plants lead a tenuous life at best.

The characteristic brownish color of most brown algae is due to the presence of a specific carotenoid pigment called **fucoxanthin.** The green pigments chlorophyll *a* and chlorophyll *c* are usually masked by the fucoxanthin. Food reserves are present in the form of a polysaccharide, **laminarin,** dissolved in the vacuolar sap. Other cell inclusions are small sacs or vesicles that are often associated with the nucleus and contain **phaeophyte tannin,** a substance believed to be a waste product of metabolism. Most vegetative cells are uninucleate, although **holdfasts** (anchoring structures at the base of the stalk) sometimes have multinucleate cells. During cell division **centrioles** that resemble those formed during mitosis in animal cells develop in many species of brown algae. The significance of this similarity is not known.

The only motile cells occurring in the Phaeophyta are zoospores

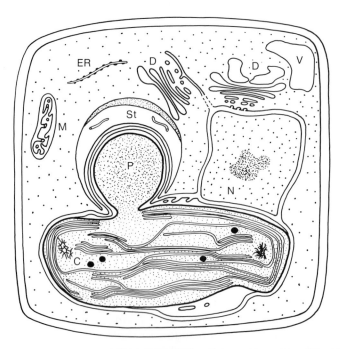

Figure 8–3 Cell structure in a brown alga. Note the close association of the nucleus (N) and the chloroplast (C). The thylakoids do not form grana, but are associated in bands, three or four in number and often extending the length of the chloroplast. Also shown are the pyrenoid (P), storage carbohydrates (St), dictyosomes (D), mitochondrion (M), endoplasmic reticulum (ER), and a vacuole (V) (Redrawn from Bouck, G. B. *Fine Structure and Organelle Associations in Brown Algae. J. Cell. Biol. 26:*523–537, 1965).

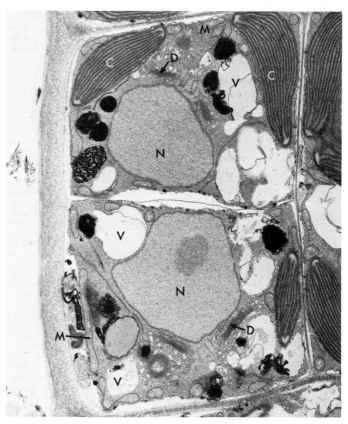

Figure 8–4 Cell structure in *Pylaiella littoralis,* a brown alga. Note the nucleus (N), chloroplasts (C), mitochondria (M), vacuoles (V), and dictyosomes (D). The thylakoids in the chloroplasts of brown algae do not form grana, but instead are associated in bands of three or four and often extend the length of the chloroplast (From Markey, D. R. A Possible Virus Infection in the Brown Alga *Pylaiella littoralis. Protoplasma 80*:223, 1974).

and gametes. Isogamy occurs in one class, oogamy in the others. The motile cells are almost always bean-shaped and have two unequal flagella that are laterally inserted. One flagellum is longer, extends anteriorly, and is **tinsellated** (i.e., it has tiny, hair-like appendages); the other is trailing and non-tinsellated.

There are no unicellular or colonial brown algae; all species have either filamentous, parenchymatous, or kelp-like bodies. Brown algae reproduce asexually both by fragmentation and by sporulation, and also sexually by isogamy, anisogamy, and oogamy. Many species produce zoospores or non-motile spores, but in advanced groups this method of reproduction has been lost. The primitive species have isogamous sexual reproduction, while the more advanced forms are oogamous.

The Isogeneratae

There are three important evolutionary series in the brown algae corresponding to the three classes of Phaeophyta, namely the **Isogeneratae,** the **Heterogeneratae,** and the **Cyclosporae.** The Isogeneratae, the most primitive brown algae, include many simple microscopic, filamentous forms. The life cycles of this series of algae typically correspond to life cycle III (see Figure 4–6), and are **isomorphic,** meaning that the alternation of generations includes 2N sporophytic plants and 1N gametophytic plants identical in appearance. An example of the Isogeneratae is the marine form *Ectocarpus.* The 2N filaments on first examination resemble a green alga. However, they produce two kinds of spore-forming structures: **mitosporangia,** which produce 2N zoospores (mitospores) by mitosis; and **meiosporangia,** which produce 1N zoospores (meiospores) by meiosis. The 2N zoospores grow into new *Ectocarpus* filaments directly, resulting in the production of additional 2N plants. The meiospores grow into 1N filaments that are very similar in appearance to the 2N ones except that in addition to mitosporangia they also form **gametangia.** These gametangia produce numerous isogametes that, once released into the water, resemble minute zoospores except that they fuse in pairs by syngamy. The zygote is again 2N and grows directly into a new 2N *Ectocarpus* filament. Thus, in *Ectocarpus,* we find a 2N sporophytic filament alternating with a 1N gametophytic filament in a typical alternation of generations.

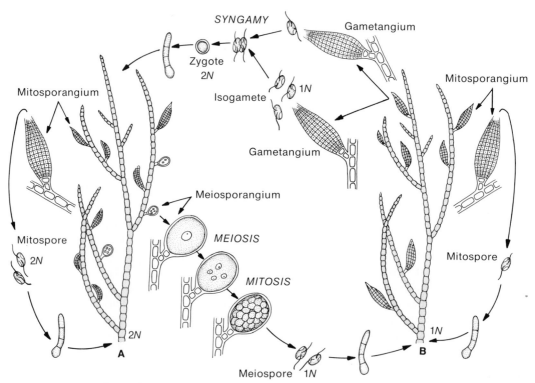

Figure 8–5 The life history of *Ectocarpus* (highly diagrammatic.). *A,* A 2N plant with meiosporangia and mitosporangia. *B,* A 1N plant with mitosporangia and gametangia.

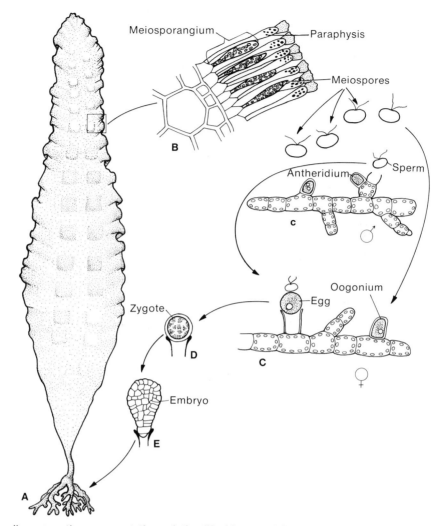

Figure 8–6 Highly diagrammatic representation of the life history of *Laminaria*. *A*, Mature sporophyte. *B*, Section of the blade of the sporophyte, showing meiosporangia. *c*, Male gametophyte with antheridia and sperm. *C*, Female gametophyte with oogonia and a partially extruded egg cell. *D*, Zygote. *E*, Embryo.

The Heterogeneratae

The second evolutionary series is the class **Heterogeneratae**, which includes the kelps and similar kinds of brown algae. One example of this group is the large marine kelp *Laminaria*. The plant grows attached to submerged rocks or other objects by rootlike holdfasts and has a stemlike portion called a **stipe** that terminates in an enlarged, bladelike **lamina**. Reproduction corresponds to life cycle III (Fig. 4–6) and involves a **heteromorphic alternation of generations,** i.e., the two phases are different in appearance. In this case one is very large, the other of microscopic size. The mature sporophyte of *Laminaria* produces masses of zoosporangia (meiosporangia) on its lamina. The zoospores are meiospores, 1N in chromosome number, and are released into the open water and soon

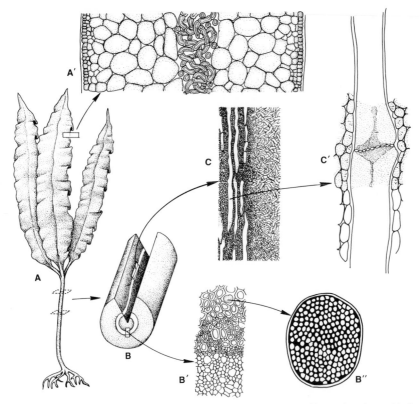

Figure 8–7 Cell structure in a kelp. *A*, The kelp plant. *A'*, Cross section of the blade of a kelp showing outer epidermal cells and internal cells of several types. *B*, Cross and longitudinal section of a stipe showing conducting cells. *B'*,Cross section of conducting region. *B"*, End view of conduction cell. *C*, Enlarged views of a conducting element. *C'*, Sieve-like end wall of a conducting unit.

develop into microscopic, filamentous gametophytes bearing gametangia. Some zoospores produce male gametophytes having **antheridia** (each containing one sperm); while others produce female gametophytes that bear a few **oogonia** (each with one egg). Fertilization occurs when the sperm swims to a partially extruded egg and combines with it to form a zygote. The zygote divides mitotically to form an embryo (young sporophyte), which shortly develops into the typical *Laminaria* plants with holdfast, stipe, and blade.

The similarity between the filamentous gametophytes of *Laminaria* and the plants of *Ectocarpus* suggests that the Heterogeneratae evolved from the Isogeneratae. Also, *Ectocarpus* has a simpler plant body and is isogamous, features considered more primitive than the more complex plant body and oogamous mode of reproduction found in the kelp.

The life and structure of a kelp show points of similarity with lives and structures observed in higher land plants. For example, the kelps are composed of several to many cell layers and the cells exhibit some division of labor, although not to the degree found in higher plants. Among the different kinds of cells found in a kelp are epidermal cells, photosynthetic cells, and in some of the larger forms, specialized food-conducting cells. These latter cells are cylindrical and arranged end-to-end. The portions of the walls where one such cell joins another are pitted, and cytoplasmic strands extend from one cell to the next. Studies of food conduction in large kelps using radioactive compounds have shown that foods may travel from the blade through the stipe at the rapid rate of about 60 centimeters per hour. Botanists believe that this similarity in structure between kelps and higher plants is a matter of either coincidence or convergent evolution. Although alternation of generations occurs in kelps and is a common feature of all higher plants, major biochemical differences between these two groups point to a more distant relationship than that between the higher green plants and the green algae. Close similarities can be seen between the life cycles of kelps and those of certain green algae, and this is probably significant from an evolutionary standpoint.

The Cyclosporae

The class Cyclosporae, the third and last series of brown algae, comprises the most advanced types. The marine rockweed *Fucus* illustrates the life history characteristic of the class. Mature rockweeds are **dichotomously branched** (forked). The vegetative plant is $2N$, but is not a typical sporophyte since it produces gametes by meiosis followed by one or more mitotic divisions; consequently, the life cycle corresponds to life cycle II (see Figure 4–6). Usually this life cycle is interpreted as one in which the gametophyte stage has been lost and the meiospores produce gametes directly. There is no alternation of generations, and eggs and sperm are the only structures in the life cycle that have the $1N$ chromosome number.

Enlargements known as **receptacles** occur on the tips of blades of reproducing plants. Within the receptacles are cavities, called **conceptacles,** in which gametes are formed. In certain species of rockweeds, the conceptacles contain both branched antheridia and globular oogonia; in other species some conceptacles on a plant contain only antheridia, while others on the same plant have only oogonia. In still other species, the conceptacles of some plants bear only antheridia, while those of other plants bear only oogonia. In any case, each antheridium produces 64 sperm by meiosis followed by four successive mitotic divisions. Each oogonium is single-chambered, and meiosis followed by one mitotic division produces eight eggs. The eggs and sperm are released from the conceptacles into the open water during high tide, and the sperm swim quickly to the eggs and bring about fertilization. The $2N$ zygote divides mitotically to form an embryo with a holdfast and eventually a new *Fucus* plant with its characteristic branching body.

The common seaweed *Sargassum,* principally a plant of warm ocean waters, also is a member of the Cyclosporae. Although its organization is more complex than that of *Fucus,* the life cycles and reproductive structures of the two are very similar.

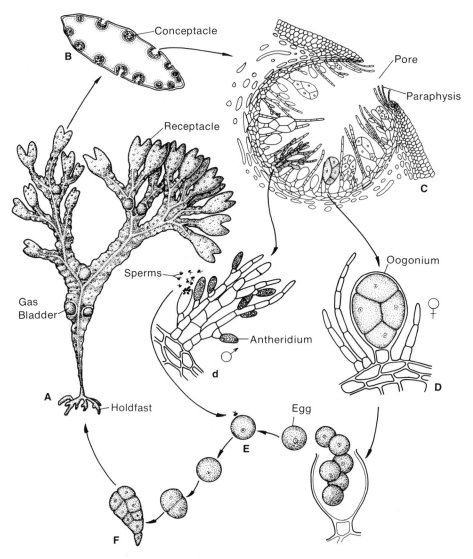

Conceptacle

B

Pore

Paraphysis

Receptacle

C

Oogonium

♀

Sperms

Antheridium

♂

d

D

Gas
Bladder

A

Holdfast

Egg

E

F

Figure 8–8 Life history of *Fucus*. *A, 2N* plant with reproductive branch tips (receptacles). *B,* Cross-section of a receptacle showing numerous cavities with external pores (conceptacles). *C,* Conceptacles of a bisexual rockweed in which male and female gametangia (antheridia and oogonia) and sterile filaments (paraphyses) are present. *D,* Oögonium containing eight eggs. *d,* Antheridial branch, each antheridium containing 64 sperm. *E,* Fertilization. *F,* Embryo (After Smith, G. M. *Cryptogamic Botany,* Volume 1. Second Edition. New York, McGraw-Hill Book Co., Inc., 1955).

Ecology of the Brown Algae

The Phaeophyta are predominantly marine organisms of cold waters of the Arctic, Antarctic, North Atlantic, and North Pacific. It has been suggested that the Arctic Sea ought to be renamed the "Sea of Laminarias" because of its vast numbers of kelps. Some brown algae, such as *Sargassum,* are common in tropical and subtropical areas, and the brown algae generally are well distributed throughout the marine environments of the earth.

Brown algae exhibit marked habitat preferences. Some, such as the rockweed *Fucus,* are found in intertidal zones growing attached to submerged rocks. Other forms are benthic, and may grow sometimes at depths as great as 100 meters if the water is clear and devoid of turbidity. Marine algae are often vertically distributed and show preferences for specific habitats that are conditioned by salinity, temperature, nature of the sea bottom, tidal character for the area, turbidity, and other factors of the environmental complex. In general, as a result of this zonation, the filamentous forms and

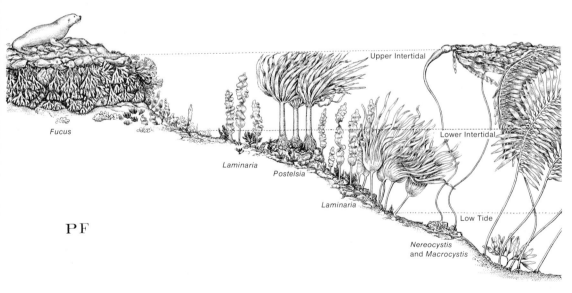

Figure 8–9 Brown algal zonation on the Pacific Coast, illustrated diagrammatically. The algae of the high tide zone are bathed but once per 24 hours, while the lower intertidal algae are flooded twice each day. Major forms are identified.

rockweeds tend to inhabit the littoral and intertidal areas, and the kelps, the deeper waters.

Unlike most algae, many of the brown algae can withstand exposure to air and direct sunlight for hours or even days and survive. All marine forms must be bathed regularly by salt water, however, since this is the manner by which the necessary minerals and water reach the cells. There is no water-conductive system such as is found in higher land plants, which would permit them to exist in a terrestrial environment for long periods of time.

Evolutionary Relationships

A number of evolutionary relationships can be postulated among the brown algae. We find isogamy, anisogamy, and oogamy

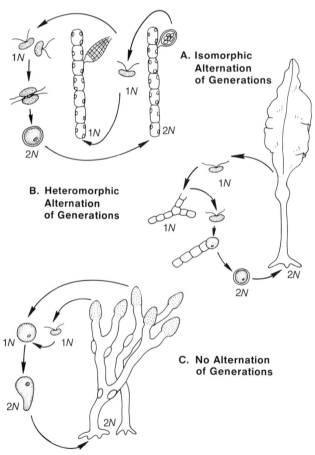

Figure 8–10 Evolutionary trends among the brown algae. *A,* Isogeneratae, showing isomorphic alternation of generations. *B,* Heterogeneratae, showing anisomorphic alternation of generations. *C,* Cyclosporae, with no alternation of generations.

in the Isogeneratae, but in the other two classes the plants are strictly oogamous. The primitive plant body, a single unbranched filament, is found in the Isogeneratae. From this has evolved the branched, filamentous type found in *Ectocarpus,* and more advanced members of the class have multi-layered plant bodies. In the Heterogeneratae, the primitive plant body is exemplified by *Laminaria,* with its single stipe terminating in a single lamina. From this it is possible to trace the elaboration of stipe and lamina in forms such as *Macrocystis* and *Nereocystis,* which have numerous laminae and more complex plant bodies.

The relationships among the Cyclosporae are less clear. The absence of the gametophyte phase makes it difficult to compare forms such as *Fucus* with any members of either the Isogeneratae or the Heterogeneratae. The cellular and plant body structure of *Fucus* is similar to that of the kelps, but the mode of reproduction in the two groups is very different. *Fucus* does not have a gametophyte phase, while the kelps have a true alternation of generations. Apparently, the Cyclosporae and Heterogeneratae have been distinct for a very long time.

It is possible that the Chrysophyta and the Phaeophyta had a common ancestral form that is now extinct. Both groups have similar pigments, and their biflagellated, tinsellated motile cells are similar (see Chapter 10 for comparative features). The evolution and development of the Phaeophyta is much more advanced than that of any of the golden algae, however, and the relationships of brown algae to other algal groups seems very remote indeed.

The fossil history of the brown algae is incomplete, and present evidence suggests that they may have evolved even as late as the Mesozoic Era. Possibly the group was present in Paleozoic times, and some fossils from that era resembling *Fucus* have been reported.

The kelps represent highly advanced algae. These large and well-organized plants have evolved holdfasts, stipes, blades, air bladders, and even primitive conductive cells and tissues. The brown algae have come closer to developing large terrestrial forms than have any other existing algal group, and they have adapted successfully to life in intertidal zones in many areas of the world.

SUMMARY

The division Phaeophyta (brown algae) includes both microscopic plants and very large forms; they are almost entirely inhabitants of salt water. Some of the large types (the kelps) are harvested by ships for use in making emulsifying agents and other commercial products.

The brown algae are classified according to life cycles into three major groups. The Isogeneratae are small algae with equal-sized sporophytes and gametophytes. *Ectocarpus,* a tiny epiphyte, is an example. The Heterogeneratae, represented by the kelps (e.g., *Laminaria*) have large sporophytes and tiny gametophytes of microscopic size. The Cyclosporae, represented by the rockweed *Fucus* and the seaweed *Sargassum* have no gametophyte generation at all.

The major groups of brown algae together with some of their more commonly known representatives are as follows:

Division Phaeophyta: The brown algae. There are about 240 genera comprising 1500 species. These are eukaryotic algae with plant bodies of varying complexities and exhibiting differing life cycles. Chloroplasts have chlorophylls *a* and *c*, fucoxanthin, and other carotenoids. The storage product is laminarin, a carbohydrate. Motile cells are present with two flagella—one tinsellated, and one whiplash. They are principally salt water plants.

CLASS ISOGENERATAE: These are characterized by isomorphic alternation of generations.

Example: Ectocarpus.

CLASS HETEROGENERATAE: These are characterized by heteromorphic alternation of generations.

Examples: Laminaria, Nereocystis, Macrocystis, Postelsia.

CLASS CYCLOSPORAE: These have no alternation of generations.

Examples: Fucus, Sargassum.

DISCUSSION QUESTIONS

1. Compare the present uses of the brown algae as compared with the green algae. Are any brown algae useful as food?
2. What is the Sargasso Sea and to what does it owe its name?
3. What is a kelp? Can you describe the general structures of these kinds of plants?
4. Explain what is meant by the "conductive cells of kelps." Do kelps have any tissues or cells comparable with those in land plants?
5. What is the basic structure of the cell of a brown alga? What are phycocolloids?
6. How does the structure of zoospores and gametes in Phaeophyta differ from those in the Chlorophyta?
7. What is an isomorphic alternation of generations? How do mitosporangia differ from meiosporangia?
8. What is a heteromorphic alternation of generations? Give an example from the brown algae.
9. How does the reproduction of *Fucus* differ from that found in *Laminaria*?
10. Describe the ecological preferences of the major groups of brown algae. Where would you expect to find kelps?
11. Are the brown algae apparently related evolutionarily to any other groups of plants? If so, identify these. Discuss the probable basis of similarity of the kelps to the land plants.

SUPPLEMENTAL READING

Chase, F. M. *Useful Algae.* Smithsonian Inst. Ann. Report, 1941, pp. 401–452.

Cheng, Tien-Hsi. Production of Kelp—A Major Aspect of China's Exploitation of the Sea. *Economic Botany 23*:215–236, 1969.

Dawes, C. J. *Marine algae of the West Coast of Florida.* Coral Gables, Florida: University of Miami Press, 1974.

Papenfuss, G. F. "Phaeophyta." *In* Smith, G. M. (ed.) *Manual of Phycology.* Waltham, Mass.: Chronica Botanica, 1951.

Smith, G. M. *Marine Algae of the Monterey Peninsula, California.* Palo Alto, California: Stanford University Press, 1944.

Taylor, W. R. *Marine Algae of the Northeastern Coast of North America,* 2nd ed. Ann Arbor: University of Michigan Press, 1957.

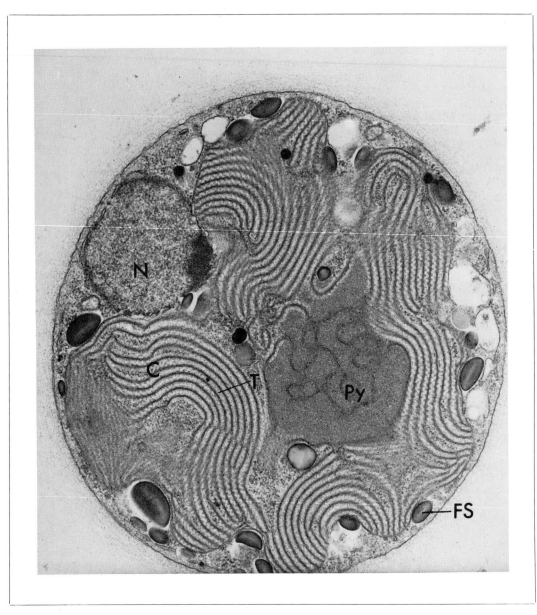

Electron micrograph of a cell of the red alga *Porphyridium purpureum,* × 15,000. C, Chloroplast; T, thylakoid; Py, pyrenoid; FS, floridean starch; N, nucleus (Photo courtesy of Dr. E. Gantt of the Smithsonian Institution Radiation Biology Laboratory).

Chapter 9

The Red Algae

RED ALGAE AS FOOD • AGAR AND THE PURE CULTURE METHOD • BIOLOGY OF THE RED ALGAE • THE LIFE OF A RED ALGA • CLASSIFICATION OF THE RED ALGAE • ECOLOGY AND DISTRIBUTION • CORAL REEFS AND CORAL-LINE ALGAE • EVOLUTIONARY RELATIONSHIPS • SUMMARY

The division Rhodophyta includes many algae that are in fact red or pinkish, although there are forms that are purple, olive-green, and other intermediate shades of color. The members of this group are often deceptively simple in appearance; some have the most intriguing life cycles known among the algae. This division is a large, fairly uniform group of over 4000 species found chiefly in warm temperate or tropical marine waters. Included are many species that are beautiful, intricately branching forms found on coral reefs, intertidal areas, or in deep water; usually they are not large, and few reach over a meter in size.

Red Algae as Food

The Rhodophyta include a number of examples of food plants that are used in various parts of the world. The red alga that is the most important edible seaweed in the United States is Irish moss, *Chondrus crispus.* Another seaweed, known as dulse (*Rhodymenia palmata*), is also used as food and in medicine, and was an important food plant during the Irish famine that lasted from 1846 to 1848. *Porphyra* is a red alga that is popular in the Far East, particularly in Japan, and is also used in Europe in making soup. It has a smooth, thin blade, and grows naturally on rocks in the littoral zone. In Japan it is cultivated on a wide scale and is called "nori" or "sushi." Bundles of bamboo or nets suspended from poles are placed in shallow tidelands, and floating *Porphyra* spores become lodged on the submerged parts. The spores germinate and grow into full size plants in about 2 to 3 months. After the crop is picked and harvested, it may be sold fresh or sun-dried before marketing.

The gemmed wave in the water, the starlight on the gem

STEPHEN VINCENT BENÉT: *Flood-tide.*

A

B

Figure 9–1 Mariculture of *Porphyra* in Japan. *A*, Ancient method of growing *Porphyra* on brush bundles. *B*, Nets used for growing *Porphyra* in place.

Illustration continued on opposite page.

The red algae are also important because of the various muci-laginous extracts that can be obtained from them. **Carrageenin** is a complex colloidal substance obtained from *Chondrus* and various other forms that are presently harvested along the North Atlantic coast. It is used in brewing, to clarify and give body to beer. It is also

C

D

Figure 9–1 *Continued*   *C,* Harvesting of the nets. *D,* Pressing the harvested *Porphyra* to make nori (From *Marine Botany* by E. Y. Dawson. Copyright © 1966 by Holt, Rinehart and Winston, Inc. Reproduced by permission of Holt, Rinehart and Winston, Inc.).

widely used in many pharmaceuticals and as a stabilizing and thickening agent in many products. It is comparable in use to the alginates of the brown algae in the manufacture of ice cream products, cheese, cosmetics, and paints. Another important phycocolloid obtained from the red algae is **agar agar,** which has played a vital role in the development of microbiology.

217

Agar and the Pure Culture Method

Robert Koch, a German physician and bacteriologist of the nineteenth century, was one of the pioneers in the science of microbiology. He was interested in the development of simple methods for growing pure cultures of bacteria. Koch first used sterilized cut surfaces of potatoes that were inoculated with bacteria. This technique was not very successful even though it was an improvement over the tedious methods then used in other laboratories. Later, he experimented with gelatin as a bacterial growth medium, but this also had some serious disadvantages, principally because the bacteria digested the gelatin and liquefied it. Moreover, gelatin tends to become liquid by itself at the temperatures required to incubate many kinds of bacteria. At that time there was working in Koch's laboratory the wife of one of his co-workers, a Frau Hesse. She had friends in the Dutch East Indies who were familiar with a substance called agar agar, which was obtained from a marine red alga growing there. Agar agar, or **agar** as it is usually called, then was used in jams and jellies, and Frau Hesse suggested that it be tried in making bacterial growth media. The results were very successful, and soon agar replaced all other methods in the laboratory. Agar is almost the perfect solidifying agent for bacterial media. Since a temperature of 100°C. is needed to melt the agar gel, it remains solid throughout the temperature range in which bacteria can be grown. Once it is melted, however, it remains liquid until the temperature drops to about 40° C. These properties make it possible to use agar in a wide variety of pure culture techniques, and it enabled Koch and other scientists to expand their studies of bacteria very rapidly. Agar is a complex carbohydrate that very few microorganisms can metabolize, so it remains a stiff gel even when many bacterial colonies are growing on it. No general substitute for agar has been found.

Gelidium is the chief source of the commercial form of agar, although it can be obtained from a number of other red algae as well. The plant is distributed widely, and has a cylindrical or flattened, pinnately branched thallus with a tough consistency. Japan produces most of the agar, where it is collected by divers. The algae are cleaned thoroughly, dried, and then spread out on bamboo racks to bleach. Afterwards the algae are boiled to extract the agar, which then is filtered from the pulpy residue. The filtrate is run into wooden troughs and allowed to cool until it hardens. Then it is cut into blocks or sticks after hardening and is ready for the market. Agar used for scientific purposes is taken through several additional refining steps, and some highly-purified types used for critical experiments sell for about sixty dollars a pound. It is used also in pharmaceuticals (such as laxatives) and as a starch substitute. Nearly every year new uses are found for this product.

Biology of the Red Algae

The plants are generally of only small to moderate size; they vary mostly from one centimeter to one meter in length, and none

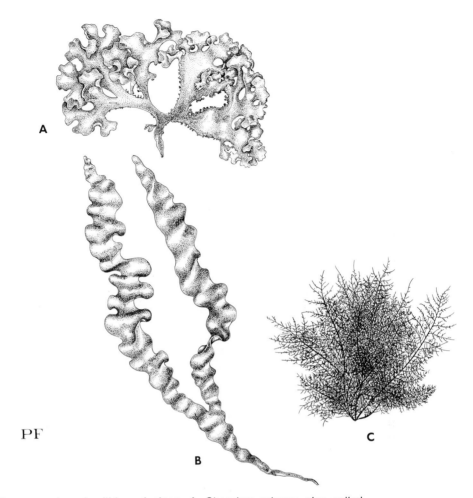

PF

Figure 9–2 Some species of edible red algae. *A, Chondrus crispus,* also called "Irish moss," a red alga found in the North Atlantic and often used in the preparation of gels used in pudding mixes and other similar products. *B, Porphyra,* a red alga of the intertidal zone. A member of the Subclass Florideophycidae, it is cultivated and harvested in Japan and used in the production of such foods as *sushi* or *nori.* There are several species. *C, Gelidium,* a red alga used in the production of *agar agar.* There also are several species of this genus that are useful to man.

reaches the size of the larger brown algae. A few species are unicellular, while most are filamentous or sheet-like in appearance. The cell wall is similar in composition to that of the green algae and consists of an inner cellulosic layer and an outer pectic layer. Complex colloidal substances in the walls and between cells, such as carrageenin and agar, are found in many species, while in others the cell walls may be impregnated with calcium carbonate, producing hard and encrusted plant forms.

The cells of red algae are typically uninucleate, although in some species cells may become multinucleate as they mature. The chloroplasts contain chlorophyll *a* and sometimes chlorophyll *d*. In addition, phycobilin pigments similar to those found in blue-green algae are present, two prominent ones being **phycoerythrin**, which

219

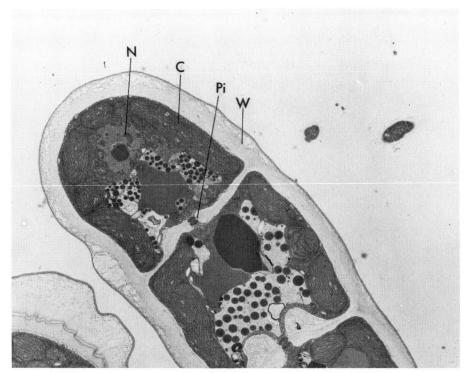

Figure 9–3 Cell of the multicellular red alga *Ptilota,* × 9180. Note the pit connections between adjacent cells (Pi), the nucleus (N), chloroplast (C), and cell wall (W) (From Scott, J. L. and Dixon, P. S. Ultrastructure of tetrasporogenesis in the Marine Red Alga *Ptilota hypnoides. J. Phycol. 9*:29–46, 1973).

is red or pink, and **phycocyanin**, which is blue. The masking effect of the phycobilins gives many Rhodophyta the characteristic red or purple coloration. Also present are carotenoid pigments. Food is stored in the form of **floridean starch**, a substance very similar to the starch found in the green algae and to glycogen, the storage product occurring in blue-green algae.

Sexually many red algae are oogamous, but there are no motile cells in any of the species. Because the reproductive structures are distinctive in Rhodophyta, special terms are used to explain the gametes, gametangia, and sporangia found in members of the division. The structure that functions much as the oogonium does in other algal groups is called the **carpogonium.** The equivalent of the antheridium in other algae is called the **spermatangium,** and the non-motile male gamete it produces is termed a **spermatium.** Gametangia may be present on one plant **(bisexuality)** or on separate male and female plants **(unisexuality).**

The one-celled carpogonium has a prolonged outgrowth called the **trichogyne.** The one-celled spermatangium contains a single spermatium. Fertilization occurs after a spermatium is released and floats to the receptive trichogyne, where it becomes attached. The nucleus of the spermatium then migrates down the trichogyne and fuses with the female nucleus in the base of the carpogonium. In most red algae the resulting 2N zygote proliferates additional 2N cells, and eventually some become 2N **carpospores.** The carpospores float freely and settle on a substrate, such as a shell of a mollusk, and develop into 2N plants that in some species are very tiny filaments, and in others are larger plants closely resembling gamete-producing individuals (gametophytes). The 2N plants are termed **tetrasporophytes** and produce **tetraspores** (meiospores) by meiosis. The tetraspores then develop into 1N gametophytes, thus completing the life cycle. A few of the simpler red algae have less specialized sex organs and may have abbreviated life cycles or no sexual stages at all; the great majority, however, exhibit alternation of generations and complex sexuality corresponding to life cycle III (Fig. 4–6).

The Life of a Red Alga

Nemalion is a marine, littoral plant composed of a mass of cylindrical, reddish-brown, jelly-like filaments that are attached by circular holdfasts to the substratum. Its name indicates the worm-like appearance of the plant body as it is seen attached to rocks during low tide. The alga produces clusters of spermatangia near the tips of short branches. Each spermatangium contains one colorless spermatium, which is released at maturity. The female reproductive structure is a cell with an enlarged basal part, the carpogonium, and a narrowed apex, the trichogyne. The nucleus of the carpogonium functions as an egg. Spermatia are carried to the trichogyne by water currents, and after they come in contact the male nucleus passes through and down the trichogyne to the egg nucleus. Fertilization results in the formation of a 2N zygote, which subsequently divides mitotically a number of times and forms cells arranged in several short filaments called **gonimoblast filaments.** These grow out from the carpogonium and produce terminal carposporangia, each containing one carpospore. When a carposporangium ruptures, a carpospore is released. A new carposporangium may form within the walls of the old one, and successive sporangia may form on the same plant.

Until quite recently, the carpospores were thought to be produced by meiosis and to grow into gametophytic *Nemalion* plants. However, it has been learned that the carpospores grow into very tiny filamentous plants, or **tetrasporophytes,** which in turn produce tetraspores (meiospores), but it remains to be proved where meiosis occurs in the formation of the tetraspores and how they develop into gametophytes. *Nemalion* is a good example of the need for on-going research into the life histories of marine plants.

Classification of the Red Algae

There are two distinct evolutionary lines in Rhodophyta that may be classified as subclasses within the division. The simplest and probably the most primitive species are members of the **Bangiophycidae,** a small group of only about one hundred species. These algae do not have distinguishable cytoplasmic connections between adjacent cells, and most have only a single chloroplast per cell. Growth takes place by cell divisions in all parts of the plant.

221

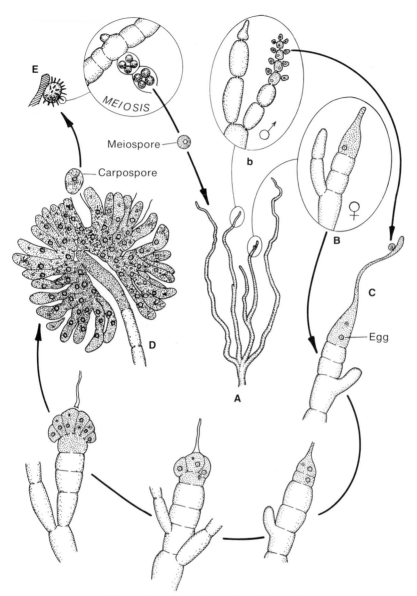

Figure 9-4 The life cycle of *Nemalion*, displayed in highly diagrammatic fashion. *A*, The gametophyte plant. *b*, The spermatangial branch of the gametophyte plant. *B*, The carpogonial branch of the gametophyte plant. *C*, Fertilization. Note the spermatium adhering to the trichogyne portion of the carpogonium (arrow). *D*, After fertilization, gonimoblast filaments are formed by mitotic divisions of the zygote; these filaments produce carpospores terminally. The carpospore grows into a minute tetrasporophyte plant (*E*), which in turn produces meiospores (tetraspores).

The reproductive organs are not well-differentiated, and in some species sexual reproduction is unknown. The unicellular red alga *Porphyridium* probably represents the most primitive kind of plant in the group, and filamentous forms such as *Goniotrichum* may be closely related to it. The culmination of this series is thought to be represented by foliose and sheet-like forms exemplified by *Bangia* and *Porphyra.* The flattish, sheet-like plant bodies of these algae

222

may be found growing attached to submerged rocks in shallow marine waters. In general, the reproduction of members of the Bangiophycidae resembles that of *Nemalion,* and carpospores may be formed that produce tiny filamentous plants. These filamentous plants produce spores that give rise, in turn, to the larger gametophyte plants.

The second major evolutionary line in Rhodophyta comprises the subclass **Florideophycidae,** with over 3900 species. In these forms there are cytoplasmic strands between adjacent cells that connect through primary pit connections. Growth occurs by division of the terminal cells, and cells typically have more than one plastid per cell. There are no unicellular forms in this series, and filamentous, foliose, and sheet-like algae are common. Multi-layered types have evolved through lateral fusion of numerous filaments. Despite the seemingly few basic differences in this series noted at the cellular level, there is wide variation in the morphological types, many having great beauty and intricate symmetry. *Nemalion* belongs in this series, as does the common marine alga *Polysiphonia.* *Polysiphonia* differs from *Nemalion* in having separate male and female gametophytes that are nearly identical in appearance, and tetrasporophytes that closely resemble the gametophytes in size and form.

The complex life cycles of many of the Florideophycidae support the conclusion that they are considerably more advanced than

Figure 9–5 *Polysiphonia.*

the Bangiophycidae. The vegetative structure is relatively simple in most forms, but the sexual cycle is often more highly specialized corresponding to life cycle III (Figure 4–6).

Ecology and Distribution

All but about 50 species of red algae are strictly marine organisms. Those few are found in moist soil or are widely distributed in freshwater springs and streams. The marine red algae are found in every ocean, including the Arctic and the Antarctic. As one passes from the polar regions into areas with warmer waters, a marked increase in species of Rhodophyta can be observed. Most are limited to zones of about 5° C. amplitude in summer temperatures, others extend to zones with 10° C. amplitude, and a few to 20° C.

There is a considerable variation in the vertical distribution of red algae. Some grow only in the intertidal zone, while others are found in the littoral region where they do not become exposed by tides. The majority of littoral marine red algae grow on rocks, but there are many that grow as epiphytes on other algae or on the few species of flowering plants that grow beneath the surface of the sea. The epiphytic forms mostly are restricted to a single host plant, usually another alga. The amount of light penetrating the water is the principal factor determining the distribution of marine red algae. Rhodophyta seldom are found below a depth of 30 meters in the North Atlantic Ocean. In Florida Bay and in tropical seas where the water is clear and the sun more directly overhead, red algae are found abundantly to a depth of 90 meters. The greatest depth at which red algae grow is about 200 meters, although less reliable reports have placed them at even greater depths.

The Rhodophyta have been successful in adapting to life in deep water where light intensities are very low, and where green, blue, and violet light prevail. This accommodation is possible because of the accessory phycobilin pigments, especially phycoerythrin. The phycobilins are very efficient absorbers of those wavelengths that penetrate most deeply beneath the surface of the water. After absorbing this light energy, the pigments contribute to the total photosynthetic activity of the cell by the transfer of energy to chlorophyll *a*. The accessory pigments make it possible for the red algae to exist in deep water regions.

Coral Reefs and Coralline Algae

Coral reefs are ridges that form in warm, shallow oceans and are created in part by the calcareous skeletons of certain animals, particularly the coelenterate coral polyps, and in part by the coralline algae. Coral polyps create a so-called "skeleton" around themselves, and as new polyps bud on the old, new skeletons are created. The coralline algae are chiefly red algae of the family Corallinaceae and certain siphonous green algae; both groups have strongly calcified plant bodies. Some groups are crustose while

224

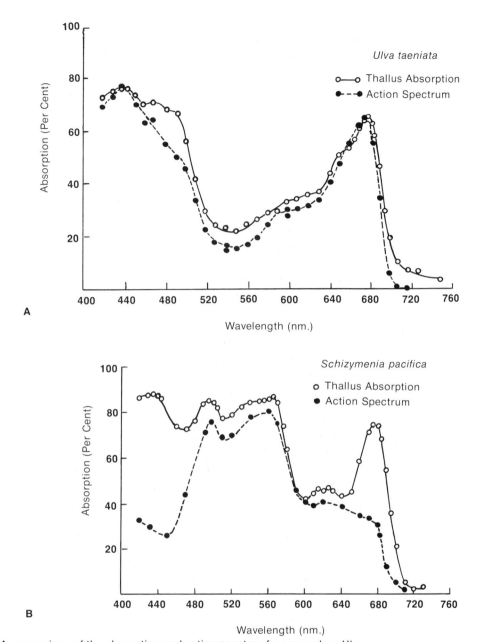

Figure 9–6 A comparison of the absorption and action spectra of a green alga, *Ulva*, and a red alga. Note the greater photosynthetic productivity of the red alga in the green range of the spectrum (520–560 nm). (From data in Haxo, F. T., and Blinks, L.R. J. Gen. Physiol. 31:414, 1950.)

others have erect, jointed thalli in which the internodes are calcified but the nodes are uncalcified. The accumulation of great masses of coral deposits, together with the accumulation of coralline algal formations, produces the coral reef. The reefs are best developed in warm, moving water, and the areas where they are best developed are the Central and Southwestern Pacific. Here the coralline algae, rather than the coral polyps, have been chiefly responsible for the upbuilding of the reef. The Great Barrier Reef of Australia is the largest formation; other reefs include the atolls of the Central Pacif-

225

ic, and in the Western Hemisphere coral reefs can be seen in the Florida Keys, the Gulf of Mexico, the Bahamas, and off the coast of Brazil. They are very interesting ecologically and are among the most beautiful natural phenomena in the world. Normally, in addition to the coralline algae a great number of other red algae are present, along with a colorful and highly varied fauna.

Evolutionary Relationships

There is a good record of fossil calcareous red algae. In some instances the remains are so well preserved that accurate identification can be made with various living forms. Some investigators believe that calcareous algae are the oldest fossils known, and they would extend the geologic history of the group from Precambrian times to the present. Coralline red algae were the most important rock builders in the Paleozoic and Mesozoic Eras, and still are today. Thus it appears conclusive that the Rhodophyta have a long and significant geological history dating at least from early Paleozoic times.

The relationships of red algae with the other algal groups is not well understood. Certainly the Rhodophyta are distinctly removed from close affinity with any other living algae, although there are some interesting similarities with the prokaryotic blue-green algae. In both groups phycobilin pigments are found, and the ultrastructural arrangement of photosynthetic lamellae is similar. Neither group has any flagellated cells. The unicellular Bangiophycidae may be related to Cyanophyceae, but there are important differences, such as the eukaryotic organization of the red algal cell. Floridean starch is very similar to the glycogen of blue-green algae. There are grounds for considering the Rhodophyta to be derived from the blue-green algae, although some phycologists consider these similarities to be the result of evolutionary convergence.

Another interesting relationship that has been proposed is that between the red algae and the sac-fungi of the class Ascomycetes. The peculiar nature of the trichogyne and its resemblance to a similar structure in the sac-fungi have caused some botanists to conclude that these two groups are related.

The origin of the red algae is lost in time, but some interesting evolutionary possibilities have been suggested, such as by symbiosis with blue-green algae (see Chapter 4). Future research may give us some of the answers to the perplexing questions raised from study of the Rhodophyta.

SUMMARY   Red algae are principally plants of warm temperate and tropical oceans, inhabiting reefs, intertidal areas, and oceanic depths to about 200 meters. Their ability to grow in such deep waters is due primarily to their phycobilin pigments, which absorb the blue, green, and violet wavelengths of light that penetrate these depths. They are economically important plants, being used as food or as thickening agents in many products. One of the most important uses is that of agar agar, a colloid produced by the red alga *Gelidium*, in bacteriological culture media.

Red algae are mostly macroscopic plants, ranging in size from one centimeter to less than a meter. Nearly all red algae exhibit an alternation of gamete-producing and meiospore-producing generations. In many species the life cycles are very complex, with sex organs unique to the Rhodophyta. None of the red algae produce motile cells; the spores and gametes are transported solely by currents of water.

Rhodophyta are ecologically important organisms. They are especially important in the formation of coral reefs. In some regions, notably in the South Pacific, coralline algae rather than coral polyps are chiefly responsible for the building up of coral reefs.

The approximately 4000 species of red algae may be classified briefly as follows:

Division Rhodophyta. There are about 400 genera comprising about 4000 species. They are eukaryotic algae with chlorophyll *a*, and sometimes chlorophyll *d*, phycobilins, and carotenoids. Floridean starch is the storage product. No motile cells are present.

SUBCLASS BANGIOPHYCIDAE. There are about 100 species.

Examples: Porphyridium, Goniotrichum, Bangia, Porphyra.

SUBCLASS FLORIDEOPHYCIDAE. There are about 3900 species.

Examples: Nemalion, Polysiphonia, Gelidium, Chondrus, Rhodymenia, and coralline forms.

DISCUSSION QUESTIONS

1. In nature where would be the best place to look for red algae?
2. What characteristics make some of the red algae valuable economically?
3. What are the properties of agar that make it useful as a bacteriological culture medium?
4. Compare the cell structure of a typical red alga with that found in the Chlorophyta.
5. How does sexual reproduction in Rhodophyta differ from that found in other algal groups?
6. What are the principal differences between the two major evolutionary series of the red algae, the Bangiophycidae and the Florideophycidae?
7. What are the differences between the general ecology and distribution of the Rhodophyta and the Phaeophyta?
8. Discuss the role of the coralline algae in the upbuilding of coral reefs.
9. The red algae share a number of similarities with the blue-green algae; list the important similarities and differences between these two groups of plants.
10. What are some of the evolutionary relationships that have been proposed for the Rhodophyta?

SUPPLEMENTAL READING

Chapman, V. J. Marine algal ecology. *Bot. Rev. 23*:320–350, 1957.

Dawson, E. Y. The Rim of the Reef. *Natural History 70*:8–16, 1961.

Dixon, P. The Rhodophyta: some aspects of their biology. *Oceanogr. Marine Biol. Ann. Rev. 1*:177–196, 1963.

Drew, K. M. Rhodophyta. *In* Smith, G. M., ed. *Manual of Phycology.* Waltham, Mass: Chronica Botanica. 1951.

Drew, K. M. Reproduction in the Bangiophycidae. *Bot. Rev. 22*:553–611, 1956.

Tseng, C. K. Agar: a valuable seaweed product. *Sci. Monthly 58*:24–32, 1944.

Red tide fish kill in Florida (Photo courtesy *Tampa Tribune*).

Chapter 10

Other Algal Groups and Summary of Algae

ECOLOGY OF PHYTOPLANKTON • RED TIDE, RED WATER • PYRROPHYTA • XANTHOPHYTA • CHRYSOPHYTA • THE DIATOMS • ECOLOGY OF DIATOMS • EUGLENOPHYTA • RELATIONSHIPS OF EUGLENIDS • EVOLUTION OF THE ALGAE • IMPORTANCE OF ALGAE • SUMMARY OF THE ALGAE

In the previous three chapters we considered the biology of the more conspicuous eukaryotic algae, and there now remains a number of additional small algal divisions of mostly unicellular forms, which generally are less conspicuous than the foregoing types. These algae belong to the divisions Pyrrophyta (**dinoflagellates** and **cryptomonads**), Xanthophyta (**yellow-green algae**), Chrysophyta (**golden-brown algae**), and Euglenophyta (**euglenids**). Most of these are components of the **phytoplankton** (the plants found in **plankton**). Plankton, in turn, is composed of all freely floating or suspended microscopic microorganisms, including **zooplankton,** the consumer organisms, and the photosynthetic **phytoplankters,** as members of the phytoplankton are called.

Ecology of Phytoplankton

Nutrients generally are adequate in aquatic habitats, although phytoplankton blooms can deplete them for a time. In particular, lack of phosphate and nitrate may be a factor limiting phytoplankton growth. Conversely, high concentrations of these minerals resulting from pollution or other sources can produce phytoplankton blooms. Depending on local conditions, other limiting factors may be the quantity of silicon, iron or manganese. Organic decomposition either of pollutants or of microorganisms tends to return the nutrient elements to the environment, and thereby to support new growth of phytoplankton.

—and all the waters that were in the river were turned to blood.
And the fish that was in the river died; and the river stank; and the Egyptians could not drink of the water of the river; and there was blood throughout the land of Egypt.

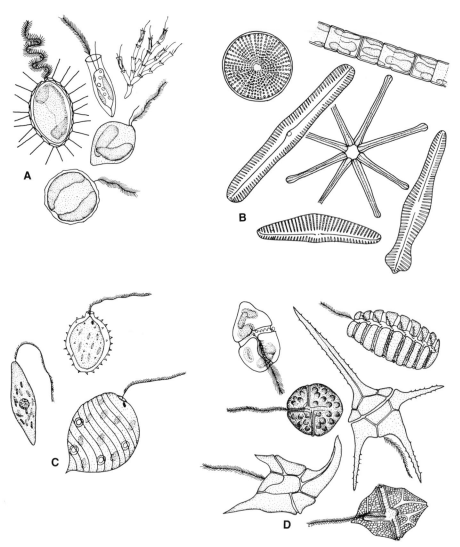

Figure 10–1 Varieties of phytoplankton (diagrammatic). *A,* Chrysophytes. *B,* Diatoms. *C,* Euglenids. *D,* Dinoflagellates. (Redrawn with some modification from Scagel, R. F., *et al. An Evolutionary Survey of The Plant Kingdom.* Belmont, Calif., Wadsworth Publishing Co., 1966.)

Upwelling of deeper water layers in lakes and oceans replenishes the supply of nutrients to upper layers by redistributing nitrogenous compounds, phosphates, and other elements. This recycling of nutrients in aquatic environments is much more rapid than in terrestrial environments; studies have shown that phosphates can be recycled up to 16 times in an aquatic habitat within a two-month period.

Of particular importance to phytoplankton are the oceanic upwellings in which cooler, nutrient-rich water is brought to the surface. Upwelling serves to replenish the nutrient supply of surface waters but is accompanied by countermovements of warmer, surface waters that carry phytoplankters downward below their optimal light intensity level (**euphotic zone**). This action tends to limit population increases and acts as a check against overpopulation. Only a relatively thin surface layer of the ocean is in the euphotic zone. Light intensity decreases as depth increases, so that at 100 meters light is reduced to about one per cent of surface intensity. Experiments have shown that phytoplankton pigments are able to absorb red light in the upper 10 meters and blue-purple light down to 50 meters. Below 50 meters phycobilins and carotenoid pigments are the principal absorbers. Light, however, is seldom so severely limiting a factor in phytoplankton productivity as are nutrient supplies.

Another factor controlling phytoplankton growth is the zooplankton, which grazes on phytoplankton. Consequently we recognize phytoplankton as the primary producers in the aquatic environment and zooplankton as the primary consumers. A number of food pyramids can be identified that are based on phytoplankton, zooplankton, small fish and **krill** (small marine animals, about 6 centimeters long, that resemble small clawless lobsters). Krill and small fish live directly on plankton and are themselves consumed by larger fish, birds, and some cetaceans (members of the whale family). Whether the food pyramid is topped by fish, birds, or mammals, the base is always phytoplankton.

Recently, the problem of mercury and DDT contamination of aquatic habitats has come to the attention of all of us. Metallic mercury is converted by bacteria into methyl mercury, a compound that enters the food chain through phytoplankton. Tuna and swordfish, as well as other animals, eat the krill, which have obtained the methyl mercury from the phytoplankton. Both of these large fish concentrate mercury in their bodies in amounts that can be dangerous to anyone eating the fish. Similar problems are now being encountered with the salmon recently introduced into the Great Lakes. DDT is a powerful insecticide, and enters the food chain in much the same way as mercury; this compound also becomes concentrated in larger animals. The concentration of DDT in fish-eating birds, such as fish hawks and pelicans, has now reached the point where it can interfere with shell formation in eggs and thus interfere seriously with reproduction. Eventually this could lead to the extinction of certain species of seabirds. Thus we see that phytoplankton populations are intimately involved in many problems relating to pollution of the aquatic environment.

Red Tide, Red Water

At times phytoplankters become so great in number that they discolor the water, making it appear reddish-brown or yellow. In some areas such algal blooms are caused by dinoflagellates, and are known as "red tide." These great blooms may reach concentrations of 500,000 to 2 million cells per liter of seawater, and occur fairly regularly in some places, causing tremendous mortality of marine life, especially among fishes, mollusks, and other animals. Red tides have occurred recently off the coasts of Florida, Massachusetts, California, Peru, Japan, and Southeast Africa. In one such catastrophe in Florida it was estimated that over one half billion fish were killed.

231

The greatest fish kills are caused by the dinoflagellates *Gymnodinium* and *Gonyaulax,* which produce a toxin that acts on the central nervous system of animals, causing death. Local ecological conditions will trigger a red tide. The danger of a red-tide outbreak is greatest when high concentrations of nutrients, especially iron, coincide with high temperatures. It is probable that there have been red tides since early geological times, and one scientist has even suggested that massive fish kills have contributed to the formation of petroleum. Petroleum is believed to be derived from organic matter, and large numbers of animals killed at the same time may have been incorporated into oil formations in the course of time.

DINOFLAGELLATES AND CRYPTOMONADS (DIVISION PYRROPHYTA)

Over 1000 species of pyrrophytes have been described, but the classification of the division is still in a state of flux. Most of the members are marine, unicellular, motile flagellates, but some are non-motile, and a few are colonial or filamentous. Both pigmented, photosynthetic forms and colorless, heterotrophic types are known. Chloroplasts are predominately golden-brown or greenish-brown, owing to the presence of a characteristic carotenoid pigment called **peridinin.** In addition, chlorophyll *a* and chlorophyll *c* are present. Food is stored in the form of starch. Many pyrrophytes have nuclei in which individual chromosomes are always visible, rather than just at metaphase as in other cells. Furthermore, the nuclear membrane remains intact dur ng cell division, leading some students of evolution to conclude that these organisms are not true eukaryotes, but have some relationships to prokaryotes.

Some pyrrophytes lack a typical cell wall, while others have cellulosic walls. Those species without a cell wall have a firm **pellicle** or sheath surrounding the protoplast. Motile forms are spoken of as "armored" or "unarmored," an armored cell having a cellulosic wall made up of articulated, sculptured plates held together in a definite pattern resembling a medieval suit of armor. The plates may be perforated with one or more pores or they may bear spines, horns, or other appendages.

The cellular structure of most pyrrophytes is related to the way in which the flagella are inserted. A long flagellum originates in a groove, called the **sulcus,** and this flagellum propels the cell. A short flagellum, lying in a groove called the **girdle,** encircles the cell and causes it to swim with a rotating motion.

The classification we have adopted recognizes two classes within the division Pyrrophyta: the **Dinophyceae** (dinoflagellates) and the **Cryptophyceae** (cryptomonads).

Dinoflagellates are among the most conspicuous of planktonic organisms. Many species exhibit **bioluminescence,** which may be defined as the emission of light from living organisms. Such species are seen as the nighttime sparkling of the bow wave of a boat or ship or the flash of a breaking wave. The light is bluish, bluish-

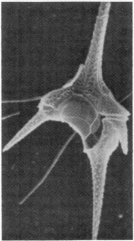

Figure 10–2 Scanning electron microscopic views of Pyrrophytes. *A, Gonyaulax. B, Ceratium.* (*A* from Anikouchine, W., and Sternberg, R. *The World Ocean: An Introduction to Oceanography.* Prentice-Hall, Inc., Englewood Cliffs, N. J., 1973; *B* from Gerking, S. *Biological Systems,* Second Edition. Philadelphia, W. B. Saunders Co., 1974).

green, green, or greenish-yellow, and results from the interactions of enzymes, ATP, and a molecule called luciferin (see also Chapter 5). Other factors also may be involved; for instance, the luminous reaction of the dinoflagellate *Gonyaulax* requires a high concentration of salt. Luminescence also occurs in the sea anemone (a marine animal), and is due to the presence of the dinoflagellates living symbiotically in the tissues of the animal.

The cryptomonads are a small group of about 100 species of biflagellated, unicellular aquatic organisms with bilaterally compressed walls. Typically, cryptomonads are photosynthetic, but heterotrophic species also occur. Their pigmentation is similar to that of dinoflagellates, and chloroplasts are characteristically yellowish-green or brown. The presence of a gullet is a distinctive feature of

233

these algae, and they are thought to have a close relationship with Protozoa.

Cryptomonads are also part of the plankton, and fluctuations in their populations are correlated with increases in nitrogenous content of the water in which they occur. Little is known of their biology, however, and further research is needed.

YELLOW-GREEN ALGAE
(DIVISION XANTHOPHYTA)

At present about 400 species are classified in the Division Xanthophyta, or **yellow-green algae.** These are found chiefly in fresh water, a few species are marine, a number grow in soil, and some live as epiphytes on trees. Their common name is based on their yellow-green color, resulting from the predominance of carotenoid pigments. The motile cells have two unequal flagella inserted apically; one flagellum is tinsellated and extends to the front, while the other is whiplash, shorter, and is trailing.

The cell walls in the Xanthophyta are composed of pectic substances and cellulose, and in some species silica also may be present. Walls often are composed of two overlapping parts that fit together, as, for example, in *Tribonema* (Fig. 10–3,A). Generally the cells are uninucleate, but multinucleate, coenocytic types also occur. Numerous disk-shaped chloroplasts are present, and contain chlorophylls *a* and *e* and carotenoid pigments. No starch is formed, but food is stored as a complex polysaccharide, **chrysolaminarin,** and in the form of oil droplets.

Reproduction is chiefly asexual, by cell division that results in the formation of various forms of motile and non-motile spores. Sexual reproduction is uncommon, although it does occur in some forms. Isogamy is seen in the genus *Tribonema,* while oogamy is found in the coenocytic, filamentous green felt alga *Vaucheria.*

GOLDEN-BROWN ALGAE AND DIATOMS
(DIVISION CHRYSOPHYTA)

Members of the division Chrysophyta appear yellow-brown or golden-brown because of the preponderance of xanthophylls, particularly fucoxanthin. Chlorophylls *a, c,* and sometimes *e* are present, but are masked by the carotenoid pigments. Food reserves are chrysolaminarin and oils. The motile cells, if present, have apically inserted tinsellated flagella, and when two are present they are unequal in length.

The Golden-brown Algae (Class Chrysophyceae)

Two distinct evolutionary lines occur in the Chrysophyta and are represented by the classes **Chrysophyceae** (golden-brown algae) and **Bacillariophyceae** (diatoms). The golden-brown algae comprise about 300 species occurring chiefly in fresh water and including

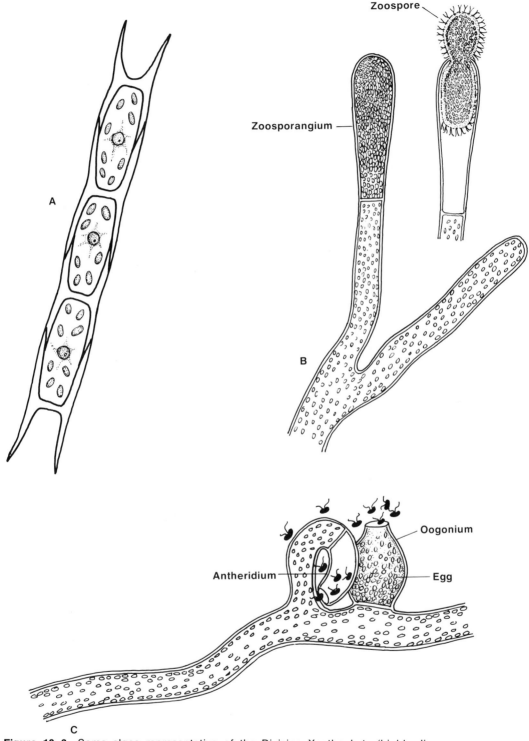

Figure 10–3 Some algae representative of the Division Xanthophyta (highly diagrammatic). *A, Tribonema. B* and *C, Vaucheria,* showing zoosporangium with escaping zoospore (*B*), and structures of antheridium and oogonium (*C*). The zoospore of Vaucheria is a compound structure with many pairs of flagella, each pair associated with one subsurface nucleus. (Redrawn from Smith, G. M. *Cryptogamic Botany,* Second Edition, Vol. I, New York, McGraw-Hill Book Co. Inc., 1955).

235

Figure 10-4 Coccoliths as viewed with the scanning electron microscope viewing chalk. *A,* × 10,000. *B,* × 6000. The chalk cliffs of Dover, England, are made of the same material (Photos courtesy of Dr. Stanley Frost).

many unicellular species. The cell wall may contain silica, and in the forms called **coccolithophores** calcified plates and disks are embedded in the wall. Coccolithophores first were described as carbonate disks, or coccoliths, from the Cretaceous Period and were thought by geologists to be of inorganic origin; later, however, they were collected from seabottom ooze and their true algal nature was determined. They are a major component of chalk deposits.

Most of the Chrysophyceae are motile, and range from amoeboid types to flagellated unicells, colonies, and non-motile filaments. Sexual reproduction is rare and when it does occur it is usually of the isogamous type. The golden-brown algae reproduce chiefly by asexual zoospores or non-motile spores. Except as components of the phytoplankton, and presence in chalk deposits, this group has little economic importance. This is not true, however, for the next group of chrysophytes, the diatoms.

The Diatoms (Class Bacillariophyceae)

Many biologists regard the **diatoms** as the most beautiful of organisms, and they have been called the "jewels of the plant world." With few exceptions diatoms are unicellular organisms. They are found in marine, freshwater, and soil habitats throughout the world. Over 5000 species have been named, and they often occur in vast numbers. One estimate gave 35 million diatoms per cubic meter of river water for certain locations in the United States.

236

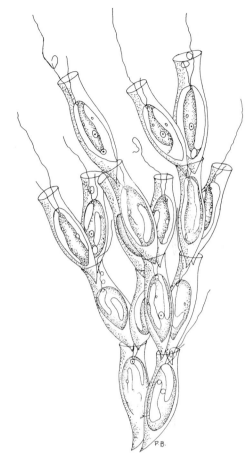

Figure 10–5 *Dinobryon,* a golden-brown alga of the Class Chrysophyceae. The cells secrete a bell-shaped envelope (or **lorica**), and adhere in colonies (From Dittmer, H. J. *Modern Plant Biology.* New York, Van Nostrand, Reinhold Co., 1972).

The diatoms are divided into two major groups, the **Centrales** and the **Pennales,** on the basis of their symmetry. The Centrales are diatoms with radial symmetry, and on surface view have a circular, triangular, or ellipsoidal form. The Pennales show bilateral symmetry and are typically rod-shaped, crescent-shaped, or wedge-shaped. Representatives of both groups are found in both fresh and marine waters, and may be studied wherever there is a naturally occurring body of water.

The diatom cell wall is called a **frustule,** and is composed of two parts that fit together much like a pill-box and its lid. The upper half, or **valve,** is called the **epitheca,** and slightly overlaps the lower valve, the **hypotheca.** The valves are composed principally of glass-like silica and are usually highly ornamented with a series of minute perforations and striations. The electron microscope shows these to be very complex and sieve-like. Motile diatoms have a fine groove, called the **raphe,** running along the frustule. At the center of the raphe is a spherical thickening, the **central nodule,** and at the end of the groove are smaller thickenings called **polar nodules.** The raphe and nodules are involved in diatom motility.

237

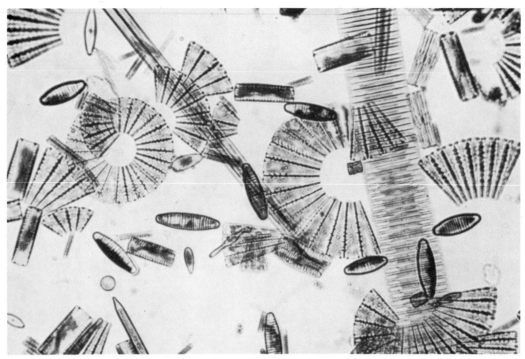

Figure 10–6 Some representative diatoms on a diatom slide (Photo from Turtox/ Cambosco, Chicago, Illinois).

Some diatoms of the order Pennales exhibit an unusual kind of motility. They have no flagella yet can be seen to glide along with a kind of halting movement. The cause of this kind of movement is not clear; it has been hypothesized that cytoplasmic streaming within the cell, along the region of the raphe, causes friction with the external environment and, hence, movement of the cell. A recent explanation is that motile diatoms secrete an adhesive from the raphe and that this swells and pushes the diatom (Fig. 10–9). It is possible that both explanations are correct.

The diatom protoplast has a single nucleus, usually in the periphery of the cytoplasm. Chloroplasts may be band-shaped, star-shaped, or may occur as numerous small, disk-shaped bodies. They vary in color from brown to olive-green or yellow. Among the more conspicuous cellular features of diatoms are numerous oil droplets, a form of stored food. Food also is stored as the complex carbohydrate chrysolaminarin.

Diatoms multiply by cell division; each daughter cell has one of its valves derived from the parent cell, but the other valve of the new frustule is produced by the daughter cell. The hypotheca of a mother cell becomes the epitheca of a daughter cell, and the new valve is always a hypotheca. This results in one of the two daughter cells remaining the same size as the parent diatom while the other daughter becomes slightly smaller. Eventually, repeated cell divisions may result in a progressive decrease in size of as much as 50 per cent. When a critical limit of diminution is reached, the diatom compensates by undergoing sexual reproduction.

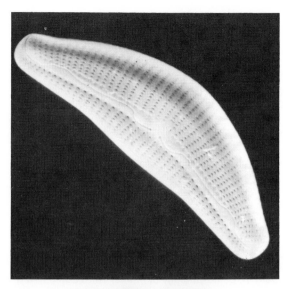

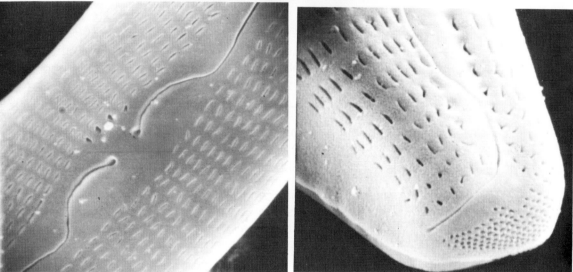

Figure 10–7 Scanning electron micrographs of a pennate diatom. Note the raphe and elaborate series of wall perforations (From Hufford, T. L., and Collins, G. B. Some Morphological Variations in the Diatom *Cymbella cistula. J. Phycol. 8*:192–195, 1972).

Most pennate diatoms exhibit a kind of anisogamy, with one amoeboid gamete moving through a mucilaginous matrix or tube to a non-motile gamete from another cell. The vegetative diatom cell is always $2N$, so meiosis occurs just before gametes are produced (life cycle II; see Figure 4–6). The zygote is a naked protoplast, termed an **auxospore,** which expands considerably and secretes a new frustule, thus forming a new vegetative cell of normal dimensions. In certain species it appears that sexual reproduction is a seasonal occurrence, reaching a peak in early summer but rare during the remainder of the year. Still another factor affecting reproduction in diatoms is the availability of silicon dioxide, which is an absolute

239

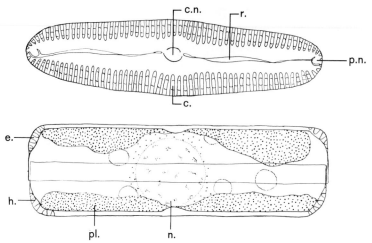

Figure 10–8 Frustule structure of a pennate diatom. c.n., central nodule; r., raphe; e., epitheca; h., hypotheca; pl., plastid; n., nucleus; p.n., polar nodule; c., costae. (From Bold, H. C. *Morphology of Plants,* Third Edition, New York, Harper & Row, 1973).

requirement for cell division since the formation of new cell walls requires silicon; the number of new diatom cells produced is proportional to the availability of silicon dioxide.

Ecology of Diatoms.   In most of the large bodies of water in temperate latitudes the abundance of diatoms and other phytoplankton follows a more or less constant cycle. Rapid increases and decreases in diatoms produce pulses of population numbers. Diatom numbers increase rapidly in the spring, decrease in the summer, and then increase again in the autumn in response to changes in environmental conditions. As the waters warm in the spring, the concentration of nutrients such as phosphates and nitrates in the upper layers are higher than at any other time of the year. When the available sunlight rises to an appropriate level there is a sudden,

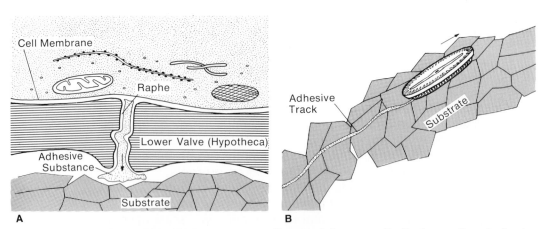

Figure 10–9 Diatom movement, illustrated diagrammatically. *A,* secretion of adhesive through the raphe. *B,* movement of a diatom leaving a track of adhesive material. (Drum, R. W., and Hopkins, J. T. Diatom Locomotion: an Explanation. *Protoplasma* *62*:1–33, 1966).

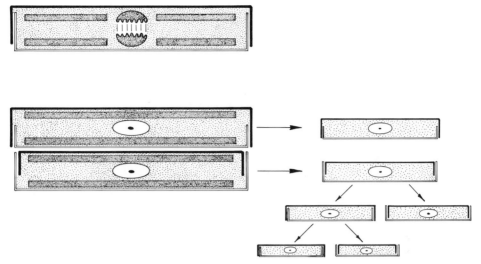

Figure 10–10 Cell division of a diatom. The inheritance of valves and the subsequent diminution of certain progeny cells are illustrated in this highly diagrammatic rendering.

tremendous increase of diatom growth. The complex of proper temperature, sufficient light, and availability of nutrients makes possible the rapid multiplication of cells. The principal growth-limiting factor is nutrient depletion, which by late spring is sufficiently advanced that diatom populations begin to decrease. The occurrence of an autumn pulse in diatom numbers is not so general as that of the spring increase. The autumn outburst begins with an increased concentration of available nutrients and ends with a decline as winter approaches.

Diatoms are among the primary producers in aquatic environments. They are excellent indicators of water pollution, and can be used as markers for particular kinds of ecological stress. The relative numbers and kinds of diatoms present in water are used to measure amounts of nitrogenous substances, mercury, DDT, and thermal pollution that may be present.

The tremendous productivity of diatoms can be seen in the large deposits of diatomaceous earth. Empty frustules of diatoms accumulated on sea bottoms for millions of years. When geological events resulted in the elevation of these deposits above sea level, they formed vast concentrations of diatomaceous earth. The most famous area is in Lompoc, California, where the strata are up to 300 meters thick and where the estimated concentration may exceed 6 million frustules per cubic millimeter. The light, soft, and crumbling material is used in a variety of ways, especially in filtration systems. It is also used in sugar refining, as an abrasive in toothpaste, and in silver polish. Interestingly, it is also used in the manufacture of reflective paint for highway pavements and in signs, to improve their visibility.

Since diatoms make excellent fossils because of their silicified walls, they are found abundantly in the geological record. The best

241

Figure 10–11 Deposits of diatomaceous earth at a quarry site near Lompoc, California (Photo Courtesy of the Johns-Manville Corporation).

fossils come from Cretaceous deposits, and these resemble closely modern species. This argues both for their antiquity and for the success of their adaptations to life.

The Euglenids (Division Euglenophyta)

In the Old Testament we read that one of the plagues of ancient Egypt was the turning of the waters to blood. Judging from scriptural descriptions of this catastrophe, it is thought that the red waters may have been due to a sudden bloom of a red-colored, unicellular organism, *Euglena sanguinea.* This **euglenid** commonly occurs in polluted waters, especially around watering troughs, springs, and streams where cattle are kept. The species is red because of the masking effect of a red pigment; however, most euglenids are green, and a few are colorless.

The euglenids are all unicellular, flagellated forms that are commonly present in fresh water but are found also in soil, brackish streams, and salt water. About 800 species have been described and are generally considered to be among the most primitive forms

Figure 10–12 Scanning electron micrographs of fossil diatoms (Photos courtesy of Dr. Stanley Frost).

in the plant kingdom. The cell is without a rigid wall, such as that found in other algae; instead, the protoplast is bounded by a grooved layer referred to as the **pellicle.** The pellicle is unlike a plant cell wall for it incorporates the plasma membrane which is outside a system of spirally-arranged rigid and proteinaceous pellicle strips.

Most euglenids have chloroplasts containing chlorophylls a and b, and carotenoids. Food is stored in the form of **paramylum,** a carbohydrate similar to starch, and oil droplets also may be present. Near the anterior end of the cell there is usually a gullet with a tube-like part and a larger posterior portion called the reservoir. A long, tinsellated flagellum projects out of the gullet from the base of the reservoir, and a shorter one lies within the gullet and is not seen by ordinary microscopy. A reddish, light-sensitive eyespot may be

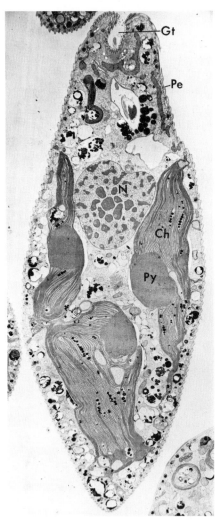

Figure 10-13 The structure of *Euglena.* Ch, Chloroplast; Pe, pellicle; Py, pyrenoid; N, nucleus; Gt, gullet (From Walne, P. L. and Arnott, H. J. 1967. The Comparative Ultrastructure and Possible Function of Eyespots: *Euglena granulata* and *Chlamydomonas eugametos. Planta* 77:325–354).

present near the base of the flagellum. The single nucleus is usually centrally located and its structure is similar to that of other eukaryotic algae.

Reproduction in the Euglenophyta is asexual only, and occurs by longitudinal division of the cell. If environmental conditions are unfavorable for growth, the cell may form a cyst as a resistant stage. Germination of the cyst produces a single motile cell. As we have noted, euglenids may experience population explosions or blooms when conditions are optimal.

Relationships Among the Euglenids. Whether the euglenids are to be considered as more plant-like or more animal-like is open to question. Many new classifications place them in a separate kingdom, the **Protista,** along with other forms of life that are not clearly plant or animal. Older classifications view the euglenids as more animal-like because of the presence of a gullet, and because some species are colorless and heterotrophic. Experiments with *Euglena gracilis* have demonstrated that photosynthetic forms can be converted into colorless, heterotrophic forms by treatment with the antibiotic streptomycin, ultraviolet light, or by using high temperatures. Apart from the absence of chlorophyll, these colorless forms are identical to the photosynthetic euglenids. So there may be a close relationship between the flagellated protozoans and the euglenids.

The similarity of pigments between the Chlorophyta and Euglenophyta may be another example of convergent evolution, rather than an indication that the two groups are closely related. Differences in reserve food, cell wall structure, and flagellar structure suggest that they are not closely related. Although colorless euglenids may have evolved from pigmented ones, primitive, heterotrophic flagellates may have been the ancestors of photosynthetic types. At the present time we can only conjecture as to which condition is primitive and which is derivative in the Euglenophyta.

Evolution of the Algae

There are some bases for considering the red algae and the blue-green algae as having a common origin. The complexity of reproduction in the red algae suggests, however, that the two groups have been divergent for a very long time. There also are similarities between the Phaeophyta, Chrysophyta, and Xanthophyta that may indicate a common origin for these groups. The relationships between the Chlorophyta and Euglenophyta are less clear, as we have seen.

Algae that are colorless are sometimes referred to as **leucophytes.** Most are unicellular organisms, usually motile, and show close relationships with certain algal groups. Except for the absence of chlorophyll, they are identical to pigmented forms. The existence of leucophytes gives us a clue to the origin of protozoa. If an organism loses its photosynthetic ability, it becomes a functional heterotroph or else it does not continue to live. Some unicellular algae are able to live without photosynthesizing by absorbing nu-

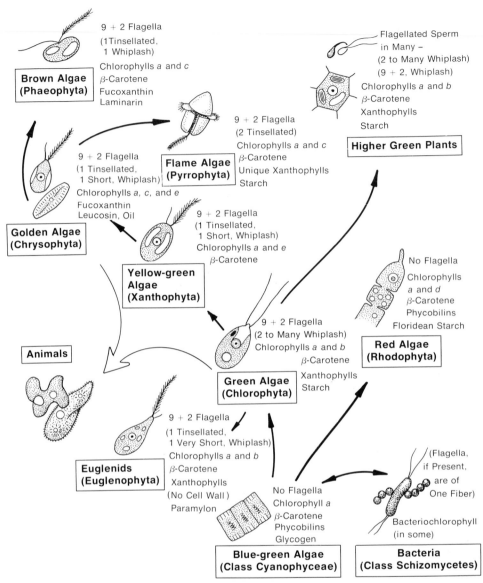

Figure 10–14 Hypothetical relationships of the divisions of algae.

trients through their cell membranes, and some can even engulf microorganisms (**phagocytosis**). Leucophytes have some cellular features that are present in ancestral forms, including pyrenoids, eyespots, and plastids. These are non-functional in heterotrophic organisms, and are not retained after a heterotrophic existence has been established.

The Pyrrophyta include a number of types that appear to bridge the gap between primitive plant and animal life. Dinoflagellates have a combination of characteristics that serve to identify members of this group. By noting such features as their unique chromosomes and distinctive flagella, it has been possible to assign a dinoflagellate ancestry to a number of protozoans. The evolution of many protozoans from algal ancestors seems to be borne out when comparisons of this kind are made.

Table 10-1 MAJOR FEATURES OF THE EUKARYOTIC ALGAE

DIVISION	CELL WALL	PIGMENTS	FLAGELLAR NUMBER AND INSERTION	CHIEF FOOD RESERVE	GENERAL ECOLOGY
Green algae (Chlorophyta)	Cellulose, pectin	Chlorophylls a and b; carotenoids	Two to many; whiplash, equal, apical	Starch	Chiefly freshwater; relatively few marine
Brown algae (Phaeophyta)	Cellulose, pectin, algin, fucoidin	Chlorophylls a and c; carotenoids, fucoxanthin	Two, lateral forward tinsellated and trailing whiplash (in reproductive cells only),	Laminarin	Chiefly marine, mostly in temperate or boreal climates
Red algae (Rhodophyta)	Cellulose, pectin, carrageenin, agar	Chlorophylls a and d; carotenoids, phyco-bilins	None	Floridean starch	Chiefly marine, mostly tropical or subtropical
Golden-brown algae (Chrysophyta)	Cellulose, pectin, often with silicon	Chlorophylls a, c, and e; carotenoids, fuco-xanthin	Various; one or two; one tinsellated, one whiplash; equal or unequal, apical	Chrysolaminarin (leucosin)	Chiefly marine, many planktonic forms
Yellow-green algae (Xanthophyta)	Cellulose, pectin	Chlorophylls a and c; carotenoids	Two, apical, unequal; long; tin-sellated; short, whiplash	Chrysolaminarin (leucosin)	Chiefly freshwater and soil, relatively few marine
Euglenids (Euglenophyta)	Absent	Chlorophylls a and b; carotenoids	One, two, or three, tinsel-lated (single row of bristles); apical or subapical	Paramylum	Chiefly freshwater, soil, relatively few marine
Dinoflagellates and cryptomonads (Pyrrophyta)	Cellulose, pectin	Chlorophylls a and c; carotenoids	Two tinsellated; one trailing, one girdling	Starch	Chiefly marine, plankton; includes luminescent forms

247

Importance of Algae

The uses of algae directly as food sources has been discussed, and their value for other uses, as in medicine, industry, and research, has also been described. By far the most important function of algae, however, is primary photosynthetic productivity, both in freshwater and saltwater environments.

SUMMARY OF THE ALGAE

In older classifications all algae were classified together with fungi and bacteria in the subkingdom Thallophyta. Research has shown, however, that the "algae" are an extremely diverse group of organisms, often having only very distant relationships with one another. Differences in cell wall structure, pigmentation, motility, reserve foods, and other features indicate that the divisions of algae are not closely related, hence the formal category Algae has been abandoned. However, for general discussion the term is useful, despite its artificiality and limitations.

Algae are typically photosynthetic; this differentiates them from all fungi and most bacteria. A few algae may be heterotrophic (e.g., the leucophytes) but it appears obvious that they are related to photosynthetic forms.

Algal groups are distinguished from each other on the basis of a number of characteristics such as (1) nature of cell wall, (2) pigments, (3) flagella, and (4) nature of food reserve. Algae are separated from the higher, green plants by (1) the unicellular nature of their sexual organs, (2) the absence of complex conductive tissues, and (3) their simple form of organization and general lack of highly specialized cells and tissues. However the green algae, more than any other algal group, closely resemble higher green plants in their cell wall structure, pigments, flagellar structure, and the presence of starch.

A classification of the groups of algae covered in this chapter follows.

Division Pyrrophyta: The *dinoflagellates* and *cryptomonads.* This division consists chiefly of unicellular algae with conspicuous chromosomes and girdling, trailing flagella. There are about 1000 species.

Examples: Gymnodinium and *Gonyaulax.*

Division Xanthophyta: The *yellow-green* algae. This division comprises about 400 species.

Examples: Vaucheria and Tribonema.

Division Chrysophyta: The *golden-brown algae* and the *diatoms.*

CLASS CHRYSOPHYCEAE: The *golden brown algae.* This class comprises about 300 species.

Example: Dinobryon.

CLASS BACILLARIOPHYCEAE: The *diatoms.* There are about 5000 species of diatoms.

Orders: Centrales (the centric diatoms), and Pennales (the pennate diatoms).

Division Euglenophyta: The *euglenids.* About 450 species are known.

Example: Euglena is a well-known example.

DISCUSSION QUESTIONS

1. If one wished to study members of the Division Xanthophyta, where would one be able to collect specimens in nature?
2. Describe in some detail the sexual and asexual reproductive cycles in the alga *Vaucheria*.
3. What are the characteristics that separate Xanthophyta from Chrysophyta?
4. Describe the two principal evolutionary lines of relationship in the Division Chrysophyta.
5. How does the structure of the cell of a diatom differ from that of most other algae?
6. Explain how diatoms reproduce and describe the role of auxospore formation in the life cycle of these algae.
7. Explain the importance of diatoms in aquatic ecosystems.
8. Why is *Euglena* classified sometimes as a plant and sometimes as an animal?
9. What appears to be the phylogenetic relationships of the euglenids?
10. Describe the typical cell structure and appearance of a dinoflagellate.
11. What causes a "red tide," and what does this phrase describe?
12. In discussing the ecology of phytoplankters, what is the significance of "upwelling"?
13. Discuss the role that leucophytes may have played in the evolution of some Protozoa.
14. Discuss the importance of algae in world ecosystems. Compare productivity of marine phytoplankters with that of agricultural plants, such as grains.

SUPPLEMENTAL READING

Blume, J. L. The Ecology of River Algae. *Botanical Review 22*:291–341, 1956.

Doyle, W. T. *Nonvascular Plants, Form and Function.* Belmont, California: Wadsworth Publishing Co., 1965.

Fogg, G. E. *Algal Cultures and Phytoplankton Ecology.* Madison: University of Wisconsin Press, 1965.

Fritsch, F. E. Chrysophyta. *In* Smith, G. M., ed. *Manual of Phycology,* Waltham, Mass.: Chronica Botanica, 1951.

Lewin, J. E. and R. L. Guillard. Diatoms. *Ann. Rev. Microbiol. 17*:373–414, 1963.

Patrick, R. L. Sexual reproduction in diatoms. *In, Sex in Microorganisms.* Washington, D.C.: American Association for the Advancement of Science, pp. 82–99, 1954.

Round, F. E., *The Biology of the Algae.* London: Edwin Arnold Ltd., 1965.

Alice in Wonderland and the caterpillar.

Chapter 11

The Fungi

KINDS OF FUNGI • THE SLIME MOLDS • THE TRUE FUNGI • CHYTRIDIO-
MYCETES • OOMYCETES • ZYGOMYCETES • ASCOMYCETES • NEU-
ROSPORA AND GENETICS • YEASTS, BREWING, AND BAKING • OTHER
USEFUL ASCOMYCETES • IMPERFECT FUNGI • LICHENS • BASIDIOMY-
CETES • HALLUCINOGENS • MYCORRHIZAE • EVOLUTION AMONG THE
FUNGI • SUMMARY

The fungi are a highly diversified group of eukaryotes that differ widely among themselves both in structural characteristics and in reproduction. Several general features, however, are shared by all, including a heterotrophic mode of nutrition, cells which are enclosed in cell walls at least at some stage in the life cycle, and the production of some type of spore, usually in large numbers.

Human existence always has been linked with fungi in a variety of ways. Fungi brought on the great potato famine that devastated Ireland in 1845 and 1846. Each year fungi cause the loss of fortunes by blights, rusts, and mildews of cereals, fruits, and vegetables. Often our prized possessions are made useless by the rotting and molding caused by fungi, which are capable of attacking and destroying nearly every organic substance known to man. They erode the cement in camera and microscope lenses, dissolve paints, attack wooden structures, rot fabrics, feed on leather and rubber, and ruin our foods. These negative aspects of fungi tend to obscure the many benefits we derive from fungi, including foods, beverages, and drugs. But most important of all is their role in nature's cycles. In an undisturbed forest the floor is carpeted with dead leaves, fallen branches, and other debris, and hummocked with the broken and uprooted trunks of dead trees. They lie in all stages of decomposition, covered by a blanket of mosses, ferns, fungal fructifications, and young plants. If one were to stumble into an old log, it would probably crumble into bits, for it may be completely riddled by the fungi and other organisms that convert its wood into humic substances and carbon dioxide. Without fungi, other forms of life would have been smothered out of existence by their own wastes

"One side will make you grow taller, and the other side will make you grow shorter."
"One side of what? The other side of what?" thought Alice to herself.
"Of the mushroom," said the Caterpillar, just as if she had asked it aloud; and in another moment it was out of sight.

LEWIS CARROLL: *Alice in Wonderland*

long ago, and the atmospheric carbon dioxide, so necessary for photosynthesis, would have been vastly depleted.

KINDS OF FUNGI

There are two groups of eukaryotic fungi, the **slime fungi** (**Myxomycota**) and the **true fungi** (**Eumycota**). The latter are the more complex in terms of numbers and kinds of organisms. The Myxomycota include two general types of fungi that differ markedly in structure and reproduction from each other, the **cellular slime fungi** and **plasmodial slime fungi**. The cellular slime fungi appear to be protozoan in nature; they retain an amoeba-like form through most of the life stages and have no flagellated cells in any stage. Spores are produced, not as a consequence of cytoplasmic divisions as in other fungi, but by the formation of walls about individual amoeboid cells. This group will not be considered further.

Plasmodial Slime Fungi (Class Myxomycetes)

The plasmodial slime fungi, or Myxomycetes, form non-cellular, multinucleate masses of naked protoplasm during the vegetative stage of their life cycle. This stage, the **plasmodium,** often is found among decaying leaves and wood in moist forests but sometimes occurs in more open areas. The plasmodium creeps along very slowly by a flowing movement of its cytoplasm and feeds on small organic particles and microorganisms in its path. Plasmodial movements are accompanied by a noticeable rhythmic and reversible "streaming" of the cytoplasm. The growth of the plasmodium occurs by the synthesis of additional protoplasm, accompanied by mitotic divisions of the nuclei.

Because the plasmodia of slime fungi consist of relatively large masses of cytoplasm, they have been used in scientific studies to determine some of the properties of living cytoplasmic material, including its consistency and streaming ability.

About 450 species of Myxomycetes are known, and may be distinguished partly by the size, color, and texture of the plasmodium as well as by the kinds of sporangia and spores that are produced. Species of plasmodia vary in size from microscopic to several centimeters in diameter, and may be white, or gray or shades of yellow, red, and violet, or black.

Environmental changes induce sporulation in slime fungi. The plasmodia may move along stems of plants, fence posts, and buildings where they form **fructifications** (sporangia, groups of sporangia, or spore masses). Fructifications vary, according to species, from little more than rounded heaps of spores to intricately formed sporangia. Meiosis is thought to occur during formation of the spores; therefore, the spores are meiospores. Cellulose and **chitin,** a nitrogen-containing carbohydrate, make up the cell walls formed during sporulation and the nature of spore formation and construction are important in relating the slime fungi to other fungal

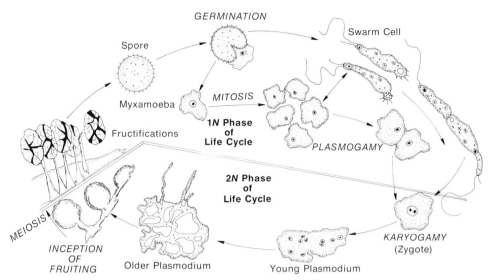

GERMINATION

Spore

Swarm Cell

Myxamoeba

MITOSIS

Fructifications

1N Phase of Life Cycle

PLASMOGAMY

2N Phase of Life Cycle

MEIOSIS

INCEPTION OF FRUITING

Older Plasmodium

Young Plasmodium

KARYOGAMY (Zygote)

Figure 11–1 Life history of a plasmodial slime mold. *A*, Multinucleate plasmodium. *B*, Sporangium. *C*, Swarm cells. *D*, Gametes. *E*, Zygote (Redrawn from Alexopoulos, C. J. *Introductory Mycology*. Second Edition. New York, John Wiley and Sons, Inc., 1966).

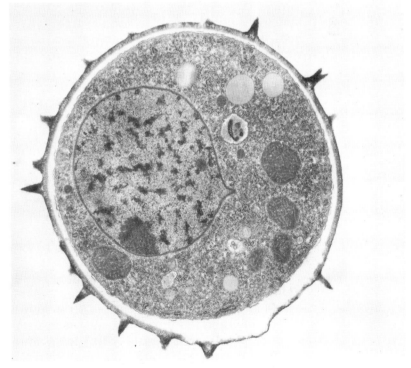

Figure 11–2 Electron micrograph of a spore of the slime mold *Stemonitis herbatica*, × 20.000 (Photo courtesy of Dr. Charles W. Mims).

groups. Walled meiospores are characteristic of both fungi and higher green plants.

When spores germinate, they produce amoeboid cells or flagellated swarm cells. The two forms are interconvertible; amoeboid cells are capable of developing flagella, and swarm cells may lose theirs and become amoeboid. After a number of mitotic divisions such cells may function as gametes, combining in pairs to form zygotes. Only the nucleus of the zygote divides further, and the result is a new plasmodium that grows as it ingests food and eventually repeats the reproductive processes described above.

One of the factors affecting sporulation in slime molds is light. For example, if a slime mold plasmodium is placed in darkness it will not produce sporangia. However, if after 18 hours of darkness it is exposed to light for five hours, sporangia will be formed. Sporangia also are formed by plasmodia kept in darkness, providing they are fed on quick-frozen plasmodia exposed to light immediately prior to being killed. This experiment indicates that a sporangium-inducing substance is produced in response to illumination. It has also been shown that slime molds will form sporangia under white, violet, or ultraviolet light, but not under green light. Nutrition also plays a part in sporulation, since plasmodia will not form sporangia on a culture medium upon which the plasmodium grows well unless the vitamin niacin is added to the culture.

Contrary to opinions held some years ago, dryness does not seem to be necessary for sporulation, since sporangia may be formed in wet cultures. Drying of the plasmodium usually results in transformation of the plasmodium into a hardened mass, or **sclerotium,** which is capable of reverting to a plasmodium under more favorable conditions of food and moisture.

THE TRUE FUNGI (DIVISION EUMYCOTA)

The **true fungi**, or **Eumycota,** have a basic filamentous organization called a **mycelium.** With but few exceptions the mycelium is composed of individual strands, the **hyphae.** These strands are often septate, that is, divided by cross walls, but, in the **algal fungi,** or **Phycomycetes,** they are non-septate and tubular. The composition of the walls of hyphae differs among the fungi. Chitin is a major wall component in most forms. Cellulose also is present in some fungal walls, and other substances such as lignin and the carbohydrate callose, are sometimes present.

The Eumycota are usually separated into five classes: the **Chytridiomycetes,** the **Oomycetes,** the **Zygomycetes,** the **Ascomycetes,** and the **Basidiomycetes.** The organization and structure of the mycelium in the first three classes are similar in that the hyphae are tubular and non-septate. This results in a **coenocytic** condition, in which the cytoplasm is continuous within the hyphal walls and is multinucleate. The Ascomycetes and Basidiomycetes, however, are not similarly coenocytic but have septate hyphae.

Two additional **form classes** have been established in the Eumycota, the **imperfect fungi** (or **Deuteromycetes**) and the **lichens** (or **Lichenes**). Form classes have been established for purposes of convenience and are artificial taxonomic groupings of plants that are incompletely known or, in the case of lichens, are symbiotic associations of two different organisms. Incompletely known plant fossils also are treated taxonomically in this way.

The first three classes of Eumycota in the past have been lumped together in one class, the Phycomycetes, a name that translated literally means algal fungi. Many of the 1100 species in the group resemble some of the simpler filamentous algae in such respects as cytoplasmic organization, structure of sex organs, spores, and gametes, as well as an aquatic mode of life. However, these similarities to the algae and to each other are probably due more to convergent evolution than to close evolutionary relationship, and for this reason they are now separated into three classes.

Class Chytridiomycetes

The members of the class Chytridiomycetes all have flagellated mitospores and gametes, and include unicellular forms that exhibit protozoan characteristics as well as hyphal forms having a true alternation of generations (life cycle III; see Figure 4–6). The latter are exemplified by beautiful microscopic fungi of the genus *Allomyces,* first discovered in India and since isolated from soils in various parts of the world.

Allomyces is readily grown in aqueous culture on boiled hempseed. Within a few days after the cultures are inoculated with the dried **resistant sporangia** from previous cultures, hempseeds will be covered with a downy growth of new hyphal filaments. The hyphae, which are coenocytic and branching, next develop male and female gametangia. The male gametangia are orange in color and are superimposed on the female gametangia. The flagellated male gametes are attracted by a substance, appropriately termed **sirenin,** which is released by the larger, flagellated female gametes (anisogamy). The resulting zygotes soon develop into branching, coenocytic plants closely resembling those that produced gametes. However, mitosporangia rather than gametangia are formed on these plants. For a time motile mitospores (zoospores) are produced, which give rise to more sporophyte plants. But as the culture ages, the later-formed sporangia develop thick, brownish walls. These are the resistant sporangia and they, upon drying and later inoculation into hempseed cultures, undergo meiosis and form flagellated meiospores, which again produce the gametophyte generation of plants.

Class Oomycetes

The Oomycetes include aquatic and terrestrial fungi having oogamous sexual reproduction and flagellated mitospores and meiospores. Some of these fungi, the **water molds,** are saprobes and parasites of fish, insect larvae, seeds, and also attack plant and animal debris; others are pathogenic to terrestrial plants. A typical water mold, the fish mold *Saprolegnia,* is often seen as an infection with cottony mycelia forming over the fins and eventually the entire

255

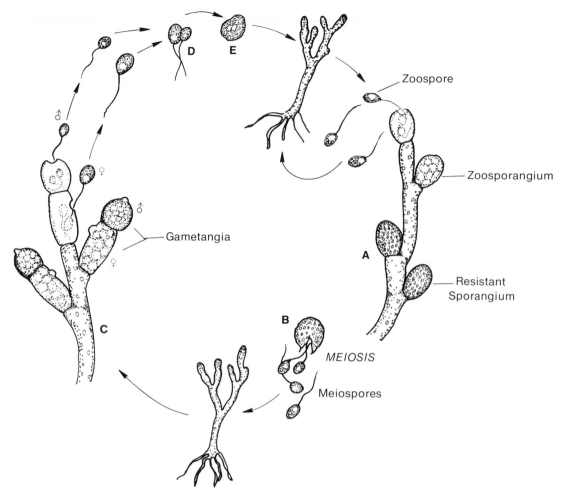

Figure 11–3 Life history of *Allomyces. A,* Sporophyte plants with mitosporangia and meiosporangia (resistant sporangia). *B,* meiosporangium producing meiospores. *C,* Gametophyte plant. *D,* Syngamy. *E,* Zygote (Modified from Emerson, R. An Experimental Study of the Life Cycles and Toxonomy of *Allomyces. Lloydia 4*:77–144, 1941).

bodies of aquarium fish. If the infection is treated early enough, by washing the infected fish in a solution of 66 milligrams of malachite green in one liter of water for ten to 30 minutes, the fish is usually saved. Since some aquarium fish are quite expensive, this treatment may be worthwhile. Most often fish mold prevails in crowded aquaria, such as those at ten-cent stores, and it often kills a number of fish before it is brought under control.

Saprolegnia produces biflagellate mitospores in elongate mitosporangia. These propagate the vegetative, infectious phase of the fungus. The sexual phase, though oogamous, is not characterized by motile gametes; rather, antheridia are formed that penetrate the oogonium wall and discharge male nuclei into egg cells. The zygotes have resistant walls and remain dormant for a time, and

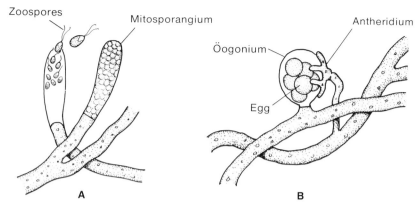

Figure 11–4 *Saprolegnia* (diagrammatic). *A,* Vegetative mycelium with a mitosporangium. *B,* Sexual reproduction (Redrawn from Smith, G. B. *Cryptogamic Botany,* Volume 1. Second Edition, New York, McGraw-Hill Book Co., Inc., 1955).

then they form flagellated meiospores and thus re-establish the vegetative phase.

Among the relatives of *Saprolegnia* and other aquatic Oomycetes are a group of terrestrial pathogens that cause such diseases of flowering plants as damping off of seedlings *(Pythium)*; downy mildew of grape *(Plasmopara)*; and the late blight of potatoes, caused by the fungus *Phytophthora infestans,* which brought about the great potato famine in Ireland in the nineteenth century.

Class Zygomycetes

Members of the Class Zygomycetes are completely lacking in flagellated cells. Included in this class are the black bread mold, *Rhizopus nigricans* (which reproduces vegetatively by means of great quantities of black mitospores) and similar fungi. *Rhizopus* and other Zygomycetes are characterized by a type of sexual reproduction known as **conjugation,** in which specialized hyphae, produced by spores of opposite mating types, fuse together. The resulting zygote develops a thick wall and becomes a **zygospore,** the characteristic meiospore of the group. When meiosis occurs, the zygospore forms a sporangium, which produces mitospores of the two mating types. From these grow mycelia capable of producing only mitospores. Conjugation and zygospore production can occur only when mycelia of the two mating types, called plus and minus, are present.

The Sac Fungi (Class Ascomycetes)

The Ascomycetes are a large class of fungi; there are at least 30,000 species and there is much diversity in form and mode of reproduction. Flagellated cells are unknown. Most Ascomycetes are mycelial and have septate hyphae, and the septa characteristically have pores so that there is cytoplasmic continuity from cell to cell. Nuclei even have been observed to pass through the pores, sometimes with great rapidity.

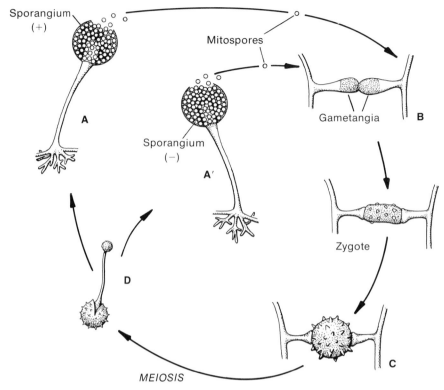

Figure 11–5 Life history of *Rhizopus nigricans*, the black bread mold. *A* and *A'*, Mycelia and mitosporangia of plus and minus mating types, respectively. *B*, Conjugation. *C*, Zygospore. *D*, Meiosis and zygospore germination.

All Ascomycetes possess a characteristic sac-like, meiospore-producing organ, the **ascus,** within which **ascospores** are formed. Ascospores are the result of sexual processes, but other sporelike cells, called **conidia,** also are produced in many Ascomycetes. In some species these may far outnumber the ascospores, and may even constitute the only mode of reproduction aside from fragmentation. Fungi reproducing solely by conidia are classified separately as imperfect fungi in the form class Deuteromycetes.

Most, but not all, Ascomycetes produce asci within a characteristic structure, the **ascocarp.** Ascocarps vary in size and shape from tiny spherical bodies to large, cup-like affairs. Regardless of ascocarp type, the typical sex organs in this group are the **ascogonium,** a receptive female gametangium, and either a male **antheridium** rather similar to that of *Saprolegnia,* or small individual cells termed **spermatia.** Fertilization occurs in two steps. The first is **plasmogamy,** in which there is a mingling of cytoplasm resulting from the transfer of one or more nuclei and some cytoplasm, either from an antheridium or from a spermatium into an ascogonium. Cells of hyphae formed prior to plasmogamy are uninucleate (**monokaryotic),** and those that develop from the ascogonium after plasmogamy are binucleate (**dikaryotic**). In other respects the life cycle is comparable to life cycle III (see Fig. 4–6). The second step in fertiliza-

258

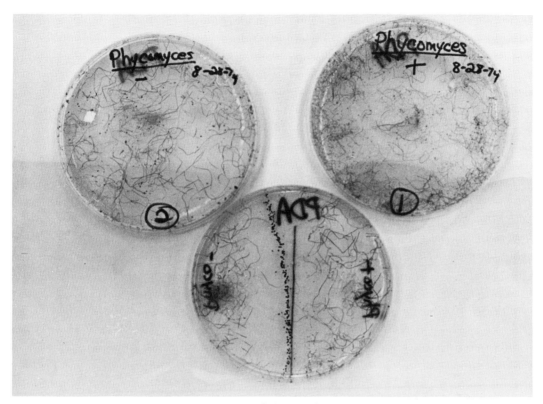

Figure 11-6 *Phycomyces blakesleanus.* Upper—Cultures of plus and minus mating types, respectively. Note the absence of conjugation. Lower—Culture plate inoculated at opposite sides with plus and minus mitospores. Conjugation has occurred along a central line where plus and minus hyphae have met one another and formed zygospores surrounded by dark-colored appendages.

tion is nuclear fusion, or **karyogamy,** occurring in terminal cells of dikaryotic hyphae (ascogenous hyphae) and following a unique process of nuclear division and septation called **crozier formation.** As a result of this process a cell is formed in which there is a 2*N* nucleus. In this cell, the **ascus,** meiosis occurs and is usually followed by one mitotic division so that the ascus comes to contain eight ascospores, each 1*N* in chromosome number.

Asexual reproduction among Ascomycetes occurs by conidia, which are spores budded off from hyphal tips rather than formed within sporangia. The conidia, sometimes called "summer spores," are a means of rapidly propagating new mycelia and are produced in various shapes and sizes. It is the color of the conidia that gives the characteristic blacks, blues, greens, pinks, and other shades to many of the molds.

Neurospora and Genetics. In an important series of experiments, Drs. George Beadle and Edward Tatum of the University of Chicago used strains of an ascomycete, the pink bread mold *Neurospora crassa*, to determine the manner in which genes are expressed biochemically. Ascomycetes are exceptionally useful organisms for biochemical genetics. It is known that in 2*N* cells of plants and animals each gene is present in duplicate form on corre-

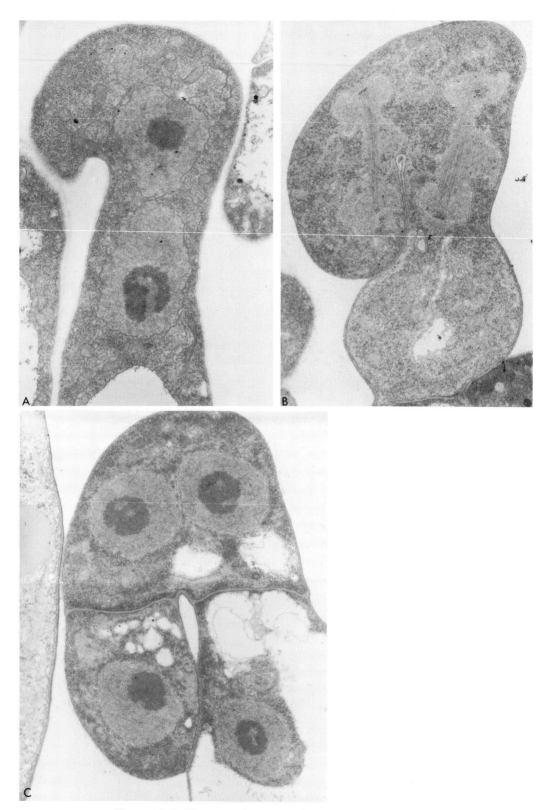

Figure 11–7 Electron microscope views of a developing crozier in an ascomycete. *A,* Dikaryotic crozier. *B,* Mitotic nuclear division in the crozier. *C,* Isolation of male and female nuclei in the tip cell of the crozier (From Hung, C.-Y., and Wells, K.: Light and Electron Microscope Studies of Crozier Development in *Pyronema domesticum. Journal of General Microbiology 66*:15–27, 1972).

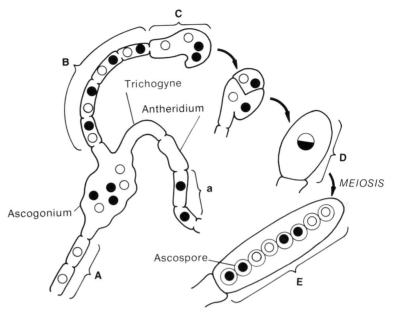

Figure 11-8 Diagram showing sexual reproduction in Ascomycetes. *A*, Monokaryon of female plant. *a*, Monokaryon of male plant. *B*, Dikaryon resulting from plasmogamy. *C*, Crozier. *D*, Karyogamy. *E*, Mature ascus.

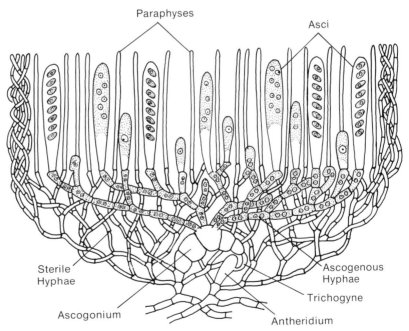

Figure 11-9 Diagram of an ascocarp. Note the relationship between the monokaryotic hyphae and the dikaryon (Redrawn from Smith, G. M. *Cryptogamic Botany,* Volume 1. Second Edition, New York, McGraw-Hill Book Co., Inc., 1955).

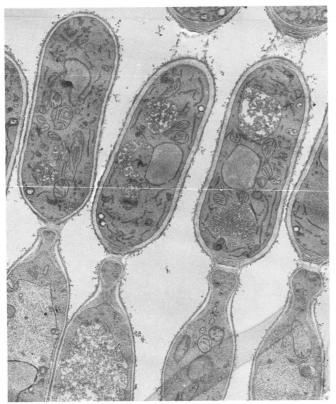

Figure 11–10 Electron micrograph of the conidia of *Metarrhizium anisopliae* (From Hammill, T. M. Electron Microscopy of Phialoconidiogenesis in *Metarrhizium anisopliae. Amer. J. Bot. 59*:317–326, 1972).

sponding positions of a chromosome pair. Such genes may differ slightly from each other in the manner in which they are expressed genetically and are termed **alleles.** Alleles may be **dominant** or **recessive.** If dominant and recessive alleles are present in the same cell, the dominant gene masks the expression of the recessive one. However, in many cases it is the recessive gene that is the most interesting to geneticists. Ascomycetes, as we have seen, exist in the monokaryotic form, the equivalent of the 1*N* state, and may be maintained as a monokaryon indefinitely in culture. Any recessive gene present is fully expressed in the absence of a dominant allele. The work of Beadle and Tatum, for which they received the Nobel Prize in 1959, involved the use of biochemical mutants of *Neurospora.* The mutants, because of the presence of certain recessive genes, were unable to make one or another of the essential amino acids. It is known that each amino acid is manufactured in the cell by way of a number of intermediate molecules, and that each step is controlled by a specific enzyme. Careful studies of mutant types of *Neurospora* have demonstrated that each gene mutation may result in a loss of one specific enzyme, and in this way the concept has been developed that genes control the synthesis of enzymes in a one for one relationship—often expressed as the "**one gene: one enzyme**" hypothesis.

Yeasts, Brewing, and Baking. Most Ascomycetes are mycelial forms with cellular hyphae and usually bear their asci within ascocarps. However, one group of Ascomycetes, the **yeasts,** have a very simple form, generally consisting of single cells rather than hyphae, and never produce ascocarps but do produce ascospores within asci.

Yeasts replicate by mitotic divisions and their cells are proliferated either by pinching off (as in budding that occurs in bread and beer yeasts), or by septation (as in other Ascomycetes). Sexual processes vary among yeasts, but all produce cells that act as gametes, uniting to form a binucleate zygote. Karyogamy, or nuclear fusion, ensues and is followed by meiosis, and sometimes mitotic division so that according to species, either four or eight ascospores develop within the zygote wall. The latter thereby functions as an ascus.

Yeasts are abundant in nature particularly where sugars are present, as in the nectar of flowers, fruit juices, saps, and other exudates from trees, and it is reasonable to believe that fermented beverages were discovered when crushed fruits were kept long enough for colonies of wild yeasts to develop and to produce alcohol.

Yeasts of the genus *Saccharomyces* are used both in baking bread and in brewing alcoholic beverages. Under conditions of limited oxygen, fermentation occurs, and alcohol and CO_2 are the byproducts. If a thick paste of flour and water is prepared and a

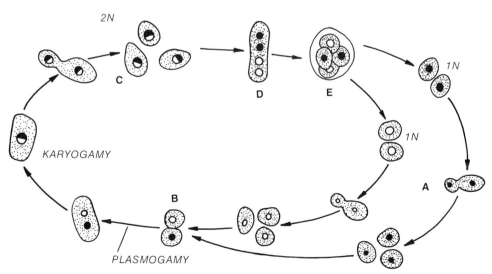

Figure 11–11 Life history of *Saccharomyces cerevisiae* represented diagrammatically. *A*, Budding 1*N* yeast. *B*, Conjugation. *C*, Budding 2*N* yeasts. *D*, Meiosis. *E*, Ascospores in ascus (Redrawn from Alexopoulos, C. J. *Introductory Mycology.* Second Edition. New York, John Wiley and Sons, Inc., 1962).

yeast culture is added, the CO_2 produced by yeast cells acting on the small amount of sugar present will cause this dough to rise. Baking stops the action of the yeast, hardens the spongy dough, and evaporates the alcohol. In olden days it was customary to keep a living yeast culture on hand, adding flour and water from time to time. This so-called "sourdough" is not at all difficult to maintain and is still used by some who prefer to make their bread the old-time way. In 1886, an American, Charles Fleischmann, found a way to compress yeast cultures into cakes, thus simplifying the process of bread-making. Formerly, most such "baker's yeast" was obtained off the thick scum of yeast cells formed on the surface of brewing vats, but today it is produced as a primary product by yeast manufacturers.

Generally speaking, alcoholic beverages are made in one or another of two ways. Sugar-containing plant parts, such as fruits, sugar beet roots, sugar cane stems, and the like are crushed, strained, and inoculated with the yeast *Saccharomyces ellipsoideus,* of which a number of strains are known. After fermentation the beverage may be aged in casks and bottled according to the product desired. Champagnes, for example, are reinoculated with yeasts and sometimes with a small amount of sugar prior to the final bottling. The result is the accumulation of CO_2, which accounts for the effervescence. Alternately, the fermented product may be distilled, as in the production of liqueurs, rums, and brandies.

Starch-containing plant parts—such as the grains of cereals and tubers of potato—may be used providing the starch is converted to sugar, since yeasts are not able to ferment starch directly. This conversion of starch to sugar may be done in several ways. Usually, partly germinated barley grains are used. As the embryo in the grain grows during germination, starch-digesting enzymes are produced, and these enzymes serve to convert the reserve starch of the grain into sugar. The action is stopped by drying the germinated grain, a procedure called malting, which kills the embryo plant but does not destroy the enzymes. Malt may be used alone to make beer or may be mixed with other starchy grains, roots, or tubers. The malt mixture is ground into a meal and water is added, allowing the conversion of remaining starch into sugar. The resulting "mash" is inoculated with the beer yeast, *Saccharomyces cerevisiae,* and allowed to ferment.

Although malt is widely used in making fermented beverages from starchy materials, other methods of starch conversion are in vogue in some regions of the world. In Japan, a rice wine called *sake* is produced using a fungus to digest rice starch prior to inoculation with yeast, and in some primitive cultures in Central and South America saliva is used to digest the starch of maize kernels. The kernels are chewed thoroughly and then expectorated into pots where fermentation by wild yeasts takes place under natural conditions.

The art of making beer is an ancient one (probably dating back at least 30 centuries), but has undergone a number of refinements in recent times. Malted barley may be used alone or with other cereals such as rice, maize, unmalted barley, and even tapioca, sugars, and syrups. The kind of water used is very important; alkaline water produces a poor beer, while the best beers are said to be made using waters containing slightly acidic sulfates. The mash is incubated for a number of hours at temperatures that vary according to the beer but are in the neighborhood of 70°C (150°F). The resulting "wort" is then boiled to sterilize it and to stop enzymatic action. Hops are usually added both for flavor and to accelerate the precipitation of undesirable residues. Only the female flowers of the hop vine, *Humulus lupulus,* are used, and these must be unfertilized since the fertilized flowers become very bitter-tasting.

The wort next is filtered through a bed of spent hops and inoculated with yeast. Two types of yeast are used. Strong English beers are produced according to a classical tradition using "top" yeasts. Somewhat milder, so-called lager beers employ strains of "bottom" yeasts first isolated in 1883 by E. C. Hansen of the Carlsberg breweries in Denmark. The fermentation continues for a week or longer at temperatures of 10° to 21°C (50° to 70°F). The green beer is then cooled and stored in large casks or vats at just over 0°C (32°F) for several months in order to improve its flavor and allow undesirable residues to settle out. Bottled beer is often pasteurized to stop further fermentation, but new techniques of ultrafiltration are now used to shortcut the aging process and remove the microorganisms that would cause souring. Such beer is sold as "draft" or unpasteurized beer, and has a much better flavor than pasteurized beer.

The procedures used in making most beverages of higher alcoholic content are similar to those used in making beer, except that the fermented mash is distilled. The distillate contains only about 20 per cent water and is about 160 proof ethyl alcohol (ethanol). Further distillation may be employed to yield a product of 190 proof (95 per cent ethanol), or the distillate may be diluted with water and then bottled or aged in casks (100 proof for bonded whiskey). Scottish malt whiskey is made with malt dried over peat fires and with water having its source in peat bogs. This accounts for its distinctive smoky flavor. Scotch whiskey is a blend of Scottish malt whiskey and diluted ethanol, and connoisseurs do not think it compares favorably with the unadulterated malt whiskey from which it is made. Other whiskeys, such as rye, bourbon, and Canadian, are made with specific cereals such as rye, maize, and barley, and are aged in oak casks.

Vodka and gin are practically pure ethanol diluted with distilled water and filtered through charcoal. The ethanol may have come from any source; in Russia and Poland, for example, it is derived from sugar beets or from potatoes. Vodka is unflavored, but gin is flavored with orris root, juniper cones ("berries"), cinnamon bark, and coriander "seed."

Actually, in many distilleries, much of the ethyl alcohol is sold in the form of 190 proof industrial alcohol and is used in numerous processes, such as in solubilizing drugs, antiseptics, and flavorings, in fuels, such as Sterno or methylated spirits (ethanol with poisonous methyl alcohol added) used in lamps and stoves. Denatured alcohol is produced by adding small amounts of highly noxious substances (for example, phenolphthalein, a powerful laxative) to ethyl alcohol.

Regarding the discovery of brewing and bread making, it appears that brewing came first. We can imagine some Stone Age woman making a broth or gruel of flour and water and then, having forgotten about it for a few days, returning to find it had acquired a new and different flavor and was mildly intoxicating. The flour would doubtless have been prepared by pounding grains with stones, and it is not unlikely that both sprouted grain and yeasts were included, along with many less essential impurities. Later, perhaps in ancient Egypt, it was discovered that the addition of a small amount of fermented material to bread dough produced a much fluffier bread. Gradually then, the procedures became refined and the art was handed down from generation to generation along with the most productive yeast cultures.

ALCOHOLISM. In terms of usage and dangerous consequences of its use, alcohol is by far the most important drug in the world today. It is a mood-altering drug; consumed in moderation, it may have a beneficial effect, relaxing tensions and producing euphoria. However, its overall effect is to depress the central nervous system. Overindulgence results in impaired motor functions and judgment. Alcohol is an addictive drug and thus produces physical and psychological dependence. It is calculated that there are 9 million alcoholics in the United States today. Less than five per cent of these conform to the "skid-row" type, but the remainder are, nevertheless, true alcoholics whose chronic indulgence impairs their ability to function in society.

Alcoholism accounts for 40 per cent of male admissions to mental hospitals, 40 per cent of court cases, and causes 800,000 automobile crashes and 25,000 deaths on American highways each year. Twenty-four per cent of alcoholics experience violent deaths, and 33 per cent of all suicides are alcoholics. These grim statistics warn us against improper use of alcoholic beverages.

Other Important Ascomycetes. In addition to those already alluded to, Ascomycetes make other contributions to human economy. Edible Ascomycetes are prized in many lands. Morels are avidly collected in the springtime in many regions of the United States and Canada, and are cooked and eaten in the same way as mushrooms. The most sought-after edible fungus is the truffle, an ascomycete that produces underground ascocarps. Oak woods are maintained in parts of Europe, particularly southern France, specifically for the growth of truffles, and specially trained dogs and pigs are sometimes used to sniff out their location, but an experienced truffle hunter requires neither dogs nor pigs.

Another ascomycete, *Claviceps purpurea*, produces the ergot disease of rye and other cereals that results in the poisoning of man and livestock known as ergotism. The alkaloids of ergot also are extracted and used in making abortifacient drugs. Lysergic acid is one of the constituents of ergot, and is an intermediate in the synthesis of LSD (lysergic acid diethylamide). In severely ergotized rye fields the

A

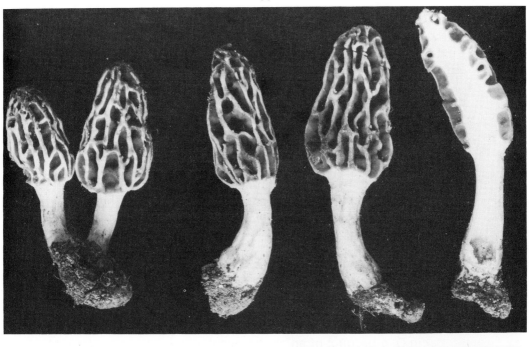

B

C

Figure 11–12 *A,* Morels, *Morchella. B,* Truffles, *Tuber. C,* A cup fungus, *Sarcosypha* (*A,* USDA Photo; *B,* from Gray, W. D. The Use of Fungi as Food, Cleveland, The Chemical Rubber Co. Press, 1970; *C,* Courtesy of Ward's Natural Science Establishment).

ergot now actually may be worth more than the grain itself; this is another interesting example in which a former liability becomes an asset.

Imperfect Fungi (Form Class Deuteromycetes)

Among the myriads of fungi are those whose sexual stages have never been observed. Since we identify fungi by their sex organs, it is necessary to place these "sexless" fungi in a separate category until such a time as someone observes their sexual stages. Because

267

the sexual stage is also called the **perfect stage,** we call these asexual fungi **imperfect fungi.** Many of them appear to be Ascomycetes on the basis of their hyphal structure and particularly their conidiophores and conidia, but a few are thought to be *Basidiomycetes.* Many species of *Penicillium* and *Aspergillus* are considered to be imperfect, including *P. notatum* and *P. chrysogenum,* which are penicillin producers, and *P. roquefortii* and *P. camembertii,* which give flavor to certain kinds of cheese. Other important imperfect fungi are pathogens; these include *Candida,* which causes a disease of the mucous membranes in humans, and *Trichophyton,* species of which produce skin infections such as so-called athlete's foot and scalp ringworm.

Antibiotics are substances produced by microorganisms such as fungi, bacteria, and a few other plants. They inhibit the growth of other microorganisms and disrupt and destroy their cells. Antibiotics vary greatly in chemical structure. Many are polypeptides (chains of amino acids) or polysaccharides. More than 80 are now in use, and thousands of others have been screened for therapeutic use but have been rejected, usually because they are found to be toxic to humans.

Penicillin, obtained from *Penicillium notatum* and *P. chrysogenum,* interferes with cell wall formation in bacteria. Actinomycin D, a product of an actinomycete (filamentous bacterium), blocks RNA synthesis. Streptomycin, also produced by an actinomycete, in-

Figure 11-13 *Claviceps purpurea* on rye (From *The Relation of Fungi to Human Affairs* by William D. Gray. Copyright (©) 1959 by Holt, Rinehart and Winston, Inc. Reproduced by permission of Holt, Rinehart and Winston, Inc.).

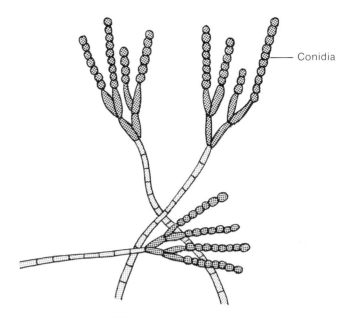
Conidia

Figure 11–14 Conidia of *Penicillium* shown diagrammatically.

terferes with the action of respiratory enzymes. Antibiotics often are quite specific with respect to the kinds of microorganisms they will attack. For example, penicillin is quite effective against Gram positive bacteria. Antibiotics effective against most pathogenic bacteria are now in use, but only a very few are known to be to any degree effective against viruses.

The microorganisms that produce antibiotics are cultured in large fermentation vats, using special nutrient media. Usually a mixture of antibiotics is produced, which must be carefully separated and purified prior to use.

The first antibiotic, penicillin, was discovered in 1928 by Sir Alexander Fleming, a British microbiologist and physician, but it was not until 1940 that Fleming, together with H. W. Florey and E. B. Chain, isolated and purified the active substance. The Nobel Prize was awarded them for this work.

One of the problems associated with the use of antibiotics is that of increasing bacterial resistance to the drugs. Either bacterial mutants are formed that are resistant, or the antibiotic kills off all but the resistant forms. In any event, repeated exposure of bacteria to antibiotics results in the development and selection of resistant bacterial strains, and this has serious consequences. Penicillin-resistant strains of the gonorrhea bacterium, *Neisseria gonorrhoeae,* have arisen in various localities, especially in Southeast Asia, and other antibiotics must now be used against them. The greatest danger is that such bacteria may develop additional resistance to other antibiotics as well, so that ultimately there remains no effective means of combating these pathogens.

Some imperfect fungi also form the fungal component (**myco-biont**) of **lichens,** interesting composite plants to be described.

Lichens (Form Class Lichenes)

For centuries lichens were thought to be individual plants; microscopic examination, however, revealed their dual nature. A lichen is part fungus and part alga. The fungus, or mycobiont, is usually an Ascomycete, but some Basidiomycete lichens and one Phycomycete lichen are known. The algal partner, or **phycobiont,** is often a blue-green alga (*Nostoc* is a common one), and occasionally a green alga. The role of each component in the association is controversial but is generally considered to be **symbiotic.** Experiments have shown that the fungus and the alga can be cultured separately and later reassembled in a functional relationship, but only if they are grown on a culture medium incapable of supporting either the fungus or the alga by itself. If the medium will support the independent growth of either one, then they will not recombine. Interestingly, the combined fungus and alga can synthesize organic compounds that neither can synthesize alone.

Lichens are found in all terrestrial life zones. The smooth bark of rain forest trees are splotched with **crustose lichens** (those of flat, crust-like form), as are rocks even in barren and rigorous climates. **Fruticose lichens** (of branching, elongate form) are repre-

Figure 11–15 A tombstone in Scotland covered with crustose lichens. Their slow growth is attested to by the date (1879) on the stone (Photo courtesy of Doug Stewart, Sycamore, Illinois).

sented by the "reindeer mosses" of the tundra and the "old man's beard" festooning trees in swamps and bogs. Still others are of the **foliose** type (of flat, leaf-like form), common in damp ravines, moist woods, and similar places.

Lichens have limited direct utility. Scottish tweed is sometimes dyed with lichen extracts, and the indicator dye litmus is obtained from a lichen. Fruticose lichens growing in the tundra and taiga are important foods for reindeer, caribou, and musk oxen, but lichens may be of greatest importance as pioneers in ecological succession. The combined abilities of a fungus (for degrading substrates) with that of an alga (for photosynthesis) permit this system to grow in the most inhospitable of environments. They are, however, quite sensitive to air pollutants, and so are seldom found in industrialized areas.

The Club Fungi (Class Basidiomycetes)

The class **Basidiomycetes,** to which mushrooms belong, includes about 13,500 species of fungi, which vary greatly in form but share a common meiospore type, the **basidiospore,** produced from a unique organ, the **basidium.** Customarily, the Basidiomycetes, or **club fungi,** are segregated into two subclasses, one in which mushrooms and similar forms with fleshy reproductive bodies called **basidiocarps** are found (the **Homobasidiomycetidae**), and a second that contains the rusts and smuts and their allies, having small gelatinous basidiocarps or lacking them altogether (the **Heterobasidiomycetidae**). Flagellated cells are lacking in the Basidiomycetes, as in the Ascomycetes.

The mushrooms are undoubtedly the only Basidiomycetes universally known by those who have not had an opportunity to study the fungi from a scientific point of view, for poisonous types have long been known, and others have been used both as food and as hallucinogens by human societies.

Hallucinogens. About 1500 B.C., the Aryans invaded India from the north, bringing with them the mysterious cult of Soma, whose ritual included use of a vision-inducing plant of unknown identity. Descriptions of the state of intoxication produced have been associated with various drug plants, but seem best to fit that induced by the fly agaric, *Amanita muscaria.* This mushroom, once thought to be a fly poison, has a long history also as an intoxicant and a hallucinogen, particularly in Eastern Europe and Siberia. One hour or so after eating *Amanita* the user is beset with trembling and twitching limbs, followed by euphoria, delusions of grandeur, and visions of the supernatural. The mushroom also causes a distortion of perspective so that things seem larger or smaller than they actually are. Lewis Carroll is said to have had *Amanita* in mind when he wrote that the Caterpillar told Alice to eat from the mushroom and "one side will make you grow taller, and the other side will make you grow shorter."

Occasionally, violent behavior occurs after eating *Amanita,* and this has led to the suspicion that the Berserkers of Viking times

271

Figure 11–16 *Amanita muscaria,* the fly agaric.

habitually ate the mushroom prior to doing acts of violence. Law in those days gave a slain man's possessions to his killers in a fair fight. Supposedly, the frenzy induced by eating *Amanita* gave members of the Berserker cult an overwhelming advantage in combat.

The Aztecs used several species of mushrooms in their religious ceremonies, among them the "sacred mushrooms," *Conocybe* and *Psilocybe. Psilocybe mexicana* is the most important of these, and is still sold in markets in some parts of southern Mexico. These mushrooms are capable of producing hallucinations, and their use is interwoven with religious ceremonies. However, there is also said to be some danger of long-term psychoses associated with their use. This, of course, is a danger in the use of any drug that affects the central nervous system.

Hallucinogens in general are composed of substances related to indole, a nitrogen-containing organic molecule. Lysergic acid diethylamide (LSD), a derivative of the fungus ergot, is an example. Such indolic substances are characterized by a very high potency and are found in nearly all hallucinogenic plants, including *Amanita, Psilocybe,* and *Conocybe,* seeds of the Mexican morning glory vine, peyote cactus, and the Congolese ordeal plant used in secret tribal initiation rites. Only the cannabinols present in marijuana and hashish are exceptions in that they are non-indolic compounds.

The way hallucinogens act physiologically is somewhat uncertain. They mimic some forms of insanity (such as schizophrenia), and it is possible that they accentuate or substitute for molecules normally present in the human body or act like molecules produced within the bodies of individuals whose biochemistry is abnormal. One possibility is that hallucinogens in some way block the action of serotonin, an indolic molecule associated with the transmission of nerve impulses across nerve synapses.

Whatever the biochemical and physiological actions of the hallucinogens prove to be, their psychedelic effects are well-known. Several profound mental aberrations are produced. Visual alterations are induced. Colors seem brighter, complex visual patterns are imagined, and surroundings have greater depth. Sounds, and even thoughts, appear to be transformed into color patterns of astonishing complexity and brilliance. Touch and hearing become much more acute than normal. The user generally achieves a highly emotional state characterized by laughter and tears, and sometimes profound depression. There seems to be enhanced rapport with one's surroundings, and even with one's own body. Inhibitions are lost and changes in attitudes toward death occur. The acceptance of one's own death seems to be one of the positive attributes of LSD and, perhaps, other hallucinogens. Cases are on record in which terminally ill patients treated with LSD have come to accept the ending of their lives with equanimity and understanding. The reluctance to discuss death as a natural occurrence is gradually being overcome in our society, and it is to be hoped that research into death attitudes will be continued and will contribute to the improvement of the human condition.

However, unsupervised use of hallucinogens can be very dangerous. Overdoses may produce long-lasting psychic disturbances. Distorted perceptions may lead to violent acts. Chromosomal damage also has been reported to occur from use of LSD, but there is no universal agreement among scientists that this is so.

Mushroom poisoning is a topic that holds a strange fascination for many people. Although it seems to be greatly overrated as a cause of death, it still must be guarded against, for some species of mushrooms are extremely poisonous. *Amanita verna,* the deadly "destroying angel," is so toxic that if one eats only a small bit of it, death due to destruction of the brain and liver ensues in three to eight days in more than 50 per cent of cases. There appears to be no really effective antidote for mushroom poisoning, but thioctic acid recently has been reported to be helpful in treating the symptoms of such poisoning. Contrary to popular opinion there are no simple tests to distinguish the dangerous mushrooms from the edible ones; one must be able to recognize the poisonous types.

Most persons are familiar with the mushrooms, bracket fungi, puffballs, and other club fungi having fleshy basidiocarps, and realize that they are decay organisms. Although such fungi are saprobes and live on dead plant material, certain of them grow on the trunks of living trees, digesting the cellulose of the dead inner wood. While such fungi usually do not attack living tissues directly, they cause immense destruction of forests. But it should be pointed out that the fungi usually invade trees that already have suffered damage either from natural causes such as lightning, wind storms, or fire, or were damaged by humans, their machinery, or their livestock.

Other basidiomycetes are highly pathogenic to plants, attacking the living tissues of many cultivated crops; such destruction is due in part to the planting of vast acreages of a single crop plant (monoculture), such as wheat or corn. Thus, the fungus has many opportunities to strike the host species at its most vulnerable stage, usually when it is a seedling, to become established, and to reinfect newly planted fields.

273

Basidiomycetes are important decay-causing organisms, and are well-known for their ability to cause wood to rot. This is a negative attribute where human possessions are concerned, but is an overwhelmingly positive influence for recycling of nutrients in the ecosystem. Basidiomycetes also are very important to many higher green plants because they form root associations, or **mycorrhizae**. These are known to be important in the nutrition of many green plants.

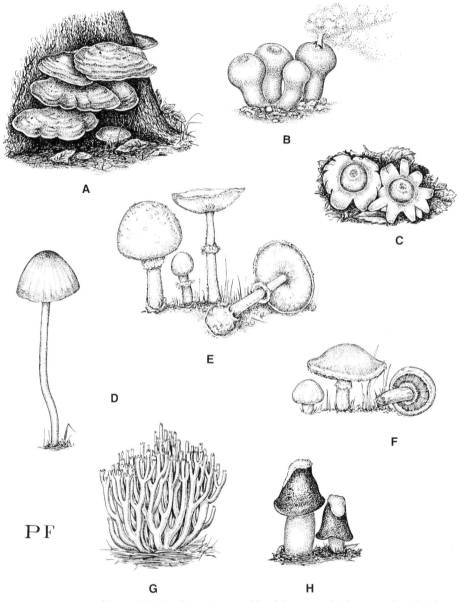

PF

Figure 11–17 Some types of basidiocarps. *A, Fomes,* a bracket fungus. *B, Calvatia,* a puffball. *C, Geaster,* an earth star. *D, Psilocybe,* a sacred mushroom. *E, Amanita verna,* the destroying angel, a poisonous species of gill mushroom. *F, Agaricus campestris,* the edible field mushroom. *G, Clavaria,* a coral mushroom. *H, Phallus,* a stinkhorn.

Figure 11–18 Rhizomorphs of wood-rotting fungi.

We may tend to think of the basidiocarp, whether it is a mushroom, puffball, bracket, or whatever, as the whole fungus, without realizing that it bears somewhat the same relationship as a fruit does to a tree. The mycelium of a mushroom often is very extensive and long-lived, and is composed typically of hyphae, which branch and intertwine, sometimes forming thick white, yellow or other-colored strings called **rhizomorphs** that run through rotting wood and humus. The hyphae are septate, but the septa are not perforate as in the sac fungi. When a basidiospore germinates, it produces a mycelium of uninucleate cells, the monokaryon. When, in the course of its growth, hyphae of such a mycelium encounter other hyphae of the same species, but of opposite mating type, they join by plasmogamy to produce the dikaryon, whose cells each contain two nuclei, one of each mating type. From this point on, growth becomes very extensive. Most mycelia are dikaryotic during the greatest part of their life span. Cells of a dikaryon often exhibit **clamp connections,** which maintain the paired relationship of the parental nuclear types. Each cell of the dikaryon contains two nuclei of opposite mating type. When nuclear division occurs, a cell containing a linear sequence (++−−) of four nuclei exists briefly until septation and a nuclear migration occurs, establishing once again unlike pairs of nuclei (+−/+−) in each new cell. The migration of

275

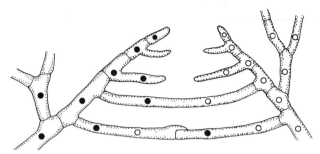

Figure 11–19 Diagrammatic illustration of the formation of a dikaryon by adjoining monokaryotic hyphae (Redrawn and modified from Smith, G. B. *Cryptogamic Botany*, Volume 1. Second Edition, New York, McGraw-Hill Book Co., Inc., 1955).

nuclei takes place through a bridging tubular structure, the clamp connection.

When conditions are suitable, as during periods of high humidity, basidiocarps are formed. These can develop very rapidly; they consist of intertwined hyphae having a felted appearance when viewed microscopically. Basidiocarps vary considerably in form, size, and even longevity. The common mushroom reproductive body is familiar to all. Mushroom basidiocarps consist of a somewhat spherical base, a stalk or **stipe,** and a cap or **pileus.** The underside of the cap is composed of thin segments, the **gills,** radiating from the stipe. It is on the surfaces of these gills that basidiospores are borne. Spores are produced in such numbers that if a cap from which the stipe has been removed is placed gill-side down on paper, a spore print will result from the deposition of millions of spores. The spore print outlines the pattern of the gills in the characteristic color of the spores. On the stipe is the ring (**annulus**), the remnant of a thin membrane, the **veil,** joined to the cap margin in the young mushroom. Poisonous mushrooms of the genus *Amanita* have a basal cup (**volva**), the remnant of an outer membrane (the **universal veil**), that covers the young mushroom.

Other basidiocarps include the perennial, woody, shelf-like bracket fungi, the spherical puffballs, and the intricate earth stars.

In certain regions of a basidiocarp, such as on the gills of mushrooms, within pores on the underside of bracket fungi, on the surface of coralloid fungi, and on the inside of puffballs, hyphal tip cells (**probasidia**) undergo karyogamy, followed by meiosis. They

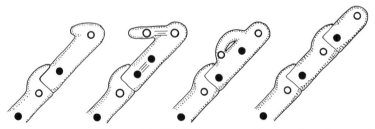

Figure 11–20 Clamp connections and nuclear exchanges in growing hyphae of a Basidiomycete shown in highly diagrammatic fashion.

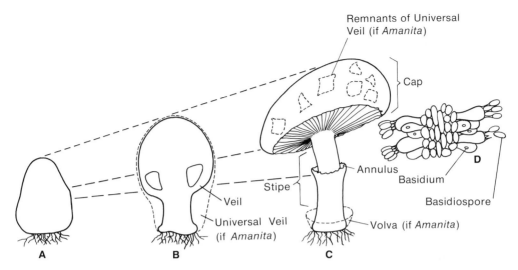

Figure 11–21 Development of the basidiocarp of a mushroom, shown in highly diagrammatic fashion. *A,* The early or button stage. *B,* Later stage in which the veil is apparent. In the poisonous *Amanita* an outer membrane, the **universal veil** also is present. *C,* Mature basidiocarp with stalk (or stipe), cap, gills, and the ring (annulus). *D,* Gill section showing basidia. In *Amanita* remnants of the universal veil are seen as patches on the surface of the cap and as a basal cup or volva.

form basidia with basidiospores. Generally four basidiospores are formed on each basidium, but exceptions are known; for example, the commercial mushroom *Agaricus campestris* forms two basidiospores per basidium. Basidiospores are produced in large numbers (by the millions in a large puffball) and are carried by the wind over long distances. Upon germination of basidiospores, monokaryotic hyphae are again established.

The life cycle just given may be considered typical of fleshy Basidiomycetes in general. However, in addition to obvious differences in the form of the basidiocarp, there may be differences in the details of plasmogamy, in basidium development, and in the number and form of basidiospores.

Although the two main groups of Basidiomycetes described earlier differ in the nature of the basidiocarp, the most important distinction between them is noted in the development and form of the basidium itself. Mushrooms and related fungi with fleshy basidiocarps have a type of basidium that is club-shaped and non-septate. Rusts, smuts, and related fungi, which either lack basidiocarps or have gelatinous basidiocarps, are characterized by possession of a basidium that is either vertically divided, transversely septate, or Y-shaped. The two types may be visualized by comparing Figures 11–22 and 11–23,*E.* Some members of this latter group, the rusts and smuts, are so well-known and of such economic importance that presentation of them is justified even in as general a text as this.

The 6000 species of rusts are all parasites of vascular plants. Among them are the white pine blister rust (*Cronartium ribicola*), the cedar-apple rust (*Gymnosporangium juniperi-virginianae*), and the wheat stem rust (*Puccinia graminis*). All of these have two hosts,

277

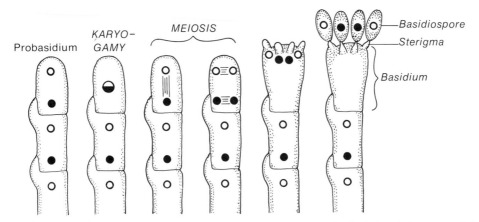

Figure 11–22 Stages in the development of a basidium (diagrammatic).

one upon which the fungus reproduces asexually, the other upon which the sexual stage of the life cycle occurs. One host of the white pine blister rust is the white pine; and the alternate host is a gooseberry or currant plant; in the cedar-apple rust, the hosts are junipers and crabapple trees; and in the wheat stem rust, the hosts are wheat and the common barberry bush.

Monocultures (such as that of wheat) are particularly prone to infection, and sometimes become devastated by rusts because of the large acreages allotted to this crop. Additionally, the overlapping of planting and harvesting that occurs on a large continent, with its regional differences in climates, presents the fungus continuously with new opportunities to parasitize young plants.

In the wheat rust, the dikaryon originates in the leaves of the common barberry (*Berberis vulgaris*) as a result of plasmogamy between **spermatia** and **receptive hyphae,** both of which are produced in small flask-like structures known as **spermagonia (pycnia)** on the upper surface of barberry leaves. Insects are attracted to a sugary liquid exuding from the spermagonium and carry spermatia to other spermagonia, thus ensuring that plasmogamy will occur between rusts of opposite mating types. After plasmogamy, male nuclei multiply in the receptive hyphae and migrate through pores in the ends of cells and thus transform the mycelium into a dikaryon, which then forms **aeciospores** (chains of binucleate conidia) in several cup-like **aecia** on the underside of the leaf. The aeciospores are carried by the wind; those that are deposited on the leaves and stems of wheat plants germinate and invade the inner tissues by way of the **stomata.** The rust mycelium deprives the cells and tissues of nutrients, with the result that the developing kernels of grain become shrivelled and worthless. As the mycelium develops it produces numerous localized tufts of rusty-red, stalked conidia, termed **uredospores** (summer spores or repeating spores). The uredospores also are carried by air currents, often to great distances, and infect other wheat plants.

As a wheat plant matures and becomes dry and brown, the

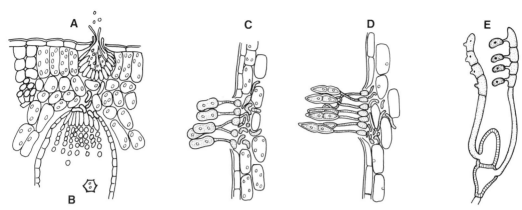

Figure 11–23 Life history of wheat rust. *Puccinia graminis* illustrated diagrammatically. On the barberry leaf: *A*, spermagonium, and *B*, aecium. On the wheat plant: *C*, **uredosorus,** and *D*, **teliosorus.** *E*, Basidia (Redrawn from Smith, G. M. *Cryptogamic Botany*, Volume 1. Second Edition. New York, McGraw-Hill Book Co., Inc., 1955).

mycelium of the rust ceases production of uredospores and begins producing **teliospores,** which are black, initially binucleate, and two-celled. Karyogamy between the two nuclei in each cell occurs as the teliospores mature, and the rust over-winters in this condition. Then in the spring, the teliospores germinate and produce a septate basidium from each cell. The basidiospores are wind-borne and infect the barberry plant. These stages are shown in Figure 11–23.

Extensive breeding programs have been undertaken to develop strains of wheat that are resistant to infection. The problem is complicated by the existence of nearly 200 physiological races of wheat rust. Gene recombination, resulting in increased pathogenicity, may occur in these races as a result of plasmogamy. Since this exchange takes place on the barberry plant, extensive campaigns to eradicate the common barberry have been carried out over the years. These efforts have met with some success; however, it appears that some genetic exchange also may occur between hyphae of different races growing on the same wheat plant, and mutations also may occur during the red rust stage so that there continues to be a need for the development of new and more resistant strains of wheat.

The smuts are a group of about 700 species of Basidiomycetes parasitizing vascular plants. The corn smut is familiar to farmers and gardeners because infected stalks, leaves, tassels, and kernels become greatly enlarged by masses of black teliospores that develop within them. The resistant teliospores survive over winter, and meiosis, basidium and basidiospore formation occur in the spring. Basidiospores producing monokaryotic hyphae again infect corn plants. Hyphae of the opposite mating type must be present in order for plasmogamy to occur and teliospores to be formed. Other smut diseases are the loose smut of oats, onion smut, and the stinking smut of wheat (bunt).

MYCORRHIZAE. Many higher plants seem to thrive best only when their roots are invaded by certain kinds of soil fungi, which form associations known as **mycorrhizae.** Many forest trees and desert plants require mycorrhizae for optimum growth and do not grow as well as they should without the fungi; some scientists even believe that the mycorrhizae are necessary for survival of most, if not all, woody plants. When soil particles containing a mycorrhizal fungus are added, such trees often show dramatic increases in their rates of growth. A number of Basidiomycetes and a few Ascomycetes, including some of the more fleshy types of both, are common mycorrhizal fungi. In forest trees, the hyphae often form a thick cylindrical sheath around young roots. In so doing, they may induce changes in the structure of the root itself, causing shortening and thickening, and sometimes a forking kind of branching quite different from the normal roots.

Isotope studies, in which radioactive minerals were added to the soil, have shown that mycorrhizae pass soil minerals on to host plant cells. Other studies have shown that mycorrhizal plants grow faster and are better able to extract nutrients from depleted soils than those lacking a fungal associate.

In the sheathing types of mycorrhizae hyphae penetrate between cells of the root epidermis and cortex, but in other mycorrhizal systems, notably those of seeds and roots of orchids, the hyphae actually penetrate the cells of the host and are digested by them. The fungus supplies the developing orchid seedling with carbohydrates and minerals, as has been shown by Dr. Lewis Knudson of Cornell University, who discovered that orchids could be grown from seeds without the fungi if they were cultured on a nutrient agar medium containing sugar and a simple mineral solution. Orchids

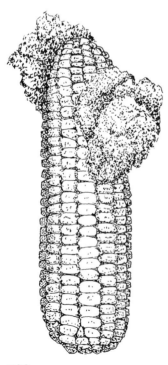

Figure 11-24   An ear of corn infected by the corn smut *Ustilago maydis.*

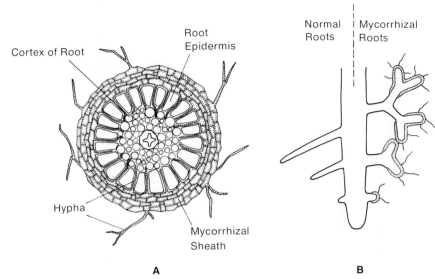

Figure 11–25 Mycorrhizal fungi of the roots of higher plants, shown diagrammatically. *A,* Transverse section of mycorrhizal root. *B,* Form of mycorrhizal and normal roots of pine (Redrawn from Harley, J. L. *The Biology of Mycorrhizae.* Second Edition. London, Leonard Hill, 1969).

now are propagated almost exclusively by Knudson's method for the reason that a much higher yield from seeds is obtained from such cultures than if the seed were to be sown in soil.

Evolution Among the Fungi

By tradition, the fungi have been included in the plant kingdom for both practical and theoretical reasons. At the introductory level it is more convenient to study them in the context of other plants than separately or with other groups of organisms. Their reproductive cycles are similar to those found in the algae, and in the structure of their cells and the nature of their organization one can find algal counterparts. With the exception of the Myxomycetes, fungal cells, like the cells of other plants, are enclosed within cell walls during the stages of their life history; even in the Myxomycetes, a cell wall is present during a part of the life cycle. However, the fungi are a diverse group and it is not at all certain whether they are more closely allied with one another or with some of the other, non-fungal groups, for example, the Protozoa.

The slime molds, especially, do not seem to be closely related to the other fungi. It is believed by some that they have evolved from a protozoan ancestry because of the amoeboid character of the plasmodium and of the gametes. However, they do produce thick-walled spores that resemble those of other fungi in structure and composition.

There is controversy as to the relationships of fungi in the Eumycota (see page 255), particularly as to the position of the Chy-

281

Figure 11–26 Orchid seedlings growing on nutrient agar. The surface of the nutrient agar in the bottle is packed with young plants.

tridiomycetes, Oomycetes, and Zygomycetes in relation to the Ascomycetes and Basidiomycetes. On the other hand there are similarities in mycelial organization, in composition of cell walls, in the formation of asexual spores or conidia, and in life processes, which argue for placing all five classes in one division, Eumycota.

The Oomycetes are thought by some mycologists to have evolved from algal ancestors, and some species are strikingly similar to certain algae, both in the structure of hyphae and in their reproductive organs; compare, for example, the alga *Vaucheria* with the fungus *Saprolegnia.* But others, such as certain of the Chytridiomycetes, lack a hyphal system, have spores and gametes with posterior flagellation (the latter not occurring in any alga), and occasionally have amoeboid stages. This group, at least, seems to have protozoan affinities and some mycologists believe them to be the base stock from which other fungi may have evolved.

There are two schools of thought on the origin of the Ascomycetes. Some believe them to have developed out of the Oomycetes since the simpler, filamentous Ascomycetes resemble such forms as *Saprolegnia* in their morphology. However, unlike the Oomycetes, none of the Ascomycetes produce flagellated cells. Moreover, the sexual reproduction of many Ascomycetes involve non-motile spermatia, and ascogonia with trichogynes, which resemble the carpogonia, trichogynes, and non-motile spermatia found in the red algae. For these reasons, it has been suggested that the sac fungi have evolved either from the red algae or that the two groups have a common ancestry.

The Basidiomyetes are generally considered to have developed from the Ascomycetes or to have a common ancestry with them. Both groups have similar dikaryotic stages. The crozier and accompanying nuclear events that precede the formation of the ascus are quite like the stages occurring in clamp formation and in the development of the basidium. The classification at the end of this chapter reflects the above assumptions.

SUMMARY

The fungi considered in this chapter are placed in two divisions: the Myxomycota (or slime fungi), and the Eumycota (literally, true fungi). The slime fungi are characterized by a vegetative, non-cellular organization, termed the plasmodium, which is generally irregular in form and moves about by streaming and flowing movements, feeding on small particles of organic material and bacteria in its path.

The Eumycota commonly have a structural organization, termed a mycelium. The mycelium is composed of filaments known as hyphae, which may be either cellular or tubular (coenocytic). Exceptions to this basic form are the yeasts, most of which are unicellular.

The Eumycota includes the classes Chytridiomycetes, Oomycetes, Zygomycetes, Ascomycetes, and Basidiomycetes. The first three of these classes include water molds, the black bread mold, the early blight of potatoes, and many others. The characteristic mycelium is non-cellular and coenocytic. Many, but not all, form flagellated gametes and zoospores; the Ascomycetes and Basidiomycetes have septate hyphae and lack flagellated stages.

The Ascomycetes, or sac fungi, have cellular hyphae and a characteristic meiosporangium known as the ascus (sac). Ascomycetes are important organisms, both in nature where they are involved in the breakdown of organic matter, and in industrial processes such as brewing, baking, cheese making, and drug production. They also include some important plant and animal pathogens.

Fungi whose sexual stages are unknown are termed imperfect fungi or Deuteromycetes. Some of these (for example, *Penicillium*) are very useful organisms in drug making and food production.

A group of plants, the lichens, are quite unique in being composed of two very different organisms; a fungus, usually an Ascomycete; and an alga, usually a blue-green species. Lichens are examples of mutualism, a type of coexistence benefiting both partners. Lichens are often ecological pioneers and are found in such rigorous environments as bare rock, arctic tundra, and deserts. They are a major component of tundra vegetation and are utilized as food by caribou, musk oxen, and other arctic herbivores. Lichens also are a source of dyes, such as litmus and the natural dyes used in making Scottish tweeds.

The club fungi (Basidiomycetes) are an interesting group that includes many useful as well as pathogenic species. Among the most remarkable of these are the sources of hallucinogenic drugs, such as the fly agaric (*Amanita muscaria*), and the sacred mushrooms of Mexico.

The characteristic reproductive organ of the club fungi is the basidium (club), which bears externally two to four basidiospores. Basidia often are found on or within fruiting bodies, the basidiocarps; however, some Basidiomycetes (rusts and smuts) lack basidiocarps. Basidiocarps range from the well-known mushroom types to puffballs, earth stars, stinkhorns, and brackets.

Certain Basidiomycetes, such as the rusts of wheat and pine, have complex life cycles that involve alternate hosts (wheat and barberry, for example). They are the cause of millions of dollars worth of damage to crops and timber every year.

Among the benefits of fungi is their role in the nutrition of forest and desert plants. Fungi compose mycorrhizae in association with the roots of these plants and have been shown to increase the uptake of nutrients by the plant.

The classification of the fungi treated in this chapter is as follows:

Division Myxomycota: The *slime molds.* These are spore-forming, heterotrophic eukaryotes, having an amoeboid form of assimilative organization and producing walled, non-motile spores.

CLASS MYXOMYCETES: The *plasmodial slime molds.* The assimilative stage is a plasmodium, and walled meiospores are formed, which germinate to form flagellated or amoeboid swarm cells (or both), and gametes.

Examples: Stemonitis, Physarum.

Division Eumycota: The *true fungi.* These are heterotrophic eukaryotes having a basic, mycelial organization. Hyphae are either coenocytic or septate, and are composed of cellulose, chitin or both. Spores various.

CLASS CHYTRIDIOMYCETES: The *Chytrids.* The mycelium, when present, is coenocytic; posteriorly flagellated zoospores and gametes are formed; reproduction is either isogamous or anisogamous.

Example: Allomyces.

CLASS OOMYCETES: The *water molds.* These are principally aquatic forms with coenocytic hyphae. Gametes are non-flagellated and oogamous. Zoospores are flagellated.

Examples: Saprolegnia, Pythium, Phytopthora, and *Plasmopara.*

CLASS ZYGOMYCETES: The *black molds.* These are coenocytic fungi lacking flagellated cells altogether; sexual reproduction is by conjugation.

Examples: Rhizopus, Phycomyces.

CLASS ASCOMYCETES: The *sac fungi.* The mycelium, when present, is composed of septate hyphae. There are no flagellated stages. Meiospores are formed in an ascus.

Examples: Saccharomyces, Peziza, Neurospora, Morchella, Tuber, and *Claviceps.*

FORM CLASS DEUTEROMYCETES: The *imperfect fungi.* These appear to be principally Ascomycetes lacking sexual stages; reproduction is mainly by conidia.

Examples: Penicillium, Aspergillus, Candida, and *Trichophyton.*

FORM CLASS LICHENES: The *lichens.* These are composite organisms consisting of a fungal and an algal component. Lichens are classified on the basis of the fungal partner (mycobiont), and most are Ascomycetes.

Examples: Usnea, Cladonia, and *Peltigera.*

CLASS BASIDIOMYCETES: The *Club Fungi.* The mycelia are composed of septate hyphae, and cell division is often accompanied by clamp formation. There are no flagellated stages; meiospores are formed upon a basidium.

SUBCLASS HOMOBASIDIOMYCETIDAE

Examples: Amanita, Conocybe, Agaricus, Geaster, Fomes,

Calvatia, Clavaria, Polyporus, Phallus, and *Psilocybe.*
　　SUBCLASS HETEROBASIDIOMYCETIDAE
　　　　Examples: Puccinia, Ustilago, Cronartium, and *Gymno-sporangium.*

DISCUSSION QUESTIONS

1. What are three features that characterize fungi?
2. What, if any, are the contributions of the slime fungi to the environment? To science?
3. How would you describe a mycelium and its relationship to hyphae and to cells?
4. Describe the mycelium of a typical phycomycete.
5. Why do you think the late blight of potatoes was such a devastating blow to the Irish people? Are potatoes such an important part of your own diet? Can you think of any modern food source whose infestation might cause a similar famine?
6. Consider a lichen growing on a rock. How does it manage to maintain its metabolism in such an apparently hostile environment? What are its requirements? How does it fulfill them?
7. What is the role of the germinating barley grain in the brewing of beer?
8. Define the term *saprobic.* How does a saprobe differ from a parasite?
9. What is the significance of that portion of the life history of the wheat rust that occurs on the barberry plant?
10. Within what structure of a mushroom or similar fleshy basidiomycete does karyogamy occur? How does this differ in the wheat rust.?
11. Why are monocultures of plants such as wheat and corn particularly susceptible to plant pathogens?
12. What are mycorrhizae? What evidence is there that they are beneficial?

SUPPLEMENTAL READING

Ahmadjian, V. The Fungi of Lichens. *Sci. Amer. 208(2)*:122–132, 1963.
Alexopoulos, C. J. *Introductory Mycology,* 2nd ed. New York: John Wiley and Sons, Inc., 1962.
Alexopoulos, C. J., and J. Koevenig. *Slime Molds and Research.* B.S.C.S. Pamphlet 13. Boston, Mass.: D.C. Heath Co., 1964.
Gray, W. D. *The Relation of Fungi to Human Affairs.* New York: Henry Holt and Co., 1959.
Gray, W. D. *The Use of Fungi as Food.* Cleveland, Ohio: Chemical Rubber Co. Press, 1970.
Gray, W. D., and C. J. Alexopoulos. *Biology of Myxomycetes.* New York: The Ronald Press Co., 1968.
Harley, J. L. *The Biology of Mycorrhizae,* 2nd ed. London: Leonard Hill, 1969.
Krieg, M. B. *Green Medicine.* Chicago: Rand McNally and Co., 1964.
Litten, W. The Most Poisonous Mushroom. *Sci. Amer. 232(3)*:90–101, 1975.
Niederhauser, J. S., and W. C. Cobb. The Late Blight of Potatoes. *Sci. Amer. 200(5)*:100–112, 1959.
Schultes, R. E. Hallucinogens of plant origin. *Science 163*:245–254, 1969.
Smith, A. H. *The Mushroom Hunter's Field Guide.* Ann Arbor: University of Michigan Press, 1958.
Wasson, R. G. *Soma, Divine Mushroom of Immortality.* New York: Harcourt, Brace and World, Inc., 1969.

Scanning electron micrograph of *Sphagnum* leaves.

Chapter 12

Mosses and Their Living Relatives

NATURE OF BRYOPHYTES • ECOLOGY OF MOSSES • MOSSES AND ARCHEOLOGY • MOSSES • LIFE CYCLES WITHOUT SEX • LIVERWORTS • THE BIOLOGY OF MARCHANTIA • HORNWORTS • ALTERNATION OF GENERATIONS • EVOLUTIONARY RELATIONSHIPS • SUMMARY

Individually the mosses and their relatives, the liverworts and hornworts, are rather insignificant plants, usually only a few centimeters tall, but they commonly grow in dense colonies so that they produce patches or cushions of green vegetation that often are quite conspicuous. Sometimes such colonies are very extensive, as in the case of peat bogs formed by the bogmoss, *Sphagnum.* Liverworts and hornworts likewise are inconspicuous as individuals, and although they too occur in colonies, these colonies are seldom as extensive as those of mosses. All three groups are members of the division Bryophyta and commonly are referred to as **bryophytes.** They are intermediate in anatomical complexity between the green algae and the higher land plants, and usually are found on land although some are true aquatic plants.

Nature of Bryophytes

The green plant we readily recognize as a moss, liverwort, or hornwort is almost always the gamete-producing, or gametophyte, stage in the life cycle. Later (after fertilization), a spore-producing or sporophyte plant is formed from the zygote, and in all cases this sporophyte plant remains attached to, and nutritionally dependent upon, the gametophyte plant. This dependence of the sporophyte generation upon the gametophyte is a unique characteristic of the bryophytes.

Another characteristic of the bryophytes is the presence of multicellular female and male sex organs known as **archegonia** and **antheridia** respectively. In contrast, the algae and fungi have unicel-

---

Moss is a Plant, that the wisest of Kings thought neither unworthy of his speculation, nor his Pen, and though in bulk one of the smallest, yet it is not the least considerable; for as to its shape, it may compare for the beauty of it with any Plant that grows.

ROBERT HOOKE: *Micrographia*, 1665.

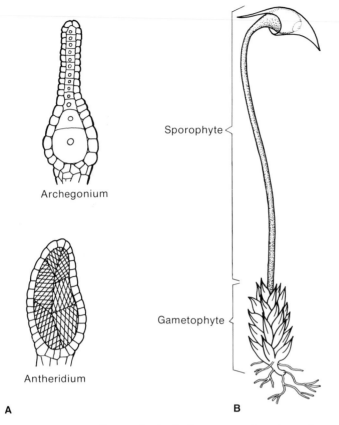

Archegonium

Antheridium

Sporophyte

Gametophyte

A

B

Figure 12-1 *A,* Structures of archegonium and antheridium. *B,* Relationship between sporophyte and gametophyte (highly diagrammatic).

lular sex organs, such as oogonia, carpogonia, and various other forms of gametangia.

Bryophytes, however, are not the only plants that have multicellular sex organs. Several other types of land plants, such as ferns, club mosses, and scouring rushes, also have antheridia and archegonia; but unlike the bryophytes, these are **vascular plants**; that is, they have specialized conduction tissues known as **xylem** and **phloem.** The bryophytes, therefore, may be defined as nonvascular, archegoniate plants. The life cycles of bryophytes, as well as all vascular plants, conform to life cycle III (see Figure 4–6); that is, all exhibit alternation of generations.

Ecology of Mosses

In Chapter 6 the ecological roles of mosses were mentioned briefly in connection with certain kinds of plant succession. Mosses (and to a limited degree their relatives, the liverworts and hornworts) are pioneers in ecological succession in all but the most arid regions of the world. They colonize the face of bare, granitic rock, lava flows, and burned-over ground in the aftermath of forest fires;

in some instances, such as in peat bogs, they are of major importance to the environment.

Peat bogs are formed by a group of mosses belonging to the genus *Sphagnum. Sphagnum* moss at first forms a border around the wet margins of ponds. Often these ponds are of the pothole variety, and were left behind by the melting of large blocks of ice in the aftermath of retreating glaciers. In time, the border of *Sphagnum* encroaches upon the pond surface to form a floating mat and eventually to close off the water surface entirely and thus create a quaking bog. Continuing growth of the *Sphagnum* and other bog plants results in the deposition of so much dead plant material that the bog finally becomes completely composed of peat, the organic residue left behind after the death and partial decay of bog plants.

Peat, when excavated and dried, has been used as a building material and as a fuel. It is still used as a popular mulch for garden plants and even as a flavoring in Scotch whiskey. In the northeastern states and in Canada extensive peat bogs in the last stages of succession often are cleared, leveled, and ditched for cranberry production. The water levels then are adjusted for summer cranberry production and for the fall cranberry harvest. Cranberry bogs are an example of productive utilization of land otherwise nonproductive agriculturally

Plant and animal remains are preserved in peat often for long periods of time because of the acidic and antiseptic properties of the peat. Pollen grains after falling on the surface of bog waters, sink to the bottom and become covered by subsequent depositions of peat, so that a record of the kinds and relative numbers of plants in the region is carried on through the centuries in the stratifications

Figure 12-2 The ecology of mosses. *A*, A *Sphagnum* bog in Wisconsin corresponding to stage *C* in Figure 12-3. *B*, Mosses in an Illinois marsh.

289

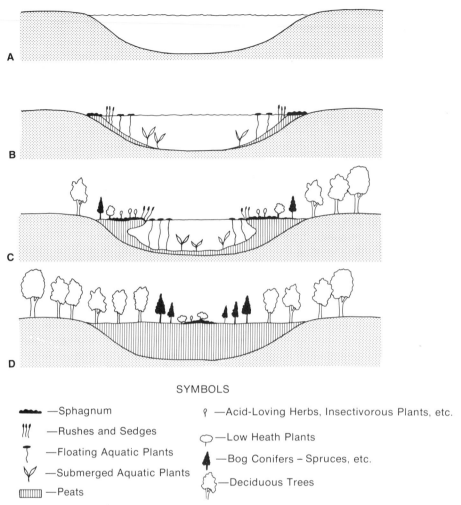

SYMBOLS

— Sphagnum   ♀ — Acid-Loving Herbs, Insectivorous Plants, etc.

— Rushes and Sedges

— Floating Aquatic Plants   ◯ — Low Heath Plants

— Submerged Aquatic Plants   ▲ — Bog Conifers – Spruces, etc.

— Peats   — Deciduous Trees

Figure 12–3 Bog succession. *A*, Post-glacial pothole pond in barren early stage. *B*, Establishment of a border of shallow water vegetation. *C*, Formation of a floating mat composed of living and dead plant material bound together by roots of bog plants. *D*, Complete closure of pond by deposited peat (Redrawn from Dansereau, P. M. *Biogeography: An Ecological Perspective*, New York, Ronald Press Co., 1957).

of the bog. By sampling the layers and identifying the pollen present in each layer it has been possible to trace the changes in climate and vegetation that have occurred in some areas over thousands of years.

Mosses and Archeology

Bogs have proved to be useful to archeologists also. In Denmark during World War II, people were forced by coal and oil shortages to resume the ancient practice of burning peat. In the process of digging the peat, a number of human bodies of great antiquity were uncovered which, because of their excellent preservation, have given an insight into the world of 2000 years ago. One body, given

Figure 12–4 A commercial cranberry bog in northern Wisconsin. *A*, Leveled and ditched peat bog in background. *B*, Dense mat of cranberries just prior to autumn harvest.

the name of Tollund Man after the region where it was found, is said to be the most perfectly preserved ancient man yet discovered. The Tollund Man is thought to have been a tribal chief. His body and other bodies were laid to rest in the sacred bogs along with articles of clothing, agricultural implements, weapons, household effects, and even musical instruments.

The Mosses (Class Bryopsida)

There are about 14,500 species of mosses occurring in a wide range of habitats. Most are found growing in humid places and some are aquatic, but others are found in deserts and are able to withstand complete desiccation, reviving and resuming growth when moisture is once again present. Typically, mosses are small plants and seldom attain a height greater than a few centimeters, although *Dawsonia,* a New Zealand moss, may reach a height of 60 centimeters. Mosses are a diverse group of plants, although they have many basic features in common. Some of the variations occurring among mosses will be described where appropriate.

As stated earlier in this chapter, mosses are characterized by an alternation of gamete-forming and spore-forming generations. The gamete-forming or gametophyte generation begins with a meiospore and is, therefore, 1*N* in chromosome number. A germinating meiospore produces a gametophyte that at first is a threadlike **protonema** resembling some of the filamentous green algae. Later, **protonemal buds** and slender filamentous cells called **rhizoids** develop. Protonemal buds are lateral outgrowths of the protonema and are composed of several cells including an **apical cell**, which by re-

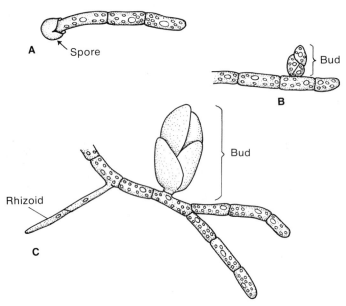

Figure 12–5 Diagrams showing steps in development of protonemata. *A,* Spore germination. *B,* Bud initiation. *C,* Protonema bud.

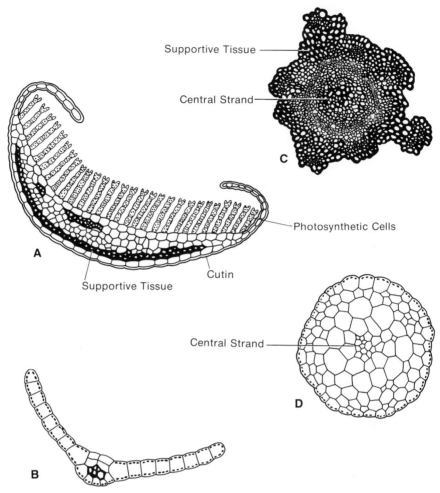

Supportive Tissue

Central Strand

Photosynthetic Cells

A

Cutin

Supportive Tissue

Central Strand

D

B

C

Figure 12–6 Structures of gametophytes of the hairy cap moss, *Polytrichum,* and *Funaria. A,* Leaf of *Polytrichum* in cross section. *B,* Leaf of *Funaria* in cross section. *C,* Stem of *Polytrichum* in cross section. *D,* Stem of *Funaria* in cross section.

peated divisions produces the leafy gametophyte plant. Protonemal buds are produced only when light is sufficiently intense (bright daylight); experiments have shown that red light is required for bud formation; therefore, the red component of daylight is effective. This ability on the part of red light to trigger certain kinds of plant development is discussed in some detail in Chapter 20.

The mature gametophytes of mosses are composed of "stems," "leaves," rhizoids, and reproductive organs. Although the moss stem has no true vascular tissue (i.e., xylem or phloem), in the stems of most (but not all) species is a central strand of cells that appears to function as a conduction system. Rhizoids, composed of filaments of cylindrical cells with oblique end walls, anchor the gametophytes to soil or rock, and also may absorb nutrients and water. The leaves, which are spirally arranged on the stem, are not highly specialized in most mosses and, except in the midrib region, are often only one

293

cell layer thick (leaves of some species are more complex; see Figure 12–6). Often such leaves lack **cutin,** a waxy substance coating the epidermis of most land plants; this explains the rapid drying-out of such mosses. However, many mosses readily survive drying and quickly revive when they are again moist. Drying-out also enables mosses to survive freezing, since ice crystals are not formed within the dried-out cells.

In general, mosses having water movement within the stem possess cutin, while those securing water by direct absorption and capillary movement lack cutin. The bog moss *Sphagnum* is of the latter form and has highly specialized leaves that consist of many large and hollow water-absorbing cells bordered by narrow, photosynthetic cells. The stems of *Sphagnum* also have specialized water-holding cells, which appear somewhat similar to chemical retorts, having flask-like bases and narrow, curving necks. These hollow cells of the stem and leaf account for the great absorbency and water-holding ability of *Sphagnum.* Once established, *Sphagnum* sometimes will form creeping upland bogs because of this ability to take up and hold moisture. The dried *Sphagnum* is very absorbent and also somewhat antiseptic; during the Russo-Japanese War and World War I it was used successfully as a filler in wound dressings.

As the development of a moss gametophyte progresses toward maturity, the cells of the stem apex cease producing leaf and stem tissues and undergo a series of changes that result in the formation of antheridia, archegonia, and **paraphyses** (sterile hairs). Both bisexual and unisexual species of mosses are known. Some of the earliest work on sex determination in plants was done using bryophytes. The spores of unisexual species produce either male or female gametophytes in equal numbers, and it was discovered (in a species of liverwort, *Sphaerocarpos*) that the spores producing female gametophytes contain a comparatively large chromosome, the X chromosome; those forming male plants had a much smaller corresponding chromosome, the Y chromosome. Since then, X and Y sex-determining chromosomes have been found in other bryophytes. If the plant is unisexual, as is the hairy cap moss often studied in botany classes, gametophyte plants have either one or the other kind of sex organ. The gametophytes of other mosses may be bisexual, some having male and female branches on the same plants (as in *Sphagnum*), or both antheridia and archegonia may be present on the same apex. However in such cases antheridia and archegonia mature at separate intervals, and this appears to ensure cross-fertilization between plants.

Antheridia are stalked, ovoid organs consisting of an outer jacket layer of cells and an inner, segmented mass of sperm-producing cells. Archegonia are stalked, flask-shaped organs consisting of a median **venter** and an elongate, cylindrical **neck** terminating in four covering cells. Within the neck there is a file of **neck canal cells** that end basally in a **ventral canal cell** located just above the large **egg cell**, which occupies the venter.

When the sex organs are mature, fertilization may take place as

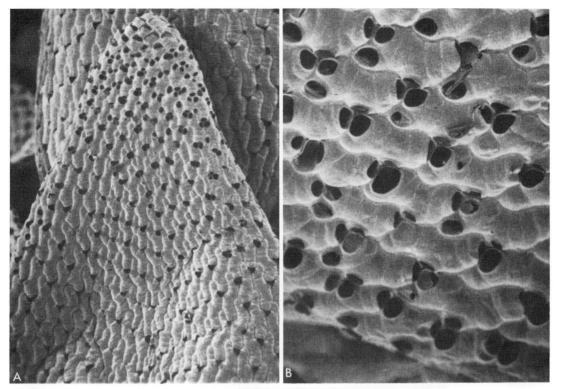

Figure 12–7 Scanning electron micrographs of a leaf of *Sphagnum*. Note that the water-holding cells are especially prominent (From Mozingo, H. N. et al. Scanning Electron Microscope Studies on *Sphagnum imbricatum*. *The Bryologist* 72:484–488, 1969. Photos by Edwin R. Lewis).

soon as the organs are in contact with water. The mature sperm are minute, biflagellate cells; they are elongate and coiled, and are released from the antheridium when it opens upon becoming wet. The covering cells of the archegonium also open upon wetting, and the liquefied contents of the neck canal cells are extruded. Also released are chemicals that induce sperm to swim in the direction of the archegonia. Such chemically induced movements are known as **chemotactic** movements. Several substances are known to induce chemotactic responses in the sperm of various bryophytes; these include sucrose (cane sugar), potassium, and proteins. Upon reaching an archegonium, a sperm moves down the neck and unites with the egg. More than one sperm may enter an archegonium, but only one unites with the egg.

The fertilized egg, a 2*N* zygote, soon undergoes a series of symmetrical divisions to form a spindle-shaped embryo, which later becomes the mature sporophyte plant. As the sporophyte grows, the archegonium also continues to expand, and becomes a **calyptra.** Although the calyptra is only a covering structure and not actually a part of the sporophyte, it is necessary for normal development of the sporophyte. If the calyptra were removed before the sporophyte were mature, an abnormal sporophyte would be formed. The mature moss sporophyte consists of a basal absorbing region termed the

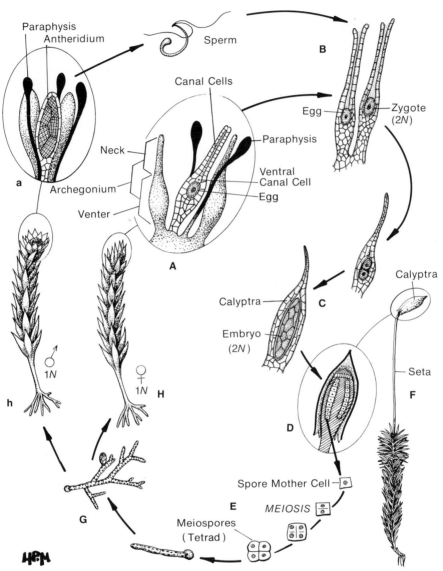

Figure 12–8 Sexual reproduction in mosses, shown in highly diagrammatic fashion. *a,* Apex of male plant showing antheridia and sterile hairs or paraphyses. *A,* Apex of female plant with archegonia and paraphyses; note neck and venter regions of archegonium and neck canal cells in longitudinal section, ventral canal cell and the egg. *B,* Fertilization; note sperm, egg, and zygote. The canal cells disintegrate prior to fertilization. *C,* Embryo sporophytes. *D,* Capsule of maturing sporophyte containing spore mother cells, which undergo meiosis (*E*) within the maturing capsule to form tetrads of meiospores. *F,* Mature sporophyte with seta and capsule partially covered by calyptra. *G,* Protonema. *h,* Mature male and *H,* female, gametophytes.

foot, a stalk or **seta,** and a sporangium or **capsule.** The seta usually has a central strand of cells that probably serves to carry food and water upwards from the foot region, and an outer zone of thick-walled supporting cells covered by an epidermis. In the mosses *Sphagnum* and *Andreaea* the seta is short and the sporophyte is elevated by the **pseudopodium,** a leafless extension of the gameto-phyte in which the foot of the sporophyte is embedded.

Although water and nutrients are absorbed by the foot region of the sporophyte from the tissues of the gametophyte plant, the sporophytes of most bryophytes are green and photosynthetic, and therefore capable of producing some of the food required for growth and development. Some mosses have very small gameto-phytes, and the sporophytes are thought to be very nearly self-sup-porting; however, none has been shown to be completely independ-ent of the gametophyte.

There is considerable diversity of form among moss capsules, but generally they have a central column of cells (the **columella**), surrounded by a region of spore-forming cells (the **spore-mother cells**). The latter are enclosed, in turn, by a wall of several cell layers, including an epidermis equipped with **stomata**. Stomata are openings in the epidermis bordered by pairs of specialized cells called **guard cells**. The guard cells are able to open and close the opening and thus regulate gas exchange between the plant and its

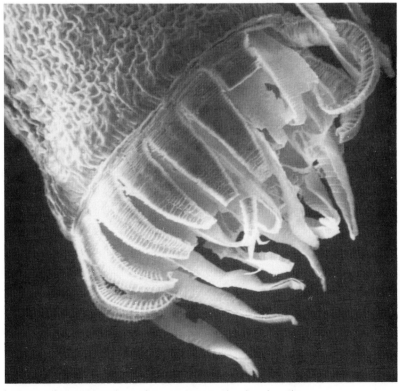

Figure 12-9 Scanning electron microscope view of a moss capsule showing the peristome teeth (Photo courtesy of Dr. James McCleary).

environment. In most mosses the tip of the capsule is covered by a lid, or **operculum**, which is shed at the time the spores are discharged. Beneath the operculum there is a circular border of teeth, the **peristome teeth**. Some mosses have two or more layers of teeth, others have only one layer; and a few lack peristome teeth altogether.

During the maturation of the capsule, the spore mother cells undergo meiosis, and tetrads of meiospores result. In unisexual mosses, two meiospores of each tetrad have Y chromosomes and the other two have X chromosomes; in bisexual mosses the meiospores lack specific sex chromosomes. In many mosses, when spores are ready to be shed, the calyptra (if present) and the operculum fall away and the spores are scattered by movements of the peristome teeth, which alternately bend and unbend upon wetting or drying. (Structures exhibiting movements of this kind in response to changes in moisture are described as **hygroscopic**.) Under dry conditions, the bending of the teeth allows spores to escape. Since dry conditions favor spore dispersal by winds and air currents, this mechanism is important in spore dissemination, and clearly qualifies as a so-called ecological strategy. Spores may germinate immediately if conditions (shade and moisture), are favorable, or may survive for several years before germinating.

The spores of the hairy cap moss are sifted out between short peristome teeth at the edge of a membranous disk over the end of the capsule; in *Sphagnum,* increasing pressure of a gas present in the capsule forces the operculum open and blows the ripe spores out into the air. The moss *Andreaea* has no operculum or peristome teeth; instead, four longitudinal slits in the side of the capsule open and close as the moisture level changes.

In addition to reproduction by spores and gametes, vegetative reproduction also occurs in mosses. This may take place in one of several ways. If the moss is a branching type, such as *Sphagnum,* branch formation followed by the death of older parts of the plant will result in the establishment of two plants. Some mosses form small, detachable branches capable of growing into new plants. Others form small, disk-like or spindle-shaped structures called **gemmae**, which are produced in groups within leafy cups, on the ends of distinctive stalks, on leaves, at the bases of stems, or even upon rhizoids, depending upon species.

Life Cycles Without Sex

One of the most interesting experiments to be done with mosses involves the removal of slices of the lower part of the capsule of certain species. This portion has more photosynthetic tissue than does any other part of the sporophyte, can be cultured in nutrient solutions, and will develop not into new sporophytes, but into protonemata. These subsequently develop into mature, functional gametophytes. Since they originated from the $2N$ cells of the sporophyte, they too are $2N$. The formation of a gametophyte directly from a sporophyte is termed **apospory** (without spore forma-

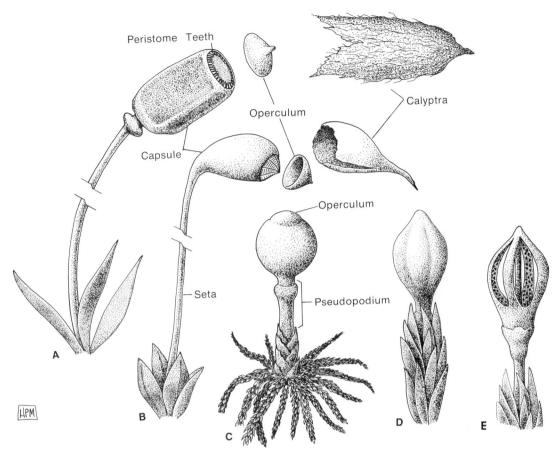

Figure 12–10 Sporophyte structures of mosses, rendered diagrammatically. *A,* The hairy cap moss. *Polytrichum. B, Funaria. C,* The bog moss, *Sphagnum. D, E, Andreaea,* illustrating dehiscence of capsule.

tion, i.e., without meiosis). Aposporous gametophytes are capable of sexual reproduction and may produce tetraploid (4*N*) sporophytes in this way. The entire process may be repeated as many as four times. The tetraploids usually are somewhat larger than the 2*N* plants, but gametophytes of higher ploidy levels are smaller. Interestingly, if apospory occurs in a species that normally forms unisexual gametophytes, the 2*N* gametophytes are bisexual. Why?

The Liverworts (Class Marchantiopsida)

Often on a walk through a damp, narrow ravine, a dense, shingle-like growth of flat, green, thumbnail-sized plants growing among the rocks in damp and shady places can be seen. These plants are **liverworts,** named for their flattened, lobed, and supposedly liver-like appearance.

Most liverworts are prostrate plants of moist habitats; a few are strictly aquatic, and there is considerable diversity in their form. The

299

Figure 12–11 Liverworts growing in a shady area on the side of a sandstone cliff in Northern Illinois.

gametophytes of some (the **leafy liverworts**) have a leafy stem and resemble mosses, although their leaf arrangement is dorsiventral rather than spiral. Others (the **thallose liverworts**) have flat, ribbon-like gametophytes.

The leafy liverworts are considered to be the more primitive members of the liverwort groups, and constitute about 80 per cent of some 280 genera and 9500 species of all liverworts. *Porella* is a common leafy type growing in temperate and tropical regions. It has delicate prostrate male and female gametophytes consisting of branching stems bearing two lateral rows of mitten-shaped leaves, a ventral row of smaller leaves, and unicellular rhizoids. The leaves lack a midrib and are but one cell layer thick. *Porella* often is studied in botany classes as a representative type.

The leaves of one leafy liverwort of temperate regions, *Frullania,* are very interesting, for they are in the form of small pitchers that function to collect and store the water trickling down the surface of stones or the bark of trees upon which it grows.

Many of the leafy liverworts are epiphytic and form colonies on stems, branches, and the large leaves of trees in tropical rain forests and elfin woodlands. Elfin woodlands are mountain cloud forests continuously enveloped in mist; the growth of bryophytes, and especially of leafy liverworts, is particularly luxuriant in this environment.

Leafy liverworts and other bryophytes grow by divisions and development of cells derived from apical cells, and so do thallose liverworts, but the latter are not organized into stems and leaves. Instead, their form is a **thallus,** a term given to any ribbon or leaf-like plant body not differentiated into a leafy stem. Although outwardly simple, the gametophytes of thallose liverworts often are internally more complex than they seem. Some, such as *Marchantia,* a common form, are composed of up to 13 different cell types and for this reason are considered to be the most specialized of all bryophytes. Other thallose liverworts have simpler thalli made up of fewer cell types.

The sporophytes of liverworts resemble those of mosses to the extent that they usually consist of a foot, seta, and capsule; however, a few consist of a capsule only, and the capsules of all lack an

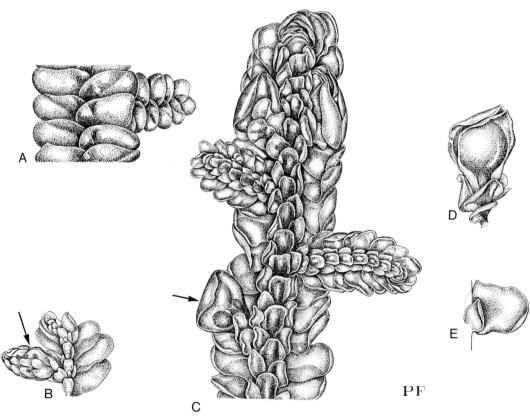

Figure 12–12 *Porella,* a leafy liverwort. *A,* Dorsal view of a portion of a gametophyte. *B,* Ventral view of a male gametophyte. The antheridia (arrow) are concealed by bracts. *C,* Ventral view of a female gametophyte showing the lateral leaves with ventral appendages, the median row of ventral leaves, and several immature sporophytes (arrow) within a perianth. *D,* A sporophyte enclosed within a perianth. *E,* Detail of a single, mitten-shaped lateral leaf showing its ventral appendage.

operculum and peristome teeth and in many cases contain highly specialized hygroscopic cells, the **elaters.** The life cycle of liverworts in overall aspect is quite similar to that of mosses, but liverworts differ in many details of structure and reproduction, as will be seen in the following example.

The Biology of Marchantia

Marchantia polymorpha is a common thallose liverwort found in moist areas, such as open woodlands and shady stream banks. It often grows very abundantly on moist, ash-laden soil following forest fires. The thallus is repeatedly forked (dichotomously branched) and is a fleshy, strap-like structure one or two centimeters wide and about four to six centimeters long. A shallow notch is seen at the tip of each branch, and a growing point composed of several apical cells is present at the base of each notch. Division of these cells gives rise to all the cells of the growing thallus.

A conspicuous midrib appears as a shallow groove on the dorsal side of the thallus and as a ridge on the ventral surface. The entire upper surface of the thallus is composed of diamond-shaped areas, each with a central air pore. These cover underlying photosynthetic chambers; several layers of storage cells containing starch, oil, and mucilage; and a lower epidermis. Three kinds of appendages are found underneath the thallus: peg rhizoids having internal, peg-like thickenings of the cell wall; smooth-walled rhizoids; and multicellular scales. The scales are thought to be protective; smooth-walled rhizoids grow directly down into the soil and function both to anchor the thallus and to conduct nutrients and water; the peg rhizoids are primarily absorptive.

Marchantia reproduces itself in several ways. As the thallus grows and repeatedly forks, older portions die and the more actively growing regions become separated and independent of each other. A more specialized kind of asexual reproduction occurs in cup-like structures containing small vegetative buds about 1 millimeter in diameter, termed **gemmae.** Drops of water falling into these cups cause the gemmae to become detached and to splash out. At the time of shedding the gemma is not dorsiventrally differentiated, but when it is free of the gametophyte rhizoids develop on the side in contact with the soil. Each gemma has two opposite growing points, and the new thallus produced by the divisions of their cells grows out in two directions. It has been shown that gemma-cups form in greatest number when days are short (10 hours or less), primarily in early spring and in the autumn.

Sexual reproduction is induced by long days (12 or more hours of light in a 24-hour cycle). *Marchantia* is unisexual, and the male and female plants produce distinctive sexual branches on their thalli. The female branches are called **archegoniophores**, and bear archegonia between the bases of finger-like projections. Antheridia are borne in pits on the disk-shaped upper parts of the **antheridiophores,** and produce numerous coiled and biflagellate

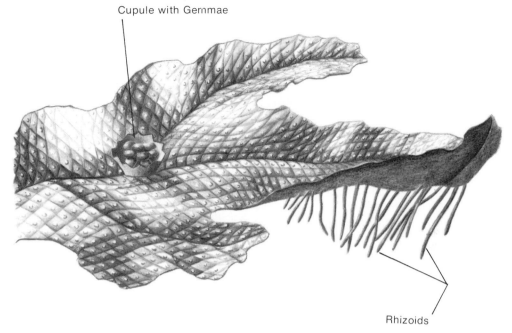

Cupule with Gemmae

Rhizoids

Figure 12–13 Vegetative thallus of *Marchantia polymorpha,* with gemma cups and gemmae (Redrawn from Parihar, N. S. *An Introduction to Embryophyta.* Vol. I., *Bryophyta,* Fifth Edition, Allahabad, India, The Central Book Depot, 1967).

sperm. Fertilization occurs when the sex organs become wet. Motion picture studies have shown that the antheridiophore acts as a splash platform in that raindrops striking it splash over to archegoniophores, carrying sperm with them. At the time of fertilization, the stalk of the archegoniophore is relatively short and the archegonia are therefore near the surface of the thallus. After fertilization, the stalk of the archegoniophore elongates. Although water is required for fertilization, it is said that it is necessary only that a film of water be present in the midrib grooves of the male and female thalli for the sperm to make their way to the archegonia. As in other bryophytes, the sperm are chemically attracted to the archegonia. A number of sporophytes may develop from the archegonia of one female gametophyte, and when mature these sporophytes consist of a foot, a short seta, and a capsule containing meiospores and elaters within a thin wall (only one cell thick).

The Hornworts (Class Anthocerotopsida)

There are about six genera and 320 species of hornworts, and these are widely distributed in the warmer regions of the world. They generally live in moist, partially shaded soil banks or wet meadows. The gametophytes superficially resemble those of thallose liverworts but do not have nearly as many cell types. Photosynthetic cells of

303

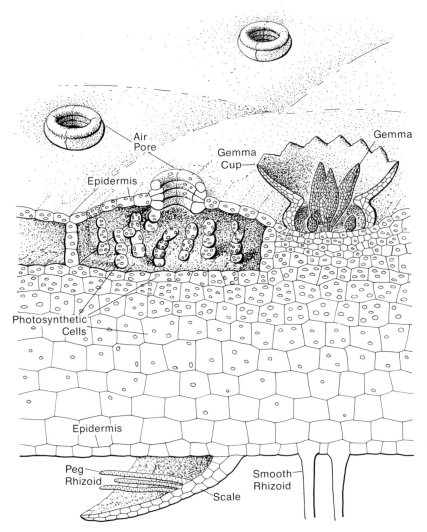

Figure 12–14 Diagrammatic transverse section of the thallus of *Marchantia,* with cell types illustrated.

most species contain a single chloroplast per cell (others have two to four) and, unlike any other bryophytes, each chloroplast has a central pyrenoid. (It will be recalled that pyrenoids are starch-forming bodies occurring in the chloroplasts of most algae.) Cavities are present in the thallus, and contain colonies of the blue-green alga *Nostoc.* These colonies apparently are of no benefit to the thallus; in fact, one study has suggested that the algae may even be slightly detrimental. Some species of hornworts possess gemmae either on the margin or the dorsal surface of the thallus.

Anthoceros, also named *Phaeoceros,* is found in moist, shady places and is the most well-known genus. It is not well adapted to dry conditions, but may be found in moist crannies among rocks; one species grows on decaying wood. The bisexual gametophyte is

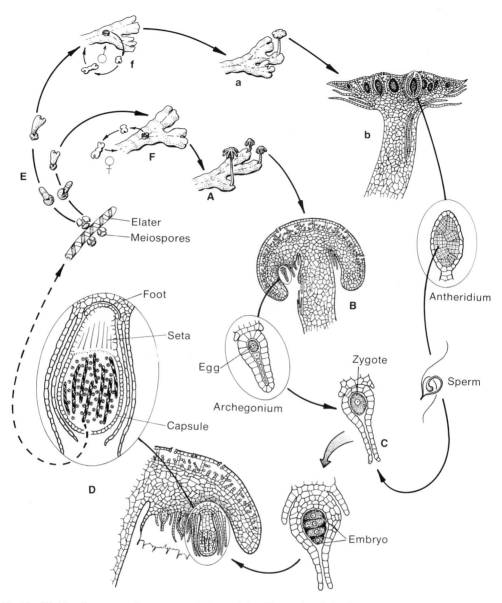

Figure 12–15 Highly diagrammatic representation of the life cycle of the liverwort, *Marchantia*. *a*, Male gametophytes with antheridial branches (antheridiophores). *A*, Female gametophytes with archegonial branches (archegoniophores). *b*, Antheridial branch in longitudinal section. *B*, Archegonial branch in longitudinal section. *C*, Fertilization. *D*, Mature sporophyte; note also the intervening developmental steps. *E*, Germinating spores. *f*, Male, and *F*, female gametophytes, respectively, reproducing vegetatively prior to initiation of development of sex organs.

dark green, usually somewhat lobed and flattened, several cell layers thick and has its archegonia and antheridia sunken in the surface of the thallus. There are no air pores or chambers.

Sexual reproduction is much like that occurring in liverworts

Figure 12–16 Scanning electron micrograph of spores and elaters of *Marchantia* (From Throughton, J. H., and Sampson, F. B. *Plants: A Scanning Electron Microscope Survey.* John Wiley and Sons, Australasia Pty., Ltd., 1975).

and mosses, and results in production of an elongated, cylindrical sporophyte having photosynthetic tissue and stomata. This sporophyte has been of great interest to botanists because of its complexity and its resemblance in some respects to those of vascular plants. Like the sporophytes of other bryophytes, it remains attached to the gametophyte as it develops (Fig. 12–17D), but unlike those of other bryophytes it has a **meristem** at its base. Meristems are regions in which cells retain a capacity for cell division indefinitely. This presence of a meristem confers upon the sporophyte of hornworts a potential for a longer active life (up to nine months in one species) than that of sporophytes of mosses and liverworts.

If the sporophyte of *Anthoceros* could somehow become detached from the gametophyte and survive, it would resemble to some extent the sporophytes of vascular plants, all of which have meristems and are nutritionally independent of the gametophyte when mature. A species of *Anthoceros* found in California nearly approaches this condition, since its sporophytes are relatively long-lived and its gametophytes become progressively more disorganized; as a result, the sporophytes are very nearly independent plants.

Alternation of Generations

Alternation of spore- and gamete-forming generations is found in nearly all groups of eukaryotic plants, and universally among higher green plants. In the bryophytes we have seen that the 1*N*, gamete-forming generation is nutritionally independent, and the sporophyte is always nutritionally dependent upon the gametophyte. In *Anthoceros,* the nature of the sporophyte has led botanists to speculate that *Anthoceros* might represent a stage toward complete independence of the sporophyte, a characteristic of higher, vascular plants. For example, the tree fern, the giant redwood, and the oak tree all are sporophytes. Their gametophytes, on the other hand, are very small and comparatively short-lived stages in the life cycle.

It has been suggested that primitive plants resembling *Anthoceros* might have developed completely independent sporophytes by losing the connection with the gametophytes and developing rhizoids or mycorrhizae-like fungi, which would allow them to obtain water and nutrients directly from the soil. If such sporophytes then were to develop vascular tissue (perhaps by differentiation of xylem and phloem in the central strand of the seta or the columella), this might constitute a starting point for evolution of vascular plants.

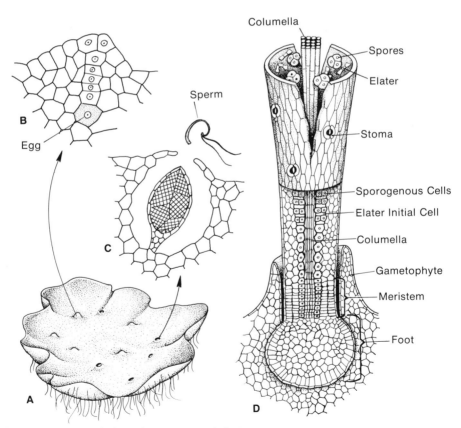

Figure 12–17 Diagrammatic rendering of structures of *Anthoceros,* the hornwort. *A,* Gametophyte plant. *B,* Archegonium. *C,* Antheridium. *D,* Sporophyte plant.

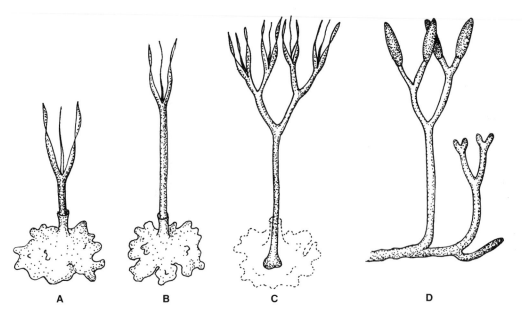

Figure 12–18 Highly diagrammatic view of the hypothetical evolution of the sporophyte generation according to the antithetic theory. *A, Anthoceros. B,* Prolongation of life of the sporophyte generation. *C,* Evolution of an independent, branching sporophyte. *D,* Primitive vascular sporophyte (refer also to Figure 13–4). (Modified from Smith, G. W. *Cryptogamic Botany,* Volume II, Second Edition. New York, McGraw-Hill Book Co., Inc., 1955).

This concept, sometimes called the **antithetic theory**, suggests that the sporophyte generation is a new generation, inserted into the life cycle by evolution from a zygote. However, we shall see in the next chapter that the discovery of ancient land plants having vascularized sporophytes and new understandings of alternation of generations and apogamy and apospory have led many botanists to look elsewhere than the bryophytes for ancestors of vascular plants.

Evolutionary Relationships

It is generally believed that mosses, liverworts, and hornworts have a common ancestry, and that the earliest bryophytes evolved from the green algae. Several characteristics of the bryophytes are thought to reflect algal ancestry. The protonemata of mosses are so similar to certain filamentous green algae that sometimes they have been mistaken for one another. The sperm of bryophytes have the same basic flagellar structure (i.e., a 9 + 2 system of internal fibers) as those of green algae, and water is required for fertilization just as it is by algae. Cellular pigmentation is almost identical in both groups; for both have chlorophylls *a* and *b*, beta-carotene, and xanthophylls. Starch is the storage product in both. One group of bryophytes, the hornworts, has chloroplasts containing pyrenoids, as do the green algae; however, bryophytes differ from algae in one important aspect—the structure of their sex organs. Most algae have unicellular sex organs; whereas bryophytes have multicellular archegonia and antheridia. There are no very good examples among the algae to indicate how these may have evolved.

Although bryophytes are composed of delicate tissues that would not be preserved as readily in the form of fossils as the harder tissues of vascular plants, remains of thallose liverworts have been found in Devonian rocks (about 360 million years old), and fossils of other liverworts are present in Carboniferous deposits (about 300 million years old). Other mosses, some of which appear related to *Sphagnum,* have been described from Permian rocks (about 280 million years old). On the other hand, vascular plants of the Silurian age (400 million years old) are known, and this seems to argue against their derivation from bryophytes. However, it is possible that bryophytes are at least as ancient as the vascular plants, although the current viewpoint is that they are not ancestral to vascular plants. It is generally believed today that all archegoniate plants share a common ancestry and that bryophytes probably are an offshoot from an evolutionary line of plants proceeding from the green algae to the vascular plants, or that they may be descendants even of early vascular plants. In the latter event, they would have lost their vascular tissue as a consequence of evolutionary simplification.

Another theory, proposed by the British botanist A. H. Church, holds that the ancestral bryophyte had similar independent leafy gametophytes and sporophytes quite similar to the gametophytes of present day mosses, and that the sporophyte has become progressively reduced and more and more dependent upon the gametophyte. Present-day sporophytes of the three groups of bryophytes are highly specialized in divergent ways, and those of the hornworts apparently have attained a higher state of development than have those of mosses and liverworts, the latter being the simplest. But it is well known that evolution may work in the direction of simplicity through reduction of complexity, as well as in the direction of increasing complexity. Thus, the sporophytes of liverworts, once considered to be quite primitive, are now thought to represent the end result of evolutionary reduction.

SUMMARY

The bryophytes are a group of plants that are largely terrestrial and characterized by independent, free-living gametophytes and attached, nutritionally dependent sporophytes. The characteristic multicellular sex organs of the group are flask-shaped archegonia (female) and club-shaped antheridia (male). Although bryophytes are predominantly land plants, they are all aquatic to the extent that water is required for fertilization, since the sperm cells are flagellated and must swim to the archegonia.

Even though bryophytes are small plants and are individually insignificant, they form dense colonies and may be ecologically important as the first plants to appear on barren areas (such as burned-over forest land, lava flows, and open water and wetlands). One such plant, *Sphagnum,* is well known for its ability to convert open-water habitats to peat bogs.

The bryophytes all show such features as autotrophic gametophytes bearing archegonia and antheridia, and non-vascular sporophytes attached to gametophytes, but three subgroups may be distinguished: the mosses, the liverworts, and the hornworts. Gametophytes of mosses have stems with spirally arranged leaves; gametophytes of liverworts either have dorsiventrally arranged leaves on branching stems (leafy liverworts) or are thallose in form. In the latter, the gametophyte is a flat, lobed thallus, a simple body not differentiated into stems and leaves. The gametophytes of hornworts also are thallose in form. Sporophytes also differ in the three groups. Those of hornworts are the most complex, those of mosses somewhat less so, and those of liverworts are of comparatively simple structure.

Because to some botanists some of the differences between them seem to be fundamental, mosses, liverworts and hornworts are occasionally classified in separate divisions. In recognition of basic similarities of sex organs, a number of similar morphological and anatomical features, and similar life cycles, the general practice is to include them all in one division.

Division Bryophyta: The small, non-vascular, archegoniate plants.

CLASS BRYOPSIDA: THE MOSSES. This class consists of about 670 genera comprising approximately 14,500 species. Members of this class have radially symmetrical gametophytes consisting of a central stem or axis and leaves with midribs. Sporophytes have stomata and may be photosynthetic.)

Examples: Polytrichum, Sphagnum, Dawsonia, Andreaea, and *Funaria.*

CLASS MARCHANTIOPSIDA: THE LIVERWORTS. There are about 280 genera and 9500 species. These are bryophytes having a dorsiventral organization of gametophyte structures. Leaves, if present, lack midribs. Sporophytes lack opercula, stomata, and columella, but have elaters.

Examples: Marchantia, Porella, Pellia, and *Frullania.*

CLASS ANTHOCEROTOPSIDA: THE HORNWORTS. There are five genera and about 320 species. This class differs from other bryophytes in that its members have a simple, thallose gametophyte and a photosynthetic sporophyte with stomata, a columella, a basal meristem, and elaters, but lack opercula.

Example: Anthoceros (Phaeoceros).

DISCUSSION QUESTIONS

1. In what fundamental respects do mosses, liverworts, and hornworts resemble each other? In what aspect do they resemble other terrestrial plants? In what important aspects do they differ from higher plants?
2. What roles do bryophytes play in ecological succession?
3. How does a peat bog develop?
4. How may fossil pollen be used in discovering the ecological history of an area?
5. What are elfin woodlands? Where do they occur?
6. Do moss plants possess any kind of conducting tissue? Elaborate.
7. What is a protonema? What may be its evolutionary significance?
8. Where are meiospores produced in mosses? What do they produce?
9. Describe an archegonium. An antheridium. What basic requirement

must be met in order for fertilization to occur? What is the significance of this from an evolutionary standpoint?

10. In what way are the leaves of *Sphagnum* specialized? What are the results of such specializations?

11. What features of a moss capsule aid in spore dispersal?

12. In what ways does the sporophyte of *Anthoceros* appear to support the antithetic theory of evolution of vascular plants?

SUPPLEMENTAL READING

Conard, H. S. *How to Know the Mosses and Liverworts.* (revised ed.) Dubuque, Iowa: Wm. C. Brown Co., 1956.

Doyle, W. T. *The Biology of Higher Cryptograms.* New York: The MacMillan Co., 1970.

Grout, A. J. *Mosses with a Hand Lens,* Newfane, Vermont: (4th ed.) A. J. Grout, 1947 (for sale at Field Museum of Natural History, Chicago, Illinois).

Parihar, N. S. *An Introduction to Embryophyta,* Vol. I. Bryophyta, 5th ed. Allahabad, India: Central Book Depot, 1967.

Thomson, V. W. *Some Common Mosses.* Audubon Nature Bulletin, Ser. 11, No. 7. New York: National Audubon Society, 1966.

Watson, E. V. *The Structure and Life of Bryophytes,* 2nd ed. London: Hutchinson University Library, 1967.

A reconstruction of a Devonian landscape from the viewpoint of science fiction.

Chapter 13

Early Land Plants

INVADING THE LAND • THE FIRST LAND PLANTS • PSILOPHYTON PRIN-
CEPS • SIR WILLIAM DAWSON • DIVISION RHYNIOPHYTA • BIOLOGY
OF RHYNIA • THE STUDY OF FOSSILS • HOMOLOGOUS THEORY • THE
SCOURING RUSHES • BIOLOGY OF EQUISETUM • THE CLUB MOSSES •
HOMOSPOROUS LYCOPODS • BIOLOGY OF *LYCOPODIUM* • HETEROSPOR-
OUS LYCOPODS • BIOLOGY OF *SELAGINELLA* • OTHER LIVING LYCOPODS
• EVOLUTIONARY TRENDS IN VASCULAR PLANTS • SUMMARY

We have noted in Chapter 3 that life began in the sea more than
3 billion years ago, a span of time so vast that it is almost in-
comprehensible to us. If we were to compare this length of time with
the distance one might walk from the Atlantic seaboard to the Pacific coast of America, then the period that the human race has been
in existence would be equivalent to the last 100 steps of the journey.
For nearly two thirds of these seemingly endless reaches of time, life
existed only in the seas. Here, environmental conditions were not as
rigorous as on land. Dissolved nutrients and, of course, water were
plentiful. Harmful radiation was effectively screened out by surface
layers of water, and reproductive dispersal of new cells was accomplished simply by drifting about.

Among the early life-forms were photosynthetic algae and for
millions upon millions of years they contributed their oxygen to the
environment so that eventually aerobic respiration became possible
and animal life came into existence.

Meanwhile the land lay bleak, barren, and devoid of life, its
contour comprised mainly of shifting sand dunes, gravel slopes,
rocky outcroppings, blackened lava flows, and eroded hills and
ravines of silt and clay. Then about one-half billion years ago sufficient oxygen had accumulated in the atmosphere to screen out the
most harmful radiation and make the land habitable.

The sun shown behind Bush, over low hills, preparing to set. The hills were bare except along the river bed, where runty little leafless Psilophyton grew in the shade of
primitive lycopods. Bush cast no shadow.
The distant sound of motor bikes, the only sound in the great Devonian silence, made
him nervous. At the fringe of his vision, a movement on the ground made him jump.
Four lobe fins jostled in a shallow pool, thrashing into the shallows. They struggled
over the red mud, their curiously armored heads lifting off the ground as they peered
ahead with comic eagerness. Bush made as if to photograph them with his wrist camera, and thought better of it; he had photographed lobe fins before.

BRIAN ALDISS: *Cryptozoic*, DOUBLEDAY, INC.

Invading the Land

We have noted in Chapter 6 that competition for space, for energy, and for the products of energy brings about the evolution of new strategies for survival among plants and animals. Doubtless the struggle for survival in the ancient seas was as keen as it is today; as a consequence, organisms capable of surviving out of water, even if only for brief periods of time between tides, floods, or rains, achieved an advantage and began the transition to a life on land. We know that no population of organisms can survive without an efficient mode of reproduction. Since early life existed and reproduced in the water it is not surprising that less advanced terrestrial forms—both plant and animal—still use water as a site for reproductive activities. Most of us are aware, for instance, that the eggs of amphibian animals are fertilized in the water, and the more primitive land plants also have retained a requirement for water in their reproduction. Even though their egg cells are retained within protective structures and are non-motile, their sperm cells are flagellated and swim freely through water en route to the egg. It is an interesting and important point that the first amphibian animals seem to have been preceded by the earliest land plants, and it is likely that a land vegetation existed before the animals moved to the land. So the harsh features of the barren earth were softened by plant life, and habitats supplying food and shelter for animal life came into being.

Recent theories of geology suggest that the land masses of the earth have drifted from place to place, so that presently some of them are thousands of miles from their locations many millions of years ago. Even though fossils of the earliest land plants are found in regions having harsh climates, we believe that such plants evolved in mild tropical regions, where an easier transition from water to land could be made. In addition to land movements, there also were major long-term climatic changes; therefore, it is possible to reconcile the present disposition of fossil plants and animals with tropical and sub-tropical environments in which they lived. If travel through time were possible, a visitor from our time to that long-ago era would likely find the most abundant life in the seas, but here and there various plant groups would be colonizing the land wherever there was sufficient water to allow them to complete their reproductive cycles. Thus, we believe, the earth eventually became the green and pleasant place it is today.

The First Land Plants

The first land plants were undoubtedly algae. They may have looked something like those algae that survive alternate wetting and drying in the intertidal zones of the sea, or they may have been simple filamentous types like the green algae that we see growing on mud flats. Comparative biochemical studies between present-day plants tend to support the belief that the higher land plants are more closely related to the green algae than to any other algal group. Un-

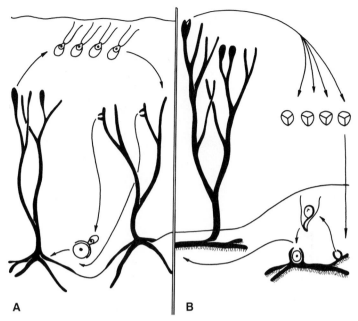

Figure 13-1 Hypothetical stages in the evolution of the first terrestrial plants. *A,* Ancestral green alga having alteration of generations and oogamy. *B,* Primitive vascular plant with upright sporophyte that produced wind-blown meiospores. The gametophyte is depicted as a prostrate plant requiring water for fertilization (Redrawn from Stewart, W. N. An Upward Look in Plant Morphology. *Phytomorphology 14*:120–134, 1964).

fortunately there exist no recognizable fossils of any transitional forms. We speculate that some of them, in adapting to life on land, developed organs (probably rhizoidal hairs) capable of extracting water and nutrients from the soil, and upright branches (which exposed more of the photosynthetic tissues to the sun's rays). An impervious epidermis enables land plants to withstand drying, and is usually accompanied by a ventilation system of pores and passageways—plants, like animals, require oxygen, and, in addition, carbon dioxide, for photosynthesis. A cutinized epidermis and stomata may have appeared rather early in land plant evolution.

Swimming, flagellated meiospores are characteristic of many green algae but are of limited usefulness on land. The development of lightweight and resistant air-borne meiospores and of sporangia atop upright branches enabled primitive plants to colonize drier habitats inaccessible to swimming spores.

Finally, since the upright growth habit is so characteristic of land plants in general and is accompanied by strengthening and supporting tissues as well as conduction (or **vascular**), tissues, we envision that some groups of early land plants developed such tissue systems and became the first **vascular plants**.

Psilophyton princeps

We have no way of knowing with any certainty when the evolutionary transition to vascular plants occurred, but we are becoming

Figure 13–2 Sir William Dawson (1820–1899) (From Dawson, J. W. *Fifty Years of Work in Canada,* London, Ballentyne, Hanson and Co., 1901).

more and more informed as to the nature of the earliest true vascular plants. In the same year that Charles Darwin published *The Origin of Species* (1859) another important contribution to the theory of evolution appeared in the form of a description of an extinct vascular plant that had been found by a Canadian geologist, William Dawson, in a quarry on the Gaspé Peninsula of Nova Scotia. Dawson named this fossil *Psilophyton princeps.* Not only was it older than any heretofore known plant, but it also was unlike most known plants; in fact, there was scepticism as to the validity of the discovery, and this persisted for more than 50 years until discovery of similar fossilized plants in another part of the world validated the earlier work.

Sir William Dawson

John William Dawson was born in 1820 to Scottish immigrant parents in Nova Scotia. As a boy, he was intensely interested in nature and collected specimens of all sorts, like many youngsters of today; however, his intelligence and curiosity carried him much farther than is typical of such youthful enthusiasms, and this led him into a distinguished career in science and education. In his thirty-fourth year he became President of McGill University in Montreal and during the next 39 years he built it into one of the great world universities.

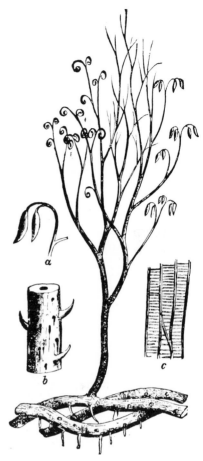

Figure 13-3 Restoration of *Psilophyton princeps* by Sir William Dawson (From Dawson, W. *The Geological History of Plants,* 1896).

In his years at McGill, Dawson accomplished a prodigious amount of work. In addition to performing administrative duties he landscaped the campus (buying the trees and shrubs with his own funds), entertained students and faculty in his home, gave twenty lectures a week, and still found time for extensive field studies. Dawson also was genuinely concerned with the education of women. In an era in which women were considered to be unsuited to intellectual pursuits, he vigorously promoted the cause of university education for women and saw to it that they were admitted to classes at McGill.

During his lifetime, Dawson wrote more than 150 articles and books. The illustration of *Psilophyton princeps* (Fig. 13–3) is from his *magnum opus, The Geological History of Plants.*

DIVISION RHYNIOPHYTA

Nearly 60 years elapsed after Dawson's discovery of *Psilophyton* before additional plants of similar nature were discovered. Then,

317

from 1917 to 1921, two Englishmen, R. Kidston and W. H. Lang, described (from the Old Red Sandstone beds near Rhynie, Scotland) two Lower Devonian vascular plants, *Rhynia* and *Horneophyton,* which, like *Psilophyton,* were rootless and leafless plants with terminal sporangia. Subsequent discoveries have added other genera to the list of primitive Paleozoic plants. One rhyniophyte, *Cooksonia,* has the distinction of being the oldest vascular plant known, since it is from the Silurian Period and thus is approximately 400 million years old.

The concept of *Psilophyton princeps,* however, has undergone a reappraisal and it is now recognized that fossil plant fragments of several different types were combined by Dawson in his original reconstruction. Only specimens corresponding to the upper part of his reconstruction are presently classified as *Psilophyton princeps.*

Biology of Rhynia

The genus *Rhynia* is represented by small rush-like plants about 20 centimeters tall. They grew in wet soil, spreading by extension of horizontal stems, or **rhizomes,** from which aerial branches arose. At a distance it would have been difficult to distinguish a Devonian marsh composed of *Rhynia* plants from a present-day marsh or pond border overgrown with rushes.

Rhynia plants had neither roots nor leaves. Patches of rhizoidal hairs occurred on their rhizomes, and it is assumed that their aerial branches were photosynthetic organs. The branches of some of the plants bore elongate sporangia with spores marked by a Y-shaped ridge (**the triradiate ridge** where each one was associated with three others in a cluster of four, or **tetrad**). This is an observation of fundamental importance, for it is evidence that such spores are meiospores and that the plant was a sporophyte.

In the center of a stem of *Rhynia,* there was a rod of vascular tissue that included a tissue type known as **xylem;** this simple arrangement constitutes a stem type known as a **protostele.** The xylem of *Rhynia,* as that of *Psilophyton* and other rhyniophytes, was composed of **tracheids,** i.e., empty, dead cells of varied form among vascular plants that serve as water-conducting elements. The tracheids of the rhyniophytes are elongate, with tapering ends and horizontal thin areas, or **pits,** in their side walls. Their pits give these tracheids a ladder-like appearance, and for this reason they are called **scalariform tracheids.** Scalariform tracheids are considered to be the most primitive type of xylem elements.

Both xylem (water-conducting) and **phloem** (food-transporting) cells make up the vascular tissues of higher plants, but the latter is not distinguishable in the rhyniophytes. It is possible that phloem cells had not evolved very far in that group. The phloem in the other primitive vascular plants discussed in this chapter is composed of elongate living cells, called **sieve cells,** having slanting end walls and perforate, sieve-like areas through which food substances flow. These sieve areas are located principally in the end walls, but are

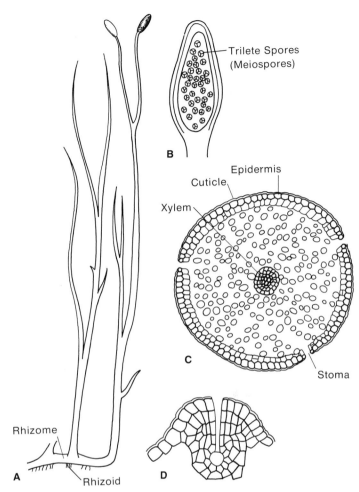

Figure 13–4 *A*, Reconstruction of *Rhynia* plant. *B*, Sporangium and spores of *Rhynia*. *C*, Cross section of *Rhynia* stem. *D*, Section of so-called archegonium of *Rhynia*. (*A, D,* redrawn from Bierhorst, D. W. Morphology of Vascular Plants, New York, MacMillan Co., 1971; *B, C,* redrawn from Smith, G. W. Cryptogamic Botany, Vol. II., Second Edition, New York, McGraw-Hill Book Co., Inc., 1955.)

present also in the lateral walls. The xylem and phloem of advanced vascular plants, particularly the flowering plants, are more complex and will be described in later chapters.

It has been reported that some *Rhynia* stems bore archegonia, but this feature is still in dispute. The structures in question resemble archegonia, but their state of preservation is not sufficiently complete for general agreement among botanists as to their true nature. However, if it turns out that these structures really are archegonia, then both the sporophytes and the gametophytes were vascularized and of similar form.

The Study of Fossils

Fossils are of three main types. One type, called a **compression,** consists of the actual tissues of a plant or animal pressed flat under such tremendous heat and pressure by overlying sediments that much of the organic matter is driven off in the form of liquid or gas, leaving behind a residue consisting mostly of carbon. Little inner cellular structure is seen in a compression, but some surface detail and the overall shape of the organism is visible. Leaves often are preserved in this way, and fish too are often amazingly well preserved. A second type, called a **cast,** has no original plant or animal matter. Mud forms a mold about the dead organism, hardens, and eventually becomes hollow when the organism decays. Then mud or other sediment seeps into the mold and hardens to form the cast. Sometimes such casts show surface details as well as the three-dimensional form of the original specimen. A third kind of fossil is the **petrifaction.** The actual cells of the organism are slowly infiltrated with mineral water and, in part, replaced by precipitated minerals; petrified wood is a good example.

It is possible to cut sections of petrified plant specimens with a rock saw and then, after grinding them until they are very thin, to study microscopically the details of cellular structure and tissue or-

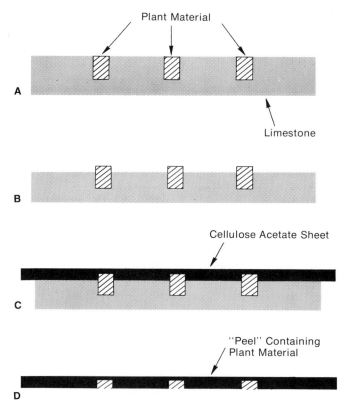

Figure 13–5 Sequences in preparation of a fossil peel, shown diagrammatically. *A,* Limestone rock containing fossil plant material is cut and ground flat. *B,* Surface is etched with HCl. *C,* Surface is flooded with solvent of plastic film (acetone). Plastic film is laid on etched surface, and adheres to fossil material. *D,* When dry, film is peeled off, taking a thin layer of the fossil plant material with it (Redrawn from *Evolution and Plants of the Past,* by H. P. Banks. ⓒ 1970 by Wadsworth Publishing Company, Inc., Belmont, California 94002. Reprinted by permission of the publisher).

ganization. An alternate and less tedious method is to etch the cut surface of a petrification with acid. This dissolves away the supporting rock material, leaving the carbonized cell material standing in relief above the surface. Acetone or a similar solvent then is applied to the etched area, and a film of cellulose acetate is laid over it. This partly dissolves the film, which then adheres to the exposed cell material. After drying the film may be pulled away; and with it will come a thin layer of carbonized fossil material. If done carefully, this etching and peeling process results in near-perfect sections of whatever structures are present. Some peels of this kind show cell structures nearly as clearly as do slides prepared from a living plant.

Homologous Theory

It will be recalled that bryophytes are non-vascular, terrestrial plants of relatively simple form, with independent green gametophytes and sporophytes that are always nutritionally dependent upon the gametophyte to which they are attached. At one time many botanists considered the bryophytes to be ancestral to the vascular plants, and considered the sporophyte generation to represent a new generation that evolved from the zygote into a multicellular, meiospore-producing plant (the **antithetic theory**). The distinction between the two generations seemed to be upheld by the discovery in the nineteenth century of meiosis and the basic 1N and 2N nature of the chromosomes of gametophytes and sporophytes. Subsequently, however, the realization that the earliest fossil vascular plants, actually older than any known fossil bryophytes, were of the sporophyte generation brought about a reappraisal of alternation of generations.

It is now generally believed that the earliest vascular plants had similar vascularized gametophytes and sporophytes; in fact, as we have noted earlier, some stems of *Rhynia* may have borne archegonia. Additionally, the fact that apogamy and apospory occur in all groups of vascular plants as well as in bryophytes is thought to support the concept that gametophytes and sporophytes are basically similar. Since these processes produce gametophytes and sporophytes with the same chromosome number, the gametophyte and the sporophyte generation cannot be differentiated on the basis of 1N and 2N chromosome number. Moreover, because each generation is capable of developing directly into the other by these two asexual processes, neither meiosis nor fertilization are necessarily distinguishing features of the two generations; rather, the gametophyte form and the sporophyte form are two expressions of the genotype (all of the genes) of the plant. Which of these forms is expressed depends on a multiplicity of internal and external conditions that activate some genes and inhibit or repress others.

The **homologous theory** of evolution of land plants contends that vascular plants evolved from ancestors (probably green algae) that had similar meiospore- and gamete-producing generations. *Ulva,* the sea lettuce, though somewhat specialized, might exemplify this algal ancestor.

THE SCOURING RUSHES
(DIVISION EQUISETOPHYTA)

Related to the rhyniophytes were primitive plants having stems with whorls of appendages. The oldest known of these is a fossil plant, *Hyenia,* which lived about the same time as *Psilophyton.* Appendages attached circumferentially at the same level on a stem constitute a **whorl,** and their whorls of appendages gave a jointed

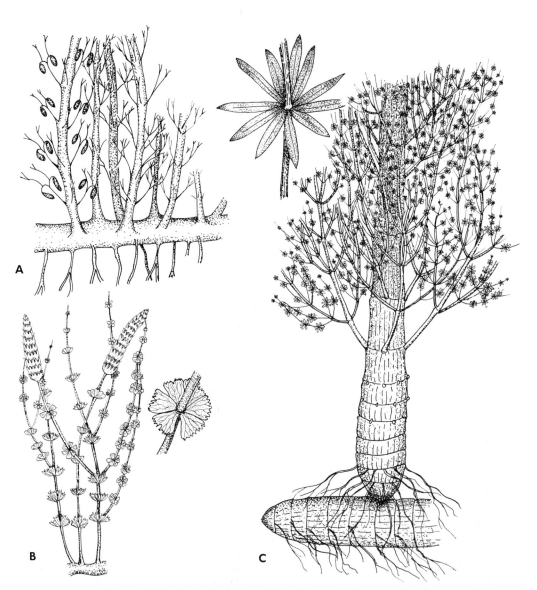

Figure 13–6 Equisetophytes of the Paleozoic Era seen in diagrammatic form. *A,* Reconstruction of *Hyenia,* a Middle Devonian species that had whorls of appendages but lacked cones. *B, Sphenophyllum,* an Upper Devonian and Carboniferous Period plant. *C, Calamites,* an Upper Devonian and Carboniferous Period plant somewhat resembling the modern-day *Equisetum.* (Redrawn from Smith, G. M. *Cryptogamic Botany,* Vol. II. Second Edition. New York, McGraw-Hill Book Co., Inc., 1955.)

appearance to this particular group of plants. This jointed appearance generally characterizes the **Equisetophyta,** including its sole surviving genus, *Equisetum.*

The Equisetophyta reached their ascendancy in the latter part of the Paleozoic Era, sometimes referred to as the Coal Age (Carboniferous Period). Two extinct genera in particular are associated with the vegetation of those times. *Calamites* was a large plant, (up to about 30 meters tall and a half a meter in diameter) superficially resembling bamboo, but in detail much like the present-day but comparatively small *Equisetum. Sphenophyllum* was a shrubby plant with whorls of multiveined leaves that were either forked or wedge-shaped. Both *Calamites* and *Sphenophyllum* had terminal cones, as does *Equisetum.*

Biology of Equisetum

The present-day equisetophytes do not constitute an ecologically significant component of any flora but are, nevertheless, interesting to us as surviving members of a major element in the vegetation of the Paleozoic Era.

The genus *Equisetum* is represented by some twenty species occurring in a variety of climates throughout the world except in Australia and Antarctica. Generally they are plants of moist areas, but some species are found in dryer habitats. *Equisetum arvense,* for example, is commonly found growing among the cinders of railway embankments. Most species are small plants less than a meter tall, but a tropical species, *Equisetum giganteum,* is six meters tall; however, it is a spindly plant (with stems about two and a half centimeters in diameter) and requires support by surrounding vegetation.

The anatomy of *Equisetum* is rather complex. Both the rhizome

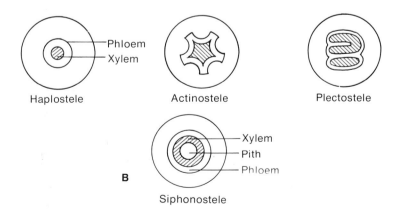

Figure 13–7 Stelar types shown in highly diagrammatic fashion.

and the upright branches have a pith that is solid at the **nodes** (a node is a point where a leaf is attached) and hollow in the **internodes** (region between two adjacent nodes). A stem with a pith is said to be a **siphonostele,** and is considered more advanced than a protostele.

All species of *Equisetum* have whorls of scale-like leaves at each node, and many species also have whorls of branches at the nodes. The vascular tissue of the stems forms a complete cylinder at each node and a ring of vascular strands in the internodes, where

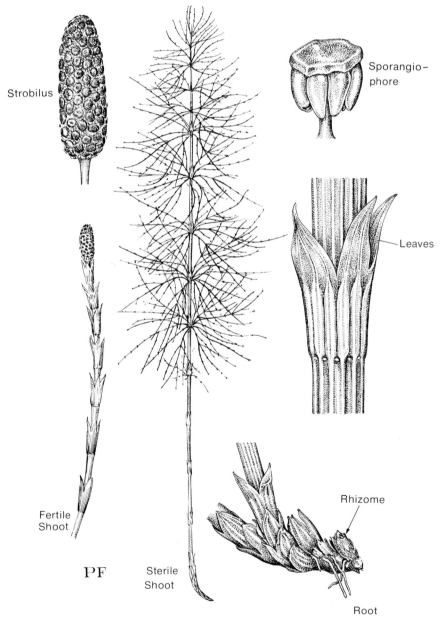

Figure 13–8 *Equisetum sylvaticum,* a species having both sterile and fertile branches produced by the underground rhizome.

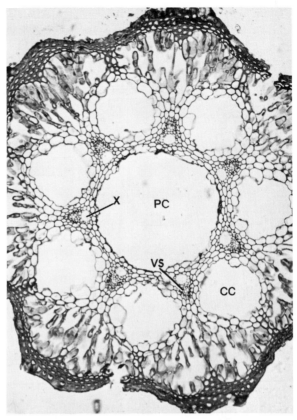

Figure 13–9 Cross section of a stem of *Equisetum*. PC, Central pith canal; X, xylem canal (carinal canal); VS, Vascular strand (vallecular canal); CC, Cortical canal (vallecular canal).

the strands are associated with a system of canals. Canals also are present in the cortex (Fig. 13–9).

At the periphery of the cortex, well-defined areas of strengthening fibers (sclerenchyma) can be discerned. Food and water storage tissue (parenchyma) occurs both in the pith and in the cortex. The outer cortical cells are photosynthetic. The epidermis is composed of a single layer of cells with walls containing silica that give the plant its characteristic harsh texture. The common name **scouring rush** refers to the former use of *Equisetum* for scouring pots and pans in the days before Brillo and Chore Girl.

Microscopic slides of plant tissues are prepared by cutting very thin slices of the plant, with a cutting machine called a **microtome**. Microtome knives have very sharp and delicate edges and become dull rather quickly when used to cut sections of *Equisetum* stem unless the stems first are soaked in hydrofluoric acid, the only effective silica solvent. Most slides of *Equisetum* used in botany classes have been prepared in this way, but it is said that specimens of *Equisetum* collected on the Keewenaw Peninsula of Michigan require no treatment with hydrofluoric acid prior to sectioning with the microtome. Evidently plants growing in this iron-rich region have a secret of mineral nutrition about which we know little.

325

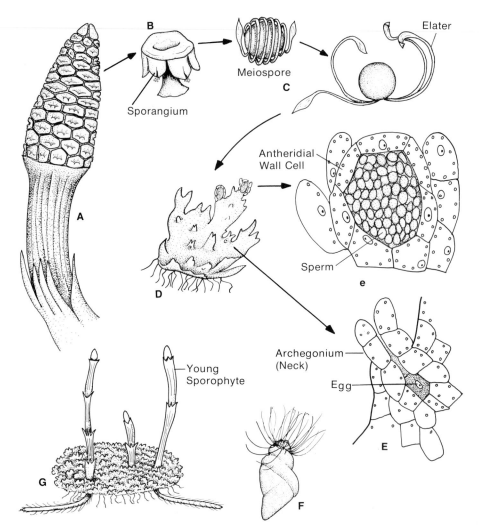

Figure 13-10 Life history of *Equisetum. A,* Sporophyte. *B,* Sporophyll. *C,* Meiospores and elaters. *D,* Gametophyte plant. *e,* Antheridium. *E,* Archegonium. *F,* Multiflagellated sperm cell (about 80 flagella are normally present). *G,* Gametophyte plant with young sporophyte plants attached.

In some branching forms of *Equisetum,* two kinds of upright stems are formed: non-green and unbranched fertile shoots bearing cones; and green, branched, sterile shoots (Fig. 13–8). Other species have unbranching, photosynthetic fertile stems, and still others have branching fertile stems. The young fertile shoots were considered a delicacy by some tribes of American Indians. They are doubtless of high food value, since proteins, starch, and oils tend to accumulate in reproductive tissues and cells of plants.

Short and slender roots occur at the nodes of rhizomes and the lower parts of aerial stems. Both stems and roots arise from single apical cells.

The cone of *Equisetum* is composed of whorls of umbrella-shaped **sporangiophores**, each bearing 8 to 10 sporangia. Short-lived green meiospores are produced in the sporangia and have hygroscopic appendages called **elaters**. There are four elaters per meiospore; these twist and coil with changes in humidity, conferring a limited mobility upon the spores and aiding in their dispersal. Some, but not all, of the fossil equisetophytes also had spores with elaters. In one experiment reported by Dr. R. W. Baxter of the University of Kansas, the meiospores of a Paleozoic equisetophyte were removed from a petrified cone, using hydrochloric acid to dissolve away the surrounding rock. The elaters of these spores, 300 million years after they were formed, still had the ability to twist and bend in response to wetting and drying.

When meiospores germinate, they form green gametophytes of irregular form that bear either antheridia or archegonia, but seldom both at the same time. Gametophytes of *Equisetum* are small, usually less than a centimeter across, but are long-lived and have been kept in culture for years. After fertilization the zygote develops into an upright sporophyte, and several may be formed on one gametophyte.

THE CLUB MOSSES (DIVISION LYCOPODIOPHYTA)

Among the rhyniophytes were some with lateral rather than terminal sporangia. The oldest of these is *Zosterophyllum,* which together with several other fossil genera probably constitute the ancestors of a group of plants, both fossil and living, collectively called the **club mosses** or **lycopods.** Lycopods also have lateral sporangia and in most instances a simple single-veined leaf type, the **microphyll**. One of the oldest lycopods is a Lower Devonian plant called *Baragwanathia.* Were it now living it might easily be taken to be one of the species of the present-day genus *Lycopodium.* The living lycopods are an extremely ancient group of vascular plants that have survived to this day without having undergone any great changes.

Many of the lycopods, both fossil and living, possess cones. This feature, together with the moss-like appearance, has given them the name *club moss.* They are, however, no more closely related to the true mosses than are any other living groups of plants. The cone of a club moss is composed of spirally-arranged **sporophylls.** Each sporophyll resembles a foliage leaf except that it bears a single sporangium on its upper surface near the base.

The sporangia of a number of the lycopods resemble those of bryophytes, equisetophytes, rhyniophytes, and most ferns in that they contain meiospores of uniform dimensions. For that reason they are said to be **homosporous**. Some other lycopods, as well as a few ferns and all seed plants, produce meiospores of two sizes, and hence are said to be **heterosporous.** As we will see, heterospory is always associated with the production of quite specialized male and female gametophytes.

Homosporous Lycopods (Class Lycopodiopsida)

There are two living genera of homosporous lycopods, *Lycopodium* and *Phylloglossum.* The 200 or so species of *Lycopodium* are worldwide in distribution, but there is only one species of *Phylloglossum,* a small plant found only in Australia, Tasmania, and New Zealand. Species of *Lycopodium,* to which the common name **ground pine** is often applied in reference to their perennial, evergreen, and usually creeping growth habit, are quite common in forests in the Northern United States and in mountainous regions. Often because of their great beauty they are gathered for Christmas decorations and sometimes are harvested for the manufacture of wreaths; all of this has caused them to become rare in many regions, but fortunately they have been designated as protected plants in some states, and it is illegal to collect them.

Biology of Lycopodium

The axis of *Lycopodium,* rhizome as well as aerial stem, is always a protostele. Several layers of **pericycle** cells surround the phloem in the stele, and it is from these cells that roots arise. The pericycle may be defined as the outer layer of the stele. It is a tissue that retains the ability to produce additional cells by mitosis, and often is involved in the formation of new roots. The roots of *Lycopodium* do not develop in any particular pattern, but are formed wherever a stem is in contact with the soil. Roots formed from stems in this way are called **adventitious roots.** Outside the stele is a cortex composed of an outer zone of photosynthetic cells, an intermediate zone of storage cells (the **parenchyma**), and a single inner cell layer, the **endodermis**. An epidermis with stomata is present outside the cortex.

Lycopodium leaves are arranged either spirally or in whorls of four. Each leaf is supplied by a single branch of xylem and phloem, called a **leaf trace**, that connects the vein of the leaf with the stele. Transverse leaf sections show a well-defined cutinized epidermis with stomata and an internal, spongy **mesophyll** composed of chlorophyllous cells (**chlorenchyma**) and numerous air spaces. The stem apex has an apical meristem composed of a number of cells, and this meristem produces all of the tissues of the stem as well as the leaves.

The arrangement of the sporophylls differs among the species of *Lycopodium.* In some species the sporophylls are scattered among the foliage leaves, while in other species they are concentrated in cones at the ends of branches. In all, the sporangia are massive and produce many bright yellow meiospores that contain oil. They are produced in such abundance that they have been harvested commercially. The harvested spores of *Lycopodium* are the "*Lycopodium* powder" of the pharmaceutical trade, once used as a dusting powder for babies' diaper rash in the days before commercial baby powder. If one rubs *Lycopodium* powder on one's hands, they will stay dry even under water. *Lycopodium* powder also was

Figure 13–11 Representative species of *Lycopodium. A, L. lucidulum.* The sporangia are located on the leaves and are distributed zonally along the stem rather than in cones. *Baragwanathia* had a very similar arrangement of sporophylls. *B, L. clavatum.* Note cones.

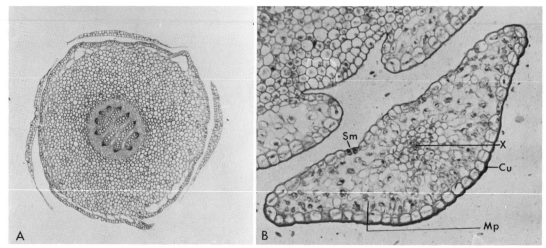

Figure 13–12 Anatomical structures of organs of *Lycopodium. A,* Transverse section of stem showing the central core of vascular tissue (stele) surrounded by the cortex. The xylem of the protostele of *Lycopodium* is rather irregular in cross section. *B,* Transverse section of the leaf (microphyll). Note the xylem (X) of the single vein, the photosynthetic tissue, the mesophyll (Mp), a stoma (Sm), and the cuticle (Cu) overlying the epidermis.

used for dramatic effects in stage productions; a pinch of powder, if tossed in the air and ignited, burns with a brilliant flash, and was used as stage lightning in dramas requiring thunderstorm effects.

Meiospores of *Lycopodium* develop into bisexual gametophytes. Some species of *Lycopodium* have photosynthetic, cushion-like gametophytes; others have tuberous, non-green underground gametophytes nourished by a mycorrhizae-like fungal association. Development varies according to species and may require anywhere from six months to 15 years before antheridia and archegonia are formed. The biflagellate sperms, when released from antheridia, show an attraction to salts of citric acid, and it is possible that such sperm attractants are secreted by the archegonia. After fertilization, the zygote develops into an embryo that remains nutritionally dependent upon the gametophyte for a time until it becomes capable of independent existence.

Heterosporous Lycopods (Class Isoetopsida)

A number of orders of lycopods with heterosporous reproduction are known. Many genera are known only from fossils, but there are three living genera: *Selaginella, Isoetes,* and *Stylites.*

Picture a deep swamp forest of magnificent trees. If somehow one were to be transported back through time to the Carboniferous Period of the Paleozoic Era, the trees most likely would be such giant lycopods as the extinct *Lepidodendron* and *Sigillaria.* Perhaps the great *Equisetum*-like plant, *Calamites,* might also be seen. *Lepidodendron* has been reconstructed by painstaking research in-

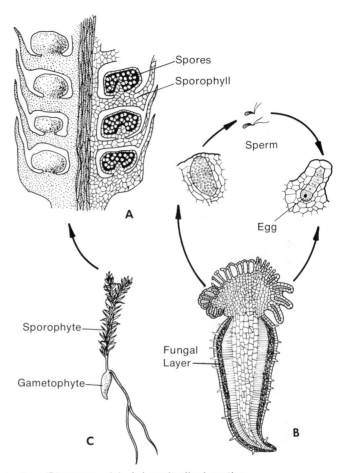

Figure 13-13 Reproduction in *Lycopodium* (Diagrammatic). *A*, Longitudinal section of cone. *B*, Underground gametophyte of *L. phlegmaria*. *C*, Young sporophyte still attached to gametophyte, with archegonium and antheridium.

volving the piecing together of fragments of leaves, roots, stems, and cones so that we have a good likeness of the tree as it actually was. When a fossil organ such as a leaf or a stem is first discovered, it is given its own generic name, the **form genus.** Later, when additional evidence accumulates, as for example, the attachment of a leaf to a part of a stem, it may become possible to reconstruct the entire plant. *Lepidodendron,* a heterosporous lycopod, specimens of which are estimated to have been as much as 40 meters tall, is composed of the following fossil form genera: stem, *Lepidodendron;* stem base, *Stigmaria;* leaf, *Lepidophyllum;* and cone, *Lepidostrobus.*

The cones *(Lepidostrobus)* of *Lepidodendron* were comparatively large (up to 30 centimeters long and 7.5 centimeters broad), and were composed of two kinds of sporophylls. **Megasporophylls** bore **megasporangia,** and each of these in turn produced eight or more megaspores. **Microsporophylls** produced numerous micro-

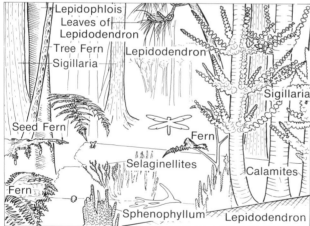

Figure 13–14 A carboniferous swamp. The large trees are *Lepidodendron* and *Sigillaria*. Also present are seed ferns, *Calamites, Sphenophyllum,* tree fern, and *Selaginellites,* the latter a counterpart of the present-day *Selaginella.* A giant dragonfly, a sow bug, and a cockroach also are visible (Field Museum of Natural History, Chicago).

spores in their **microsporangia.** Aside from their large dimensions, the arrangement of the sporophylls and the essential details of reproduction were not greatly different from those found in the modern genus *Selaginella.*

Figure 13-15 Coal miner in Nova Scotia uncovering a fossil stem of the giant club moss, *Sigillaria* (From Dawson, W. The *Geological History of Plants,* 1896).

Biology of Selaginella

Selaginella includes about 600 species, largely of tropical distribution, but a number of temperate species also are known. They vary in size; many are only a meter or less in length, and some are only a few centimeters tall, but a few tropical forms may have erect branches as much as two or three meters tall and may extend horizontally for many meters. Most species are found in moist woodlands but others occur in dry habitats, and a desert species, *Selaginella lepidophylla* (the resurrection plant), is able to withstand complete drying over long periods and revives when moisture is again present. The ecology of plants that are able to survive complete drying out is just now being discovered. At least some of them undergo complete dissociation of their cytoplasmic organization; yet within a few hours after a rainfall their chloroplasts are reconstituted and they become green and photosynthetic once again.

In general, the organization of tissues in *Selaginella* is similar to that described for *Lycopodium.* As in *Lycopodium,* a protostele is present, and some species may have more than one per stem, a condition known as **polystely.** The leaves are microphylls and are unusual in that their cells contain only one or two chloroplasts, each

333

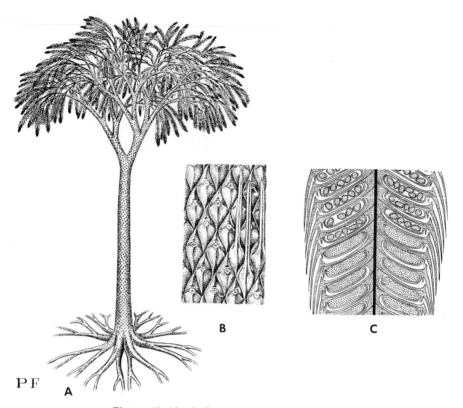

PF

Figure 13–16 *A*, Reconstruction of a giant club moss, *Lepidodendron. B*, Enlargement of the stem surface showing the pattern of leaf scars. *C*, Longitudinal section of the pendant cone showing microsporangia and megasporangia (*C*).

with several pyrenoids. The only other archegoniate plants having pyrenoids are *Anthoceros* and *Isoetes.* In addition, the leaves are equipped with a peculiar appendage, the **ligule,** which is a small, tongue-like structure occurring on the adaxial (upper) surface. There is no positively known function for the ligule, but it has evolutionary significance, for it relates the living heterosporous lycopods *(Selaginella, Isoetes,* and *Stylites)* to the extinct genera that also were ligulate *(Lepidodendron, Pleuromeia,* and some others). The leaves of upright species of *Selaginella* are spirally arranged; those of prostrate species are in a modified spiral of two lateral rows of alternate larger leaves and two median dorsal rows of smaller scale-like leaves.

Roots in most species of *Selaginella* are found in the angles of stem branches. In most cases a specialized root, the **rhizophore,** develops from the stem and in turn bears a tuft of several branch roots.

Reproduction seems complex to those not familiar with heterospory. All *Selaginella* species have cones and these usually are of a mixed type, with both microsporophylls and megasporophylls. The sporophyte, therefore, is **monoecious.** Each microsporophyll bears one microsporangium on its upper surface and megasporophylls similarly bear megasporangia. A microsporangium contains nu-

Figure 13–17 *Selaginella canaliculata,* a vining tropical species.

merous small microspores; a megasporangium usually contains four megaspores.

A microspore develops into a male gametophyte, or **microgametophyte,** totally contained within the microspore wall. The microgametophyte consists of a single **prothallial cell** (thought to be equivalent to the multicellular gametophyte of such plants as mosses, liverworts, *Lycopodium,* and others), and an antheridium containing several hundred biflagellate sperm cells.

Megaspores develop into female gametophytes or **megagametophytes**. They begin their development within the megasporangia but mature after they have been shed. The end result is a multicellular female gametophyte consisting of an inner mass of starchy tissue and a portion projecting outside the spore wall where it has opened along the triradiate ridge. This expanded part develops rhizoids as well as archegonia. After fertilization, the zygote develops into an embryo resembling that of *Lycopodium.* Details of reproduction are presented in Figure 13–19.

335

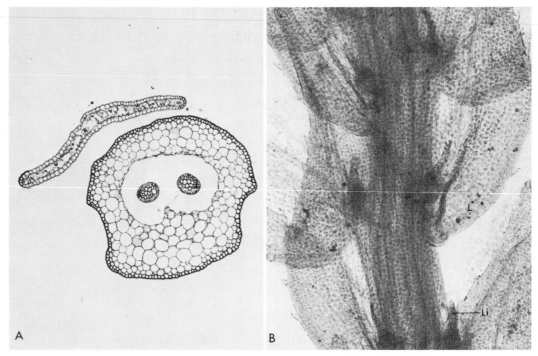

Figure 13–18 *A,* Transverse section of a stem of *Selaginella kraussiana,* a species having two protosteles (i.e., exhibiting polystely). A cross section of a leaf is also included. *B,* Cleared specimen of *Selaginella,* showing a portion of the stem and several leaves (L), each with a ligule (Li) on its upper surface near the base.

Other Living Lycopods

Two other living heterosporous lycopods—*Isoetes* and *Stylites*—are known. These differ from the other living lycopods in the structure of their leaves and stems, and in the organization of the root systems, but they show some remarkable similarities, on a very much reduced scale, to *Lepidodendron* (similar stem bases, rootlets, and sporangia).

There are about 40 species of Isoetes, a dozen or so in the United States. They have very short stems but have elongate leaves that give the plant a rush-like appearance and account for the common name "quillwort." Their height, with leaves included, ranges from 5 to 50 centimeters. *Stylites,* a genus of two species discovered in 1957 in the high Andes of South America, resembles *Isoetes* in most respects, but differs in that it has a more elongate stem.

The life history of *Isoetes* and *Stylites* is very much like that of *Selaginella* and will not be described; however, the structure and organization of the sporophylls is somewhat different. Both kinds of sporophylls are present on the same plant; in fact, all the leaves are sporophylls, although a varying number become sterile as a result of abortion of the sporangia during their development. For this reason it is said that the leafy part of the plant really consists of a single

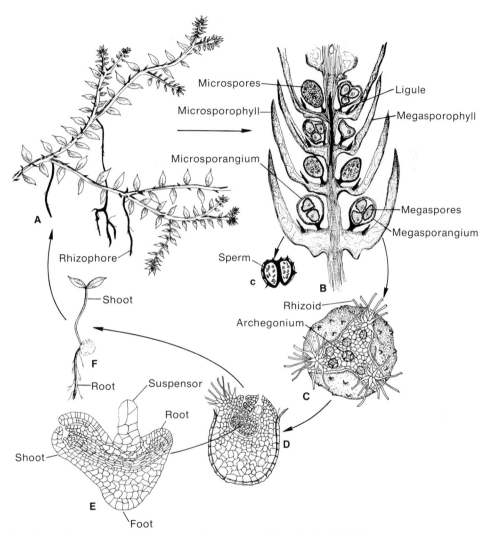

Figure 13–19 Generalized and semi-diagrammatic representation of the life history of Selaginella. *A*, Mature sporophyte. *B*, Cone. *c*, Microgametophyte in section. *C*, Megagametophyte protruding through the opening in megaspore wall provided by separation along the triradiate ridge. *D*, Megagametophyte in cross section. *E*, Embryo. *F*, Young sporophyte (**sporeling**) still attached to megagametophyte (After Smith, G. M. *Cryptogamic Botany,* Volume II, Second Edition, New York, McGraw-Hill Book Co., Inc., 1955).

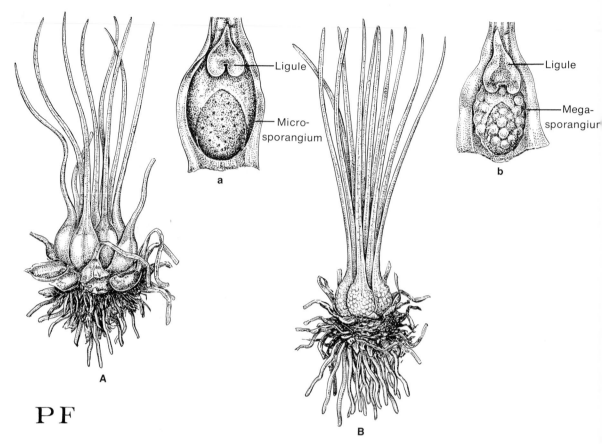

PF

Figure 13–20 *Isoetes*, the quillwort. *A*, Drawing of plant showing outer whorls of microsporophylls. *a*, Adaxial view of microsporophyll showing the microsporangium partially covered by a sheathing membrane. *B*, Same plant as in *A*, but with outer microsporophylls removed and megasporophylls visible. *b*, Adaxial view of megasporophyll showing megasporangium.

cone. The very short stem has a lobed base with spirally attached rootlets, and resembles a diminutive stem base of *Lepidodendron*.

Evolutionary Trends

While we have indicated certain evolutionary trends among the plants described in this chapter, some further general observations are in order.

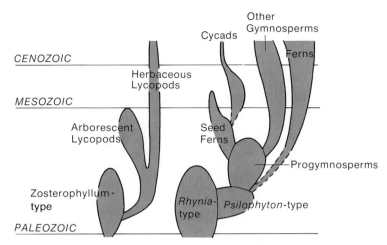

Figure 13-21 A recently suggested theory concerning the evolution of vascular plants, suggesting descent from primitive Devonian rhyniophytes (Redrawn with modifications from Banks, H. P. *Evolution and Plants of the Past.* Belmont, Calif., Wadsworth Publishing Co., Inc., 1970).

On the basis of present fossil evidence, the concept of a group of early vascular plants with gametophytes and sporophytes that were anatomically and morphologically similar, and differed mainly in possessing antheridia and archegonia in the one case and meiosporangia in the other, is emerging. This concept is formalized in the homologous theory. If this idea turns out to be correct, then we must conclude that the relatively simple non-vascularized gametophytes of the Equisetophyta, the Lycopodiophyta, and, as we shall see, the ferns and seed plants, have evolved by reductional changes.

Because these early vascular plants, represented by *Psilophyton, Rhynia,* and others, had independent sporophytes, we now tend to disbelieve the once-popular theory that vascular plants are descendants of mosses, evolved by progressive independence and isolation of a dependent sporophyte generation (the antithetic theory). It now seems more likely that both bryophytes and vascular plants have evolved in different directions from algal ancestors having independent, autotrophic gametophytes and sporophytes. The bryophytes, however, constitute an evolutionary dead end, since they have not given rise to any of the major groups of vascular plants.

Apparently two groups of early land plants had arisen by the onset of the Devonian Period. One group, represented by *Rhynia, Psilophyton, Cooksonia,* and others, bore terminal sporangia; a second group bore lateral sporangia. It has been suggested that the group with terminal sporangia gave rise to such higher plants as ferns and seed plants, and perhaps the Equisetophyta. Those with lateral sporangia, exemplified by *Zosterophyllum,* were the progenitors of the Lycopodiophyta, which are characterized by the lateral sporangia at their leaf bases.

339

SUMMARY
It is a matter of considerable importance that vascular plants are the oldest terrestrial plants known to us. Their state of preservation, even after 400 million years, shows us that nearly all of the basic anatomical and morphological features associated with the present-day vascular plants had evolved early in the Paleozoic Era. Among these features are stems having a cortex and stele, the latter containing xylem and phloem; well-developed multicellular meiosporangia; and, probably, gametangia. Only in the reproductive processes of more recent plants do we see further great advances, such as flowers and seeds.

The earliest vascular plants gave rise to several groups of plants, including the Equisetophyta (scouring rushes) and Lycopodiophyta (club mosses). These two groups flourished in the Paleozoic Era, reaching their ascendancy in the Coal Age (Carboniferous period) and now, much diminished, are represented in one case by the single genus, *Equisetum,* and in the other case by only five genera. These surviving plants seem to have but limited ecological impact, although *Equisetum, Lycopodium,* and *Selaginella* may be locally significant as pioneers in ecological succession. Their economic aspects are almost nil.

A classification of the major plant groups covered in this chapter follows:

Division Rhyniophyta: No genera survive. They were leafless, rootless, homosporous vascular plants.

Examples: Psilophyton, Rhynia, Horneophyton, Cooksonia, and *Zosterophyllum.*

Division Equisetophyta: The *scouring rushes.* There is one living genus of about 20 species. Their characteristics include: jointed stems, whorls of leaves at the nodes, and sporangia borne on sporangiophores, usually in cones.

Examples: Extinct genera include *Hyenia, Calamites,* and *Sphenophyllum.* The living genus is *Equisetum.*

Division Lycopodiophyta: The *club mosses.* There are five living genera comprising about 640 species. They are homosporous or heterosporous plants; leaves are microphylls arranged spirally on stems; sporangia are on upper surfaces of leaves at their bases; cones are often present.

CLASS LYCOPODIOPSIDA: The *homosporous club mosses.*

Examples: Living genera are *Lycopodium,* and *Phylloglossum;* extinct genera include *Asteroxylon, Baragwanathia,* and *Protolepidodendron.*

CLASS ISOETOPSIDA: The *heterosporous club mosses* and related forms.

Examples: Living genera are *Selaginella, Isoetes, Stylites,* while extinct genera include *Lepidodendron* and *Pleuromeia.*

DISCUSSION QUESTIONS

1. Dawson's concept of *Psilophyton princeps* later was revised by other workers. Why?
2. What is meant by the term *form genus*? Give several examples.
3. How are cellular details observed in petrified plants?
4. What is a protostele?
5. What features distinguish the two lines of earliest vascular plants discussed in this chapter?

6. What evidence is there for the viewpoint that the *Lycopodium* type may have survived from Paleozoic times with little change?
7. What is meant by *hygroscopic?* Give an example.
8. Two members of the Equisetophyta, one living and one extinct, resemble each other in many respects. Name the two and state one feature in which they differ.
9. Where in nature might one look for *Selaginella, Lycopodium, Stylites, Equisetum,* and *Psilophyton?*
10. Name five tissue types found in the stems of vascular plants. What are functions of each?
11. Briefly describe the homologous theory and its significance with respect to plant evolution.
12. Give a concise statement (of one sentence) defining heterospory and its possible evolutionary significance.

SUPPLEMENTAL READING

Andrews, H. N., Jr. *Studies in Paleobotany.* New York: John Wiley and Sons, Inc., 1961.

Arnold, C. A. *An Introduction to Paleobotany.* New York: McGraw-Hill Book Co., Inc., 1947.

Banks, H. P. *Evolution and Plants of the Past.* Belmont, California: Wadsworth Publishing Co., Inc., 1970.

Bierhorst, D. W. *Morphology of Vascular Plants.* New York: MacMillan Co., 1971.

Chaloner, W. G. The Rise of the First Land Plants. *Biol. Rev. 45:*353–377, 1970.

Dawson, J. W. *Fifty Years of Work in Canada.* London: Ballentyne, Hanson and Co., 1901.

Delevoryas, T. *Morphology and Evolution of Fossil Plants.* New York: Holt, Rhinehart and Winston, 1963.

Foster, A. S., and E. M. Gifford, Jr. *Comparative Morphology of Vascular Plants,* 2nd ed. San Francisco: W. H. Freeman and Co., 1974.

Cyathea australis, a tree fern.

Chapter 14

Ferns and Fork Ferns

FORK FERNS • FERNS • IMPORTANCE OF FERNS • THE FERN LEAF • ANATOMY OF STEMS AND LEAVES OF FERNS • BIOLOGY OF A FERN • HOW TO GROW A FERN • WATER FERNS • EVOLUTIONARY TRENDS • SUMMARY

Ferns are of interest to many of us. They are usually not very "assertive" plants; they have no flowers to catch the eye, and they generally are short plants (at least in temperate climates), lacking the majestic proportions of some of the seed plants. On the other hand, ferns are more highly organized than the mosses and club mosses studied earlier; they also have more complex leaves and stems, and show a much greater variability in size and structure.

Ferns have considerable scientific appeal to both the amateur and the professional biologist, as we shall see. Only through study of them in their native surroundings can it be realized how much they add to the environment, both aesthetically and ecologically.

In the previous chapter several groups of plants known to us principally in fossil form were examined. Only a few of these plants have survived to the present time. But now we will consider two additional groups of vascular plants that are familiar to us mainly on the basis of living genera and species, the **fork ferns** and the **ferns**. The fork ferns are completely unknown in the fossil record; the ferns, although well represented by fossils, constitute a rich and varied element of modern floras.

FORK FERNS (DIVISION PSILOTOPHYTA)

Until quite recently it was customary to group in the single division Psilophyta such fossil plants as *Psilophyton* and *Rhynia* with two living genera of plants, the fork ferns *Psilotum* and *Tmesipteris*. Dawson gave *Psilophyton* its name because he thought it resembled *Psilotum* (see Chapter 13), and in fact there are several

---

Here is the fern's frond unfurling a gesture,
Like a conductor whose music will now be pause,
And the one note of silence
To which the whole earth dances gravely-

Ferns by TED HUGHES. FROM THE NEW YORKER BOOK OF POEMS, VIKING PRESS, 1969.

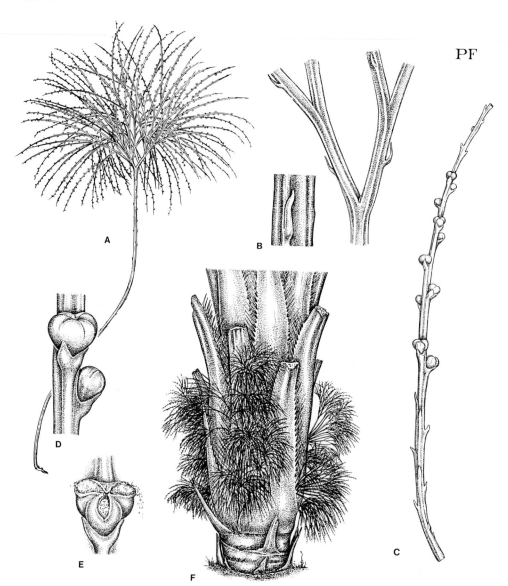

Figure 14–1 The fork fern, *Psilotum nudum*. *A*, An aerial branch. *B*, Details of stem structure. *C*, Stem with sporangia. *D*, Enlarged view of sporangia. *E*, Sporangial dehiscence. *F,* Clumps of *Psilotum* growing among the leaf bases of a large palm trunk.

similarities between the two plants. However, the sporangia of *Psilotum* and *Tmesipteris* are borne on very short, lateral stalks rather than terminally, as in *Psilophyton* and other rhyniophytes. Also, it has not been resolved whether the upright parts of the fork ferns are to be interpreted as stems or as complex leaves. If the latter is the case, it would be more appropriate to include *Psilotum* and *Tmesipteris* with the ferns in the division **Polypodiophyta**, for ferns are characterized in part by their complex leaves, or **fronds**. This grouping has been made in at least one classification; however, the argument is quite involved, and until the question is finally settled to the satisfaction of most botanists, it appears advisable to place *Psilotum* and *Tmesipteris* in a separate division, **Psilotophyta**.

The species of *Psilotum* are small plants (less than 20 centimeters tall), and are found growing in soil or as epiphytes, often among the fibrous roots at the bases of palm trunks. Two species are scattered about the world in the tropics and subtropics, including the Southeastern United States. The 10 or more species of *Tmesipteris* are small, pendant epiphytes and are restricted to Australasia and New Zealand. They grow in wet, subtropical and tropical forests, and sometimes are quite abundant on the fibrous trunks of tree ferns.

Both *Psilotum* and *Tmesipteris* resemble the rhyniophytes both in size and in certain other aspects. They are homosporous and rootless, and their protostelic rhizomes bear rhizoidal hairs. The aerial branches of *Psilotum* are dichotomously branched throughout and bear tiny, veinless appendages, and are in part protostelic and in part siphonostelic (see Fig. 13–7). However, the aerial parts of *Tmesipteris* are much less like those of the rhyniophytes, for they are unbranched or have but one dichotomy, are siphonostelic, and bear leaves. The leaves have only a single vein and usually are interpreted as microphylls.

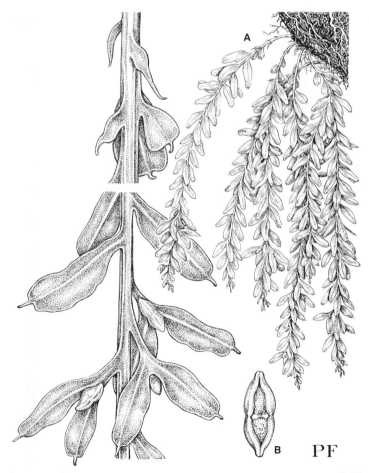

Figure 14–2 *A, Tmesipteris. B,* Sporangium of *Tmesipteris.*

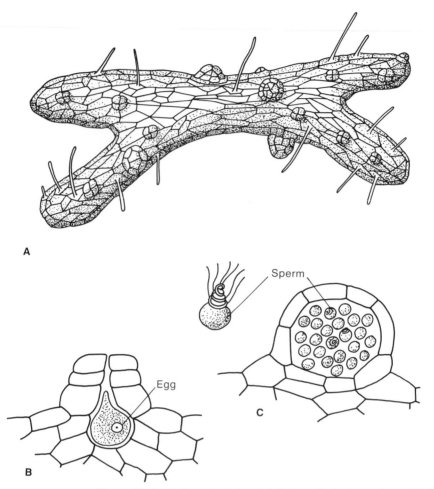

Figure 14–3 *A*, Gametophyte of *Psilotum*. *B*, Archegonium of *Psilotum*. *C*, Antheridium of *Psilotum*. The gametophytes of *Tmesipteris* are similar, but lack a stele. The gametophytes of both species are perennial, underground, and saprobic, owing to their association with mycorrhizae-like fungi. (Diagrammatic.)

The life histories of both *Psilotum* and *Tmesipteris* are quite similar to those of species of *Lycopodium* having subterranean gametophytes. There has been much interest over the years in the gametophytes of *Psilotum* because the larger and presumably older ones have a stele that is complete with xylem and phloem and is surrounded by an endodermis. Furthermore, the gametophytes are somewhat stem-like and are dichotomously branched. These features are considered to support the concept of basic similarity of gametophytes and sporophytes proposed in the homologous theory of plant evolution.

Neither *Psilotum* nor *Tmesipteris* is sufficiently abundant to have any significant impact on the environment, nor is either of much economic importance. The former is often grown in college greenhouses for classroom use, and both are bought and sold by biological supply houses. They are, however, important plants to the botanist; for, as we have seen, they give insight into the relationships between sporophytes and gametophytes. It is also possible, when the fossil record becomes more complete, that their position as primitive survivors of much older fossil plants may be clarified.

FERNS (DIVISION POLYPODIOPHYTA)

Among the approximately 9000 species of ferns are many that are important members of plant communities and a number that are pioneers in succession. Overgrazed pastures in Great Britain and elsewhere sometimes are invaded by the bracken fern, which poses a problem for the farmer since its presence in hay may cause poisoning of livestock.

Following the devastation of forest fires, when the land is barren and subject to erosion by wind and water, thick stands of bracken appear and provide ground cover, in the shade of which delicate seedlings of conifers become established. In the north woods of America fire-breaks, roadsides, and clearings for electrical transmission lines and ski lifts quite often develop a ground cover of bracken ferns.

In the tropics, ferns of many kinds are common, particularly in the disturbed habitats we call jungles. Tree ferns are typical of jungle growth, as is the climbing fern *Gleichenia,* known for having the longest leaves of any land plant (up to 50 meters). These leaves have an indeterminate pattern of growth; that is, they continue to elongate indefinitely and have long-lived, terminal meristems. In fact, *Gleichenia* and some other members of the family Gleicheniaceae become pests, invading fields and orchards, choking out desired plants, and making almost impenetrable thickets. The Hartford fern, a native of Eastern North America, also has indeterminate leaf growth.

Most of us are perhaps more familiar with ferns in connection with gardens and landscaping or in floral displays, but a walk in a rich temperate woodland or a visit to the tropics soon convinces one of the great variety to be found among the ferns and the way in which they have become adapted to diverse ecological situations. Aside from floriculture and horticulture, ferns have little economic utility. The roots of some species are gathered and used as a base upon which to grow orchids, and in some parts of the world, including North America, the young coiled leaves (**fiddleheads**) of some species are cooked and eaten. In Eastern North America, fiddleheads of the ostrich fern are a favorite food of connoisseurs of natural foods.

The characteristics that set ferns apart from other lower vascular plants (i.e., the non-seedbearing vascular plants) include leaf structure, stem anatomy, and sporangium location and development. Although no single character or even group of characters serves exclusively to distinguish and set apart all the ferns from other plants, it is possible to list some key features generally associated with the ferns: the prevalence of large, branching leaves

347

Figure 14-4 Bracken fern on an old burn.

(**fronds**), the coiling of young fronds (fiddleheads), the sporangia borne on fronds in clusters called **sori**, and stems that are usually siphonostelic.

The Fern Leaf

Probably most of us visualize the ferns as plants with large, lace-like leaves; generally, this is correct. However, some ferns have simple, strap-like leaves and a few are so reduced as to look like anything but ferns (see Figure 14–22). As noted above, the young leaves are coiled; this coiling is known technically as **circinate vernation**, and it enables us to recognize ferns and distinguish them from most other plants. In addition, ferns have what the late F. O. Bower, a famous botanist from the University of Glasgow, called "general purpose leaves," that is, leaves that function both as photosynthetic organs and as sporophylls.

A typical fern frond consists of a basal stalk (the **petiole**), and a blade portion, usually subdivided into leaflets. The median extension of the petiole in the blade portion of the leaf is called the **rachis,** which in turn bears leaflets (or **pinnae**). A leaf of this type is called a **compound leaf**. If the pinnae are further subdivided, the leaf

Figure 14–5 *Dicksonia*, a tree fern.

Figure 14–6 *Gleichenia.*

349

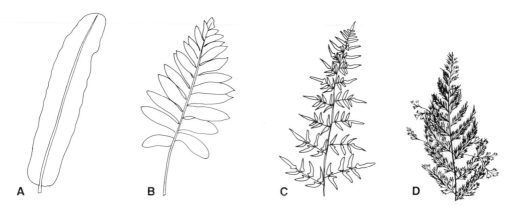

A B C D

Figure 14–7 Fern leaf types. *A*, A simple leaf. *B*, A pinnately compound leaf. *C*, A bipinnate leaf. *D*, A tripinnate leaf.

is said to be **bipinnate**, and the leaflets are termed **pinnules**; if again divided, the leaf is said to be **tripinnate**.

In Chapter 13 (Figure 13–7) it was said that the protostele is considered to be the primitive vascular system; from these, steles with a pith (siphonosteles) have evolved. In some siphonosteles the

Figure 14–8 Fiddlehead of the tree fern, *Cyathea cooperi*.

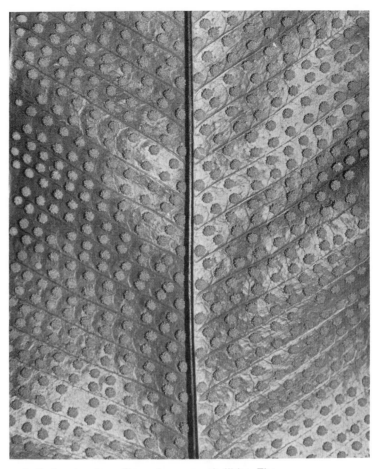

Figure 14-9 A portion of a sporophyll of a strapfern, *Campyloneuron phyllides*. The sori are naked, and they lack indusia. Note the distinct aggregation of sporangia in sori.

xylem and phloem are in the form of a closed cylinder except at points where branches occur. Here, where the continuity of the vascular cylinder is interrupted by the departing xylem and phloem supplying the branch, the branch is associated with a parenchymatous area called a **branch gap**. Fern stems not only have branch gaps, but also have **leaf gaps,** or sites of interruption in the cylinder of xylem and phloem where a vascular strand departs in the form of a **leaf trace** to serve as the vascular connection of a leaf. The two kinds of gaps are thought to be homologous; that is, to have a common evolutionary origin. This particular homology is explained by the theory that broad, multiveined leaves (**megaphylls**) found in fossil ferns and present-day ferns are evolutionary derivatives of the branching stems of certain primitive vascular plants known as **preferns.**

Anatomy of Stems and Roots of Ferns

There is considerable variation in the anatomy of stems of ferns, ranging from protosteles to complex siphonosteles. In many ferns,

351

Figure 14–10 Sterile and fertile pinnules of *Ankyropteris glabra,* a fern-like Paleozoic plant. The pinnules correspond approximately to drawings *D* and *G* in Figure 14–11. One cannot recognize a clear distinction between stems, branches and leaves in *Ankyropteris* and related forms (After Eggert, D. A. *Amer. J. Bot. 50*:379–387,1963, and Eggert, D. A., and T. N. Taylor. *Paleontographica 118B*:52–73, 1976).

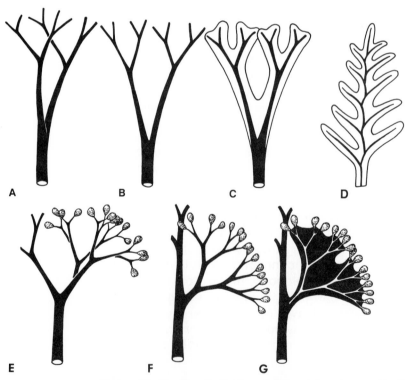

Figure 14–11 Hypothetical evolution of fern leaves (*A–D*) and sporophylls (*E–G*). *A*, A branch system with dichotomies in two planes. *B*, Flattening or planation of dichotomies. *C*, Webbing of dichotomies by photosynthetic tissues. *D*, Rearrangement of dichotomies to form lateral pinnae (overtopping). *E*, Branch system similar to *A*, but having terminal sporangia. *F*, Planation combined with overtopping. *G*, Webbing so as to form a fern-like sporophyll with marginal sporangia (Redrawn with permission from Stewart, W. N.: An Upward Outlook in Plant Morphology. Phytomorphology *14*:120–134, 1964).

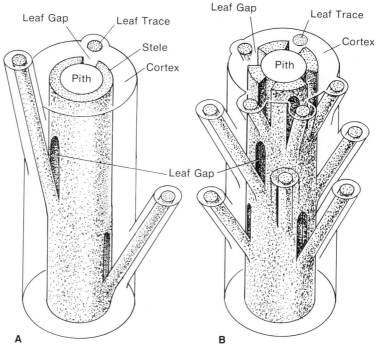

Figure 14–12 Highly diagrammatic representation of two types of fern steles. *A*, Siphonostele with non-overlapping leaf gaps. *B*, Siphonostele with overlapping leaf gaps, or so-called dictyostele.

the leaves are so closely spaced that their leaf gaps overlap. In such cases the cylinder of xylem and phloem appears to be discontinuous or "dissected"; hence, the term **dissected siphonostele** or **dictyostele.** To further complicate matters, it is not uncommon to find ferns in which there are two or more dictyosteles that are concentric.

The stems of many ferns, including familiar ones such as the bracken fern, are in the form of horizontal rhizomes; others are upright, and those of tree ferns may be 10 or more meters tall and have fronds 3 or 4 meters long. All the tissues of the stem arise as a result of divisions of a three-sided apical cell and its derivatives. Regardless of its form or size, the fern stem lacks a lateral meristem (cambium) and does not undergo secondary thickening. This is especially evident upon examination of the trunk of a tree fern. The lower part of a tree fern stem, formed when the plant was young, is narrower than it is at the top, but it is clothed in a mantle of tough, interlacing, adventitious roots. This mantle of roots may be as much as a meter in diameter, and makes the trunk appear much more bulky than the actual diameter of the stem itself. Blocks and rods of this fibrous material are often carved into planters and supports of various shapes and used for growing orchids, bromeliads, ferns, and other plants.

Fern roots arise from the pericycle layer of the stem and force their way through the cortex to the outside. The fern root tip, like the fern stem tip, has a single three-sided apical cell that produces all the other cells. Examination of transverse root sections shows why

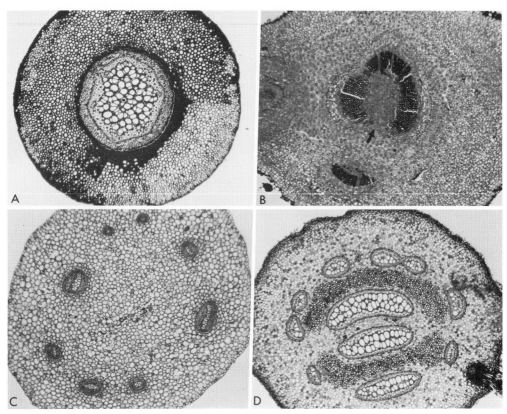

Figure 14–13 Stelar types among the ferns. *A*, Transverse section of the rhizome of *Gleichenia*, a protostele. *B*, Transverse section of the rhizome of *Botrychium*, a siphonostele; arrow points to a leaf gap. *C*. Transverse section of the rhizome of *Polypodium*, a dissected siphonostele (or dictyostele). *D*, Transverse section of the stem of *Pteridium*, a polycyclic type consisting of two concentric dictyosteles.

fern roots are so tough and fibrous—the inner cortex consists of thick-walled fiber cells. Like most plant roots, the roots of ferns are protostelic; unlike those of many seed plants, however, the roots of ferns never undergo any secondary thickening.

Biology of A Fern

The morphological and anatomical features just described pertain to the sporophyte generation, which in ferns might be said to be the dominant generation since it is larger and more complex than the gametophyte generation. However, there is great variation both in form and in growth of fern sporophytes; included are the tiny, epiphytic, filmy ferns so delicate that they exist in nature only in the depths of rain forests, the large and robust tree ferns, the strap-like forms, the vining types (such as *Gleichenia,* which covers entire hillsides), and the diminutive water ferns.

Fern sporangia also are varied. A few ferns have massive sporangia that produce thousands of spores, but most are delicate and thin-walled and produce a definite number of spores, usually 16

Figure 14–14 Tree fern trunk used as a planter for bromeliads. The thick mantle of adventitious roots comprises the bulk of the trunk, from which sections such as this are cut.

to 64. There also is considerable variation in the development and arrangement of sporangia in the sori. Some sori are discrete circular aggregates of sporangia and may be "naked", as in Figure 14–9, or covered by a shield-like structure called the **indusium** (Fig. 14–16). Others may be more or less confluent, as in *Pteridium* (Fig. 14–19B); many other variations are known.

In the bracken fern, *Pteridium,* often studied in botany classes, the sori are confluent along the leaflet margins and are covered by an indusium consisting of a recurved outer membrane that is contiguous with the leaf margin and a less conspicuous inner membrane. The developing sporangia each contain 16 **spore mother cells,** which undergo meiosis to produce 64 spores. At maturity the sporangium consists of a stalked, thin-walled sac with a vertical row of cells, the **annulus,** encircling about three-fourths of the sporangium. At the distal end of the annulus (the end farthest from the stalk) there is a lateral strip of delicate cells, the **stomium**. When

355

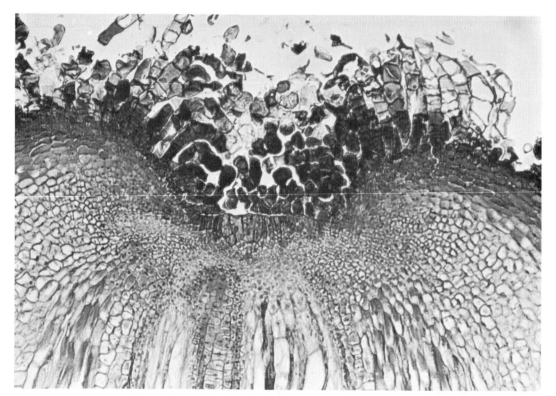

Figure 14–15 Longitudinal section of the root tip of a fern. Note the apical cell and its derivatives.

the sporangium is ripe, its drying brings about an increasing tension in the thick-walled cells of the annulus. This tension causes the annulus to become recurved, and thus opens the sporangium at the stomium. A rapid recoil action of the annulus then occurs, which flings the spores much as one would throw a handful of stones.

The spores of ferns are carried by air currents, sometimes for great distances. Charles Darwin collected air samples during his voyage on H.M.S. Beagle and discovered that spores of mosses and ferns were carried hundreds of miles out to sea. The great abundance of ferns on the Malayan Archipelago is said to be due not only to the tropical climate but also to extensive spore dispersal during the monsoon season.

If a spore chances to land in a moist place, it will germinate and produce a gametophyte plant. Some fern gametophytes are perennial and underground (resembling those of *Psilotum*), but most are found above ground and are short-lived, green, and photosynthetic. The typical fern gametophyte is a small (less than one centimeter in diameter), heart-shaped plant called the **prothallus** (plural: prothallia), and is anchored to the soil by rhizoids.

Archegonia and antheridia are present on the underside of a prothallus; formation of antheridia usually precedes archegonium initiation. It has been shown that, when spores of bracken germi-

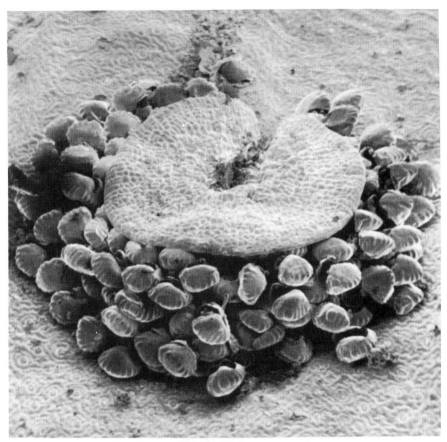

Figure 14–16 Scanning electron micrograph of a sorus of the Boston fern, *Nephrolepis exaltata.* Note the shield-like indusium partially covering the numerous stalked sporangia. The annulus, which functions as a dehiscence mechanism, is visible on some sporangia. Note also the form of the epidermal cells and the stomata visible in the surrounding epidermis (Photo courtesy of Argonne National Laboratory).

nate, a few prothallia grow faster than others. These secrete a substance, named **antheridogen,** that causes antheridia to form on the slower growing neighboring prothallia. In addition to antheridogen, the faster growing prothallia also produce within themselves an antheridial inhibitor that causes these prothallia to become solely archegoniate. However, if fertilization from sperm of antheridiate prothallia does not occur, antheridia eventually form on the archegoniate prothallia and self-fertilization can occur. Antheridogens produced by fern gametophytes exhibit many of the characteristics of **gibberellic acid**, a well-known plant growth hormone; gibberellic acid itself will cause antheridia to form, even on fern prothallia so young that only a few cells are present.

The antheridia of advanced ferns (such as *Pteridium*) are especially interesting; their walls consist of only three cells—two ring cells and a cover cell. About 30 to 50 multiflagellated sperm are produced within each antheridium. Archegonia commonly are present near the apical notch of the prothallus. Following fertilization, the zygote

357

Figure 14–17   A portion of a sporophyll of a maidenhair fern, *Adiantum trapeziforme.* The sori are marginal and are covered by an indusium formed by a portion of the leaf margin (a false indusium).

develops into an embryo that remains attached to and dependent on the gametophyte until roots develop and the shoot begins to form leaves, whereupon the young sporophyte becomes fully independent and the gametophyte dies.

One of the interesting aspects of fern life cycles is the existence of gametophytes far removed from their parent sporophytes. The reason for this wide dispersal is that fern spores, being small and light in weight, as we have noted, are carried great distances by winds. One such gametophyte, known as the **Appalachian game- tophyte**, grows as far north as Northern Ohio; its sporophyte is a subtropical fern known only in Florida. The gametophytes of several tropical ferns are similarly dispersed and seem able to withstand the colder climates that are fatal to the sporophytes. Some such game- tophytes form colonies by vegetative propagation. They produce gemmae consisting of one to ten cells, small enough to be dis- persed by air currents; in the case of one species, the gametophytes are found in South Carolina, but the nearest place where sporo- phytes are found is Cuba—about 800 miles away.

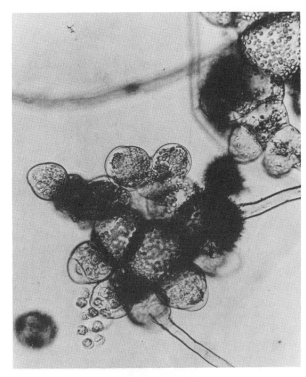

Figure 14–18 Antheridia induced by gibberellic acid on very young fern prothallia (From Voeller, B. R. Gibberellins: Their Effect on Antheridium Formation in Fern Gametophytes. *Science 143*:373–375, 24 January 1964. Copyright 1964 by the American Association for the Advancement of Science).

Ferns are noted for their capacity for apogamous and aposporous reproduction. Many can be induced to form aposporous gametophytes and apogamous sporophytes under experimental conditions. For example, fern gametophytes will form sporophytes apogamously if they are cultured on nutrient media containing sugar. However, there are several species of ferns that regularly reproduce by apospory and apogamy under natural conditions. They have evolved mechanisms of spore production without meiosis. In one case the sporophytes produce spore-forming cells (sporocytes), which then divide by mitosis to form spores having the same chromosome number as the sporophyte plant. The prothallia produced by these spores are asexual and form sporophytes by apogamy. There is, therefore, an alternation of prothallia and sporophytes having identical chromosome numbers. Similar cases also are known to occur among other ferns.

How To Grow a Fern

Ferns can be bought at the florist or garden shop and grown as houseplants or outdoors in the garden, but one of the most interesting ways to grow them is to start with the spores.

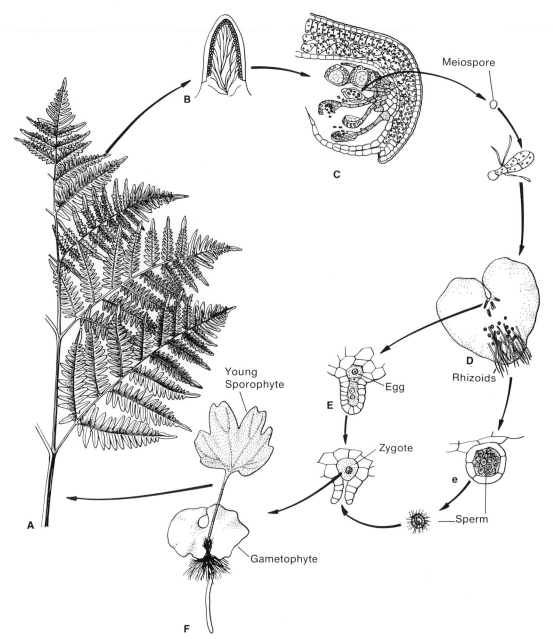

Figure 14–19 Life history of *Pteridium aquilinum*, the bracken fern. *A*, Sporophyte plant. *B*, Fertile pinnule. *C*, Section of a sorus. *D*, Gametophyte plant viewed from beneath. *e*, Antheridium and sperm. *E*, Archegonium. *F*, Gametophyte with young sporophyte.

Pick some fronds of the fern you wish to grow; you may select several species if you wish. Be sure that they have mature but unopened sporangia in their sori. Fold these fronds in a clean sheet of paper and set them aside for a day or so. This should result in a fine dusting of spores on the inside surface of the paper.

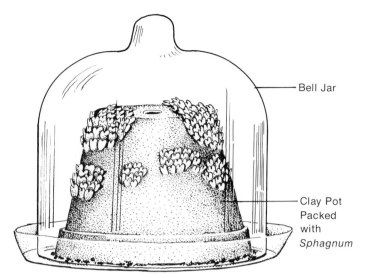

Bell Jar

Clay Pot
Packed
with
Sphagnum

Figure 14-20 Chamber set up for growing fern spores.

In the meantime an ordinary clean unglazed clay pot, about three inches in diameter, has been packed with *Sphagnum* moss and inverted in an enamel baking pan or an old china dish. Fill the pan with water; distilled water or rainwater is best. Hard water or water from copper or galvanized pipes (i.e., most household water) may contain enough impurities to be injurious; copper and zinc are especially to be avoided. Also obtain a glass or plastic jar large enough that it can be inverted over the clay pot. Attractive bell jars can be made from glass jugs with special sawing kits available from hobby shops.

Gently dust the fern spores over the surface of the moist clay pot and replace the covering bell jar. Place the culture chamber in indirect light and be sure to maintain water in the pan or dish—it must never dry out. Within ten days to two weeks prothallia will appear on the pot, and shortly a lush growth of gametophytes will be seen. Next, young sporophyte plants will appear. When these have developed root systems they may be removed—gently—to a pot or tray containing a moist mixture of peat, sand, and soil (a standard potting mixture will do if it contains sufficient humus). Cover this with a bell jar, plastic cake cover, or similar cover, and take the same care as with the spore culture. The young fern plants should grow very nicely and may be planted later in a shady garden spot. The soil should be loamy. Add peat and sand if the soil is heavy and clayey. The pH should be neutral or slightly acid. Soil test kits are not expensive and may be purchased at any good garden shop.

Ferns also may be grown as houseplants. Many do well in hanging baskets lined with sphagnum and containing a good potting mixture. Remember that ferns require humic soil, diffuse light, and pure water.

Water Ferns

The **water ferns** include two groups of heterosporous plants. One group comprising three genera *(Marsilea, Regnellidium, and Pilularia)* includes aquatic plants of moderate size with rhizomes that grow in mud and shallow water. Their erect leaves are on the order of 20 centimeters in length; *Marsilea* species have four leaflets, *Regnellidium* has two, while *Pilularia* species have none at all. Five species of *Marsilea* occur in the United States and there are about 60 others, many of them in Australia. There is only one species of *Regnellidium,* and it occurs in Brazil. The six species of *Pilularia* are widely distributed throughout the world.

The second group of water ferns is represented by two genera, *Azolla* and *Salvinia*; the first has six species, the second about 10. The species of both genera consist of small, floating plants and are represented by species growing in the Southern United States.

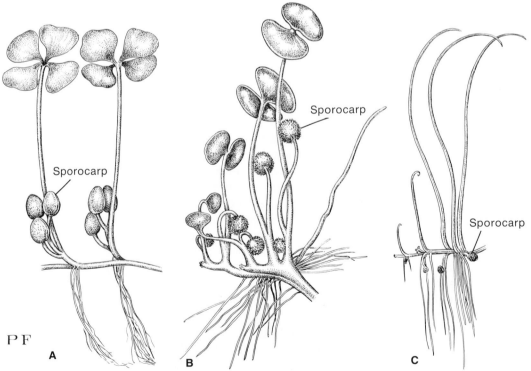

P F

A

B

C

Figure 14–21   *A, Marsilea. B, Regnellidium. C, Pilularia.*

Figure 14–22 *A, Salvinia. B, Azolla.*

All of the water ferns bear sporangia within resistant capsules called **sporocarps.** The sporocarps of all three genera—*Marsilea, Regnellidium,* and *Pilularia*—are thought to be homologous, with a single fertile leaflet that has become permanently enfolded and has developed a hard outer layer. The sporocarps of *Azolla* and *Salvinia* are cup- or vase-like and are homologous, with a single sorus and its enveloping indusium.

Sporocarps of *Marsilea* are often studied in botanical classes, and provide an interesting means of observing events in the life cycle of a heterosporous plant. Within a day or so one may observe the liberation of free-swimming sperm and the development and fertilization of eggs in archegonia, and still another day or so later the appearance of young sporophytes. Each lateral half of a sporocarp bears rows of sori; each sorus is composed of megasporangia and microsporangia. A ring of mucilaginous material, the **sorophore,** is present within the sporocarp and, if the sporocarp wall is abraded and the sporocarp placed in water, within about 20 minutes the sorophore imbibes water and swells, forcing the two halves of the

363

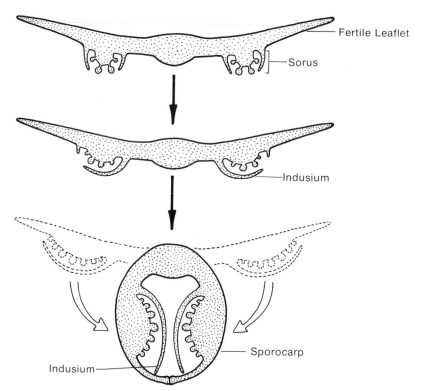

Figure 14–23 Diagram showing possible evolution of a sporocarp of *Marsilea* by the enfolding of a fertile leaflet. (Redrawn from Smith, G. M. *Cryptogamic Botany,* Volume 2, Second Edition, New York, McGraw-Hill Book Co., Inc., 1955.)

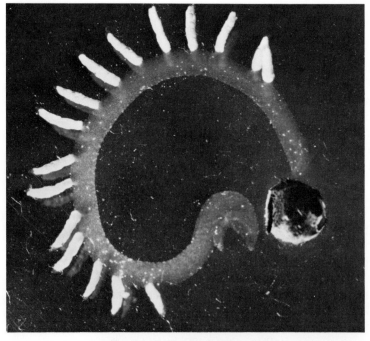

Figure 14–24 Sporocarps of *Marsilea* after water imbibition and extrusion of sorophore. The sori contain both megasporangia and microsporangia (Courtesy Carolina Biological Supply Company).

sporocarp apart. The sorophore then is extruded, carrying the attached sori with it. In about twelve hours the microspores develop into mature microgametophytes and release their multiflagellated sperm. At the same time, the megagametophytes mature within the megaspore walls and a single archegonium is formed on the portion projecting outside of the spore wall. Fertilization then occurs, and young sporophytes develop.

Evolutionary Trends

The living ferns, as we have seen, exhibit considerable structural and ecological diversity, and several evolutionary lines are apparent. The water ferns, for example, have evolved heterospory independently of other groups, such as the lycopods and the seed plants. Fossils indicate that this may have occurred as early as the Late Paleozoic Era, and equally ancient diversifications appear to have occurred in other fern lineages. Yet the ferns are an ecologically thriving and, by most criteria, a highly successful group of modern-day plants.

It is generally believed that most, and perhaps all, present fern groups have evolved from those ancient vascular plants we call **preferns.** Some of these were contemporary with the rhyniophytes, which they resembled in their leaflessness, forking branches, and terminal sporangia, and we conjecture that the characteristic leaf type of the ferns, the megaphyll, may have evolved by elaboration of the prefern branch system.

SUMMARY

Two groups of plants have been discussed in this chapter. One of these, commonly referred to as the fork ferns, bears a resemblance to the ancient vascular plants, the Psilophytes. There are but two genera of fork ferns: *Psilotum,* a genus of rather wide distribution in tropical and subtropical regions; and *Tmesipteris,* found only in Australasia and New Zealand. *Psilotum* is of particular interest to botanists because it possesses vascularized gametophytes as well as sporophytes; this finding is considered evidence in support of the homologous theory of evolution.

The ferns, a much larger and more varied group than the fork ferns, range from very small, heterosporous water ferns *(Azolla* and *Salvinia)* only a few millimeters in size to tree ferns 10 or more meters tall. Except for the water ferns, all are homosporous plants. Ferns play an important ecological role as pioneers in ecological succession; the bracken fern, *Pteridium,* which grows so quickly as a ground cover after forest fires, is a good example.

Ferns have a long evolutionary history, and abundant fossils are known from the Paleozoic Era as well as from more recent times. However, they stand today as eminently successful modern plants, for there are numerous species of ferns in all parts of the world. The evolutonary relationships of ferns, as well as their diversity, is reflected in the classification that follows.

Division Psilotophyta: The *fork ferns.* There are two living genera, no known fossils. Sporophytes are homosporous and root-less but with rhizoidal hairs. The sporangia are lateral, the stems either leafless or with microphylls. The sporophytes and gametophytes branch dichotomously. Gametophytes are underground, sometimes vascularized.

Examples: Psilotum and *Tmesipteris.*

Division Polypodiophyta: The true ferns. There are about 300 living genera comprising 9000 species. The division is made up of modern-day and extinct plants with sporophytes characterized by a variety of stelar types, adventitious roots, megaphyllous leaves, and circinate vernation. The sporophylls have sporangia usually aggregated in sori. They are generally homosporous, but the water ferns are heterosporous. Gametophytes vary, and include perennial, non-green underground types, and above-ground photosynthetic prothallia.

Examples of living genera: Azolla, Dicksonia, Campylo-neuron, Nephrolepis, Marsilea, Pilularia, Cyathea, Pteridium, Polypo-dium, Gleichenia, Botrychium, Salvinia, and *Adiantum.*

DISCUSSION QUESTIONS

1. What characteristics are shared by *Psilotum* and *Psilophyton*?
2. What is significant about the anatomy of the gametophyte of *Psilotum*?
3. Define apogamy and give an example.
4. List four characteristics that, taken together, help to set the ferns apart from the other plant groups studied thus far.
5. Briefly outline steps in the hypothetical evolution of fern fronds.
6. What is the significance of the leaf gap in understanding the homology of the fern leaf?
7. What is the relationship between plants as weeds and plants as ecological pioneers? Give examples of ferns that illustrate this topic.
8. What is the Appalachian gametophyte?
9. What mechanisms and natural phenomena are involved in the dispersal of fern spores?
10. Where would one expect to find fern gametophytes?
11. What is the function of antheridogen?
12. Briefly compare the reproductive cycle of *Marsilea* with that of *Pteridium.*

SUPPLEMENTAL READING

Andrews, H. N., Jr., *Studies in Paleobotany.* New York: John Wiley & Sons, Inc., 1961.

Bierhorst, D. W. *Morphology of Vascular Plants.* New York: The Macmillan Co., 1971.

Cobb, B. *A Field Guide to the Ferns and their Related Families.* Boston: Houghton Mifflin Co., 1956 (includes lycopods and equisetophytes).

Delevoryas, T. *Morphology and Evolution of Fossil Plants.* New York: Holt, Rinehart and Winston, 1963.

Parihar, N. S. *An Introduction to Embryophyta; Vol. 2. Pteridophytes,* 5th ed. Allahabad, India: Central Book Depot, 1967.

Sporne, K. R. *The Morphology of Pteridophytes.* London: Hutchison and Co., Ltd., 1962.

Wherry, E. T. *The Southern Fern Guide.* Garden City, New York: Doubleday and Co., Inc., 1964 (includes lycopods).

Whittier, D. P. The Value of Ferns in an Understanding of the Alternation of Generations. *Bioscience 21*:225–227, 1971.

Seed cone of *Macrozamia mooreii.*

Chapter 15

Early Gymnosperms—Seed Ferns, Cycads, and Cycadeoids

SEED PLANTS • GYMNOSPERMS • PROGYMNOSPERMS • SEED FERNS • DIS-
COVERY OF MOTILE SPERM CELLS IN GYMNOSPERMS • CONTINENTAL DRIFT
AND THE CYCADS • PRESENT-DAY CYCADS • BIOLOGY OF A CYCAD • ECOLOGY
OF CYCADS • CYCADEOIDS • EVOLUTIONARY TRENDS • SUMMARY

We have seen that the early vascular plants and their living descendants—the ferns, club mosses, and scouring rushes—retained a
vestige of their aquatic ancestry in their need for water in fertilization; the free-swimming male gametes are reminiscent of the remote
algal progenitors of the land plants. It is interesting to note that
animals too show a similar relationship, for amphibians also require
water to convey their motile sperm to the egg cell. Let us examine
this analogy a bit further. Reptiles, birds and mammals have no need
of water to carry their sperm to their egg cells; nevertheless, their
sperm cells are flagellated and motile, and, once introduced into the
female reproductive tract, swim under their own power to the egg. Is
there an equivalent in plants to this?

Perhaps 300 million years or more ago, when the first reptiles
were making their way on earth, plants also were developing independence of water in their fertilization. The device that made this
possible was the **seed**, and the plants that evolved the seed we
know as the **seed ferns**. We have only fossils of seed ferns to in-
struct us as to their reproductive processes, but fortunately there
survives to this day a small and ancient group of primitive seed
plants, the **cycads**. The reproductive structures of cycads allow us
to make a number of educated guesses as to the way male gametes
of plants changed from free-swimming to captive cells in the reproductive processes of advanced land plants.

It will be recalled that the female gametophytes of such he-

I am the Chigua grown
on the shore of the sea
After the formation of the world
and I put forth shoots from the earth
I asked of myself
what food would I be

Cook the Chigua well
Watch out for the emetic effect
Take care lest happen to you
what happened to Tenorio.

COLOMBIAN FOLK POEM TRANSCRIBED BY DR. VICTOR M. PATIÑO,
TRANSLATED BY DR. JULIA F. MORTON.

terosporous plants as *Selaginella* (a lycopod) and *Marsilea* (a fern) are contained within the megaspore wall, except for a projecting part bearing archegonia prior to fertilization and an embryo after fertilization. The cells of such female gametophytes are rich in stored food and serve as sources of nourishment for the young sporophytes that develop from the embryo. The megaspore wall encloses most of the female gametophyte and embryo and acts as a "survival package;" it can be transported by wind or water, and if it lands in a likely spot its embryo will grow into a new plant. Thus gametophytes of this kind with their embryos seem to be functionally seed-like.

It is believed widely that seed plants evolved from ancestors with life cycles resembling those of *Selaginella*, *Marsilea*, and similar

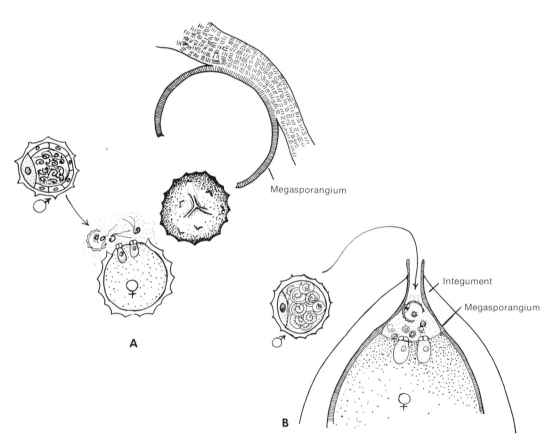

Megasporangium

Integument

Megasporangium

A

B

Figure 15–1 Highly diagrammatic representation of the hypothetical evolution of the seed. *A,* Condition in a heterosporous, nonseed-bearing plant in which free gametophytes occur. *B,* Hypothetical primitive seed plant differing in mode of reproduction from *A* in that the female gametophyte is retained within the megasporangium. The megasporangium, in turn, is enclosed within an integument. The male gametophytes are pictured as completing their development within the confines of the megasporangium but, unlike modern-day seed plants, have not formed pollen tubes. See also Figures 15–20 and 16–16.

plants, because all seed plants are heterosporous, and also because fossils have been discovered that exemplify stages in seed evolution.

SEED PLANTS

Most persons use the term *seed* in a functional sense rather than technically, and some structures that are called seeds may be something different; for example, a wheat "seed" is really a fruit. Precisely speaking, a seed is a complex assembly of tissues, including one or more outer layers (called **integuments**) enclosing a megasporangium (sometimes called the **nucellus**), stored food, and an **embryo**. Prior to fertilization, before an embryo is present, the structure composed of the megasporangium and integument is termed the **ovule**.

Gymnosperms

Most biology students have read of Robert Brown, a Scottish botanist who often is mentioned as the discoverer of the cell nucleus, or in connection with the movements of colloidal particles known as *Brownian movement.* However, we wish to acknowledge him here as the first botanist to distinguish between gymnosperms and flowering plants.

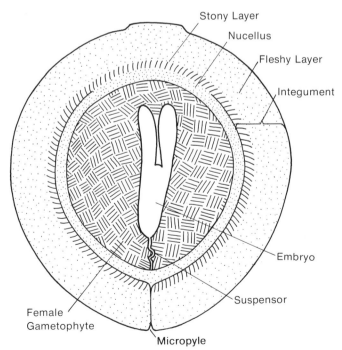

Figure 15–2 Highly diagrammatic representation of a longitudinal section of the seed of a gymnosperm. The female gametophyte consists principally of stored food.

371

Figure 15–3 Portrait of Robert Brown (1773–1858). (From Cronquist, A. *Introductory Botany,* Second Edition. Copyright 1971 by Harper & Row).

Robert Brown began his professional career as a military surgeon and subsequently became a botanist, and participated in one of the pioneering voyages to Australia. He made so many remarkable scientific discoveries that his works fill the pages of three large volumes; among these were his observations on the nature of the gymnosperm seed.

There are two major groups of seed plants, **gymnosperms** and **flowering plants**. Gymnosperms are often described as plants having ''naked seeds,'' while flowering plants are said to be plants that have their seeds enclosed within fruits; however, there are other differences as well, and the two groups are distinguished from each other by a number of characteristics that are introduced here and in later chapters.

Progymnosperms

As far as we know, gymnosperms evolved from a group of Devonian plants referred to as **progymnosperms**. The progymnosperms had frond-like branches resembling those of the preferns. In addition, they had a type of xylem generally associated with gymnosperms; that is, xylem composed of tracheids with **bordered pits**. (A bordered pit is a thin area between adjacent xylem cells, ringed on each side by cell wall material so that superficially it has a

372

doughnut appearance.) One of the progymnosperms, *Archaeopteris*, until recently was thought to be a prefern. This fossil consisted of foliage only, and was not associated with stems. Then it was discovered by Dr. Charles Beck of the University of Michigan that its foliage belonged with certain petrified tree trunks having tracheids with bordered pits, and it was classified as a progymnosperm. *Archaeopteris* was a large tree with a trunk nearly two meters in diameter, and its overall appearance may have been similar to such present-day gymnosperms as pines and cypresses.

We see in *Archaeopteris* two characteristics generally associated with gymnosperms: xylem composed of tracheids with bordered pits, and woody stems that often have extensive amounts of xylem.

The nature of the reproductive organs of progymnosperms is not well understood. Microspores and megaspores are associated with some species of *Archaeopteris*, and others had spores of only one size and may have been homosporous, but it is also possible that they were pollen-producing plants. Moreover, primitive seeds have been found with *Archaeopteris* in some deposits. Although such seeds are not attached to *Archaeopteris* fossils, it is thought possible that some forms of this plant may have borne seeds.

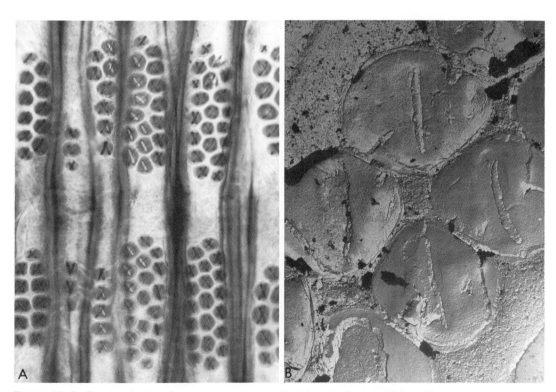

Figure 15-4 Bordered pits of a progymnosperm. *A,* A longitudinal, radial section showing a wood ray and a number of tracheids, × 2400. *B,* Electron micrograph of several bordered pits, × 330 (From Beck, C. B. The Appearance of Gymnospermous Structure. *Biol. Rev. 45*:379–400, 1970).

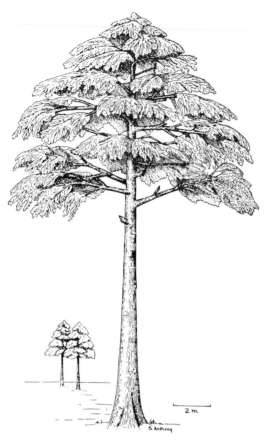

Figure 15-5 A restoration of *Archaeopteris* (From Beck, C. B. Reconstruction of *Archaeopteris*, and Further Consideration of its Phylogenetic Position. *Amer. J. Bot.* 49:373–382, 1962.)

Seed Ferns (Class Lyginopteridopsida)

When fossils from the Paleozoic coal beds were first studied a century or so ago, scientists were impressed by the abundance of fronds, which at that time were thought to be those of ferns. Subsequently, it was discovered that seeds were attached to some of these leaves, and so the specimens were named **seed ferns**. Some seed ferns were small trees and some were clambering vines; the existence of the latter is deduced from the dimensions of fossil stems and leaves; plants with large fronds and slender stems probably would have required support, as do present-day tropical vines.

The seeds of seed ferns varied in size from 4 or 5 millimeters to as much as 11 centimeters in length, and were attached to leaves in several ways. In some species, seeds were borne at the tips of leaves; in others, they were attached at the margins of leaflets; and in still others, they grew from the rachis of fronds. Pollen-bearing organs also were attached to seed-fern fronds, and these often were compound structures composed of several to many elongate microsporangia. There has been some speculation on the manner in which pollination and fertilization occurred, but a recent description

374

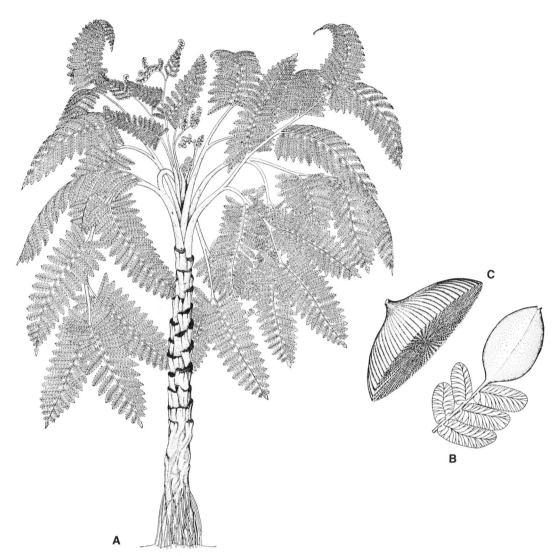

Figure 15–6 *A,* A reconstruction of a seed fern, *Medullosa noei,* which in life was about 5 meters tall. *B,* A large seed fern seed, attached terminally to a part of a frond. *C,* A microsporangiate organ of *Medullosa,* composed of many longitudinally united microsporangia (From *Morphology and Evolution of Fossil Plants* by Theodore Delevoryas. Copyright © 1962 by Holt, Rinehart and Winston, Inc. Reproduced by permission of Holt, Rinehart and Winston, Inc.).

of fossil pollen tubes in an ovule of a seed fern suggests that it resembled that occurring in living gymnosperms, in particular among a group of very ancient but still living plants, the **cycads.**

The Cycads (Class Cycadopsida)

The Discovery of Motile Sperm Cells in Gymnosperms. In 1884 the great German botanist Edward Strasburger reported that

375

the pollen tubes of seed plants conveyed male gametes to the vicinity of the egg and thus effected fertilization. In nearly all seed plants these male gametes are themselves non-motile and consist of nuclei surrounded by only a small layer of cytoplasm and a plasma membrane; in fact, for a dozen years after Strasburger's discovery, it was thought that non-motile sperm were typical of all seed plants. Then much excitement was aroused among botanists in 1896 when two Japanese microscopists, working independently, announced their discovery of flagellated, motile male gametes in two different kinds of seed plants, the maidenhair tree (*Ginkgo biloba*), and the sago palm *(Cycas revoluta)*. This achievement has been described as the most significant botanical discovery of the last decade of the nineteenth century.

The discovery of motile sperms in the maidenhair tree preceded that of sperm motility in the sago palm by only a few months. Oddly enough, the principal discoverer was not a renowned and highly-trained scientist, but a rather humble plant illustrator and technician named Sakugoro Hirase, who worked in the botanical laboratories of the Imperial University in Tokyo. He sought to understand the process of fertilization in *Ginkgo,* then not well understood, and so he taught himself microscopy. He observed a cell with a snail-like coil of flagella in pollen tubes growing within maturing

Figure 15-7   The discoverers of flagellated cells in seed plants. *A,* Sakugoro Hirase (1856–1925). *B,* Seiichiro Ikeno (1866–1943) (Photos courtesy of Y. Ogura, Tokyo, Japan).

Figure 15–8 The sago palm, *Cycas revoluta*. This picture, taken in about 1900, shows the actual plants upon which Ikeno made his observations of spermatozoids. These plants are still growing in the Kagoshima Perfectural Museum gardens south of Tokyo (Photo courtesy of Y. Ogura, Tokyo, Japan).

seeds (ovules); this cell was the motile sperm. Meanwhile, the other Japanese botanist, Seiichiro Ikeno, had been studying reproduction in *Cycas revoluta* and found similar but larger male gametes. Coincidentally, a young American botanist, H. J. Webber, who was studying the reproduction of the Florida cycad *(Zamia integrifolia)* also found flagellated male gametes, and described his observations in several papers published in 1897. Thus we see another example of the curious coincidences in science in which several individuals, working quite apart from each other, arrive at essentially the same conclusions at approximately the same time.

Such coincidental discoveries, however, are not so mysterious if we reflect for a moment on the nature of scientific progress, which depends more on the efforts of many individuals whose findings and interpretations are freely exchanged than upon inspired individual works of genius. The motile male gametes, or **spermatozoids,** of the maidenhair tree would not have been discovered without the patient work of the earlier botanical microscopists so briefly mentioned in Chapter 4.

Since the days of Hirase, Ikeno, and Webber, spermatozoids

have been discovered in all other cycad genera, but in no other group of seed plants; nevertheless, this discovery is of great scientific value, for it links the seed plants with the lower vascular plants, all of which have spermatozoids.

Continental Drift and the Cycads. The living cycads are true relics of the past; fossil remains dating from early Mesozoic times are known, and only ten genera, scattered about the world, presently survive. At their peak in the Mesozoic Era, they coexisted with dinosaurs, advanced seed-ferns, and early conifers. Fossil cycads are found in regions where they no longer occur and where present climates are far too rigorous for present-day cycads

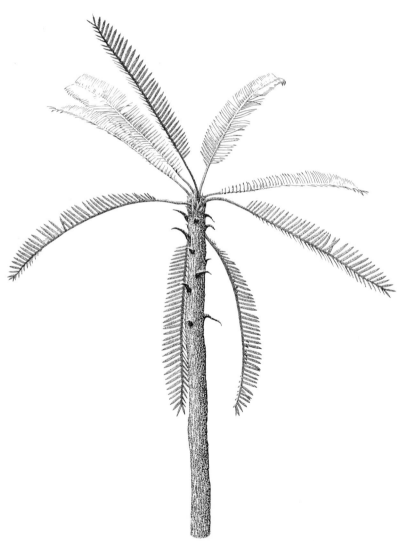

Figure 15–9 A Triassic cycad, *Leptocycas gracilis,* the most completely-known Mesozoic cycad, as reconstructed by Dr. Theodore Delevoryas of the University of Texas (From Delevoryas, T., and Hope, R. C. *A New Triassic Cycad and its Phyletic Implications. Postilla,* Peabody Museum, Yale University Press).

to endure, such as Greenland, Alaska, and Siberia. An explanation for both their past occurrence in places where they no longer grow as well as their present scattered distribution is the theory of **continental drift**.

Francis Bacon (1561–1626) was the first scientist to point out the fit between the outline of the Atlantic coastlines of Europe, Africa, North America, and South America. However, it was not until 1915 that the German geologist Alfred Wegener introduced the theory of continental drift, in which the continents were considered to be rafts of lighter rock floating on heavier, semi-fluid rock. Wegener conceived that there once existed a super-continent (which has been named **Pangaea**), composed of our present continents. Pangaea existed until the Triassic Era, when it began to split apart into two great land masses, **Laurasia** in the northern hemisphere and **Gondwanaland** in the southern hemisphere. Toward the end of the Mesozoic period the two land masses became further dissassociated, with Africa, South America, Antarctica, and Australia separating from each other but Eurasia and North America remaining united. Subsequently, in the Cenozoic Era, they too began slowly to drift apart. A ridge in the ocean floor, the mid-Atlantic ridge, marks the region of separation, and similar oceanic ridges have been found between the other continents.

At first Wegener's theory of continental drift was not taken seriously; it was not until the 1960's that it began to receive wide support. However, more than 30 years ago, at a time when Wegener's hypothesis was generally not accepted, the French botanist Henri Gaussen recognized continental drift as a possible explanation for the widely scattered, discontinuous distribution of Paleozoic seed-fern fossils, as well as the present puzzling occurrence of cycads in Australia, South Africa, Malaysia, and the Caribbean region, including Florida, Mexico, Central America, and Northern South America. Such widely scattered distribution of plants whose seeds are too large, heavy, and dense to be carried great distances by birds, winds, or water had been an enigma. Gaussen, noting the distribution of fossil cycads during the Mesozoic Era, suggested that the ancestors of present-day cycads once occurred in several parts of Pangaea and then were separated by continental drift.

Thus we see that the theory of continental drift, once scorned by many scientists but now receiving wide acceptance, may explain the present-day distribution of those ancient plants, the cycads, and also clarify discontinuities in the occurrence of other plants and animals as well.

Present-day Cycads

Commercially, cycads have little value except as ornamentals—some species, principally *Cycas revoluta* and *Cycas circinalis,* are widely used in landscaping in the tropics and subtropics. The fronds are sometimes gathered, dried, and dyed dark green for use as funeral palms. The seeds of *Cycas* are gathered and eaten in some regions of the world, and at one time the export of *Cycas* from

379

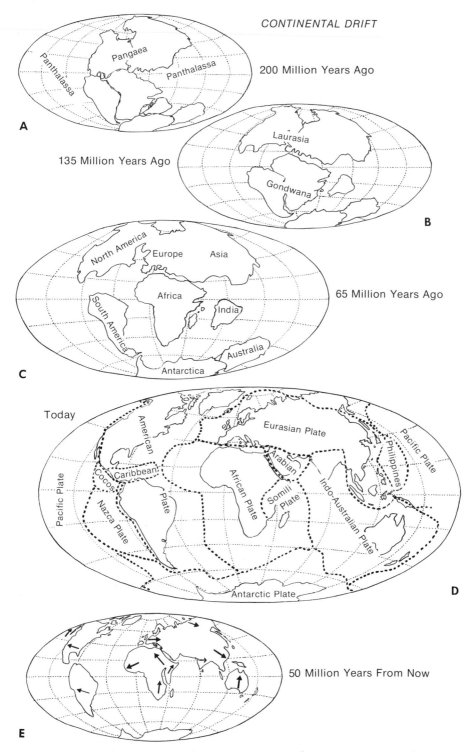

Figure 15–10 Continental drift. *A,* The supercontinent Pangaea of the Triassic Period, about 200 million years ago. *B,* Break-up of Pangaea into Laurasia (Northern Hemisphere) and Gondwana (Southern Hemisphere) 135 million years ago in the Cretaceous Period. *C,* Further separation of land masses, which occurred in the Tertiary Period, 65 million years ago. Note that Europe and North America are still joined and that India is a separate land mass. *D,* The continents today. *E,* Projected positions of the continents in 50 million years.

Japan was a crime punishable by death, because the plant was so highly regarded as a famine food. A meal prepared from cycads of the genus *Encephalartos* was used by certain African tribes to prepare an alcoholic beverage, and fleshy underground stems of several species of *Zamia* (termed *Chigua* by South American Indians) have been used as a source of starch in Florida, the Caribbean, and South America. At the turn of the century, a small mill in Miami extracted *Zamia* starch and sold it as "arrowroot flour." This product is no longer available and is not the same as West Indian arrowroot flour, a product of a flowering plant.

Great care must be taken in preparing cycad meal, whether from stems or from seeds, since it contains a neurotoxin capable of producing paralysis and death. Cycad foliage also contains this neurotoxin, and it has poisoned livestock in some areas. In addition, a potent carcinogen, **cycasin,** has been isolated from the stems and seeds of cycads. Since both these toxins are water soluble, they may be removed from meal by repeated rinsing, and the product apparently is safe if properly handled.

Figure 15–11 Bonsai trees of *Cycas revoluta*. Bonsai trees are produced by a dwarfing process that produces miniature trees of great charm and beauty. The more highly prized specimens may be 100 or more years old. Mr. Satake, a Japanese businessman whose hobby is bonsai, is shown with some of his most valuable specimens (Photo courtesy of W. H. Hodge).

Zamia is the only cycad native to the United States, and occurs in Southern Florida roughly from Gainesville south into the Keys. However, a number of other genera and species have been introduced as ornamentals and are found in gardens, principally in Florida and California. *Zamia* is one of the smallest cycads, having a short but fleshy underground stem, a long tap root, and leathery, pinnately compound leaves usually less than one meter long.

Transverse sections of a *Zamia* stem show a wide pith region surrounded by a rather narrow zone of xylem and phloem, and a broad cortex. Although other cycad stems are much more massive, all have a somewhat similar distribution of tissues. Even if cycads were not extremely slow-growing plants, the scanty wood and abundance of parenchyma would still make them valueless as sources of lumber.

Cycads have, in addition to a tap root, secondary roots, and adventitious roots that develop at the base and even on aerial parts of the stem. Certain of these roots, known as **ageotropic** roots because they do not grow downward in response to gravity, and present near the surface of the soil, are closely branched, nodular, and contain colonies of the nitrogen-fixing blue-green alga, *Nostoc.* Cycads are rather easily damaged by excessive applications of fertilizers, and it seems likely that their nitrogen requirements are met at least partially by their association with *Nostoc.*

Figure 15-12   An uprooted specimen of *Zamia.*

Figure 15-13 Cross-section through an old stem of a sago palm. The narrow, dark rings of tissue are xylem. Note the wide pith region in the center of the stem and the massive outer layer of cortical tissue.

Figure 15-14 Nodular roots of a cycad (at arrow). Such roots grow horizontally and even upward, and therefore are described as **ageotropic**.

383

The leaves of *Zamia* and other cycads are arranged helically on their stems, and usually a new crown of leaves is formed each year. The leaves are compound in all the living genera; they are singly compound except in the genus *Bowenia*, where bipinnate leaves occur. Cycad leaves are tough and leathery because of the presence of considerable amounts of internal fibrous tissue **(sclerenchyma)**. Some species have spines on their leaves; *Encephalartos horridus,* a South African form, is so spiny that it is actually dangerous. Most of the cycads that have above-ground stems retain an armor of leaf bases long after the leaves themselves are shed, and the age of a specimen can be estimated by counting the number of leaf bases and dividing by the average number of new leaves formed per year; this is the only accurate clue to age, since annual xylem rings are not formed. One very old cycad plant in western Australia has recently been estimated to be five thousand years old. If this can be verified, then this plant is one of the more ancient living organisms in the world. Because cycads grow so slowly, they never attain the dimensions of faster growing trees, such as the redwoods and *Eucalyptus.* An illustration of this slow growth is seen in Figure 15–16.

Figure 15–15 *Macrozamia.* Note the palm-like appearance and the spiral pattern of leaf scars on the trunk of this Australian cycad.

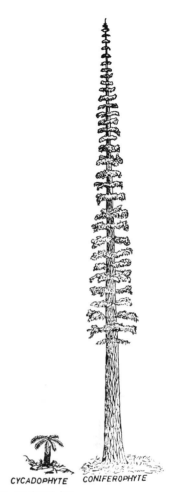

CYCADOPHYTE   CONIFEROPHYTE

Figure 15-16 A comparative study illustrating the maximum height attained by cycads contrasted with the tallest conifers (From Chamberlain, C. J. *Gymnosperms, Structure and Evolution*. New York, The Johnson Reprint Corp., 1965).

All living cycads bear cones. The two kinds of cones, seed cones and pollen cones, are borne on separate plants; thus, cycads are dioecious. The seed cones of cycads are consistently larger than the pollen cones, and those of some species of *Encephalartos, Macrozamia,* and *Dioon* may be as much as a meter long and weigh up to 40 kilograms (88 pounds). Seed cones also tend to be very colorful; those of *Encephalartos ferox* are a striking bright red-orange, and the seeds of nearly all the cycads are brightly colored, ranging from yellow to a deep red. Pollen cones range in color from rusty brown to bright yellow.

The cones of cycads are composed of sporophylls arranged helically about a central axis; pollen cones bear microsporophylls, and seed cones, megasporophylls. The microsporophylls have many large microsporangia on their undersurface. In most of the cycads, each megasporophyll bears two ovules prior to pollination and fertilization. The term *ovule* is sometimes used interchangeably with

385

seed; however, correct usage of these terms dictates that *ovule* denote prefertilization stages, and *seed* denote post-fertilization development, when an embryo is already present.

Megasporophylls of the genus *Cycas* differ from those of all other living cycads in that they may bear up to eight ovules each and are not aggregated in cones but instead are arranged in a helix about the stem in the same way as leaves. Moreover, the megasporophylls of *Cycas* are themselves rather leaf-like, as were those of some of the fossil cycads. For this reason it is thought that they represent the primitive sporophyll condition among cycads.

Comparison of megasporophylls from several genera of cycads (Fig. 15–19) points to a gradual reduction both in width of sporophyll blade and in number of ovules present. Each leaf-like megasporophyll of *Cycas revoluta* bears four or more ovules, while the other species of *Cycas* shown have smaller blades. Sporophylls of

Figure 15–17 The cones of some cycads. *A*, Pollen cone of *Zamia integrifolia*. *B*, Seed cone of *Zamia integrifolia*. *C*, Seed cones of *Dioon spinulosum*. *D*, Seed cone of *Encephalartos ferox*.

Figure 15–18 Megasporophylls of *Cycas media*. The megasporophylls of members of the genus *Cycas* are borne in a loose whorl (in the same fashion as foliage leaves) rather than in a tight cone, as in the case of other cycads.

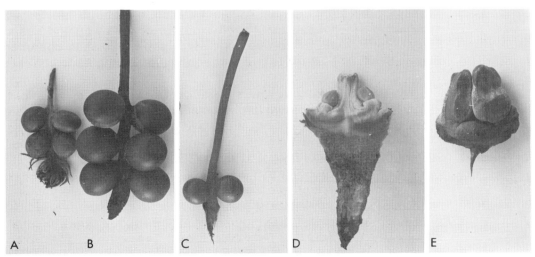

Figure 15–19 A comparative study of cycad megasporophylls. *A, Cycas revoluta. B, Cycas circinalis. C, Cycas media. D, Dioon spinulosum. E, Macrozamia mooreii.*

387

Dioon are only slightly leaf-like, and those of *Macrozamia* and *Zamia* have peltate megasporophylls that bear only two ovules. This series illustrates both the leaf-like nature of cycad megasporophylls and their relationship with the now-extinct seed ferns.

Biology of *Zamia*. The life history of *Zamia* is most often chosen to represent the cycads, not only because it has been studied rather extensively but also because material is readily available for class use. In Florida, the cones of *Zamia* begin to appear on the stem apex in early summer. While the pollen cones are still very small, microsporangia develop on the lower surfaces of microsporophylls. These microsporangia contain microspore mother cells, which in turn produce tetrads of microspores. During the summer and autumn the microspores develop thick walls and divide mitotically to form three-celled **microgametophytes** (male gametophytes). The entire assemblage of wall and microgametophyte constitutes a mature pollen grain. These pollen grains are released in December and are dispersed by the wind. They are very numerous, and many are carried to and deposited on the megasporophylls of neighboring seed cones.

Meanwhile the seed cones of *Zamia* also have undergone a series of developmental changes. Each megasporophyll bears two ovules. Within an ovule a megasporangium produces four megaspores by meiosis. Only one of these survives, to form a **megagametophyte** (female gametophyte). The ovule at the time of pollination consists of an outer layer, the **integument,** a **megasporangium** (also called a **nucellus**), and a developing megagametophyte.

The process of pollination involves adherence of pollen grains to a drop of sticky, mucilaginous fluid that fills the **micropyle.** This fluid is produced by the breakdown of some cells of the megasporangium just beneath the micropyle. As the fluid dries it shrinks and carries the pollen grains with it, depositing them within the **pollen chamber,** a receptive region within the megasporangium. The pollen grains then germinate, and pollen tubes slowly develop over a period of about five months. Meanwhile, the female gametophyte continues to grow, and also matures at about the same rate as the male gametophyte. At the time of fertilization the female gametophyte occupies most of the interior of the ovule and has at its micropylar end a cup-like depression, the **fertilization chamber,** beneath which lie three to five **archegonia** containing large egg cells (nearly 2 millimeters long).

As the pollen tubes grow, several cell divisions occur, culminating in the formation of two large, flagellated sperm cells. Cycads are especially remarkable in that they have motile male gametes within their pollen tubes; among all the living seed plants, only they and *Ginkgo biloba* have flagellated sperm. The sperm cells of cycads are so large (400 micrometers in one species of *Zamia*) that they may be seen with the unaided eye and are the largest motile male gametes known among higher plants. In organization, cycad sperm resemble those of ferns except that they may be perhaps ten times as large. There are about 12,000 flagella per cell. These are of the typical eukaryote 9 + 2 pattern and are attached to a spiral band that encircles the anterior end of the cell.

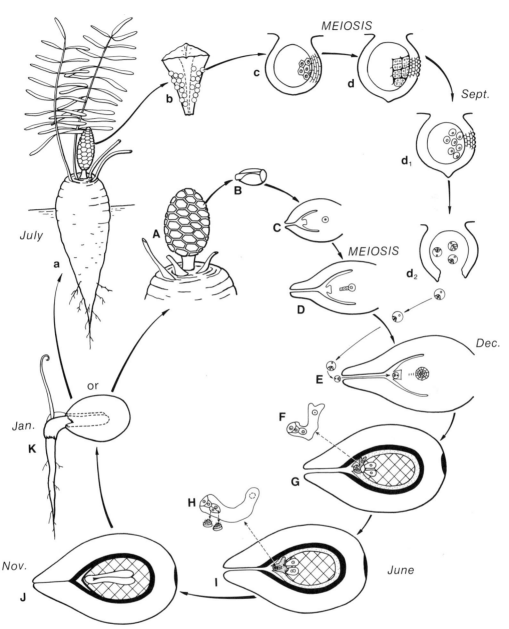

Figure 15–20 Life history of *Zamia*. *a*, Pollen plant. *b*, Microsporophyll. *c*, Young microsporangium with microspore mother cells. *d*, Microsporangium containing microspore tetrads. *d₁*, Microspores. *d₂*, Three-celled pollen (immature male gametophytes). *A*, Seed cone. *B*, Megasporophyll. *C*, Ovule with megaspore mother cell. *D*, Tetrad of megaspores, one of which is functional. *E*, Pollination, showing pollen in pollen chamber and young megagametophyte. *F*, Developing pollen tube (microgametophyte). *G*, Mature megagametophyte. *H*, Mature microgametophyte. *I*, Fertilization. *J*, Mature seed with embryo. *K*, Germinating seedling (Redrawn from Norstog, K., et al. *Laboratory Exercises in Plant Biology.* Burgess Publishing Co., 1971).

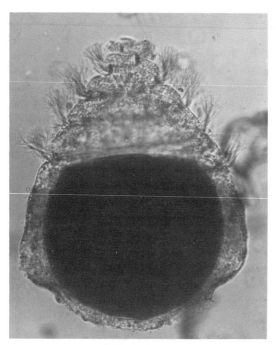

Figure 15–21 The flagellated sperm cell of *Zamia,* × 200. (From Norstog, K., and Overstreet, R. Some observations on the Gametophytes of *Zamia integrifolia. Phytomorphology 15*:46–49, 1965).

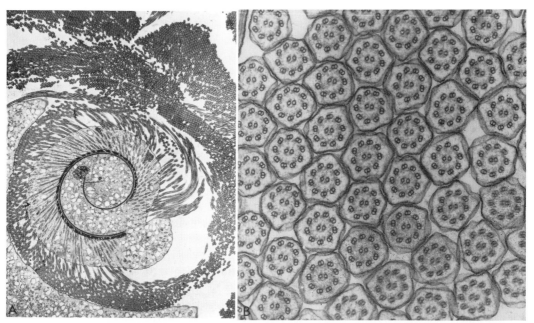

Figure 15–22 Electron micrograph of the male gamete of *Zamia. A,* Anterior end of a sperm cell, showing attachment of flagella. *B,* Transverse section of flagella. (From Norstog, K., Fine Structure of the Spermatozoid of *Zamia*: The Vierergruppe. *Amer. J. Bot. 61*:449–456, 1974).

Just before fertilization the sperms become active and move about in the pollen tubes. The tubes then burst and release the sperms, which swim about briefly in the liquid of the fertilization chamber. This liquid probably comes from the burst tubes, but some may also be produced by the archegonia. Each archegonium has four neck cells that project into the fertilization chamber, and these open precisely when the sperms are freed from the pollen tubes.

Several sperms may enter each archegonium but only one enters the egg cytoplasm, where it loses its flagella. The sperm nucleus then combines with the egg nucleus in the first mitosis. Subsequent cell divisions and growth of the embryo produce an embryo equipped with a long and highly coiled **suspensor** and two seed leaves (**cotyledons**). The role of the suspensor seems to be to push the embryo deep within the female gametophyte.

Nearly a year after pollination the seed cone breaks apart and the brilliant red-orange seeds drop to the ground at the base of the parent plant. Some germinate in place, but others may be dispersed by animals. A large scarab beetle is said to plant *Zamia* seeds in Florida by burying them 5 to 45 centimeters deep within a distance of a meter or less from the parent plant.

Perhaps the greatest value of the cycads to humans is the insight they provide into the mode of reproduction that most likely was characteristic of the earliest seed plants, including the seed ferns. Because of their motile male gametes the cycads are a connecting link between such vascular plants as the ferns and lycopods, which must depend upon environmental water for the transport of their free-swimming male gametes, and the advanced seed plants (described in chapters that follow), in which sperms are non-flagellated and non-motile.

Ecology of Cycads. Most genera and species of cycads grow in humid regions and are usually found in shady forest habitats.

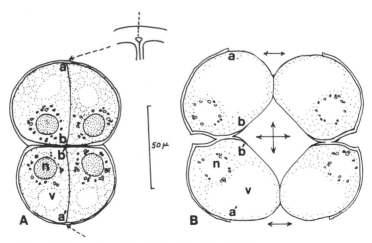

Figure 15–23 Mechanism of opening of the neck cells of *Zamia* at fertilization. *A*, Transverse section of neck cells prior to fertilization. *B*, Neck cells at time of fertilization (From Norstog, K., Role of Archegonial Neck Cells of *Zamia* and other Cycads. *Phytomorphology* 22:125–130, 1972).

391

However, some of the Australian, Mexican, and African forms *(Macrozamia, Dioon,* and *Encephalartos)* grow in xeric conditions. These may have stiff, almost thorn-like leaflets and thus resemble some of the other plants of desert thornscrub vegetation (including *Yucca, Acacia,* and *Agave).* In most regions where they occur they are relatively uncommon, and may be only locally abundant; in no case do they appear to be the dominating species. Because of their scarcity, it is regrettable that few attempts have been made to protect them.

The Cycadeoids (Class Bennettitopsida)

The cycadeoids are an interesting and rather enigmatic group of extinct Mesozoic plants, in that they were cycad-like in general form

Figure 15-24 Reconstruction of *Cycadeoidea,* a fossil cycad. The short, squat trunk and pinnately compound leaves of many of the cycadeoids are reproduced here. The reproductive cones in this model appear flowerlike; they are correctly located, but more recent evidence suggests that the microsporophylls were not so spreading as shown here, but instead were much more compact (Field Museum of Natural History, Chicago).

but their cones, at least in some cases, produced both pollen and ovules, so that in a general way they resembled flowers. Although these cones have been called "flowers" by some botanists, the cycadeoids are true gymnosperms, for their ovules are exposed, not enclosed within fruits. At one time it was suggested that flowering plants may have evolved from the cycadeoids, but this viewpoint has lost favor because of important anatomical and morphological differences between the two groups.

A large collection of cycadeoid material was assembled in the Peabody Museum of Yale University by Dr. George Wieland in the early years of this century. Wieland discovered a large number of petrified cycadeoid trunks near the Black Hills of South Dakota. These peculiar short and squat petrifactions were being depleted in this and other regions by collectors, some of whom apparently were under the impression that they were taking home petrified beehives. To curb these depredations Dr. Wieland filed a homestead claim on about 300 acres containing the richest deposits. He then turned his claim over to the National Park Service, which still maintains it under the name Fossil Cycad National Monument, a misnomer since the fossils actually are not cycads.

EVOLUTIONARY TRENDS

The cycadophytes described in this chapter include the seed ferns, cycads and cycadeoids, and they appear to be a more cohesively related group of gymnosperms than some of those to be considered in the next chapter. It is thought that the cycads are descended from seed ferns and that the cycadeoids may be more closely related to cycads than to other gymnosperms. On the other hand there are differences that separate the groups, and future studies may show their independent evolution, perhaps from the progymnosperms. Not only have cycadeoids been proposed as hypothetical flowering plant ancestors, but certain advanced Mesozoic seed ferns have also been suggested for this role. The latter may be the more likely candidates, but there are no known connecting links between the flowering plants and the gymnosperms, and such proposals are generally regarded as being quite speculative.

SUMMARY

The earliest seed plants belonged to a group of plants known as gymnosperms. Gymnosperms are plants that bear naked seeds, unlike the seeds of flowering plants, which are enclosed within fruits of a variety of types.

We do not know just how seed plants originated, but very possibly they evolved from some heterosporous, fern-like ancestor. The megaspores of such plants as *Selaginella* resemble seeds in that they develop megagametophytes containing stored food and have embryos that live from this food as they develop into young sporophytes. They might be described as "functionally seed-like." However, a seed is a more complex structure consisting of several layers, including an outer integument, a megasporangium, a megagametophyte, and an embryo.

Seed ferns are gymnosperms of the late Paleozoic and Mesozoic Eras. They were especially abundant during the Carboniferous period, and contributed to the coal deposits so characteristic of that period. Seed ferns are completely extinct, but the cycads, a primitive group of gymnosperms represented by a handful of genera, still live in several regions of the world.

Cycads are palm-like plants with relatively short, thick, usually unbranched trunks, and compound leaves. The leaves are thick and leathery in most of the species. All cycads bear cones, which are often quite large and are of two types—pollen cones and seed cones—borne on separate plants. Only one cycad occurs within the continental borders of the United States: *Zamia integrifolia,* the Florida cycad.

A classification of seed ferns, cycads and related plants follows:*

Division Pinophyta. These are primarily woody plants bearing "naked" seeds, often in cones. Collectively they are termed gymnosperms.

CLASS LYGINOPTERIDOPSIDA: The *Seed Ferns.* All are extinct.

Example: Medullosa.

CLASS CYCADOPSIDA: The *Cycads.* There are ten genera comprising about 120 species.

Living genera: Cycas, Bowenia, Ceratozamia, Dioon, Encephalartos, Microcycas, Macrozamia, Lepidozamia, Zamia, and *Stangeria.*

CLASS BENNETTITOPSIDA: The *Cycadeoids.* All are extinct.

Examples: Cycadeoidea, Williamsoniella.

---

*NOTE: We have not placed *Archaeopteris* in the above classification because it is not known definitely to have been a seed plant. It has been placed by some authors in a class of progymnosperms, the Aneurophytopsida.

DISCUSSION QUESTIONS

1. What is a seed, and in what ways does a seed differ from a mature female gametophyte of *Selaginella?*
2. What characteristics of *Archeopteris* indicate a gymnosperm relationship?
3. Why was the Carboniferous Period termed the age of ferns? What might be a more correct designation?
4. Identify the regions of the world where cycads occur today, and name one cycad occurring in each region.
5. How might one account for the present scattered distribution of cycads in the world?
6. Why are cycads not considered to be important sources of wood for lumber?
7. What problems are encountered in the use of cycads for food?
8. How is pollination affected in *Zamia?* What is the time lag between pollination and fertilization?
9. Describe the mature male and female gametophytes of *Zamia.*
10. Differentiate between an ovule and a seed.
11. What evolutionary implications, if any, do you see in the structure of male gametes of cycads?
12. In what important way do cycadeoids differ from cycads? Why have cycadeoids been proposed as ancestors to the flowering plants?

SUPPLEMENTAL READING

Andrews, H. N. Early Seed Plants. *Science 141*:925–931, 1963.

Beck, C. B. The Appearance of Gymnospermous Structure. *Biol. Rev. 45*:379–400, 1970.

Chamberlain, C. J. *The Living Cycads.* Chicago, Ill.: University of Chicago Press, 1919.

Chamberlain, C. J. *Gymnosperms: Structure and Evolution,* 3rd reprinting. New York: The Johnson Reprint Corp., 1965 (original edition published in 1934).

Pant, D. D., and B. Mehra. *Studies in Gymnospermous Plants; Cycas.* Allahabad, India: Central Book Depot, 1962.

Sporne, K. R. *The Morphology of Gymnosperms.* London: Hutchinson and Co., Ltd., 1965.

The sugar pine, *Pinus lambertiana* (Photo courtesy of W. H. Hodge).

Chapter 16

Conifers, Ginkgo, and Gnetopsids

NATURE OF CONIFERS • ECOLOGY OF CONIFERS • BIOLOGY OF PINES • GINKGO • GNETUM, EPHEDRA, AND WELWITSCHIA • EVOLUTIONARY TRENDS • SUMMARY

Conifers are woody gymnosperms. Many of them are trees, and some are shrubs; most are evergreen and needle-leaved (for example, pines, spruces, and cedars). As their name indicates, they bear cones; in most instances, both pollen cones and seed cones are present. While a few genera (such as *Taxus* and *Podocarpus*) lack seed cones, even these have pollen cones. The conifers are world-wide in distribution and are very important ecologically and economically.

A single week's issue of the *Chicago Tribune* has been said to use up 400 acres of Canadian coniferous forest in its production. This is only one of a number of large newspapers; when other newspapers, other paper products (such as cellophane, toilet paper, towels, and napkins), rayon automobile tires, lacquer paint, photographic film, explosives, and many other materials are considered, the drain on the forests of the world is very great. Not all of our wood products come from coniferous forests, but it is estimated that 85 per cent of the lumber in the United States is of coniferous origin, and 80 per cent of our houses are constructed of pine, redwood, cypress, fir, or cedar (all of which are conifers), and the poles for telephone, telegraph, and electric power lines and highway guard rails are usually of pine or some other conifer.

The first homes built by the earliest immigrants to the shores of North America were constructed either of stone or wood. Visitors to the reconstructed Plymouth Colony in Massachusetts may be surprised to see that the huts of the pilgrims were not log cabins but were made of wattle and daub (plastered mud and sticks). The log cabin was introduced to the North American colonies later by Swedish settlers. It caught on quickly and became the accepted mode of pioneer construction. The tall and straight trunks of conifers were the material of choice for building log houses.

"I went to the woods because I wanted to live deliberately, to front only the essential facts of life, and see if I could not learn what it had to teach, and not, when I came to die, discover that I had not lived."

HENRY DAVID THOREAU: *Walden.*

Figure 16–1 A log house in a Michigan lumber camp. The large logs probably are of white pine.

As soon as they could afford it, settlers replaced their rude log cabins with more imposing houses constructed of hewn and sawn lumber. These usually were constructed on the "beam and post" principle, with a framework of heavy beams. Oaks and other hardwoods were used for this framework, and beams and boards were held together with wooden pegs because nails were scarce and could be driven into the tough wood only with difficulty.

Next came the invention of the steam-powered sawmill and the extensive logging of the great coniferous forests that stretched from New England through the Lake States, and from California to the Pacific Northwest. At the same time, passage of the Homestead Act in 1862 brought on a rush of immigration from Europe and a rapid expansion of population in the Western United States. The settlers in the prairie regions had few forests near them and relied on the sawmills of the East for cheap lumber. At about this time, nail-making machinery came into use and, as a result, a new type of home construction, the "balloon frame," which used much lighter material, i.e., 2 × 4's of pine instead of heavy oak beams, was developed. All of these events led to a destruction of the pine woods from Maine to Minnesota, which were gone by World War I. Today, we rely mainly on the coniferous forests of the Pacific Northwest and the second growth pinelands of the Southeast for lumber. Despite assurances that our supplies of timber are sufficient for the future, we see evidence to the contrary in the rapidly rising cost of lumber, the increasing use of substitutes for wood, and the almost total absence of fine, knotless boards such as those obtainable from the white pine.

The Nature of Conifers (Class Pinopsida)

Conifers are found in both the Northern and Southern Hemispheres, and range in distribution from subarctic to tropical regions. The most extensive coniferous forests of the world are found in the Northern Hemisphere, principally in Canada and Siberia where they constitute the predominant trees of the boreal forest ecosystem. Conifers generally are characterized by their simple leaves, ranging from the single-veined, scale-like or needle-like types to the broad

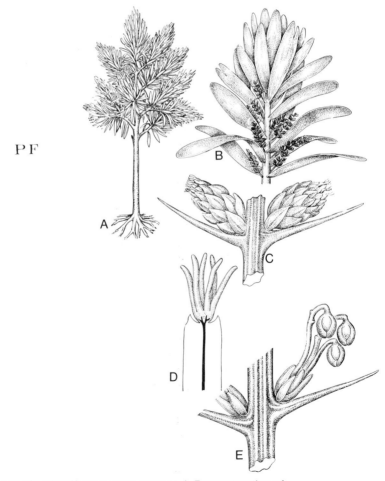

P F

Figure 16–2 *Cordaites,* a genus of carboniferous gymnosperm. *A,* Reconstruction of the entire plant. *B,* Fertile branch bearing compound strobili. *C,* Polliniferous cones in the axils of bracts. *D,* Microsporophyll with terminal microsporangia. *E,* Portion of a compound ovuliferous strobilus (Redrawn in part from Chamberlain, C. J. *Gymnosperms, Structure and Evolution* (Reprint Edition) New York, Johnson Reprint Corp., 1965).

399

"lancehead" forms with multiple venation. Some conifers are deciduous, but many more are evergreen, retaining their leaves for as long as five years before shedding them. Conifers are uniformly woody perennials, and the tree form is highly characteristic. Their wood is composed of tracheids having bordered pits, and since their seeds are "naked," they are gymnosperms.

The conifers appear to have evolved separately from the seed ferns and cycads, although both groups probably share a common ancestry among the progymnosperms. Well-defined conifers coexisted with seed ferns in the Paleozoic Era; among them were a number of species of *Cordaites,* all of which are now extinct. *Cordaites,* a large cone-bearing tree with strap-shaped leaves and stems up to 30 meters tall and a meter in diameter, formed great forests during the Carboniferous Period. A number of species and related genera have been described, some with leaves as much as 15 centimeters wide and one meter long. It is believed that modern conifers are descended from these and other forms known to us now only as fossils.

Ecology of Conifers

Conifers are found in a variety of habitats, ranging from very humid rain forests (where, for example, some species of *Podocarpus* thrive), to dry semi-deserts (where junipers are found). Generally, we think of them as xerophytes, i.e., plants capable of growing in rather dry climates. For instance, the northern coniferous forest region of North America and Northern Eurasia is characterized as a relatively dry environment. Surface moisture is in the form of ice and snow for much of the year, and relative humidity may be quite low. Most conifers are evergreen and retain their leaves through such dry periods; they may exhibit leaf modification that tends to reduce water loss. The surface-to-volume ratio is low in needle-leaved types such as pines, firs, spruces, and junipers. The vascular tissue of such leaves may be surrounded by an endodermis that restricts the movement of water out of the xylem and the photosynthetic tissue is compact with few intercellular spaces, which further restricts water movement. Finally, the stomata of needle leaves usually are sunken below the leaf surface, which is thought to reduce transpiration (the diffusion of water vapor from the interior of leaves through stomata).

Western North America is said to have the most interesting formation of conifers in the world. Among the New World conifers is *Sequoia,* named for an Indian chief who invented an alphabet and taught his tribe to read; the California Big Tree, *Sequoiadendron,* known to be the largest living thing; firs (including the balsam fir, often used as a Christmas tree); the Douglas fir, champion lumber tree of the Pacific Northwest; the many species of pines, spruces, and junipers; and many others. In other regions of the world, there are equally magnificent conifers. There are more species of pines (over 90) than there are any other genus of conifers, and these are almost completely restricted to the Northern Hemisphere.

Figure 16–3 The bunya bunya, *Araucaria cunninghamia* (Photo courtesy of Royal Botanic Garden, Melbourne, Australia).

Podocarpus, the genus with the second largest number of species (about 70), is principally a Southern Hemisphere conifer. When the first exiles from British prisons landed on Norfolk Island in the South Pacific, they must have been impressed by the towering *Araucaria,* commonly known as Norfolk Island pine. The bunya bunya, another species of *Araucaria* found in Australia, is equally magnificent, as are species of the Kauri pine, *Agathis,* of New Zealand. Conifers were widespread in the Mesozoic era (225–65 million years BP). *Araucaria,* mentioned above, is among the oldest of the surviving Mesozoic conifers; huge petrified trunks of Araucarian trees are to be seen in the Petrified Forest National Park in Arizona (Fig. 16–4).

One of the most interesting botanical events in recent years was the discovery in 1945 of the dawn redwood in remote valleys of Central China. Strangely, fossils of this tree had been found and described just four years earlier in Japan. Since then, other fossil remains of this genus have been found in the Northern Hemisphere, and it is thought to have been widespread in the Tertiary Period (some 60 million years ago). Seeds of the dawn redwood were collected and distributed in 1948 by the Arnold Arboretum of Harvard University, and trees grown from those seeds are to be seen

401

Figure 16–4 Petrified trunk of *Araucaryoxylon,* a Triassic Period araucarian tree (United States Department of the Interior, National Park Service Photo).

now at botanical gardens around the world. The average height attained by these trees in the past 20 years is about 20 meters and many of them have been producing cones and seeds for the last dozen years.

The largest trees known to man are conifers. The giant cypress of Tule, 15 miles south of Oaxaca, Mexico, is 16 meters in diameter at its base and the largest of the California big trees are 11 meters in diameter and about 100 meters tall; but neither of these is the tallest. That distinction goes to specimens of the California coastal redwood, which attain heights of 110 meters. Among the flowering plants, only some species of Australian *Eucalyptus* approach these dimensions. Officially, the tallest *Eucalyptus* tree is about 100 meters tall, but there are unverifiable reports of one tree, cut down in logging operations in the 1800's, that allegedly was 120 meters tall.

Biology of Pines. Although there is considerable variation among the conifers, there is also sufficient similarity that all are recognizable as such, even by botanically inexperienced individuals. Pines are the conifers most often chosen for study in botany classes, probably because they are the most widely distributed of the conifers in the Northern Hemisphere, and so more is known about their structure and life history than of any other genus.

The stems of pines are strongly **monopodial,** with a well-developed columnar trunk and smaller lateral branches, some of which occur in whorls marking the termination of each year's longitudinal growth. The branches of pines are of two distinctive types, **long shoots** and **short shoots.** The long shoots form the main stem and branches of the tree. The short shoots develop on long shoots in the axils of scale-leaves, and bear clusters of two to five needle-like leaves. In the pines the short shoots produce only one set of leaves and these may last several years, but the larch which has deciduous leaves borne on short shoots, produces a new set each year and the short shoots continue to grow from year to year and are often quite conspicuous. Other conifers, such as spruces and firs, have only long shoots.

The stem of a young pine is composed of a central pith sur-

Figure 16-5 A specimen of the recently discovered dawn redwood (*Metasequoia glyptostroboides*), growing in the Arnold Arboretum of Harvard University. The tree is about 25 years old (Photo courtesy of Arnold Arboretum).

403

Figure 16–6 The big tree of Tule, near Oaxaca, Mexico, *Taxodium mucronatum* (Photo by Dr. Gary J. Breckon).

Figure 16–7 *Pinus lambertiana,* the sugar pine of the Western United States (Photo courtesy of W. H. Hodge).

Figure 16–8 Comparison of the long and short shoots of larch and pine. *A,* Larch. *B,* Pine. Note the presence of leaf-bearing short shoots.

rounded by a circle of vascular strands. Outside of this is a cortex made up of parenchymal tissue enclosed by an epidermis. During the first year of life of a young pine, a layer of cells develops between the xylem and phloem of the vascular strands and in the parenchymal tissue between the strands. This layer, the **vascular cambium,** produces additional xylem and phloem by mitotic division. The xylem formed by the cambium consists principally of tracheids with bordered pits. Parenchymal cells also are formed, and these may participate in the formation of **resin ducts** extending both longitudinally and laterally in the xylem. Resin ducts also may be present in the phloem and in the cortex. Copious amounts of resin are produced in some pine species, and are the source both of rosin and turpentine. Forests of longleaf pines in the Southeastern United States are tapped for their resin.

Also present in the xylem and phloem are laterally-extending bands of tracheids and parenchymal cells. These bands, or **rays,** appear differently in cross-sections and longitudinal sections of pine stems (Fig. 16–9), looking like spokes in a wheel in cross-sections, appearing in end view in longitudinal sections that pass through the outer part of a stem (tangential sections), and in side view in radial-longitudinal sections (longitudinal sections passing through the center of a stem).

405

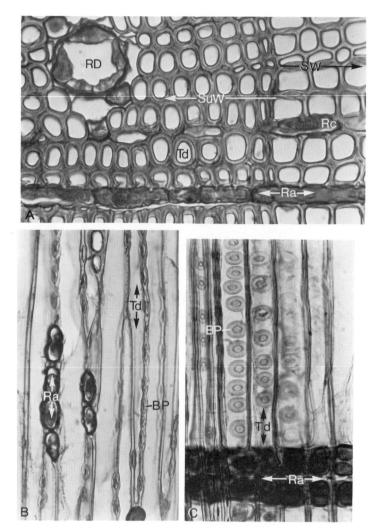

Figure 16–9 Sectional views of a pine stem. *A,* Transverse section of a portion of the xylem showing summerwood (SuW) and springwood (SW), and including a ray (Ra), ray cell (RC), resin duct (RD), and numerous tracheids (Td). *B,* A tangential, longitudinal section showing a ray (Ra) in end view, tracheids (Td), and bordered pits (BP). Note that in a tangential section the bordered pits appear in side view. *C,* A radial, longitudinal section in which the rays (Ra) are seen in side view, while the bordered pits appear in face view.

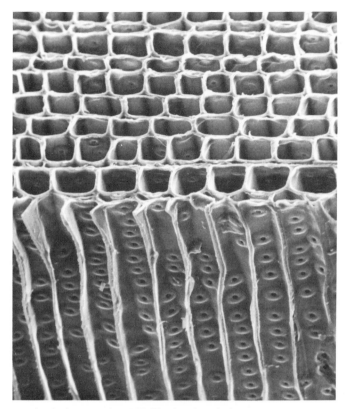

Figure 16–10 Scanning electron micrograph of pine wood, × 275. The bordered pits of tracheids are clearly seen (Photo courtesy of Institute of Paper Chemistry).

The phloem of the pine stem consists primarily of food-transporting cells called **sieve cells.** Sieve cells are elongated cells, usually with rounded or slanting ends and lateral, porous areas, or **sieve plates,** where there is intercellular continuity of cytoplasm. The sieve cells of conifers have nuclei (unlike those of the flowering plants; see Chapter 18), and live for a year or so and then are incorporated into the layers of the outer **bark**. The bark consists of all the tissues outside the cambium, and includes living and dead phloem, cortex, and **cork**. Cork is a tissue composed of cells having walls impregnated with wax and a fatty substance called **suberin,** and is formed by cell divisions of the **cork cambium.** A cork cambium develops in the cortex of a young stem as it begins to produce increments of xylem and phloem. In particular, production of xylem exerts pressure from within against the outer stem tissues, disrupting the epidermis, cortex, and older phloem. As the stem grows, new layers of cork cambium are formed and continually provide additional protective layers of cork.

With the majority of gymnosperms, marked seasonal variations in temperature and rainfall occur each year of their lives; as a consequence, periods of greater and lesser growth occur. In temperate regions, the spring and early summer are periods of great

407

cellular activity and growth, whereas slower growth occurs in later summer and early fall, and little or no growth takes place in winter. These changes in rate of growth are most obvious in the xylem. The tracheids formed in spring and early summer are relatively large and numerous compared to those of later summer; hence, the terms "**spring wood**" and "**summer wood**." Each year's increment of spring wood and summer wood is readily apparent as an **annual ring**, with the number of annual rings present corresponding to the age of the tree. Not all conifers attain great ages, but some individuals of the California big tree are known to be more than 2000 years old, and the bristlecone pine of Nevada apparently is the oldest living organism known, at 5000 years. However, a recent estimate places the age of the Tule cypress of Mexico at 6000 years but this requires further study.

The roots of conifers develop from the primary root, or **radicle**, of the embryo and form a branching tap-root system. Young roots are composed of a core of xylem and phloem surrounded by cortex and epidermis. They lack a pith, and thus are protostelic. A vascular cambium is formed in older roots, and their subsequent development is very similar to that of older stems. Reference has been made in Chapter 11 to mycorrhizal associations, and these seem to be characteristic of the roots of most, if not all, conifers.

The needle-like leaves of pines are rather specialized organs, and as we have said earlier, show such adaptations to xeric condi-

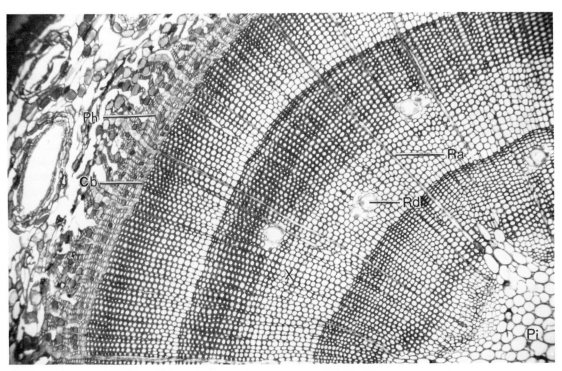

Figure 16–11 Transverse section of a three-year-old pine stem showing annual rings, × 50. Ph, phloem region; Cb, cambium region; X, xylem; RD, resin duct; Ra, ray; Pi, pith.

Figure 16–12 Scanning electron micrograph of a cross section of pine wood, × 50. *A,* Spring wood. *B,* Summer wood (Photo courtesy of Institute of Paper Chemistry).

tions as a thick cuticle, sunken stomata, and a low surface-to-volume ratio. A single vascular strand, surrounded by a conspicuous endodermis, occupies the center of the leaf. Other conifers have similar leaf structures, but some, such as *Podocarpus* and *Agathis,* have broad leaves with dichotomous venation. The latter usually are found in more mesic regions.

Pine sporophytes are monoecious and have both seed and pollen cones. The tree is the 2N sporophyte generation. The seed cones develop *in place of* long shoots; that is, the central cone axis is equivalent to a long shoot, while the cone scales each take the place of a short shoot. Pollen cones, on the other hand, develop *on* long shoots, and each cone takes the place of a single short shoot. Because of this interpretation, and for other reasons based principally on the study of extinct conifers, the seed cones of pines and those of other conifers, are considered to be composite or **compound cones**, unlike the simple cones of cycads.

The microsporophylls of pollen cones each bear two microsporangia on their lower surface. Seed cones do not have megasporophylls but are composed of a system of **bracts** arranged spirally along the cone axis. A cone scale, considered to represent a much-modified short shoot, is present in the axil of each bract. In pines, each cone scale bears two ovules on its upper surface. As the

409

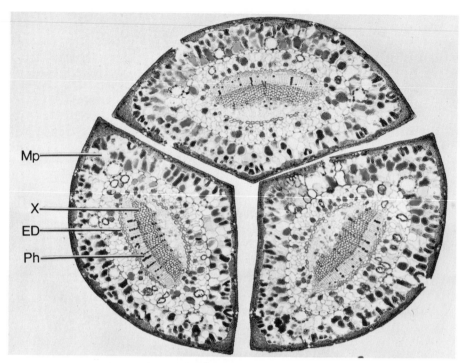

Figure 16–13 Cross sectional view of a pine leaf showing various structures. X, Xylem; Ph, phloem; ED, endodermis; Mp, mesophyll (chlorophyllous tissue) (Courtesy Carolina Biological Supply Company).

Figure 16–14 Pine cones. *A*, Cluster of pollen cones. *B*, Seed cones at time of pollination.

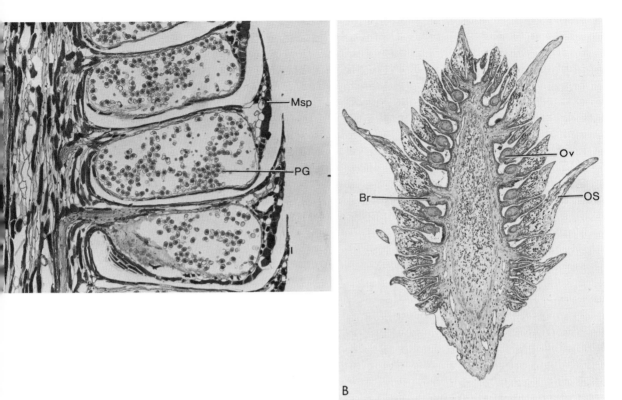

Figure 16–15 Longitudinal sections of pine cones: *A,* Portion of a pollen cone showing microsporophylls (Msp) and pollen grains (PG) × 50. *B,* Ovuliferous cone showing ovules (Ov), ovuliferous scales (OS) and bracts (Br), × 20.

ovules mature, accessory wings are formed, and these aid in the dispersal of seeds by air currents.

The reproductive cycle of the pine is similar to that of cycads in many respects. Many immature male gametophytes or pollen grains develop from 1*N* microspores within a microsporangium. The pollen grains are windborne, and some are carried to developing ovules where they adhere to drops of micropylar fluid and are drawn into the ovules. Within each ovule, a female gametophyte develops from a 1*N* megaspore. As in the cycads, four megaspores are produced in a megasporangium but only one is functional. Concurrently with the growth of the female gametophyte, male gametophytes form pollen tubes in the megasporangial tissue and these grow in the direction of the archegonia, eventually discharging two non-flagellated sperms into the egg cytoplasm. One sperm disintegrates, while the other unites with the egg nucleus. The embryo that develops from the fertilized egg is polycotyledonous (with eight to 10 cotyledons) and has a long suspensor. The female gametophyte, composed of starchy tissue, nourishes the growing embryo and later supplies food to the growing seedling. The female gametophytes of the piñon pine are collected and eaten by Indians of the Southwest, and sometimes are available in delicatessens and specialty food shops; they are flavorful, if somewhat resinous.

The seed cones of pine require about two years to mature. Initially, pollen cones develop in the spring and pollen is shed in late

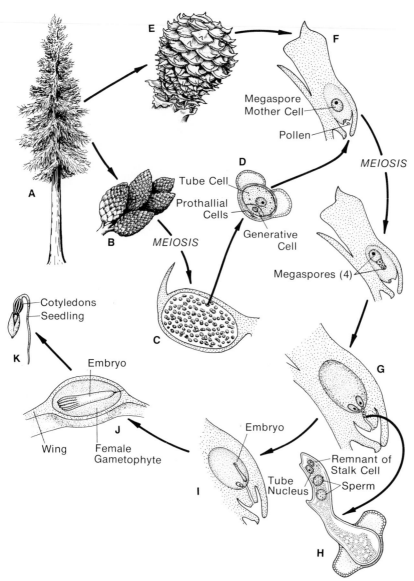

Figure 16–16 Life history of the pine. *A*, Mature sporophyte. *B*, Pollen cones. *C*, Microsporophyll and microsporangium. *D*, Pollen at time of shedding. *E*, Seed cone with cone scales. *F*, Longitudinal section of cone scale with developing ovule at time of fertilization. *G*, Mature female gametophyte (megagametophyte). *H*, mature male gametophyte (microgametophyte). *I*, Section of seed with developing embryo. *J*, Section of mature seed. *K*, germinating seed.

spring. Seed cones also are formed in spring and ovules develop and are pollinated in late spring. Male and female gametophytes mature during the ensuing months and fertilization occurs the next spring. The seed develops through summer and fall, overwinters, and is mature the third spring.

Mature pine cones differ in the manner in which their seeds are shed. The cones of some species open immediately and the seeds germinate with little delay. Others require such heat that the cones will open and shed their seeds only after an exceptionally hot day or after a forest fire; this mode of germination ensures the survival of at least some progeny in the wake of a serious fire. Even after the seeds germinate, conifer seedlings differ in their environmental requirements; for example, some will grow only in the shade of other plants, while others require open conditions and maximum sunlight.

Although the conifers represent an ancient line of gymnosperms, they must be considered to be one of the more successful plant groups of the present, since they are so widespread. We next consider a few survivors of once widespread groups of other gymnosperms including *Ginkgo,* a well-known horticultural plant, and the gnetopsids, a small assemblage of strange and morphologically puzzling genera and species.

Ginkgo (Class Ginkgoöpsida)

Plants of the Class Ginkgoöpsida were widespread in the past, and their fossil record goes back some 200 million years to the Triassic Period. Today only *Ginkgo biloba* remains, and it is doubtful whether there are any natural populations anywhere on earth. Most, if not all, *Ginkgos* are in captivity, so to speak, and they are widely planted both for decoration and, in China and Japan, for their edible seeds. *Ginkgo* tends to be tough and hardy under most conditions and is a valued horticultural species. Studies have shown it to be remarkably resistant to insect and fungal attack. The wood, though brittle, is resistant to boring insects and has been used to make insect-proof cabinets. Even the leaves appear to repel certain insects and have been used as bookmarks to ward off silverfish and other inhabitants of books. The wood is used also for the manufacture of chessmen and lacquerware in the Orient.

As was noted in Chapter 15, Mr. S. Hirase discovered the motile sperm of *Ginkgo* in 1896. *Ginkgo* and the cycads are the only seed plants known to have flagellated motile gametes, although we suspect that seed ferns and primitive conifers may have had similar sperm cells. The huge *Ginkgo* tree upon which Hirase made his discovery still stands on the campus of the University of Tokyo.

Ginkgo, like pine and larch, has both long shoots and short shoots. Like those of larch, the short shoots are perennially active and bear a new set of deciduous leaves each year. The leaves are bilobed and fan-shaped, with dichotomous venation. Commonly, *Ginkgo* is called the maidenhair tree because of a superficial resemblance of its leaves to the leaflets of the maidenhair fern (see Figure 14–17).

Like the cycads, *Ginkgo* is dioecious. Its ovules usually develop in pairs at the ends of short, forked stalks that are borne on the short shoots of seed trees. Pollen trees have paired microsporangia that occur on short shoots in rather loosely structured pollen cones or **catkins**. Pollination occurs in the spring, and fertilization takes place the following autumn, often after the ovules have been shed. The embryo develops while the seed lies on the ground. Mature

413

Figure 16-17 The *Ginkgo biloba* tree from which Hirase gathered his findings, as it looked about 1908. This tree is still growing on the campus of the University of Tokyo (Photo courtesy of Y. Ogura, Tokyo, Japan).

seeds have a fleshy outer layer that emits a very disagreeable odor, like rancid butter; for this reason, seed trees are often cut down after they begin to produce seeds.

Gnetum, Ephedra, and Welwitschia (Class Gnetopsida)

Three genera—*Gnetum, Ephedra* and *Welwitschia*—are unique among living gymnosperms because they have flower-like compound pollen cones, ovules with two integuments, and **vessels** in their wood. The latter are tube-like xylem elements composed of cylindrical xylem cells positioned end to end, with perforate or open end walls; they are unknown in any other gymnosperms, but are a characteristic component of the xylem of flowering plants. In most other respects the three genera are as unlike one another as they are unlike other gymnosperms.

The 40 or so species of *Gnetum* are mostly tropical vines, although a few are trees or shrubs. They are found in the valley of the Amazon River, in West Africa, and in Asia from India to Malaya. *Gnetum* is remarkable in its resemblance to many of the flowering plants. It has opposite leaves that are broad and net-veined, and its reproductive organs look somewhat flower-like, although its ovules are naked as they are in other gymnosperms.

414

Figure 16-18 *A,* Twig from a seed tree of *Ginkgo* bearing several mature seeds. *B,* Twig from a pollen tree of *Ginkgo* bearing a loosely organized pollen cone, or **catkin.**

The approximately 35 species of *Ephedra* are shrubby desert plants found in Europe and Africa along the Mediterranean Sea, in Southwestern United States, Mexico, and from Persia eastward into China. The stems of *Ephedra* are angular and photosynthetic and its leaves are minute and few in number so that the plant is reminiscent generally of a large *Equisetum*. *Ephedra* has been used in this country to prepare a beverage (which accounts for its common name, Mormon tea), and a Chinese species is the source of the widely used alkaloid drug ephedrine, used in the treatment of asthma and hay fever.

There is only one species of *Welwitschia,* and it too is a desert plant found only in the extremely dry regions of coastal Southwest Africa. Its deep tap root is said to extend downward for several meters to subsurface water. *Welwitschia* is without a doubt the most bizarre plant in the world; it consists of a short, broad, woody stem that is mostly underground, except for a concave, disk-shaped crown that is covered over with thick cork. The mature plant has been likened to a large woody carrot. Some very old specimens of *Welwitschia* have crowns over 1 meter in diameter and are about 2000 years old. A pair of thick and leathery apron-like leaves, the only leaves ever produced by the plant, grows from the periphery of the crown. These last throughout the life of the plant and become quite tattered as they sprawl over the surface of the soil.

Ecologically, *Welwitschia* is a very interesting plant. It lives in some of the driest deserts on earth, among these one region in which there may be no measurable precipitation for four or five years at a

Figure 16–19 *Gnetum,* a gymnosperm found in tropical and subtropical Asia. Note how similar the foliage is to that of some flowering plants, such as some magnolias. The seeds are bright red (Photo courtesy of Dr. James McCleary).

time. However, in such areas this plant occurs along the sea coast, in the fog belt. Apparently nightly fogs are a major source of water, especially for young plants lacking deep root penetration. The spreading leaves are thought to collect water condensing on them and to take in this water through the stomata, which are reported to remain open at night and to be closed during the daytime. This is contrary to the stomatal action of many other plants, in which the stomata are open during the daylight hours. However, no critical experiments have yet been performed to determine exactly how *Welwitschia* manages its water uptake, utilization, and conservation.

Because the Gnetopsida have features found also among flowering plants, some botanists have suggested that they represent an ancestral gymnosperm type from which flowering plants have evolved. Their reproductive organs have been called "flowers," but in all cases the ovules are "naked" and pollination is typically gymnospermous, with pollen being deposited at the entrance of the micropyle and drawn inwardly by shrinkage of the micropylar fluid. Most botanists now believe that these similarities to flowering plants are coincidental, the result of parallel evolutionary processes.

Figure 16–20 *Ephedra*, a desert plant.

Figure 16–21 Reconstruction of *Welwitschia*, showing its habitat in the desert of Southwest Africa. The model in the foreground is of a plant bearing seed cones, while the one above and to the right is a replica of a plant bearing pollen cones (Field Museum of Natural History, Chicago).

417

Evolutionary Trends

The pinopsids are believed to be of ancient lineage, with origins in the Paleozoic Era among the progymnosperms. Since some of the early gymnosperms (such as *Cordaites*) co-existed with the seed ferns and cycads, it is probable that they evolved *with* them rather than *from* them. *Ginkgo biloba* and its antecedents are sometimes included with the conifers in a single class; however, early conifers occurred in the Triassic Period together with trees having leaves closely resembling those of *Ginkgo biloba;* therefore, these two groups have had separate identities for a considerable time. They do, however, share a number of similar anatomical characteristics (such as similar wood structure and tree-like form) as well as reproductive characteristics. The unique, flagellated sperms of *Ginkgo* and the cycads, on the other hand, have suggested a relationship to the cycadophytes. Nevertheless, this is seen as a common trait, shared by all of the most primitive gymnosperms and perpetuated in *Ginkgo* and the living cycads, and not evidence of a direct linkage between the latter.

The relationship of the gnetopsids to the rest of the gymnosperms is very obscure, and their fossil record is quite fragmentary and consists only of some fossilized pollen of fairly recent vintage.

SUMMARY

The conifers are cone-bearing gymnosperms of world-wide distribution and ecological and economic importance. They evolved during the Paleozoic Era and were widespread in the Mesozoic Era. All conifers are woody plants, and the Tule cypress of Mexico and the California Big Tree are the largest plants known. The wood of conifers is composed of tracheids with bordered pits; the phloem is composed of sieve cells. In many of the conifers, especially those of the Northern Hemisphere (pines, spruces, firs and cedars), the leaves are needle-like and evergreen, and show xerophytic adaptation.

Most conifers have both pollen and seed cones on an individual plant. The tree is the sporophyte generation, and microspores and megaspores are formed by meiotic division. Microspores develop into male gametophytes (pollen tubes) and megaspores form female gametophytes with archegonia. Both kinds of gametophytes reach their mature state of development following pollination. Pollen tubes penetrate the archegonia where the non-motile sperm cells are discharged. Following union of male and female nuclei in the egg, embryos are produced and, eventually, mature seeds. The reproductive cycle of *Pinus* requires two years for completion.

Several genera of plants related to conifers occur in various regions of the world. *Ginkgo* is a living fossil, descended from widely occurring fossil genera and species of the late Paleozoic and Mesozoic Eras; it resembles the cycads in that both have motile, flagellated sperms. *Gnetum, Ephedra,* and *Welwitschia* are rather bizarre plants having such advanced features as vessels and, in the case of *Gnetum,* the overall appearance of a broad-leaved, flowering plant.

The classification of these plants and related forms follows:

Division Pinophyta: The gymnosperms.

CLASS PINOPSIDA: (The conifers) There are approximately 55 living genera, with 575 species. They are living and extinct seed plants characterized by simple scale, needle, or strap-like leaves, commonly with a single vein but occasionally with multiple, dichotomizing venation. The tree-form predominates and most are large woody plants. The reproductive organs usually are in cones.

Examples: The extinct genera include *Cordaites* and *Araucarioxylon,* and some living genera are *Pinus, Abies, Picea, Sequoia, Juniperus, Cupressus, Sequoiadendron, Podocarpus, Metasequoia, Agathis,* and *Araucaria.*

CLASS GINKGOÖPSIDA: There is only one living species. The Ginkgoöpsida include gymnosperms that exhibit many characteristics in common with conifers, including two shoot types, tracheids with bordered pits, a monopodial tree form, and simple leaves. The latter, however, are fan-shaped with multiple, dichotomizing venation. The male gametophytes produce flagellated sperms similar to those of cycads.

Example: *Ginkgo biloba.*

CLASS GNETOPSIDA: There are three living genera with about 75 species. These plants have growth habits quite unlike that of the foregoing gymnosperms. The ovules have two integuments, and all possess compound pollen cones that appear flower-like.

Examples: *Gnetum, Ephedra,* and *Welwitschia.*

DISCUSSION QUESTIONS

1. How may one differentiate between conifers and seed ferns? Between conifers and cycads?
2. What are some commercial uses of coniferous trees?
3. Name three genera of conifers wholly or largely confined to the Northern Hemisphere, and three of the Southern Hemisphere.
4. What is meant by the term *primary tissue?*
5. Define the cambium in terms of location, cellular type, and function.
6. Compare the leaves of *Cordaites* and those of *Pinus.*
7. What relationship exists between the monopodial growth habit of conifers and their commercial uses?
8. What is meant by cellular differentiation? Give an example.
9. What is the relationship between the dimensions of tracheids in pines and other trees and seasonal and climatic variations?
10. Give one single characteristic that exclusively distinguishes *Ginkgo* from all of the conifers.
11. Cycads are dioecious; *Pinus* is monoecious; but both have separate seed and pollen cones. Explain.

SUPPLEMENTAL READING

Berry, J. B. *Western Forest Trees.* New York: Dover Publications, Inc., 1966.

Chamberlain, C. J. *Gymnosperms, Structure and Evolution,* 3rd reprinting. New York: Johnson Reprint Corp., 1965 (original edition, 1934).

Foster, A. S., and E. M. Gifford, Jr. *Comparative Morphology of Vascular Plants,* 2nd ed. San Francisco: W. H. Freeman and Co., 1974.

Harrar, E. S., and J. G. Harrar. *A Guide to Southern Trees,* 2nd ed. New York: Dover Publications, Inc., 1965.

Major, R. T. The *Ginkgo,* the Most Ancient Living Tree. *Science 157:*1270–1273, 1967.

Muenscher, W. C. *Key to Woody Plants,* 6th ed. Ithaca, New York: Cornell University Press, 1950.

Petrides, G. A. *A Field Guide to Trees and Shrubs.* Boston: Houghton Mifflin Co., 1958.

Sargent, C. S. 1922. *Manual of Trees of North America,* 2nd ed. New York: Dover Publications, Inc., 1965 (reprint; original edition, 1922).

Sporne, K. R. *The Morphology of Gymnosperms.* London: Hutchinson and Co., Ltd., 1965.

Flowers of *Couroupitia guianaensis*, the cannonball tree (Courtesy Fairchild Tropical Garden).

The Flowering Plants

Botanists and zoologists alike are in agreement that the advent of flowering plants in the late Mesozoic Era, about 100 million years ago, resulted in an explosion of plant and animal life forms. Why was this so? The answer lies in the nature of the flowering process: its rapidity; its requirement for cooperation by bees, birds, and even mammals in the pollination process; in the formation of fruits and seeds high in food value; and in the dispersal mechanisms, evolved by these flowering plants, which depend upon animals to a major extent for their effectiveness. Mammals and birds (but mammals mostly) replaced the reptiles of the earlier Mesozoic Period and were able to do so because of their more rapid, warm-blooded metabolism. High metabolism is supported by foods rich in energy, precisely the kind supplied by fruits and seeds of flowering plants. The grasses that carpet the earth today are flowering plants. They have exerted a stabilizing influence over the environment since first they appeared and began to spread in the early part of the Cenozoic Era. All our livestock exists because of grass. Almost all our foodstuffs, certainly all those we consider to be staples, are the products of flowers. For these reasons, we can say that without flowers there would be no human race.

"Without the gift of flowers and the infinite diversity of their fruits, man and bird, if they had continued to exist at all, would be today unrecognizable. Archeopteryx, the lizard bird, might still be snapping at beetles on a sequoia limb; man might still be a nocturnal insectivore gnawing a roach in the dark. The weight of a petal has changed the face of the world and made it ours."

LOREN EISELY: *The Immense Journey.* RANDOM HOUSE, 1957.

FLOWERING PLANTS (DIVISION MAGNOLIOPHYTA)

The division Magnoliophyta, to which flowering plants belong, is the largest of all plant divisions, with more than 300 families and 275,000 known species. Flowering plants are placed in two major classes, the **Magnoliopsida,** also called **dicotyledons ("dicots")** and the **Liliopsida** or **monocotyledons ("monocots").** These two classes are separated from one another on the basis of their embryo structure, the form of their flowers, and their stem and leaf anatomy. The Magnoliopsida is the larger of the two groups, with more than 225,000 species compared with about 50,000 species of Liliopsida.

Economics of Flowering Plants

The cereal plants—wheat, maize (corn) and rice—which form the basis of agriculture for all modern societies, are monocotyledons of the class Liliopsida. Most vegetable and fruit crops are dicotyledons (Magnoliopsida), as well as such important medicinal plants as *Digitalis,* a heart stimulant, and *Rauwolfia,* used in the treatment of hypertension. Other useful members of the Magnoliopsida are *Coffea* (coffee) and *Thea* (tea). Cocoa is made from an extract of cocoa beans, the seeds of the cacao tree *(Theobroma cacao)*; and

Table 17–1
COMPARISON OF LILIOPSIDA AND MAGNOLIOPSIDA.

LILIOPSIDA (MONOCOTYLEDONS)	MAGNOLIOPSIDA (DICOTYLEDONS)
Single cotyledon (none in orchids).	Usually two cotyledons.
Endosperm commonly present in the mature seed.	Endosperm often absent in the mature seed.
Leaves usually parallel-veined.	Leaves usually pinnately or palmately veined.
Cambium usually absent.	Cambium present.
Floral parts typically occurring in threes and sixes or their multiples.	Floral parts generally are in fours, fives, or their multiples.
Plants generally herbaceous; a few families have genera of wood-producing plants.	Many families have genera of woody plants.
Vascular bundles in stem are typically scattered.	Vascular bundles in stems are usually arranged in a ring.
Roots are adventitious and fibrous.	Root system usually consists of one or more primary roots (taproot) and secondary roots.

the original formula for a popular soft drink contained an extract of the leaves of the Andean plant, coca *(Erythroxylon coca),* a source of the narcotic drug cocaine. Another ingredient was prepared from the cola nut *(Cola nitida).* Although this beverage no longer contains coca extract, it still retains the name of the coca plant.

The aesthetic role is sometimes neglected in discussions of the importance of flowering plants. Not only are flowering plants highly desired for interior decoration and landscaping, but one of the most popular outdoor activities in the United States is gardening. Horticultural botany is one of the most popular of hobbies.

To satisfy these and other needs, the search for new species of flowering plants is a major botanical pursuit. Plant exploration is currently in progress in tropical America, Asia, and Africa, and new plant discoveries are made each year. Exotic plants are continually being collected abroad, transplanted to this country, carefully propagated, and finally introduced to the market. Many newly introduced species also are subjected to pharmacological screening for use in foods and as drugs. One recent discovery is the so-called miracle berry *(Synsepalum dulcificum)* of the Sapote family (Sapotaceae). The berries of this shrub have been used by West African tribes as a sweetening agent for many years. Recent research has shown that the active principle is a protein rather than a carbohydrate. This protein desensitizes the acid receptors of the tongue but does not interfere with the sweet receptors. The sweetening power is so great that even extreme dilutions of the chemical cause substances to taste sweet; lemons, for example, taste as sweet as oranges. A natural, low calorie sweetener would be a desirable substitute for some of the chemicals presently in use as sweeteners. As yet, however, the miracle berry has not been put into commercial use, but it exemplifies the importance of plant exploration and plant introduction.

The Nature of the Flower

The characteristic feature of all the Magnoliopsida is the reproductive structure called the **flower**. Strangely, so common a structure is subject to a good deal of misinterpretation. For example, the sunflower is not a flower but an aggregate of flowers or an **inflorescence.** The "flowers" of the poinsettia and the dogwood consist mostly of the highly colored leaves, and the true flowers of the plants are the rather inconspicuous greenish-yellow structures that are seen at the center of an array of red, pink, or white **bracts.** There are many other examples of similar confusion. What, then, are flowers? Morphologically, the flower may be defined as a short shoot that bears highly-specialized sporophylls—an accurate, albeit unromantic, definition.

In some plants, such as the waterlily and *Magnolia,* the flowers are borne singly, but in many other cases flowers are produced in clusters or inflorescences of various kinds. In such cases, the flower stalks of the inflorescence are called **peduncles**, and the tip of a

P F

Figure 17–1 The largest flower, *Rafflesia,* is a leafless parasite that may be found on the stems of a tropical vine. It is native to Malaysia. The flowers may be as large as 1 meter in diameter, and give off the odor of carrion; as a result, this plant is pollinated by insects that are attracted to carrion.

peduncle, to which the floral parts are attached, is called the **receptacle.**

Whether they occur singly or in clusters, typical flowers are composed of outer, sterile, **accessory parts** called **sepals** and **petals** and fertile inner structures called **essential parts;** all are attached to the receptacle. Sepals collectively make up the **calyx,** which often provides protection for the more delicate inner portion of the flower. Sepals usually are green but sometimes may be colored and thus resemble petals. Petals collectively make up the **corolla** and often are highly colored and attractive to insects and sometimes small birds. The calyx and corolla together constitute the **perianth.** Variation in the number, color, and shape of perianth parts is the basis for the many different forms of flowers occurring in the Magnoliophyta. Basic flower patterns of the Magnoliopsida (dicots) and the Liliopsida (monocots) are different. Dicot flowers have petals and sepals occurring in fours or fives or their multiples; monocot flowers have perianth parts generally in threes or multiples of three.

The essential parts of the flower are called the **androecium** (or **stamen**), and the **gynoecium** (or **pistil**). Each stamen morphologically is a highly modified microsporophyll. Each microsporophyll has three parts, the **microsporangium** or **anther** (pollen sac), the **filament** supporting the microsporangium, and the **connective,** a part that joins the filament and the microsporangium.

Initially a microsporangium or anther contains a number of cells with large nuclei, the **microspore mother cells**, which are $2N$ in chromosome number. Each microspore mother cell undergoes meiosis and produces a tetrad of microspores, each with a single $1N$ nucleus. This stage is quickly followed by a single mitotic division of the microspore nucleus and forms an immature **microgametophyte,** or male gametophyte. The developing microgametophyte now con-

424

tains two 1 *N* cells. One of these, the **generative cell**, later divides to form two sperm cells; the other cell is called the **tube cell**. Typically, when the young microgametophyte is at the two-celled stage, it is called the **pollen grain**, and it is at this stage that pollen is released from the microsporangium.

The gynoecium, or **pistil,** is made up of one or more highly modified megasporophylls called **carpels**, and consists of three distinct parts, the **ovulary** (ovary) which contains ovules, the **stigma**, and the **style**. If an ovulary is cut transversely, one to many **locules** or chambers can be observed. Ovularies with two or more locules are derived from simple pistils that have become united through evolution. Each component of a compound pistil is a carpel. Simple ovularies are thought to have evolved from a simple, leaf-like organ, the megasporophyll, on whose margins ovules were borne. By the infolding of this structure at its midrib, followed by lateral fusion, the simple ovulary came from a single megasporophyll, the ovules being borne in two rows where the margins of the megasporophyll are conjoined. The area of ovule attachment in the ovulary is known as the **placenta.** In flowering plants with compound ovularies, the form of attachment of ovules on the placenta (placentation) is an important character that distinguishes various groups.

Variation in Floral Structure

Although the typical flower consists of four principal parts (calyx, corolla, androecium, and gynoecium), there are many variations in floral structure. The perianth may have **radial symmetry** and be considered **actinomorphic** (star-shaped) if the parts are of similar size

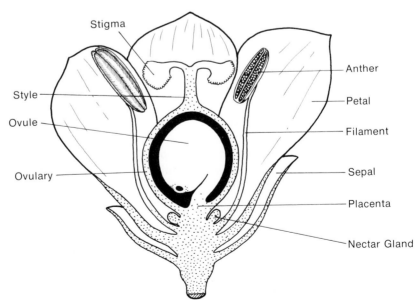

Figure 17–2 The structure of a flower, represented highly diagrammatically.

425

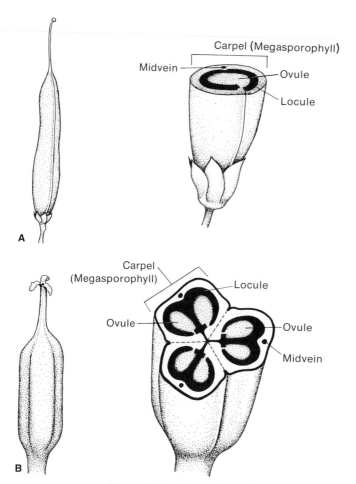

Figure 17–3 Comparison of simple and complex pistils. *A*, Simple pistil, with ovulary composed of one carpel. *B*, Pistil with a compound ovulary composed of three carpels.

and shape. Flowers in which some of the parts are larger or of different shape than the others have **bilateral symmetry** and are considered **zygomorphic flowers.** Both kinds of perianths are common.

The perianth may either be composed of only one whorl of parts or may be missing altogether, in which latter instance the flower is said to be apetalous or naked. Flowers with conspicuous perianths are often insect or bird pollinated, while naked or apetalous flowers are frequently wind pollinated. Perianth parts may also be free (i.e., not united with other perianth parts in the same whorl); or they may be wholly or partly united, referring to the cohesion of parts that form a united calyx or a united corolla. The position of the ovulary may be **superior** to the floral parts (**hypogyny**), or may be surrounded but free of the floral cup formed by the basally-united floral parts (**perigyny**), or the ovulary may be **inferior**, i.e., united with the basally fused floral parts (**epigyny**).

How to Identify Flowers. Recognition of flowering plants is a pastime that many people find very satisfying. But how does one go about identifying an unknown flower? The vegetative parts of different plants often look much the same to most of us so we depend on the flower for identification; this is also how professional botanists identify flowering plants.

A number of books are available to the interested student of flowering plants for use in discovering the names of plants. These books range from the simple "how to know" types to very complete and technical compendia. Many states have published guidebooks to local and regional flowering plants, so there is no dearth of informative and interesting reference works. Nearly all books pertaining to flowering plants and their identities use "keys" to identify particular plants. The flower is considered to be the most reliable and diagnostic plant structure, so the keys ask a series of questions about flower structure among these: Does the flower have both sepals and petals? How many stamens are present? How many carpels compose the pistil? Such information, together with leaf and stem characteristics, is usually sufficient to identify an unknown plant. In addition, many wild-flower books have color photographs, drawings, and diagrams to supplement the technical descriptions.

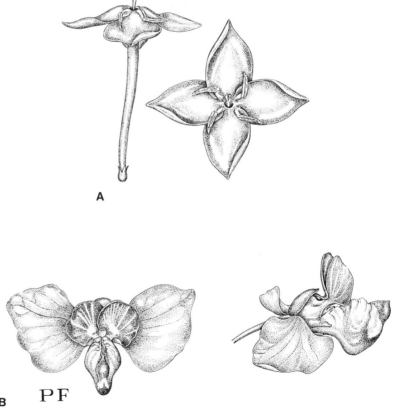

Figure 17–4 Variations in floral symmetry. *A*, Flower of the yellow *Ixora (Ixora chinensis)*, having radial symmetry and equal parts (an example of **actinomorphism**); *B*, Flower of purple milkwort (*Polygala grandiflora*), with bilateral symmetry and united parts (an example of **zygomorphism**).

427

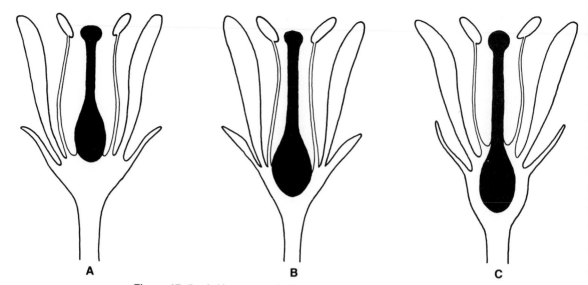

Figure 17–5 *A*, Hypogyny. *B*, Perigyny. *C*, Epigyny. See text for explanation.

Pollen and Pollination

Each kind of flowering plant has its own distinct kind of pollen, and it is possible to identify many plants by the character of their pollen. For instance, pollen obtained from ancient bogs and prehistoric human habitations can be used to determine the kinds of plants that were present in those times. The range of pollen variation is enormous. In the acanthus family (Acanthaceae), a group of largely tropical species, can be found a variety of shapes, sizes, and sculpturing of pollen grains; this is also true in other plant groups. It is not always clear what the significance of these variations may be from the evolutionary point of view. Wind dispersed pollen typically is smooth and dry, while pollen carried by insects is often bristly, rough, or sticky. Most kinds of pollen grains have conspicuous pores or furrows that are thin places in the pollen grain through which the pollen tube grows. One of the common types of pollen grains is the **tricolpate** form, which is so called because of the three-furrowed outer wall of the grain. Typically, the pollen wall consists of two layers: an outer one called the **exine,** which has the characteristic markings such as pores and furrows; and an inner layer, the **intine**, which bulges through the pores at the time of pollen tube germination.

Pollen usually is released from anthers through longitudinal slits that develop in the microsporangium, or sometimes from special pores at the top of the anther. The grains are carried from the anther by wind, rain, or small animals, and some flowers have evolved special adaptive mechanisms that permit a high degree of control of pollen transfer. The flowers of the attractive mountain laurel of the Appalachian mountains have reflexed stamens wedged in small pockets of the corolla. If slight pressure is applied to the corolla, as by a visiting insect, the anthers are suddenly released and pollen is catapulted

428

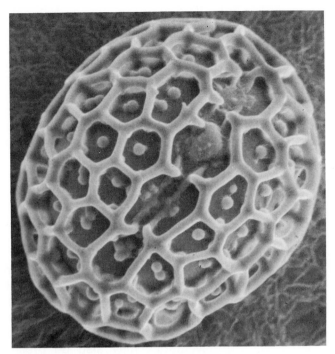

Figure 17–6 *Eranthemum* (Acanthus family) pollen as viewed with a scanning electron microscope, × 1000.

explosively onto the insect's back. A similar mechanism may be observed in alfalfa and in some orchids. Milkweed flowers have special pollen-bearing structures, called **pollinia**, that become entangled in the feet of visiting insects and so are carried from flower to flower.

Of course, it is possible that pollen grains of another species may be carried to the stigma of a plant. How does a flower recognize its own kind of pollen and receive it while rejecting the pollen of other species? Recent studies have shown that there are chemical interactions between stigma and pollen somewhat like the immune

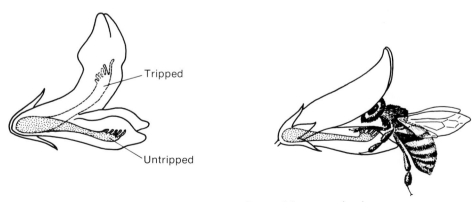

Figure 17–7 Structure of the alfalfa flower. The stamens have a trigger mechanism that is tripped by a visiting bee; pollen is then deposited on the insect's body (Redrawn from *Plant Science: An Introduction to World Crops,* Second Edition, by Jules Janick, Robert W. Schery, Frank W. Woods and Vernon W. Ruttan, W. H. Freeman and Company. Copyright © 1964).

429

reactions that take place when animal bodies are invaded by bacteria or other foreign bodies. A pollen grain secretes a protein within a few minutes of its arrival on the stigma of another flower. The flower, if it recognizes the pollen protein, becomes receptive to the growth of the pollen tube; otherwise, it reacts to the pollen protein by blocking the entry of the pollen tube into the tissues of the pistil. It does this by plugging up the cells in the vicinity of the foreign pollen with **callose,** a carbohydrate material. Interestingly, it is the pollen proteins of the ragweed and other such plants that cause allergic reactions in humans.

Nectaries and Fragrances

Nectar is the sugary liquid sought and collected by insects and other small animals. It is produced by many kinds of flowers in floral structures called **nectaries.** Nectaries are usually specialized parts of the base of petals, but they also may be formed as a ring of tissue near the base of the ovary. Generally, they are thought to have been derived from the reduction and modification of a whorl of stamens or petals. The sugar content of nectar may vary from 25 per cent to 75 per cent, but even lower levels are sufficient to attract animals.

Nectaries may also be present outside the flower. In *Thunbergia,* a vining plant from India, extrafloral nectaries apparently serve to attract ants. The ants protect the flower from depredations by so-called robber bees, which attempt to drill holes in the base of the corolla in their search for nectar.

In simple flowers, the nectaries are often accessible to a wide variety of insects, while specialized flowers have modifications that protect both nectar and pollen. In such flowers, rows of hairs or

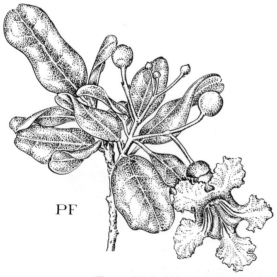

PF

Figure 17–8 Honey guides in the flower of *Catalpa.* Many insect-pollinated flowers have variously colored streaks on the petals that function as guides to the nectaries.

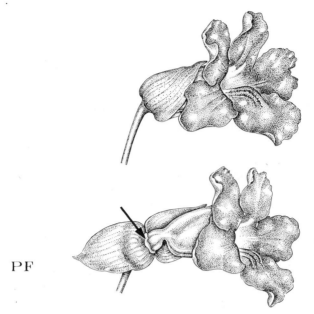

PF

Figure 17-9 Extrafloral nectaries (arrow) of *Thunbergia.* The accessory nectaries of *Thunbergia* are located externally at the base of the flower and are visited by ants that serve to protect the flowers from nectar thieves. Note also that the flowers have obvious honey guides.

bristles, fragrances, distinctly colored areas, and various other kinds of signals function as honey guides, and this results in some control of the pollinator. Nectar "thieves," such as the robber bees of the *Thunbergia,* are those small animals that bypass the controls evolved by plants and obtain nectar without transferring pollen, as by puncturing the base of the corolla.

Pollinators are attracted to flowers by many kinds of fragrances and odors that vary from very pleasant ones, such as those produced by gardenias and roses, to very repulsive ones that smell like rotting flesh. Air samples containing the fragrance of orchid flowers have been collected and analyzed for their chemical nature. The main constituents are menthol, wintergreen, vanilla, and clove oil in various combinations. If a piece of filter paper is saturated with the appropriate combination of these chemicals and then placed in a tree, bees are attracted to the paper as though the fragrance had been produced by the orchid.

Ecology of Flowers

Botanists have classified flowers on the basis of the kind of pollen agent involved, such as bee flower, beetle flower, moth flower, bat flower, fly flower, wind flower, and water flower. Certain highly specialized flowers are pollinated by only one kind of animal. For instance, one orchid has flowers that look like female wasps and are attractive to male wasps (see Figure 6–10); night-blooming cacti

431

are pollinated by moths, and the sausage tree of tropical regions also blooms at night, and its flowers are pollinated by bats.

Flowers may also be studied in relation to climatic conditions and to particular adaptations of pollinators. Bee flowers, such as snapdragons and mints, generally are found in dry and open parts of the temperate zones. Flies are more common pollinators in high mountain and arctic areas, but also serve as pollinators in the tropics. Beetle-pollinated plants, such as waterlilies and magnolias, are common in the warm temperate and tropical zones, while moth and bat pollination is common in the tropics. Bright orange, yellow, and red colors in flowers (such as in eucalyptus trees and in members of the pineapple family) are often adapted to bird pollination. Long, tubular flowers with brightly colored corollas are thought to have evolved along with nectar-gathering birds having long, curved bills. In cold temperate areas and polar regions where animal pollinators cannot survive, pollination is brought about by wind. Grasses, sedges, and willows are familiar examples of plants that are pollinated in this manner. Submerged flowering plants, such as certain pondweeds *(Zannichellia),* rely on water currents to carry pollen to receptive stigmas.

Breeding Systems in Flowering Plants

Most flowering plants are monoecious, and this is considered to be a primitive condition, while dioecious plants are considered to be a sign of evolutionary advancement. The flowers of a monoecious plant may have both stamens and pistils and thus be **monoclinous,** or the plant may be **diclinous,** having separate staminate and pistillate flowers. Examples of monoecious, monoclinous plants are the *Magnolia,* rose, poppy, and lily. Examples of monoecious, diclinous plants are maize, birch, oak, melon, and cucumber. Dioecious plants bear either staminate or pistillate flowers and obviously never are monoclinous. Some examples are willow, poplar, and holly.

Jack-in-the-pulpit usually has staminate flowers produced on one plant and pistillate flowers on another and therefore is dioecious. However, sex reversal can occur if environmental conditions vary. If plants are grown under arid conditions, the plants are all staminate, but if plants are then grown in moderate conditions, they will revert to production of pistillate flowers only. Papaya plants will behave in a similar fashion.

Breeding systems are basically of two kinds, either **autogamous,** in which the flower is pollinated by its own pollen, or **allogamous,** in which the flower is pollinated by pollen of another flower. **Hybridization** is cross-pollination between different races or different but closely related species, and is common in plants. **Homogamous** breeding systems are those in which the anther and stigma mature at the same time, thereby favoring self-pollination, while in **dichogamous** ones, maturation occurs at different times, and thereby ensures cross-pollination. Some members of the orchid family and the sunflower family are dichogamous. **Cleistogamy,** in

Figure 17–10 *A,* The bee-pollinated flower of the orchid, *Oncidium. 1.* Bee gathering nectar touches adhesive pollen sac, which becomes attached to its head. *2.* Bee then transfers pollen to stigmatic surface of next orchid flower visited (*3*), and picks up second pollen sac. *B,* Bat-pollinated flowers of the African sausage tree, *Kigelia pinnata.* The flowers are pollinated at night by bats. Note that the structure of the flower is such as to provide a landing platform for the bat as it seeks nectar and that the pistil and stamens are placed so as to facilitate pollen transfer. *C,* Wind-pollinated flowers of *Panicum,* a grass. Note in the enlarged drawing of the flowers that the stigma is feathery and that the stamens have slender filaments. Wind-pollinated flowers often are apetalous and inconspicuous.

433

which seeds form without the flower opening and coming into bloom, occurs in many plants (among them violets and *Oxalis*) and is an extreme form of autogamy. Cleistogamous flowers often look like those that open normally but are smaller and less conspicuous.

Fluctuating environmental factors may prevent normal open flowering, which is called **chasmogamy.** Areas in which such climatic instability persists are inhabited by a greater proportion of plants having the ability to produce cleistogamous flowers. Factors such as lack of sufficient water, the presence of both drought and heat, or excessive heat, result in floras consisting of species that are self-pollinating and cleistogamous, because pollinating insects cannot live under such conditions. This has been seen in such normally insect-pollinated groups as the legume and milkwort families. Also, **seasonal cleistogamy,** with chasmogamous flowers present in the spring and cleistogamous flowers present in the summer ensures production of a constant high level of seeds, and has been an important breeding system in flowering plants among many families. Specific examples of seasonal cleistogamy are seen in the mint (*Lamium*), the yellow sorrel grass (*Oxalis*), the acanth (*Ruellia*), and many grass species such as the needle grass (*Stipa*). Such a breeding system permits the species to produce seeds through cross-fertilization of chasmogamous flowers that may be adapted to new or changing environmental conditions. Cleistogamy ensures the production of large numbers of seeds that are identical genetically to their parent since they are formed as the result of self-fertiliza-

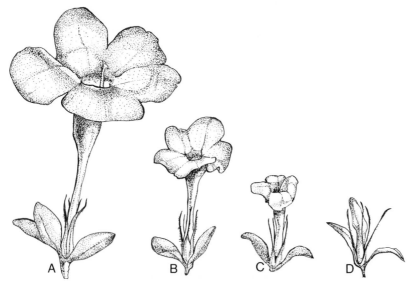

Figure 17–11 Flower forms in *Ruellia caroliniensis*. Considerable variation in both flower form and breeding behavior is exhibited by this species. The flowers drawn here were seen in one Florida population. *A*, A typical large chasmogamous flower. *B*, A miniature chasmogamous flower. *C*, A semi-cleistogamous flower. *D*, A completely cleistogamous flower (From Long, R. W.: Floral Polymorphy and Amphimictic Breeding Systems in *Ruellia caroliniensis* (Acanthaceae). *Amer. J. Bot. 58(6)*:525–531, 1971).

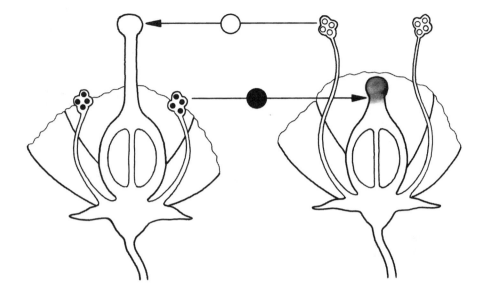

HPM

Figure 17-12 Heterostyly in the common primrose. The flowers are self-incompatible, but intercross readily. Both kinds of flowers produce offspring with short and long styles in equal numbers. Pollen compatibility is indicated by shading (Redrawn from Solbrig, O. *Principles and Methods of Plant Biosystematics*. New York, MacMillan Co., 1970).

tion; therefore, these plants will be as well-adapted to their environment as their parent, and there will be no defective offspring, as may occur in cross-fertilizing systems. **Facultative cleistogamy** (including seasonal cleistogamy) is one of the most successful breeding systems that flowering plants have evolved.

Another interesting example of breeding systems is the one called **heterostyly.** In primrose there are two kinds of flowers, one with long styles and short stamens, and the other with short styles and long stamens. Pollination can occur only between short styled and long styled flowers because an insect visiting one type of flower picks up pollen on its body and then brushes against the stigma of the other type, but not against the stigma of the first kind. Heterostyly involves floral modification that tends to ensure cross-fertilization and prevent self-fertilization.

Biology of the Flowering Plant

The function of the flower is sexual reproduction, and this is initiated when pollen is transferred to a receptive stigma. The pollen begins germination on the stigma with the formation of a germ tube that grows out through one of the pores or furrows of the exine and penetrates the surface of the stigma. As mentioned earlier, during the early development of the pollen tube the generative nucleus of the pollen grain divides to form two sperm nuclei. As the tube grows down the style, the sperm nuclei follow just behind the tube nucleus, which has preceded them into the pollen tube.

435

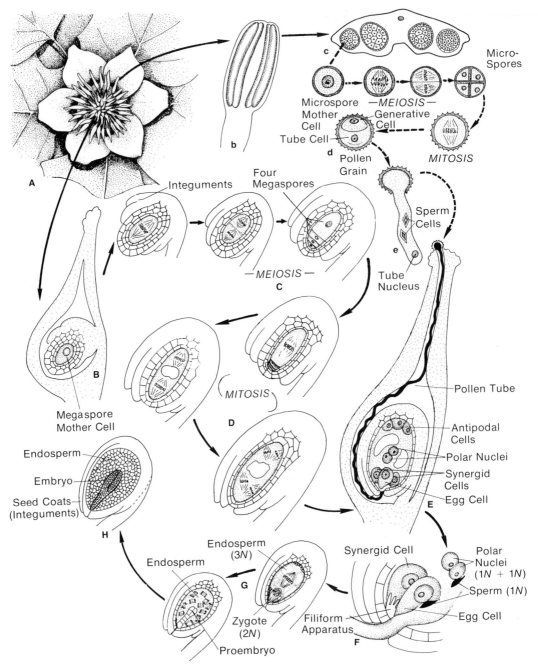

Micro-Spores

Microspore Mother Cell

MEIOSIS

Generative Cell

Tube Cell

Pollen Grain

MITOSIS

Sperm Cells

Tube Nucleus

Integuments

Four Megaspores

MEIOSIS

C

b

c

d

e

A

B

Megaspore Mother Cell

MITOSIS

D

Pollen Tube

Antipodal Cells

Polar Nuclei

Synergid Cells

Egg Cell

E

Endosperm

Embryo

Seed Coats (Integuments)

H

Endosperm

Endosperm (3N)

G

Zygote (2N)

Proembryo

Synergid Cell

Filiform Apparatus

F

Polar Nuclei (1N + 1N)

Sperm (1N)

Egg Cell

Figure 17–13 The life history of a flowering plant, rendered highly diagrammatically. *A*, The flower of the sporophyte plant. *b*, The microsporophyll or anther. *c*, Stages in microsporogenesis (meiosis). *d*, The mature pollen grain, an immature microgametophyte. *e*, Germinating pollen on microgametophyte (pollen tube). *B*, A megasporophyll (carpel) or simple pistil containing a developing ovule. *C*, Stages in megasporogenesis *(meiosis)*. *D*, Development of the megagametophyte or embryo sac. *E*, Pistil, ovule, and mature megagametophyte (embryo sac) at time of fertilization. *F*, Fertilization. One sperm unites with the egg, while the second sperm unites with the combined polar nuclei. *G*, Stages in the development of the embryo and endosperm in the maturing seed. *H*, Seed containing an embryo and cytoplasm.

The ovulary develops simultaneously with the anther and the formation of pollen. Ovules form inside the ovulary along the placenta, generally forming either a single or a double row. A longitudinal section through the ovule in early development shows two layers of cells, the **integuments,** surrounding a mass of undifferentiated parenchymal cells, the **megasporangium** or **nucellus.** The integuments enclose the ovule completely except for a minute opening (the **micropyle**), usually located near the point of attachment of the ovule to the placenta. Later one of the nucellar cells enlarges and becomes the **megaspore mother cell.** This cell undergoes meiosis and forms four daughter cells with the reduced or $1N$ chromosome number. These cells are the **megaspores.** In most cases three of them begin to shrivel and become disorganized so that only one survives. The single megaspore next begins to enlarge within the megasporangium. The megasporangium nourishes the remaining megaspore and provides the necessary food for its growth into the **megagametophyte** or **female gametophyte (embryo sac).**

Typically, the megaspore divides in three successive mitotic divisions to form a female gametophyte composed of seven cells, six of which contain single nuclei with the $1N$ chromosome number, while the other cell, the **central cell**, has two nuclei and is $1N + 1N$. As this growth takes place, the megasporangium becomes absorbed by the developing female gametophyte.

Near the micropyle is another cell, the **egg.** Two cells, the **synergids**, are immediately adjacent to the egg; the egg and the two synergids are referred to frequently as the **egg apparatus**. The central cell is the largest of the female gametophyte; it contains the two **polar nuclei**, and after fertilization forms the food supply of the seed. The remaining three cells, the **antipodals**, have no known function.

Although the developmental sequence outlined above is typical of about 80 per cent of flowering plants, other patterns of megasporogenesis and embryo sac development are known. One of these is typical of members of the lily family, and is of particular importance to students because it frequently is studied in botany classes. The reason for its continued use seems to be partly traditional and partly because slides of lily reproduction are much more easily prepared and show the developmental stages more clearly than do those of many other plants. All four megaspore nuclei participate in embryo sac formation in the lily family, and the embryo sac, though composed of seven cells, has a $3N + 1N$ central cell and $3N$ antipodals. The egg cell and the synergids are $1N$.

After pollination, the pollen tube grows into the ovulary and penetrates the micropyle, in the process destroying one of the synergid cells. At the base of each synergid is a finger-like structure, the **filiform apparatus**, which is thought to contain a pollen tube attractant, probably calcium. One of the two sperms in the pollen tube enters the egg to form the zygote, while the other sperm enters the central cell and combines with the two polar nuclei to form a $3N$ nucleus ($5N$ in the lily). The fertilized central cell later divides many times

A

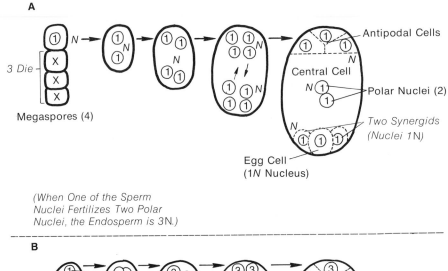

3 Die

Megaspores (4)

Antipodal Cells

Central Cell

Polar Nuclei (2)

Two Synergids
(Nuclei 1N)

Egg Cell
(1N Nucleus)

*(When One of the Sperm
Nuclei Fertilizes Two Polar
Nuclei, the Endosperm is 3N.)*

B

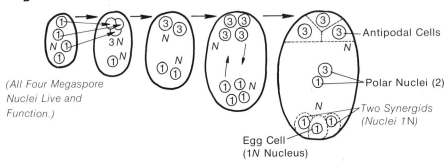

*(All Four Megaspore
Nuclei Live and
Function.)*

Antipodal Cells

Polar Nuclei (2)

Two Synergids
(Nuclei 1N)

Egg Cell
(1N Nucleus)

*(When One of the Sperm Nuclei Fertilizes
the 3N + 1N Polar Nuclei, the Endosperm
is 5N.)*

Figure 17–14 A comparison of the typical embryo sac development found in most flowering plants with that occurring in members of the lily family. *A*, Most common type. *B*, Type found in lily.

and becomes the **endosperm.** The zygote forms an embryo for which the endosperm furnishes a supply of food. The process described here is considered typical for most flowering plants, although variations in cell number, chromosomal makeup, and fertilization processes do occur. In summary, in flowering plants during sexual reproduction there is **double fertilization**, which results in a $2N$ zygote and a $3N$ endosperm cell ($5N$ in the lily). Double fertilization is unique to the Magnoliophyta and is generally believed to be a state of evolutionary advancement.

There are several patterns of embryo development in flowering plants, but typically the embryo passes through certain proembryonic phases. In dicots the zygote divides first to form an embryo composed of a **basal cell** and a **terminal cell.** The terminal cell of this pair undergoes divisions that result in the formation of an octant of cells arranged in a sphere. At the lower (or micropylar) position of this sphere, the **radicle** and the **hypocotyl** form and the upper part forms the **cotyledons** and **epicotyl** of the mature embryo. The cotyledons appear first as two bulging regions that begin to elongate when the embryo is approximately 100 micrometers in length and, when the embryo is about 400 micrometers in length, differentiating tissues (including xylem and phloem) become apparent. Depending on species, the basal cell undergoes several or more divisions to form a **suspensor**. Monocot embryos go through similar early embryonic stages, but the full-term embryos differ considerably in structure from dicot embryos.

The dicot embryo often elongates until it reaches the end of the embryo sac, and its continued growth results in a folding over of the cotyledons. At this stage, the **epicotyl** becomes visible as a minute conical-shaped mass of cells between the cotyledons. The growth of the embryo often results in the absorption of the endosperm, and in many instances it has been completely utilized by the time the embryo has matured. There are, however, examples of development in which the embryo remains small and consists of only a few cells while the endosperm makes up the bulk of the seed. In orchids (which are monocots), the embryo remains very small (generally from 100 to 200 micrometers long) when the seed is mature, and the endosperm is almost non-existent. Orchid embryos in nature depend on mycorrhizal-like fungal associations for nourishment (see Chapter 11), but can be grown artificially on nutrient agar in the absence of any fungus.

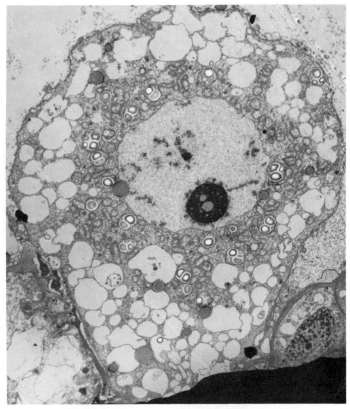

Figure 17–15   Zygote of barley, a monocot, × 3700. Note how much larger the zygote is than the adjacent cells. (From Norstog, K., Early Development of the Barley Embryo: Fine Structure. *Amer. J. Bot. 59*:123–132, 1972).

The Fruit

As the embryo develops, the enclosing integuments harden and become the **testa,** or seed coat. The developing seeds are within the ovulary, and as the embryo and seed mature, the ovulary, with other tissues in some cases, becomes the **fruit.** The changes in the shape, size, and appearance of the ovulary are usually brought about by hormonal changes stimulated by pollination and fertilization. The ovulary wall becomes the **pericarp** in fruits, and typically is made up of three more or less distinct layers: the **endocarp**, a layer immediately enclosing the seed; the **mesocarp**, a layer that is often fleshy or fibrous in texture, and an outer layer, the **exocarp**, which is often skin-like in character.

Fruits may have other parts of the flower included in their structure. The apple, for example, has a floral tube that grows around the ovulary and becomes the fleshy, edible portion of the fruit, while the core represents the true ovulary. Shapes, colors, textures, and numbers of seeds of fruit vary greatly. Generally, flowering plants either produce fleshy fruits or dry fruits depending on their pericarp

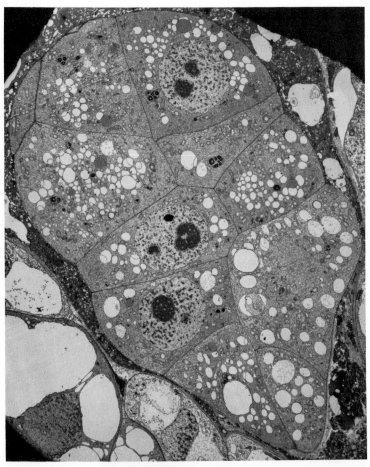

Figure 17–16 Proembryo of barley, × 3250. Proembryos are often characterized by a high order of cellular symmetry and a low degree of cellular specialization (From Norstog, K., Early Development of the Barley Embryo: Fine Structure. *Amer. J. Bot. 59*: 123–132, 1972).

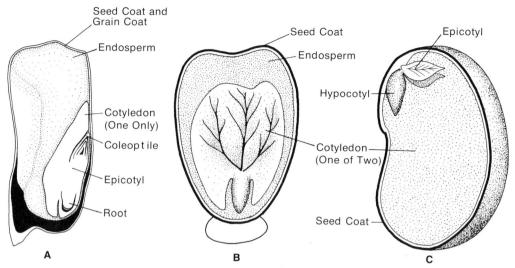

Figure 17–17 The structure of seeds. *A,* Grain of maize, a dry fruit containing a single seed. *B,* Seed of castor bean, a dicot type having persistent endosperm. *C,* Seed of bean, a type that lacks endosperm in the mature seed.

development. The kind of fruit formed usually is quite characteristic for each particular family of plants, and knowledge of types of fruit is very helpful in identifying and classifying plants (see Table 17–2).

Fruit and Seed Dispersal. Most new plants have greater chances of survival to maturity if they grow at some distance from their parent plant, since in that way competition for light, space, and nutrients may be less severe (see Chapter 6). Various kinds of fruit and seed dispersal mechanisms have evolved in flowering plants, and these may depend on explosive fruit dehiscence or on the help of animals, wind, or water. Typically, the whole fruit with its ripened seeds is transported from the parent plant, but sometimes the entire plant may be transported, or in other cases only the seeds are dispersed. The tumbleweed is blown about during much of the year on the Western plains, shedding its seeds as it tumbles about.

For the sake of convenience, we may examine the matter of dispersal mainly as the function of fruit. Many flowering plants develop fleshy fruits that are attractive to, and eaten by, birds and mammals. The indigestible seeds of such fruit are passed through the alimentary tract of the animal, eventually germinating wherever they are deposited in fecal material (perhaps the reader has noticed that many kinds of plants spring up in abundance along fences). Cherry trees, in particular, show this sort of dissemination pattern because birds deposit the seeds while perching after eating the cherries. Fruit and seeds also may be carried externally by animals. The mistletoes, which are parasitic plants, are an interesting example of this. Their fruits are sticky and adhere to the beaks of birds. The birds then wipe the seeds onto the branches of host plants, and the germinating mistletoe seeds grow into the tissues of the host and the plant becomes established.

441

Table 17–2
CLASSIFICATION OF FRUITS.

1. **SIMPLE FRUITS.**   Consist of a single ripened ovulary.
    I. *FLESHY FRUITS.*   Most or all of the pericarp is fleshy and soft at maturity.
        1. **Berry.**   Pericarp fleshy throughout, or almost completely so (*examples:* grape, tomato). Other types of berries are the **Hesperidium,** with a leathery rind (*examples:* citrus fruits) and **Pepo,** with a thick, hard rind (*examples:* pumpkin, watermelon).
        2. **Drupe.**   Exocarp thin, mesocarp thick and fleshy, endocarp strong and hard and enclosing one to three seeds. (*examples:* peach, olive, cherry, coconut).
    II. *DRY FRUITS.*   Pericarp dry and hard or often brittle at maturity.
        A. DEHISCENT   (splitting open along definite lines or at definite points at maturity):
            1. **Legume.**   Consists of one carpel that splits open along two lines (*example:* pea).
            2. **Follicle.**   Consists of one carpel that splits along one line (*example:* milkweed).
            3. **Capsule.**   Derived from two or more united carpels split in various ways (*examples:* lily, tulip, snapdragon).
            4. **Silique.**   Derived from two united carpels that separate at maturity (*examples:* cabbage, mustard).
        B. INDEHISCENT (not opening at maturity and containing usually only one or two seeds):
            1. **Achene.**   One-seeded, seed separable from fruit (*examples:* sunflower, dandelion).
            2. **Samara.**   One- or two-seeded, achene-like, but pericarp bearing a flattened wing-like outgrowth (*examples:* maple, ash, elm).
            3. **Nut.**   One-seeded fruit similar to achene but with very hard, thickened pericarp (*examples:* acorn, chestnut, hazelnut).
            4. **Caryopsis** (grain).   One-seeded with seed coat united to the inner surface of the pericarp (*examples:* corn, wheat, oats).
2. **AGGREGATE FRUITS.**   Derived from a cluster of several to many ripened ovularies produced by a single flower and borne on the same receptacle. The individual ovularies may develop into drupes (*examples:* raspberries, blackberries), achenes (*example:* buttercups), or other types of simple fruits.
3. **MULTIPLE OR COMPOUND FRUITS.**   Derived from a cluster of several to many ripened ovularies that are produced by several flowers closely formed on the same inflorescence. The individual fruits may be drupes, berries, or nutlets (*examples:* mulberry, pineapple, osage orange, breadfruit, fig).
4. **ACCESSORY FRUITS.**   Formed as structures that are made up of ripened ovularies plus tissues of some other floral part, such as the receptacle or calyx. The accessory tissues may make up most of the fruit (*example:* as in the strawberry, in which the fruit is made up of many small achenes borne on a succulent, edible receptacle; or as in the apple and pear, in which the mature ovulary or so-called core is surrounded by the enlarged and edible receptacle and calyx tissue. The latter type of fruit is called a **pome.**

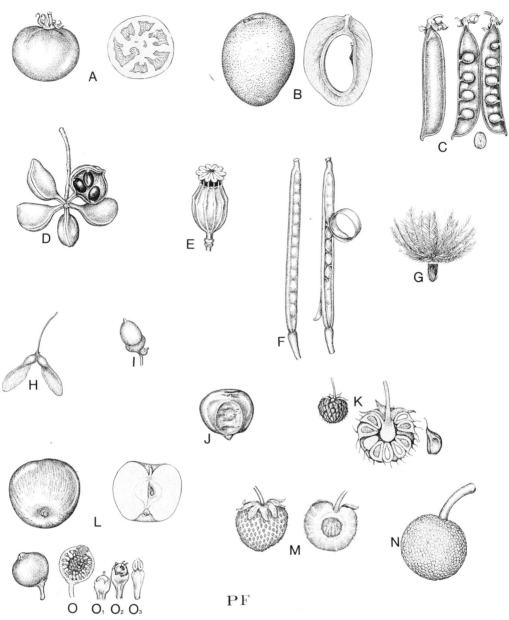

Figure 17-18 Types of fruit. *A* and *B,* Fleshy fruits derived from one ovulary. *A,* Tomato, a berry. *B,* Mango, a drupe. *C* to *J,* Dry fruits derived from one ovulary. *C,* Garden pea, a legume. *D, Sterculia* fruit, a follicle. *E,* Poppy fruit, a capsule. *F,* Mustard fruit, a silique. *G,* Dandelion fruit, an achene. *H,* Maple fruit, a samara. *I,* Oak fruit, a nut. *J,* Maize fruit, a grain or caryopsis. Fruits derived from several to many ovularies of one flower include *K,* the raspberry, an aggregate fruit. *L* and *M,* Fruits derived from one or more ovularies plus the receptacle and, in some cases, the calyx. *L,* Apple, a type of accessory fruit called a pome. *M,* Strawberry, an aggregate-accessory fruit. *N* and *O,* Fruits derived from the ovularies and receptacle of many flowers. *N,* Breadfruit, a multiple fruit. *O,* A multiple fruit type known as a syconium (fig) in which the flowers are borne within the involuted, fleshy receptacle. *O_1,* The single fruit, *O_2,* The pistillate flower, *O_3,* The staminate flower.

Many flowering plants form dry fruits, which may be either dehiscent or indehiscent. Dehiscent fruits split open naturally at maturity and release seeds in the process, while indehiscent fruits remain closed at maturity. Fruits of maple, elm, and ash are winged, indehiscent dry fruits adapted to wind dispersal; such fruits are called **samaras**. Another familiar example of a wind-dispersed fruit is that of the common dandelion. It has a tuft of hairs that serves as a tiny "parachute." Other indehiscent fruits are adapted to animal dispersal and have prickles, hooks, or barbs that attach to an animal's fur; for example, the cocklebur, beggar's tick, and Spanish needles. All of these have small hooks or tooth-like projections. Animals may harvest indehiscent, dry fruits, bury them, or otherwise store them and then neglect to eat them. For instance, acorns and other types of nuts may be gathered by squirrels and other small animals, buried, and abandoned. Later these may germinate into new plants. Finally, many indehiscent fruits are so lightweight that they are dispersed easily by air and water. The coconut has been widely distributed throughout the tropics because its fruit is lighter than water and can float in the ocean for great distances without damage to the embryo within.

The milkweed has a dehiscent fruit known as the **follicle**. When the follicle is mature and dry, it opens and releases hundreds of seeds, each of which has a silky tuft of hairs that catches the wind. Other examples of dehiscent fruits are the **legume** found in members of the pea family and the **silique** of the mustard family. Some plants have developed dehiscent, explosive fruits that suddenly burst as a result of pressure buildup in the ovary wall. When the fruit ruptures, seeds may be thrown for several feet from the parent plant. The touch-me-not is a familiar example of this kind of plant.

Still other fruits and seeds seem to have no special adaptation to the method of dispersal, but are accidentally picked up by wind, water, or animal agents. The fruits of many grasses and sedges are very small and are easily carried about on the feet of animals or blown by the wind. Such small and light seeds are easily transported, and several forms of dispersal may occur.

Once seeds have been scattered, other factors become important in plant reproduction. The availability of suitable soil, the temperature, the presence of moisture and light (or their absence), and the ability of the seed to compete successfully with other plants are factors of vital importance as regards the establishment of the new plant. The reproductive potential of most flowering plants is enormous (since most of them produce immense quantities of seeds) but only a few seeds grow to maturity.

Plants differ greatly in the manner in which they grow to maturity. Some do so rather rapidly, forming flowers and completing their life cycles in one year or less (**annuals**); others form flowers in the second year; these are called **biennials. Perennial** plants may form their flowers in the first year after seed germination, but live and reproduce for an indefinite number of years before they die.

Factors Affecting Flowering

Some plants produce flowers only in the spring and remain in the vegetative condition for the remainder of the year. Other plants bloom only in the late summer or fall and are vegetative in the spring. Botanists have long been interested in discovering the reasons why plants produce flowers only at certain times of the year, but it is only recently that some answers have been obtained. Research has shown that a precise interaction of environmental and physiological factors determines when flowers will be formed. One of the most significant factors is the relative length of the days and nights, a phenomenon called **photoperiodism**.

Research on photoperiodism has demonstrated that some plants are **short-day plants**; in such plants, flowers are initiated when daylight falls below a certain critical number of hours, usually less than 12 to 14 hours. Short-day plants include chrysanthemums, soybeans, ragweed, strawberries, and poinsettias. A second group of plants produces flowers only when the photoperiod equals or exceeds a minimum length of time, usually 12 to 14 hours. Such plants are termed **long-day plants**, and include spinach, henbain, plantain, and some cereals. Another group is composed of plants, called **intermediate-day plants**, that fail to flower when daylight is either too short or too long; and a fourth group of plants, apparently not affected by photoperiodicity, are called **day-neutral** plants. Some common day-neutral plants are tomatoes, cucumbers, cotton, and numerous weeds. This ability of flowering plants to synchronize their flowering with the seasons of the year is of immense ecological significance, for it enables plants to reproduce during periods when optimal conditions exist for the reproduction of the species.

It has long been suspected that hormones were involved in the formation of flowers, and a flower hormone called **florigen** was postulated that somehow was able to transform a vegetative bud into a flower bud. Research has shown that a substance is synthesized in the leaf and is translocated to the bud where flower induction takes place. Thus far, however, florigen has not been isolated, although other hormones that affect flowering have. One in particular, **gibberellin** (see Chapter 20), is known to promote flowering in some plants. Long-day plants can be brought to flowering, even under short-day regimens, by applications of gibberellin. However, gibberellins apparently have no effect on short-day plants, and even inhibit flowering in some species.

Another important factor affecting flowering is temperature. The influence of daily temperature changes on plant growth and development has been called **thermoperiodism.** The optimal temperatures during the day for growth of plants are different from those at night. Tomatoes develop fruits best when the daytime temperature is around 26° C. and the nighttime temperatures are between 17° C. and 20° C. Peppers flower best at high temperatures, while beets flower best at low temperatures. However, thermoperiodism, unlike photoperiodism, is not a flower-inducing process. Temperature affects the rate and vigor of vegetative growth and fruit formation, but has less effect on the initiation of flowers.

Figure 17-19 Effect of photoperiod on the flowering of poinsettia, a short-day plant. The plant with flowers was maintained on a short-day schedule (less than 11 hours of light per 24 hours); the other plant was grown under long day conditions (Photo by Jane K. Glaser).

The balance of available phosphorous and nitrogen also influences flowering. If the nitrogen in the soil is high, plants usually respond with vigorous vegetative growth but very few flowers. On the other hand, an overabundance of phosphorous in relation to nitrogen may cause flowering to occur before adequate vegetative growth has been accomplished.

Origin and Relationships of Flowering Plants

The origin of flowering plants has long been a source of controversy. In the nineteenth century Darwin referred to their evolution as "an abominable mystery," and so it remains today. Some botanists have maintained that flowering plants originated from **seed ferns,** while others have suggested origin from a fossil gymnosperm group called **cycadeoids**. The cycadeoids produced a cone that superficially resembled a flower; however, differences between the structure of the cones of cycadeoids and that of flowers, together with differences in the anatomy of the stems, have led scientists to conclude that the cycadeoids and flowering plants are neither closely related nor derived from a common ancestor.

The conifers also have been proposed as ancestors, since they have cones that superficially resemble apetalous or "naked" flowers found in some groups of flowering plants. The "Amentiferae," a group of flowering plants with naked flowers arranged in catkins (birches and willows), and the **gnetophytes**, a group of gymnosperms possessing vessels and flower-like strobili, were once considered to be the direct line of evolution from conifers to flowering plants. Later, detailed anatomical studies demonstrated that neither the Amentiferae nor the gnetophytes are likely ancestors of flowering plants, and these theories have since been abandoned.

Fossil remains that are unquestionably of flower parts are found in the lower Cretaceous Period of the Mesozoic Era, also known as the age of dinosaurs and gymnosperms; and even older pollen and wood, similar to modern species of flowering plants, have been reported from the Jurassic Period. By the end of the Cretaceous Period, flowering plants were highly diversified and many modern groups (including *Magnolia*, maple, sassafras, and oak) were present. Later, in the Tertiary Period of the Cenozoic Era, a second major burst of magnoliophyte evolution occurred and many of the dominant forms of plant life in the Mesozoic Era either disappeared altogether or were greatly reduced in numbers.

The search for the ancestors of flowering plants and for primitive flowering plants eventually led to the discovery of some interesting plants in the South Sea Islands, and these have given us considerable insight into the evolution of flowers.

The Primitive Flowering Plant

Dr. Albert Smith, formerly of the New York Botanical Gardens, spent part of the year 1934 collecting plants in the Fiji Islands. Among the many tropical species that he collected was one that he could not identify as a member of any known family of flowering plants; furthermore, no one was able to suggest where to place the new species in the known list of plant families. Later, the Harvard botanist and plant anatomist I. W. Bailey discovered that the unknown plant was identical to a specimen of a flowering tree collected in 1941 by a botanist named Otto Degener. Bailey classified it as a member of the order Ranales, a group of families including the *Magnolia* family (Magnoliaceae) and the buttercup family (Ranunculaceae). The plant itself was named *Degeneria* in honor of its collector, and Bailey also established a new family, the Degeneriaceae. *Degeneria* produces solitary flowers, each of which has a perianth in which the sepals and petals are very similar to each other and are spirally arranged on a short floral axis. The stamens are not differentiated into filament, anther, and connective, but may best be described as broad microsporophylls with four slender, elongated sporangia embedded in the lower surface of the sporophyll. Near the top of the floral axis are **staminodes**, or sterile microsporophylls. The pollen grains are smooth and ellipsoidal and have a single furrow (i.e., are of the monocolpate type). The carpel of *Degeneria* is single and indehiscent. During flowering, the carpel resembles an inwardly folded, three-veined sporophyll in which the veins, placentas, and the two rows of numerous ovules are at some distance from the edge of the megasporophyll. Significantly, the edge of the carpel is not infolded or united during developmental

447

stages, but rather tends to flare apart (i.e., it is leaf-like). During flowering, the epidermal layers of two adjacent surfaces of the megasporophyll are separated by many loose, interlocking, short glandular hairs. Therefore, the stigmatic surfaces of the carpel are not terminally localized as they are in typical flowering plants, but rather extend along the upper surfaces of the carpel close to the placenta. The carpel matures into an oblong, ellipsoidal, smooth, leathery fruit that bears numerous seeds in two rows.

Whatever may have been the origin of flowering plants, botanists today believe the earliest magnoliophytes looked something like *Degeneria*. Modern plants with flowers resembling those of *Degeneria* (with undifferentiated perianth, many simple stamens, and many simple pistils) are considered primitive species. Advanced or modified plants are those having definite perianth parts, or even vestigial perianth parts, few stamens, and compound pistils. At the present time, however, we have no clear idea as to what group was directly ancestral to these primitive flowering plants.

Why were the flowering plants so successful when they appeared in the Cretaceous Period? How did it happen that the magnoliophytes surpassed all other plants and have come to be the dominant form of plant life? To answer these questions, we must examine the special features of flowering plants that make them biologically unique, especially in comparison with their closest competitors, the gymnosperms.

The success of flowering plants is related closely to the degree of advancement seen in the flower. The development of carpels that protected the ovules probably gave flowering plants an evolutionary advantage over those seed plants, such as cycads and conifers, in which the ovules were borne in the open. Injury to ovules by insects and other animals may have been more likely to occur in gymnosperms than in the flowering plants.

The formation of flowers normally is quite rapid, and pollination takes place quickly. Pollen tube growth takes far less time in flowering plants, and reproduction is more efficient than in most gymnosperms (recall that in pines, two years are required for the production of mature seeds). In annuals, the whole life cycle is completed in one year, and in many species of flowering plants seeds are produced by individuals during the first few weeks of growth. By comparison with the length of time it takes a conifer to grow, become mature, produce cones and seeds, it becomes obvious that magnoliophytes have outreproduced the gymnosperms.

Another advantage that flowering plants have is a result of their anatomical characteristics. Flowering plants possess vessels in their xylem that make them more effective in water conduction, while most gymnosperms have xylem composed solely of tracheids. Although tracheids are effective water-conducting elements, they are not as efficient as vessels. Flowering plants also tend to have much broader leaves and so have a greatly increased capacity for photosynthesis in comparison to the needle-like or scale-like leaves of most gymnosperms. The greater efficiency of vessels in the xylem

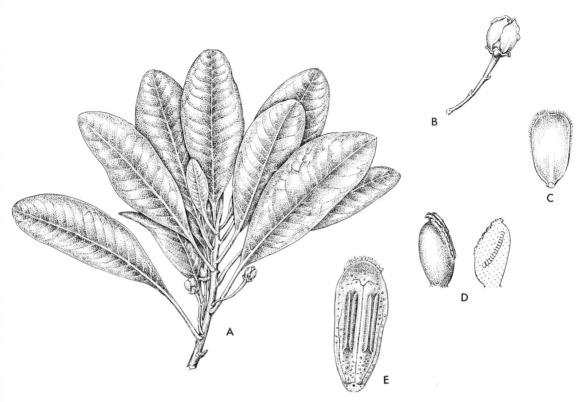

Figure 17–20 *Degeneria*, a primitive flowering plant. *A*, Branch with flowers. Note simple pinnate leaves. *B*, The flower. *C*, The petal. *D*, Pistil composed of one carpel. *E*, The stamen. Note its resemblance to a petal, and the location of the microsporangia (Redrawn from Bailey, I. W., and A. C. Smith. Degeneriaceae, A New Family of Flowering Plants from Fiji. *J. Arnold Arboretum 23*:356–365, 1942).

providing ample water to broad leaves results in increased photosynthesis and food production. Thus it seems that efficient and abundant food production is the basis for the efficient reproductive cycles occurring in magnoliophytes. Ample food manufacture makes it possible for seeds to be better supplied with food reserves, and more efficient in competition with gymnosperms.

The evolutionary success of magnoliophytes also rests on their adaptability to a wide range of environmental conditions. Leaves, stems, and flowers have become modified in many ways in accommodation to particular ecological requirements. For instance, leaves may be large or they may be reduced to mere scales; they may be photosynthetic organs or they may be modified into traps that catch small animals. Stems may be structures that support leaves, or they may be modified into photosynthetic structures, or even into thorns or tendrils. Flowers, as we have seen, are modified in many ways related to pollination mechanisms and fruit and seed dispersal.

SUMMARY

The division Magnoliophyta includes two large groups of flowering plants, the monocotyledons (or monocots), and the dicotyledons (or dicots). Together, the members of these two classes compose more families and species of plants than all the other divisions of the plant kingdom in their entirety.

Most of our important economic plants are flowering plants; among these are nearly all of our food plants and most of our drug, timber, fiber, and fuel plants. All of these plants share a common characteristic, namely the possession of flowers and fruits. We do not know how, where, or even when flowering plants originated, although there is fossil evidence that indicates their presence in the Mesozoic Era. Perhaps they evolved from seed ferns, but there are no known connecting links.

Primitive flowering plants have been discovered in recent years, and these have leaf-like and sporophyll-like flower parts. Thus, we can see a relationship to the pollen and seed-bearing structures of gymnosperms. In more advanced flowers, we often find adaptations to all sorts of ecological situations, such as complex flower-insect pollinator mechanisms and various kinds of seed dispersal structures and mechanisms. This ecological flexibility exhibited by flower plants may be a clue to their great success in competition with other plant groups.

About 275,000 species of flowering plants are presently known and new ones are being discovered nearly every day. The following classification is a very brief summary of this important division.

Division Magnoliophyta: The flowering plants. There are about 275,000 species making up 300 families. They are plants in which double fertilization and formation of endosperm occurs. Most species have closed carpels that form fruits from ripened ovularies.

CLASS MAGNOLIOPSIDA: The *Dicotyledonae* or *Dicots*. Two cotyledons (seed leaves) are present in the seed, the stem is dictyostelic with functioning cambium, leaves usually have special type of venation appearing net-veined, and floral parts occur usually in fours or fives or their multiples.

Examples: Magnolia, Nymphaea (the water lily), *Digitalis* (the foxglove), *Rauwolfia, Coffea, Thea,* cotton, oak, hickory, ash, maple, clover, dandelion, primrose, birch, legumes, milkworts.

CLASS LILIOPSIDA: The *Monocotyledonae* or *monocots*. One cotyledon (seed leaf) is present in the seed of these plants, the stem is polycyclic and there is no functional cambium; the leaves are parallel-veined; and floral parts are usually in threes or multiples of three.

Examples: Triticum (wheat), *Zea* (maize), *Oryza* (rice), *Saccharum* (sugar), orchids, sedges, jack-in-the-pulpit, palms.

DISCUSSION QUESTIONS

1. What are the main characteristics of the flowering plants that distinguish them from other divisions of the plant kingdom?
2. Prepare a list of economically important magnoliophytes. How many of them are monocots? How many are dicots?
3. Describe the parts of the flower from the standpoint of their function. If there are essential parts of the flower, what are their non-essential parts?
4. With what are the androecia and gynoecia homologous in the reproductive structures of pine? Of *Selaginella*? Of *Marsilea*?
5. In what ways may pollen be transferred to the stigma of a flower?
6. What are the functions of the nectaries? List several floral modifications that serve as "signals" to animal pollinators.
7. Discuss some floral modifications that apparently have evolved in response to the pollination system.
8. Explain what is meant by describing the pollen tube as the microgame-

tophyte and the embryo sac as the megagametophyte. Are flowering plants heterosporous? Explain.

9. Describe the events leading to the formation of the zygote and the 3*N* endosperm nucleus. What is "double fertilization"?

10. Outline the important breeding systems in Magnoliophytes, clearly differentiating between those that promote inbreeding and those that promote outbreeding.

11. Discuss some of the factors affecting the formation of flowers in the Magnoliophyta.

12. What is the function of the fruit? Give some examples of different kinds of seed dispersal methods that plants have evolved.

13. What is presently considered to be an example of a primitive flowering plant? What are the floral characteristics of the plant?

14. How do you explain the success of the Magnoliophytes over the other seed plants?

SUPPLEMENTAL READING

Benson, L. *Plant Classification.* Boston: Heath, 1957.

Cronquist, A. *Evolution and Classification of Flowering Plants.* Boston: Houghton Mifflin, 1968.

Dodge, P. *Plants that Changed the World.* Boston: Little, Brown & Co., 1959.

Good, R. *The Geography of the Flowering Plants,* 3rd ed. London: Longmans, Green and Co., 1964.

Grant, V. The Flower Constancy of Bees. *Botanical Review, 16*:379–398, 1950.

Jensen, William A. Fertilization in Flowering Plants. *Bioscience, 23*:21–27, 1973.

Just, T. Gymnosperms and the Origin of Angiosperms. *Botanical Gazette, 110*:91–103, 1948.

Mason, H. L. The Concept of the Flower and the Theory of Homology. *Madroño, 14*:81–95, 1957.

Van der Pijl. *Principles of Dispersal in Higher Plants.* New York: Springer-Verlag, 1969.

USEFUL FIELD GUIDES TO FLOWERING PLANTS

Britton, N. L., and A. Brown. 1913. *An Illustrated Flora of the Northern United States and Canada.* New York: Dover Publications, Inc., 1970 (reprint in paperback, three volumes; original edition, 1913).

Fernald, M. L. Gray's Manual of Botany, Eighth Edition, New York, American Book Co., 1950.

Hylander, C. J., and E. F. Johnston. *The Macmillan Wild Flower Book.* New York: Macmillan, 1954.

Long, R. W., and O. Lakela. *A Flora of Tropical Florida.* Miami, Florida: University of Miami Press, 1971.

Munz, P. A., and D. D. Keck. *A California Flora.* Berkeley, California: University of California Press, 1973.

Peterson, R. T., and M. McKenny. *A Field Guide to Wildflowers of Northeastern and North Central America.* Boston: Houghton-Mifflin Co., 1968.

Weber, W. A. *Rocky Mountain Flora.* Boulder, Colorado: Colorado Associated University Press, 1972.

Adansonia digitata, the baobab tree (Photo courtesy of W. H. Hodge).

Chapter 18

Structure and Function in Flowering Plants

THE EMBRYO • SEED GERMINATION • THE STEM • SHOOT DEVELOPMENT • STEM TISSUES AND THE PRIMARY BODY • STEM CELLS AND THEIR FUNCTIONS • TRANSLOCATION • CONDUCTION • TRANSPIRATION • SECONDARY GROWTH IN STEMS • CRIMINALS, FOSSILS, AND STEM ANATOMY • WOODY MONOCOTYLEDONS • STEM MODIFICATIONS • THE LEAF • LEAF FORM • LEAF ARRANGEMENT • LEAF DEVELOPMENT • LEAF ANATOMY AND FUNCTION • AUTUMN COLOR • THE ROOT • ROOT DEVELOPMENT • ROOT TISSUES • ROOT FUNCTIONS • PLANT PROPAGATION FROM STEMS, LEAVES, AND ROOTS • PLANT MOVEMENTS • SUMMARY

The growth of a flowering plant is an interesting but often misunderstood phenomenon. A seedling does not simply expand into an adult plant; rather, it grows by addition of new structures. If, then, we wish to find the cells and tissues of the young plant, we must look deep within the adult, for these tissues are embedded under layer upon layer of more recently formed cells and tissues. Growth by addition of layers is a characteristic found invariably in flowering plants. Even those of short life span, such as the common garden annuals, demonstrate this mode of growth; new tissues are formed and added to the old and, as has been pointed out in Chapter 2, this is one of the principal differences between the development of plants and animals.

On the other hand, even though the growth processes of flowering plants are continuous throughout the life of the plant, the overall pattern of growth is established in the embryo. In this respect plants and animals are alike, and for this reason the organization of the young plant must be studied to understand the organization of the mature plant, just as animal embryos are studied to learn the derivation of the tissues of the adult. However, we must recognize that there are some important differences in form among various plants, both in the organization of embryos and seedlings and in the mature plant. For example, there are short-lived soft green plants as well as long-lived woody plants; there are monocotyledons with unique embryos

---

The best and greatest of all trees is Yggdrasil,
its branches spread o'er all the world,
and reach up above heaven.
Three roots sustain the tree.
One root is in Hel,
under the second root is the well of Mimir
in which knowledge and wisdom are concealed,
the third root is in heaven.

SCANDINAVIAN MYTHOLOGY

and other characteristics, and dicotyledons with their own characteristic structures; finally, there are many modifications and adaptations in the roots, stems, and leaves of plants in both groups.

The Embryo

When we look at a large, mature plant, such as an oak or a palm, it is difficult to understand how only a single cell—the zygote—could have produced such a complex organism. However, analysis of the development of plant forms shows that plant growth is progressive and stepwise, and therefore comprehensible.

In many plants, the first division of the zygote is transverse, and establishes the polarity of the future plant; that is to say, the embryo develops a top and a bottom, or an axis. In other plants, the first cell divisions of the embryo appear to be random, but shortly thereafter the embryo becomes elongate and an axis becomes apparent. More importantly, the meristems of the shoot and root tips are formed. Once this has occurred, the later transformation of the embryo into the mature plant is largely a matter of the continued cell division in the terminal meristems and the differentiation in cells produced.

The full-term plant embryo consists of a short axis with either one or two cotyledons; the species are referred to as **monocotyledons** or **dicotyledons**, respectively. The part of the embryo above the cotyledons is the **epicotyl** and that below the cotyledons is the **hypocotyl**. The hypocotyl ends in a meristematic region that differentiates into the embryonic root or **radicle**. During germination, the hypocotyl often elongates very rapidly, lifting the epicotyl and cotyledons above the soil; the bean seedling is a good example. In other cases (as in peas), the epicotyl elongates and the cotyledons remain buried in the soil. Anatomically, the hypocotyl is considered to be the first stem unit of the plant.

The cotyledons in dicots serve as food storage structures and

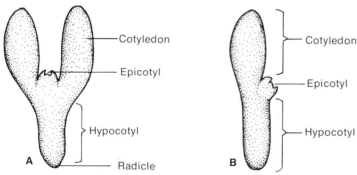

Figure 18–1 Highly diagrammatic view of basic embryo types. *A,* Embryo of a dicotyledon (Magnoliopsida). *B,* Embryo of a monocotyledon (Liliopsida). In the dicot embryo, the cotyledons usually function as food storage organs, and sometimes as photosynthetic organs. In the monocot embryo the cotyledon is non-photosynthetic and absorptive, and the radicle is late in developing (grass embryos are more complex; see Figure 18–2).

provide energy necessary to maintain the germinating plant, and in some instances they also carry on photosynthesis. Generally they are shed soon after the seedling becomes established. In monocots, the single cotyledon serves as an absorbing and conducting structure, and transfers the stored food in the endosperm to the young seedling.

Functionally, the role of the embryo is twofold: (a) it reestablishes the organization of the plant following sexual reproduction and genetic recombination; and (b) as noted in Chapter 17, the

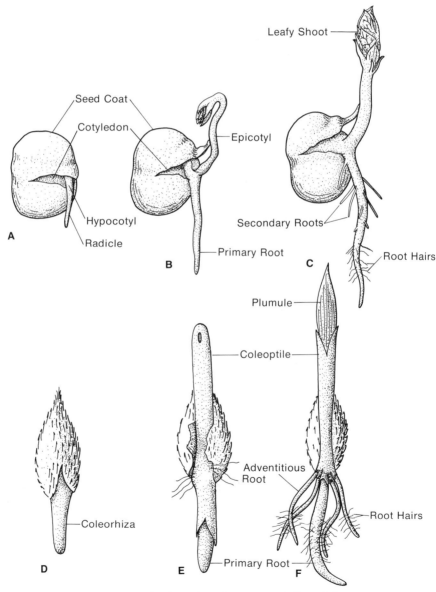

Figure 18–2 Seeds and seedlings. *A,* Longitudinal section of a pea seed. *B* and *C,* Successive stages in the germination of the garden pea. *D,* Longitudinal section of an oat grain. *E* and *F,* Successive stages in the germination of an oat grain.

455

embryo is part of a dispersal device, the seed. In this latter role the strategy of **embryo dormancy** often is displayed; the embryo may remain inactive for a considerable length of time before it germinates.

Seed Germination

The germination of seeds depends on such environmental factors as presence of oxygen, moisture, and light, as well as proper temperature. Required also is a supply of energy, which is furnished by food stored in the cotyledons or in the endosperm, if present. Light for photosynthesis is necessary after the seedling becomes established, although during the early stages of germination light may actually inhibit seedling growth.

Seeds absorb quantities of water, become hydrated, and swell. The seed coat splits open as a result of this swelling, and the embryo begins to grow into a seedling. The radicle emerges and grows downward into the soil, and a root system becomes established. Enzyme activity is greatly increased, and food stored in the endosperm or in the cotyledons is digested and transported to the rapidly growing tips of the embryonic axis.

How does the complex arrangement of tissues and organs in the mature plant come about? The architecture of the mature plant evolves progressively as a consequence of the development of shoot and root apices initially formed in the embryo. Longitudinal sections of such root and shoot tips show the presence of active **apical meristems** in which repeated cell divisions occur. The new cells formed continue to divide for a time and also become enlarged to form a region of cell elongation. Just behind this area is a region in which cells become specialized and mature, thus giving rise to the various tissue types present in stems and roots. These regions of cell division, elongation, and specialization are not precisely delimited but instead overlap, so that both cell division and cellular specialization are found in the elongation zone.

THE STEM

Shoot Development

As already noted, stems grow and develop from the top down so that a cell formed by division in the apical meristem occupies a progressively more basal position as the cells of the shoot apex divide and add new cells to the summit of the plant. It is therefore possible to follow the fate of cells from their origin in the apical meristem, through zones of elongation and maturation, to their final destiny as fully mature and often highly specialized members of one or another of the plant's tissue systems.

In the growing shoot are present three basic tissue types: the

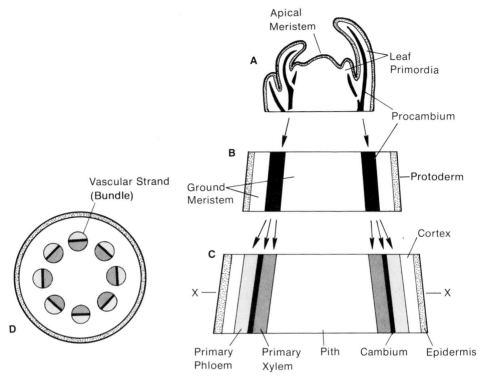

Figure 18–3 Highly diagrammatic representation of the organization of the young shoot of a dicotyledon. *A*, The apical region, composed of meristematic cells. *B*, Region of continuing cell division, cell elongation, and differentiation of basic tissue types. *C*, Region of cell specialization and maturation. *D*, Cross section of *C* at X–X. Note that the vascular strands (or bundles) form a ring.

protoderm, the **ground meristem**, and strands of **procambium.** These, in turn, give rise to other tissues; the protoderm forms the epidermis, the ground meristem forms the parenchyma of the pith and cortex, and the cells of the procambium differentiate into the xylem and phloem and, in dicots, into the cambium of the vascular strands (**vascular bundles**) as well. In dicotyledons these vascular bundles are arranged in a circle, but in monocotyledons they are rather evenly distributed throughout the stem or, in some cases, in several rings. For this reason, the stem structure of monocots and dicots appears quite different, although the basic tissue types are much alike.

Examination of a shoot apex from which surrounding appendages (such as young leaves and bud scales) have been removed reveals a dome-like mound of non-specialized cells—the apical meristem—surrounded by regularly spaced smaller mounds, the **leaf primordia**. The spacing of the leaf primordia, which has a characteristic pattern in each species of plant, determines the ultimate leaf arrangement, or **phyllotaxy**, of the mature stem.

Stems of young, developing plants also can be described as consisting of a linear series of **nodes** and **internodes**. Nodes are

457

specific points along the stem where leaves and buds are attached, while the portion of the stem between adjacent nodes is called the internode. Growth in length and stem curvatures are dependent on cell elongation and cell multiplication in internodes.

Terminal and lateral (or **axillary**) buds are present in the young stem. Buds are exceptionally good examples of nature's skill in packaging. If a bud is examined microscopically, it will be seen to contain an apical meristem below which are several nodes; each node will, in turn, bear both a miniature leaf and a partly formed axillary bud. Some buds, called **mixed buds**, also bear immature flowers as well as leaves, while others have only flowers. Plants that remain soft and green during their life (**herbaceous plants**) have dynamic buds that are always growing and producing new leaf, bud, and stem growth. Woody plants, especially those of temperate regions, usually have protected buds that remain quiescent or **dormant** during part of the year. Such buds often have an outer layer of scale leaves (or **bud scales**, as they are called). When a bud elongates and forms a leafy stem or branch in the springtime, the bud scales are shed, leaving **bud scale scars** at the base of the newly formed stem. Where several years' growth has occurred in a stem, the portion of a stem between adjacent bud scale scars represents one year's growth.

Stem Tissues; the Primary Body

The shoot that develops from the epicotyl at first contains only **primary tissues**. These primary tissues are the **epidermis, cortex, primary xylem, primary phloem, pith,** and **pith rays (medullary rays),** and together they are referred to as the **primary body.**

Externally, a young stem is relatively soft and usually green, and carries on some of the same functions as leaves. Stomata are present in the epidermis, and chloroplasts, although absent in all epidermal cells except the guard cells of stomata, are found in the cells just beneath the epidermis. The epidermis functions chiefly to prevent evaporation of water from the soft, watery tissues within, and to protect the more delicate cells immediately beneath itself. Generally, the epidermis is a single layer of cells covered with a waterproof cuticle composed of a fatty substance, **cutin**; in addition, a coating of wax may be secreted in varying amounts. The carnauba wax palm of South America produces harvestable amounts of carnauba wax, used in manufacture of such high grade waxes as automobile waxes and polishes.

Stem Cells and Their Functions

Beneath the epidermis of a dicot stem are several layers of cells that make up the **cortex**. The outermost layers of the cortex often are composed of **collenchyma cells** and there also may be groups of **sclerenchyma cells** scattered throughout this region. Collenchyma

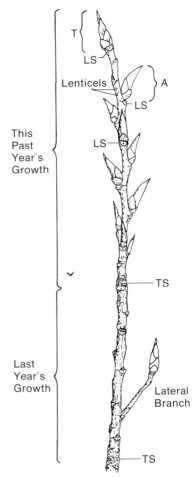

Figure 18–4 External form of a young cottonwood stem. T, terminal bud; TS, bud scale scars of previous year's terminal bud; A, axillary bud; LS, leaf scar showing point of attachment of last year's leaf.

cells are thick-walled, elongated living cells; sclerenchyma cells are thick-walled, lignified, usually dead cells, sometimes varying considerably in shape. In young stems, many of the outer cortical cells are photosynthetic, but the primary function of the cortex is storage of food and water.

Within the cortex is the **stele**, a region composed of vascular bundles, rays, pith, and sometimes a **pericycle**. The latter, if present, is the outermost region of the phloem, and may be the site of fiber formation. The outermost part of each vascular bundle is made up of a complex tissue, the **primary phloem**. Four principal cell types are found here (**sieve tube elements, companion cells, phloem fibers,** and **parenchyma**), but only the sieve tube elements carry on the principal function of the phloem, which is food conduction. Sieve tube elements lack nuclei and form continuous columns of

459

cells, the **sieve tubes,** in which the cytoplasm is continuous and extends through perforations called **sieve plate pores**. Accompanying each sieve element is a smaller, nucleated companion cell, which is believed to have a correlative function in connection with the conduction of food in the sieve tubes. It has been noted in earlier chapters that the phloem of non-flowering vascular plants is composed of sieve cells, and companion cells are not present.

The phloem parenchyma cells are associated with later formation of cork in perennial stems, while the fibers strengthen the conductive tissue and provide mechanical support. In some plants, such as hemp and flax, the phloem fibers are made into rope and linen, respectively, for commercial use.

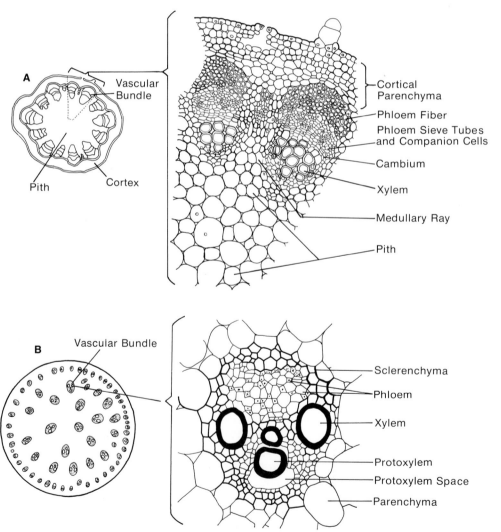

Figure 18–5 Diagrammatic cross sections of herbaceous stems. *A*, Stem of clover, a dicot, termed a **eustele,** or interpreted as a form of dictyostele. *B*, Stem of maize (corn), a monocot., termed an **atactostele** or interpreted as a polycyclic dictyostele.

Translocation

The movement of foods through the phloem sieve tubes is known as **translocation**. The actual mechanism of translocation is poorly understood, even though much study and experimentation have been done. Translocation rates can be measured by calculating the amount of food moving through the peduncle into a growing fruit, such as a squash or pumpkin. It has been found that conduction of food through the phloem is rapid; quantities as great as 1.7 grams per hour and flow rates as high as 155 centimeters per hour have been reported.

Several theories have been postulated to account for the high rates of translocation occurring in plants. Perhaps the most favored of these is called the **mass flow theory,** which, in brief, states that sugars and other solutes in the phloem move as a result of a diffusion pressure gradient resulting from differences in solute concentrations between the top and the bottom of the stem, with solutes being added at the top of the phloem column by photosynthesis and withdrawn at the bottom by stem and root cells. However, the flow of solutes in phloem also requires that phloem cells be living, and will not occur if the cells are killed. It appears, then, that metabolic as well as physical processes are involved in translocation.

Conduction

The **primary xylem** is the other complex tissue in the vascular bundle. Two kinds of water-conducting cells are present: **tracheids,** which are long, tapered cells with lateral pits, and **vessel elements.** The latter are usually of greater diameter than tracheids, and are typically cylindrical cells in which the end walls have virtually disappeared at maturity. Vessel elements lie end to end to form continuous tubes, known as the **vessels**. Tracheids and vessel elements die at maturity and function only as conductive cells after the protoplasm has disappeared from the cell. Their main function is the conduction of water and dissolved substances, mainly minerals.

Transpiration

The movement of water and solutes in the xylem has been the subject of much research. Generally the path taken by water is upward from the roots, through the stems, and then into the leaves. In the leaves, some of the water is used in photosynthesis, but much more moves out through the stomata in the form of water vapor. In this process, **transpiration,** the departing water molecules are believed to exert traction on the columns or strands of water in the xylem elements of the stem and roots. This traction is called **transpiration pull,** and can be demonstrated experimentally by cutting a stem of a small plant at its base and connecting it to a glass tube containing water. Then, if a current of warm air is blown gently over the leaf surfaces, water will be observed to flow through the glass tube into the stem. However, transpiration pull by itself does

461

not seem to account completely for water movement. Under some circumstances, the roots seem to exert a positive pressure (**root pressure**) capable of moving water and solutes up into stems, and also the cells of the root and stem may act like lamp wicks or blotting paper (via **capillarity**), and transport water considerable distances.

Vessel elements are more efficient than tracheids in conduction because of their larger size and absence of end walls. Tracheids are found in all groups of vascular plants, but with few exceptions vessels are found only in the flowering plants. In addition to vessels and

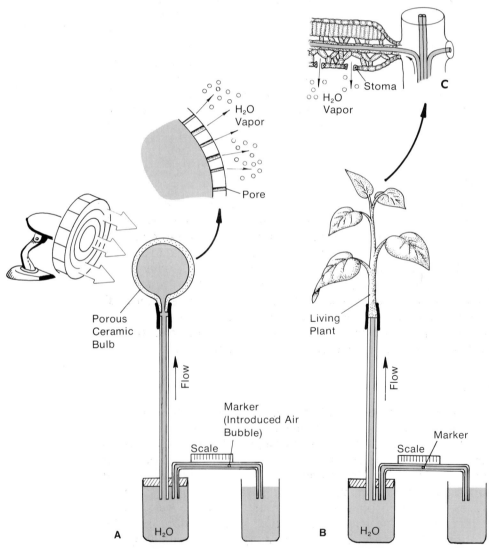

Figure 18–6 An experiment demonstrating transpiration. *A,* An atmometer. Water evaporating from the surface of the porous ceramic bulb exerts tension on the column of water in the capillary tube. *B,* A transpirometer, in which a living plant substitutes for the porous bulb of the atmometer. *C,* Diagram showing water movement in a plant leaf.

tracheids, the xylem tissue also contains living parenchyma cells and fibers. The latter are dead cells with thick, lignified walls; they are mechanically supportive in function, adding strength to the vascular bundles and to the stem (as do phloem fibers when present).

The pith and rays of stems are composed of parenchyma cells. These cells are rather unspecialized and often highly vacuolated. The function of the pith is chiefly storage of food, while ray cells function in the lateral transport of food, water, and solutes.

Secondary Growth in Stems

Secondary growth consists of the lateral addition of new layers of xylem and phloem, and results in an increase in plant girth. Such growth generally is restricted to dicotyledons, and is rarely encountered in monocotyledons. In the typical dicot, as in gymnosperms, a cambium is present. Originally it forms between the xylem and phloem in each vascular bundle, and later it develops also in the parenchyma between the bundles so that a complete cylinder of cambial tissue is produced. Most of the cell divisions are parallel to the stem surface, so that the thickness of the stem is increased, but a few also occur at right angles to the usual planes of division, which adds to the circumference of the cambium and keeps pace with the increasing diameter of the stem.

As cambial cells divide, they alternately produce xylem cells toward the interior of the stem and phloem cells outwardly. About 25 to 30 per cent of all cambial derivates are phloem cells, as compared with about 70 to 75 per cent that are secondary xylem cells. These cells are called **secondary tissues** because they are formed after the general architecture of the stem has been formed by the primary tissues, and because the cambium that produces the secondary tissues is itself a primary tissue type.

The presence of an active cambium is responsible for the transformation of a green herbaceous seedling into a woody shrub or tree. Eventually the secondary tissue produced by the cambium replaces the primary tissues, and in older woody plants the epidermis, cortex, and phloem are crushed or obliterated through the growth of secondary tissue. The principal secondary tissues are the **secondary xylem, secondary phloem,** and the **xylem** and **phloem rays**. The cells of these tissues are similar to those of the primary body, both in structure and function.

As stems become older a new secondary tissue system, the **periderm,** arises in the outer cortex just beneath the epidermis. Periderm is a complex tissue composed of outer, suberized cells (the **cork cells**), and dividing cells (the **cork cambium**). Typically, the outer surface of the stem becomes rougher and loses its green color as the periderm continues to develop. **Lenticels** (small raised areas either circular or ellipsoidal in outline) form openings in the periderm. Underneath the lenticels is a loosely arranged tissue with many intercellular air spaces. This tissue, together with the lenticels,

463

functions in gas exchange, replacing the function of the stomata, which are lost with the epidermis.

In woody perennial plants, the continuing activity of the cambium produces more and more xylem. This causes the outward displacement of the phloem and cortex. As a result, these tissues tend to become crushed and broken. As this occurs, new layers of periderm are formed in the cortex and older phloem so that the stem eventually becomes enclosed by thick layers of cork. The phloem, the remaining cortical cells, and the periderm constitute the **bark**.

Upon examination of an older stem in cross section, the older xylem toward the center can often be seen to be darker in color than the outer, younger xylem, because xylem cells become infiltrated with various substances such as tannins, resins, gums, oils, and certain kinds of pigments as they age. These alterations result in loss of function by tracheids and vessels and the death of xylem parenchyma. This inner xylem region is called the **heartwood**.

In certain tree species the heartwood may decay, resulting in the familiar hollow tree; in other species, the heartwood is very hard and resistant to destruction. Xylem surrounding the heartwood is generally lighter in color and consists of functioning conducting cells. This part of the stem is referred to as the **sapwood**. The inner layers of sapwood are constantly being changed into heartwood so the heartwood area is progressively expanding in size. In very old trees, the cylinder of heartwood may be a meter or more in diameter, while the sapwood is only a few centimeters wide.

As in the conifers (see Chapter 16), the most conspicuous features of transverse sections of woody stems of flowering plants are the **annual rings** composed of **spring wood** and **summer wood**. These concentric bands of secondary xylem are usually formed each

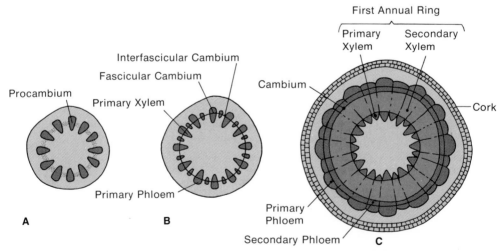

Figure 18–7 Development of the secondary body in stems. *A,* Young stem composed of primary tissues. *B,* Development of the interfascicular cambium. *C,* Older stem with secondary tissues (Redrawn from Wilson, C. E., Loomis, W. E., and Steeves, T. A. *Botany*, Fifth Edition, New York, Holt, Rinehart and Winston, Inc., 1971).

Figure 18–8 Heartwood and sapwood. The dark, interior region is heartwood, the lighter-colored outer zone of wood is sapwood. Note within both zones the presence of annual rings composed of darker-colored summerwood and lighter-colored spring-wood.

year in temperate tree species. In the tropics, similar rings often correspond to seasonal changes in rainfall or to annual cycles of growth and flowering. Secondary phloem does not occur in annual rings because the cells typically function for one season and then are crushed or obliterated by expansion from within by the next year's growth of xylem. Eventually much of the older phloem is incorporated into the cork and, if the tree lives long enough, finally becomes sloughed off as the inner tissues continue to expand.

The structure of wood (xylem) may better be understood by viewing a stem that has been cut at different angles. A cut across a stem produces a **transverse section,** or **cross section**. In this kind of section the xylem rays radiate from the pith like the spokes of a wheel. Longitudinal sections are made either at right angles to the xylem rays (**tangential section**) or parallel to the rays (**radial section**). In a tangential section the rays are observed in end view and appear elliptical in shape. In a radial section, the rays appear in side view. In both kinds of longitudinal sections the vessels and tracheids are seen in lateral view, and the pitting of their walls is visible. Longitudinal cuts of wood often produce boards showing beautiful configurations caused by the patterns of the annual rings and rays in such sections. We speak of these patterns as the "grain" of the wood.

Criminals, Fossils, and Stem Anatomy. A knowledge of stem anatomy has been used in some unusual ways. In 1932, the infant son of Charles A. Lindbergh, the man who made the first solo flight across the Atlantic Ocean, was kidnapped and killed. The most damaging piece of evidence that led to the conviction of the man accused of the crime, Bruno Hauptmann, was the ladder used in the kidnapping. A botanist from the United States Department of Agri-

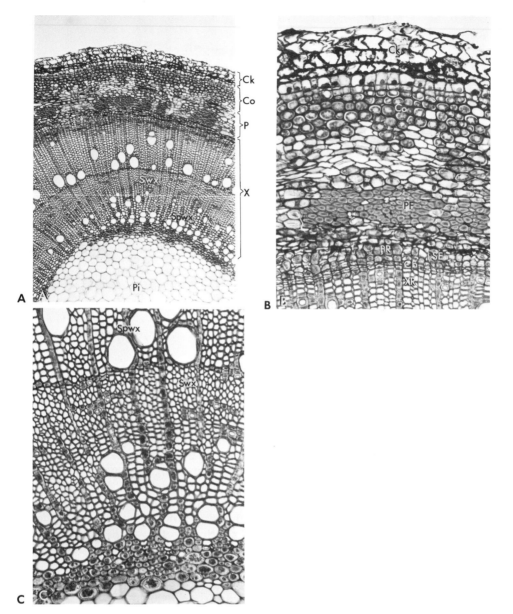

Figure 18–9 Cross section of the stem of ash (*Fraxinus*), a woody dicot. *A*, Cross sectional view, illustrating the general structure and zonation of the stem. *B*, Enlarged view of the outer part of *A*, including the cork, phloem, and cambium. *C*, Enlarged view of the inner part of *A*, showing the structure of the xylem. Cb, Cambium; Ck, cork; Co, cortex; Ph, phloem; Pi, pith; PF, phloem fibers; PR, phloem ray; SE, sieve elements and companion cells; SX, summer wood (xylem); SpX, spring wood (xylem); X, xylem; XR, xylem ray.

culture showed by microscopic examination that the ladder was homemade of birch, Douglas fir, and two kinds of pine, and had never been used before the crime. One rail on the ladder was found to match a floorboard from Hauptmann's attic, and it was proved that the rail and board were originally from the same piece of wood.

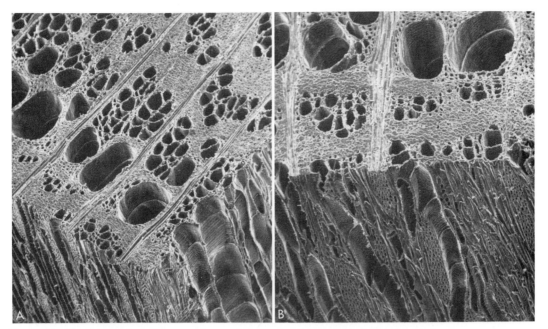

Figure 18–10 A scanning electron microscopic study of the wood of the elm. Note especially the structure of the vessels. *A,* × 95. *B,* × 150 (Photos courtesy of Institute of Paper Chemistry).

The comparative structure of annual rings in trees has been used to date extinct cultures. This is done by matching ring patterns found in logs of abandoned villages with a master tree ring sequence from very old but recently cut trees. Specific cases of dating by **dendro-archeology** or **dendrochronology** are the Cliff Dwellers' ruins, Mummy Cave and Pueblo sites in the Southwestern United States. Hundreds of areas have been dated by this method. Similarly, climates of past ages have been determined by studying the relative width of annual rings after having learned the approximate age of the tree by counting the number of rings (**dendroclimatology**). The rings are widest in years where favorable climate for growth occurred and narrowest in the poor years. By comparing tree ring patterns from trees sampled over large areas, it is possible to gain information about past climates. Dendroclimatology has become an important tool in the study of past climatic conditions.

Woody Monocotyledons

The stems of monocotyledons may be quite soft and succulent (as in lilies, cattails, and young asparagus) or they may be hard and tough (as in bamboo and palms). In the latter especially, numerous strengthening fibers (sclerenchyma) are present in a zone beneath the epidermis and surrounding the vascular bundles. There is no cambium or secondary body in herbaceous monocots and most woody monocots, and typically there is no prolonged growth in girth. In large monocots (such as palms), the increase in stem diameter occurs by division of cells in a region called the **primary**

467

Figure 18–11 Some woody monocotyledons having tree forms. *A*, The pony-tail palm, *Beaucarnea*, a member of the lily family. *B*, The Australian grass-tree, *Xanthorroea*, also related to lilies. *C*, A pandanus or screw pine tree, *Pandanus*.

thickening meristem, located just below the shoot apex. However, a few woody monocots have a cambium-like meristem that produces secondary growth.

Stem Modifications

The remarkable variation in form of flowering plants is partly due to differences and modifications in stem structure. Some of these modifications may result in stems, or portions of stems, that resemble other structures; for example, some plants have flattened, photosynthetic stems resembling leaves and only after careful examination of their development and anatomy is it possible to understand their true nature.

Many stem modifications enable plants to reproduce asexually. **Stolons** (or runners) are long, slender stems that grow from the parent plant horizontally over the surface. When a node touches the ground, a shoot and roots may develop at the point of contact. This shoot, in turn, may send out additional stolons so that eventually a network of plants becomes established. A familiar example of a plant having this form of reproduction is the strawberry.

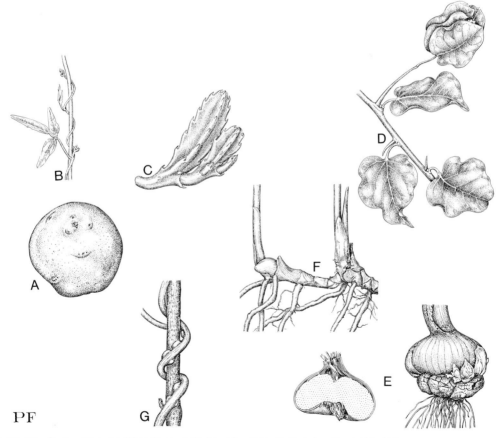

PF

Figure 18–12 Some stem modifications. *A*, Tuber of potato. *B*, Twining stem of a vine, genus *Vignia*. *C*, A leaf-like stem or cladode of *Stapelia*. *D*, Axillary buds of *Bougainvillaea* which may form either a thorn or a branch. *E*, A flattened underground stem or corm of *Gladiolus* with longitudinal section at left. *F*, Rhizome of edible ginger. *G*, Twining stem of *Cassythea* with parasitic suckers.

469

Another common modification is the underground, horizontal stem, or **rhizome**. Although rhizomes are sometimes mistaken for roots, they have nodes, internodes, and reduced, scale-like leaves. Many perennial herbs have rhizomes that enable them to survive the winter; these species send up new aerial stems and leaves when spring returns. Many grasses grow in this way.

A short, fleshy, terminal enlargement of a rhizome, called a **tuber**, is a familiar stem modification. The tuber of a white potato is a short, thick stem with nodes, and internodes. The "eyes" are in fact composed of vestigial leaves and axillary buds. If a potato is cut up, each piece with an eye can reproduce a new plant by the development of the bud.

Many plants produce **bulbs** and **corms.** Bulbs are very short stems surrounded by many overlapping, fleshy leaves. The terminal bud develops into the new shoot, while the leaves, rich in stored food, provide the shoot with necessary growth requirements. The onion is a familiar example of a bulb. Corms are sometimes bulb-like in general appearance but are actually short squat stems, often spherical in outline, with only thin, scaly leaves present. The gladiolus is an example of a plant that produces corms.

Other stem modifications include the **thorn,** a sharp, pointed structure produced by a lateral bud, and the **tendril,** which serves to anchor vines and clambering plants. An example of a very familiar plant having tendrils is the grape vine; many other vine-like plants also possess tendrils. It is well to note that some kinds of tendrils are derived not from the stems, but from leaf parts.

THE LEAF

In no other group of plants is there such a variety of leaf forms as there is among the flowering plants. Leaves vary in size from less than a centimeter (in chickweeds) to nearly 20 meters in some of the large palms, and there also are many bizarre types. The floating leaf of the giant Victoria water lily is large enough to support the weight of a small child. The leaves of the insectivorous plants, such as the Venus' fly trap and the pitcher plants, are highly specialized and function as insect traps. Other leaf modifications include the spines of the black locust and barberry and the tendrils of pea plants. Such specialized structures may occupy a portion of a leaf, or may even replace the entire leaf.

In Chapter 17 we noted that the two classes of flowering plants are distinguished on the basis of leaf structure, among other characteristics. Monocotyledons (Liliopsida) typically have simple leaves with **parallel venation**, and dicotyledons (Magnoliopsida) exhibit a branching venation, termed **net** or **reticulate venation**. Dicotyledons may have either simple or compound leaves. In general these are useful distinctions, although there are a few monocots with branching venation and compound leaves.

Figure 18–13 Leaves of flowering plants. *A,* The leaves of the American oil palm (*Scheelia*) are among the largest found in flowering plants, measuring nearly 20 m. long. *B,* The large, floating leaves of the Victoria water lily (*Victoria*) are able to support the weight of a small child. *C,* The trumpet-like leaves of *Nepenthes*, the pitcher plant, capture insects (*C* courtesy of W. H. Hodge).

471

Leaf Form

Although the leaf of the maize plant (a monocot) is markedly different from that of an oak tree (a dicot), and even more divergent types could be cited, many of these differences can be accounted for by analyzing the way in which leaves develop. Leaves exhibit a basic developmental pattern regardless of their final growth-form.

A typical leaf consists of a blade (or **lamina**) with a median vein (or **midrib**) and a stalk (or **petiole**). Sometimes there is a small pair of appendages (called **stipules**) located at the petiole base, and leaves normally are associated with axillary buds located on the stem immediately above the base of the petiole.

Leaves of flowering plants are either **simple,** i.e., they consist of a petiole and one blade, or **compound,** i.e., they have several to many leaflets (or pinnae) attached to the petiole in a variety of ways. Simple leaves may differ in the patterns of their venation; they may be **pinnate** (with a midrib and lateral branch veins), or **palmate** (i.e., having several diverging major veins). Other differences may be

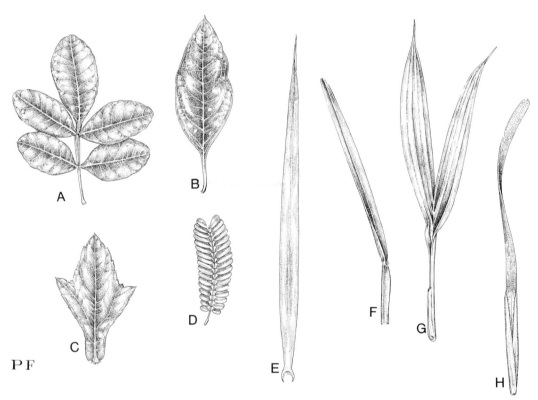

PF

Figure 18–14 *A–D,* Leaves of some dicots. *E–H,* Leaves of some monocots. *A,* Pinnately compound leaf of *Schinus terebinthifolius,* the Brazilian pepper, a species of Anacardiaceae. *B,* Simple pinnate leaf of *Citharexylum fruticosum,* a species of Verbenaceae. *C,* The simple, palmately veined leaf of *Wedelia trilobata,* of the Compositae. *D,* The pinnately compound leaf of *Abrus precatorius,* known as the rosary pea, a species of Leguminosae. *E,* Leaf of a woody monocot, *Dracaena emarginata,* of the Agavaceae. *F,* Leaf of the centipede grass, *Eremochloa ophiuroides. G,* Leaf of a species of *Sphaeradenia,* a genus of Cyclanthaceae. *H,* Leaf of an aquatic monocot, *Thalassia testudinum.*

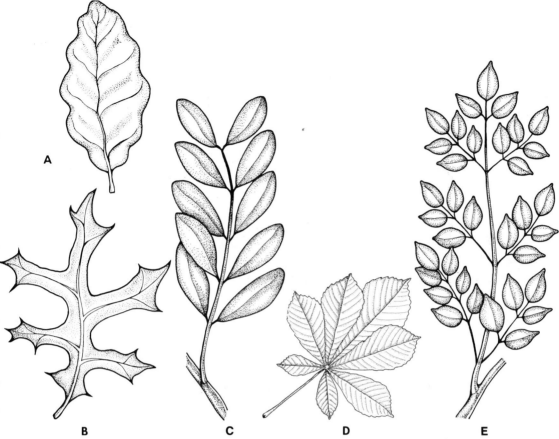

Figure 18–15 Variations in leaf form. *A,* Typical simple leaf, pinnate venation. *B,* A pinnately lobed leaf. *C,* A pinnately compound leaf. *D,* A palmately compound leaf. *E,* A doubly compound or bipinnate leaf.

observed, such as in the leaf margins, which may be smooth, toothed, or scalloped; and in leaf surfaces, which may show many types of surface features including hairs, scales, and glands.

The compound leaf-form is seen in many flowering plants, and ranges from the **pinnately compound** type, as exemplified by the ash tree and the walnut, to **palmately compound** types, as found on the horse chestnut tree and the Virginia creeper vine. Compound leaves are sometimes confused with leafy branches but are readily distinguished if it is remembered that leaves have axillary buds at their bases but leaflets do not.

Leaf Arrangement

Examination of stem-leaf relationships quickly reveals that the placement of leaves on stems is regular rather than random, and is capable of mathematical formulation. There are three basic patterns of leaf arrangement, or **phyllotaxy**: one in which an opposed pair of leaves is present at each stem node; a second in which three or more leaves occur per node; and a third, in which only one leaf is

473

found at each node. These are designated as **opposite, whorled,** and **alternate,** respectively. In the opposite type, each leaf pair is at right angles to the pairs immediately above and below, and whorled leaves also are arranged in such a way that leaf positions are not superimposed on those immediately above and below. Thus, when viewed from above, the leaves appear to be in vertical rows. Four rows are observed when the arrangement is opposite and more occur when leaves are whorled. The simplest arrangement of alternate leaves is seen in cases where the leaf at one node is opposite to those just above and below it; this arrangement is called **distichous**. Alternate leaves have a helical arrangement on the stem and describe one or more turns before a leaf position is superimposed upon one above or below it. This is not so apparent in the distichous type, but is readily seen when more leaves occur per complete turn. In the example in Figure 18–17 there are two turns before two leaves are found to be superimposed. The phyllotaxy of this plant is said to be 2/5; that is, there are two turns and five leaves before the pattern is repeated.

The functional significance of phyllotaxy seems to be one of efficient deployment of leaf surface for light absorption; plant breeders have become interested in phyllotaxy as a means of achieving greater photosynthetic efficiency in crop plants. Growing corn plants in close rows in order to increase the yield per acre has caused corn geneticists to select strains with optimal leaf size and leaf angles, to maximize light absorption. Such modification of plant form has been called **genetic engineering.**

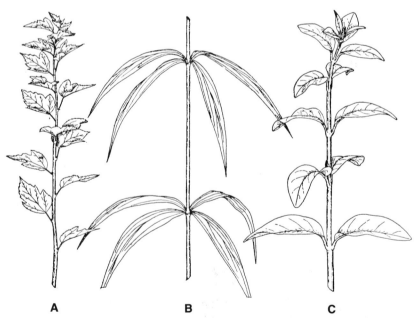

A   B   C

Figure 18–16 Patterns of leaf arrangement. *A*, Alternate. *B*, Whorled. *C*, Opposite (From Weatherwax, P. *Botany*, Third Edition. Philadelphia, W. B. Saunders Company, 1956).

Figure 18-17 Phyllotaxy of a young tobacco plant as viewed from above, 2/5 phyllotaxy. Note that leaves numbered 1 and 6 are superimposed (Photo courtesy of Jane K. Glaser).

Leaf Development

The arrangement of leaf primordia about the apical dome of the shoot apex determines the phyllotaxy of the plant. Stated in developmental terms, the apical meristem controls phyllotaxy. Experiments have been done in which the youngest discernible leaf primordium was removed surgically. In such cases, the next leaf primordium to appear will be nearer to the site of the removed primordium than it would normally have been. Such experiments have led to a hypothesis—the **field theory**—stating that each primordium has an inhibiting zone about it that prevents the next primordium from developing in close proximity. The width of this zone would determine the spacing of primordia, and thus produce a distinctive phyllotaxy. However, the nature of the inhibition is unknown. It might be due to a specific inhibiting substance, to an interaction of substances, or to draining of nutrients from the immediate vicinity of the developing primordium so as to prevent the initiation of a new primordium within certain distances. Since specific phyllotaxies are associated with species, genera, and even families of flowering plants, the pattern of leaf initiation must be under strict genetic control.

Leaves are organs of determinate growth; that is, unlike most stems and roots (which can grow indefinitely), they have a finite growth period. As leaves develop, they exhibit a basic pattern that is quite uniform among plants in general, regardless of final leaf

475

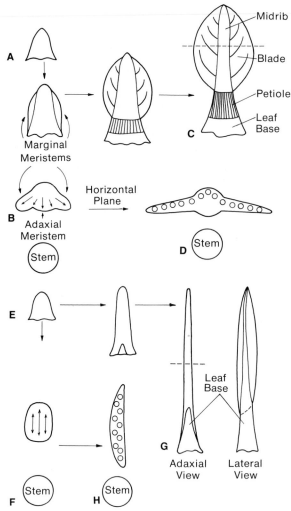

Figure 18-18 Patterns of leaf development. *A,* Leaf primordium. *B,* Typical leaf development shown in cross-sectional view. *C,* Typical mature leaf having a dorsiventral blade and a petiole. *D,* Cross section of a typical leaf showing its relationship to the stem. *E,* Leaf primordium of a sword leaf, which initially closely resembles the primordium of any typical leaf. *F,* Cross section of a developing sword leaf. Note that in addition to longitudinal growth, adaxial growth (i.e., growth toward the stem) also occurs. *G,* Mature sword leaf, as in *Iris. H,* Cross section of a sword leaf showing relationship to the stem (Redrawn from Kaplan, D. R., Leaf, *The McGraw-Hill Yearbook of Science and Technology,* 1970).

shape. This development is dependent upon cell division in several meristematic zones of the growing leaf, including tip, basal region, and intermediate region. The leaf blade develops as a pair of wing-like outgrowths produced by marginal meristems. Dr. Donald Kaplan, working at the University of California at Berkeley, has shown that the characteristic form of mature leaves of species is determined by the relative growth rates of the different meristematic zones during development of the leaves. By way of illustration, suppression of the marginal meristems and increased growth in the leaf tip would result in production of a long cylindrical leaf, while the combination of a highly active marginal meristem and a less active axis region would produce broad and even circular leaves, as seen in lily pads. The sword-shaped leaves of *Iris* and *Gladiolus* may be interpreted as the result of a suppression of the marginal meristems and relatively greater adaxial growth of the leaf axis (i.e., growth toward the stem; see Figure 18–18).

Leaf Anatomy and Function

The typical foliage leaf of a flowering plant has a dorsiventral organization. The petiole contains one or more vascular bundles (or veins), which branch out in the blade of the leaf. The xylem usually is in the upper (adaxial) part of the bundle; the phloem, in the lower (abaxial) part. Surrounding each major bundle in the leaf blade is a layer of parenchyma cells known as the bundle sheath. The sheath cells are thought to be involved in conduction of substances from the vascular tissues to other leaf tissues and vice versa. They also produce starch grains and in certain plant species the sheath cells have unique chloroplasts that are involved in a form of photosynthesis called the **C-4 pathway** (see Chapter 5).

The leaf is covered on both sides by a cutinized epidermis composed of pavement-like cells that usually lack chloroplasts. Interspersed at regular intervals among the other epidermal cells are pairs of guard cells that form the stomata, which control the exchange of gases between the leaf interior and the outside atmosphere.

Stomata normally are open during daylight hours and closed at night, but exceptions are known. Cacti and some other desert plants have their stomata open at night. The mechanism of opening is based on osmotic relationships of the guard cells. The stomata are

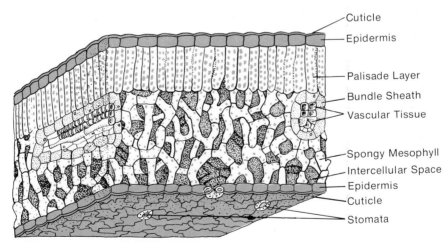

Cuticle
Epidermis
Palisade Layer
Bundle Sheath
Vascular Tissue
Spongy Mesophyll
Intercellular Space
Epidermis
Cuticle
Stomata

Figure 18–19 Highly diagrammatic rendering of the anatomy of a dicot leaf (Redrawn from *Botany,* Fifth Edition by C. E. Wilson, W. E. Loomis, and T. A. Steeves. Copyright © 1971 by Holt, Rinehart and Winston, Inc. Reproduced by permission of Holt, Rinehart and Winston, Inc.).

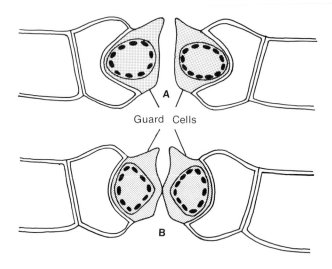

Guard Cells

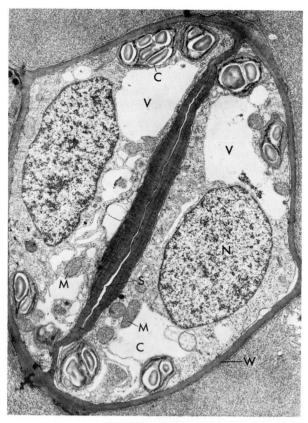

C

Figure 18-20 *A* and *B*, Diagrammatic representations of cross sections of guard cells of the bean leaf. × 5200. The section is parallel to the leaf surface. Note vacuoles (V), stoma S (Sm), mitochondria (M), chloroplasts (C), nuclei (N), and cell wall (W), which is particularly thick along the borders of the stoma. (*A* and *B* redrawn from *Botany,* Fifth Edition by C. E. Wilson, W. E. Loomis, and T. A. Steeves. Copyright © 1971 by Holt, Rinehart and Winston, Inc. Reproduced by permission of Holt, Rinehart and Winston, Inc.; *C* Courtesy of Steven H. Sanchez).

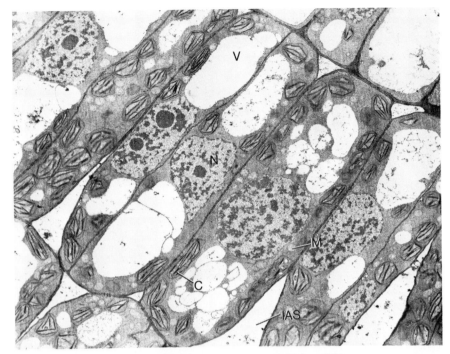

Figure 18–21 Electron micrograph of the palisade cells of a young bean leaf, × 6000. C, Chloroplast; M, mitochondrion; N, nucleus; V, vacuole; IAS, intercellular air space (Photo courtesy of Paul Umbeck).

open when the guard cells are turgid and closed when the guard cells are flaccid. Whether the guard cells are turgid or flaccid depends on whether water moves into or out of them from adjacent epidermal cells. Guard cells have chloroplasts, and photosynthesis is either directly or indirectly involved in stomatal opening through changes in sugar concentrations in the guard cell vacuoles. However, the relationships are complex. Many factors bring about stomatal opening and closing, among these light intensity, temperature changes, CO_2 concentrations, wind, and potassium ion levels. Despite considerable research, there is no completely satisfactory explanation of the mechanism of stomatal opening.

Water may enter a leaf directly through the leaf surface, but most of the time it is taken up by the roots and enters the leaf via the xylem. The arrangement of veins in a leaf is such that few cells are far removed from vein endings. The movement of water within the plant also depends in part on the leaves. As stated earlier in this chapter, water vapor leaving the leaf through open stomata exerts a pull on the water in the cell walls and intercellular spaces, and this tension is transmitted through the xylem to water entering the roots (**transpiration pull**). Transpiration pull is thought to be a major factor in water movement within vascular plants; however, transpiration is not in itself essential for metabolic processes in plants, for sufficient water is available under ordinary conditions to support photosynthesis and other life processes whether or not transpiration is occurring.

479

Figure 18-22 *A*, Guttation in the leaves of young corn plants. *B*, Guttation in the leaves of the tomato, *Lycopersicon esculentum* (*A* from Weatherwax, P. *Botany*, Third Edition. Philadelphia, W. B. Saunders Company, 1956; *B* from *Botany,* Fifth Edition by C. E. Wilson, W. E. Loomis, and T. A. Steeves. Copyright © 1971 by Holt, Rinehart and Winston, Inc. Reproduced by permission of Holt, Rinehart and Winston, Inc.).

Sometimes liquid water exudes from leaves under conditions that check transpiration, most often during periods of coolness and high humidity. In this process, called **guttation,** water may move out of leaves either through stomata or through special secretory structures known as **hydathodes**.

The photosynthetic tissue, or **mesophyll**, within the blade of most dicot leaves has a dorsiventral arrangement. One or more layers of columnar cells form the **palisade** just beneath the upper epidermis. Beneath the palisade is a more loosely arranged tissue system, the **spongy mesophyll**, which is composed of large, irregu-

480

larly shaped cells. Between these cells is a system of air spaces that is continuous with the outside atmosphere when the stomata are open. Typically, the cells of the palisade and spongy mesophyll contain large vacuoles and numerous ellipsoidal chloroplasts arranged peripherally in the cytoplasm (See Chapter 4). The chloroplasts, in turn, contain grana made up of stacked membranes termed thylakoids. Sclerenchyma cells are found within leaves also, and include bundles of fibers as well as the large, branching types (the **sclereids**) found in some plants.

Autumn Color

Leaf senescence is often accompanied by the brilliant reds and yellows of fall coloration. These autumnal hues are due partly to the loss of chlorophylls, which otherwise mask the orange and yellow carotenoids of the chloroplasts, and also to the accumulation of a class of pigments called **anthocyanins** in the vacuoles of leaf cells just prior to abscission. Anthocyanins are produced by conversion of sugars during cool fall weather, and are particularly pronounced when damp conditions prevail and there have been no killing frosts.

THE ROOT

At the beginning of this chapter it was observed that an embryonic structure, the radicle, is present at the tip of the hypocotyl. The radicle forms the first root (**primary root**) of the young plant. In many plants the primary root continues to grow and persists throughout the life of the plant in the form of a **tap root** system. In others, including the monocots, the primary root does not last very long and its functions are soon taken over by adventitious roots developing usually from the lower part of the stem (**fibrous root** system). The function and structure of roots and shoots overlap to some extent, but the primary function of root systems is distinct in most plants. Roots typically are the principal means by which water and minerals are absorbed from the soil. In addition to absorption and conduction, roots also serve to store reserve food and water and to anchor the plant. They also may provide support for aerial structures in the form of stilt or prop roots or the holdfasts of some vines.

Root Development

Root tips resemble stem tips in their zonation. The tip region contains an apical meristem covered by a protective mass of cells, the **root cap**. Root cap cells are rubbed or sloughed off as the root tip grows through the soil, but the apical meristem replaces lost cells by cell division. Nothing resembling the root cap occurs in stem tips.

Just as in stem tips, there is present in root tips a region of

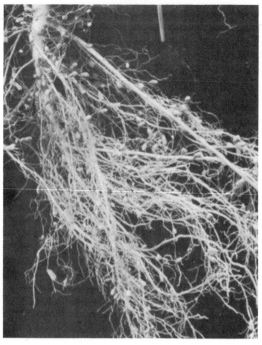

A

B

Figure 18-23 Root types. *A*, Taproot system of clover, a dicot. The secondary roots have nodules containing nitrogen-fixing bacteria. *B*, Fibrous, adventitious roots of banana, a monocot (*A*, USDA Photo; *B*, from *Botany*, Fifth Edition by C. E. Wilson, W. E. Loomis, and T. A. Steeves. Copyright © 1971 by Holt, Rinehart and Winston, Inc. Reproduced by permission of Holt, Rinehart and Winston, Inc.).

cellular elongation; here cells become larger as cell walls stretch and protoplasmic contents expand, and gradually these cells become specialized and merge into the region of cell maturation. The organization of the root is much simpler than that of the stem. Leaves and buds are lacking, and in most cases the vascular system is protostelic. Branch roots are initiated internally, unlike stem branches (which develop from lateral buds).

Root Tissues

The region of cell maturation in roots can be identified as that area where specific types of tissues become evident. Cross-sections of the root in this region show an outer epidermis having some cells elongated into root hairs. The structure of the root epidermis is similar to that of the epidermis in stems, although no cuticle is present and there are no stomata. Within the epidermis is the cortex, a region usually larger in volume than that observed in stems and composed of parenchyma cells that often contain an abundance of starch grains. The inner boundary of the cortex is composed of the **endodermis,** a conspicuous one-layered sheath with cells characterized by **Casparian strips**. Casparian strips are thickenings in the lat-

482

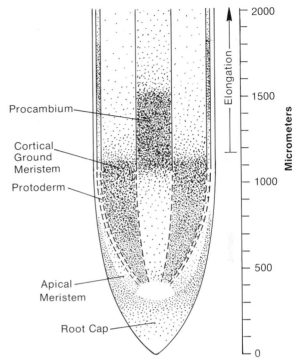

Figure 18-24 The root tip, shown highly diagrammatically. The relative number of cell divisions in each zone corresponds to the intensity of the shading. (Redrawn from Wilson, C. E., Loomis, W. E., and Steeves, T. A. *Botany*, Fifth Edition. New York, Holt, Rinehart and Winston, Inc., 1971).

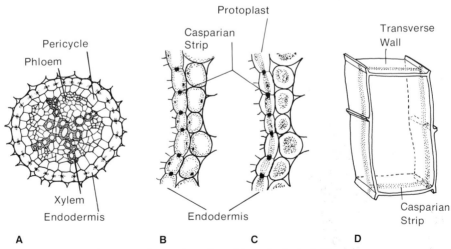

Figure 18-25 The endodermis of a root of morning glory (*Convolvulus*). A, Transverse section of the stele and endodermis, showing arrangement of Casparian strips. B, Endodermis, showing normal relationship of protoplasts to cell walls. C, Endodermis after treatment with alcohol. Note that shrunken protoplasts adhere to the Casparian strips only. D, Endodermal cell, showing a Casparian strip (Redrawn and modified from Esau, K. *Plant Anatomy*, Second Edition, John Wiley and Sons, Inc., 1965).

483

eral walls of endodermal cells. They contain both lignin and suberin and are waterproof. The plasma membrane adheres to the Casparian strip, with the result that water and solutes moving into or out of the center of the root must pass through the selectively permeable plasma membranes of the endodermal cells rather than through their walls; thus, the endodermis functions to control the water movement of the root.

Within the endodermis of the root is a layer of pericycle tissue. The cells of this tissue have the capability of becoming meristematic and forming part of the vascular cambium of the root, as well as forming branch roots.

The vascular tissues of the root lie within the pericycle. Xylem cells are present in the center of the root and usually show a starlike form in cross-section. The star may have three, four, or five arms (**triarch, tetrarch,** or **pentarch** respectively), or even more arms **(polyarch),** or there may be a simple two-armed pattern (**diarch**).

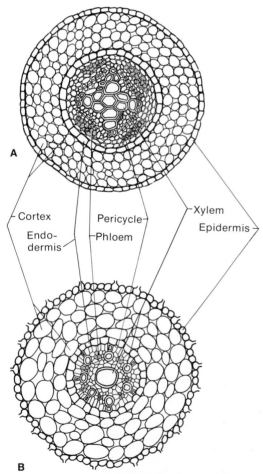

Figure 18–26 Diagrammatic representation of cross sections of roots. A, Root of a dicot. The xylem of this root has a tetrarch configuration. B, Root of a monocot. Redrawn from Wilson, C. E., Loomis, W. E., and Steeves, T. A . Botany, Fifth Edition. New York, Holt, Rinehart and Winston, Inc.).

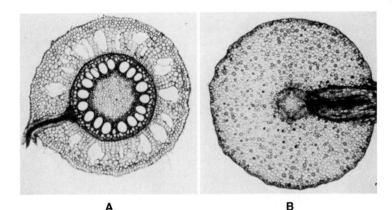

A   **B**

Figure 18–27 The origin of branch roots. *A,* Maize. *B,* Willow. The branch roots originate when certain cells of the pericycle become meristematic and form an apical root meristem complete with a root cap. The new branch root then grows out through the cortex and epidermis. Adventitious roots, on the other hand, develop within stems, and typically arise in the parenchyma between vascular bundles in young stems, or from the cambium in older stems (From Weatherwax, P. *Botany,* Third Edition. Philadelphia, W. B. Saunders Company, 1956).

The roots of monocotyledons tend toward the polyarch configurations and in some a pith may be present. The primary phloem is located between arms of primary xylem, and occurs as distinct groups of cells. In most dicotyledons a vascular cambium arises from residual procambial cells between the xylem and phloem as the root matures. This cambium functions in the same manner as the vascular cambium in stems forming secondary xylem, phloem, and rays. The roots of monocotyledons lack a cambium and do not develop secondary tissues. Eventually the roots of dicots may become quite woody; annual rings are present, and a thick cork may be formed. The older root thus may closely resemble an older woody stem.

Root Functions

Certain epidermal cells form **root hairs**. These elongate and become closely intertwined with soil particles as they grow. The root hairs secrete viscous substances that help maintain this close contact with the soil. Recent studies using electron microscopy have shown that among these secretions are very fine fibers about the same diameter as cilia (about 200 nanometers). These fibers, the **rhizoplane fibers,** probably conduct nutrient elements from the soil particles to the root cells.

Root hairs grow rapidly and generally live for a short time, usually only a few weeks or months. Large numbers of root hairs serve to increase the total surface area of the root tip enormously with little change in total root volume, thus greatly increasing the surface-to-volume ratio. About 90 per cent of all plant absorption takes place through root hairs. Plants that are transplanted often

485

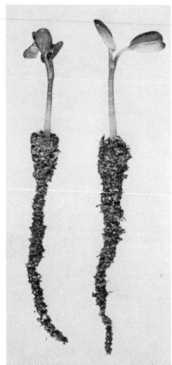

Figure 18–28 Root hairs. *Left,* Radish seedlings, grown in moist air. *Right,* Radish seedlings grown in soil; note soil particles adhering to the hairs. It is now known that very fine fibers about 200 nm. in diameter, called **rhizoplane fibers**, extend into the soil from the surface of the hair cells (From Weatherwax, P. *Botany*, Third Edition. Philadelphia, W. B. Saunders Company, 1956).

have their fragile root hair systems damaged; this results in great loss in capacity for absorption. For this reason transplanted plants must be kept heavily watered until new root hairs are formed.

Root systems may become very extensive, even in small herbaceous plants. A single rye plant was found to develop over 14 million rootlets and over 14 billion root hairs in two cubic feet of soil after only four months of growth. The total surface area of the root hairs was about that of a tennis court. The roots and root hairs of plants form an intricate, fibrous branching pattern that effectively exploits soil space. It can easily be understood why plants with extensive root systems provide excellent ground cover and help prevent soil erosion.

Soil water contains minerals in solution. Both water and solutes pass through epidermal surfaces, much of these through the surfaces of root hairs. From the epidermis, water and solutes move from cell to cell in the cortex, finally passing into the xylem. Several processes are involved in these movements; among these are **osmosis, active absorption** (see Chapter 4), and **transpiration pull.**

It should also be noted that in many green plants the function of

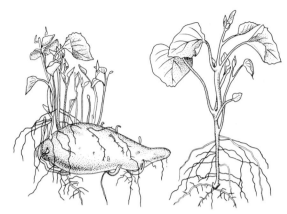

Figure 18–29 Propagation by cuttings in the sweet potato (*Ipomoea batatus*). The tuberous root is shown producing new shoots and adventitious roots in water (From *Botany*, Fifth Edition by C. E. Wilson, W. E. Loomis, and T. A. Steeves. Copyright © 1971 by Holt, Rinehart and Winston, Inc. Reproduced by permission of Holt, Rinehart and Winston, Inc.).

root hairs is often taken over by certain fungi that invade the growing root tip and penetrate the surface tissues. These combinations of roots and fungi are known as mycorrhizae (see Chapter 11). Absorption of water and minerals from the soil may take place through fungal hyphae that later transfer the materials into the root. An intimate, mutualistic association comes about between a fungus and a flowering plant comparable to that of an alga and a fungus in the composition of a lichen.

An important root function in many plants is the storage of reserve foods and water. Carbohydrates, including sugars and starch, are the foods commonly stored. One of the common root modifications is the fleshy tap root, such as we see in carrots, beets, and radishes. The sugar beet, which is presently gaining greatly in importance because of shortages in the world sugar market, contains 15 to 20 per cent sugar. Some plant roots contain valuable drugs, such as the storage roots of the Mexican yam *(Dioscorea)* which contain steroid substances from which contraceptive drugs ("the Pill") are manufactured.

PLANT PROPAGATION FROM STEMS, LEAVES, AND ROOTS

Many plants are reproduced by means of **cuttings**. A small piece of stem or root or a fleshy leaf is cut off and the cut end is placed in water or such suitable propagating mixture as moist soil, sand, or vermiculite. In a short time (usually from a few days to a few weeks) adventitious roots begin to form from the cutting. Root formation

487

Figure 18–30 A graft union in avocado. In this old tree the scar of the union between the scion (upper) and stock (lower) is still visible.

can often be stimulated by the application of a growth hormone, such as indoleacetic acid (IAA), to the cut end. Many of our common ornamental and food plants are grown from cuttings since this is the fastest way of producing a new plant. Moreover, it insures that the new plant will be exactly like the parental plant from which the cutting was taken, with all its desirable features. For example, geranium and coleus are grown commonly from stem cuttings by simply cutting off the branch tips and placing the cut ends in moist sand. African violet and *Sedum* are grown from leaf cuttings placed directly in water or in moist sand or vermiculite.

Various species of flowering plants can be reproduced quickly and dependably by grafting, although generally this technique is used primarily with economically valuable woody plants. Nearly all important varieties of fruit and nut trees are propagated by grafting. The technique involves transferring a piece of a branch (called the **scion**) of one plant to the rooted and growing stem of another plant (called the **stock**). An incision is made in the stock so as to place cambial tissues of both scion and stock in contact, and then the two are carefully bound together. The graft will take if the cambial tissues of the stock and scion are compatible. Eventually, the scion becomes unified with the stock plant and resumes growth. Grafting combines the excellent vegetative growth characters of one plant (usually of the stock) with excellent fruit or flower yield (usually of the scion) to produce a plant that is superior to ungrafted plants of the same kind. For instance, several varieties of oranges grown in Florida are all grafted to the same kind of stock, the sour orange. Although the sour orange is not used for its fruit, it produces a vigorous, resistant root system that is ideal for healthy vegetative growth. When scions of varieties of oranges desirable as food are grafted on the sour orange, an improved tree is produced. This procedure is the basis for the citrus industry in Florida.

PLANT MOVEMENTS

Although stems, leaves, and roots often appear to be completely immobile, time-lapse photography has demonstrated that they are in almost ceaseless motion. Generally, the movements can be considered of two kinds—**growth movements** and **turgor movements.** Growth movements come about as the result of different rates of growth; cells in one part of a structure grow faster than those in a different part, which causes a change in direction of growth. In contrast, turgor movements come about as the result of changes in the turgor of cells of the affected structure.

Growth movements can further be classified into **tropisms, nu-**

Figure 18–31 Phototropism in young radish plants: The plants at the left were grown in darkness. At right are the same plants placed near a window for a half an hour. (From Weatherwax, P. *Botany,* Third Edition. Philadelphia, W. B. Saunders Company, 1956.)

tations, and **nastic movements.** Tropisms involve a growth response to external stimuli that come from a particular direction, and the direction of the stimulus determines the direction of the movement. Roots and stems exhibit tropisms; i.e., they can bend or curve in response to environmental stimuli. Various tropisms are named on the basis of the kind of stimulus involved; for example, tropisms that occur in response to light are called **phototropisms.** The response to gravity is called **geotropism.** Stems are typically positively phototropic; that is, they grow or bend in the direction of the light stimulus, but they are negatively geotropic, and bend away from the center of gravity. In contrast, roots exhibit positive geotropism and bend or curve down towards the earth, but they are negatively phototropic. There are, however, plants that possess non-geotropic roots (i.e., are **ageotropic**). The coralloid roots of cycads in which blue-green algae are found are of this type, as are rhizoids. Rhizomes, the horizontal, subsurface stems of grasses and other plants, are laterally geotropic. Tendrils of pea plants and other vines curl about objects with which they come in contact. This touch response is called **thigmotropism.** A special kind of phototropism, known as **heliotropism,** is seen in sunflowers; the heads of the sunflowers follow the sun, from east to west, every day.

Other tropisms are **hydrotropism** (response to water) and **chemotropism** (response to certain chemical compounds). The physiological bases of tropism will be explained further in Chapter 20.

Time lapse photographs show that stems also exhibit random waving motions known as **nutations.** Nutations are not tropisms but are autonomous spiral growth movements. They are especially pronounced in some types of twining vines, morning glories, sweet potatoes, and bindweeds.

Nastic movements are plant responses to stimuli that are independent of the direction of origin of such stimuli. Some of the so-called "sleep" movements of plants are nastic movements. The response of the tentacles of the insectivorous sundew *(Drosera)* is a nastic response. After small insects are attracted to the brightly-colored leaves of sundew, the hair-like tentacles of the leaf wrap themselves around the insect prey and eventually enzymes produced by the leaf bring about its digestion. The quick movement of the tentacles is a turgor response.

Turgor movements are more characteristic of leaves. The effective cells are structurally different from surrounding cells, and are usually more numerous in the **pulvinus** or swollen petiole base of leaves or leaflets. Rapid changes in the turgor of these cells due to water movement can result in drooping or closing of the leaf. The rolling of the leaves of certain grasses during drought is caused by changes in turgor and the collapse of tissues that maintain the normal expansion of the leaf.

Perhaps the best known example of turgor movement is in the sensitive plant *Mimosa pudica,* which has leaves and leaflets that quickly droop when touched or otherwise stimulated by shock or sudden heat (Fig. 18–32). The affected leaves and stems generally

490

Figure 18–32 The sensitive plant, *Mimosa pudica.* Same plant before (*left*), and after (*right*), application of touch stimulus.

require about 20 minutes to recover their turgor. Some other plants also show very fast movement, such as the Venus fly-trap and certain legumes. The mechanism is not completely understood, although it appears that hormones affecting the differential turgor of certain cells are involved (see Chapter 20).

SUMMARY

A number of differences can be observed between roots and shoots, not only in respect to their function but also in regard to their origin and structure. The shoot is derived from the epicotyl and consists essentially of nodes and internodes. In early development, the vascular tissues are formed in narrow strands called vascular bundles. Branches, leaves, and flowers arise from buds, leaf primordia, and flower primordia. Young stems of dicotyledons have well-developed pith that function as food storage zones.

Leaves of flowering plants are remarkable for their diversity, yet all seem to share a common developmental pattern. The different shapes that mature leaves assume result from differential rates of growth in the several meristematic regions of the young leaf.

Not only does leaf form vary from plant to plant, but many different arrangements of the leaves on stems also occur (phyllotaxy). These are of three main types: opposite, whorled, and alternate, and these types are characteristic of species, genera, and even families of plants. Examination of a growing stem apex shows us that the distinctive leaf arrangement of a plant is established at the time of leaf initiation. Leaf primordia develop at time-space intervals, which later on are manifested in the phyllotaxies of mature leaves.

Foliage leaves of most plants have dorsiventral symmetry, although other symmetries, exemplified by cylindrical and sword-shaped leaves, are known. The supporting framework of a leaf is the vascular system, which branches out in the leaf blade in a number of distinctive patterns. These are of diagnostic importance in classification. Parallel venation, for instance, is typical of monocot leaves, whereas net venation is characteristic of dicots.

491

The photosynthetic tissue of leaves, the mesophyll, contains chloroplasts, which are the sites of photosynthetic reactions in the plants. The chloroplast membrane structures, or grana, are the sites of the pigment systems that convert light energy into chemical energy in the light reactions.

In regard to structure, development, and tissue types, roots are generally similar to stems; however, there are no nodes or internodes in roots, no epidermal stomata, and usually no pith. The root tip is covered by a root cap. Higher up on the root, root hairs are formed in great numbers. Branches arise from within the root, specifically from the pericycle. The vascular tissue of roots is not found in discrete bundles as in the stem, but rather the xylem and phloem occur in alternating radii of the typical herbaceous dicotyledonous root.

Many plants can be propagated by cuttings and by grafting. Small pieces of the plant that are used for propagation may be rooted in water or in other media. Grafting makes possible the production of superior forms of many fruit and nut trees, as well as many ornamental species, and is widely practiced in horticultural botany.

Although roots, stems, and leaves appear to be immobile, they are constantly in slow motion. Plant movements are classified as tropisms, nastic movements, or turgor movements, according to the nature of the plant response and the mechanism that brings it about. Plant hormones appear to be involved in most plant movements.

DISCUSSION QUESTIONS

1. What part(s) of the flowering plant embryo develop(s) into the shoot? Into the root? What part(s) of the embryo contain(s) stored food?
2. List the primary tissue types found in stems of herbaceous dicotyledonous plants. Describe the function of the cortex; of the pith; of the sieve tubes; of the vessels; and of the fibers.
3. Define phyllotaxy.
4. What mathematical ratio expresses the phyllotaxy of a plant with a helical (alternate) leaf arrangement in which every third turn finds a ninth leaf position superimposed on a first leaf position?
5. Explain how to distinguish between one leaflet of a compound leaf and a simple leaf on a leafy branch.
6. What is meant by the phrase the secondary body? List the secondary tissues in the stem of a woody dicotyledonous flowering plant.
7. Where does the cork tissue come from and what function does it have in the woody stem?
8. Clearly differentiate between transverse section, radial section, and tangential section in regard to the appearance of the vascular ray in these three sections.
9. Compare the arrangement of primary tissues in the transverse section of a herbaceous dicotyledonous root with that of a herbaceous stem.
10. Branches from stems come from the growth of lateral buds. How do branch roots develop?
11. List some important root crops of economic importance.
12. What kind of plant movement is described by the term tropism? What is phototropism?

SUPPLEMENTAL READING

Biddulph, S., and O. Biddulph. The Circulatory System of Plants. *Sci. Amer.* *200*:44–49, 1959.

Esau, K. *Plant Anatomy.* Ed. 2. New York: John Wiley & Sons, Inc., 1965.

Jane, F. W. Botanical Aspects of Wood Science. *Vistas in Botany 11*:1–35, 1963.

Salisbury, F. B., and C. Ross. *Plant Physiology.* Belmont, California: Wadsworth Publishing Co., Inc., 1969.

Schulman, E. Tree Rings and History in the Western United States. *Economic Botany, 8*:234–250, 1954.

Steeves, T. A., and I. M. Sussex. *Patterns in Plant Development.* Englewood Cliffs, New Jersey : Prentice-Hall, Inc., 1972.

Williams, S. Wood structure. *Sci. Amer. 188*:64–68, 1953.

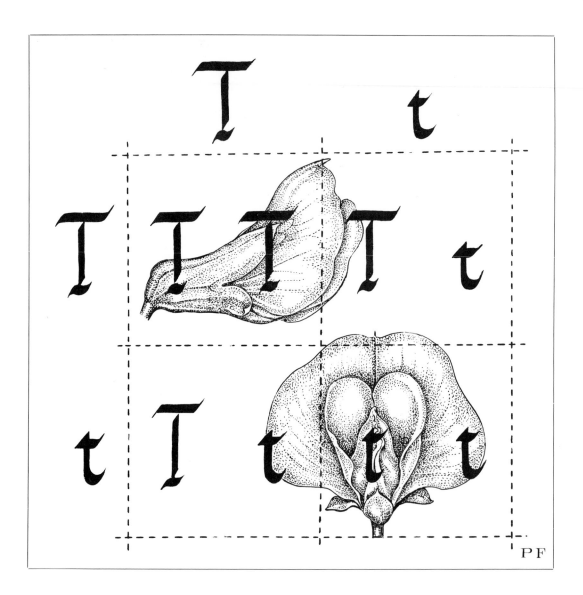

Chapter 19

Plant Heredity

THE MONOHYBRID CROSS • THE DIHYBRID CROSS • INCOMPLETE DOMINANCE • MEIOSIS AND CHROMOSOME BEHAVIOR • REDISCOVERY OF MENDEL'S LAWS • THE ORIGIN OF GENETIC FACTORS • GENE LINKAGE • QUANTITATIVE INHERITANCE • CYTOPLASMIC INHERITANCE • CHEMICAL BASIS OF INHERITANCE • REGULATION OF GENE EXPRESSION • CYTOGENETICS • PLANT BREEDING AND IMPROVEMENT • SUMMARY

One cold evening in February of 1865, a meeting was held by the Society of Natural Science in Brunn, Austria (now Brno, Czechoslovakia). The meeting took place in a small classroom with about 40 persons in attendance. They had gathered to hear a paper entitled *Experiments in Plant Hybridization,* to be given by an Augustinian monk and local high school teacher, Gregor Mendel. There had been a great deal of interest in hybridizing plants ever since the German botanist Kolreuter (1733–1806) demonstrated the function of pollen and ovules and developed a successful method for the control of artificial hybridizations. It took Mendel about an hour to present his talk about studies on the common garden pea, *Pisum sativum.* From 1856 to 1864 Mendel observed the results of hybridization upon single, specific characters in over 10,000 individual plants. Earlier he collected 34 more or less distinct varieties of the pea, and fortunately had chosen a self-fertilizing plant in which the varieties bred true to type. He selected 22 varieties for his experiments, and these showed constant pairs of sharply contrasted differences, such as fruit shape, fruit color, seed shape, and stem height. In the simplest cases the peas differed from one another by only one character or by a pair of characters.

The Monohybrid Cross

In one of his experiments, Mendel crossed a tall variety of pea (that reached heights of up to 2 meters) with a dwarf variety that was

---

"My experiments with single characters all lead to the same result: that from the seeds of the hybrids, plants are obtained half of which in turn carry the hybrid characters (Aa), the other half, however, receive the parental characters A and a in equal amounts."

GREGOR MENDEL, 1869

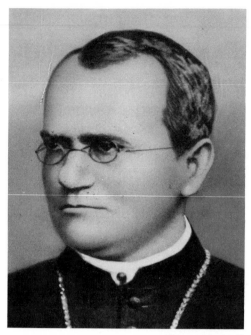

Figure 19–1 Gregor Mendel (Photo courtesy of The Bettmann Archive).

usually only one-half meter tall. He expected hybrids of intermediate height, but to his surprise all the plants were tall. Mendel allowed the tall hybrids to self-pollinate, and among the second generation hybrids there was a ratio of about 75 per cent tall plants to 25 per cent dwarf plants. The actual count was 787 tall to 277 dwarf plants, or about a 3-to-1 ratio of tall to dwarf. When he allowed the dwarf plants to self-pollinate, he found that the third generation of hybrids were all dwarf, but when the tall plants were allowed to self-pollinate, about one-third produced tall pea plants in the third generation, while about two-thirds produced tall and dwarf plants in approximately a 3-to-1 ratio. Mendel reported to the audience that in all cases the first hybrid generation (the F_1 or **first filial generation**) was uniform in appearance, and that one of the two parental characters, the **dominant** or stronger one, was found in all the hybrid plants. In the cross between the tall and dwarf, the tall factor (indicated by T) was dominant over the dwarf one (indicated by t). The character not seen in the F_1 generation was the **recessive** character, which seemed to disappear in the hybrid. Mendel formulated his first law, the **law of uniformity** (or law of dominance), which states that all individuals of an F_1 generation will be equal and uniform. The 3-to-1 ratio that he observed in the second generation hybrids (**the F_2 generation**) led him to derive his second law, the **law of segregation**, referring to the separation of dominant characters from recessive characters so that each gamete will receive only one or the other of a pair of factors controlling a specific trait.

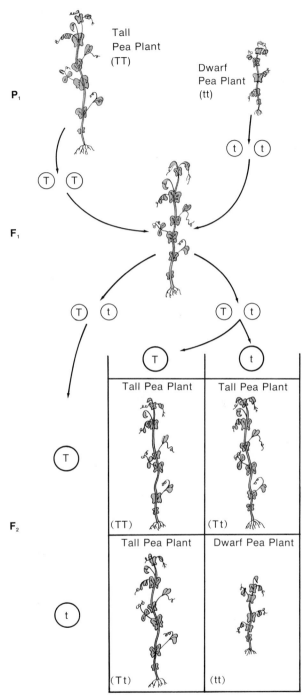

Figure 19–2 A monohybrid cross in garden peas involving genes for plant height. The Punnett's square method is utilized to illustrate the assortment of characters in the F₂ generation.

The Dihybrid Cross

The third law that Mendel presented that evening was an explanation of the results of hybridizations he made between plants that differed from each other by two pairs of hereditary characters. In one example, he crossed a variety of pea that had round, yellow seeds with a variety that had wrinkled, green seeds. The F_1 hybrid generation was uniform; all the plants had round, yellow seeds. However, when he allowed the plants to self-pollinate, the F_2 hybrids produced showed all possible combinations of the parental characters, and always in particular ratios. Of the 556 hybrid plants, 315 were round and yellow, 101 were wrinkled and yellow, 108 were round and green, and 32 were wrinkled and green, or ratios of approximately nine round-yellow to three round-green, to three wrinkled-yellow, to one wrinkled-green. From these results he concluded his third law, the **law of independent assortment.** He suggested that the factors sorted independently of one another during the production of gametes, and thus the gametes of all the possible combinations combined independently of one another.

We can understand how Mendel obtained these ratios by using a technique called the **Punnett square** (see Figure 19–3). All the possible gametes of one parent are arranged along one side of a checkerboard, while the gametes of the other parent are placed along the side perpendicular to the first side. As in the case of the monohybrid cross, the gamete carrying the dominant trait is symbolized by the capital letter (in this case R for round), while the gamete carrying the recessive trait is symbolized by the small letter r (for wrinkled). Similarly, the dominant trait for seed color is represented by the capital letter Y (for yellow), while the recessive character is represented by the small letter y (for green). Since gametes are $1N$, each factor is represented by a single symbol. When the gametes are combined to form the zygote there will be two factors present, since the zygote is $2N$. The genetic constitution of the hybrid is called the **genotype**. If the two factors affecting a character are identical (e.g. RR), the individual is described as having a **homozygous** genotype for that character. If the factors are dissimilar (e.g., Rr), the individual is said to be **heterozygous**. The appearance of an individual results from the interaction of the genotype and its environment and is called the **phenotype**. Thus, the genotype of the zygote determines whether the seed will be smooth, wrinkled, yellow, or green, while the actual appearance of the seed is its phenotype.

Let us again examine the Punnett square for the dihybrid cross. Remembering that round and yellow are dominant factors, then the number of times that plants with the round and yellow phenotype are formed is nine; the number of times that plants are round and green is three; the number of times that plants are wrinkled and yellow is three; and, the number of times that plants are wrinkled and green is one; therefore, the phenotypic ratio as originally reported by Mendel for the dihybrid cross is 9:3:3:1.

Mendel explained his experiments and observations to an ap-

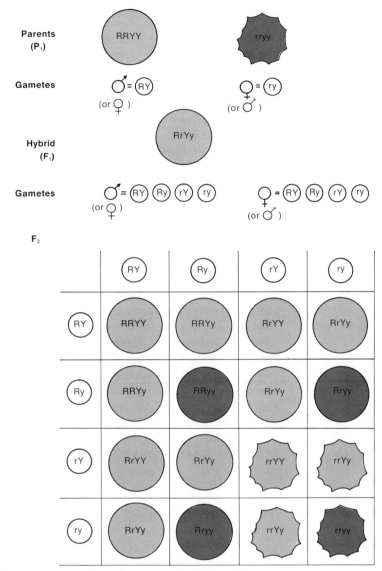

Figure 19–3 A dihybrid cross in garden peas. Genes for seed color and seed form are involved.

preciative audience, many of whom were his personal friends. Nevertheless, they were astonished at this account of numerical ratios and hybrids; nothing like it had ever been postulated before. He concluded his paper by promising to give a final talk at the next meeting of the Society, to present a theory to explain the behavior of the hybrids.

At the next meeting, Mendel stated that he believed that living individuals were made up of distinct hereditary characters transmitted from one generation to the next by factors. Hybrids combine these factors, but when gametes are formed the parental factors separate. Each gamete contains only one of the two factors of a pair. Through

499

combinations of different kinds of gametes, the law of segregation and the law of independent assortment can be explained.

After Mendel read his paper, there were no questions or discussion from the audience. Slowly the small crowd dispersed without realizing that they had witnessed the announcement of one of the greatest scientific achievements in history. Mendel was not discouraged, however; he told a friend, "My time will come." His paper was published in the Proceedings of the Natural History Society of Brunn in 1866, and he sent copies to many of his scientific correspondents, including the famous botanist from Munich, Karl Naegeli (1817–1891). Naegeli had also been experimenting with plant hybridization and should have been greatly interested in Mendel's results; instead, he completely ignored the paper and never made any mention of it in his own work. Naegeli advised Mendel to experiment with other plants such as the hawkweed, the plant with which Naegeli was then working. It is now known, that hawkweed does not reproduce sexually, but only appears to do so; the reproductive process of hawkweed is called **apomixis,** which may be defined as the formation of seeds without fertilization. It is not surprising, then, that Mendel was unable to confirm his earlier work with peas when his laws were applied to hawkweed, since the typical ratios of offspring with dominant and recessive characters cannot be observed with hawkweed. Probably Mendel experimented also with other plants in which dominance was modified, and incomplete dominance or intermediate dominance was observed. Results such as these would tend to appear to negate Mendel's original proposition, and probably caused him to doubt his own theories. As a result, his work was soon forgotten, and when he died in 1884 the many pupils and mourners attending his funeral never knew that a great scientist had passed away.

Incomplete Dominance

Mendel worked with only seven pairs of traits, and these segregated independently and apparently by pure chance. Six of these pairs are now known to be on different chromosomes, and the seventh is linked so loosely with one of the other pairs that the linkage was not noticeable in his experiments (gene linkage is explained on pp. 508 and 509). Mendel was also the first to observe **incomplete dominance**. He showed that the time of flowering in peas was subject to the same laws of segregation as the other traits but that there was no dominance; instead, the flowering time of the hybrid was intermediate between that of the two parents. In many species, the factor for flower color does not show simple dominance; for example, in snapdragons, if plants bearing red flowers are crossed with those having white flowers, the F_1 generation will produce pink flowers.

Later studies on hybridization demonstrated that hereditary factors also existed in forms other than simply dominant or recessive ones; we call such forms **alleles.** Precisely, an allele is one of the

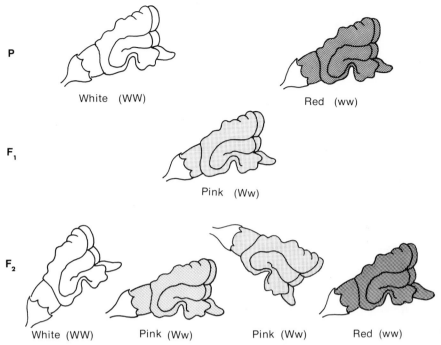

P

White (WW)   Red (ww)

F$_1$

Pink (Ww)

F$_2$

White (WW)   Pink (Ww)   Pink (Ww)   Red (ww)

Figure 19–4 Incomplete dominance in the snapdragon. Neither the genes for white (W) nor those for red (w) are dominant; when both are present, flowers with pink petals result. (Redrawn from Burns, G. W.: *The Science of Genetics: an Introduction to Heredity*, New York, The MacMillan Co., Inc., 1972).

two or more alternative forms of a factor that may occupy the same site on a chromosome, though not simultaneously. In some cases several alleles control the expression of one or a number of forms of the same character; these are referred to as **multiple alleles.** In some instances whole series of such alleles may exist, with one allele dominant over many recessive forms. In particular recombinations the genetic effect may resemble that of simple incomplete dominance.

Meiosis and Chromosome Behavior

The theoretical explanations so clearly given by Mendel were based on the idea that a mechanism existed in organisms that resulted in the distribution and combinations of factors. Today we refer to these factors as **genes** and we understand the mechanism to be associated with the behavior of the chromosomes during meiosis.

Chromosomes were first observed by the German botanist Wilhelm Hofmeister (1829–1877) as early as 1848, but he did not understand their real function in the cell. However, the suspicion that the chromosomes were the carriers of hereditary material began to develop in the latter half of the nineteenth century. In 1885 the great German plant cytologist Edward Strasburger (1849–

501

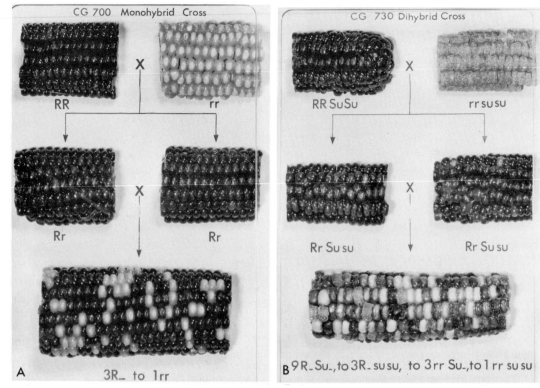

Figure 19–5 Genetic segregation in corn. *A*, A monohybrid cross involving genes for color of kernels. *B*, A dihybrid cross involving genes for kernel color and texture (Courtesy Carolina Biological Supply Company).

1912) suggested that the chromosomes in fact were the bearers of hereditary material because they were the only material in the cell that divided quantitatively equally and were present constantly in all living cells. The role of the nucleus and the chromatin network was beginning to be understood.

In previous chapters it was noted that during sexual reproduction the zygote is formed by the union of sperm and egg. Every plant that originates by sexual reproduction begins its existence as a single cell, and the hereditary traits that develop are the result of the genes present in the gametes. We know that most hereditary characteristics are carried from one generation to the next by the chromosomes of the cell. Each species has present in its nuclei a characteristic complement of two sets of chromosomes derived from the parents, one set from the male parent and one from the female parent. The chromosomes of a given pair are called **homologous chromosomes**, or homologues, because they are very similar structurally and contain genes that control the same physiological and morphological characters of the plant. The location on the chromosomes of these genes, the **locus** (plural **loci**), is the same for each homologue. Although the number of chromosomes varies considerably in plants—from a low of four in the aster-like herb

Haplopappus to a high of over 1200 in the fern *Ophioglossum* — the number is usually fairly low (between 10 and 60).

The multicellular plant body that develops from the zygote is a 2N structure; its living cells contain two sets of homologous chromosomes. These chromosomes are copies of the originals that were brought together at the time of fertilization and then faithfully replicated through thousands of successive mitotic divisions (see Chapter 4).

Meiosis always involves the separation of paired homologous chromosomes, so that each daughter cell has only half as many chromosomes as did the mother cell, while in mitosis only the chromatids separate during cell division, with the number of chromosomes in the daughter cells remaining the same as in the mother cell; this is the principal difference between meiosis and mitosis. In meiosis this separation of homologues occurs in the first division (**meiosis I**) and is followed quickly by the second division (**meiosis II,** the latter accomplishing a separation of the chromatids of each chromosome in a division similar to mitosis. Thus meiosis involves both a reduction in chromosome number and a division of the chromatids. The nucleus of each of the four daughter cells has one-half the chromosome number of the original mother cell and is therefore 1N (see Chapter 4 for additional information).

The most important part of meiosis is **prophase I**. In prophase I, each chromosome becomes visibly double and homologous chromosomes associate in pairs. At this stage, each chromosome pair is composed of four chromatids, with each chromosome composed of two chromatids. Two important events take place at this stage in meiosis: **chromosome pairing** (or **synapsis**) and **crossing over**. When homologous chromosomes associate, they come together and pair in a zipper-like fashion, and lie parallel to each other throughout their entire length. Each locus lies exactly opposite the same locus on the homologous chromosome. Matching segments of homologous chromatids may be exchanged by crossing over during prophase I. Cytological evidence of this is the **chiasma** (plural **chiasmata**), the visible point on chromatids where crossing over has occurred. These events occur while the chromosomes are shortening and thickening, and prior to their moving to the cell equator at metaphase.

At **metaphase I**, the chromosome pairs are aligned across the middle of the cell, and spindle fibers are seen attached to the **centromeres**. In **anaphase I** the homologous pairs separate in what is known as **disjunction,** and move to opposite poles. Disjunction is the cytological basis for the genetic law of segregation. In **telophase I**, two daughter cells can be recognized, but after a short **interphase** when the nuclei appear to be in a quiescent period, the daughter nuclei soon pass into **prophase II,** and the second division of meiosis is initiated. During **metaphase II** the sister chromatids of each chromosome separate (similar to mitosis), and in **anaphase II** these chromatids move toward the opposite poles. Thus in **telophase II** we now see four daughter cells, each with the 1N chromosome number. Each of these cells becomes a meiospore, which potentially can give rise to a gametophyte. (See Figure 19–6.)

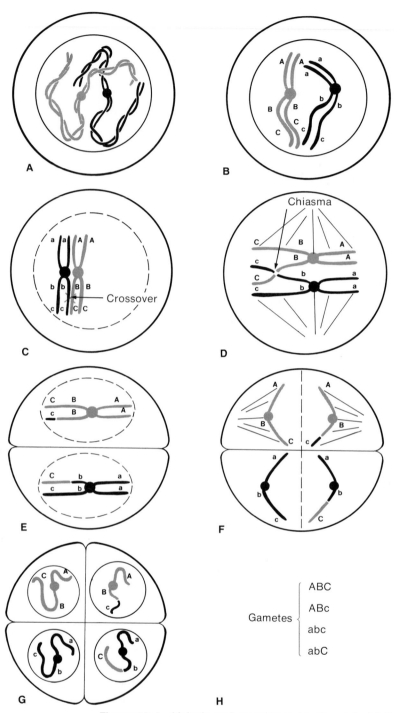

Figure 19-6 Meiosis and crossing over, shown in highly diagrammatic fashion. *A*, Early prophase. *B*, Mid-prophase. *C*, Synapsis. *D*, Metaphase I. *E*, Telophase I. *F*, Anaphase II. *G*, Telophase II.

It was noted that when heterozygous F_1 plants (Tt) are allowed to self-pollinate, about 75 per cent of the plants in the F_2 generation are tall and the remaining 25 per cent are dwarf. This ratio can be understood after considering the process of meiosis and fertilization. The two homologous chromosomes that carry genes T and t move to opposite ends of the cell during telophase I. Each gamete that is derived from the daughter cell carries only one gene (either T or t), and the two kinds of gametes are present in equal numbers. The proportion of each genotype that can be expected in the F_2 generation can be determined by using the Punnett square, which shows all possible combinations of the gametes in the squares. When the plants are permitted to self-pollinate, the gametes on the side of the square are the same as those along the top, and so the square appears as in Figure 19–2. So about 25 per cent of the F_2 plants have the genotype TT and are homozygous for tallness; 50 per cent have the genotype Tt and are also tall; the remaining 25 per cent have the genotype tt and are dwarf. Successive generations after self-pollination by the TT plants would produce offspring that are all tall; self-pollination of the tt plants would produce only offspring that are dwarf. But selfing the heterozygote Tt would again produce the 75 per cent: 25 per cent (3:1) phenotypic ratio of homozygous tall (1), to heterozygous tall (2), to homozygous dwarf (1).

A **test cross** or backcross can be made by crossing the heterozygous F_1(Tt) with one of the original homozygous parents. When Tt is backcrossed to the parent that is homozygous for the dominant factor (TT), the offspring of the cross will be 50 per cent homozygous tall (TT) and 50 per cent heterozygous tall (Tt). In other words, all the offspring of this kind of test cross will be tall. If the F_1 is backcrossed, however, to the parent that is homozygous for the recessive trait (tt), then the ratio of phenotypes in the offspring will be 50 per cent heterozygous tall (Tt) to 50 per cent homozygous dwarf (tt), or a ratio of 1:1.

The genetic significance of meiosis comes from the reshuffling and reassortment of genes through the random separation of homologous chromosomes at anaphase I; this is the physical basis of the genetic law of independent assortment. Crossing over brings about a further reassortment of genes.

The control of most phenotypic characteristics is the function of genes, all of which are located on chromosomes. In the garden pea a gene pair controlling seed color is on one pair of chromosomes, while a gene pair controlling seed shape is on a different chromosome pair. Chance alone dictates which single genes (and chromosomes) for seed shape and color are contained in each gamete.

Rediscovery of Mendel's Laws

As was noted earlier, after Mendel published the results of his plant hybridization studies and formulated his genetic laws, his work was quickly forgotten. During this time the theories of the French naturalist Lamarck (1744–1829) were still widely held. Lamarck maintained that hereditary variations were due to direct effects of the environment and the inheritance of changes were affected by need and use. Although Charles Darwin did not specify how variations originated in his *The Origin of Species,* he tacitly accepted Lamarckian views. Darwin assumed that the mode of inheritance was some form of blending of parental traits. In 1868 he proposed his **pangenesis hypothesis**, which supposed that material units or gemmules that represented individual hereditary characteristics were formed by different parts of the body. They were then collected in reproductive cells (by methods not explained by Darwin) and then passed on to the offspring, where they brought about the trait as it had been in the parent.

In 1900 Hugo DeVries (1848–1935), a professor of botany who was working on hybridization experiments at the University of Amsterdam, reached conclusions that paralleled those proposed by Mendel 35 years earlier. Then he accidentally discovered Mendel's soon-to-be-famous paper in the obscure journal in which it had been published. A German botanist named Karl Correns (1864–1933) also rediscovered Mendel's paper independently of DeVries two months later. He had been performing hybridization experiments on peas in 1899 and had reached about the same interpretation as Mendel had. The third "rediscoverer" was the Austrian Erich Tschermak-Seysenegg (1871–1962), who by 1900 had independently discovered Mendel's Laws in his hybridization experiments of 1898.

The English naturalist William Bateson is probably most responsible for the early publicity for Mendel's work. He read the paper in 1900, quickly realized its significance, promptly announced the discovery to English biologists, and then showed how the laws extend to animal inheritance as well. He wrote the first textbook in genetics and defended Mendelism to its critics. The science of genetics began dramatically in 1900, and laboratories all over the world took up the scientific study of heredity.

In a little known sidelight of the history of genetics, there was a graduate student at Columbia University in 1900 named Walter Sutton, who postulated what the laws of heredity would be if it were assumed that the hereditary determiners or factors were on the chromosomes. He figured out the laws of segregation and independent assortment, and—just when his paper was ready for publication—Mendel's original work was rediscovered!

The Origin of Genetic Factors

It has been noted that, from his early experiments, Mendel postulated that factors brought about the hereditary traits observed in the offspring; these are now referred to as genes. One of the important questions that interested the early geneticists was: How did alleles originate? Biologists today believe that they arise from a **mutation** of the existing gene. A mutation is a specific, permanent change in a gene, but a broader definition would include any

Figure 19-7 Chlorophyll-less maize plants. This is a lethal mutant in this species (From Burns, G. W. *The Science of Genetics: An Introduction to Heredity,* Third Edition. © 1976 by George W. Burns, Delaware).

changes in chromosome structure that would result in a change in phenotypic characteristics. Thus, changes in gene location, gene number, chromosome structure, or chromosome number, might bring about a genetic effect and would be called a mutation.

The first to observe a mutation was Thomas Hunt Morgan of Columbia University, who discovered the experimental value of the fruit fly, *Drosophila,* and carried on extensive genetic experiments with it. Since the life cycle of the fly is relatively short, results of crossing studies can be observed sooner than with peas or other flowering plants. It was not until 1927, however, that the mechanism for experimentally inducing mutation was discovered at the University of Texas. Hermann J. Muller announced in his paper, *Artificial Transmutation of the Gene,* that mutations in fruit flies could be caused by x-ray radiation, and that this rate of mutation was over 1500 times the normal rate. Later, other agents—such as temperature, ultra-violet rays, and certain chemicals—were shown also to be able to induce mutations.

Gene Linkage

Mendel observed characteristics as determined by seven pairs of genes, and deduced from his hybridization studies that each gene separated and assorted independently of the others. Soon after the rediscovery of Mendel's laws in 1900, genetic research demonstrated that the conclusions regarding independent assortment were not valid in peas if more than seven pairs of genes were considered. Groups of genes were discovered that acted as if they were linked together. Morgan first clearly explained **linkage** and showed its significance in genetics. The correlation of linkage groups with chromosomes was made, and the cytological basis for Mendel's results was confirmed. The garden pea has a 2N chromosome number of 14, or seven pairs of chromosomes. Six of the characters that Mendel studied were on different chromosomes. If that had not been the case, he would not have been able to deduce his law of independent assortment, because some genes would have been linked to others on the same chromosome. Mendel was either extremely lucky or extremely knowledgeable in choice both of plant and of exactly the right characters and the right number of characters for study.

After linkage groups were discovered, the concept of independent assortment of genes was dropped in favor of the concept of independent assortment of chromosomes. Genes are linked together on the same chromosome and move together during meiosis, but they are independent of the assortment of other chromosomes. Today Mendel's work is viewed as evidence for the independent as-

Figure 19-8 Thomas Hunt Morgan (1866–1945) (Photo courtesy of The Bettmann Archive).

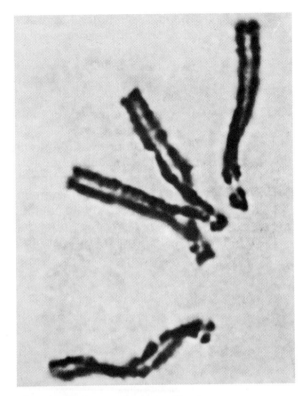

Figure 19–9 A chiasma resulting from X-ray–induced genetic crossing over (From Cronquist, A. *Basic Botany.* New York, Harper & Row, 1973).

sortment of chromosomes rather than for the independent assortment of genes or factors.

Soon after linkage groups were recognized, it was discovered that linkage was not always complete. Genes that normally showed up in one group might appear in another. The reason for this was also explained by Morgan. During prophase I, chromosomes were observed to form cross-shaped figures, and Morgan reasoned that genetic crossing over took place then. The result of crossing over is the exchange of genes between homologous chromosomes and the genetic result is that linkage groups are not fixed. The rate of crossing over will vary, but it makes for a significant amount of genetic recombination. The rearrangement of genes in the chromosome increases the amount of genetic recombination possible in the organism.

Quantitative Inheritance

Another important discovery of the early twentieth century was that groups of genes can also act together to affect a single character. Although each gene is a separate unit with one or more alleles, all the genes of a series can interact to bring about a particular expression of a character. Flower color and form are usually con-

509

trolled by such gene interaction. If all the genes are present in a certain form, the expression will be at its maximum. For instance, a dark red flower may result when all the genes are present in the same form. If all the genes are present in the other form, a white corolla will be produced. Intermediate color forms, ranging from dark red to light red, to pink, light pink and white will be formed; intensity of color will depend on the relative number of genes and the forms in which they occur. This kind of inheritance is called **quantitative inheritance** or **multiple factor inheritance,** and the many genes that contribute to such hereditary expression are called **polygenes**. This is the explanation for most cases of **continuous variation** as observed in many characters in plants.

The broad effect that genes may have can also be illustrated through study of the phenomenon known as **pleiotropy**, the capacity of a single gene to affect more than one character. Some genes af-

Figure 19–10 Quantitative inheritance in tobacco corolla tube variation as a result of multiple factor inheritance. The parents are at 1 and 2, the F_1 is at 3, and the F_2 generation is represented by numbers 4–9 (From East, E. M. *Botanical Gazette 55*: 177–188, 1913).

fect enzymes that are important to many characters of the organism. For instance, any change in a gene that provides an enzyme involved in lignin synthesis may also cause a large number of other effects on the plant.

Cytoplasmic Inheritance

In addition to those characters known to be transmitted by chromosomes, a few are known to be passed from one generation to the next through the cytoplasm. Cytoplasmic characters are generally maternal in origin, since the egg carries much more cytoplasm than the sperm.

One of the best documented instances of cytoplasmic inheritance in plants is that involving the character of the plastids of the primrose. A yellow-leafed form of this plant contains less than the normal amount of chlorophyll. Pollen from this plant does not transmit the yellow-leaf character to the offspring; however, seeds from the yellow-leaf plant will produce yellow-leaf offspring regardless of the color of the parent contributing the pollen.

A similar example of cytoplasmic inheritance occurs in the four o'clock plant. Three forms of the plant are known: normal green, variegated (i.e., having both green and non-green tissue in the same leaf), and yellow. The plastids of the yellow form are without chlorophyll, while the chloroplasts of the green form have the normal amount of chlorophyll. Cells in the leaves of the variegated form have either normal or yellow plastids. Occasionally a single plant will produce branches that exhibit all three forms. All the offspring of crosses between the different forms are phenotypically identical to the egg-producing (seed) parent, except when the seed parent is of the variegated form. The pollen has no effect on the leaf color pattern of the offspring. In crosses involving the variegated seed parent, the offspring will be of all three forms in an irregular ratio. The eggs produced by the variegated parent have either, or both, normal chloroplasts or yellow plastids, because these are distributed unequally in the cytoplasmic divisions preceding egg formation, since the segregation of cytoplasmic organelles in mitosis is random.

Cytoplasmic genetic mechanisms have been reported also in algae and fungi, as well as in various animal groups, and it can be generally assumed that they are of widespread occurrence.

The Chemical Basis of Inheritance

It was noted in Chapter 4 that the most important constituent of the chromatin of the plant cell nucleus was nucleic acid. Nucleic acid occurs in two forms—deoxyribose nucleic acid (DNA), and ribose nucleic acid (RNA). DNA is more abundant in the nucleus, and RNA is more abundant in the cytoplasm. The existence of nucleic acid has been known for over 100 years, but not until the 1930's was it suspected that DNA was genetically the most important part of the chromosome. In 1953 James D. Watson and F. H. C. Crick assembled all information available and produced the first structural model of DNA. Watson and Crick showed that the DNA molecule was a double helix or coil with regular cross-connections between the two spiral members (see Figure 19–11). Each member consists of nucleotides with the phosphate-ribose connection making the main strand for each helix; the associated nitrogenous bases make the cross-connections (by hydrogen bonds). These bases are the **purines**: **adenine** (**a**), and **guanine** (**g**), and the **pyrimidines**: **cytosine** (**c**), **thymine** (**t**), and in RNA **uracil** (**u**) (see also Chapters 3 and 4).

DNA is self-replicating; normally each double helical strand forms another double helical strand identical to the first. The chemical replication is not absolutely infallible, and mistakes occur. There are genes known that can cause the rate of such errors to increase.

If an error in DNA replication occurs, the error is repeated in later replications of the new strand of DNA. The DNA has been modified, and a mutation is said to have occurred. For instance, the insertion or deletion of a single nucleotide would change the coding for an amino acid and thereby affect the coding from the point of insertion (or deletion) to the end of the strand; this would, in turn, cause the DNA to code for a different protein. Thus, a single nucleotide could have a great effect on the coding. Probably any

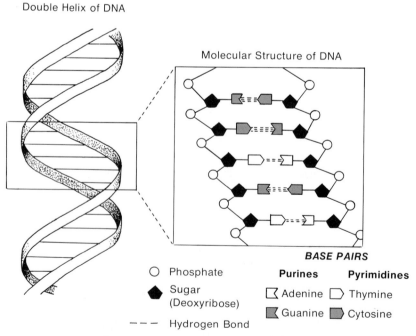

Double Helix of DNA

Molecular Structure of DNA

BASE PAIRS

○ Phosphate

◆ Sugar (Deoxyribose)

– – – Hydrogen Bond

Purines   **Pyrimidines**

Adenine   Thymine

Guanine   Cytosine

Figure 19–11   Double helix structure of a portion of a DNA molecule (Redrawn from Gerking, S. D. *Biological Systems*, Second Edition).

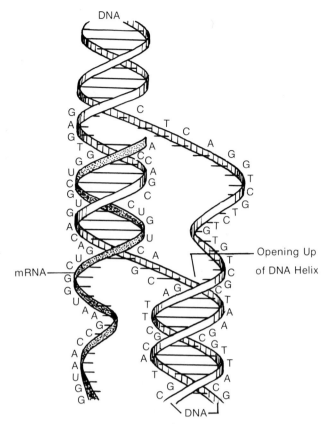

Figure 19-12 Synthesis of messenger RNA. Messenger RNA is synthesized as a copy of one strand of the double helix of DNA.

new protein originating in this way would either interfere with the function of other proteins or would have no effect. This is true in most cases; rare is the mutation that confers an advantage to the organism. Nucleotide substitution would more likely have some adaptive value for the organism than would a mutation caused by insertion or deletion of nucleotides. Substitution would have a less drastic effect on the coding. Although the probability that a given mutation may be beneficial to the organism is very low, some mutations do have the potential of becoming adaptive and hence beneficial to the plant. Substitution mutations appear to make up the principal raw material from which the evolutionary process is built.

In biochemical terms, then, what is a gene? A gene is part of a molecule of DNA, and it functions by controlling the production of a specific protein molecule. The protein may function as structural material, or it may be an enzyme. The character of cells and organs, whether on the level of structure, function, or form, is the result of a very complex series of enzymatic interactions. Each character is influenced by a number of genes and each gene affects a number of characters.

513

Proteins are linear polymers of amino acids held together by peptide bonds. A polymer is a chemical compound made up of a long chain of repeating units. A peptide bond is a chemical linkage between carbon and nitrogen atoms. Proteins can differ from one another structurally in numerous ways, depending upon the number, kind, and sequence of amino acids in the chain. There are 20 different protein amino acids. These may be joined together in any sequence so that the number of combinations theoretically possible is beyond comprehension. The specifications for combinations that will produce specific protein molecules with specific properties are all encoded in the sequence of nucleotides of the DNA molecule. The effect of an insertion or deletion of a nucleotide is the production of a protein molecule having properties different from those of the protein originally encoded. The alteration of the protein molecule would then be observable as a mutation of the phenotype.

The nucleotide sequence in DNA is not converted directly into an amino acid sequence; rather, the DNA molecule controls the synthesis of **messenger RNA (mRNA)**, which functions as the intermediary. The synthesis of mRNA is similar to that for DNA. The two chains that make up the DNA molecule separate, and on one of these strands the ribonucleotides are synthesized with the sequence ordered by the way in which the bases of mRNA become paired with those of the DNA. The DNA strand thereby functions as a template and the ribonucleotides are linked into a chain; the RNA strand then separates from the DNA strand.

The sequence of nucleotides of the mRNA strand determines the placement of specific amino acids in a protein molecule. This **transcription** of information from DNA to mRNA takes place typically in the cell nucleus, although protein synthesis occurs in the ribosomes associated with the endoplasmic reticulum (the rough endoplasmic reticulum) or in the free ribosomes of the cytoplasm. It is necessary, then, that the mRNA move from the nucleus to the ribosomes through the nuclear membrane pores. When the mRNA becomes attached to the ribosomes, the synthesis of proteins begins. The amino acids present in the cytoplasm are transferred to the ribosomes and then joined together to form a polypeptide chain. In this part of protein synthesis, molecules of **transfer RNA (tRNA)** transport amino acids to mRNA, which positions them and, with the aid of enzymes, joins them by means of peptide bonds to form a polypeptide.

When growth of the polypeptide chain is complete, it dissociates as a protein from the ribosome and mRNA complex. These steps, in which the arrangement of a code of nucleotides of mRNA directs the formation of a specific protein molecule, are called **translation**. In summary, it can be said that the chemical basis of gene action involves the transcription of DNA into the message of mRNA in the nucleus, followed by translation in the cytoplasm of the mRNA message into a particular protein.

With this understanding of the chemical basis of heredity, we can now redefine the gene as that part of the DNA helix that controls

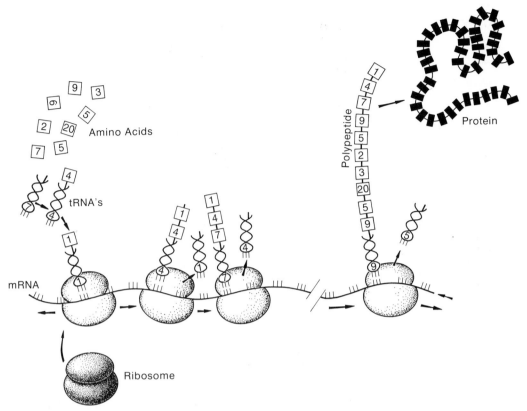

Figure 19–13 Translation of a genetic message into protein by mRNA and ribosomes, utilizing amino acids and tRNA.

the synthesis of a specific type of mRNA. The control by genes of the kinds of mRNA determines the kinds of polypeptide chains that are formed to make up the proteins of the cell. The particular sequence of bases in mRNA, occurs always in threes, and is a code for a particular amino acid. For instance, in 1961 it was discovered that a uracil-uracil-uracil sequence (abbreviated UUU) was the coding (or **codon**) for the amino acid phenylalanine; eventually, it was possible to work out the base sequences for all the amino acids. Later it was shown that a particular amino acid can be controlled by several different codons; the amino acid valine, for example, has four codons: GUU, GUA, GUC, and GUG.

We might visualize mRNA as having a comb-like structure. The ribose and phosphate units could be said to compare to the back of the comb, while the bases compare to the teeth. Starting at the end of the comb, each successive set of three teeth (bases) make up a particular codon, which controls the synthesis of a specific amino acid. The amino acids are associated into polypeptide chains in the sequence determined by mRNA and tRNA. The mRNA does the encoding, while the tRNA provides the appropriate amino acids one by

515

AMINO ACID	FIRST TWO BASES	THIRD BASE
Alanine	GC	A, C, G, or U
Arginine	AG	A or G
	CG	A, C, G, or U
Asparagine	AA	C or U
Aspartic acid	GA	C or U
Cysteine	UG	C or U
Glutamine	CA	A or G
Glutamic acid	GA	A or G
Glycine	GG	A, C, G, or U
Histidine	CA	C or U
Isoleucine	AU	A, C, or U
Leucine	CU	A, C, G, or U
	UU	A or G
Lysine	AA	A or G
Methionine	AU	G
Phenylalanine	UU	C or U
Proline	CC	A, C, G, or U
Serine	AG	C or U
	UC	A, C, G, or U
Threonine	AC	A, C, G, or U
Tryptophan	UG	G
Tyrosine	UA	C or U
Valine	GU	A, C, G, or U
Terminus	UA	A or G
	UG	A

Figure 19–14 The RNA genetic code.

one. The ribosomes control the attachment of amino acids on the elongating polypeptide chain.

Regulation of Gene Expression

The characteristics of a plant are determined by the DNA present in the genes and acting through enzymes and other proteins. The synthesis of particular substances, such as suberin or lignin, depends on the activities of specific genes. This would appear to mean that different cells have different kinds of DNA since certain parts of the plant often contain special substances, but this is not the case. Because mitosis reproduces and sorts out the chromosomes very precisely, each new cell receives an identical set of chromosomes and genes; as a result, all of the nuclei in a plant contain identical DNA, with but minor exceptions. It is necessary, then, to assume that during the development of the individual some genes are "turned on" to transcribe their information, while others are "turned off," or **repressed**. It is the manner in which transcription and repression are controlled that determines what kind of cell is formed and how it functions.

An explanation of a mechanism for **gene repression** was developed by two Frenchmen, François Jacob and Jacques Monod, working at the Pasteur Institute in Paris with the colon bacterium, *Escherichia coli*. They received the Nobel Prize in 1965 for this work. In *E. coli,* several genes are responsible for the synthesis of a team of enzymes controlling the entry of the sugar, lactose, into the cell, and its subsequent breakdown. In the Jacob-Monod model, this team of genes, called **structural genes**, is associated with a controlling, non-structural gene called the **operator gene**. The latter, together with the team of structural genes, make up a functional genetic unit known as the **operon**.

What keeps the operon from making enzymes continuously, whether lactose is present or not? Another gene, the **repressor gene**, produces a repressor protein that binds to the operator gene and inactivates or represses the operon (Fig. 19–15). However, if lactose is present it binds to the repressor protein, preventing it from binding to the operator gene. Thus, the operon is not repressed and the enzymes for lactose breakdown will be synthesized, but only when lactose is present.

The DNA in eukaryotes is arranged differently from that in bacteria (see Chapter 4); therefore, the Jacob-Monod model, which is based on the bacterial cell, may not be applicable. But it is thought that the inactivation (or repression), as well as the activation (or **derepression**), of genes in eukaryotes is to an extent analogous to that in prokaryotes. It is known that gene repressor proteins (or **histones**), are present on certain regions of chromosomes and repress the genes of those regions. The differentiation of cells in eukaryotes

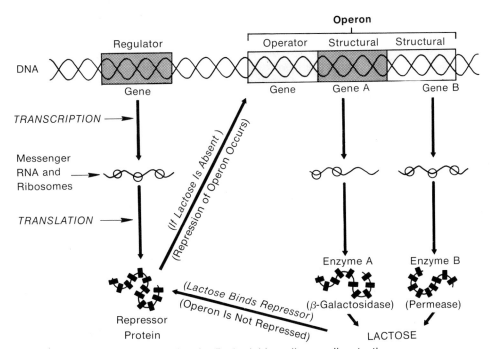

Figure 19–15 The regulation of gene action in *Escherichia coli* according to the Jacob-Monod hypothesis.

probably results from the repression of different sets of genes in different cells.

Cytogenetics

The study of chromosomes in relation to reproduction and evolution is called **cytogenetics**. Breeding behavior in plants often is associated with structural and numerical changes in chromosomes. Such changes are easily observed in young anthers. Microspore mother cells may be squeezed out onto a microscope slide and stained in a drop of carmine dye. Application of a cover slip flattens the cells, and the dyed chromosomes then may be observed with a microscope. Such preparations, known as *squashes,* enable botanists not only to count the chromosomes but also to observe their form and even to study their behavior during meiosis.

One of the more interesting phenomena studied in plant cytogenetics is polyploidy. Among many plant species are individuals and populations exhibiting varying chromosome numbers. For example, the dock plant, *Rumex,* has a base chromosome number of 10. Such base numbers are called **genomes** (abbreviated X). Therefore, in docks the base number is $X = 10$. Among the docks are diploid plants ($2X = 20$), tetraploid plants ($4X = 40$), and even higher numbers up to 200 ($20X$) have been found in this species. Plants having such doubling and redoubling of the basic chromosome number are known as **autopolyploids** or **autoploids**. Although autoploids occasionally occur in nature, as in the docks, they also are produced by plant breeders. This is done by briefly exposing the shoot apex to **colchicine**, a product of the autumn crocus, *Colchicum autumnale.* Colchicine has the property of being able to arrest the formation of the mitotic spindle while still permitting chromosomal replication, so that the chromosome number per cell doubles. If the plant is carefully rinsed free of colchicine, subsequent mitotic divisions will be normal but all of the new cells will be $4X$, or tetraploid. Tetraploids often are larger than the parental diploid type and, in some cases, are of value in horticulture and agriculture. For example, large snapdragons (called by the trivial name *tetrasnaps*) are popular and are sold by many seed companies. Tetraploid tomatoes bearing large fruit also have been produced by the process described above. Despite these successes, autoploids usually are of limited economic value, because chromosome synapsis and segregation in meiosis tend to be irregular and thus result in an uneven distribution of homologous chromosomes in the gametes. Such scrambled assortments of chromosomes produce reproductive abnormalities and sterility. Actually, most natural autoploids are completely sterile and are propagated solely by vegetative means.

Another type of polyploid, the **allopolyploid** or **alloploid,** is common in nature and is able to reproduce with few of the difficulties found in autoploids. Let us consider two related plants, perhaps of different genera but of the same family. Sometimes such plants are capable of cross-pollination and produce hybrids, but in nearly all cases these are sterile, because the chromosomes of the two parental genomes are so different that during flowering of the hybrid they remain unpaired throughout meiosis and, as a result, only sterile seeds are produced. However, if chromosome doubling occurs in the hybrid prior to flowering, each genome is duplicated and normal meiosis occurs. A fertile plant of this type is called an allopolyploid, or alloploid. Many natural alloploids are known and a few have been produced artificially. A well-known artificial alloploid was produced

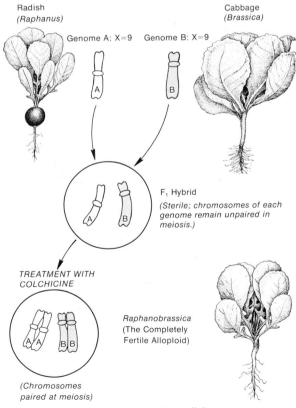

Radish
(*Raphanus*)

Genome A: X=9

Genome B: X=9

Cabbage
(*Brassica*)

F₁ Hybrid
(*Sterile; chromosomes of each genome remain unpaired in meiosis.*)

TREATMENT WITH COLCHICINE

Raphanobrassica
(The Completely Fertile Alloploid)

(*Chromosomes paired at meiosis*)

Figure 19–16 Alloploidy in the artificial intergeneric cross between the radish (*Raphanus*) and the cabbage (*Brassica*), represented diagrammatically.

by breeding the radish *(Raphanus)* with the cabbage *(Brassica).* The nine radish chromosomes (represented by R) are quite different from the nine cabbage chromosomes (B), and the radish-cabbage hybrid (RB) was found to be sterile. However, when the hybrid was treated with colchicine to double its chromosomes, a perfectly fertile plant (RRBB) was produced. This new plant, named *Raphanobrassica,* showed similarities to both parents in its appearance but possessed none of their desirable characters.

A number of natural alloploids are of considerable economic value. For example, wheat has three genomes (A, B, and D) and each has been traced to different wild relatives. Chromosomal doubling that occurred long ago resulted in domestic wheat having AABBDD genomes and embodying desirable characters of all three wild ancestors. Domestic cotton is a fertile alloploid originating from

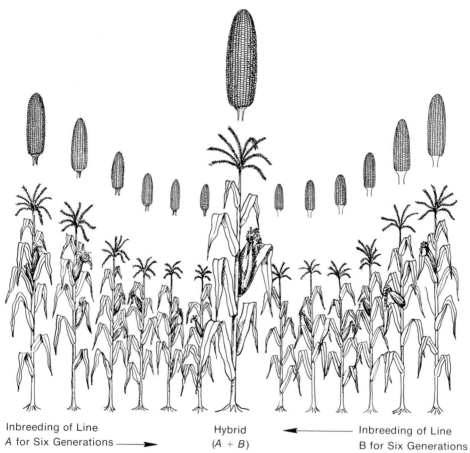

| Inbreeding of Line
A for Six Generations ──────▶ | Hybrid
(A + B) | ◀────── Inbreeding of Line
B for Six Generations |

Figure 19–17 Inbred and hybrid maize *(Zea mays).* The production of a hybrid from two inbred lines is illustrated (Redrawn with modifications from Baker, H. G. *Plants and Civilization,* Second Edition. Belmont, Calif., Wadsworth Publishing Co., Inc., 1970).

two wild cotton species, and domestic tobacco is of similar ancestry.

Many other kinds of chromosomal behavior are studied by cytogeneticists, including translocations (exchange of portions of non-homologous chromosomes) and inversions (reversal of a part of a chromosome), among others. All of these, as well as autoploidy and alloploidy, are known to be involved in plant evolution.

Plant Breeding and Improvement

The rediscovery of Mendel's laws and the development of the science of genetics has had a most profound effect on plant breeding. In 1876, Darwin summed up the knowledge of heredity at the time as far as plant breeding was concerned in his book, *The Effects of Cross- and Self-Fertilization in the Vegetable Kingdom.* The deleterious effect of self-fertilization on animals and plants was understood, but it was not until the early twentieth century that the application of breeding experimentation on plant improvement could be practiced on a wide scale. Hybridizations, such as those of E. M. East and Donald Jones, demonstrated that maize could be inbred for six or seven generations until finally there was no further reduction in vigor and size. When these highly inbred plants were hybridized with other inbred varieties, very vigorous, large-sized, large fruited plants were formed. This led to the origin of hybrid maize and resulted in the most significant improvement in American agriculture at that time. The term **heterosis** was used to describe the return of full size and vigor that was obtained after crossing inbred lines that had reached the limits of decrease in size. The heterosis concept has been the direct result of our knowledge of plant heredity.

In addition to maize, every other valuable crop in the Western Hemisphere has been improved by careful breeding and selection experiments based on the laws of heredity. New varieties of wheat with greatly increased resistance to cold and to pathogens have been developed by plant breeders working in the agricultural experiment stations of the United States and Canada. These laboratories, in cooperation with their respective governmental research agencies, are continually producing new crop varieties with higher productivity, greater resistance to pathogens and other parasites, and other desirable qualities. Thus far, the spectacular advances in plant breeding have been in temperate agriculture; results in tropical agriculture have not been so successful.

SUMMARY

Although the basic laws of inheritance were discovered over 100 years ago, the scientific community at that time was not ready to accept or to understand their significance. Gregor Mendel fortunately had worked with a plant that enabled him to derive the fundamental rules governing the inheritance of traits by offspring from their parents in the classical monohybrid and dihybrid ratios. Cytological discoveries in the latter half of the nineteenth century led to an understanding of the physical basis of the genetic mechanism. The relationship between meiosis and inheritance began to be suspected, and when Mendel's paper was rediscovered in 1900, many facts began to be understood for the first time. The apparent exceptions to Mendel's laws were shown to be due to incomplete dominance, quantitative inheritance, and linkage. Mutation was shown to be the chief cause of variation and the origin of alleles. In recent years the study of the chemical basis of inheritance has been the chief interest of many geneticists. Many practical applications have been made from the knowledge of genetics, including crop improvement, especially with the production of new hybrid varieties of such plants as maize (*Zea mays*).

DISCUSSION QUESTIONS

1. What were the results in Mendel's hybridization experiments that led him to formulate his *law of uniformity* and *law of independent assortment*?
2. Mendel was not able to verify his results in peas when he experimented with other plants such as hawkweed. What do we know about garden peas that made it possible for Mendel to produce such clear interpretations of the monohybrid and dihybrid crosses?
3. Explain clearly the difference in chromosome behavior in meiosis as compared to mitosis. What are homologous chromosomes?
4. What is the cytological basis of Mendel's *law of independent assortment*?
5. Explain the relationship between linkage group and chromosome. What cytological event can bring about a change in a particular linkage group?
6. What other theories had been proposed, prior to the rediscovery of Mendel's paper, to account for variation and inheritance?
7. Explain the meaning of the term allele. How do alleles originate in organisms?
8. We now know there are seven pairs of chromosomes in garden peas. If Mendel had worked with more than seven pairs of characters, would he have been able to draw the same conclusions from his experiments as he originally reported? Why or why not?
9. What is the chemical basis of inheritance? Which component of the chromosome is the bearer of genetic information?
10. How does the inheritance of characters controlled by polygenes differ from those controlled by a single factor? Give an example of what is called quantitative inheritance.
11. Describe how DNA operates in the synthesis of proteins from amino acids. Explain the Jacob-Monod hypothesis of gene regulation.
12. Heterosis has been applied to the results of crossing inbred lines of plants. In maize, what results and what practical applications have been made of this knowledge?

SUPPLEMENTAL READING

Beadle, G., and M. Beadle. *The Language of Life.* Garden City, New York: Doubleday and Co., Inc., 1966.

Burns, G. W. *The Science of Genetics.* New York: The Macmillan Co., 1972.

Crick, F. H. C. On the Genetic Code. *Science 139*: 461–464, 1963.

Iltis, H. *Life of Mendel.* New York: W. W. Norton and Co., 1932.

Peters, J. A. (ed.) *Classic Papers in Genetics.* Englewood Cliffs, N. J.: Prentice-Hall. 1959.

Ravin, A. W. *The Evolution of Genetics.* New York: Academic Press, Inc., 1965.

Stebbins, G. L. From Gene to Character in Higher Plants. *American Scientist 53*:104–126, 1965.

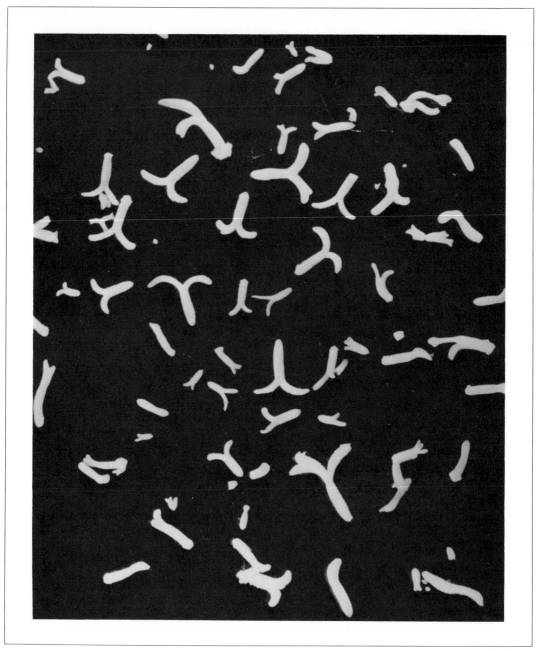

Embryoids formed in a tissue culture of cells of carraway (*Carum carvi*) (From Ammirato, P. V. *Botanical Gazette, 135*:328–337, 1974).

Chapter 20

The Control of Plant Growth and Development

PLANT HORMONES • **AUXINS** • **ETHYLENE** • **GIBBERELLINS** • **CYTOKININS** •
ABSCISIC ACID • **GROWTH RETARDANTS** • **HERBICIDES AND DEFOLIANTS** •
PHOTOPERIODISM • **PLANT TISSUE AND ORGAN CULTURE** • **PROTOPLAST**
CULTURES • **SUMMARY**

There has always been intense interest among botanists regarding methods for controlling plant growth. The beginning of our modern view of what makes plants behave the way they do can be traced to some interesting experiments by Charles Darwin. The observation that the first leaf, or coleoptile, of young grass seedlings bent toward a light source excited his curiosity. It has been noted in Chapter 18 that growth curvatures of this kind are called phototropisms, that is, responses caused by exposure to unilateral light. Microscopic examination shows that this bending of the coleoptile is due to greater cell elongation on the shaded side of the plant than on the side in direct light. Darwin wondered what part of the coleoptile perceived light. He found that if a cylinder of tinfoil were placed about the lower parts of the coleoptile so that its tip remained exposed to light, the coleoptile bent toward the light as it elongated; however, if the tip of the coleoptile were covered with a small tinfoil cap, no curvature took place. Therefore, he concluded that the tip region of the coleoptile is most sensitive to light in the phototropic response. This can be shown also by cutting off the coleoptile tip. When this is done, the coleoptile no longer is phototropic.

PLANT HORMONES

If we had been discussing animals, we might be inclined to believe that some kind of nervous response is involved in tropisms

---

Whilst observing the accuracy with which the cotyledon of this plant became bent toward the light of a small lamp, we were impressed with the idea that the uppermost part determined the direction of the curvature of the lower part.

CHARLES R. DARWIN: *The Power of Movement in Plants.*

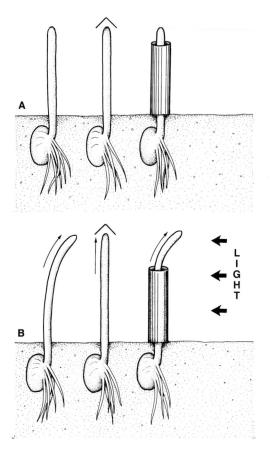

Figure 20–1 Experiments of Darwin, in which the tip of the grass coleoptile was shown to be the light receptor in the phototropic growth response (Redrawn from Gerking, S. D. *Biological Systems*, Second Edition, Philadelphia, W. B. Saunders Co., 1974).

and other plant movements. For many years after Darwin's experiments with grass coleoptiles, it was not clear what made plants move. Slowly the suspicion grew that tropisms were caused by chemical growth substances or hormones rather than by nerve action.

Most of the early experiments dealing with growth movements were done with oat seedlings, which grow rapidly and produce well-developed and uniform coleoptiles. The coleoptile is present in embryos and seedlings of all grasses and is a modified leaf enclosing the first true leaves and protecting them during the emergence of the shoot from the soil. It is a short-lived organ, and its growth during germination occurs mainly by elongation of cells already present in the embryo plant.

Some time after Darwin's discovery, Peter Boysen-Jensen in Denmark and A. Paal in Hungary were able to confirm Darwin's observations. From 1910 to 1913, Boysen-Jensen performed experiments showing that, while the ability for a phototropic response was lost by amputation of the coleoptile tip, it could be recovered when the tip was replaced on the stump (or when the tip was replaced but with a thin block of gelatin inserted between it and the stump—but not with the interposition of a thin wafer of mica instead of gelatin). This suggested that a chemical, or possibly an electric current, was produced in the coleoptile tip and diffused into adjacent tissues where a response was induced. Paal, in experiments from 1914 to 1919, showed that recovery of the response did not occur when the tip was separated from the stump by cocoa butter, mica, or platinum foil. These early workers concluded, therefore, that the substance was water soluble (because it diffused through gelatin), but not fat soluble (because it did not pass through cocoa butter). Had it been an electrical phenomenon, it should have been transmitted across

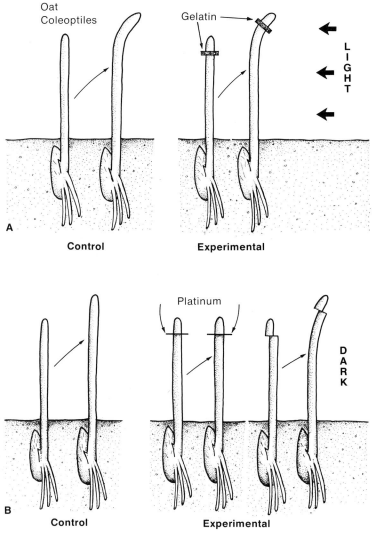

Figure 20–2 Experiments of Boysen-Jensen (A), and Paal (B).

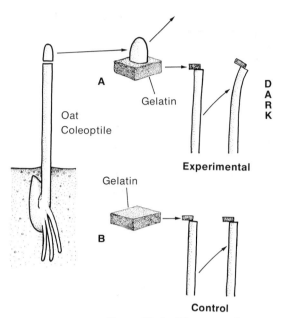

Figure 20-3 Diagrammatic summary of Went's experiment with the oat coleoptile.

the platinum foil. Paal also showed that in either dark or uniform light if the coleoptile tip was placed on one side of the stump, bending occurred away from that side.

In the late 1920's a young plant physiologist named Fritz Went was working in his laboratory in Utrecht, Netherlands. As a result of discussions with fellow researchers, he became interested in the controversy whether phototropisms and geotropisms could best be explained by a nerve-electrical theory or by a chemical growth substance theory. From earlier work by Boysen-Jensen and Paal, Went was persuaded that a growth substance was involved rather than an electric current.

In a key experiment, he cut the tip from an oat coleoptile and placed the severed tip on a small block of gelatin for one hour. He then discarded the tip and placed the gelatin on one side of the coleoptile stump. The experiment was carried out in the absence of light or in very weak red light, to which coleoptiles are insensitive. When the gelatin block was placed on one side of the coleoptile, the structure began to bend as if it were exposed to normal light coming from the side opposite the gelatin block. The cells immediately beneath the gelatin began to elongate more rapidly than those on the opposite side, and curvature of the coleoptile resulted. This experiment demonstrated conclusively that a chemical substance had been absorbed by the gelatin from the severed tip, and it was this substance that was responsible for the bending movement; there was no electrical stimulus.

Auxins

Went named the substance absorbed by the gelatin **auxin**, a term now applied to any substance that is active in making oat coleoptiles bend. The significance of Went's experiments was that it was the first indisputable proof that plant growth substances existed, and it led directly to our modern concepts of plant hormones.

Later studies have indicated that the tropism resulting from unilateral exposure to light does not involve the destruction of an auxin in the illuminated side of a coleoptile or stem; rather, the exposure to light causes a lateral displacement from the side exposed to light to the side in darkness. The amount of cellular elongation occurring in plants is proportional to the concentration of auxin; therefore, the migration of auxin to the shaded side results in greater cell elongation, whereas the lowered concentration on the light side produces a lesser cellular elongation.

Geotropisms also can be explained by auxin distribution. When a plant is placed on its side, auxin accumulates in the cells on its lower side. In stems, this increased concentration produces a proportionately greater cellular elongation on the under side and the stem grows upward. Roots, however, are many times more sensitive to auxin than are stems. The increased auxin concentration on the lower side of a root is sufficient to inhibit cellular elongation, while the reduced concentration on the upper side stimulates elongation; thus, the root grows downward. Note that in both cases the downward migration of auxin is in response to the same stimulus, gravity.

In 1934 a German botanist, F. Kögl, found that an organic molecule, **3-indoleacetic acid**, acted as an auxin when applied to plants. Later, Kögl and an American, Kenneth Thimann, found that this molecule, commonly termed **IAA,** was present in plants, and was a naturally occurring auxin.

IAA has been found to participate in a number of plant growth responses. It is involved in the setting of fruit, and can bring about the development of unpollinated flowers so that seedless fruits are formed. When leaf blades are cut off so that only petioles attached to stems remain, an abscission layer (a layer of thin-walled cells) is formed at the petiolar base and in a few days the petiole falls off. However, if IAA is applied to the petiole stump, an abscission layer does not form and the petioles remain attached. As long as the leaves are green and healthy, IAA is present naturally within them, and thus suppresses the development of abscission layers. Although other factors also control abscission, IAA is a principal factor. Fruits may absciss before they are fully developed or ripe; this is known as **early drop**, and is a problem in orchards. It has been found that early drop can be controlled by spraying the developing fruits with an auxin. IAA is also involved in the process of cell division, in the differentiation of xylem cells, in the suppression of lateral buds in stems having apical bud dominance, and in a number of other natural processes.

Synthetic auxins have been produced and found to have proper-

Figure 20-4 Formation of adventitious roots through use of indolebutyric acid (IBA). *Left*, Untreated control. *Right*, Holly cutting treated with IBA (USDA photo).

ties similar to IAA, and in some cases to be much more active than IAA. Among these are **indolebutyric acid** (IBA), used to stimulate root development in cuttings; and **alpha naphthalene acetic acid** (NAA), used to control fruit set in unpollinated flowers such as hothouse tomatoes, to control early fruit drop, and to regulate time of flowering in the pineapple. Other synthetic auxins **(2,4,-dichlorophenoxyacetic acid, 2,4-D,** and **2,4,5-trichlorophenoxyacetic acid, 2,4,5-T)** are used as herbicides and defoliants. There is no question that auxins have become major factors in agriculture, horticulture, and plant research in all countries of the world.

Ethylene

"One rotten apple will spoil a barrel" states an old proverb. This is literally true, not only of apples but of other kinds of fruit, for over-ripe fruits produce a gaseous product capable of inducing over-ripeness in adjacent fruits. The story of the discovery of the action of this gas and of its identity is one of many fascinating accounts of progress in botanical research.

When manufactured coal gas, known as "city gas", was used for illuminating purposes, it was found to have some unusual effects on plant growth. Gas leaks in the vicinity of plants produced atypical development. For example, leaking street lamps sometimes caused unequal lateral expansion of stem cells and the loss of geotropisms in adjacent shade trees so that weird-looking forms resulted. Unripened fruit, such as green bananas in warehouses, ripened much too rapidly when exposed to leaking illuminating gas, and other responses—such as premature flowering in certain plants—have been noted. The component in illuminating gas producing these effects is a simple organic molecule, **ethylene** (C_2H_4). Now it is recognized that ethylene also is a natural plant product and often acts as a plant hormone. Ripe fruits produce ethylene, which in turn induces ripening and more ethylene in adjacent fruits. Such actions of ethylene appear to be related to IAA, for it has been found that IAA stimulates ethylene synthesis in plants, and many auxin effects can be duplicated by exposing plants to ethylene.

The most important commercial use of ethylene is in the control of fruit ripening. Bananas shipped from South America normally are picked green, stored in ships for transport to North America, and treated with ethylene gas while in transit in order to bring them to the precise stage of ripening for the market. Conversely, premature ripening in stored fruit can be suppressed to a degree by careful

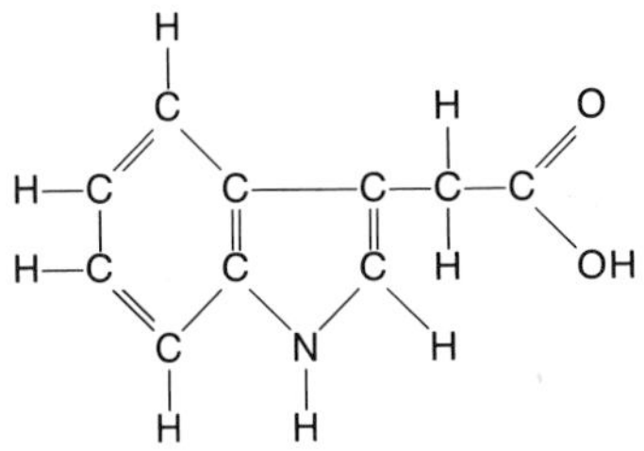

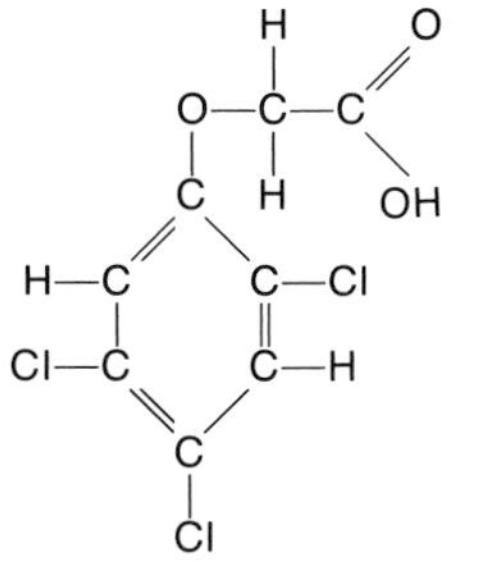

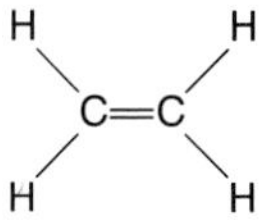

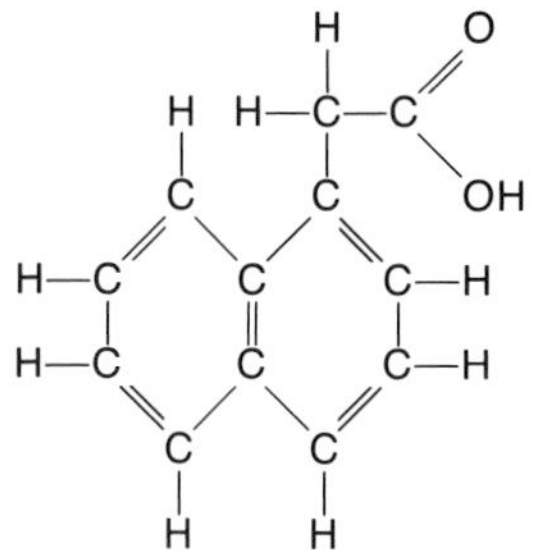

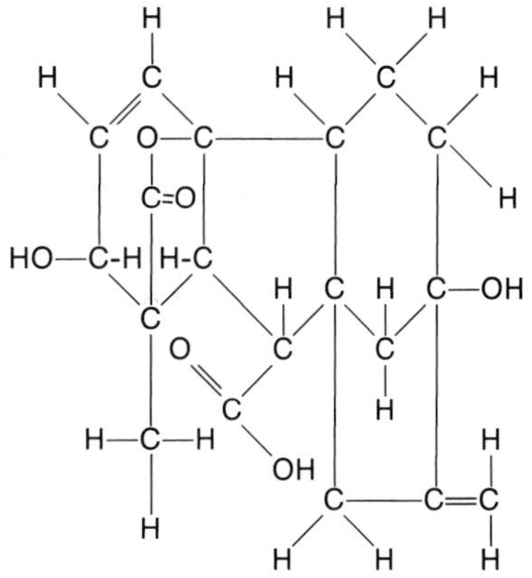

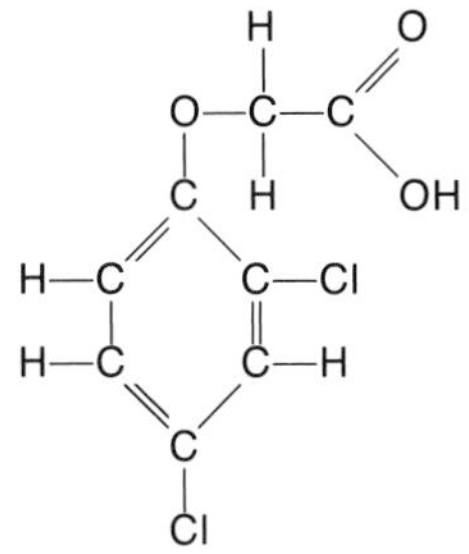

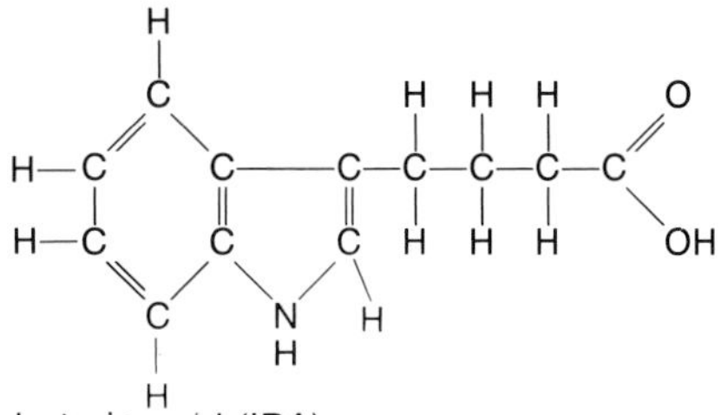

Figure 20–5 Structural formulas of some commonly dealt-with plant hormones.

531

ventilation of the warehouse to remove the ethylene formed by the fruit, or by exposure of the fruit to carbon dioxide, which counteracts the effect of ethylene.

Gibberellins

For a number of years it was thought that the only naturally occurring plant hormones, or **phytohormones**, were auxins. Then Japanese botanists isolated another class of phytohormones from a fungus infection of rice plants. Rice farmers in Japan were familiar with a disease of rice they termed **baka nae** (literally "foolish seedling"), in which the plants became very tall and spindly. Actually, work on this disease began about the time Went and others were experimenting with auxin, but this was generally unnoticed by botanists in other countries. Dr. E. Kurasawa, a prominent Japanese botanist, found that extracts of the fungus causing baka nae, *Gibberella fujikuroi*, when applied to healthy plants, brought about the excessive elongation characteristic of diseased plants. Later (in 1935), a biochemist, Dr. T. Yabuta, crystallized this substance and named it **gibberellin**. Perhaps because of World War II, it was not until 1950 that interest in gibberellin became widespread in Europe and the Americas. Now it is recognized that there are at least 37 different gibberellins occurring naturally in plants, and a variety of important plant responses have been found to be regulated by such gibberellins.

In the study of plant genetics, we have become familiar with a type of dwarfing first discovered in peas by Gregor Mendel, and controlled by a recessive gene. Dwarf pea plants may be only one-tenth as tall as their normal counterparts; however, if such dwarfs are treated with one of the gibberellins, such as **gibberellic acid**, the dwarf plants become as tall as normal plants. Other genetic dwarfs respond in the same way. This has led to the conclusion that the mutant gene causing dwarfness does so either by controlling gibberellin production in the plant or by somehow blocking its action. The dwarf maize plant is a popular species for the study of gibberellin-induced elongation and is a sensitive indicator of gibberellin concentrations in natural plant extracts.

Gibberellins have also been shown to be able to induce flowering in certain plants that normally do not flower unless they are subjected to specific environmental conditions. For example, certain long-day plants (i.e., plants that require a relatively long daily light period to flower) will flower after treatment with gibberellic acid despite the absence of a long light period, and some biennials that normally require a low-temperature interval will begin to flower after treatment with gibberellic acid despite the absence of such a low-temperature interval. Gibberellic acid also can induce the germination of some types of dormant seeds (dormant lettuce seeds, for example).

One of the most interesting and widely studied examples of the involvement of gibberellins is in the germination of barley. In Chapter 11 it was stated how barley seeds are allowed to germinate

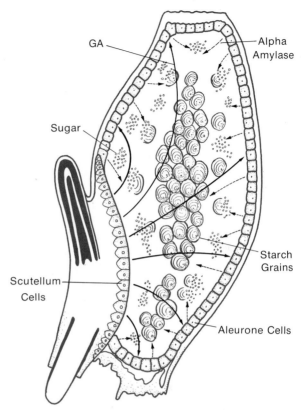

Figure 20-6 The action of gibberellic acid in the germination of barley grains (highly diagrammatic). Following water imbibition, cells of the scutellum (cotyledon) produce and secrete gibberellic acid (GA). The gibberellic acid, in turn, activates the synthesis of starch-digesting enzymes (amylases) in the living cells of the aleurone layer of the endosperm. The amylases are secreted into the starchy endosperm, where the hydrolysis of starch to sugar occurs.

for a few days and are then dried for use in brewing. This process, known as malting, is done so that germination enzymes will be produced, among these **alpha amylase**. Alpha amylase digests starch to its constituent glucose molecules, which then may be fermented by yeasts. It has been learned that when a barley embryo imbibes moisture and germination ensues, the embryo secretes gibberellins. These gibberellins diffuse into the endosperm of the grain and trigger the production of alpha amylase by a layer of cells known as the **aleurone**. This is a typical hormone action and has received the attention of physiologists and biochemists in many lands.

Cytokinins

Some years ago a plant physiologist at the University of Wisconsin, Dr. Folke Skoog, and a post-doctoral student, Dr. Carlos Miller, were studying the effects of nucleic acids on the growth of plant cells in culture on a nutrient medium (**tissue culture**). One sample of nucleic acid that had been stored on a shelf for a rather long time produced some dramatic growth responses, including stimulation of cell division and the production of shoots. The experiment was repeated using fresh nucleic acid; nothing happened. Upon examination of the older sample it was discovered that during storage a substance had been formed spontaneously that acted as a phytohormone. This substance was purified and named **kinetin**. Kinetin is not a natural plant product, but it closely resembles naturally occurring molecules that also act as cell division factors and development stimulators. One of these, called **zeatin**, is present in the kernels of *Zea mays.* These kinds of phytohormones now are called **cytokinins**. They are thought to be present in the cells and tissues of all higher plants. Cytokinins have been shown to promote leaf expansion in developing buds and to inhibit leaf senescence (leaf aging) by preventing chlorophyll decomposition and protein destruction. In this regard they may be considered as "juvenile hormones", because they serve to counteract normal aging processes. Cytokinins also interact with auxins in cell division and with gibberellins in regulating some aspects of dormancy and germination.

Abscisic Acid

In recent years, plant hormones have been discovered that have an inhibiting effect on plant growth and development. One of these is **abscisic acid,** originally found by Drs. Addicott and Smith at the University of California, Davis, in developing cotton fruits where it causes abscission, and in England by Drs. Wareing and Cornforth in the buds of birch trees where it is associated with bud dormancy. When abscisic acid is applied to an actively growing twig of a woody plant, elongation of internodes ceases, some of the leaves develop abscission layers and fall away, young developing leaves form scale leaves rather than foliage leaves, and the terminal bud becomes much less active. These are much the same responses seen in normal twigs toward the onset of winter, when they enter dormancy; therefore, abscisic acid may be described as a dormancy-inducing hormone. It is now known to have a number of different effects on plant growth, promoting flowering in some short day plants, inducing dormancy in barley grains, and counteracting the effect of gibberellin on the aleurone tissue. Recent studies by Dr. P. Ammirato at Rutgers University have shown that abscisic acid also controls the development of plant embryos in tissue cultures. It seems to have a normalizing effect on their growth. Whether its effects are due to its inhibitory influence on other plant regulators or whether it also acts directly as an embryo growth factor is not well understood at this time.

Growth Retardants

A number of synthetic molecules have been found to retard plant growth without otherwise affecting the health of plants. One of

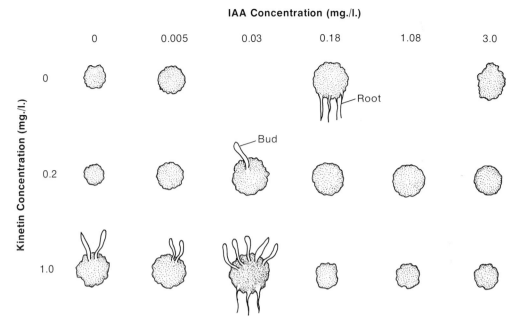

IAA Concentration (mg./l.)

Kinetin Concentration (mg./l.)

Figure 20-7 The effect of cytokinin on growth of tobacco cells. The combined (synergistic) effect of increasing auxin concentrations (top line) and increased cyto-kinin (left) is evident. High auxin levels with low cytokinin levels favor cell division, while medium concentrations of both auxin and cytokinin promote both cell division and production of adventitious buds and roots. (Redrawn from Skoog, F., and Miller, C. Chemical Regulation of Growth and Organ Formation in Plant Tissues Cultured *in Vitro. S. E. B. Symposium 11*:118–131, 1957).

these substances, **AMO-1618**, suppresses stem elongation. It was so named because it was the 1618th chemical tried in a series of exper-iments. Others, given such trivial names as **CCC** and **phosphon,** have similar effects. Growth retardants may act by blocking the ac-tion of gibberellins. One retardant, **tri-iodobenzoic acid (TIBA),** may act by blocking the movement of auxin in stems. Growth retardants are used commercially for the production of short-stemmed house plants (such as chrysanthemums) and the formation of bushy rather than tall crop plants. Soybeans may be treated with retardants to suppress stem growth; increased fruit production seems to accom-pany such suppression. Apparently, nutrients that ordinarily would go into stem growth are used instead in the growth of fruits and seeds.

Herbicides and Defoliants

Certain plant growth regulators may be quite toxic to plants in higher concentrations; 2,4-D is a well-known example of a growth

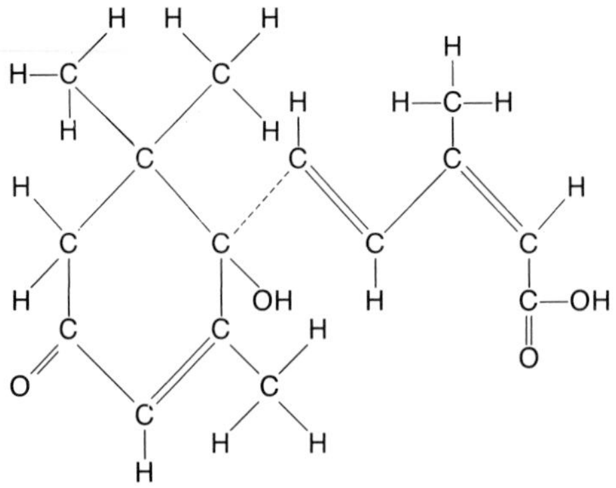

Abscisic acid (ABA)

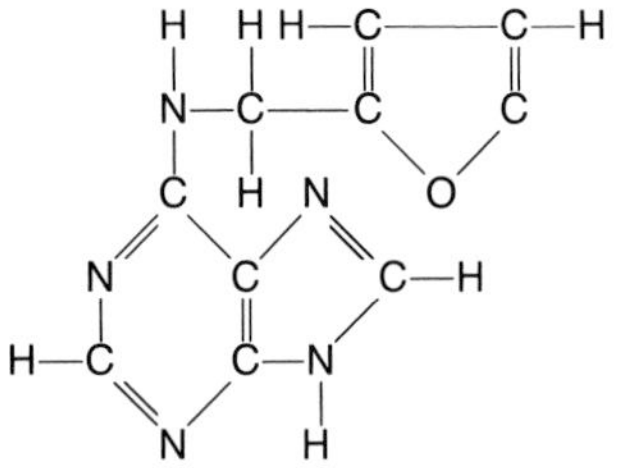

6-Furfurylamino purine
(KINETIN)

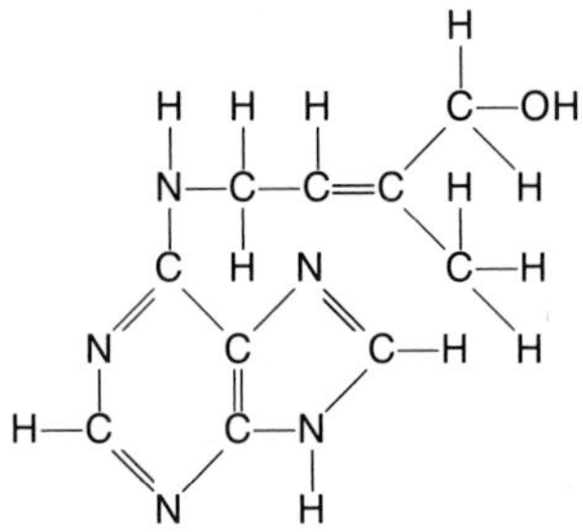

6-(4-Hydroxyl-3-methyl but-2-enyl)
amino purine (ZEATIN)

Figure 20–8   The structural formulas of kinetin, zeatin, and abscisic acid.

regulator with such potential. It is a growth promoter when present in extremely low concentrations, but higher concentrations of 2,4-D (0.05 to 0.1 per cent), are capable of killing most broad-leaved (dicotyledon) plants. Narrow-leaved plants (primarily grasses) are usually not affected. The biological explanation for this selective toxicity is unknown, but the fact that it does occur has made 2,4-D and related compounds substances of inestimable importance in agriculture and environmental plant relationships.

The use of 2,4-D as a lawn weed killer is widespread. Cereal crops are almost universally sprayed with 2,4-D or 2,4,5-T to control weeds, most of which are broad-leaved plants (note that all cereals are grasses). The use of such weed killers in fields has been called *chemical cultivation.*

Substances of this kind also may be used as defoliants. Cotton fields are sprayed with chemicals that kill the leaves and cause defoliation, leaving just the bare stems and the bolls; as a result, mechanical harvesting of the cotton is much easier. Another, considerably more sinister use of defoliants is their employment in warfare. The United States military forces in Viet Nam sprayed many square miles of tropical forests and rubber plantations with defoliants; in addition, use of defoliants was followed by application of napalm in order to burn the partially dried vegetation and thus per-

536

Figure 20–9 Tall, untreated chrysanthemums and short chysanthemums treated with AMO-1618, a growth retardant (USDA photo).

manently destroy large areas of vegetation. Many American botanists, including some who had contributed greatly to research on plant hormones, actively protested this indiscriminate use of such chemicals in warfare, not only because of the damage to the environment but also because of the destruction of food needed by noncombatants.

PHOTOPERIODISM

In 1920, two botanists working with the United States Department of Agriculture, then in Washington, D.C., W. W. Garner and H. A. Allard, reported that the flowering of an unusually robust variety of tobacco called "Maryland mammoth" was controlled by day length. Unlike other varieties, this variety did not bloom during the summer, but in autumn, when some plants were moved into a greenhouse to escape frost, they began to flower. It was found that these plants required a short day length in order for flowers to be formed. Now it is recognized that many species of plants require rather specific day lengths, or **photoperiods,** if flowers are to form. However, not all of these have the same requirements, as was noted in Chapter 17; they may vary greatly in length of light period required for initiation of flowering. Some, the **short-day plants** (Maryland mammoth is one),

537

do not flower if the light period exceeds a certain, critical number of hours; others, the **long-day plants,** require a light period greater than a certain critical number of hours for flowering to take place. The critical photoperiod is not necessarily shorter in short-day plants than in long-day plants. In fact, some short-day plants have a greater critical photoperiod than do some long-day plants. The important point is that the photoperiod *must be less* than the critical length in short-day plants if they are to flower, and *greater* than the critical length in long-day plants. For example, the critical light period in oats, a long-day plant, is nine hours, while that of the chrysanthemum, a short-day plant, is 15 hours. In most cases, however, the critical period is about the same in both long-day and short-day plants; i.e., about 11 to 13 hours.

A small number of plants, among these some varieties of sugar cane, are said to be **intermediate-day plants**. They fail to flower when the photoperiod is either too long or too short. Still others, the **day-neutral plants**, apparently are not affected by the length of the photoperiod.

The photoperiodic response in plants is a very interesting example of the relationship between a plant and its environment. It would indeed be strange if all plants in the world flowered and set seed at the same time. The competition among them would be fierce. Photoperiodic flowering responses in plants result in very precise timing of reproductive events. These are closely correlated with the plant's position in an ecosystem so that competition for light, water, and nutrients among germinating seeds is minimized.

Study of photoperiodic requirements of plants has shown that the dark period is perhaps a more important factor in regulating flower initiation than is the light period. A short-day plant, growing under short-day conditions, has a concurrent requirement for long-night conditions. This can be demonstrated very effectively by interrupting the dark period with a flash of light. This so-called "light-break" often is sufficient to prevent formation of flowers. Although the light-break does not significantly affect the total length of exposure to either light or darkness, its effect illustrates the need for a period of uninterrupted darkness. Long-day plants, on the other hand, have no requirement for darkness, and will usually flower under continuous light. How do plants regulate their developmental patterns in response to light and darkness? Research has shown that a pigment, **phytochrome**, is active in many photoperiodic effects in plants.

The research that led to the discovery of phytochrome was initiated in the United States Department of Agriculture at Beltsville, Maryland in the early 1950's by a physical chemist, Dr. Sterling B. Hendricks, and a botanist, Dr. Harry A. Borthwick. Physiological as well as biochemical and biophysical studies have indicated that many aspects of plant growth and development are controlled by this pigment. It exists in two forms: **Pr,** which has an absorption maximum of approximately 660 nanometers (nm) (red light); and **Pfr,** with an absorption maximum near 730 nm (far-red light). Absorption of the appropriate wave-length by either form converts it to the

Figure 20-10 Photoperiodism in the cocklebur (*Xanthium*), a plant commonly used in photoperiodic experimentation. Both plants in the photograph are only 5 weeks old. The plant at left, maintained on a photoperiod of 8 hours of light per 24 hours, has flowered and bears maturing fruit; the plant at right, however, was maintained on a photoperiod of 16 hours of light per 24-hour period, and has no flowers (Photo by Jane K. Glaser).

other form. When Pr, the red-absorbing form (which is blue-green in color), is irradiated with light (red being the most effective), it is converted to the Pfr form. When Pfr, the far-red absorbing form (which is light-green in color), is irradiated with far-red light, it is converted to the Pr form. These conversions are rapid, and occur in just a few seconds. However, Pfr is the unstable form of the molecule and will revert spontaneously to the Pr form after several hours if kept in darkness.

This slow conversion to Pr in darkness is of importance because it is the normal mechanism by which phytochrome is converted to the Pr form in nature, and is responsible for the effectiveness of the dark period in photoperiodic control of flowering as well as many other responses. In a short-day plant, phytochrome in the Pr form is required for flowering. When night-length is long enough for all the Pfr present at the end of the day to be converted to Pr, the plant will flower. If during the night plants are exposed to a flash of light, then the conversion process is upset and insufficient Pr is accumulated for flowering.

Using extracts of phytochrome, which is present in very low concentrations in plants, plant physiologists have been able to show

539

that when a molecule of phytochrome absorbs light, subtle changes in its configuration take place. These subtle changes result in the conversion of Pr to Pfr. The leaves are the principal site of light reactions of phytochrome under normal conditions, and therefore, the effects produced by red and by far-red light originate in the leaf. A hypothetical phytohormone, **florigen**, has been postulated as the product of phytochrome action, but has never been isolated or characterized chemically.

There are other phytochrome-mediated responses known in plants, and in every case the response is dependent upon the form of phytochrome in the plant and upon the relative duration of the two forms. All phytochrome-mediated responses have identical or nearly identical light wave length requirements or action spectra. In each case, the biological responses may be reversed by irradiation with either red or far-red light. One interesting phytochrome-mediated response is that of lettuce seed germination. If seeds of the so-called "Grand Rapids" variety of lettuce are moistened and exposed to light, they will germinate; if kept in continual darkness, however, they will not germinate, even though moistened. This appears to be a survival response. Many thousands of seeds are produced by a single lettuce plant, and a considerable number are covered by enough soil to shield them from all light. These will germinate only if the soil is disturbed so that they are exposed to light, and if moisture is also present. This insures that there will always be some seeds in reserve even when weather and other conditions may have prevented plant growth and flowering over a period of several years.

The following examples illustrate the control of specific growth responses by the two forms of phytochrome. The Pr form of the pigment induces flowering in short-day plants while preventing flowering in long-day plants, causes stem elongation, prevents leaf expansion, and prevents germination of light sensitive seed. When the pigment is in the Pfr form, all these responses are reversed; i.e., the Pfr form induces flowering in long-day plants but prevents flowering in short-day plants, prevents etiolation, induces leaf expansion, and induces germination of light sensitive seed.

PLANT TISSUE AND ORGAN CULTURE

We have spoken of the culture of plant cells and tissues in relation to the discovery of cytokinins. Plant tissue culture is an interesting and important frontier in modern botanical research. It is concerned with the culturing of organs or pieces of tissue, surgically removed from living plants, and aseptically grown in sterile nutrient culture media. For example, a tiny slice of carrot tissue can be cultured in a nutrient solution, where its cells will continue to grow and divide. Eventually some cells in this growing tissue mass, or **callus**, will become specialized and form shoots and roots. At least some of

540

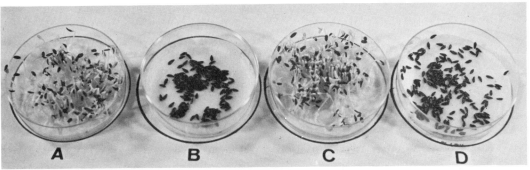

Figure 20–11 Light and dark responses in lettuce seeds. Seeds of the variety Grand Rapids in dish A were maintained in white light from a fluorescent tube; those in dish B were kept in darkness; those in dish C were kept in darkness except for a 15 minute exposure to red light; and those in dish D were kept in darkness except for a 15 minute exposure to red light followed by a 15 minute exposure to far-red light. Total length of the culture period in each case was 48 hours.

these shoots and roots will be associated in the form of small plantlets, or **embryoids,** which in turn can be transferred to other kinds of media capable of promoting internode elongation and leaf expansion; eventually this "test-tube" plant can be moved into soil, where it may grow into a mature flowering plant. Imagine the implications if we could sever whole organs or pieces of animal tissue and grow these in culture in the same manner as is possible with plant tissues!

The first successful cultures of a detached plant organ were reported in 1922 by Dr. W. J. Robbins of the New York Botanical Gardens. He discovered that tomato root tips could be cultured if given an energy source (i.e., a carbohydrate), a supply of minerals, yeast extract, and if the roots were grown aseptically in a sterile solution to prevent the growth of bacteria and other microorganisms. Later (in 1939), Dr. P. R. White of the Rockefeller Institute showed that when isolated tomato roots are given simple materials such as sucrose, certain inorganic salts, vitamins (three of the B vitamins are a satisfactory substitute for yeast extract), and a trace of the amino acid glycine, they can be cultured perpetually by repeated transfers of lateral root tips to fresh media. Dr. White successfully grew his isolated tomato roots for over 30 years and through more than 1000 successive transfers. Today roots of many other species in addition to tomato have been successfully used in tissue culture, and a few (such as those of the bindweed, *Convolvulus*) have grown into plantlets in culture.

One of the most significant advances in the study of plant growth regulation was reported by Dr. F. C. Steward at Cornell University. Dr. Steward studied individual phloem cells from carrot roots, growing them in a sterile medium containing coconut milk. Coconut milk was used because it is the natural nutrient supply of the coconut embryo and has been found to contain substances that support the growth of other kinds of plant cells. Some of the carrot cells

541

began to grow, and organized themselves first into embryoids and then into normal mature carrot plants with roots and shoots. Such plants have been placed in soil, have matured, and have developed flowers. This experiment established the concept of **totipotency** of plant cells—that *isolated plant cells have the complete hereditary information necessary to program an entire plant's development.* Cells from other plant species have been found to react in much the same manner when cultured on suitable nutrient media.

One of the practical uses of plant tissue culture is the growing of virus-free plants such as potato, geranium, and *Gladiolus.* Such plants are propagated largely by vegetative means (cuttings, tubers and corms) and over the years have become infected with viruses that reduce their productivity without actually killing the plants. When tissue cultures are established from virus-free parts of the plant (such as the terminal meristem, which usually is virus-free), new plants can be established by obtaining buds or embryoids from these tissue cultures and, when these develop into small plants, by transplanting them to soil. A procedure for production of virus-free geranium and *Gladiolus* plants, developed by Dr. A. C. Hildebrandt, a plant pathologist working at the University of Wisconsin, is shown in Figure 20–13.

An exciting new discovery in the control of plant development is based on the culture of immature anthers removed from flower buds and placed in culture on suitable nutrient media. The first successful cultures of this kind were done by Drs. S. Guha and S. C. Mahesh-

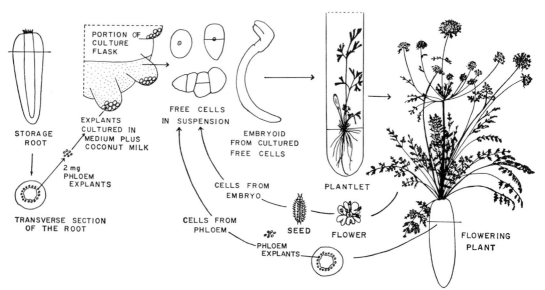

Figure 20–12 Steps in the development of single, cultured carrot cells into embryoids, and, finally, into mature, flowering plants. The procedures illustrated diagrammatically here were developed by Professor F. C. Steward of Cornell University (From Steward, F. C., et al., Growth and Development of Cultured Cells. *Science 143*: 20–27, 1964. Copyright 1964 by the American Association for the Advancement of Science).

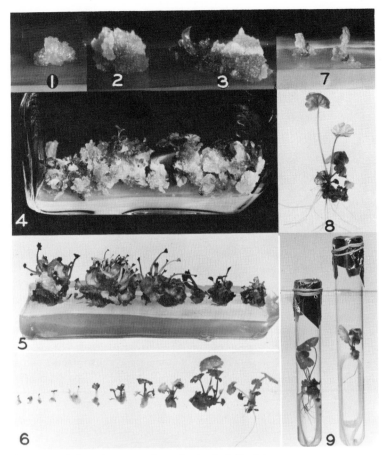

Figure 20-13 Steps in the development of virus-free geranium plants. *1–3,* Excision, culture, and growth of a Tissue derived from a virus-free part of an infected plant. *4–6,* Induction of bud development in the cultured tissue. *7,* Abnormal buds, which sometimes occur, may be discarded. *8,* A plantlet formed in tissue culture has roots lacking root hairs. *9,* Development of root hairs by culturing plantlet on filter paper wicks. (From Pillai, S. K., and Hildebrandt, A. C.: Induced Differentiation of Geranium Plants from Undifferentiated Callus in Vitro. *Amer. J. Bot. 56(1):*52–58, 1969).

wari of the University of Delhi, India, using *Datura* (jimson weed) plants. In these cultures, the pollen formed a tissue and gave rise to buds, roots, and eventually new plants. Since pollen is 1*N* in chromosome number, the resulting plants were 1*N* also. Further experiments in raising 1*N* or haploid plants from anther cultures have been done with tobacco, tomato, and other species. These experiments have been most successful when plants belonging to the family Solanaceae *(Datura,* potato, tobacco, tomato) have been used. One of the most productive methods has been developed by Drs. Jean and Colette Nitsch of Gifs-sur-Yvette, France. By adjusting the components of tissue culture media, the Nitsches induced the direct formation of embryoids from microspores of tobacco anthers, and grew haploid plants from these which eventually flowered. The

543

Figure 20–14 Vigorous, large-flowered, virus-free geranium plant (left) grown from meristem culture of commercial virus-infected and stunted plant (such as the one on the right). Both plants are of comparable age. (From Pillai, S. K., and Hildebrandt, A. C. *Proc. Third Int. Cong. Plant Cell and Tissue Culture*, London, England, 1974).

haploid plants were about one-third smaller than the normal 2*N* plants and were sterile. However, when embryoids were cultured on media containing cytokinins, chromosome doubling occurred, so that 2*N* plants (or **doubled haploids**) were produced, and these were fertile.

What use might be made of such haploid plants? We have noted in Chapter 11 that the advantage of using the fungus *Neurospora* in genetic research is that the monokaryon carries but one set of chromosomes. Therefore, any mutation or other change in the genes of the plant is immediately expressed and its effect noted. The same is true in haploids of flowering plants. Moreover, if a truly homozygous fertile plant (i.e., one in which each gene is duplicated on sister chromosomes) is desired, it is necessary only to double the chromosomes of the haploid plant according to the procedures outlined above or by treatment with chromosome doubling agents such as colchicine. Owing to heterozygosity prevalent in most natural 2*N* plants and to crossing over during meiosis, such purity of genotype is normally not attainable by standard plant breeding procedures; in fact, it would take years even to approach homozygosity through selective breeding. Anther culture and haploid plants offer a short cut to production of pure-line plants. It is noteworthy that the production of lysine-rich barley strains has already been achieved in Denmark through haploid culture. Lysine is an essential amino acid in human nutrition and is often deficient in plant

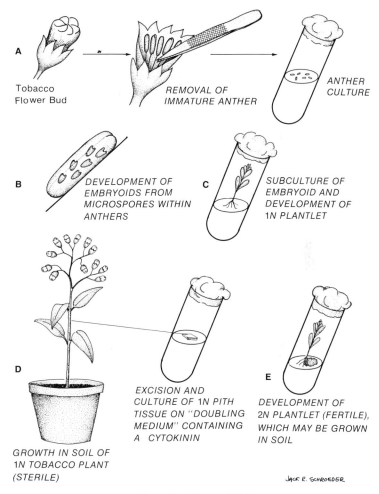

Figure 20-15 Steps in the formation of plants from cultured anthers of tobacco. *A*, Cultured anthers. *B*, Formation of embryoids from microspores. *C*, Development of 1*N* (haploid) plants. *D*, Induction of chromosome doubling with a cytokinin. *E*, Development of 2*N* plants (i.e., doubled haploids) (After Nitsch, J. P. Experimental Androgenesis in *Nicotiana. Phytomorphology 19:*389–404, 1969).

proteins used as food. Its increase in plant products is highly significant in this day of malnutrition and protein deprivation in many regions of the world.

PROTOPLAST CULTURES

Another significant breakthrough in plant development is the culture of **plant protoplasts.** Protoplasts are single cells from which the walls have been removed by treatment with the enzymes pectinase and cellulase. Such cells are obtained from any tissue source capable of being grown in culture. Protoplasts have been obtained

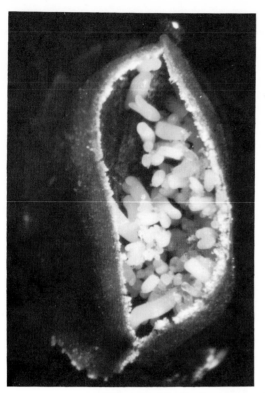

Figure 20–16 Photomicrograph of an anther of tobacco cultured on media capable of inducing the development of embryoids from microspores (Photo courtesy of Dr. Colette Nitsch).

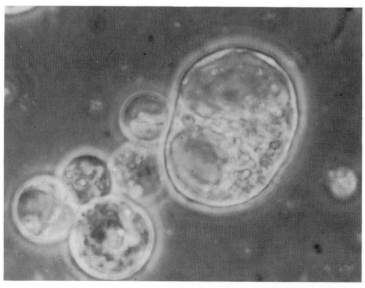

Figure 20–17 A suspension culture of plant protoplasts. Some protoplasts have divided and have formed cell aggregates (Photo courtesy of Dr. Gary Howland).

from leaf mesophyll and from tissue cultures of tobacco, tomato, and some other species.

Once the cell walls are removed, plant cells become very sensitive to osmotic changes, and they may burst unless the osmotic pressure of the surrounding medium is carefully adjusted. The protoplasts will remain naked as long as cellulase and pectinase are present, but if they are transferred to an enzyme-free medium, new walls are formed shortly and the cells often begin to divide and may even develop into plants.

One very important feature of plant protoplasts is the ability to fuse together prior to wall formation. Usually the nuclei of fused cells remain separated in their combined cytoplasm, but occasionally the nuclei also fuse, producing a **somatic hybrid**. Recently Dr. Peter Carlson and his associates, working at Brookhaven National Laboratory, New York, succeeded in obtaining a hybrid plant by combining the protoplasts of two different species of tobacco *(Nicotiana langsdorffii* and *N. glauca)*. Carlson also has found that albino protoplasts of tobacco will take up isolated chloroplasts when these are added to the cells and will adopt them as their own. In this way albino plants may be transformed into green plants.

What is the future of protoplast culture and fusion? First of all, it promises to be a very quick means of obtaining hybrid plants, for protoplast fusion can be done in a matter of hours, whereas the production of hybrids by the usual breeding methods may require a year or more in raising plants to maturity, cross-pollinating them, and waiting for seeds to set. Moreover, intergeneric crosses might someday be possible. Suppose, for example, that haploid protoplasts of tomato, tobacco, and potato (all of the family Solanaceae) could be fused and their combined chromosomes doubled to produce a fertile plant. Might it then be possible to have multipurpose plants bearing tomato fruit, potato tubers, and tobacco leaves? This is doubtless an extravagant dream, but it is likely that by protoplast fusion some characters may be introduced to form new kinds of plants. For example, if the capacity to form nitrogen-fixing root nodules could be transferred from legumes to other crop plants, the present fertilizer shortages might be alleviated. And what of chloroplast transplants? We have noted that some plants, such as sugarcane, have highly efficient chloroplasts that utilize a high-energy photosynthetic pathway, the C-4 pathway. Might it be possible to transplant such chloroplasts into crop plants now lacking them? This suggestion has received some consideration from developmental botanists.

Another way in which cells in culture have been manipulated is through the direct transfer of genes. Drs. Peter Gresshoff and Colin Doy, working at the Australian National University, have succeeded in transferring a bacterial gene (the *lac*operon of *E. coli*) into tomato cells, and as a result have changed the nutritional requirements of the cultured cells. The direct introduction of individual genes has long been a dream of plant geneticists.

Many possibilities for the development of new kinds of plants are receiving the attention of plant breeders and developmental botanists throughout the world. Malnutrition is rampant in many parts

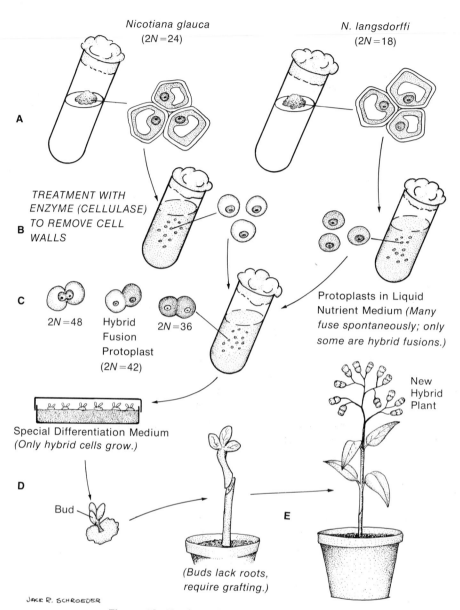

Nicotiana glauca
(2N=24)

N. langsdorffi
(2N=18)

A

*TREATMENT WITH
ENZYME (CELLULASE)
TO REMOVE CELL
WALLS*

B

C

2N=48   Hybrid
Fusion
Protoplast
(2N=42)

2N=36

Protoplasts in Liquid
Nutrient Medium *(Many
fuse spontaneously; only
some are hybrid fusions.)*

New
Hybrid
Plant

Special Differentiation Medium
(Only hybrid cells grow.)

D

Bud

E

*(Buds lack roots,
require grafting.)*

JACK R. SCHROEDER

Figure 20–18 A method for obtaining hybrid plants from protoplasts. *A,* Culture of
cells from two species. *B,* Removal of cell walls by enzyme treatment. *C,* Combining
of the two kinds of protoplasts to obtain fusion. *D,* Isolation of fusion products and
induction of cell division followed by bud formation. *E,* Grafting of bud onto stock
of one of the parental plants. *F,* Maturation of hybrid. (Based on Carlson, P. S., The Use
of Protoplasts for Genetic Research, P.N.A.S. (U.S.A.), *70:*598–602, 1973).

of the world, particularly because of protein shortages. Because
animals are at the small end of the food chain funnel, animal protein
is insufficient to support the present world population. Plant proteins, unfortunately, are not always satisfactory substitutes because
either they are lacking in certain essential amino acids or they con-

tain suboptimal amounts. There is little doubt that new and highly nutritive plant proteins will become available as a result of basic plant research now in progress. The results will be far reaching.

SUMMARY

We have now examined a number of areas of current research interests in plant biology but we have by no means exhausted the subject. This sampling has shown that modern botanists are interested in a wide variety of both pure and applied subjects, and related to a number of other scientific disciplines. We have seen that one of the most active and promising research areas continues to be in the field of agriculture. Programs designed to produce crop plants with higher yields and higher food values are in progress in many parts of the country. The recent successes of the "green revolution" attest to the importance of this aspect of botanical research.

The study of plant regulation has been of interest to botanists for over 40 years, but still there are many unsolved riddles. The role of plant hormones in controlling plant movement and plant behavior has been the subject of continuing investigation in many laboratories across the country. Auxins, gibberellins, cytokinins, abscisic acid, and ethylene gas have all been shown to function in regulating plant growth and other plant activities.

Another important plant regulator system is that based on the natural, light-sensitive molecule phytochrome. Phytochrome in the leaves of plants is known to measure light, and in some presently unknown way it thereby controls flowering. Phytochrome also is active in controlling germination, leaf expansion, stem growth, and other plant activities.

Organ and tissue culturing has been studied in plants for over 30 years. Yet recent advances in the culture of anthers, pollen grains, and microspores to induce haploid plants, production of wall-free plant cells by enzyme treatment, fusion of such protoplasts, and chromosome doubling, have revolutionized the prospects of plant breeding. Even more exciting are the possibilities of the direct transfer of such organelles as chloroplasts and mitochondria from plant cell to plant cell, and even the direct transfer of genes across species barriers.

DISCUSSION QUESTIONS

1. Describe Darwin's experiments with the grass coleoptile and the conclusions to be drawn from these experiments regarding plant growth movements.
2. Plants respond to the direction of light, to the stimulus of gravity, to day-length, to touch, and to a variety of other environmental signals, yet they do not have nerve tissues. Explain.
3. Describe how changes in cell elongation result in tropisms.
4. What is a principal difference in effect on plant development of gibberellins and abscisic acid?
5. What is a role of the gas ethylene in natural plant development?
6. Explain in terms of the state of phytochrome how a "light-break" at night might affect flowering in a short-day plant.
7. In what plant activity is the leaf pigment phytochrome involved?
8. Discuss the significance of organ and tissue culture in the study of plant development.
9. What advantages might plant breeders derive from haploid plants?
10. What is meant by protoplast culture? What is its significance?

549

SUPPLEMENTAL READING

Baffey, P. M. Herbicides in Vietnam: AAAS Study Finds Widespread Devastation. *Science 171*: 43–49, 1971.

Bonner, J., and J. E. Varner. *Plant Biochemistry.* New York: Academic Press, Inc., 1965.

Carlson, P. S. 1973. The use of protoplasts for genetic research. *Proc. Nat. Acad. Sci. (U.S.A.) 70(2)*:598–602, 1973.

Cocking, E. C. Plant cell protoplasts – isolation and development. *Ann. Rev. Plant Physiol. 23*:29–50, 1972.

Galston, A. W., and P. J. Davies. Control Mechanisms in Plant Development. Englewood Cliffs, N.J.: Prentice-Hall, Inc., 1970.

Steward, F. C. *Plants at Work.* Palo Alto, California: Addison-Wesley Publ. Co., Inc., 1964.

Torrey, J. G. Development in Flowering Plants. New York: The Macmillan Co., 1967.

Westling, A. H. Ecological Effects of Military Defoliation on the Forests of South Vietnam. *BioScience 17*:893–898, 1971.

Glossary

Abscisic acid a plant hormone having growth-inhibiting action. It promotes abscission and is associated with the onset and maintenance of dormancy.

Abscission the detachment of an organ, such as a leaf or a floral part, as a consequence of cell separation in an abscission zone.

Absorption spectrum (of chlorophyll) the wavelengths of light actually absorbed by chlorophyll.

Accessory parts the sterile, outer parts of the flower.

Achene a small, dry, one-seeded indehiscent fruit in which the seed coat is not adherent to the pericarp.

Actinomorphic having radial symmetry, with floral parts of similar size and shape.

Actinomycetes a group of filamentous bacteria. They reproduce by fission, arthrospores and/or conidia. Some cause diseases of plants and animals, and some (e.g., *Streptomyces*) produce useful antibiotics.

Action spectrum (of chlorophyll) the photosynthetic response to a spectrum of light.

Active absorption the uptake of substances by a cell from the environment by processes that require the expenditure of energy by the cell.

Adaxial next to the axis; dorsal; turned toward the axis.

Adenine one of the main purines found in DNA and RNA.

Adenosine triphosphate (ATP) a compound containing three high-energy phosphate groups; ATP loses a phosphate group when cellular energy is released; ADP is formed when such energy is liberated.

Adventitious root root other than the primary root or a branch of the primary root; often occurring on stems.

Aeciospore a yellow, single-celled, binucleate spore of the rust fungus formed in a special cluster or cup-like structure called the aecium.

Aecium (plural, *aecia*) (1) a cup-like structure produced on certain plants by rust fungi, in which binucleate single-celled spores are borne; (2) a globular, cup-shaped, tubular or irregular fungus fruit-body that bursts through the epidermis of the host. Typically it consists of surrounding sterile fungus membrane called the peridium, which encloses the fertile portion, which produces chains of aeciospores.

Aerobe a plant depending on free oxygen for its life processes.

Aerobic requiring oxygen for respiration.

Aerobic respiration the oxygen-dependent form of respiration.

Agar-agar a gelatin-like material, made from seaweeds, that is frequently used as a base for laboratory culture media.

Ageotropic not responding to gravity.

Aggregation state of soil in which mineral particles of various sizes, ranging from clay to sand, are bound into clumps.

Akinete nonmotile reproductive cell formed without true cell formation or rejuvenescence.

Aleurone (1) protein granule of globulins and peptones found in ripe seeds; (2) the outermost layer of the endosperm in cereals rich in gluten.

Aleurone layer a layer of aleurone grains found in the periphery of most seeds.

Algal fungi common name for Phycomycetes; members of this group resemble certain of the green algae in structure and method of reproduction.

Algin the magnesium-calcium salt of alginic acid, found in inner cell-wall of the brown algae, and used commercially in the manufacture of confectionery and synthetic fibers.

Allele one of the two or more alternate genes that may exist at a particular locus on a chromosome. An organism may be homozygous for some alleles and heterozygous for others.

Allogamy mode of reproduction in which a flower is pollinated by pollen from another flower.

Alloploid (Allopolyploid) a polyploid resulting from interspecific hybridization and subsequent chromosomal doubling.

Alpha amylase an enzyme that digests starch to its constituent glucose molecules.

Alternate applied to the arrangement of the leaves or buds that occur singly at a node.

AMO-1618 a synthetic compound that retards stem elongation.

Anabolism constructive or synthetic phases of metabolism, such as photosynthesis, assimilation, and the synthesis of proteins.

Anaerobe an organism ordinarily living in the absence of free oxygen.

Anaerobic respiration a type of respiration, found only in bacteria, in which the hydrogen released in glycolysis is combined with the bound oxygen of inorganic compounds.

Anaphase the stage in mitotic division at which chromosome sets migrate toward the spindle poles.

Angiosperm the classical or traditional name for the flowering plants.

Anisogamy reproducing by motile gametes of similar form but dissimilar size. The smaller usually is considered the male, the larger, female.

Annual a plant in which the entire life cycle is completed in a single growing season.

Annual ring an annual growth layer, as seen in cross section. The term applies primarily to wood grown in the temperate zones.

Annulus (1) in gill fungi, a ring on the stalk, the remnant of the partial or inner veil; (2) in ferns, a specialized ring of cells around the sporangium.

Anther the pollen sac or microsporangium of a flower.

Antheridium (plural, *antheridia*) the male sex organ producing microgametes, which are usually motile, but in some of the Oomycetes, the antheridium contacts the oogonium into which it produces a fertilization tube and through which the cell contents of the antheridium pass. It is multicellular in cryptogams.

Antheridiophore a special male branch found in some of the Marchantiales and bearing one or more antheridia.

Antheridogen substance secreted by certain fern prothalli and causing antheridia to form on neighboring prothalli.

Anthocyanin one of a class of pigments in flowers and fruits, varying from pink to blue according to the acidity of the cell sap; it is generally a water-soluble glucoside but sometimes is in a crystalline or amorphous form.

Antipodal one of three (and sometimes more) cells of the mature embryo sac, located at the end opposite the micropyle. They are usually functionless and are believed to be vestigial.

Antithetic theory the theory that explains alternation of generations as the gametophyte and sporophyte being distinct; the gametophyte represents the primitive aquatic phase, while the sporophyte is secondary, having arisen from the germinating zygote concurrent with migration from an aquatic to a terrestrial habitat. Deals with the alternation of morphologically unlike generations, that is the generations are not homologous.

Apetalous flower flower in which the perianth is missing.

Apical meristem (1) the meristematic cells at the tip of a stem or root from which all the tissues of the mature axis are ultimately formed; (2) the group of actively dividing cells found at or near the tip of a stem, root, or sometimes a leaf. The apical meristem originates from a single cell in the Polypodiophyta and from a group of cells in the seed plants, and brings about an increase in length by forming the primary plant body.

Apogamy reproduction without the fusion of gametes, and usually without meiosis. The term may include any form of vegetative reproduction.

Apomixis (1) development of an embryo vegetatively, in the absence of fertilization in a species that normally reproduces sexually; (2) reproduction without the fusion of gametes and usually without meiosis.

Apophysis (plural, *apophyses*) (1) an enlargement of the seta below the theca of certain mosses; (2) the sterile tissue at the base of a moss capsule.

Apospory (1) the production of a 2N gametophyte from the sporophyte as a result of the absence of meiosis; (2) suppression of spore formation with the prothallus developing directly from the sporophyte.

Apothecium (1) the fructification, seen in some Ascomycetes, that is flattened or cup-shaped with the asci on the upper surface in a palisade-like layer, usually mixed with sterile hyphae; (2) a disk-like, cup or bowl-shaped fruit body borne on lichens and discomycetous fungi. The spores are borne on the inner surface and are exposed while the ascospores are maturing.

Archegonium (plural, *archegonia*) the female reproductive organ in bryophytes, pteridophytes, and some gymnosperms, composed of a narrow upper portion pierced by a canal enclosing one or more neck cells that in turn lead to a basal dilated portion containing one egg.

Archegoniophore the archegonial receptacle; the branch which bears the archegonia in liverworts.

Ascocarp the structure in which asci are formed.

Ascogenous hyphae the hyphae growing from the zygote of the Ascomycetes. Several ascogenous hyphae develop from each zygote and each hypha bears several asci.

Ascogonium (plural, *ascogonia*) the female sex organ of the Ascomycetes which, after fertilization, produces the ascogenous hyphae; the cell or group of cells of the Ascomycetes fertilized by the antheridium.

Ascomycete a fungus whose spores are borne in an ascus.

Ascospore (1) a spore produced as the result of sexual fusion and subsequent reduction division in the Ascomycetes; (2) a spore formed in an ascus and characteristic of Ascomycetes.

Ascus (plural, *asci*) (1) in Ascomycetes, a large sac-like cell, usually the swollen tip on a hyphal branch in the ascocarp within which ascospores (typically eight in number) are developed; (2) a sac-like cell in the perfect stage of an ascomycete, in which the ascospores are produced.

Atactostele a stelar type exhibited by members of the Liliopsida, in which the vascular bundles are in several concentric rings or have a random distribution.

Autocolony the product of a mother cell in coenobic algae; the formation of a colony of algal cells by synchronized division or cleavage of a mother cell.

Autogamy reproduction in which the flower is pollinated by its own pollen.

Autolysis enzymatic self-digestion or dissolution of tissue or other part of an organism.

Autoploid (Autopolyploid) a polyploid resulting from self-duplication of the genome.

Auxin a growth-promoting substance in plants; it is a hormone produced in the tips of plants, and it travels through the plants from cell to cell.

Auxospore a rejuvenescent spore produced under adverse environmental conditions by some diatoms. It forms as a result of shedding the cell wall followed by enlargement of the cytoplasm and formation of a new cell wall.

Axillary occurring in the axil of a leaf.

Bacillus (plural, *bacilli*) a rod-shaped bacterium.

Bacteriophage a virus that infects bacteria.

Bark any or all tissues outside the cambium.

Basidiocarp the basidia-producing fructification of the Basidiomycetes.

Basidiospore a sexual spore, loosely attached to the tip of a basidium, and characteristic of Basidiomycetes.

Basidium (plural, *basidia*) (1) the club-shaped structure characteristic of certain fungi, at the tip of which spores (usually four) are produced on short, slender stalks; (2) a structure composed of one to four cells upon which spores are borne externally in Basidiomycetes.

Benthic (1) living on or near the bottom of a large mass of water; (2) living and generally attached to the bottom of aquatic habitats.

Berry a simple fleshy fruit, such as a grape or tomato.

Betacyanin the purple-colored pigment of flowers.

Biennial a plant that normally requires two growing seasons to complete its life cycle. Vegetative growth occurs the first year, and flowering and fruiting occur in the second year.

Bilateral symmetry condition in which symmetry in one plane exists, as in certain flowers.

Biological oxidation process by which food is chemically oxidized, resulting in the breakdown of organic material and the release of energy.

Biomass (1) the quantity of plankton substance in weight; (2) the total living organic matter, usually on an oven-dry weight basis.

Biome (1) a large community of plants and animals, characterized by its particular type of dominant vegetation and its associated animals (e.g., tundra); (2) biotic communities; communities that are similar as regards climate, soil, and life-forms.

Biosphere the part of the atmosphere and geosphere where life exists; that part of the land and air that influences vegetative growth and is affected by it.

Bipinnate leaf a compound leaf that has its main segments pinnately divided.

Bisexuality condition in which an organism is capable of the function of both sexes.

Bloom (1) dense growth of planktonic algae, giving a distinct color to the water body; (2) an exceptionally abundant growth of planktonic algae during hot weather.

Bordered pit a thin area in the wall between two vessels or tracheids surrounded by overhanging rims of thickened walls.

Boreal forest one of the three major zones in North America, in the northern part of the world.

Bract (1) A modified leaf found usually just below a flower or an inflorescence; (2) a small, rudimentary leaf.

Branch gap an area of parenchyma developing in a siphonostele immediately above the vascular tissue that enters a branch.

Bromeliad a member of the family Bromeliaceae, which are mostly tropical and epiphytic. Pineapple and Spanish moss are included in this family.

Bud scale modified leaf or stipule forming a part of a covering that protects the contents from dessication or other injury.

Bud scale scar a scar encircling the twig and caused by the fall of bud scales of the terminal bud after the previous year's growth.

Bulb a very short stem surrounded by many overlapping, fleshy leaves.

Bundle scar a trace within a leaf scar produced by a vascular bundle; a mark on the surface of a leaf scar denoting former attachment of the bundles of a leaf to those of a stem.

C-4 pathway a cycle found in a few tropical and temperate plants; characterized by using higher light intensities to fix CO_2 than does the Calvin cycle.

Callose a carbohydrate, deposited seasonally or permanently on sieve plates, or upon cells or in tissues.

Callus (1) a mass of parenchymatous cells formed by plants over a wound; (2) an abnormally thickened part as the base of a cutting from which roots develop.

Calvin cycle a widely occurring dark reaction in plants; photosynthesis in which CO_2 is affixed to a 5-carbon sugar molecule and subsequently reduced to form other sugars.

Calyptra (1) the cap or lid covering the developing spore case of a moss and formed by the enlargement of the archegonium after fertilization; (2) a membranous cap on the sporangium of liverworts or mosses derived from the archegonial wall.

Calyx the collective term for sepals.

Cambium (1) the cylinder, strip, or layer of meristematic cells that divide to produce cells that ultimately form a permanent tissue; (2) the thin layer of formative tissue beneath the bark of dicots and gymnosperms from which new wood and bark originate.

Capillarity the movement of a liquid due to surface forces; it is especially observable in capillary tubes.

Capsule (1) the theca or spore case of mosses and ferns; (2) the part of a bryophyte sporangium that contains the spores.

Cardinal temperatures the minimum, optimum, and maximum temperatures affecting plant growth. The minimum temperature is that point at which growth begins; the optimum temperature is that point at which growth is best; and the maximum temperature is that point at which growth stops.

Carotenoid (1) the collective name for the red and yellow pigments in plastids; (2) one of the yellow and orange pigments in chloroplasts.

Carpel a highly modified megasporophyil found in flowering plants.

Carpogonium (1) the female reproductive organ of some algae and some common fungi; (2) the female sex organ of the *Floridiophycidae*.

Carpospore (1) a spore formed at the end of a filament and developed from a carpogonium; (2) a rounded, uninucleate, non-motile spore formed from the direct or indirect division of the zygote of the Rhodophyta.

553

Carrageenin   the hydrocolloid of red algae.

Caryopsis   a dry, indehiscent, one-seeded fruit in which the seed coat is completely fused to the pericarp.

Casparian strip   a band of suberized material around the radial walls of the individual cells of the endodermis in their primary condition.

Cast   a type of fossil that results from the filling of a cavity originally formed by plant tissues that later decayed.

Catkin   (1) a specialized type of inflorescence in which several flowers are borne on a single stalk, usually pendant, and consisting either entirely of staminate or entirely of pistillate flowers; (2) a pendulous spike with many simple, usually unisexual flowers. It is usually bracteate, and falls as a unit when the pollen or seeds have been shed.

Cauliflorous   (1) flowering on the trunk or on specialized spurs from it or from the larger branches; (2) bearing flowers on old stems.

CCC   cycocel, an antigibberellin that inhibits induction.

Cell-plate   an initial partition between two sister cells, formed *de novo* in the cytoplasm in association with the spindle fibers as part of the terminal stage in typical mitotic cell division in most plants.

Cell theory   theory stating that all organisms are made up of cells and cell products.

Cell wall   the non-living, usually cellulosic covering layer of the plant cell.

Central cell   cell of the embryo sac containing the primary endosperm nuclei.

Central nodule   in the Bacillariophyceae, the structure to which the raphe attaches.

Centriole   cytoplasmic organelle of some algal flagellates and most animals, from which the microtubules of the mitotic spindle appear to originate.

Centromere   (1) a minute body believed to have directive influence in nuclear division; (2) the self-propagating particle in the chromosome whose activity in protein organization determines certain movements of the chromosome.

Chaparral   (1) the xerophytic scrub vegetation consisting of such plants as dwarf oaks, currants, buckeye, and roses; (2) any dense, impenetrable thicket composed of stiff thorny shrubs and dwarf trees.

Charophyceae   a class of green algae (chlorophyta) characterized by calcified filaments that have nodes and internodes.

Chasmogamy   the quality of having flowers that open before pollination.

Chemical evolution   (of the earth's atmosphere) the theory of development of the earth's atmosphere from an early one in which free oxygen is absent to that of the present.

Chemosynthetic   (1) synthesizing organic compounds by energy derived from chemical changes or reactions in place of reactions, as in respiration; (2) forming organic material by means of energy derived from chemical change, in contrast to the transfer of energy by complex chemical reactions, as in respiration.

Chemotactic   capable of reacting to a chemical stimulus; said of living organisms.

Chemotaxis   sensitivity and reaction of cells or organisms to chemical stimuli.

Chemotropism   movement or growth resulting from a chemical stimulus.

Chiasma   (1) the exchange of material between chromosomes during nuclear division, a crosswise fusion at one or more points of paired chromosomes or chromatids that are twisted about each other in meiosis; (2) the joint between two chromatids of two homologous chromosomes, where an exchange of chromatic material takes place.

Chitin   (1) a major constituent of fungal cell walls, made up of N-acetyl-2-glucose amine units; (2) a hard substance characteristically found in insects and having the same composition as fungal cellulose.

Chlorenchyma   (1) an unlignified tissue containing chloroplasts; (2) tissue whose cells contain chlorophyll.

Chlorophyll a   the fundamental green pigment of photosynthesis; localized on the chloroplast, and of composition $C_{55}H_{72}O_5N_4Mg$.

Chloroplast   a chlorophyll-containing plastid.

Chromatid   one-half of a doubled chromosome before the two portions separate.

Chromatin   a nuclear material (usually a nucleoprotein) that stains deeply with basic dyes.

Chromoplast   a pigmented plastid that does not contain chlorophyll; carotenoids are among the pigments usually present.

Chromosome   gene-containing filamentous body in the cell nucleus that becomes conspicuous during mitosis and meiosis; the number of chromosomes per cell is constant for each species.

Chrysolaminarin   the food reserves in chrysophytes; made up of a β-1,3–linked polyglucan.

Chrysophyceae   algae with golden-brown pigmentation, classified in the division chrysophyta.

Chytrid   one of the Chytridiales, the simplest parasitic or saprophytic fungi. The plant body is unicellular, never forming a true mycelium. Most or all of the plant body forms a sporangium or gametangium. There may be several reproductive organs. There is no alternation of generations; asexual reproduction is by anteriorly uniflagellate zoospores, most of which lack a nuclear cap, while sexual reproduction is by flagellate isogametes.

Cirinate vernation   curled arrangement of leaves and leaflets in the bud, the result of more rapid growth on one surface.

Cisterna (plural, *cisternae*)   flattened tube or bag of the endoplasmic reticulum.

Citric acid cycle   see *Krebs cycle*.

Cladium (plural, *cladia*)   small, detachable branch of a moss capable of becoming a new plant.

Clamp connection   (1) an outgrowth from the ultimate cell of a hypha, forming a connection by fusion with the penultimate cell, which is formed during cell division. Found in all Basidiomycetes except the Uredinales; (2) a small protuberance attached to the walls of two adjoining cells in the hypha of a fungus mycelium, covering the septum between the cells like a clamp.

554

Cleistogamy breeding system in which the seed forms without the flower opening.

Cleistothecium an ascocarp which remains closed and produces its spores internally.

Climax community (1) the plant association permanently established in any given habitat; (2) a stable community that does not undergo change unless the surroundings change.

Club fungus member of the class Basidiomycetes.

Club mosses members of the Lycopodiophyta.

Coccolithophore a member of the Coccolithophoridaceae, which possess plates of calcium carbonate embedded in the gelatinous envelope.

Coccus (plural, *cocci*) a bacterium having spherical or almost spherical form.

Codon the coding triplet of mRNA.

Coenobium colonial aggregation of independent protistan cells held together by a common sheath, with cells arranged in an orderly pattern.

Coenocyte (1) a multinuclear plant body enclosed within a common wall; (2) a bit of cytoplasm with many nuclei not separated by walls; (3) a multinucleate, vegetative protoplast.

Coenzyme a biological catalyst, of smaller molecular size than an enzyme, that must cooperate with an enzyme to produce its effect.

Colchicine an alkaloid obtained from the root of the autumn crocus, used to induce artificial polyploidy.

Collenchyma the first-formed mechanical or strengthening tissue of stems. It is composed of elongated cells that are thickened only at the angles by material heavy in cellulose.

Columella (plural, *columellae*) a central sterile column extending into a sporangium, as in mosses.

Companion cell a small, specialized parenchyma cell associated with the sieve-tube elements of flowering plants.

Compound leaf a leaf divided into two or more parts or leaflets.

Compression a plant fossil formed by the exertion of pressure by the weight of accumulated sediments upon plant organs such as leaves.

Conceptacle (1) a superficial cavity, opening outward, within which gonidia are produced; the reproductive cavity in the receptacle of *Fucus;* (2) a flask-shaped cavity in the thallus of the Fucus in which the sporangia develop.

Conidium (plural, *conidia*) (1) asexual, thin-walled spores produced by abstriction from the summit of a conidiophore; an asexual spore developed on mycelium or hypha of a fruit body; a dust-like spore that is disseminated into the air; (2) an asexual spore cut off from the end of a hypha.

Conjugation the union of two similar, non-flagellated cells or protoplasts.

Connective the structure that joins the filament and the microsporangium (anther).

Consumer an animal that derives its energy directly from plants.

Continental drift theory suggesting the separation of the continents from a single land mass, with resulting movement to produce the separate land masses as they exist today.

Continuous variation a series of minute variations; variation shown by such slight individual differences between member specimens belonging to the same lineage that one specimen may shade into another.

Cork a secondary tissue produced by a cork cambium; polygonal cells, nonliving at maturity, with walls infiltrated with a waxy or fatty material resistant to the passage of gases and water vapor.

Cork cambium a lateral meristem producing cork in woody and some herbaceous plants.

Cork cell a dead, suberized cell that is protective and impervious to gases and water vapor.

Corm short, squat, often spherical stem having only thin, scaly leaves.

Corolla the second (from the bottom) of the series of floral organs; composed of petals.

Cortex the outer primary tissues of the stem or root, extending from the primary phloem to the epidermis and composed chiefly of parenchyma cells.

Costa (plural, *costae*) (1) general term for midrib or veins; (2) a rib or valve of a diatom; (3) a ridge or midrib of a frond or leaf.

Cotyledon a seed leaf of a plant embryo.

Crista (plural, *cristae*) inwardly directed fold of the inner wall of a mitochondrion.

Crossing over (of chromosomes) (1) the interchange of genes usually linked in inheritance, probably due to the exchange of corresponding segments between corresponding chromatids of different chromosomes; (2) the exchange of corresponding segments of two chromatids of homologous chromosomes during meiosis. This is caused by the breaking and reunion of the chromatids and results in the independent segregation of the genes.

Crozier the hook formed by an ascogenous hypha prior to ascus development.

Crustose (1) having the thallus closely and tightly fixed to the substratum; (2) crust-like or closely attached to the substratum and lacking a distinct cortex.

Cutin the waxy substance that impregnates the walls of epidermal cells and causes them to be almost impermeable to water; the substance, allied to suberins, that repels liquids from passing through the cell walls.

Cycad members of the Cycadopsida, which have unbranched stems and a terminal crown of long, leathery, compound leaves.

Cycasin a potent carcinogen isolated from stems and seeds of cycads.

Cyclosis a flowing movement of the peripheral cytoplasm in certain types of plant cells, especially in the mesophyll.

Cycocel an antigibberellin that inhibits induction.

Cytochrome one of a series of pigmented iron-containing protein molecules. Some function in electron transfer during respiration; others are active in photosynthesis.

Cytogenetics the science of chromosome behavior in relation to inheritance.

Cytokinin one of a group of growth regulators that promote cell division.

Cytosine one of the two main pyrimidines found in DNA.

Dark reaction a complex reaction that takes place during the photosynthetic process. Carbon dioxide is fixed to form sugars by combination with hydrogen. This is a complex reaction, and takes place in the stroma of the chloroplast (see Chapter 5).

Daughter colony the result of asexual reproduction, in which a new colony forms within the parent, as in *Volvox*.

Day-neutral plants plants that are independent of day length, and thus can bloom under conditions of either long or short days.

Decompound leaf a compound leaf in which the leaflets are made up of distinct parts.

Dehiscence spontaneous opening of a structure to liberate seeds.

Dendro-archaeology see *dendrochronology*.

Dendrochronology the dating of trees by observation of annual growth rings in the trunks.

Dendroclimatology determination of past climates by study of relative widths of annual rings.

Denitrifying bacteria soil bacteria that break down nitrites and nitrates anaerobically to produce gaseous nitrogen.

Desert (1) a region with little precipitation and, consequently, with scant vegetation, such as a steppe, tundra, dune, and fellfield; (2) places where rainfall is often less than 10 inches per year, with extreme temperature fluctuations. Most of the vegetation is restricted to living only during the very short rainy season.

Desmids aquatic, free-floating algae characterized by a median constriction that divides the cell into two equal halves.

Diatoms unicellular microscopic forms of algae with a regularly shaped cell wall of silica; also known as Bacillariophyceae.

Dichogamy breeding system in which the anther and stigma mature at different times, thus favoring cross-pollination.

Dichotomously branched branched by the division or forking of an axis into two more or less equal branches.

Dicotyledon a flowering plant with embryos having two seed leaves or cotyledons.

Dictinous having unisexual flowers.

Dictyosome see *Golgi body*.

Dictyostele a siphonostele with numerous and elongate leaf gaps and branch gaps, such that the primary vascular tissue forms a ring of vascular bundles.

Diffusion the movement of molecules from regions where they are abundant to regions where they are less abundant.

Dikaryotic (1) having hyphae made up of segments, each of which contain two nuclei, as some Basidiomycetes; (2) having cells containing two $1N$ nuclei that divide simultaneously, as some fungal hyphae.

Dinoflagellate a member of the class Dinophyceae; these are mostly unicellular, having cellulose walls with interlocking plates.

Dioecious (1) having microsporangiate and megasporangiate organs on separate individuals; (2) having the staminate and pistillate flowers on separate individuals.

Diploid having two sets of homologous chromosomes: $2X$.

Disjunction the separation of the chromosomes at anaphase, particularly at the first mitotic division.

Dissected siphonostele siphonostele divided deeply, into narrow lobes.

Distichous arranged in two vertical rows.

DNA hybridization an experimental technique involving the pairing of strands of DNA and/or RNA.

Dominant allele a gene that expresses itself in the phenotype to the exclusion of the expression of another allele.

Dominant parental character the prevalent character in a hybrid; the member of an allelomorphic pair that manifests itself wholly or partly to the exclusion of the other member of the pair.

Dominant species a species that controls the habitat, strongly influencing what other species may exist within the community.

Dormant in a state in which metabolic processes, especially respiration, are slowed.

Double fertilization the process in flowering plants that results in a $2N$ zygote and a $3N$ ($5N$ in lily) endosperm cell.

Drupe a simple, fleshy fruit in which the inner part of the ovary wall develops into a hard, stony, or woody endocarp, as in the peach.

Ecological succession a series of changes in vegetation types generally leading to a stable plant community.

Ecosystem (1) the complete ecological system of an area, including the plant, animal, and other environmental factors; (2) an all-inclusive term characterizing a living community and all the factors of its nonliving environment.

Egg a cell near the base of the embryo sac and closest to the micropyle of flowering plants.

Egg apparatus the functional female nucleus and the two synergids in the embryo sac of an angiosperm.

Egg cell the oösphere or gynogamete; the female gamete.

Elater (1) a sterile, elastic, spirally twisted, hygroscopic, filament found mixed with the spores of some liverworts and assisting in the expulsion of the spores from the spore case; (2) an elongated, spirally thickened cell derived from the sporogenous tissue and sometimes aiding in spore dispersal.

Electron carriers molecules that transfer electrons from coenzymes to electron acceptors.

Embryoid a small plantlet.

Endocarp the layer of the pericarp that immediately encloses the seed.

Endodermis the single layer of cells surrounding the vascular tissue of certain plants; it is usually present in roots, but may be lacking in some stems.

Endoplasmic reticulum cytoplasmic network of membranes adjacent to the nucleus and making up a part of the submicroscopic structure of the protoplasm.

Endosperm the nutritive material in the seed.

Endospore (1) a spore formed inside a mother cell; (2) an asexual spore; (3) the innermost layer of the wall of a spore.

Energy subsidy the amount of fuel used to run machinery to harvest crops.

Envelope, nuclear the outer, bounding membrane of the nucleus.

Epicotyl the part of a seedling stem above the cotyledons.

Epidermis the outermost layer of cells of the leaf and of young stems and roots.

Epigyny state or condition of having the ovulary surrounded by and united with the floral parts.

Epiphragm the membrane stretching across the top of and closing a moss capsule and bordered by the peristome teeth.

Epiphyte (1) a green plant, attached to or dependent upon another plant for physical support, but able to manufacture its own food; an air plant; (2) a plant growing on another plant but not deriving any nourishment from it.

Epitheca the outer, older layer of the half-wall of diatoms and dinoflagellates.

Equational division the second division in meiosis.

Essential parts the fertile, inner structures of flowers.

Ethylene (C_2H_4) a regulator hormone, influencing cell division and producing other effects; an auxin.

Etiolation abnormal elongation and blanched condition produced by darkness or disease.

Euglenid one of a group of green or colorless flagellates, usually with two flagella per cell. Their mode of sexual reproduction is unknown, they are unicellular, with definite nuclei, and most have plastids.

Eukaryote cell type of plants and animals other than the bacteria and blue-green algae; such a cell has a nucleus surrounded by a nuclear membrane.

Euphotic zone the top layer of a sea or lake through which light can penetrate, allowing photosynthesis to take place; usually about 100 meters deep.

Eustele the stelar type found in members of the Magnoliopsida, in which a ring of vascular bundles is present. Also interpreted as a type of dictyostele.

Eutrophication state of lakes associated with excessive soluble nutrients and low oxygen concentrations.

Exine the outer wall of the pollen grain. It has the characteristic markings such as pores and furrows.

Exocarp the outer, often skin-like layer of the pericarp.

Exoenzyme an enzyme produced by a plant and exuded into the surrounding area where it breaks down potential food material which can then be assimilated by the plant.

Exotic (1) not native; e.g., an exotic plant is a plant that is not indigenous to a particular area.

Eyespots a pigmented spot, found in some motile forms of the dinoflagellate algae; and believed to be light sensitive.

Facultative (1) incidental; not necessary; (2) having the power to live under different conditions.

Facultative cleistogamy a plant that can have either chasmogamic flowers or those that do not open during pollination.

FAD (flavin adenine dinucleotide) a coenzyme that carries hydrogen from one compound to another.

Female gametophyte an individual of the 1N generation, producing the gametes called eggs.

Fermentation anaerobic respiration consisting of a series of complex oxidation-reduction reactions; hydrogen is released in glycolysis and combines with pyruvic acid to form alcohol, lactic acid, or other products.

Fibrous root system root system in which the roots are finely divided.

Fiddlehead the coiled, immature fern frond.

Filament the structure that supports the microsporangium.

Filiform apparatus a fingerlike ingrowth of the synergid associated with the attraction and penetration of the pollen tube into the embryo sac during fertilization in flowering plants.

First filial generation (F_1) the first generation of a cross between two individuals (the latter called the *parent generation*).

Fission (1) the cleavage into new organisms or cells; (2) the division of one-celled organisms into two equal parts during asexual reproduction; (3) reproduction by splitting of the nucleus and cytoplasm into equal parts.

Fixation (Photosynthesis) the process of producing carbohydrates by adding hydrogen to carbon and oxygen.

Flagellum (plural, *flagella*) (1) a whiplike, locomotory organ, typically consisting of an axoneme and a sheath; (2) the thread-like organ of locomotion on bacteria.

Flavonoid a group of chemical pigments, consisting of anthocyanins and anthoxanthins; flavone is a form of anthoxanthin.

Floridean starch (1) a solid carbohydrate resembling starch, staining reddish or brown with iodine, and formed by red algae as a product of assimilation; (2) an insoluble carbohydrate storage product found in red algae.

Florigen a hormone, presumed to be produced during photosynthesis, that stimulates flower production.

Flower a reproductive structure characteristic of the Magnoliophyta.

Foliose (1) having the nature or appearance of a leaf; e.g., lichens with a leafy form and layered structure; (2) flat and leaflike.

Follicle a dry fruit derived from a simple pistil and opening along only one side.

Food chain the path along which caloric energy is transferred within a community (from producers to consumers to decomposers).

Food web the complex of intertwining food chains in a community.

Foot (1) the lower part of the embryo sporophyte of the Bryophyta (it remains embedded in the gametophyte); (2) the portion of a sporophyte that fastens it to the gametophyte and absorbs materials from the gametophyte.

Form genus the generic name given to a fossil organ when first discovered.

Frond a leaf of a fern.

Fructification (1) a fruiting body; (2) a complex spore-bearing structure of definite form.

Fruit the mature ovary, including embryo and seed.

Fruit set relative number of fertile fruits formed by a plant.

Frustule the diatom cell wall.

Fruticose lichen lichen in which the thallus is attached to the substratum at one point only by a narrow base, thus growing upward as a simple shrub-like body.

Fucoidin a sulphated polysaccharide serving as the amorphous matrix for the cells of *Fucus*.

Fucoxanthin (1) the brown pigment characteristic of the brown algae; (2) the carotenoid that gives the brown color to the Phaeophyta. The light absorbing power is nearly that of chlorophyll.

Gamete (1) a reproductive cell of either sex prior to conjugation (the union of gametes produces a sexual spore or zygote); (2) a 1N cell in sexual fusion.

Gametophyte a gamete-producing plant.

Gametophyte generation a gamete-producing generation; phase of life cycle that alternates with a sporophyte phase.

Gemma (plural, *gemmae*) (1) a group of cells serving for asexual reproduction and found in some algae, fungi, and bryophytes; (2) a small, multicellular body produced by vegetative means and able to separate from the parent plant and form a new individual.

Gene (1) one of the units of inherited material carried on a chromosome; (2) the hereditary unit that controls the appearance of definite characters.

Gene repression the inhibition of gene transcription by a specific repressor protein, as proposed by the Jacob-Monod hypothesis.

Generative nucleus one of the nuclei in the microgametophyte. It later divides to form two sperm nuclei.

Genus (plural, *genera*) a group of closely related species that can be distinguished from other groups.

Geotropism movement toward the earth in reaction to gravity.

Gibberellic acid see gibberellin.

Gibberellin a group of growth-promoting substances found widely in plants and first isolated from the fungus *Gibberella*. They increase general physiological activity (e.g., they increase cell length and promote germination and flowering).

Gill a plate on the underside of the cap in the Basidiomycetes.

Girdle (1) the overlapping edge of one of the two valves in diatoms; (2) a transverse groove on the dinoflagellates and on the zoospores of the immobile genera of the Dinophyceae.

Glycolysis respiratory process during which glucose is anaerobically broken down to pyruvic acid.

Glyoxisome membranous vesicle containing certain enzymes of the glyoxylate cycle.

Glyoxylate cycle a metabolic process occurring in plant cells, converting 2-carbon molecules into carbohydrates and other molecules.

Gnetophyte a member of the Gnetopsida, a division of gymnosperms.

Golden-brown algae see *Chrysophyceae*.

Golgi body a cytoplasmic organelle playing a role in the manufacture of certain cell secretions.

Gondwanaland the southern hemisphere of the supercontinent Pangaea until the Triassic Era.

Gram's stain a stain devised by Hans C. J. Gram that distinguishes bacterial cells containing or lacking a magnesium salt of a particular type of RNA from others.

Granum (plural, *grana*) a functional unit of a chloroplast; it is the smallest particle capable of performing photosynthesis.

Grassland plant community in which herbs (mostly grasses or sedges) are dominant, and woody plants are either lacking or are dwarfed and inconspicuous.

Greenhouse effect the effect of the atmosphere on the earth's surface in maintaining surface temperatures of the earth much higher than they otherwise might be (the atmosphere acts like a glass pane and radiates the sun's long waves).

Ground meristem the partially differentiated meristem that gives rise to the cortex, pith rays, and pith.

Guanine one of the two principal purines in DNA and RNA.

Gullet a longitudinal groove present in some dinoflagellates and euglenids.

Guttation the exudation of liquid water from plant leaves.

Gymnosperm a seed plant bearing seeds in open receptacles.

Halophyte (1) a plant growing in a saline habitat; (2) a plant living in soil containing saltwater in sufficient amount that a physiological drought exists.

Haploid the 1N or gametic number of chromosomes.

Haustorium (1) a specialized branch or organ of a parasite that penetrates the host tissue and absorbs nutrients and water; (2) an absorptive structure of a fungus mycelium or a modified root or shoot of a higher plant that serves as an attachment to obtain food through penetration of the host cells.

Heartwood nonliving and commonly darker-colored wood surrounded by sapwood.

Heliotropism the tendency of certain growing organs to respond to the stimulus of sunlight by movement or curvature.

Herbaceous plant a nonwoody plant.

Herbivore a plant eater.

Hesperidium a berry with a leathery rind (e.g., a citrus fruit).

Heterocyst a distinctive cell that sometimes occurs in the filaments of certain algae.

Heteromorphic alternation of generation having morphologically distinct sporophyte and gametophyte generations.

Heterosis increased vigor resulting from the union of genetically different gametes and assumed to be due to special recombinations of dominant and recessive genes.

Heterosporous producing large megaspores that give rise to the female gametophyte, and small microspores that give rise to the male gametophytes.

Heterostyly mode of reproduction in which there

are two kinds of flowers and pollination can occur only between two different kinds of flowers.

Heterothallic self-incompatible in reference to syngamy; i.e., producing gametes that are incapable of fusing and producing a zygote so that they are dependent on the gametes of another organism of the same species (cf. *homothallic*).

Heterozygous possessing both the dominant and the recessive genes of an allelomorphic pair.

Holdfast the basal part of an algal thallus that serves as an attachment to a solid object; it may be unicellular or composed of a mass of tissue.

Homogamy mode of reproduction in which the anther and stigma mature at the same time, and thus favor self-pollination.

Homologous chromosome (*homologue*) (1) one of a pair of chromosomes, one maternal and one paternal, that contain identical inherited characters; (2) genes found on identical loci.

Homologous theory theory that proposes the origins of the sporophyte as a modification of the gametophyte, not as a new phase introduced into the life cycle.

Homosporous producing only one kind of meiospore; producing spores of the same size.

Homothallic self-compatible in reference to syngamy; i.e., able to produce gametes capable of fusing and producing a viable zygote and thus being independent of the gametes of other individuals of the species (cf. *heterothallic*).

Homozygous (1) having received identical genes, one from each parent, for a particular character; (2) having identical genes at the same locus on each member of a pair of homologous chromosomes.

Hormogonium (plural, *hormogonia*) a short filament of blue-green algae (separated from adjacent parts by modified cells) capable of a gliding motion and of development into independent colonies capable of reproduction.

Humus (1) the organic matter in the soil formed by the decomposition of plant and animal remains. It contains a large number of elements necessary for plant growth, and its colloidal nature improves the texture of the soil and its water-retaining capacity; (2) the mixture of decayed vegetation and soil found in many forests and fields, decaying organic matter in the soil, and the mold or soil formed by the decomposition of vegetable matter.

Hybridization cross-pollination between different races or different but closely related species; common in plants.

Hydathode a water-secreting gland found on the edges and tips of the leaves of many plants.

Hydrologic cycle the circulation of water through a system extending from 10 miles above the earth to about one half mile below the surface of the oceans, sustained by solar energy.

Hydrophyte (1) an aquatic plant of any kind; (2) a plant adapted to living in water, especially, a vascular plant.

Hypha (plural, *hyphae*) a filamentous structural unit of a fungus. A meshwork of hyphae forms a mycelium.

Hypocotyl the short stem of an embryo seed plant; it is the portion of the axis of the embryo seedling between the attachment of the cotyledons and the radicle.

Hypotheca the younger of the two valves in the cell wall of a diatom.

Imperfect fungi (1) the group of fungi with septate hyphae for which the knowledge of the life cycle is incomplete and for which no sexual stage is known; (2) fungi having septate hyphae but producing no known sexual stage.

Incomplete dominance an intermediate expression of a character in a hybrid, usually favoring the expression of a dominant character by one of the parents but without complete masking of the recessive character.

Indehiscent remaining closed at maturity, as many fruits.

Indolebutyric acid (IBA) a plant hormone used to stimulate root development in cuttings.

Indusium an epidermal outgrowth covering the sorus in ferns.

Inferior ovulary an ovulary surrounded by and united with the fused parts of the calyx and corolla. syn. epigyny.

Inflorescence the distinctive arrangement of flowers on a plant.

Integument (1) one or more cell layers covering the ovule and leaving only a small pore, the micropyle. (2) The covering or testa of a seed.

Intercalary (1) lying between other bodies in a row or placed somewhere along the length of a stem, filament, or hyphae; (2) said of a meristem occurring between non-dividing tissue.

Internode (1) the space between nodes or phalanges; (2) the stem between successive nodes.

Interphase (1) the resting stage between mitotic cell division; (2) the resting stage that may occur between the first and second meiotic divisions.

Intine the inner layer of the pollen wall.

Isogamete one of two gametes of opposite sex type that are structurally alike.

Isogamy the sexual union of two like gametes.

Isogeneratae class in the division Phaeophyta in which the sporophyte and gametophyte are alike.

Isomorphic alternation of generations a life cycle in which the two alternates are morphologically similar.

Isotope one of two or more forms of an element, each form of which is distinguished from the other or others by its atomic weight.

Jungle (1) a low or thin forest; (2) any impenetrable thicket or tangled mass of vegetation; (3) any dense intermingled growth.

Karyogamy (1) the fusion of two sex nuclei following the fusion of protoplasts; (2) the union of two nuclei, especially gametic nuclei.

Kelps the largest of the brown algae, usually

559

consisting of expanded leaf-like blades connected by a stalk to a holdfast.

Kinetin group of chemical substances having a significant influence in the stimulation of cell division. They are structurally similar to adenine.

Krebs cycle the long, complicated series of reactions that results in the oxidation of pyruvic acid to hydrogen and carbon dioxide. The hydrogen, held on hydrogen carrier molecules, then goes through the oxidative phosphorylation and terminal oxidation processes.

Krummholz type of forest characteristic of certain alpine regions of Southern Europe, in which the knee pine or the mountain pine is the predominating tree.

Lamella (plural, lamellae) a layer of protoplasmic membrane observed in the protoplast, particularly in and between the grana of the chloroplasts.

Lamina (plural, laminae) (1) the flattened part of a leaf; any flattened part of a thallus; (2) the blade or extended part of a leaf; the leafy portion or blade of the frond.

Laminarin a polysaccharide storage product found in the brown algae.

Laurasia the hypothetical northern hemisphere of the super-continent Pangaea, which existed until Triassic times.

Law of independent assortment law stating that the random combination of characters in the offspring is the result of the random alignment of the chromosomes on the equator of the spindle at the reduction division; their combination in eggs and sperms is random, and union at fertilization is independent. This law applies only when the genes affecting such characters are on separate chromosomes.

Law of segregation law stating that in each individual the genes occur in pairs, and in the formation of gametes the members of each pair separate and pass into different gametes, so that each gamete has only one of each type of gene.

Law of uniformity Mendel's first law, which states that all individuals of the F_1 generation will be equal and uniform.

Leaf gap an interruption in the continuity of the primary vascular cylinder above the departure of the leaf trace or traces. This break is filled with parenchyma tissue.

Leaf primordium a miniature leaf in a bud.

Leaf trace a vascular bundle that connects the vascular tissues of the stem with those of the leaf.

Leafy liverworts also called scale mosses; bodies typically dorsiventral and composed of an axis bearing leaflike expansions.

Legume a type of dry fruit developed from a simple pistil and opening along two sides.

Lenticel (1) a small breathing pore in the bark of trees and shrubs, it is a corky aerating organ which permits gaseous diffusion between the plant and the atmosphere; (2) a pore in the periderm of a woody stem, packed with a loose aggregate of cells derived from the phelloderm and acting as an organ of gaseous exchange.

Leucophyte a colorless alga.

Leucoplast an unpigmented plastid.

Lichen a cryptogam composed of an alga and a fungus in intimate association, the fungus usually being an ascomycete but rarely a basidiomycete; (2) a composite plant consisting of an alga and a fungus in intimate association.

Life cycle I a life cycle found in many algae in which the only $2N$ stage is the zygote and meiosis is zygotic.

Life cycle II a life cycle found in some algae (and most animals) in which meiosis is gametic.

Life cycle III a life cycle found in some algae and fungi and in all higher plants in which $1N$ and $2N$ plant generations alternate and meiosis is sporic.

Life-form (1) the form of a plant determined by the position of its resting buds (if any), in respect to the surface of the soil; (2) the characteristic form and structure by which a plant is adapted to cope with various conditions of the environment; e.g., size, habit of growth.

Light reaction part of photosynthesis occurring in the grana and entailing the separation of water in the presence of light and chlorophyll; also called the *Hill reaction*.

Lignin a complex substance present in substantial quantities in wood.

Ligule (1) a strap-shaped corolla bract of the ray flowers in composites; (2) a flattened membrane arising from the base of the leaves of some lycopods; (3) a membrane at the junction of the leaf-sheath and leaf-base of many grasses.

Linkage the physical segregation of genes on a single chromosome, resulting in their frequent association in inheritance of characters.

Lithophyte (1) a plant found growing on rocks and stones; (2) a plant found growing on rocky ground.

Liverwort a member of the Marchantiopsida; liverworts are usually inconspicuous and live in moist environments.

Locus (plural, loci) (1) the position of a particular gene on its chromosome; (2) the position of a gene on a chromosome in a linkage group or on a chromosome map.

Long-day plant a plant that needs alternating periods of comparatively prolonged periods of light and relatively brief periods of darkness for the proper development of flowers and fruits.

Lorica the bell-shaped testa, or envelope, secreted by the chrysophyte *Dinobryon*.

Luciferase an oxidizing enzyme that acts on luciferin to cause luminosity.

Luciferin the substance oxidized by luciferase, causing luminosity; a group of various substances essential in the production of bioluminescence.

Lycopod a member of the Lycopodiophyta.

Lycopodiophyta a division of vascular plants of microphyllous nature, generally bearing sporangia in strobili.

Lysosome membrane-bound structure functioning in the storage of many digestive enzymes.

Major essential elements those chemical elements required by plants in large amounts and producing a deficiency if absent for a few days. Included among these are carbon, hydrogen, oxygen, nitrogen, phosphorus, potassium, calcium, sulfur, magnesium, and iron.

Mangrove (1) a community of tropical plants found in the swampy lands and estuaries along the coasts, and composed of several genera of which *Rhizophora* is the most common; (2) an association of plants of the muddy swamps at the mouths of rivers and elsewhere in the tropics, over which the tide flows daily, leaving the mud bare at low tide.

Medullary rays (1) the strands of connective tissue, made up of parenchymatous cells, separating the vascular bundles and extending from the pith to the bark or pericycle in woody dicots and gymnosperms (they conduct food and water transversely); (2) a sheet of parenchyma running radially through the vascular tissue of a stem or root. They are concerned with food storage and lateral conduction of food materials, water, and the like.

Megagametophyte the gametophyte produced by the megaspore.

Megaphyll a leaf derived from a branch system, often associated with a leaf gap in the stele and having a branching vein system; opposite of microphyll (q.v.).

Megasporangium (plural, *megasporangia*) the sporangium in which megaspores are produced by division of sporogenous tissue.

Megaspore the larger spore produced by heterosporous plants. It produces a megagametophyte.

Megasporophyll a leaf-like plant organ that bears or encloses megasporangia; a carpel.

Meiosis the two divisions during which the chromosomes are reduced from the 2N to the 1N number.

Meiosis I the first, reductional division of meiosis.

Meiosis II the second, equational division of meiosis.

Meiospore a spore produced by meiosis within a sporangium; it is always 1N.

Meristem any embryonic tissue in plants capable of giving rise to additional tissues.

Mesic said of an environment in which plants are adapted to average or moderate moisture conditions.

Mesocarp the layer of the pericarp that is often fleshy or fibrous in texture.

Mesophyll the soft tissue (parenchyma) that is between the upper and the lower epidermis of the leaf and is chiefly concerned with photosynthesis.

Mesosome specialized membranous structure in the bacterial cell; may have some function in cell division.

Metabolism sum total of catabolic and anabolic chemical processes occurring within a living organism.

Metaphase (1) the stage in mitosis during which the chromosomes aggregate in the equatorial region of the spindle, divide longitudinally, and the daughter chromosomes move toward the poles of the spindle; (2) stage in mitosis or meiosis at which the chromosomes become arranged on the equator of the spindle.

Metaxylem (1) the later-formed primary xylem having pitted tracheary elements; the central wood as distinguished from the peripheral xylem strands; (2) primary xylem which is derived from the procambium. The cells are heavily lignified and have reticulate thickening or pitted walls; in consequence, they cannot be stretched.

Microbody any of several ellipsoid cytoplasmic organelles in the size range of 0.2 to 0.6 micrometer long bounded by a single unit membrane.

Microfilament a small cytoplasmic fiber composed of protein and associated with cyclosis.

Microflora (1) the microscopic flora of a given locality; (2) the microscopic plants (e.g., fungi and bacteria) of an organ or body region.

Microgametophyte (1) the individual gametophyte that bears only male sex organs; (2) the gametophyte which produces microgametes.

Microphyll (1) leaves with a single central vein, especially the Lycopodiophyta; (2) a small leaf.

Micropyle the opening in the integuments of the ovule.

Microsporangium (plural, *microsporangia*) (1) the structure in which microspores are developed; (2) an anther sac.

Microspore mother cells those cells that undergo meiosis to produce microspores.

Microsporophyll (1) a leaf bearing a microsporangium; may be highly modified, (e.g., the stamens of flowering plants); (2) a small leaf-like structure bearing microspores; a stamen.

Microtubule a cytoplasmic organelle in the form of an elongate, very slender tube.

Middle lamella thin membrane separating two adjoining cells, and serving to cement them together.

Midrib the differentiated midaxis of a thallus or leaf.

Mitochondrion a cytoplasmic organelle serving as site of respiration.

Mitosis a form of nuclear division characterized by complex chromosome movements and exact chromosome duplication.

Mixed buds buds that produce both leaves and flowers.

Mixed grass prairie the middle grassland biome of North America, having grasses 2 to 4 feet tall.

Monoclinous bisexual; having stamens and carpels in the same flower.

Monocotyledon a flowering plant with one seed leaf or cotyledon; one of the two great groups of angiosperms.

Monoculture growth of a single kind of plant only over large areas of land.

Monoecious having both microsporophylls and megasporophylls.

Monokaryote a cell with a single 1N nucleus.

Monoploid having one set of chromosomes.

Monopodial having one continuous main stem or axis, with growth at the apex in the direction of previous growth. The lateral structures of like kind are produced beneath the apex in acropetal succession.

mRNA RNA produced in the nucleus and moving to the ribosomes where it determines the order of the amino acids in a polypeptide.

Mucoprotein conjugated protein containing an acid mucopolysaccharide.

Multiple alleles a series of three or more alternative forms of a gene occupying a single locus on a chromosome; genes produced by a number of mutations of different natures at the same locus.

Multiple factor inheritance inheritance involving two or more factors, all of which are needed to produce a certain result in inheritance.

Mutation (1) sudden variation in an inherited character resulting from an abrupt change in the genotypic nature other than normal segregation or crossing over; (2) the sudden alteration of the chemical structure of a gene, or the alteration of its position on the chromosome by breaking and rejoining of the chromosomes. Mutations occur naturally, but may be induced artificially by irradiation.

Mutualism (1) form of symbiosis in which both parties derive advantage without sustaining injury; commensalism; (2) a form of biological interaction in which both organisms must associate together for continued success of both.

Mycelium (plural, *mycelia*) (1) a hypha; the plant body of a fungus; a mass of thread-like structures which constitute the thallus of a fungus; (2) collectively, the vegetative hyphae of a fungus.

Mycobiont the fungal partner in a lichen.

Mycorrhiza (plural, *mycorrhizae*) (1) the association of a fungus with the roots of a higher plant for mutual benefit; (2) the association between a fungus and the roots of a plant. It is probably symbiotic, but may be a weak form of parasitism.

Myxomycetes class in which plasmodial slime molds are placed.

Myxomycota division in which slime molds are placed.

NAD (nicotinamide adenine dinucleotide) hydrogen acceptor molecule in respiration.

NADP (nicotinamide adenine dinucleotide phosphate) a hydrogen acceptor molecule in photosynthesis.

Nastic movement response to external stimuli in which the nature of the reaction is independent of the direction from which the stimulus comes.

Neck canal cell one of the central cells of the central canal in the neck of an archegonium.

Nectary the floral structure that produces a sugary liquid capable of attracting insects and other small animals.

Net venation the pattern of venation in which the branching veins in the leaf or leaflet form a network.

Node point at which a leaf is attached.

Non-sister chromatids chromatids of one homologous chromosome with respect to the chromatids of the other homologue in synapsis.

North American prairie (1) the grass country east of the Rocky Mountains; (2) the grassland area dominated by the tall prairie grasses as distinguished from the short grass plains.

Nucellus (1) the megasporangium; (2) the central tissue of the ovule, containing the embryo sac and surrounded by the integument(s).

Nucleolus an RNA-containing body within the nucleus of a cell.

Nucleoplasm the granular matrix of the nucleus.

Nucleotide a subunit of a nucleic acid (RNA or DNA) composed of either a purine (adenine, guanine) or a pyrimidine (thymine, cytosine, or uracil), plus a sugar and phosphoric acid.

Nucleus (plural, *nuclei*) a body present in all cell types except prokaryotes and consisting of external nuclear membrane, interior nuclear sap, and chromosomes and nucleoli suspended in the sap.

Nut a one-seeded fruit in which the fruit wall is hard, stony, or woody at maturity.

Nutation (1) any rotating or rhythmic movement in plants or plant organs caused by growth or a stimulus such as light; (2) the lateral swaying of the tip of a growing organ.

Obligate parasite a parasitic organism that is unable to live free of its host.

Octoploid having eight sets of chromosomes.

Oögamy (1) fertilization of a large, non-motile female gamete by a small, motile male gamete; (2) the conjugation of two dissimilar gametes.

Oögonia (1) female sex organs in the thallophytes and oomycetes containing one or more oospheres; (2) a cell giving rise to oöcytes, directly or by mitosis.

Oösphere (1) an unfertilized female gamete; (2) the large, non-motile, fertile gamete of some algae and fungi.

Oöspore (1) the final stage of development after the fusion of unlike gametes in the Oomycetes; (2) the thick-walled, resting zygote formed from a fertilized oösphere.

Operculum (1) a lid; (2) the upper portion of a circumscissile capsule; in mosses, the lid covering the capsule.

Opposite one of the two terms applied to leaves or buds occurring in pairs at a node, in relation to the other.

Orbital the space within which an orbiting electron may move in an atom.

Organelle specialized part of a cell with specialized structure and serving a specific function.

Osmoregulation the control of solute or solvent in response to diffusion through differentially permeable membranes of a cell.

Osmosis the movement of molecules by diffusion through a selectively permeable membrane (such as the cell membrane). It is a physical process and does not require directly the expenditure of energy by the cell (see *diffusion*).

Ovary see *ovulary*.

Ovulary that part of a flower that contains the ovules.

Ovule (1) the nucellus that contains the embryo sac and is enclosed by one or two integuments and that, after fertilization and subsequent development, becomes a seed; (2) the unfertilized young seed in the ovary; the megasporangium of a seed plant that later develops into a seed.

Oxidation the loss of electrons from an atom or a molecule; in biology, an energy-releasing process.

Oxylophyte an acid-loving plant.

Paleobotany the scientific study of plant fossils.

Paleoecology (1) the ecology of geological periods; (2) a field of ecology that reconstructs past vegetation and climate from fossil evidence.

Palisade a leaf tissue composed of columnar chloroplast-bearing cells with their long axes at right angles to the leaf surface.

Palmate venation presence of veins in a leaf arising from the base of the leaf and radiating outward.

Palmately compound leaf compound leaf in which the leaflets are attached at the tip of the petiole.

Pangaea the hypothetical original single land mass from which all the present continents are believed to have formed.

Pangenesis hypothesis obsolete theory proposing that small, exact, invisible copies of each body organ and component are transported by the blood to the sex organs and incorporated into gametes.

Parallel venation pattern in which the principal veins of a leaf are parallel, or nearly so.

Paramylum a substance resembling starch and found in granules in the Euglenophyta.

Paraphysis (plural, *paraphyses*) (1) the sterile hairs growing around or among reproductive structures, and found in some algae, Ascomycetes Basidiomycetes, and mosses; (2) sterile filaments occurring in the fructification of many lower plants.

Parasexuality a kind of genetic exchange process found in some cells involving exchange of DNA but not of chromosomes.

Parasite (1) a plant or animal living on or in another organism (the host) and deriving nourishment from the host and living at the latter's detriment; (2) a plant or animal requiring a living plant upon which to live and from which to derive sustenance.

Parenchymatous composed of thin-walled, living cells arranged in more than one layer.

Parthenogenesis production of spores or seeds without fertilization (see also *apomixis, apogamy*).

Peat (1) an accumulation of plant matter that is only partly decomposed because of a lack of oxygen that prevents the bacteria that cause decomposition from living; (2) a carbonaceous substance formed by the partial decomposition in water of various plants, especially mosses of the genus *Sphagnum*.

Pectin a complex organic compound that is present in the intercellular layer and primary wall of plant cell walls.

Peduncle the flower stalk of the inflorescence.

Pelagic community biome in the open ocean: a floating community.

Pellicle the structurally complex outer membrane of certain cells, including euglenids.

Pepo a berry with a thick, hard rind (e.g., watermelon).

Perennial a woody or herbaceous plant living for more than two years, and not dying after once flowering.

Perfect stage (1) the sexual stage in the life-cycle of a fungus, at which spores are produced by sexual fusion; (2) state of pleomorphic fungi in which spores are produced as a result of some sort of sexual process or morphologically similar spores are formed by parthenogenesis.

Perianth the outer envelope of a flower, made up of calyx and corolla.

Pericarp the ovary wall consisting of three distinct layers in fruits.

Pericycle (1) a cylinder of vascular tissue, three to six cells in thickness, lying immediately inside the endodermis of a root and consisting of parenchyma and sometimes fibers; (2) a layer of nonconducting cells one or more layers thick at the periphery of the stele.

Periderm the composite layer consisting of cork cells, cork cambium, and sometimes parenchymatous cells and replacing the epidermis in organs undergoing secondary growth.

Peridinin (1) an alcohol-soluble, reddish pigment in the chromatophores of the Dinophyceae; (2) coloring matter found in some algae.

Perigyny having the ovulary surrounded by but free of the floral cup.

Peristome (1) a single or double row of hygroscopic teeth found in the opening of the spore case or capsule of mosses and assisting in ejection of the spores; (2) a fringe of elongated teeth around the mouth of the capsule of a moss. The teeth are formed from the remains of unevenly thickened cell walls.

Perithecium a round or flask-shaped fruit body of certain Ascomycetes and lichens. It has an internal hymenium of asci and paraphyses and an apical pore (ostiole) through which the ascospores are discharged.

Permafrost perennially frozen ground characteristic of regions above the Arctic Circle and in Antarctica.

Peroxisome a microbody that contains enzymes that break down hydrogen peroxide and in which the glyoxylate cycle and photorespiration can occur.

Petal one of the units of the corolla of the flower.

Petiole the stalk of a leaf.

Petrifaction type of plant fossil in which the original cellular tissues are retained and are impregnated with mineral compounds.

Pfr the form of phytochrome that has an absorption maximum near 730 nm (far-red light).

Phenotype (1) a group of individuals similar in appearance but not necessarily in genetical constitution; (2) the type of organism produced by the reaction of a given genotype with the environment.

Phloem vascular tissue that conducts synthesized foods in vascular plants. It is characterized by the presence of sieve tubes, and in some plants companion cells, fibers, and parenchyma.

Phloem fiber element of sclerenchyma present in the phloem and probably serving to support the sieve tubes.

Phloem parenchyma layer of thin-walled cells in the phloem whose primary function is the storage of starch, other foods, water, or tannins and resins.

Phosphon antigibberillin causing growth retardation.

Photon a quantum of light; a discrete amount of light energy.

Photoperiod the relative length of time that a plant is exposed to light, especially as it affects the life cycle and physiological processes of the plant.

Photoperiodism (1) the response of a plant to the amount of light received by it, noted by influence on the vegetative and reproductive processes (plants often exhibit a definite response to their particular optimum daylengths); (2) the effect of alternating light and dark periods on the growth and formation of flowers and fruits.

Phototropism (1) the tendency shown by most plants to turn their aerial growing parts toward the greater light; (2) the growth curvature of a part of a plant in response to light.

Phycobiont the algal partner of a lichen.

Phycocyanin (1) a bluish coloring matter found in certain marine algae; (2) the blue pigment found in the chloroplasts of the Rhodophyta and distributed through the cells of the Cyanophyceae.

Phycoerythrin (1) a red pigment formed by the red and blue-green algae; (2) the red pigment of the Rhodophyta. It is found in the cell-sap, is protein in nature, and is soluble in water.

Phyllotaxy arrangement of leaves on the stem.

Phytochrome light sensitive pigment believed instrumental in the initiation of flowering.

Phytohormone a hormone produced by a plant or one used to stimulate plant growth.

Phytoplankters the plankton algae largely concentrated in the upper few meters of the sea.

Phytoplankton (1) floating pelagic plant organisms; floating microscopic plants; (2) plants of the plankton.

Pileus (plural, _pilei_) the cap of the mushroom basidiocarp and that of certain ascocarps.

Pinna a primary division (leaflet) of a pinnately compound leaf.

Pinnate venation structural arrangement in which veins arise from each side of a common axis, like the barbs of a feather.

Pinnately compound a compound leaf with the leaflets arranged along the sides of a common axis.

Pinnule the individual leaflet of a bipinnately compound leaf.

Pistil the female reproductive structure of the flower.

Pit (1) a small sharply-defined area of a plant cell wall that remains unthickened when the rest of the wall thickens; (2) a thin, localized area in the wall of a cell or other plant structure.

Pith (1) the soft tissue, in the interior of a stem, that often disappears so that the stem becomes hollow; (2) central core of parenchymatous cells in stems and some roots.

Pith ray vascular ray.

Placenta the area of ovule attachment in the ovary.

Plankton (1) the more or less free-floating animals and plants living near the surface of a sea or lake; (2) the free-swimming or passively floating organisms of bodies of water.

Plasma membrane (1) a thin membrane surrounding the cytoplasm or a cell organelle consisting of fat and protein; in contact with the plant cell wall, and thus responsible for the restricted penetration of many substances into the cell; (2) the ectoplasm or the outer layer of the cytoplasm forming the limiting membrane of a protoplast.

Plasmodesma (plural, _plasmodesmata_) the fine cytoplasmic strand interconnecting adjacent cells in many plant tissues.

Plasmodial slime fungi see _Myxomycota_.

Plasmodium (1) the plant body of a slime mold; (2) a body of plurinucleated protoplasm exhibiting amoeboid motion in myxomycetes.

Plasmogamy the fusion of cytoplasm, in contrast to fusion of the nucleoplasm.

Plastid a cytoplasmic, often pigmented body of cells; the three types are leucoplasts, chromoplasts, and chloroplasts.

Pleiotropy (1) simultaneous influence of more than one character in the offspring by one factor; (2) the production of more than one physiologically uncorrelated effect by one gene, attributed to the initiation of two or more chains of reactions by one gene.

Plurilocular gametangia multicellular gametangia of the Phaeophyta producing laterally biflagellate gametes.

Plurilocular mitosporangia mitosporangia that generate $2N$ zoospores by mitosis.

Pneumatophore a specialized root that grows upward into the air from roots embedded in the mud, and, being of loose construction, makes gaseous exchange possible for the submerged roots.

Polar nodule a spherical swelling at each end of the raphe or groove in diatoms.

Polar nucleus one of two nuclei, each one derived from an opposite end of the embryo sac, and later becoming centrally located. The polar nuclei fuse at about the time the pollen tube enters the embryo sac.

Pollen chamber a small cavity formed in the apex of the nucellus in gymnosperms in which the pollen grains lodge after pollination. It is here that the pollen slowly develops and ultimately brings about fertilization.

Pollinium a mass of pollen grains held together by a sticky substance and transported as a whole during pollination.

Polygenes genes whose differences or mutations are too slight to be identified by their individual effects in an individual and which are, therefore, presumed to have only a small effect on the selective advantages of the individual.

Polyploid having more than two sets of homologous chromosomes.

Polyribosome the complex of ribosomes associated with a single strand of messenger RNA.

Polysome aggregation or cluster of ribosomes.

Polystely having more than one stele.

Pome an accessory fruit with a leathery endocarp (e.g., apple).

Pr form of phytochrome that has an absorption maximum near 660 nanometers (red light).

Predatory of, pertaining to, or characterized by plundering; practicing rapine; pillaging.

Preprophase band a band of microtubules encircling the meristematic plant cell within the plasma membrane.

Primary body the part of the plant formed directly from cells cut off from the apical meristem.

Primary phloem (1) the phloem formed from a procambial strand, consisting of protophloem and metaphloem, and present in a primary vascular bundle; (2) the first year's phloem, which develops from the procambium.

Primary root the emergent or emerged embryonic root or radicle.

Primary succession ecological succession beginning with a barren substrate in which no prior vegetation has become established.

Primary thickening meristem a meristematic region in the shoot apex of certain plants, among them the palms, that produces lateral expansion of the stem.

Primary tissues cells derived from the apical and subapical meristems of root and shoot; opposed to secondary tissue which is derived from a cambium.

Primary wall first wall produced by a developing cell, and usually associated with living protoplasts.

Primary xylem (1) primary wood formed without cambial activity; (2) xylem formed from a procambial strand and present in a primary vascular strand. It consists of protoxylem and metaxylem.

Procambium the primary meristem giving rise to vascular tissue.

Producer organism an organism that produces organic matter for itself and other organisms by photosynthesis.

Progymnosperm member of an extinct group of plants, the prototypes of the gymnosperms.

Prokaryote (1) cells of bacteria and blue-green algae having no nuclear membrane, no plastids, no mitochondria, and no lysosomes; (2) a cell lacking the internal membranous structures characteristic of eukaryotes.

Prophase the preliminary stages in mitosis and meiosis; the stage in cell division prior to metaphase during which the chromosomes appear in the nucleus after the interphase.

Proplastid an embryonic plastid that divides and grows.

Prothallial cells (1) the two cells in *Cycad*, one of which gives rise to the antheridial cell; (2) a single cell cut off early in the division of a microspore of some heterothallic pteridophytes. It represents the vegetative tissue of a male gametophyte.

Prothallus the free-living or independent gametophyte generation of ferns and other lower vascular plants.

Protoderm outer cell layer of primary meristem; it gives rise to the epidermis.

Protonemia (plural, *protonemata*) the green, filamentous gametophyte in mosses that later produces leafy sexual branches.

Protonemal buds the processes from the protonema that later form the conspicuous, visible moss plant.

Protoplasm the living material of the cell.

Protostelic having essentially a solid core of xylem surrounded by a cylinder of phloem, the simplest type of vascular arrangement.

Protoxylem (1) the first-formed xylem having tracheary elements characterized by annular or spiral thickening; (2) the xylem derived from the apical growing part (its elements are extensible and become partly thickened before elongation is complete).

Pseudopodium (plural, *pseudopodia*) a leafless stalk of the gametophyte of the Sphagnaceae (it bears the sporophyte and remains short until the sporophyte is mature, then elongates).

Pulvinus (plural, *pulvini*) the enlargement of a petiole or of the stalk of a leaflet at the point of attachment.

Puncta (plural, *punctae*) a marking on a valve of a diatom.

Punnett square a chart constructed to conveniently show the possible results of gametic pairings.

Purines bases containing two carbon-nitrogen rings.

Pycnia (1) term applied to the spermagonium of the Uredinales; (2) a spermagonium.

Pyramid of numbers expression of the total biomass of a community in the form of a pyramid, such that the dominant species (at the top) are of a lesser number and biomass, while life-forms at successive levels are of greater biomass and quantity.

Pyrenoid a small mass of refractive protein occurring in or on chlorophyll structures in some lower plants, and concerned with the formation of carbohydrates.

Pyrimidine a base containing one carbon-nitrogen ring.

Rachis a main axis, such as that of a compound leaf.

Radial section a view of wood exposed by a longitudinal cut along the radius.

Radial symmetry presence of more than one plane of symmetry.

Radicle the embryonic root; the portion of the embryo below the cotyledons; the canticle.

Raphe a slit-like line running longitudinally on the valve of a diatom; it bears a nodule at each end and one in the middle.

Ray the non-vascular tissue developed in a stele.

Receptacle the tip of the peduncle to which parts of a flower are attached.

Receptive hyphae elongate periphyses of the spermagonia in Basidiomycetes.

Recessive allele a gene that has no effect on the phenotype; a masked gene.

Recessive parental character (1) of characters, those not evident in a hybrid, owing to the domination of the other character; i.e., a character which seems to disappear in crosses; (2) the relationship of two allelomorphs such that the single gene heterozygote does not resem-

565

ble one of the two homozygous parents because its effect is masked by the dominant allelomorph.

Reduction gain of electrons by an atom or molecule, as by addition of hydrogen or removal of oxygen.

Reductional division the process by which the number of chromosomes in a cell is reduced from $2N$ to $1N$.

Reservoir an intercellular space, often containing resin, essential oil, or some product of metabolism.

Resin duct a tube-like cavity lined with living cells that secrete resin into the canal; present in pines.

Resistant sporangia sporangia found in some fungi, that are thick-walled and are thus able to withstand extreme environmental conditions.

Reticulate venation branching, rebranching, and anastomosis of veins.

Retort cells cuticular cells of *Sphagnum* having an outward curved apex.

Rhizoid (1) a single-celled or multicellular, hair-like structure at the base of a moss "stem," and on the underside of liverworts and fern prothalli, serving for anchorage, and, in the moss, holding water by capillarity; (2) a hair-like structure or outgrowth of many mosses and thallophytes.

Rhizome the underground, horizontal stem that has internodes and reduced, scale-like leaves.

Rhizomorph (1) a root-like hypha of certain fungi; (2) a root-like organ composed of many united strands of hyphae, in agarics and some other fungi.

Rhizophore (1) a leafless branch in some club mosses from which roots arise; (2) the stem base in Lepidodendrales.

Ribosome (1) a macromolecule containing protein and RNA, seen as a dense particle in electron micrographs, and found in all types of cells in which protein is being synthesized; (2) a small particle of nucleic acid and protein that can occur on the endoplasmic reticulum.

Ribulose diphosphate the 5-carbon sugar taking part in photosynthesis.

RNA hybridization

Root descending portion of a plant that serves to fix it in soil and absorbs and conducts water and nutrients to other parts of the plant.

Root cap a thimble-shaped mass of parenchyma cells that covers the root apex and protects it from mechanical injury.

Root hairs one of the tubular outgrowths of epidermal cells of the root in the zone of maturation.

Root pressure the pressure developed in roots that causes guttation and exudation from cut stumps.

Rough endoplasmic reticulum a formation of ribosomes lining the outer surfaces of the endoplasmic reticulum.

Samara a dry fruit bearing wings useful in dispersal, as in the maple.

Saprobe a plant living on and deriving its food from dead organic matter.

Sapwood outer part of the wood of a stem or trunk, usually distinguished from the heartwood by its lighter color.

Scion a portion of a shoot used for grafting.

Sclereid a short sclerenchyma cell having heavily lignified cell walls.

Sclerenchyma elongated cells with tapering ends and thick secondary walls; they are usually nonliving at maturity, and serve as supporting tissue.

Sclerotium (plural, *sclerotia*) (1) a compact mass of fungal hyphae, often with a thickened rind (they are organs of perennation, and may give rise to fruiting bodies; (2) of Myxomycetes, the firm, resting condition of a plasmodium.

Seasonal cleistogamy production of cleistogamic flowers during one season, and chasmogamic flowers during another.

Secondary phloem (1) the phloem formed by the activity of the cambium; (2) the part of the bark formed by the cambium; it is composed of permanent tissue developed from a fascicular cambium.

Secondary root a branch of the primary root.

Secondary succession ecological succession occurring in a disturbed substrate, as after a fire.

Secondary wall innermost wall formed inside the primary cell wall.

Secondary xylem (1) secondary wood; (2) xylem derived from the cambium.

Seed a structure formed by seed plants following fertilization. In conifers, it consists of seed coat, embryo and female gametophyte storage tissue.

Seed ferns the fern-like fossil plants that lived in the Carboniferous Period.

Semicell (1) one of the two halves of a cell of a desmid; (2) one-half of a desmid.

Sepal one of the units of the calyx.

Septum (1) a wall between two adjoining cells; (2) any kind of wall or partition.

Seta (plural, *setae*) (1) the multicellular stalk that bears the capsule of liverworts and mosses; (2) a hollow outgrowth from a cell; a slender straight prickle or bristle.

Sheath a tubular envelope; the base of a leaf that wraps around the stem, as in grasses.

Short-day plant a plant in which the onset of flowering is brought about by relatively brief periods of illumination, followed by relatively long periods of darkness.

Short grass prairie the westernmost grassland biome of North America, having grasses 0.5 to 1.5 feet in height.

Short shoot (1) a spur, or dwarfed fertile branch; (2) a small shoot, borne in the axile of a scale leaf, and bearing the foliage leaves.

Sieve cell long, slender cell having perforations in its wall: a phloem element.

Sieve plate perforated end wall connecting two sieve elements.

Sieve plate pores perforations in the end walls of sieve tubes.

Sieve tube conducting element of phloem composed of cells known as sieve tube elements.

Sieve tube element one of the component cells of the sieve tube of flowering plants.

Silique special type of capsule or pod of a cruciferous plant developed from an ovary of two united carpels, which dehisces at maturity.

Simple (leaf) an undivided leaf; opposed to a compound leaf.

Siphonostele (1) a hollow cylindrical stele with or without pith; (2) a stele in which the xylem and phloem form concentric cylinders around a central pith.

Siphonous series the third main evolutionary series among the Chlorophyta.

Sirenin (Chap. 11) a chemical sperm-attracting substance secreted by female gametes of certain fungi.

Sister chromatids the two chromatids composing a chromosome; term usually used with reference to synapsis in meiosis.

Slime fungi see *Myxomycetes.*

Smooth endoplasmic reticulum endoplasmic reticulum, the outer surface of which is not lined by ribosomes.

Sorophore the sorus stalk in Marsileales.

Sorus (plural, *sori*) (1) a powdery mass of soredia on the surface of a lichen thallus; (2) a cluster of sporangia with a cover (in ferns); (3) a group of antheridia on male fronds of marine algae; (4) a fruiting structure in certain fungi, especially the spore-mass of rusts and smuts.

Spermatangium (plural, *spermatangia*) the male sex organ of the Rhodophyta; an antheridium.

Spermatium (plural, *spermatia*) (1) a non-motile, male sex cell, present in red algae, and in some Ascomycetes, some Basidiomycetes, and some lichens.

Spindle a structure, formed during mitosis, and associated with the movement of the chromosomes to opposite poles.

Spindle fiber an individual structure, formed during mitosis, that is associated with the movement of the chromosomes to the poles.

Spirillum (plural, *spirilli*) a bacterium with a strongly spiral shape.

Spirochaetes elongated, spirally-twisted organisms that move by flexing the body, not by flagella. Some are free-living and others are parasitic in animals and man; they are usually classified with the Bacteria.

Spongy mesophyll a leaf tissue composed of loosely arranged, chloroplast-bearing cells; also called *spongy tissue.*

Sporangiophore a structure that bears one or more sporangia.

Sporangiospore (1) a spore produced in the sporangium; (2) a spore, especially a non-motile spore formed within a sporangium.

Spore mother cell a 2N cell that undergoes meiosis and produces (usually) four 1N cells (spores) or four 1N nuclei.

Sporeling a young plant produced by germination of the spore.

Sporocarp a hard, nut-like structure containing sori of heterosporous sporangia in ferns.

Sporophyll a spore-bearing structure.

Sporophyte a spore-producing organism; the phase of the life cycle that alternates with a gametophyte phase.

Springwood the wood formed in spring, when xylem cells grow larger and thus form a lighter portion of the annual ring.

Stamen the male reproductive structure of the flower.

Staminode sterile microsporophyll.

Stele the primary vascular structure of a stem or root, together with any tissue that may be enclosed.

Stem apex the meristematic region of the stem.

Stigma the part of the pistil, distal to the ovary, that receives the pollen.

Stipe a supporting stalk, such as the stalk of a gill fungus or the leaf stalk of a fern.

Stipule an appendage on either side of the basal part of a leaf of some species of plants.

Stock that part of a stem that receives the scion in grafting.

Stolon a long, slender stem that grows from the parent plant horizontally across the surface of the ground.

Stoma (plural, *stomata*) a pore in the epidermis of plants, present in large numbers, particularly on leaves, through which gaseous exchange takes place.

Stomium the lip cell region of the sporangium in ferns.

Stonewort a member of the Charophyceae; characterized by apical growth and branches in whorls.

Stratification (1) the grouping of vegetation in a wood into two or more well-defined layers differing in height, as in trees, shrubs, and ground vegetation; (2) classification of the plants in a plant community according to life-form.

Streaming (of cytoplasm) see *cyclosis.*

Stroma the connective tissue network supporting the epithelial portions of an organ.

Style the structure joining the stigma and the ovary in a flower.

Suberin a complex fatty or waxy substance found in cork cell walls.

Substrate (1) the solid object to which a plant is attached; (2) the material in or upon which a fungus grows or to which it is attached; the matrix; (3) the nutritive medium in which a cell or organism grows.

Succession (1) the sequence of plant formations; (2) the progressive change in the composition of a plant population during development of vegetation, from initial colonization to the attainment of the climax community.

Sulcus a furrow; a groove in the wall of pyrophytes.

Summerwood the summer growth of wood, in which the xylem cells are smaller and form the denser, darker layer of the annual ring.

Superior ovulary ovulary borne above the insertion of the floral parts.

Suspensor (1) a hypha supporting a zygospore; (2) a structure in the embryo of seed plants that pushes the terminal part of the embryo into the endosperm and probably also absorbs nutrients.

Symbiont (1) an organsim that lives in a state of symbiosis; (2) an organism living in physical association with another, typically with benefit to both.

Symbiosis (1) the living of two or more orga-

567

nisms in close association, resulting in mutual benefit; (2) the living together of dissimilar organisms in a state of mutualism.

Symbiotic (1) living in a beneficial partnership; (2) living in close association with one or more organisms to their mutual benefit.

Synapsis pairing of homologous maternal and paternal chromosomes early in meiosis.

Synconium a multiple fruit having flowers borne within an involuted receptacle, e.g., the fig.

Syncytium a multinucleate mass of protoplasm without differentiation into cells; a plasmodium; a coenocyte.

Synergid one of two ephemeral cells lying close to the egg in the mature embryo sac of the ovule of flowering plants.

Syngamy fertilization; the fusion of gametes to form a zygote.

Synusiae (1) life forms associated in growth and habitat but distinct as to affinity; (2) an ecological unit based on the life-forms of plants growing in company.

Taiga (1) a wet woodland soil in Siberia; (2) a broad northern belt of vegetation dominated by conifers; also a similar belt in mountains just below alpine vegetation.

Tall grass prairie the easternmost grassland biome of North America, having grasses 5 to 8 feet in height.

Tangential section a section of wood in which the wood is exposed by a longitudinal cut at right angles to the vascular rays.

Taproot a short, tapering main root from which arise smaller, lateral branches.

Teliosorus (plural, *teliosori*) a collection of hyphae bearing conidia known as teliospores, and found in rusts such as wheat rust.

Teliospore (1) a thick-walled rust spore that produces a promycelium when it germinates; (2) a thick-walled spore consisting of two or more cells and formed by a rust fungus toward the end of the growing season. Such spores can remain dormant for some time and then germinate to give one or more promycelia on which the basidiospores are formed.

Telophase a stage in mitotic division during which the two daughter nuclei form; it is usually accompanied by partitioning of cytoplasm.

Temperate, deciduous forest plant community as found in Eastern North America, and typically having trees that form two layers; with several layers of shrubs and herbs below.

Tendril modification of the stem of vines or clambering plants, serving to secure support.

Terminal cell that cell found at the tip of a young embryo.

Test cross (1) a back cross of the diheterozygote to a double recessive in order to test linkage; (2) a cross of a double or multiple heterozygote to the corresponding double or multiple recessive. It is used to estimate linkage relationships to behavior.

Testa the seed coat, made up of the hardened integuments.

Tetrad (1) a group of four spores formed by meiosis within a spore mother cell; (2) a group of four structures (e.g., pollen grains) that remain together until they reach maturity.

Tetraploid having four sets of homologous chromosomes.

Tetrasporangium the cell in red algae in which tetraspores are formed.

Tetraspore one of four non-motile spores produced in the tetrasporangium.

Tetrasporine series the second main evolutionary line of the Chlorophyta; individual species contain a multicellular plant body in which the thallus may be branching or non-branching.

Tetrasporophyte stage in life cycle of a red alga; it is produced by diploid carpospores and reproduces by production of tetraspores.

Thallose liverwort a conspicuously lobed liverwort in which growth occurs at apical regions.

Thallus a simple, unicellular or multicellular, sometimes large plant body that is never differentiated into stem, leaf and root.

Thermoperiodism the influence of daily temperature changes on plant growth and development.

Thigmotropism a growth (twining) movement resulting from contact with a solid object.

Thorn sharp, pointed structure that comes from the development of a lateral bud.

3-indoleacetic acid (IAA) a plant hormone that causes elongation of cells when present in suitable concentrations.

Thylakoid an individual photosynthetic lamella, often stacked to form grana within the chloroplast.

Thymine one of the two main pyrimidines in DNA.

Tinsellated flagella flagella with slender lateral fibrils extending out from the central shaft.

Tissue culture the growth of detached pieces of tissue in nutritive fluids under conditions that exclude bacteria and fungi.

Totipotent a cell or tissue capable of regenerating an organ or an entire individual.

Toxin any complex poisonous substance produced by bacteria or other forms of living organisms.

Trace element an element needed in a very small amount for healthy growth and development. Most trace elements are metals that are involved in the structures of enzyme complexes.

Tracheid an elongated, thick-walled conducting and supportive cell of wood, having tapering ends and pitted walls without true perforations.

Translation process in which a particular nucleotide sequence on an RNA molecule gives rise to a particular amino acid sequence with the help of the ribosomes.

Translocation the movement of food through phloem sieve tubes.

Transpiration the loss of water vapor from a plant, especially through the stomata.

Transpiration pull movement of water upward through the stem of a plant caused by evaporation of water from the leaves (with resulting differences in pressure), osmosis, and the cohesion of water.

Transverse section (1) a section of an organ or an organism exposed by making cuts at right angles to the long axis; (2) a section of wood cut transversely to the long axis.

Trichogyne (1) a thread-like extension of the carpogonium in red algae that receives the male cell; (2) a unicellular or multicellular organ projecting from a female sex organ and receiving the male gamete or male nucleus before fertilization.

Trichome (1) a short filament of cells; (2) a hair-like outgrowth of the epidermis, as a hair or bristle; (3) in the Cyanophyta, a single row of cells that, with their sheath, make up the filament.

Tricolpate having three germ furrows, as in pollen grains.

Tri-iodobenzoic acid (TIBA) compound used to cause fruit set under otherwise adverse conditions.

Trilete spores spores with triradiate ridges marking the points at which they were associated with three others in a tetrad.

Tripinnate said of a pinnately compound leaf, having pinnately divided leaflets, that in turn are pinnately divided.

tRNA smaller RNA molecules that unite with specific amino acids and align them on messenger RNA in the formation of polypeptides.

Trophic levels successive levels of nourishment in the food chains of a community.

Tropical rain forest a complex community composed of a hundred or more dominant tree species. The dominant trees are usually very tall, and their interlacing tops form dense canopies that intercept much of the sunlight and rainfall.

Tropical savannah (1) grass country broken by patches of forest or copse; (2) a more or less leafless forest during the dry season, rarely evergreen, xerophilous, usually less than 20 meters high, park-like, very poor in undergrowth, lianas and epiphytes, and rich in grass.

Tropism response to an external stimulus in which the direction of movements is usually determined by the direction from which the stimulus comes.

Tube nucleus one of the nuclei of the microgametophyte. It directs the tube down the pistil to the egg.

Tuber morphologically short, fleshy, terminal enlargement of a rhizome.

Tundra (1) cold desert characterized by the scanty, xerophytic vegetation in which mosses and lichens are dominant; (2) cold, northern, treeless desert that is flat or gently undulating.

2,4-Dichlorophenoxyacetic acid (2,4-D) a synthetic auxin used as an herbicide and defoliant.

2,4,5-Trichlorophenoxyacetic acid (2,4,5-T) a synthetic auxin used as an herbicide and a defoliant.

Unilocular meiosporangia organs producing $1N$ zoospores in the Phaeophyta.

Unisexuality condition in which an organism has only one sex.

Universal veil in *Amanita,* an outer membrane enclosing the young fruiting body; its remnant is the cup or volva.

Upwelling movement of ocean waters so as to bring the cold waters from the depths to the surface.

Uracil one of the two main pyrimidines in RNA.

Uredosorus collection of hyphae bearing conidia known as uredospores; found in rusts such as wheat rust.

Uredospore an orange or brownish spore formed by rust fungi when growth is vigorous. It serves as a means of rapid propagation and gives rise to a mycelium, which may produce more uredospores or, later in the year, teliospores.

Vacuole a small, usually spherical space within a cell, bounded by a membrane and containing fluid, solid matter, or both.

Valve (1) one of the two halves of the cell wall of a diatom; (2) one-half of the silicified membrane of a diatom in side view.

Vascular bundle a strand-like portion of the vascular tissue of a plant, composed of xylem and phloem.

Vascular cambium the meristematic zone or cylinder, one cell thick, that produces secondary phloem and xylem.

Vascular plant a plant containing xylem and phloem.

Venter that part of an archegonium that contains the egg cell.

Ventral canal cell nonfunctional, unwalled cell that lies in the venter of an archegonium above the egg, of which it is a sister cell.

Vesicle a sac-like structure attached to the margins of dictyosomes, and thought to contain cell wall substances and participate in the formation of the cell plate.

Vessel a tube-like structure of the xylem, composed of cells placed end to end and connected by perforations.

Vessel element one of the cells composing a vessel.

Volutin (1) metachromatic granules in the yeast cell occurring in the nuclear vacuole; (2) stored food substances in fungi, especially in yeasts.

Volva remnants of the universal veil at the base of the stalk of a gill fungus.

Volvocine series the first of the main evolutionary series in Chlorophyta; led to the production of a motile colonial form.

Water mold an aquatic member of the Oomycetes.

Water net common name for *Hydrodictyon.*

Whiplash flagella flagella that are smooth and lack external fibrils; as opposed to tinsellated flagella (q.v.).

Whorl one of several appendages attached circumferentially at the same level on a stem.

Xerarch succession (1) succession beginning on land where conditions are very dry; (2) a plant succession originating in a dry habitat and becoming more mesic in its successive stages.

Xerophyte a plant that can live where the water supply is scanty or there is physiological drought.

Xylem tissue that conducts water from roots upward and consists of tracheids, vessels, and other cell types; in bulk, it forms wood.

Xylem parenchyma parenchymatous cells occurring in xylem apart from those present in the vascular rays.

Yeast one of several species of ascomycetous

fungi in which an extensive mycelium is not produced, so that the plant body is usually unicellular.

Yellow-green algae members of the Chrysophyta, having an excess of beta-carotene.

Zeatin Cytokinin isolated from *Zea* (corn, or maize).

Zooplankton small animals floating or drifting near the surface of the ocean.

Zoosporangium (plural, zoosporangia) (1) a sporangium in which zoospores are pro-duced; (2) a spore case containing zoospores.

Zoospore (1) an asexual spore, which is motile by one to many flagella; (2) a motile asexual spore or swarm spore.

Zygomorphic flower a flower with only one plane of symmetry.

Zygospore an encysted zygote, as found in *Spirogyra.*

Zygote the cell resulting from the sexual fusion of two gametes; a fertilized egg.

Index

Page numbers in **boldface** indicate illustrations; those followed by (t) indicate tables.